SCI 论文写作与投稿
Writing and Submission of SCI Papers

梁福军　著

机械工业出版社

本书旨在多方位建立科技论文分类和 SCI 论文体系，系统讲述 SCI 论文的内容与结构、写作方法与步骤、写作规则与技巧，并辅以大量实例分析和点评，有很强的针对性和实用性。

本书共分 9 章，涵盖科技论文分类、概念链、SCI 论文体系（价值、结构、语言、质量、过程和评价六大体系）、SCI 论文主体写作，SCI 论文辅体写作，SCI 论文中量、单位、插图、表格、数学式的使用，SCI 论文投稿与发表流程，国际知名投审稿系统 EM（Editorial Manager）投稿流程示例。

本书是在作者长期工作实践经验积累的基础上，结合 SCI 论文写作要求及有关标准、规范，分析众多国际顶尖期刊论文实例撰写而成的。

本书适于作为硕士、博士研究生的学术论文特别是英文论文写作的教材，也可作为各类研究人员、大学生论文写作的参考、自学用书和科技写作、编辑的培训教材，还可作为科研、技术和科普领域的科技工作者，期刊、图书和新媒体的编辑，以及从事英文写作教学、研究的专家、学者和教师的参考书或工具书。

图书在版编目（CIP）数据

SCI 论文写作与投稿/梁福军著．—北京：机械工业出版社，2019.8
（2024.1 重印）
ISBN 978-7-111-62910-8

Ⅰ．①S… Ⅱ．①梁… Ⅲ．①科学技术-论文-写作 Ⅳ．①H152.2

中国版本图书馆 CIP 数据核字（2019）第 110923 号

机械工业出版社（北京市百万庄大街 22 号　邮政编码 100037）
策划编辑：韩效杰　　责任编辑：韩效杰　刘琴琴
责任校对：张　薇　　封面设计：鞠　杨
责任印制：单爱军
北京虎彩文化传播有限公司印刷
2024 年 1 月第 1 版第 8 次印刷
184mm×260mm·24.5 印张·605 千字
标准书号：ISBN 978-7-111-62910-8
定价：69.00 元

电话服务　　　　　　　　网络服务
客服电话：010-88361066　　机　工　官　网：www.cmpbook.com
　　　　　010-88379833　　机　工　官　博：weibo.com/cmp1952
　　　　　010-68326294　　金　书　网：www.golden-book.com
封底无防伪标均为盗版　　　机工教育服务网：www.cmpedu.com

序 一
FOREWORD ONE

Writing a high-quality scientific paper and having it published in a highly ranked SCI journal is not only a required task for researchers to fully develop their careers, but also an effective way to disseminate results through the research community to make value-added contribution to existing knowledge, as well as to reach a broad audience to raise public awareness of their research and inspire future generation of researchers. However, successful production of a written product for submission to an SCI journal is not easy, especially for those novice researchers. It requests substantial effort and advanced writing skills. Dr. Liang's book *Writing and Submission of SCI Papers* provides beginning authors with very helpful guidelines that help them to achieve success when writing and submitting manuscripts to SCI journals.

This book is all about teaching the style and conventions of authoring papers for SCI journals and suggesting the best practices for successfully getting research manuscripts published. Readers of this book will acquire knowledge of a broad range of the entire process in the context of planning, structuring, writing, submitting, and revising research papers for SCI journals. The readers will also be exposed to real examples of publishing papers in top-ranked journals. Insiders' perspective on the editorial processes at SCI journals and the strategies to maximize the chances of being published in those journals are also offered.

After reading this book, especially through the many examples it provides, the readers will learn more about how to write different sections of the main body of a scientific paper, which includes but not limited to introduction, background, methodology, results and discussion, and conclusion; how to write an abstract, create reference list, and add an acknowledgement section for your paper; how to design visually appealing figures and tables and use them as an effective way to communicate your primary findings; as well as how to format your paper make it more appealing to journal editors. Detailed information about peer review and editorial decision making process adds extra value to this book.

This book is very helpful for those early-career scientists, including graduate students, who are relatively new to writing and publishing papers. It can be used for either teaching or self-learning. For English language scholars and students, inclusive of scientific journal editors, this book is also a most recommended reference.

Yucheng Liu, Ph. D., P. E.
Jack Hatcher Chair Professor and Graduate Coordinator
Fellow of American Society of Mechanical Engineers
Department of Mechanical Engineering
Mississippi State University
December 9, 2018

序 二
FOREWORD TWO

  SCI 论文是现代与未来科技工作者与国际学术界和同行进行交流、学习、评定和发展自己的手段和工具，也是科学技术研究完整体系中不可缺少的一个重要环节。SCI 论文写作是硕士、博士研究生和青年科技工作者应具备的基本功。因此，梁博士撰写的《SCI 论文写作与投稿》教材的出版非常及时，适应和满足了中国科技研发与国际学术交流同时迅猛发展的需要。

  记得二十年前，我在哈尔滨工业大学开始做"长江学者特聘教授"的时候，就已认识到 SCI 论文写作是当时博士生和青年教师培养和科研能力提高的一个主要瓶颈。于是，我连续多次在学科和学院里组织了有关 SCI 论文写作与投稿的讲座，获得了积极的效果，虽然当时讲座内容只是个人论文发表经历和经验的总结，远不够系统和规范，但我对广大研究生和青年教师的需求与所存在问题的体会还是相当深刻的。今天，梁博士所著的《SCI 论文写作与投稿》一书，把我们过去的经历和经验进行了系统、规范和创造性的归纳和总结，并以国际名刊（如 *Nature*、*Science*、*Cell* 等）发表的论文作为实例进行阐述和讲解，很有代表性和科学性。我相信需要进行 SCI 论文发表的广大科技工作者一定能认可该书，阅读使用该书一定能够起到事半功倍的作用。该书一定会成为高校、科研院所师生特别是硕士、博士研究生的重要工具书，也会成为许多青年科技工作者的案头必备参考书。

  任何学科与学术体系的建立和发展，与其相关学科领域中学术论文及思想的实时发表、丰富交流和广泛传播是分不开的。对每位科技工作者及在校硕士、博士研究生来说，其 SCI 论文发表、学术著作出版和各自学术体系的建立是一个相辅相成、循序渐进、不断完善的发展过程。我坚信梁博士的新著将会成为能帮助我们撰写和发表高水平论文论著、归纳和总结学术思想的实用的教材和工具书。

英国布鲁内尔大学制造系统首席教授

哈尔滨工业大学特聘教授

《国际先进制造技术》（IJAMT）欧洲编辑

程凯（Kai Cheng）

2018-12-18

序 三
FOREWORD THREE

近些年，我国在科技发展方面投入大量资金，极大地促进了我国科学研究的快速发展和技术的持续进步，许多领域已由与国际水平跟跑、并跑状态进入并跑、领跑状态，大量优秀科研成果不断涌现。目前，我国科技工作者每年发表在SCI期刊的论文数量已经超过美国，成为世界上发表SCI论文数量排名第一的国家，值得国人骄傲和自豪。

然而，过去我国高校通常较少专门设置科研论文写作课程，对科研论文写作的教育投入不足或重视不够，学生在校期间没有受到系统、专门的论文写作训练，不少学生不论是在在校期间撰写科研论文、学位论文，还是在毕业后走上工作岗位撰写科研专著、学术论文，通常难以写出合规、得体的论文，论文因写作质量问题常被科技期刊拖延出版或作退稿处理。

同时，我国科技期刊的专业编辑也需全面掌握科技论文的写作规范和技能，以更好地指导作者撰写、修改论文，从而使科技期刊刊登的论文高质量地出版，易于获得更为广泛的交流和更加有效的传播。

我作为长期从事科技期刊出版和传播的专业编辑，深深感受到让作者提高论文的写作水平和让科技期刊编辑全面懂得科技论文写作技能的重要性。

梁福军博士所著的《SCI论文写作与投稿》一书，是我目前所看到的在学术论文写作方面内容最全面、最具体的著作。这本书的主题鲜明、结构合理、层次清晰，内容包括论文价值、结构、语言、质量、过程和评价六大体系，论文主体、辅体写作，论文中量、单位、图、表、式使用，论文投稿、发表流程，以及EM投稿流程示例。各章讲解都较为细致、全面，几乎涉及高水平学术论文写作的全部内容，同时又列举了大量具有代表性的名刊论文实例，大大增强了说服力。

相信该书既是一部经典的专著，也是一部实用的教材。

科技导报社副社长、副主编　史永超

2018-12-18

前 言
PREFACE

SCI（Scientific Citation Index）论文已在多个方面发挥着重要作用，比如它在日益全球化的科学研究中成为国际科学交流的重要方式和国际同行相互了解的主要渠道，其发表数和被引量成为评价或衡量研究成果水准的国际通用标准及招聘、晋升、考核和评奖等的重要指标，其发表的期刊及数量成为博士学位申请获得的必要条件，也是出国深造者联系国外导师让其了解自己的最佳窗口……。因此，SCI 论文在科技工作者心目中的地位往往很高。对于中国来说，发表 SCI 论文，可以向世界展示中国的基础科研实力，提高中国在世界科学界的地位，使中国学者在国际舞台上拥有话语权。

SCI 论文如此高端，是缘于其至上的内容价值，还是其优美的表述语言？有人认为，对 SCI 论文写作，中国作者大多面临英语能力欠佳的缺陷，尤其对于年龄大和专业性强的作者来说，内容也许根本不是问题，而英语往往成为影响其成果发表的重要因素。这种说法有道理，但过分强调语言，忽略了内容，或许对那些母语（如中文）写作能力强而英语写作能力相对差的作者来说是对的，但对内容空洞、结构欠缺的论文的作者来说，也许至多说对了一半。另外，顾名思义，SCI 论文就是被 SCI 索引数据库收录的期刊（SCI 期刊）所刊登的论文，而 SCI 期刊多是英文期刊，这样就有很多优秀的非英文期刊不在 SCI 之列。不同国家都有其母语的大量优秀期刊，这些期刊未被 SCI 收录，但其刊登的论文就不是好论文了吗？因此，将 SCI 论文列为高水平论文没有错，但它并不等同于高水平论文，只能说它是高水平论文的一个子集。况且，SCI 索引数据库不只收录英文语言的文章，对其他语言的文章也有收录的，只不过在数量上较少而已。因此，不能认为 SCI 论文全是英文论文。

其实，即使对于同样的内容，不管用什么语言写，所写论文的应有内容和结构是相同的，这是从论文的科学本质来说的；只是用一定结构呈现一定内容的语言形式不同罢了，这是从论文的语言形式来说的。有不少知名科学家，包括一些诺贝尔奖获得者，从来没有在 SCI 期刊甚至英文期刊上发表过论文，更谈不上在高影响因子的 SCI 期刊发文了，而他们仅在自己本土"不怎么知名"的期刊发表了重大发现和原创成果，正是这些非 SCI 论文和期刊成就了其学术权威和获奖辉煌。因此，论文的价值在于内容，在于将原创的客观事物变成语言文字，而不在于用来表达客观事物的语言文字的类别。

从这个意义讲，SCI 论文的高大上首先应归于其价值，其次才是语言；若首先归于语言而忽视价值，那就本末倒置了。一篇论文如果没有发表价值或价值较低，其语言即使再地道、优美，也不能成为好论文，倒是可能因为被某个影响不大的 SCI 期刊刊登了而成为 SCI 论文，进而进入"好"论文之列了。

鉴于此，SCI 论文不应仅从字面来理解。它至少应有两层含义：价值高（内容好，结构合理，内容铸就价值，结构呈现内容）；语言好（语法通，逻辑顺，修辞巧）。对于一篇论文，价值高是其成为 SCI 论文的充分条件，而语言好是其成为 SCI 论文的必要条件。笔者对 SCI 论文写作进行系统研究，将其分为内容篇和语言篇，内容篇在本书讲述，语言篇在另一

前　言

本著作《英语科技论文语法、词汇与修辞》讲述。

本书中还分享了笔者对 SCI 论文及其评价体系的一些知识、观点，希望对包括科技期刊编辑在内的广大科技工作者正确认识 SCI 论文、SCI 期刊及 SCI 影响因子的作用与局限有一些参考意义；同时还分享了 SCI 论文的投稿与发表流程，希望对作者加强流程意识、把控投稿流程和提升论文质量有实战、实用意义。

笔者水平和能力有限，疏漏之处在所难免，诚请广大读者批评指正！

梁博士讲堂公众号（drliangwechat）是笔者分享写作心得的园地，敬请关注。

梁福军

2019-6-18

目 录
CONTENTS

序一
序二
序三
前言

第1章 绪论 1
  1.1 科技论文基本知识 1
    1.1.1 科技论文的特点 1
    1.1.2 科技论文的分类 4
    1.1.3 科技论文概念链 9
  1.2 SCI论文的分类 10
    1.2.1 按学科或专业方向 10
    1.2.2 按期刊栏目或文体 10
  1.3 SCI论文价值体系 12
    1.3.1 原创性 12
    1.3.2 重要性 14
    1.3.3 新颖性 15
    1.3.4 巧妙性 17
    1.3.5 交叉性 17
    1.3.6 可读性 19
  1.4 SCI论文结构体系 19
    1.4.1 论文总体结构 19
    1.4.2 原创论文主体结构 20
    1.4.3 综述主体结构 22
    1.4.4 常见短文介绍 23
  1.5 SCI论文语言体系 24
  1.6 SCI论文质量体系 25
  1.7 SCI论文过程体系 26
    1.7.1 论文形成过程 26
    1.7.2 写作准备阶段 28
    1.7.3 写作进行阶段 31
  1.8 SCI论文评价体系 32
    1.8.1 SCI论文 32
    1.8.2 SCI期刊 33
    1.8.3 影响因子观 37

第2章 SCI论文主体写作 42
  2.1 层次标题 42
  2.2 题名 45

目　录

- 2.2.1　题名写作要求 ……………………………………………………… 45
- 2.2.2　题名内容表达 ……………………………………………………… 47
- 2.2.3　题名结构表达 ……………………………………………………… 49
- 2.2.4　题名语言表达 ……………………………………………………… 51
- 2.2.5　题名形式表达 ……………………………………………………… 55
- 2.2.6　眉题规范表达 ……………………………………………………… 55
- 2.2.7　系列题名问题 ……………………………………………………… 56

2.3　引言 …………………………………………………………………… 56
- 2.3.1　引言内容及结构 …………………………………………………… 57
- 2.3.2　引言写作要求 ……………………………………………………… 57
- 2.3.3　引言写作方法 ……………………………………………………… 59
- 2.3.4　引言写作实例 ……………………………………………………… 59
  - 2.3.4.1　实例一 …………………………………………………… 60
  - 2.3.4.2　实例二 …………………………………………………… 61
  - 2.3.4.3　实例三 …………………………………………………… 63
  - 2.3.4.4　实例四 …………………………………………………… 64
- 2.3.5　不规范引言实例 …………………………………………………… 65
  - 2.3.5.1　实例一 …………………………………………………… 65
  - 2.3.5.2　实例二 …………………………………………………… 66
  - 2.3.5.3　实例三 …………………………………………………… 67

2.4　材料与方法 …………………………………………………………… 68
- 2.4.1　材料与方法内容及结构 …………………………………………… 68
- 2.4.2　材料与方法写作要求 ……………………………………………… 69
- 2.4.3　材料与方法写作方法 ……………………………………………… 70
- 2.4.4　材料与方法写作实例 ……………………………………………… 72
  - 2.4.4.1　实例一 …………………………………………………… 72
  - 2.4.4.2　实例二 …………………………………………………… 74
  - 2.4.4.3　实例三 …………………………………………………… 78
  - 2.4.4.4　实例四 …………………………………………………… 80

2.5　结果与讨论 …………………………………………………………… 82
- 2.5.1　结果与讨论内容及结构 …………………………………………… 82
- 2.5.2　结果与讨论写作要求 ……………………………………………… 83
- 2.5.3　结果与讨论写作方法 ……………………………………………… 86
- 2.5.4　结果与讨论写作实例 ……………………………………………… 88
  - 2.5.4.1　实例一 …………………………………………………… 88
  - 2.5.4.2　实例二 …………………………………………………… 93
  - 2.5.4.3　实例三 …………………………………………………… 104

2.6　结论 …………………………………………………………………… 107
- 2.6.1　结论内容及结构 …………………………………………………… 107
- 2.6.2　结论写作要求 ……………………………………………………… 108
- 2.6.3　结论的句型 ………………………………………………………… 108
- 2.6.4　结论写作实例 ……………………………………………………… 110
  - 2.6.4.1　实例一 …………………………………………………… 110
  - 2.6.4.2　实例二 …………………………………………………… 111
  - 2.6.4.3　实例三 …………………………………………………… 112

2.6.4.4 实例四ㆍㆍㆍㆍㆍㆍㆍㆍㆍㆍㆍㆍㆍㆍㆍㆍㆍㆍㆍㆍㆍㆍㆍㆍㆍㆍㆍㆍㆍ 113
2.6.4.5 实例五ㆍㆍㆍㆍㆍㆍㆍㆍㆍㆍㆍㆍㆍㆍㆍㆍㆍㆍㆍㆍㆍㆍㆍㆍㆍㆍㆍㆍㆍ 114

第 3 章 SCI 论文辅体写作ㆍㆍㆍㆍㆍㆍㆍㆍㆍㆍㆍㆍㆍㆍㆍㆍㆍㆍㆍㆍㆍㆍㆍㆍ 117

3.1 署名ㆍㆍㆍㆍㆍㆍㆍㆍㆍㆍㆍㆍㆍㆍㆍㆍㆍㆍㆍㆍㆍㆍㆍㆍㆍㆍㆍㆍㆍㆍㆍㆍㆍ 117
3.1.1 署名体例格式ㆍㆍㆍㆍㆍㆍㆍㆍㆍㆍㆍㆍㆍㆍㆍㆍㆍㆍㆍㆍㆍㆍㆍㆍㆍㆍ 117
3.1.2 人名惯用写法ㆍㆍㆍㆍㆍㆍㆍㆍㆍㆍㆍㆍㆍㆍㆍㆍㆍㆍㆍㆍㆍㆍㆍㆍㆍㆍ 120
3.1.3 单位名称表达ㆍㆍㆍㆍㆍㆍㆍㆍㆍㆍㆍㆍㆍㆍㆍㆍㆍㆍㆍㆍㆍㆍㆍㆍㆍㆍ 122
3.1.4 署名细节表达ㆍㆍㆍㆍㆍㆍㆍㆍㆍㆍㆍㆍㆍㆍㆍㆍㆍㆍㆍㆍㆍㆍㆍㆍㆍㆍ 123
3.2 摘要ㆍㆍㆍㆍㆍㆍㆍㆍㆍㆍㆍㆍㆍㆍㆍㆍㆍㆍㆍㆍㆍㆍㆍㆍㆍㆍㆍㆍㆍㆍㆍㆍㆍ 125
3.2.1 摘要的作用ㆍㆍㆍㆍㆍㆍㆍㆍㆍㆍㆍㆍㆍㆍㆍㆍㆍㆍㆍㆍㆍㆍㆍㆍㆍㆍㆍ 125
3.2.2 摘要内容及结构ㆍㆍㆍㆍㆍㆍㆍㆍㆍㆍㆍㆍㆍㆍㆍㆍㆍㆍㆍㆍㆍㆍㆍㆍㆍ 126
3.2.3 摘要的类型ㆍㆍㆍㆍㆍㆍㆍㆍㆍㆍㆍㆍㆍㆍㆍㆍㆍㆍㆍㆍㆍㆍㆍㆍㆍㆍㆍ 129
3.2.3.1 报道性摘要ㆍㆍㆍㆍㆍㆍㆍㆍㆍㆍㆍㆍㆍㆍㆍㆍㆍㆍㆍㆍㆍㆍㆍㆍㆍ 129
3.2.3.2 指示性摘要ㆍㆍㆍㆍㆍㆍㆍㆍㆍㆍㆍㆍㆍㆍㆍㆍㆍㆍㆍㆍㆍㆍㆍㆍㆍ 132
3.2.3.3 复合性摘要ㆍㆍㆍㆍㆍㆍㆍㆍㆍㆍㆍㆍㆍㆍㆍㆍㆍㆍㆍㆍㆍㆍㆍㆍㆍ 133
3.2.4 摘要的语法ㆍㆍㆍㆍㆍㆍㆍㆍㆍㆍㆍㆍㆍㆍㆍㆍㆍㆍㆍㆍㆍㆍㆍㆍㆍㆍㆍ 134
3.2.4.1 摘要的时态ㆍㆍㆍㆍㆍㆍㆍㆍㆍㆍㆍㆍㆍㆍㆍㆍㆍㆍㆍㆍㆍㆍㆍㆍㆍ 134
3.2.4.2 摘要的语态ㆍㆍㆍㆍㆍㆍㆍㆍㆍㆍㆍㆍㆍㆍㆍㆍㆍㆍㆍㆍㆍㆍㆍㆍㆍ 135
3.2.4.3 摘要的人称ㆍㆍㆍㆍㆍㆍㆍㆍㆍㆍㆍㆍㆍㆍㆍㆍㆍㆍㆍㆍㆍㆍㆍㆍㆍ 136
3.2.4.4 摘要的句式ㆍㆍㆍㆍㆍㆍㆍㆍㆍㆍㆍㆍㆍㆍㆍㆍㆍㆍㆍㆍㆍㆍㆍㆍㆍ 136
3.2.5 摘要的效能ㆍㆍㆍㆍㆍㆍㆍㆍㆍㆍㆍㆍㆍㆍㆍㆍㆍㆍㆍㆍㆍㆍㆍㆍㆍㆍㆍ 138
3.2.6 摘要写作方法ㆍㆍㆍㆍㆍㆍㆍㆍㆍㆍㆍㆍㆍㆍㆍㆍㆍㆍㆍㆍㆍㆍㆍㆍㆍㆍ 141
3.2.6.1 摘要写作步骤ㆍㆍㆍㆍㆍㆍㆍㆍㆍㆍㆍㆍㆍㆍㆍㆍㆍㆍㆍㆍㆍㆍㆍㆍ 141
3.2.6.2 各个部分写作ㆍㆍㆍㆍㆍㆍㆍㆍㆍㆍㆍㆍㆍㆍㆍㆍㆍㆍㆍㆍㆍㆍㆍㆍ 143
3.2.7 摘要写作实例ㆍㆍㆍㆍㆍㆍㆍㆍㆍㆍㆍㆍㆍㆍㆍㆍㆍㆍㆍㆍㆍㆍㆍㆍㆍㆍ 144
3.2.7.1 实例一ㆍㆍㆍㆍㆍㆍㆍㆍㆍㆍㆍㆍㆍㆍㆍㆍㆍㆍㆍㆍㆍㆍㆍㆍㆍㆍㆍ 144
3.2.7.2 实例二ㆍㆍㆍㆍㆍㆍㆍㆍㆍㆍㆍㆍㆍㆍㆍㆍㆍㆍㆍㆍㆍㆍㆍㆍㆍㆍㆍ 145
3.2.7.3 实例三ㆍㆍㆍㆍㆍㆍㆍㆍㆍㆍㆍㆍㆍㆍㆍㆍㆍㆍㆍㆍㆍㆍㆍㆍㆍㆍㆍ 146
3.2.7.4 实例四ㆍㆍㆍㆍㆍㆍㆍㆍㆍㆍㆍㆍㆍㆍㆍㆍㆍㆍㆍㆍㆍㆍㆍㆍㆍㆍㆍ 146
3.2.7.5 实例五ㆍㆍㆍㆍㆍㆍㆍㆍㆍㆍㆍㆍㆍㆍㆍㆍㆍㆍㆍㆍㆍㆍㆍㆍㆍㆍㆍ 147
3.2.7.6 实例六ㆍㆍㆍㆍㆍㆍㆍㆍㆍㆍㆍㆍㆍㆍㆍㆍㆍㆍㆍㆍㆍㆍㆍㆍㆍㆍㆍ 147
3.2.8 不规范摘要修改ㆍㆍㆍㆍㆍㆍㆍㆍㆍㆍㆍㆍㆍㆍㆍㆍㆍㆍㆍㆍㆍㆍㆍㆍㆍ 148
3.2.8.1 实例一ㆍㆍㆍㆍㆍㆍㆍㆍㆍㆍㆍㆍㆍㆍㆍㆍㆍㆍㆍㆍㆍㆍㆍㆍㆍㆍㆍ 148
3.2.8.2 实例二ㆍㆍㆍㆍㆍㆍㆍㆍㆍㆍㆍㆍㆍㆍㆍㆍㆍㆍㆍㆍㆍㆍㆍㆍㆍㆍㆍ 150
3.2.8.3 实例三ㆍㆍㆍㆍㆍㆍㆍㆍㆍㆍㆍㆍㆍㆍㆍㆍㆍㆍㆍㆍㆍㆍㆍㆍㆍㆍㆍ 150
3.2.8.4 实例四ㆍㆍㆍㆍㆍㆍㆍㆍㆍㆍㆍㆍㆍㆍㆍㆍㆍㆍㆍㆍㆍㆍㆍㆍㆍㆍㆍ 151
3.2.9 摘要与结论比较ㆍㆍㆍㆍㆍㆍㆍㆍㆍㆍㆍㆍㆍㆍㆍㆍㆍㆍㆍㆍㆍㆍㆍㆍㆍ 153
3.3 参考文献ㆍㆍㆍㆍㆍㆍㆍㆍㆍㆍㆍㆍㆍㆍㆍㆍㆍㆍㆍㆍㆍㆍㆍㆍㆍㆍㆍㆍㆍㆍ 157
3.3.1 参考文献的概念ㆍㆍㆍㆍㆍㆍㆍㆍㆍㆍㆍㆍㆍㆍㆍㆍㆍㆍㆍㆍㆍㆍㆍㆍㆍ 157
3.3.2 参考文献的类型ㆍㆍㆍㆍㆍㆍㆍㆍㆍㆍㆍㆍㆍㆍㆍㆍㆍㆍㆍㆍㆍㆍㆍㆍㆍ 158
3.3.3 参考文献标注法ㆍㆍㆍㆍㆍㆍㆍㆍㆍㆍㆍㆍㆍㆍㆍㆍㆍㆍㆍㆍㆍㆍㆍㆍㆍ 158
3.3.3.1 按顺序编码制标注ㆍㆍㆍㆍㆍㆍㆍㆍㆍㆍㆍㆍㆍㆍㆍㆍㆍㆍㆍㆍㆍㆍ 158
3.3.3.2 按著者–出版年制标注ㆍㆍㆍㆍㆍㆍㆍㆍㆍㆍㆍㆍㆍㆍㆍㆍㆍㆍㆍㆍ 160

3.3.4　参考文献表组织 ··· 162
　　　　3.3.4.1　按顺序编码制组织 ··· 162
　　　　3.3.4.2　按著者–出版年制组织 ··· 163
　　3.3.5　参考文献著录项目 ·· 164
　　　　3.3.5.1　专著 ··· 164
　　　　3.3.5.2　专著的析出文献 ··· 168
　　　　3.3.5.3　连续出版物 ·· 170
　　　　3.3.5.4　连续出版物的析出文献 ·· 171
　　　　3.3.5.5　专利文献 ··· 173
　　　　3.3.5.6　普通电子资源 ··· 173
　　　　3.3.5.7　特别电子资源 ··· 175
　　3.3.6　参考文献引用规则 ·· 176
　　3.3.7　参考文献著录细则 ·· 177
3.4　致谢和作者贡献 ·· 179
3.5　作者介绍 ·· 185
3.6　附录 ·· 185
3.7　出版信息 ·· 186
　　3.7.1　论文 DOI ··· 186
　　3.7.2　日期信息 ·· 188
　　3.7.3　附加信息 ·· 188
　　3.7.4　利益声明 ·· 189
　　3.7.5　作者信息 ·· 190
　　3.7.6　版权许可 ·· 190

第 4 章　SCI 论文量和单位使用 ··· 191
4.1　量和单位使用基本原则 ··· 191
4.2　量和单位规范使用 ·· 193
　　4.2.1　量名称 ·· 193
　　4.2.2　量符号 ·· 195
　　4.2.3　单位名称 ·· 197
　　4.2.4　单位符号 ·· 197
　　4.2.5　词头 ·· 201
　　4.2.6　法定单位 ·· 202
　　4.2.7　量纲匹配 ·· 203
　　4.2.8　行文统一 ·· 203
4.3　量和单位使用常见问题 ··· 203
4.4　名刊量和单位实例分析 ··· 204
　　4.4.1　*Nature* 实例 ·· 204
　　4.4.2　*Science* 实例 ··· 208
　　4.4.3　*Cell* 实例 ··· 211
　　4.4.4　*Light*：*S&A* 实例 ··· 213
　　4.4.5　*Cell Research* 实例 ··· 214

第 5 章　SCI 论文插图使用 ·· 216
5.1　插图的分类 ·· 216
　　5.1.1　单图和组合图 ·· 216

5.1.2 坐标图 ·· 220
　　5.1.2.1 线形图 ·· 220
　　5.1.2.2 条形图 ·· 222
　　5.1.2.3 点图 ··· 226
5.1.3 构成比图 ··· 227
5.1.4 示意图 ·· 228
　　5.1.4.1 结构图 ·· 228
　　5.1.4.2 原理图 ·· 230
　　5.1.4.3 功能图 ·· 232
　　5.1.4.4 流程图 ·· 233
　　5.1.4.5 网络图 ·· 235
5.1.5 记录谱图 ··· 237
5.1.6 等值线图 ··· 238
5.1.7 计算机输出图 ·· 238
5.1.8 照片图 ·· 240
5.2 插图的构成及表达 ··· 242
5.2.1 图序和图题 ·· 243
5.2.2 图例 ·· 244
5.2.3 图注 ·· 244
5.2.4 标目 ·· 244
5.2.5 标值线和标值 ·· 246
5.2.6 坐标轴 ·· 246
5.3 插图使用一般原则 ··· 246
5.4 插图规范设计制作 ··· 248
5.4.1 设计制作细节 ·· 248
5.4.2 图中线型选取 ·· 249
5.4.3 图形符号使用 ·· 249
5.4.4 图形布局设计 ·· 249
5.4.5 插图幅面确定 ·· 253
5.5 线形图规范设计制作 ··· 253
5.5.1 曲线设计制作基本方法 ·· 253
5.5.2 线形图设计制作技巧 ··· 253
5.5.3 线形图设计制作要点 ··· 255

第6章 SCI 论文表格使用 ·· 256
6.1 表格的基本名称 ··· 256
6.2 表格的结构分类 ··· 257
6.3 表格的构成及表达 ·· 262
　6.3.1 表序和表题 ·· 262
　6.3.2 表头 ·· 264
　6.3.3 表体 ·· 265
　6.3.4 表注 ·· 265
6.4 表格使用一般原则 ·· 266
6.5 表格规范处理 ··· 267
　6.5.1 表格幅面确定 ·· 267

6.5.2	表格拆分、合并、增设和删除	268
6.5.3	表格排式转换	269
6.5.4	表格项目头设置	271
6.5.5	复式表头使用	272
6.5.6	栏目取名	273
6.5.7	表格数值表达	277
6.5.8	表文排式及标点符号使用	279
6.5.9	表中图及式子处理	280
6.5.10	表格与文字配合	281
6.5.11	卡线表转换为三线表	281
6.5.12	三线表项目栏配置	283

第7章 SCI论文数学式使用 287

- 7.1 数学式的特点 287
- 7.2 数学式表达要求 288
  - 7.2.1 正文排式 288
  - 7.2.2 符号注释 288
  - 7.2.3 式子编号 290
  - 7.2.4 式前用语 291
  - 7.2.5 自身排式 292
  - 7.2.6 排式转换 294
  - 7.2.7 矩阵和行列式 295
  - 7.2.8 合理转行 296
  - 7.2.9 式中乘除号 302
  - 7.2.10 式后标点 302
  - 7.2.11 式中字体 303
  - 7.2.12 式子完整性 303
- 7.3 数学式表达的严谨性 303
- 7.4 数学式使用实例 305
  - 7.4.1 实例一 305
  - 7.4.2 实例二 306
  - 7.4.3 实例三 306
  - 7.4.4 实例四 307
  - 7.4.5 实例五 308

第8章 SCI论文投稿与发表 310

- 8.1 投稿与发表流程 310
  - 8.1.1 写作完成阶段 310
  - 8.1.2 整体流程示意 311
  - 8.1.3 详细流程概述 311
- 8.2 期刊选择 312
  - 8.2.1 客观评估论文 312
  - 8.2.2 综合考虑期刊 314
- 8.3 投稿准备 317
  - 8.3.1 阅读投稿须知 317

8.3.2　继续修改论文 ··· 319
　　8.3.3　撰写投稿信 ·· 321
　　8.3.4　*Nature* 投稿准备 ··· 323
8.4　投稿 ··· 323
　　8.4.1　在线投稿 ·· 323
　　8.4.2　邮件投稿 ·· 324
　　8.4.3　邮寄投稿 ·· 324
　　8.4.4　注意事项 ·· 325
　　8.4.5　*Nature* 投稿 ·· 326
8.5　审稿 ··· 327
　　8.5.1　编辑初审 ·· 327
　　8.5.2　专家选择 ·· 328
　　8.5.3　同行评议 ·· 328
　　8.5.4　编辑决定 ·· 331
　　8.5.5　*Nature* 审稿模式 ·· 334
8.6　修稿 ··· 334
　　8.6.1　编辑加工 ·· 334
　　8.6.2　作者修改 ·· 334
　　8.6.3　运用修稿技巧 ·· 335
　　8.6.4　语言润色 ·· 336
　　8.6.5　撰写修稿信 ·· 336
　　8.6.6　投修改稿 ·· 339
8.7　录用和发表 ··· 339
　　8.7.1　制图 ··· 340
　　8.7.2　生产 ··· 340
　　8.7.3　校对 ··· 340
　　8.7.4　发表 ··· 342
　　8.7.5　版权转让 ·· 342
8.8　论文处理绩效 ··· 343
　　8.8.1　时间机制 ·· 343
　　8.8.2　质量机制 ·· 344

第 9 章　EM 投稿流程示例 ·· 346

9.1　投稿 ··· 346
9.2　查稿 ··· 357
9.3　修稿 ··· 359
9.4　生产 ··· 362
9.5　订购 ··· 363
9.6　校对 ··· 366
9.7　订购确认 ·· 371
9.8　发表 ··· 371
9.9　查询 ··· 371

参考文献 ··· 372
后记 ··· 376

第1章 绪 论

SCI（Scientific Citation Index）论文是指那些被 SCI 索引数据库收录的期刊（SCI 期刊）所刊登的论文，属于高水平科技论文，它们除具高水平科技论文的所有特点外，还有价值较高、结构完整、语言准确、质量过硬和形成较难等显著特性。价值来源于内容，内容用语言表达，语言用结构呈现，价值、结构、语言和过程共同铸就论文的质量。作者只有熟悉科技论文的基本知识（如特点、分类和概念链），懂得 SCI 论文的分类，了解 SCI 论文的价值、结构、语言和质量体系，掌握写作方法、熟悉写作过程、注重写作质量、扎实开展研究、认真细致撰写、反复推敲修改，才能写出、写成、写好 SCI 论文。作者还应了解 SCI 论文的评价方法，知道对 SCI 论文的评价与 SCI 论文本身的高水平是两个不相同的概念。

1.1 科技论文基本知识

1.1.1 科技论文的特点

科技论文的水平有低有高，高水平的自然有其特殊属性，大体呈现出以下几个特点。

1. 创新性

创新性是科技论文的灵魂和价值的根本所在，是衡量论文学术水平的重要标志。科技论文的创新性是指做出或突破了前人没有做出或突破的发明或创造，在理论、方法或实践上获得新的进展或突破，体现出与前人不同的新成果（如新思想、新理论、新方法、新技术等），而且必须是作者本人或本团队研究的结果，其理论水平、实践成果和学术见解达到某区域、某时段的最高水平。一篇论文如果在其研究领域内，理论上有发展，方法上有突破，作者有自己独到的见解，提出了新的观点、理论和方法，那么就是创新性论文。

创新是有程度的，是相对于人类已有知识而言的。首创性（原创性）是创新性的最高形态，要求论文所揭示的事物本质、属性、特点及其运动所遵循的规律或规律的运用是前所未有、首创或部分首创的，是有所发现、发明、创造和前进的，而不是对前人工作的复述、模仿或解释。首次提出、首次发现是属于创新程度最高的，对某一点有发展属于一定程度的创新，而基本上重复他人工作就不属于创新。实际中有很多课题是通过引进、消化、移植国内外已有的先进科技和理论来解决本地区、行业、系统的实际问题的，只要对丰富理论、促进生产发展、推动科技进步等方面有积极效果，报道这类成果的论文也应视为有一定程度的创新。

创新性这一特点使科技论文的写作与教科书（讲义）、实验报告、工作总结等的写作有较大不同。教科书的主要任务是介绍和传授已有知识，能否提出新的内容并不十分重要，主要读者是外行人、初学者，强调系统性、完整性和连续性，常采用深入浅出、由浅入深和循序渐进的写法。实验报告、工作总结等则要求把实验过程、操作内容和数据，所做工作和采用方法，所得成绩和存在缺点，工作经验和体会等较为详细地写出来，也可将与别人重复的工作写进去（这里并不否认某些实验报告或工作总结在某一点或某些方面也有新意）。科技论文却显然不同，要求报道的内容必须是作者自己的最新研究成果，而基础性知识、与他人重复性研究内容、一般性具体实验过程和操作、数学推导、比较浅显的分析等都不应写进来。

2. 学术性

学术性也称理论性，是科技论文的主要特征，即科技论文有一定的学术价值。它以学术成果为表述对象，学术见解为论文核心，在科学实验（或试验）的前提下阐述学术成果和学术见解，揭示事物发展、变化的客观规律，探索科技领域中的客观真理，推动科学技术的发展。有无学术性以及学术性是否强，是衡量科技论文有无价值和价值大小的标准。

学术不是一般的认识和议论，而是思维反复活动和深化的结果，是系统化、专门化的学问，是具有较为深厚实践基础和一定理论体系的知识。学术性就是指有无学术以及学术水准怎样，因此也是一个有程度的概念，至少包括以下两方面含义：一是从一定理论高度分析和总结由实验、观测或其他方式所得到的结果，形成一定的科学见解，提出并解决一些具有科学价值的问题；二是用事实和理论对自己所提出的科学见解或问题进行符合逻辑的论证、分析或说明，将实践上升为理论。

学术的本质在于创新，有创新，才可能有学术。一篇论文有学术性，就是说它有创新的内容，就叫学术论文。这里牵扯一个时间的问题，首发时（如今年）是创新，过后（如几年后）就未必是创新了。一篇论文发表时是学术论文，过后就未必是了；发表时不是学术论文，也许到后来被发现有学术性，也是可能出现的极端情况。可见，论文的学术性具有鲜明的时间性，看一篇论文是否具有学术性，不仅看内容上的，还要考虑时间要素。

科技论文有自己的理论系统，对较多事实、材料进行分析、研究，由感性认识上升到理性认识。通常具有论证或论辩色彩，其内容符合历史唯物主义和唯物辩证法，符合"实事求是""有的放矢""既分析又综合"的科学研究方法。其写作过程就是作者在认识上的深化和在实践基础上进行科学抽象的过程，所报道的发现或发明不但具有实用价值，更具学术价值。一篇论文如果只是说明解决了某一实际问题，讲述了某一技术和方法，学术价值还是不够的。从事科学研究特别是工程技术的研发人员，应善于从理论上进行总结与提高，写出学术性论文。

3. 科学性

科学性是科学技术的重要属性，必然也是科技论文的基本要求。对于科技论文，内容客观、真实、准确，不允许弄虚作假，能经得起他人的重复和实践检验；论点鲜明、论据充分、论证严谨，能反映出作者的科学思维过程和所取得的科研成果；要以精确可靠的数据资料为论据，经过严密的逻辑推理进行论证，理论、观点要清楚明白，有说服力，经得起推敲和验证。作者应尽可能基于实验数据和相关文献，以最充分、确凿有力的论据作为立论依据，不带个人偏见，不主观臆造，切实从客观实际出发，得出符合实际的结论。

科技论文无论所涉及的专题大小如何，都应有自己的前提或假说、论证素材和推断结论；通过推理、分析提升到学术理论的高度，不要出现无中生有的结论和无序的数据，而要巧妙、科学地揭示论点和论据之间的内在逻辑关系，达到论据充分、论证有力。

科技论文的科学性主要表现在内容、形式和过程三个方面：

（1）科技论文的内容是科学研究的成果，其科学性是客观存在的自然现象及其规律的反映，是人们进行生产劳动、科学实验的依据，其观点、论据和方法均要受到社会实践的检验，不能凭主观臆断或个人好恶随意地取舍素材或得出结论，必须将足够、可靠的实验数据或现象观察作为立论基础，观点正确无误、论据真实充分、方法准确可靠（可靠指整个实验过程是能够经得起复核和验证的）。

（2）科技论文的形式是其内容的结构呈现，其科学性体现在结构清晰、行文严谨，符合思维一般规律，逻辑通顺严密，语言简洁明确，格式较为规范。写作要求是：①表达概念、判断必须清楚明白、准确恰当，不含糊其辞、不模棱两可，通常不能像文学创作那样用含蓄、夸张、反语等修辞手法来增强论文的可读性；②尽量不用容易产生歧义的词语，而要用明确的修饰语加以限制，以避免读者误会和影响对论文的理解；③尽量不用华丽的词藻来描述和带感情色彩的语句来表意，通常不用比拟、双关、借代、反语等修辞手法；④语言表达规范准确，使用准确的术语、标准的量名称及法定计量单位，数据、文字、符号以及插图、表格、式子等的表达均应准确、简洁、规范。

（3）科技论文的过程是其形成的整个过程，其科学性要求作者在研究和写作中要有科学态度和科学精神，在从选题、收集材料、论证问题，到研究结束、形成正式论文的一系列过程中，都要用实事求是的态度对待一切问题，踏踏实实、精益求精，不可草率马虎、武断轻言，更不可伪造数据、谎报成果甚至抄袭剽窃。

4. 规范性

规范性是科技写作不同于文学创作或人文写作的一个重要特点，它是科技论文的标准化特性和结构特点。科技论文要求脉络清晰、结构严谨、前提完备、演算正确、符号规范、语言通顺、图表清晰、推断合理、前后呼应、自成系统，规范性这一特点决定了论文的行文具有简洁平易性，即要用准确的专业术语或通俗易懂的语言表述科学道理，做到语句通顺，表达准确、鲜明、协调，语言自然而优美，内容深刻而完备。

撰写科技论文是为了交流、传播和储存新的科技信息，最终让他人方便地使用这些信息。因此科技论文必须按一定的体例格式来写作，要有很好的可理解性和可读性，在文字表达上，语言准确、简明、通顺，层次分明、条理清楚，论述严谨、推理恰当；在技术表达上，正确使用名词术语、量和单位，正确表达数字、符号和式子，科学设计插图、表格，规范引用（标注和著录）参考文献。不规范的论文会影响其可理解性和可读性，最终将降低其发表价值，甚至使读者对其真实性和可靠性产生怀疑，而产生厌烦情绪。

5. 法规性

科技论文发表是给别人看的，具有广阔的宣传性、指引性，因此就不能无约束、无纪律地任性写作。科技论文要以遵纪守法、不损害国家和民族利益为前提，这就是科技论文的法规性，表现在政治性、法律性和保密性几个方面。

科技论文主要讲述科技内容，一般很少有政治方面的表达，但有时也会涉及一些政治性问题。例如：讲述科技发展方向和服务对象时，可能涉及国家经济、科技政策；提到某些国家和地区时，可能涉及国家领土主权和对外关系问题；翻译国外科技论著时，可能遇到其中某些提法与国家法律、方针、政策相抵触以及不合国情之处。科技论文如果在这些方面出现问题，就会犯政治性错误。

科技论文如同私人财产一样，一经发表就受到国家法律的保护，作者在拥有版权的同时又负有多方面的责任（中国宪法、民法通则、著作权法、专利法、商标法等对知识产权有明确的规定，著作权是知识产权的一种重要类别）。对于论文内容，政治上要符合国家法律法规，科学上要经得起实践检验，道德（伦理）上要保证不存在抄袭剽窃。

科学研究是为探索真理，揭示事物存在、发展的客观规律，其成果是对整个人类的贡献，其本身没有保密问题。但是，不同国家有各自的利益，为了维护国家的安全和利益，科技论文也需保守国家机密。比如在中国，科技论文写作须遵守《中华人民共和国保守国家秘密法》《科学技术保密规定》及有关条例的规定，在一定时间和范围内施行保密，有些项目虽不属保密范围，但受专利法的保护。世界上其他国家也是这样做的。

科技论文中不能引用秘密资料和内部文件，不能发表尚未公布的国家和地区计划。引用全国性的统计数字应以国家政府和权威部门正式公布的为准。未经公布的国家特有资源和尚未公开的工艺、秘方，还没有的新发明、重大科技成果和关键技术，各项专利，与国防和国家安全有关或涉及国家重大经济利益的项目，以及医疗秘方、疫情、发病率、死亡率等，都属于保密范围，应谨慎对待、妥善处理。

6. 伦理性

科技论文的伦理性问题近年来有增多的趋势，对这个问题的关注也似乎越来越多，在各种相关会议、场合一般不会缺少这方面的报告、讨论，有些期刊的领导或编辑还专门发文讲述这个问题。一般认为，期刊的编辑是发表高质量论文的关键，与期刊的编委会和同行专家共同来保障期刊发文的质量，但实际发文中还是出现了这样那样的伦理或学术不端问题。期刊出版商一般会强烈要求其期刊成员加入出版伦理委员会（The Committee on Publication Ethics，COPE），让编辑了解其工作机制，致力于对各种学术不端行为指控的处理，以保证研究内容的完整性。

期刊出版单位为保证期刊出版质量，通常会在其《作者须知》（《投稿须知》《征稿简则》）中写上伦理声明，规定作者对其所投稿件的研究工作的完整性应承担的伦理责任。伦理声明聚焦作者伦理和职业道德一般原则，还可实时修改，一般包括三个方面：①潜在的利益冲突（Potential conflicts of interest）；②涉及人类和（或）动物的研究（Research involving human participants and/or animals）；③知情告知（Informed consent）。

目前，期刊出版单位常使用 CrossCheck 软件来检查伦理问题（在审稿系统中安装 CrossCheck 软件）。CrossCheck 是 CrossRef 的一个创新软件，旨在帮助出版单位来查证稿件（稿件的各个版本，包括原稿和修改稿）的原创性。CrossCheck 包含两个产品：学术出版物数据库 CrossCheck；基于此数据库来检查权威原创的网络工具 iThenticate。

有关内容见 COPE 官网（http：//publicationethics.org/）。

1.1.2 科技论文的分类

科技论文可从多个角度进行分类，如图 1-1 所示。

按学科领域，科技论文分为自然、社会、思维、人体等类或基础、农业、工业、医药等类，自然类分为基础、应用等类，社会类分为语言、经济等类……，其中每个子类、子子类还可继续往下细分。

按发挥作用，科技论文分为学术、技术和学位类。学术论文发表学术成果，通常是某一学术课题在理论、实验或观测性上具有新的科学研究成果或创新见解的科学记录，或是某种原理应用于实际中取得新进展的科学总结，起着公布成果、交流信息、丰富科学理论、推动科技发展的作用。技术论文报道工程技术应用成果，通常是应用已有理论来解决设计、技术、工艺、设备、材料等具体技术问题而获得的先进、实用和科学的手段和方法，对技术进步和生产力提高起直接推动作用。学位论文用来申请学位而向学位授予单位提交，要求作者详细论述，充分表达研究成果，并反映其知识获取和科学研究的能力，又可分为学士论文、硕士论文和博士论文三类。学术论文篇幅适中，比学位论文精练、比技术论文深厚。

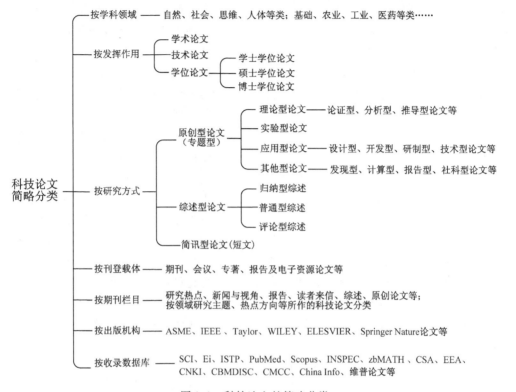

图 1-1 科技论文的简略分类

按刊登载体，科技论文分为期刊、会议、专著、报告、电子资源论文等类。期刊论文是最重要、最多的一类；会议论文成为科技人员们发表论文的第二重要园地，会议论文发文较多，评审把关不那么严格，因此在质量上往往比期刊论文逊色不少；专著、报告等也会刊登论文，对应的论文就是专著论文、报告论文；目前电子资源论文越来越普遍。

按期刊类别，科技论文分为原创、综述、来信、热点等类。原创类期刊主要登原创论文，可加上少量综述；综述类期刊一般只刊登综述；混合类期刊刊登的文章类别较多，通常设置几个栏目，将类别相同的文章组织在一起。SCI期刊的代表性栏目有研究热点、新闻与视角、报告、读者来信、综述、原创论文或按领域研究主题、热点方向等所作的分类（如交叉与前沿、机构与机器人、智能材料、运载工程、仪器与测试技术、再生能源与工程热物理等）。

科技论文还可有按出版机构的分类，如ASME、IEEE、Taylor、WILEY、ELESVIER论文，相应的期刊为ASME、IEEE、Taylor等期刊；还可有按收录数据库的分类，如SCI、Ei、ISTP、PubMed、Scopus、INSPEC、zbMATH论文，相应的期刊为SCI、Ei、ISTP等期刊。

对作者具体写作最直接相关的应是按研究方式（或内容）的科技论文分类，下面稍详细讲述。

从大的类或层面来说，科学研究有的是以具体客观事物为研究对象，探究其本质、运行机制和存在方式，进而获得其科学研究的新成果，这类成果即为原创类成果，用来完善或补充现有科学技术，对应的论文即为原创型论文（也称专题型论文）；有的是以已有研究成果（主要为文献资料）为研究对象，分析某领域或研究点的研究现状、发展规律、存在问题和前景展望，进而获得科学研究发展的新成果，这类成果即为综述类成果，用来指导科学技术发展，对应的论文即为综述型论文；有的不以获得科学研究或科学研究发展的新成果为目标，而是用来发布科研信息、发表评论认识、共享科研发现或展现技术技巧，这类内容具有资讯的性质，对应的论文为简讯型论文（简讯型短文，平常多称简讯型文章）。

从中间的类或层面来说，科技论文也有不同的分类。比如原创型论文中，有的是先提出某种假说，然后进行数学推导、逻辑推理或用实验结果进行检验，往往以论述或论证为中心，提出新理论或补充和发展原理论或否定原理论，这类论文即为理论型论文；有的是通过实验来发现新现象、寻找科学规律或验证某种理论和假说，实验结果的科学记录和总结可作为研究成果，这类论文即为实验型论文；有的应用现有成熟的理论、方法、技术来改进现有事物或产生新事物，即进行发明和创造，虽然可能没有重大原创，却具有先进性、实用性和科学性，有一定的创新性，这类论文即为应用型论文。

从小的类或层面来说，科技论文还可有不同的分类，如理论型论文有论证、分析、推导等类，应用型论文有设计、开发、研制等类，简讯型论文有简讯和简报类。

1. 原创型论文

原创型论文（Original Paper 或 Original Article）又称研究型论文或原创论文、研究论文，也称专题型论文，是指对具体问题如理论、实验（试验）、技术方案、设计方法等予以完整阐述，给出目前没有的新理论、新方法，或设计新试验、给出新方案。此类论文用来对某一领域、学科或某项工作等发表议论（立论和驳论），通过分析论证，提出创新理论、观点或试验发现等。

原创型论文写作要求：完整报道最新研究成果，阐述新理论、新见解、新技术、新产品、新工艺及最优解决方案等。

（1）理论型论文

理论型论文一般以某学科范畴中某课题或论题的纯粹抽象理论问题为研究对象，基于对相关成果的严密理论推导和分析，概括和总结已有理论，探讨客观对象内在规律，提出正面思想、主张、观点和见解，建构新理论。理论推导是运用理论对事物内在规律进行推导并求解，需借助数学式来推导和证明。理论分析是用计算方法结合定理、定律等理论依据分析实际问题，强调原理上可行，实践上是否可行还有待进一步验证。

理论型论文写作要求：追溯理论发展过程，提炼理论框架，分析已有理论，比较各种理论优劣；考查一个理论的内部与外部的一致性，理论本身是否自相矛盾，以及理论与实验观测结果是否矛盾；通常需要建立数学模型或给出计算方法。

理论型论文按具体研究方式可分为论证、推导和分析等类。

1）论证型论文。主要对基础科学命题作论述与证明，如对基础学科（数学、物理、化学、天文、地理、生物等）及其他众多应用学科的公理、定理、原理、原则、模型或假设的建立、论证及其适用范围、使用条件进行讨论。写作要求：议论要素完备，论点鲜明，论据充分，论证合理，结果可信。

2）推导型论文。主要对所提出的新假说由数学推导、假设、证明和逻辑推理来得到新理论（包括定理、定律和法则）。写作要求：数学推导科学准确，逻辑推理严谨严密，定义和概念准确可靠，所得的结论无懈可击。

3）分析型论文。主要对已有理论和新假说（新的设想、原理、模型、机构、材料、工艺、样品等）作理论分析，对已有理论进行完善、补充或修正。写作要求：论证分析严谨，数学运算正确，资料数据可靠，结果、结论可信，通过了实验验证。

(2) 实验型论文

实验型论文主要是为检验某一科学理论或假说，或为发明创造，或为解决实际问题，有计划、目的地进行，做好科学实验，再辅以调查与考察、检阅与分析、模拟与想象等环节，如实记述实验材料与方法、严格记录实验过程，准确呈现实验结果，得到系统的观测现象、实验数据或效果效能等较为重要的原始资料，并给予归纳、总结和分析，得出创新性结论。准确齐备的原始资料往往是进一步深入研究的依据与基础。

实验型论文写作要求：以科学实验为前提，包括实验的设计、实施、研究（实验是创立理论的基础和先导，是发现和检验真理的依据）；介绍实验目的，说明实验的材料、方法和过程，展现实验的结果（记实性），对结果分析、讨论，归纳、总结科学规律；对根据已知和可靠的科学事实进行推导、猜测而提出新假说（创见性）进行验证，保证其科学性（确证性）。

实验型论文不同于一般的实验报告，写作重点应放在研究上，追求的是可靠的理论依据、先进的实验方案、创新的实验方法、适用的测试手段、准确的数据处理、严密的分析论证及可信的结果与结论，而非实验材料的罗列叠加和实验过程的流水明细。

(3) 应用型论文

应用型论文是将已有研究成果（包括别人或作者自己）应用于研发新事物或解决实际问题，包括对象设计、软件开发、技术研究、系统集成、算法改进、工艺完善、技术改良、产品研制、材料发展、模拟仿真等，多由从事应用型研究（如设计、开发）的科技人员来撰写。

依据具体工作的类别，可对此类论文分类。例如：以设计结果为主体内容的称为设计型论文，如对某工程、技术和管理问题所做的计算机程序设计，对某系统、工程方案、机构、产品等所做的计算机辅助和优化设计等；以开发结果为主体内容的称为开发型论文，如对某产品、系统、技术、配方、材料的某个功能的实现、改进，或某具体问题的解决而开发出来的功能模块、结构组件、控制系统、算法程序、源代码、系统平台、应用软件、新型配方、改进方法等；以研制出完整或相对完整的独立实体产品为主体内容的称为研制型论文，如实现某种用途或用于某场合的实体机器、设备、设施、工具、仪器、仪表、艺术品、材料、药品及其组件、部件或成分；以使用某种技术而获得新成果为主体内容的称为技术型论文，如某种工艺、算法、模型、流程或方案等的应用。

应用型论文写作要求：内容有新意、有创意，计算结果准确合理，模型建立和参数选择合理，编制的程序能正常运行，研制的产品经过实验、生产和使用证实，调制、配制的物质或材料要经过使用考核等。

(4) 其他型论文

科技论文还有一些类型，属于原创型，但不好说是理论型、实验型还是应用型，既可能属于其中的一种，也可属于几种的融合。下面列举几类。

1) 发现型论文。此类论文主要用来记述被发现事物的背景、现象、本质、特性、运动变化规律及人类使用这种发现的前景。发明型论文是发现型的特殊形式，用来阐述所发明的装备、系统、工具、材料、工艺、模型、配方等的功效、性能、特点、原理及使用条件等。

2) 计算型论文。此类论文主要用来提出和讨论不同类型（包括不同边界和初始条件）的数学或物理方程的数值计算方法，数列或数字运算方法，计算机辅助设计（CAD）方法，计算机在不同领域的应用原理、数据结构、操作方法，或进行收敛性、稳定性、精度分析等。其内容往往能成为计算机软件进一步开发的基础。有的计算型论文可列为推导型论文。

3）报告型论文。科技报告有两类：描述某项科学技术研究的结果、进展或一项技术研制、实验、评价的结果；论述某项科学技术问题的现状和发展。前一类仅是结果的陈述，没有"论"的要素，不能算是科技论文；后一类是现状和发展的议论和认识，明显含有"论"，可算作科技论文。报告型论文就是指以上第二类科技报告，既有结果又有认识的科技报告当然也属科技论文。

4）社科型论文。科学研究的对象有的属于自然科学或工程技术范畴，但对其撰写的论文采用了类似于社会科学的表述方式，即用调查研究所得的可信事实或数据来论证新观点，这类论文称之为社科型论文。在科学和学科越来越交叉和融合的时代，科技的范畴已大大拓展，早已不是过去那种纯自然的科学观了，请读者参看 1.2 节中有关 Nature 出版集团（NPG）期刊（论文）的学科分类。

2. 综述型论文

综述型论文（Review）也称综述论义，简称综述，是将已发表的文献资料作为原始素材（研究对象）进行研究而撰写的论文。综述包括"综"和"述"两个方面："综"是作者对所写专题相关的现有大量素材进行归纳整理、综合分析，使材料更加精炼、明确，更有层次和逻辑性；"述"是评述，是对"综"的结果作较为全面、深入、系统的论述和评价，提出在特定时期内某领域或研究点的演变规律和发展趋势。可见，综述是对某一专题、领域的历史背景、前人工作、争论焦点、研究现状与发展前景等，以作者自己的观点所写成的严谨而系统的评论、资料性科技论文。它有几个显著的特点：①对某领域或研究点的研究历史、现状、进展及未来趋势（内容）进行综合、可靠的分析和详细、系统的阐述（过程），得出结构性、趋势性、前瞻性、指导性结论（结果）；②资料充分详实，总结系统全面；③结论或观点明确，指出存在的问题和未来发展的方向；④篇幅长，参考文献较多；⑤有高屋建瓴和权威性的观点，多由领域和行业领军人物或权威专家撰写。

综述较为特殊，所做分析和评价是在已有文献的基础上进行的，要求作者博览群书，综合介绍、分析、评述特定学科和专业领域的最新研究成果和发展趋势，表明作者自己的观点，对发展做出科学预测，提出较中肯的意见和建设性建议，但并不要求在研究内容上具有首创性。一篇好的综述通常提出或介绍某些未曾发表过的新资料和新思想，具有权威性和指导性，对所讨论学科的进一步发展能够起到指导与引领作用。

依据文献资料范围，综述可分为大综述、小综述，前者是对整个领域的相关文献资料进行总结，后者是对与作者自己研究课题（某研究点）直接相关的文献资料进行总结。根据搜集的原始文献资料数量、提炼加工程度、组织写作形式及学术水平的高低，综述可分为归纳型（资料整理型）、普通型和评论型（综合研究型）三类。

（1）归纳型综述。这是作者将搜集到的文献资料进行整理归纳，按一定顺序分类排列，使其互相关联、前后连贯，而撰写成的具有一定条理性、系统性和逻辑性的综述。它能在一定程度上反映出某一专题、领域的当前研究现状与进展，但较难有作者自己的见解和观点。

（2）普通型综述。这是具有一定学术水平的作者，在搜集较多文献资料的基础上撰写成的系统性和逻辑性比较强的综述，行文中能表达出作者自己的观点或倾向性。它对从事某专题、某领域工作的读者有一定的指导意义和参考价值。

（3）评论型综述。这是某领域较高学

术水平和较高造诣的作者，在搜集大量文献的基础上，对原始文献资料归纳整理、综合分析，而撰写的反映当前该领域研究进展和发展前景的议论性综述。其逻辑性强，有较多作者自己的见解和评论，对读者研究工作有普遍指导意义。

综述型论文写作要求：资料全而新，有足够的代表性（时间、内容上），作者立足点高、眼光远，问题综合恰当、分析在理，意见、建议中肯，题目稍大（可能笼统），引文较多，篇幅较长。

综述反映出某一专题、领域在一定时期内的研究工作进展情况，将该专题、领域及其分支学科的新的进展、发现、趋势、水平、原理和技术等较全面地呈现出来，使读者特别是从事该专题、领域研究的读者受益，因此往往成为教学、科研和生产的重要参考资料。

理论型、综述型论文在结构上类似，但前者主要引用那些对建构理论有作用的资料，而后者引用的资料就宽泛多了，只要对表述某种研究现状和发展趋势有用的就可引用。

3. 简讯型论文

简讯型论文以简讯、简报为主，快速报道最新科技成果或行业资讯，同时加进个人主观评价和认识。这类论文篇幅短，简明扼要，严格讲可能不属于学术范畴，但在SCI期刊上有增多的趋势，对科技发展的作用越来越大，在科学评价、学术引证方面也有重要作用，而且其中包含个人认识和评价，因此将其列为学术范畴也是有道理的。但要注意，这类文章是指加进（发表）个人观点的那类，而纯粹新闻资讯的那类就不属论文范畴，更谈不上学术了。

简讯型论文报道内容较广，各领域、学科及其中的各层面、方面都可用来报道，具体类别较多。

1.1.3 科技论文概念链

科学技术（科技）依靠知识的继承、交流和传播而发展，科技工作者发表论文是实现继承、交流和传播的主要方式。作为科学研究（科研）的结果，科研成果要用科技论文来表述与传播，科技论文则是科研成果的标志，是科技信息传递、存储的重要载体。科学、技术、科研、科研成果和有关概念环环相扣、紧密关联，组成一个概念链体系，如图1-2所示。

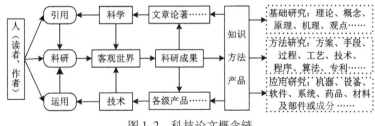

图1-2 科技论文概念链

人通过科研认识和改造客观世界，获得科研成果。科研成果有两类，思想认识上的文章论著（如论文）和生产实践上的各级产品等，前一类进入学问体系成为科学，后一类用来改造客观世界成为技术。人在科研中，引用科学（如写论文时引用别的论文中的理论、知识、见解、观点等），运用技术（如制定方案、做实验、结果记录、讨论、分析、研发），形成对客观世界的新的认识和改造客观世界的新的能力。科技论文的生命力在于发表后对科技进步所产生的促进、推动作用，因此对论文的评价也非常重要。

用来发表的科研成果大体上包括知识、方法和产品三个层面，知识是对客观世界的认识，方法是认识和改造客观世界的手段，产品是改造客观世界的工具。知识包括理论、概念、原理、机理、机制、观点、认识等，大体对应基础研究；方法包括方案、手段、过程、工艺、技术、程序、算法等，大体对应方法研究；产品包括机器、设备、仪器、仪表、系统、软件、药品、材料及部件或成分等，大体对应应用研究。

1.2 SCI 论文的分类

下面按目前 SCI 期刊的学科或专业方向及期刊栏目或文体，对 SCI 论文进行简单分类。

1.2.1 按学科或专业方向

SCI 期刊有明显的学科或专业方向属性，同领域期刊的学科或专业方向可以相同，也可以不同。例如：*Nature* 和 *Science* 几乎涵盖了自然、社会的所有学科和专业方向；*Cell* 主要针对实验生物学，主要有 cell biology、stem cells、new molecule、totipotency、cell biology、biochemistry and molecular biology、biology、iPS cells（induced pluripotent stem cells）、poly adenylate（polyA）tail 等学科和专业方向；*Cell Research* 主要有 stem cells、iPS cells、cell biology、cell apoptosis、plant biology、molecular genetics、plant epigenetics、immune cell、omics、cell differentiation、RNA、cell signaling pathway、medicine、miRNA、signal transduction 等；*Light：Science & Applications* 主要有 small-scale optics、optical material processing、optics in life science and the environment、special optics、optical data transmission、optical measurement、optical materials、manufacture of optical elements、organic optoelectronics、guided light 等。

以 Nature 出版集团（NPG）为例，2018 年其旗下大约有 150 种期刊，虽然期刊间在学科或专业方向上可能有重叠，但各期刊报道范围或侧重不同，其论文涵盖 biological sciences、health sciences、social sciences、earth and environmental sciences、humanities、physical sciences、business and commerce、scientific community and society 八大学科方向，每个大类下又包括多个子类（子类总计 100 多个，有的子类可能兼属几个类别），见表 1-1。

1.2.2 按期刊栏目或文体

SCI 期刊通常按其栏目或文体来组织刊发论文（按文体设置栏目，或按栏目组织论文），类别相同的集中在同一组内，在期刊目录上设置栏目，在论文页面显著位置（书眉线上方或下方）注明文体（有的仅在论文首页注明）。原创类期刊主要刊登原创论文加少量综述，综述类一般只刊登综述，混合类可以刊登多种文体。下面大体看看一些名刊的栏目或文体。

Nature 的常见栏目或文体有 Editorial、Opinion、News、News & Views、News Feature、News in Brief、Research Highlights、Article、Reviews Article、Book Review、Books & Arts、Correspondence、Erratum、Letter、Matters Arising、Miscellany、Obituary、Scientific Correspondence、Supplement to Nature 等。

Science 的常见栏目或文体有 This Week in *Science*（Research in *Science* Journals）、Editorial、Editors' Choice（This Week in Other Journals）、Products & Materials、In Brief、In Depth、Feature、Working Life、Letters、Policy Forum、Perspectives、Research Articles、Reports 等。

Cell Research 的常见栏目或文体有 Editorial、Letter、Review、Original Articles、Letters to the Editor 等。

Light：Science & Applications 的常见栏目或文体有 Editorial、News and Views、Research Highlights、Reviews、Original Articles、Letters to the Editor 等。

第1章 绪 论

表1-1 NPG 期刊（论文）的学科方向（2018）

Biological sciences	Health sciences	Social sciences	Earth and environmental sciences
• Biochemistry • Biological techniques • Biophysics • Biotechnology • Cancer • Cell biology • Chemical biology • Computational biology and bioinformatics • Developmental biology • Drug discovery • Ecology • Evolution • Genetics • Immunology • Microbiology • Molecular biology • Neuroscience • Physiology • Plant sciences • Psychology • Stem cells • Structural biology • Systems biology • Zoology	• Anatomy • Biomarkers • Cardiology • Diseases • Endocrinology • Gastroenterology • Health care • Health occupations • Medical research • Molecular medicine • Nephrology • Neurology • Oncology • Pathogenesis • Rheumatology • Risk factors • Signs and symptoms • Urology	• Anthropology • Business and management • Complex networks • Criminology • Cultural and media studies • Development studies • Economics • Education • Environmental studies • Finance • Geography • History • Language and linguistics • Politics and international relations • Psychology • Science, technology and society • Social policy • Sociology	• Biogeochemistry • Climate sciences • Ecology • Environmental sciences • Environmental social sciences • Hydrology • Limnology • Natural hazards • Ocean sciences • Planetary science • Solid Earth sciences • Space physics
Humanities	Physical sciences	Business and commerce	Scientific community and society
• Complex networks • Cultural and media studies • Health humanities • History • Language and linguistics • Literature • Medical humanities • Philosophy • Religion • Theatre and performance studies	• Astronomy and planetary science • Chemistry • Energy science and technology • Engineering • Materials science • Mathematics and computing • Nanoscience and technology • Optics and photonics • Physics	• Agriculture • Business and industry • Developing world • Energy and society • Forestry • Geography • Scientific community • Social sciences • Water resources	• Business and management • Economics • Finance • Information systems and information technology • Operational research

Cell 的栏目设置较为特别，它是在传统的期刊栏目或文体类别上提升一级设置为按某种视角来分类的栏目名称，这样相同文体就可能分布到不同栏目下了（不同于常规的相同文体集中在相同栏目下）。例如，2018年 *Cell* 某期的栏目设置是：Leading Edge：Stem Cells（含文体 Review）、Free Featured Article（含文体 Article）、Free Featured Leading Edge、Trending（含文体Article、Resource）、Metabolism（含文体Perspective、Review、Minireview、Primer）。

学术期刊还经常出版专刊、专栏（Special Issue、Special Column），这是目前学术期刊的一种常态，常在期刊栏目中增加相应的栏目名称，如"Special Issue：Composite Materials"，再在该栏目下放置各类文体，如Introduction to Special Issue、Reviews 和Article 等。

SCI 期刊中除 Reviews 和 Original Articles 外，其余的文体多数是资讯类的，能吸引大众眼球，引起广泛关注，通常不是研究人员或普通作者的自由投稿，而多由期刊的编辑和记者撰写或邀请别人来撰写。作者应了解栏目、熟悉文体、对症下药、有的放矢、按文体要求写作，最终提高写作的目的性、针对性及投稿的有效性和录用率。

1.3 SCI 论文价值体系

SCI 论文有四个显著特征，一是价值高（内容好）；二是结构好；三是语言好；四是质量高。价值是目标，结构是形式，语言是材料，质量是保障，过程是落实（行动），这每一项都是一个系统（价值体系、结构体系、语言体系、质量体系、过程体系），加起来便形成一个更大的系统，描绘出 SCI 论文的壮丽蓝图。

SCI 论文的价值在于其有用性，对提高人们认识、改造世界的水平和能力有较大影响和作用。它引用了最新实验数据、理论资料，对原有材料进行最新整理，提出、解决或创造了前人所没有的普遍性新理论、新技术和新工艺。它能发前人所未发，在科学理论、方法或实践上获得新进展或新突破，富有创造性、科学性，有很大价值；或能在前人基础上有所发现、发明，富有一定创造性，有较大价值；或能为人类知识和技术宝库增加新的库藏，无论创新程度如何，只要有所创新，就有价值。

笔者根据 Nature 内容为王的选文标准，将 SCI 论文的价值概括为六个方面，它们之间相互作用和影响，形成一个以原创性为核心的价值体系，如图1-3 所示。

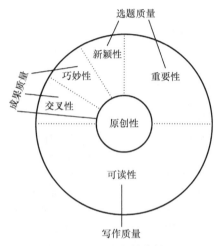

图1-3　SCI 论文价值体系

1.3.1 原创性

原创性即原始性，指论文的研究成果必须是作者自己独立工作的结果，是他人或自己没有发表过的，其核心部分的任何内容都没有在其他出版物发表过或向其他出版物投过稿。原创性强调是否首次报道，重在首创，是 SCI 论文价值体系的核心要素（第一重要要素），在人类认识和改造世界的征途中发挥着相当重要的作用。

从古至今不知有过多少个科学理论创建和技术发明，无不闪耀着辉煌的原创光芒。例如：

1953 年 5 月 25 日，美国科学家 Watson（沃森）和英国科学家 Crick（克里克）在 Nature 上发文，报告了重要发现——"两条以磷酸为骨架的链相互缠绕形成了双螺旋结构，氢键把它们连结在一起"，首次提出 DNA 双螺旋模型，阐明复杂 DNA 分子的二级结构。

1965 年，英国 Mckenzin（麦肯齐）和美国 Morgan（摩根）首次在 Nature 发文，提出板块构造说，并讨论其在球面运动的几何学问题，形成一种新的大陆漂移说，认为大陆板块是被动地伏在构造板块之上受地幔对流的影响作难以控制的运动，延伸了海底扩张说。

1997 年 2 月 27 日，英国科学家 Wilmut（威尔穆特）在 Nature 发表了利用成年哺乳动物体细胞核移植技术培育出克隆羊多莉的研究论文，在世界生物技术领域引发了强烈的轰动。

在 Nature 原创发文的还有：1932 年 Chadwick（查德威克）的中子发现（discovery of the neutron）；1960 年 Maiman（梅曼）的激光发现（demonstration of the laser）；1973 年 Lauterbur（劳特布尔）的磁共振成像（magnetic resonance imaging）；1990 年 Burroughes（伯勒德）等的聚合物发光二极管（Polymer LEDs）……。这样的例子不胜枚举，加起来汇聚成今天这座宏伟的科技大厦。

原创为何如此重要呢？不妨看看日本诺贝尔奖"井喷"现象及其给予的启示。①

日本从 1949 年第一次获诺奖到 2018 年，已有 27 位诺奖得主，出现了诺奖"井喷"现象。日本获诺奖人数虽然较多，但发表在 Nature、Science 等国际顶尖期刊的论文并不多，有些还未发表在高影响因子的期刊上，甚至还没有发表在英文期刊上。这其中的原因是什么呢？

2001 年，日本出台"第二个科学技术基本计划"，明确提出"50 年要拿 50 个诺奖"的目标。计划一提出就反响强烈，科学家认为科研有不确定性，不能像生产丰田汽车一样来生产诺奖。诺贝尔化学奖得主、名古屋大学野依良治教授公开批评政府没有头脑。出人意料的是，从 2001 到 2018 年，日本已有 18 人获诺奖，平均每年拿下一个，计划进行时间尚未过半，已经完成了超出目标 1/2 的数量（其中在 2000 年前拿到的只占 1/3）。按诺奖评选规则，最后有一个调查过程，进入此过程的日本科学家数量很大，说明日本未来获诺奖的前景光明。

1932 年，25 岁的大阪大学讲师汤川秀树从事科研教学工作，并同时备战攻读博士学位。1935 年，他在日本本土学术期刊《日本物理 - 数学会刊》发表论文"论基本粒子的作用"，首次提出介子理论，预言介子的存在。1938 年，他获物理学博士学位。1946 年，他在京都大学创办了日本本土刊物《理论物理学进展》，向国外推介日本理论物理学的研究成果，帮助日本科学家克服因国际竞争和语言障碍等对发表创新思想不利的因素。1949 年，他获诺贝尔物理学奖。

1973 年，汤川秀树的两名年轻助教小林诚和益川敏英合作，在《理论物理学进展》发表论文"弱相互作用可重整化理论中的 cp 破坏"，提出著名的小林 - 益川模型，解释了弱相互作用中的电荷宇称对称性破缺。2008 年，小林诚和益川敏英获诺贝尔物理学奖。从该刊国际学术界逐渐看到汤川秀树本人的高水平学术论文以及一批日本科学家的原创性研究，可以说是这本期刊最终培养出多个物理学诺奖得主。

有趣的是，益川敏英虽是科学家，但不懂英文，既不会用英文交流，也不能在英文刊发表文章，几乎不看国外期刊，他获诺奖后的第一个要求是领奖时可否讲日语，也就在那时，他才办了人生第一本护照出了一次国。那么这样的科学家也能折下科学桂冠，是否有点奇怪呢？

诺奖评选有个特别规则——某研究进入诺奖评审程序时，评奖委员会一定要了解其当时的真实情况或原始记录，不管用什么语

---

① 这部分内容较多引用参考文献 [8]。

言记录,是否发表或发表在哪里,只要谁最先提出,当时记录了,就会被认定。其中,尊重"原创"是核心。可见日本出现诺奖"井喷"现象,绝非偶然,也不奇怪,是原创起了作用。

那么日本诺奖"井喷"现象能给予我们什么启示呢?笔者认为至少有以下方面值得借鉴。

1)研究人员应沉下心来多做原创研究,多思考基本的科学问题。新媒体发展快速,原创机会增多,研究人员应及时记录科学发现和灵感。有了大数据,可开展数据驱动型或大数据科研,写论文能产生原创,分析数据也能产生原创。

2)从学术研究的内容与质量而言,论文用什么语言写并无差别,各种语言的论文都要内容上有新发现、写作上遵守规范、表述上讲求条理……,而 SCI 期刊多是英文期刊,除英文外的其他语言期刊(非 SCI 期刊)还大量存在,从这个意义上讲,期刊和论文无 SCI 之分。

3)鼓励年轻学者多做原创研究,也可为办刊所借鉴,如 Nature、Science 等名刊顺应科学、学科发展,不断创刊、合作办刊来扩大规模和提升影响的办刊模式,丰富的栏目设置、独到的论文内涵、严格的审稿选稿制度等,都是我们应该学习的可贵之处。

4)中国期刊国际化正在路上,英文刊更占优势,但只要增强自信,中文刊国际化也是没有问题的,目前正是大好时机。中国影响力高的期刊要保持风格、品牌,多为年轻学者成长创造条件,比如对年轻学者的论文实施倾斜政策,为研究生论文写作进行培训等。

5)中国学者发表论文越来越多,但原创论文相对较少。管理者喜欢用影响因子(IF)这一硬指标进行评价,但评价造成的负面效果远远超出 IF 自身的内涵。过分依赖 IF 反映出管理者自信不足,不能通过自己的眼睛来判断,而是通过他人的标准来评价,事实上只有科学家最了解科学工作本身。相信唯 IF 评价是一个历史阶段产物,从量到质转变有个过程,但这个怪象迟早会退出历史舞台。

6)日本科研规模总体较小,但在科研人才培养方面有借鉴之处,如大力倡导学习国外先进经验、允许学生用英文撰写学位论文、为有原创精神的学生大开绿灯等。

7)一位接待过诺奖评委的日本科学官员曾说过:"如果中国科学家获诺奖,很可能最早出现在女性身上,因为中国女科学家的地位、规模及科研热情超过了任何一个国家。"中国首位获诺贝尔拉斯克医学奖的屠呦呦确是女性,印证了这位官员的说法。

8)中国科学家获诺奖是很有希望的。中国女性从事科研的规模不仅名列前茅,而且还有一批女科学家在默默地帮助别人,因此中国科学家中的女性更有优势获诺奖。

有的读者会有疑惑,本书是讲述 SCI 论文的,这里偏偏似乎在否定 SCI,这不是自相矛盾吗?其实,笔者完全没有否定 SCI,而是否定现实中的唯 SCI 的唯 IF 评价。SCI 的评价体系本来有很多指标,管理部门为何不均衡考虑,而只对 IF 情有独钟呢?还有那么多高水平的非 SCI 论文,为何将 SCI 论文置于其他期刊之上呢?SCI 评价本是针对期刊的,为何偏偏有人用来评价论文呢?笔者在本书开始就已经对 SCI 论文作过描述,它是高水平论文的一个子集,高水平是它的一个显著特征,原创性以及后面几个其他特征均为所有高水平论文的必备特征,更不用说是 SCI 论文了。所以,SCI 论文的高水平与 SCI 期刊的评价是两回事。

1.3.2 重要性

重要性指论文的内容至少对同一领域的研究人员有重要参考价值。实际中很多投稿未经审稿就被退稿,并非因为学术论点错误,而是因为其关键内容远未达到最终应有的研究结果，往往只是一个新概念形成的中间步骤，产生不了实际作用，谈不上什么重要性。重要性与原创性紧密相关，有原创性必有重要性，有重要性不一定有原创性。例如以下示例中，原创性尽显光芒，而重要性也必相随。

Watson、Crick提出的DNA双螺旋模型，显示出DNA分子在细胞分裂时能自我复制，能完善地解释生命体为繁衍后代，物种要保持稳定，细胞内必有遗传属性和复制能力的机制。这是生物学领域的一座里程碑，标志着分子生物学时代的开端，怎样评价其重要性都不过分[一]。

Mckenzin、Morgan提出的板块构造说是海底扩张说的具体延伸，是一种新的大陆漂移说。随后于1968年，他们和法国的Lepichen（勒比雄）基于大陆漂移说、地幔对流说和海底扩张说，进一步把陆地和海底统一起来考虑，认为洋底和陆地都是岩石圈的一个组成部分，提出一种全新的大陆板块学说[二]。此学说是20世纪地球理论最伟大的发现，可以说是地球科学在20世纪60年代的一场活动地球革命，其重要性可见一斑。

Wilmut提出的克隆羊原理和技术，因用于克隆人是完全可能的，故立即在世界范围内包括中国掀起了一场以"克隆人"为中心议题的轩然大波。无论是政府首脑还是平民百姓，无论是本领域专家还是哲学、社会学家，都纷纷卷入了这场所谓的克隆热潮之中，争论的问题涉及自然、社会、科技、政治、法律、哲学、伦理、道德、价值乃至精神、信念等广泛领域，其重要性不言而喻。

目前中国的研究论文很多，但原创的不多。原创确实来之不易，当然，衡量论文的价值也不能只看原创，因为如果只看原创，那么可能就没有多少论文来发表了。但我们应该首先鼓励论文的原创性，其次再去倡导论文的重要性。论文没有原创性可以原谅，但没有重要性则是不应该的，重要性是SCI论文价值体系的第二重要要素。

1.3.3 新颖性

新颖性就是有新意，指论文报道的内容鲜为人知，非公知公用、模仿抄袭的，有别人学习和借鉴之处，但不要求必须是原创的。若是模仿，也应仿中有变；若是老问题，也应老中有新，都应从"新"的角度阐明问题（古方今用、老药新用、旧法改进等）。新颖性要求论文的内容至少包含某种新鲜的成分、结果，既可以是对以前人们未知的某种现象的描述，也可以是向以前被人们广为接受的某个假设提出质疑，或是其他新的思路、方法、技术等。

新颖性和原创性都强调"新"，但前者在于一般的新鲜和实用，至少能给读者带来一点新意和收获；后者则在于特别的创造和发明，带来的是学术贡献。新颖性是SCI论文价值体系的第三重要要素。

例如，一篇发表在 *Chinese Journal of Mechanical Engineering*（Vol. 28, No. 2, 2015）上题目为 "Overall Evaluation of the Effect of Residual Stress Induced by Shot Peening in the Improvement of Fatigue Fracture Resistance for Metallic Materials" 的学术论文[三]，内容上有新颖性。为了理解方便，下面给出这篇文章的摘要。

Abstract：Before 1980s, the circular suspension spring

[一] 当时Watson、Crick都是名不见经传的小人物，Crick只有37岁，连博士学位还没有。1962年，这两位获诺贝尔奖。

[二] 大陆漂移说和海底扩张说分别由德国气象学家Wegener（魏格纳）和美国科学家Hess（赫斯）提出。

[三] 作者为Wang Renzhi（Metal Physics Laboratory, Beijing Institute of Aeronautical Materials）和Ru Jilai（Metal & Chemistry Institute, China Academy of Railway Science）。

in automobile subjected to torsion fatigue load, under the cyclic normal tensile stresses, the majority of fatigue fracture occurred was in normal tensile fracture mode (NTFM) and the fracture surface was under 45° diagonal. Because there exists the interaction between the residual stresses induced by shot peening and the applied cyclic normal tensile stresses in NTFM, which represents as "stress strengthening mechanism", shot peening technology could be used for improving the fatigue fracture resistance (FFR) of springs. However, since 1990s up to date, in addition to regular NTFM, the fatigue fractures occurred of peened springs from time to time are in longitudinal shear fracture mode (LSFM) or transverse shear fracture mode (TSFM) with the increase of applied cyclic shear stresses, which leads to a remarkable decrease of FFR. However, LSFM/TSFM can be avoided effectively by means of shot peening treatment again on the peened springs. The phenomena have been rarely happened before. At present there are few literatures concerning this problem. Based upon the results of force analysis of a spring, there is no interaction between the residual stresses by shot peening and the applied cyclic shear stresses in shear fracture. This means that the effect of "stress strengthening mechanism" for improving the FFR of LSFM/TSFM is disappeared basically. During shot peening, however, both of residual stress and cyclic plastic deformed microstructure are induced synchronously like "twins" in the surface layer of a spring. It has been found for the first time by means of force analysis and experimental results that the modified microstructure in the "twins" as a "structure strengthening mechanism" can improve the FFR of LSFM/TSFM. At the same time, it is also shown that the optimum technology of shot peening strengthening must have both "stress strengthening mechanism" and "structure strengthening mechanism" simultaneously so that the FFR of both NTFM and LSFM/TSFM can be improved by shot peening.

此文针对汽车上使用的承受扭转疲劳载荷的圆柱悬架簧在使用中出现的疲劳断裂，阐述"交变正应力作用"下的正常现象（正断型疲劳断裂），从"外施交变切应力提高"下的反常现象（切断型疲劳断裂）切入，由受力分析及研究结果，驳斥了传统上仅用"喷丸应力强化机制"来解释正断型疲劳断裂的错误做法，进而不能解释切断型疲劳断裂产生的真正原因。最后得出喷丸强化工艺只有同时具备"应力强化机制"和"组织结构强化机制"，才能提高正断型和切断型的疲劳断裂抗力。这是对传统相关认识和做法的否定，内容上有新意，有实用价值，符合论文对新颖性的要求（该文为分析型论文，无实验内容）。该文发表后，反响较大，其价值得到印证。下面摘抄本文发表后作者 Wang Renzhi 先生收到的三封读者反馈邮件：

1）The purpose of this letter is to notify you, on behalf of the Organizing Committee, to be Speaker at the upcoming 3rd *International Conference and Exhibition on Mechanical & Aerospace Engineering* which is being organized in collaboration with *the International Association for Hydrogen Energy*, USA on Oct 05-07, 2015 San Francisco, USA.

2）Acquiring that you have enjoyed a high reputation and once shared your work in *CJME*, which titled … on shot peening strengthening principle; fatigue fracture resistance; strengthening mechanisms of fatigue fracture; classification on fatigue fracture mode, here Science Publishing Group, an international publisher who currently owns more than 700 Special Issues sincerely invites you to propose a Special Issue in your specialized field as the Lead Guest Editor.

3）I have had an opportunity to read your paper …on *CJME* and can tell from your work that you are an expert in this field …. I am the editorial assistant of *Mechanical Engineering Research* …. We are calling papers for the coming issues, it is a great pleasure to invite you to contribute your best knowledge and research. Your contribution will help us to establish a high standard.

第一封邮件邀请作者在某学术会议作报告（Speaker）；第二封邮件邀请作者作某专刊的高级客座编辑（Lead Guest Editor）；第三封邮件邀请作者为某期刊撰稿（calling papers for the coming issues）。这些事实充分表明该文有新意，具有发表价值，是一篇不错的实用性论文。

1.3.4 巧妙性

巧妙性指优先考虑研究工作的新颖、别致、技巧性，由简单路径、巧妙改进方法等而得到可靠、可信的结果，以及将一个领域的知识巧妙应用于另一领域。巧妙性其实也包含一个"新"义，但更侧重"巧妙""特别""艺术"。巧妙性是 SCI 论文价值体系的第四重要要素。

英国赫瑞-瓦特大学（Heriot-Watt University）副教授孔宪文博士在 Chinese Journal of Mechanical Engineering（Vol. 30, No. 1, 2017）发表了题为"Standing on the Shoulders of Giants: A Brief Note from the Perspective of Kinematics"一文，从机构运动学的角度简析了及时掌握研究现状的重要性及挑战。该文先介绍机构运动学随着人类需求的变化而演变及其与相关学科、技术的相互影响，接着以机构运动学的两个案例强调了掌握研究现状的重要性。

案例一：对心曲柄滑块机构滑块最大速度的位置。该问题早于 19 世纪末为满足内燃机的开发需求而得到很好的解决。未能掌握此研究现状使得若干研究人员在此后 100 多年里仍在花费时间与精力寻求该问题的解析解，并在一些权威期刊上发表了数篇论文。

案例二：并联机器人机构的构型综合。K. H. Hunt 于 1973 年发表的关于等速联轴器设计的论文看似与并联机器人机构无关，但连接两平行轴的等速联轴器实质上就是三自由度平动并联机构。不熟悉等速联轴器或未能及时认识到等速联轴器与并联机器人机构的上述联系，使得多名研究人员在 21 世纪初用不同数学方法重新得到与 Hunt 的上述论文中相同的三自由度移动并联机构。

孔博士的这篇论文在分析了上述两个不同历史时期典型案例的成因后，指出掌握研究现状既需要不同学科之间的合作，又需要同一学科内不同学科方向之间的合作。

该文将研究者在 19 世纪末后的 100 多年里仍花费气力寻求案例一问题的解析解，在 21 世纪初用不同数学方法寻求案例二问题的解析解这种本不必要付出的劳动，巧妙地归结于是由于他们未能掌握这些实际上早已解决的研究现状所致，进而得出学科间、学科内不同学科方向之间合作的重要性。孔博士学术功底深厚，了解学科历史及研究现状，他勤于思考，善于发现问题和探求缘由，善于总结，以巧妙的手法找到了问题的症结，该文是论文巧妙性的杰作。

笔者曾经发文一篇，用相似性理论来分析 RMS（可重构制造系统）的多工艺路线，巧妙地建立了基于相似性理论的 RMS 多工艺路线模型，并成功开发出相应的软件系统。该文将相似性理论运用于 RMS 建模，形成了它的巧妙性。

实际中，论文的巧妙性可体现在很多方面，如参数的设置、算法的改进、路线的优化、理论的提炼、结构的设计、技术的应用、场景的模拟等。写作中用好巧妙性，可带给读者一种愉悦和创作灵感，也即一种"新"意。巧妙性往往包含新颖性，但新颖性不一定有巧妙性。巧妙性用好了，是一种艺术。看来，写作也是一门艺术。

1.3.5 交叉性

交叉性指论文的内容能让本领域和其他

领域的读者都感兴趣并且都能看懂，很多读者会对自己领域之外的研究工作有浓厚的兴趣。交叉性主要是从论文的学科覆盖面及读者的专业背景和层次来说的，是 SCI 论文价值体系的第五重要要素。

以 Nature 为例，回顾一下它的创刊与学科交叉性的问题，以加深对论文交叉性的认识。

Nature 论文报道世界范围内影响最广泛的重大进展，应能让非专业人员容易看懂，如物理学进展能让生物学家看懂，反之，生物学进展能让物理学家看懂。(Nature paper reports the most significant advances that have the widest implications. Significance should be readily appreciated by non-specialists, which means, the significance of physics papers should be readily apparent to biologists, and, the significance of biology papers should be readily apparent to physicists.)

Nature 的使命是发表研究领域中最重要的进展。对于主要面向物理学家而非生物学家的物理学重大研究进展，主要面向遗传学家而非其他领域科学家的遗传学重大研究进展，该怎么刊登呢？依此类推，还有材料学、免疫学、化学、神经学等，都面临这样的问题。(Nature's mission statement is to publish the most important advances in research. But what about important advances in physics whose principal appeal is to other physicists, but not biologists? What about advances in genetics whose principal appeal is to geneticists? Or materials science, immunology, chemistry, neuroscience … ?)

这样，Nature 的研究类子刊就诞生了。这类期刊的论文报道该刊所覆盖研究领域的重大进展。这些进展应能让非专业人员看懂，一个领域的进展应能让另一领域的研究人员看懂。(Nature research journal paper reports the most significant advances within the discipline it covers. Significance should be readily appreciated by non-specialists. The significance of papers in one specialty should be apparent to researchers in another.)

然而，Nature 及其研究类期刊的空间毕竟有限，仅刊登影响最广泛的重大研究进展。对适于一个领域的专业人员同时又适于其他领域的专业人员的重要进展，该如何刊登呢？结果只能是创办多学科、多领域交叉类期刊，如 Nature Communications、Scientific Data 和 Scientific Reports 等。(Only limited space in Nature and the Nature Research journals. Only the MOST important research with the WIDEST implications can be published. What about important advances in specialists areas of research whose principal appeal is to other specialists? The solution …)

交叉类期刊刊登有影响或改变领域内人的思想潜力的重大进展，关注的是新观点、新见解和新技术，广泛的需求并不是发表论文的先决条件，而要有伟大的科学发现。(Reports significant advances that have potential to influence thinking in a field. New ideas, new insights and new technologies. Broad appeal isn't a prerequisite for publication! Great science is!)

从 Nature 的创刊需求和结果来看，在论文写作和投稿时，作者一定要树立学科观、领域观，想清楚论文内容适合的读者范围、层次，弄明白涉及不同学科领域（领域差异）以及同一学科领域不同层次的人员（人员差异）。对于交叉学科领域，论文写作一定要考虑领域差异；对于同一学科领域，论文写作要考虑人员差异（专业还是非专业），不同领域的人员、相同领域的不同人员阅读论文的需求和能力并不相同。这就要求写论文应对症下药，按读者层次来写。

例如，2017 年发表在 Nature Communica-

tions 的一篇题目为 "High-resolution adaptive optical imaging within thick scattering media using closed-loop accumulation of single scattering" 的原创论文，内容上有交叉性，适合物理、光学、测量、仪器等相关领域的专业人员和非专业人员参考。下面给出这篇论文的摘要，请读者自行阅读体会。

Abstract：Thick biological tissues give rise to not only the multiple scattering of incoming light waves, but also the aberrations of remaining signal waves. The challenge for existing optical microscopy methods to overcome both problems simultaneously has limited sub-micron spatial resolution imaging to shallow depths. Here we present an optical coherence imaging method that can identify aberrations of waves incident to and reflected from the samples separately, and eliminate such aberrations even in the presence of multiple light scattering. The proposed method records the time-gated complex-field maps of backscattered waves over various illumination channels, and performs a closed-loop optimization of signal waves for both forward and phase-conjugation processes. We demonstrated the enhancement of the Strehl ratio by more than 500 times, an order of magnitude or more improvement over conventional adaptive optics, and achieved a spatial resolution of 600 nm up to an imaging depth of seven scattering mean free paths.

1.3.6 可读性

可读性是从写作质量来讲的，指论文表述条理性强，可理解性强，读者易读、易懂、易消化、易接受。再好的内容最终都是通过语言表达出来的，若所用语言缺乏可读性就不能准确全面地表达内容，进而影响论文的价值。可读性涉及因素较多，与论文结构和语言要素都有关，但其中最核心的是逻辑要素。逻辑不通时，其他要素用得再好也起不了本质作用，而只有逻辑通了，其他要素才会派上用场。可见，写作中思维的逻辑性胜过写作的语言本身和语言风格。（逻辑要素与其他要素也是互为依存的，其他要素用得不好时，当然也会影响逻辑要素。）

写作本质上是一个认识过程，包括由客观事物到人的主观认识的"意化"过程，以及从人的主观认识到书面表现的"物化"过程。意化过程中常出现"意不符物"，即主观认识未能完全、正确地反映客观事物，而物化过程中又容易言不达意，即不能完整、准确地反映作者的观点，结果是因为这两次偏差，写作结果或多或少地偏离了客观事物。从某种程度上说，此问题可用"逻辑欠缺"来解释，即意化、物化过程中都缺少正确的逻辑。意化中，应使用思维语，讲求表达的逻辑性；物化中，应使用文字语，也要讲求表达的逻辑性。写作中如果将这两个层面的逻辑性把握好，就能达到语言对内容的准确、有条理的表述，最终获得理想的可读性。

论文即使有好的内容，但如果可读性不好，那么其价值就会受到影响，严重时内容和价值会被淹没，失去发表价值。可读性是 SCI 论文价值体系的第六重要要素。不过，可读性是写作层面，其他 5 个要素是内容层面，这是可读性与其他要素的最大不同。

1.4 SCI 论文结构体系

1.4.1 论文总体结构

SCI 论文的结构是由其各个组成部分紧密关联而形成的统一整体，从开头、中间到结尾均要达到首尾连贯、层次分明、逻辑严密和条理清楚。同类型的 SCI 论文一般具有相同或相近的结构，但由于研究的内容、方法、过程、成果等的不同，其结构不可能完全相同甚至差别较大。笔者将 SCI 论文的结构概括为由主体和辅体两部分组成，如图 1-4 所示。

主体是论文的核心内容。辅体是围绕主

体的辅助信息，虽是辅助性的，但也非常重要。有的论文还有附录部分，用于表述在主体中不便于表述的内容，可看作主体的附件，多位于论文的最后[①]。

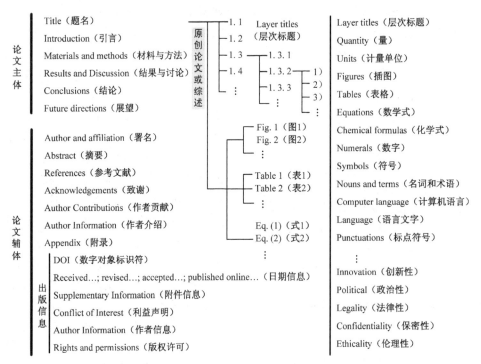

图 1-4　SCI 论文结构体系

主体主要有题名、引言、材料与方法、结果与讨论、结论、展望等，以及内含的层次标题、量、单位、插图、表格、数学式等。辅体主要有署名、摘要、参考文献、致谢、数字对象标识符、日期信息等，以及内含的量、单位、数学式等[②]。辅体的结构基本差不多，但主体的结构差异或大或小。这就是说，SCI 论文结构的差别主要体现在主体上。有人将论文主体中引言后面、结论前面的组成部分称为论文的正文。

SCI 论文分为长文和短文两大类，长文主要包括原创论文和综述，短文主要包括编辑社论、研究热点、读者来信等，不同文体在辅体结构上大同小异，而在主体结构上往往差别较大。以下大略给出这些类别的结构对比示意图，如图 1-5 所示。

1.4.2　原创论文主体结构

Original Paper 又称 Original Article，简称 Article（原创论文），是原创研究的详细报告，主要面向领域内读者（科学家或研究人员）较为详细地报道作者自己研究课题的实质进展及所取得的重要研究成果，注重原创性，有重要的学术影响，参考价值较大。篇幅通常 8 页以上（20～30 页也并不少见），插图数量不限，引文通常 30 篇以

---

① 期刊编辑通常认为附录对论文发表后的被引不起任何作用，而且占用较多的版面，故不提倡论文有附录，即使作者的投稿中有，录用后修改时编辑也会删除或建议作者删除。

② 这里给出的论文结构中没有包含 Keywords（关键词）。关键词通常是科技论文辅体的重要组成部分，但由于读者在查找论文前看不到论文，也就无从知道论文上所列的关键词。*Nature*、*Science*、*Cell* 和 *Cell Research* 的论文中已没有 Keywords 这一项了。

上。这里给出的数字只是大略的说法，视领域、期刊和内容等不同有所差异，具体是多少要看目标期刊的具体要求，不可一概而论作硬性规定。

原创论文主体结构包括引言、正文、结论和参考文献。

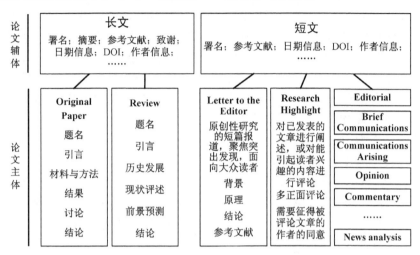

图1-5　SCI长文和短文结构大略对比

1. 引言

引言又称前言，主要针对某一研究主题（领域、范围）进行相关文献综述，回顾过去到现在关于该主题已经进行过的研究，写明研究现状，指出存在的问题或不足，引出本文研究的重要性，清楚交待研究目的和作用，并说明本研究相较于过去研究的不同。篇幅通常较长，因为太短了不大容易写清某一主题的研究现状。

2. 正文

（1）材料与方法。写明用什么做研究（所用的材料，包括材料来源、性质、数量、选取、设备型号、制造商、实验时间、季节等）和怎样做研究（所用的方法，包括仪器设备、实验条件、测试方法、处理事项等）。实验细节应尽可能详写，主要是让其他人有办法按这些信息复制（重复）实验。

具有可复制性是所有实验成功的必要条件，因此这部分内容显得特别重要，是作者充分展示研究成果的一个重要环节，也是论文中容易写好的部分。

（2）结果和讨论。结果回答发生或得到了什么，即研究出什么，如由实验、观测、计算、仿真等得到的数据、曲线图等。全文的一切结论由结果得出，一切议论由结果引发，一切推理由结果导出，因此结果构成正文的核心。理论上讲，在论文的各个组成部分中，结果可能是最短的，因为很多数据资料可直接用图表表示。另外，结果毕竟是一种客观结果，列示时不宜加进个人主观色彩，不宜对其进行任何评论和说明（有关内容应放在讨论中）。

讨论用来对结果进行分析、论证、总结，给出具体认识、意见和建议，说明研究结果的意义和重要性，阐述与前人研究结果的异同，如果有些结果不理想，未达到预期目标，则对观察到的差异及可能出现的意外情况进行解释。最后还要总结一下，根据研究结果表明作者自己的见解，指出研究的局限性，提出日后可继续完善、改进研究工作。

3. 结论

对全文进行总结，篇幅较短，综合说明

全文结果的科学意义，反映由实验、观测、调查等得到的结果，以及由推理、判断、归纳等逻辑分析所得到的学术总见解，如提出建议、研究设想、改进意见、尚待解决的问题等。结论是整个论文的最高点，也往往是决定论文能否录用的重要依据之一。

4. 参考文献

论文中凡是引用前人（包括作者自己过去）已发表的文献中的观点、数据和材料等，都要在文中引用处予以标明，并在文末列出参考文献表。引文通常30篇左右为宜，而且近年的文献不应缺少。阅读参考文献是论文撰写的起点，参考文献引用是否合适（包括内容、数量、时间）往往成为论文能否写成、写好的关键要素。

Nature 原创论文基本写作要求：结构上由研究背景、原理、讨论和结论组成，篇幅不超过5页，引文不超过50篇，摘要不超过150个单词；正文一般3 000个单词，前面可有500个单词的引言；小标题不超过6个单词，各级标题不超过40个字符；图表5或6个。

1.4.3 综述主体结构

Review（综述）用来对某个问题的历史背景、前人工作、争论焦点、研究现状和发展前景等进行评论，分为大综述（领域文献总结）和小综述（与作者自己研究课题直接相关的文献总结）。通常有两种写法：①以汇集文献资料为主，辅以注释，客观而少评述（某些发展较活跃的学科的年度综述就属于此类）；②着重评述，通过回顾、观察、分析、归纳、总结和展望提出合乎逻辑、具有启迪和指导性的看法、结论或建议。综述通常10页以上，插图数量原则上是不限的，小综述的引文通常在60篇以上，大综述的引文通常超过120篇。

综述主体结构基本与原创论文相同，但侧重不同。原创论文注重研究方法的科学性和结果的可信性；而综述侧重有关研究主题（领域、专题）的详细信息资料，不仅要指出发展背景和工作意义，还应有作者的评论意见，指出研究成败、得失的原因，不仅要写明研究动态与最新进展，还要基于评述来预测发展趋势和应用前景。二者的引言、结论侧重面不同，写法上差异较大；二者的正文结构也不同，原创论文常有讨论，而综述应有展望或前景预测。

综述主体结构包括以下部分。

1. 引言

引言将读者导入综述主题，主要叙述综述的目的和作用，概述主题的有关概念和定义，简述所选主题的历史背景、发展过程、研究现状、争论焦点、应用价值和实践意义，同时还可限定综述的范围，使读者对综述主题形成初步印象。引言可长可短，长一点可能更加有效。

2. 正文

正文没有必须遵循的固定模式，由作者按综述的内容自行设计创造。一般可根据内容的多少分成几个大的部分，各部分标上简短而醒目的层次标题。各部分的区分标准多种多样，如按问题、按原理、按方法、按论点、按年代、按发展阶段等。

（1）历史发展。按时间顺序简述主题的来龙去脉、发展概况及各阶段的研究水平。

（2）现状评述。重点论述当前国内外的研究现状，着重评述已解决和未解决的问题，提出可能的解决途径；指出存在的争论焦点，比较各种观点的异同并做出理论解释，亮明作者的观点；详细介绍有创造性和发展前景的理论和假说，并引出论据，指出可能的发展趋势。

（3）前景预测。通过纵横对比，肯定主题的研究水平，指出存在的问题，提出可能的发展趋势，指明研究方向，揭示研究捷径，为专题研究或行业发展提供指导。

3. 结论

对全文进行总结，篇幅较短。可根据对正文的论述，提出几条语言简明、含义确切的意见和建议；也可对正文的主要内容做出扼要的概括，并提出作者自己的见解，表明作者赞成什么和反对什么。对于篇幅较小的综述，可不单独列出结论，而是在正文各部分内容的后面用简短的几句话对全文进行高度概括。

4. 参考文献

参考文献是综述的原始素材和基础，引用足够的、有代表性的、年代较为均衡的参考文献是写好综述的前提条件。引文数少则60篇，多则120篇以上，没有硬性规定。

1.4.4　常见短文介绍

1. Editorial

Editorial（编辑社论、编者按、卷首语）主要由期刊的主编、副主编、编辑、客座编辑等来撰写，内容包括学科进展和现状、学术观点和视野、研究热点和难点、期刊发展规划和年度计划、本期安排和介绍、专刊专栏策划和说明等。通常1或2页，可有1或2幅插图，还可有少量的引文。对有此栏目的某期期刊来说，一般只刊登一篇这样的文章。

Editorial 是由期刊的"编辑"而非自由投稿的作者来写的，似乎放在这里讲不合适。但笔者认为，目前SCI期刊往往聘用从事科学研究的知名专家、学者做期刊的编辑（主编、副主编、客座编辑等）。实际中会有一些人员承担双重角色，既是从事科研撰写论文而投稿的作者，也可能是某（些）期刊聘用的某种级别的编辑或兼职编辑，因此他们有撰写 Editorial 的任务或机会，需要懂得或了解 Editorial 的写作要求。

2. Research Highlight

Research Highlight（研究热点、前沿）主要由研究领域的专家、学者或学术权威来撰写，内容包括学科进展、研究现状、学术评论等，可能涉及某领域、学科或某领域、学科的某个方面的研究热点、前沿。通常由期刊编辑部邀请目标人士，对其期刊已发表（多指在线发表）的文章进行阐述，或对能引起读者兴趣的内容进行评论（多为正面评价），例如对文中的某个观点、原理、方法、技术等进行正面评价或从文章整体进行正面评述。通常1~4页，最好有1或2幅插图，可有适量的引文。对有此栏目的某期期刊来说，一般刊登少量这样的文章。

3. Letter to the Editor

Letter to the Editor 或 Letter（读者来信，短论文）是原创性研究的短篇报道，聚焦突出发现，没有讨论部分，通常对领域内、外的读者都适用，即一般读者也能看懂。常由作者对其自己的原创论文（没有被录用的原创论文）进行删减、压缩和修改而成，内容通常是研究成果正式详细报道出来之前的简短报道。通常4个页码以内，最好有插图，可有适量的引文。

Nature 对此类文章的写作要求：结构上由研究背景、原理和结论组成，篇幅不超过3页，引文不超过30篇，引言不超过180个单词，正文一般1 500个单词，图表3或4个。

4. 其他

SCI期刊还可能有其他栏目，不同期刊的栏目设置可能有较大的差异，其下短文类别自然不尽相同。以 *Nature* 为例，它设置有很多栏目，用多样化的栏目满足多层次的读者的需求，以灵活的文体激发作者的写作灵感。其栏目除以上介绍的几种外，还包括以下几类：

Brief Communications（简讯）：非正式、读者面广的精品版块，常由审稿人或编辑对 Letter 缩减而成，但不是已发表 Article 或 Letter 的前期报道或附录，常配一个小幅面插图或表格。

Communications Arising（短评）：属于

简讯栏目,是对 Nature 已发表的综述或原创论文的阐述及能引起读者兴趣的评论。提交前,应先送交被评论文章的作者,允许对方 2 周内答复。双方通信的复印件同时提交,即使对方无回复也要提交。不接收对除 Nature 外的其他期刊发表的文章的短评。

Opinion(观点):由 Nature 不同国家的编辑撰写,传达期刊自己的声音,其观点有真正的国际性。

News(新闻):由 Nature 全球记者每周提供的科学界最新消息,用全球观点观察事物,有独特的公正性。

News & Views(新闻和观点):向公众交流科学新闻,是所有媒体上就科学研究进行评论的仿效最广和最受尊敬、欢迎的论坛,深受读者喜爱。

Briefings(简报)和 News analysis(新闻分析):对某个热门或敏感话题进行更加深入的分析,让读者了解公众眼中的科学问题。

Correspondence(通信):评论新闻和其他非正式内容,或用来继续某一辩论。

Commentary(评论):对有争议、热门和受到广泛关注的话题进行评价,为那些对科学感兴趣但其自身又不一定是科学家的读者开设。

这类文章多数是新闻、消息类的,刊登后能吸引大众眼球,引起较为广泛的关注,通常不是研究人员或普通作者的自由投稿,而多由期刊的编辑、记者或邀请他人来撰写。作者要按文体要求写出文体合适的文章,提高文章的投稿有效性和录用率;而编辑要规划期刊,开设合适的期刊栏目,组约或撰写文体合适的文章,办好期刊。

按目前 SCI 期刊影响因子的计算规则,除 Review 和 Original Article 以外的其他所有类型的文章,是不计入发文分母的,但对它们的引用是计入引用分子的。因此 SCI 期刊应作好定位,有计划地多发资讯类文章,这样对提升其影响因子和影响力大有帮助。不过,这涉及期刊的学术定位问题,也不是一般编辑能决策的。

1.5 SCI 论文语言体系

SCI 论文同其他论文一样,形式上是一堆密密麻麻的语言文字,表面上看这些语言文字无组织、无规律,实际上却是按种种规则组合起来的一个有组织的语言体系,如图 1-6 所示。

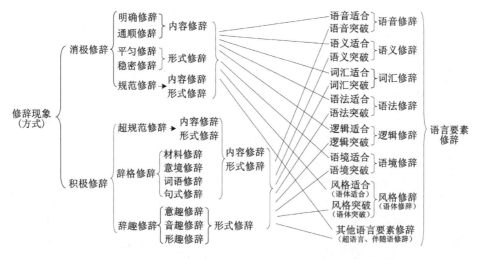

图 1-6 SCI 论文语言(修辞)体系

SCI 论文涉及语音、语义、词汇、语法、逻辑、语境等各种语言要素，写作时应调整这些要素使其"适合"，即符合语言基本要求，如语音适合、语义适合、语法适合等；同时还可突破，如语音突破、语义突破、语法突破等，突破就是语言艺术。各种"适合"和"突破"将语言要素关联起来，形成一个有机统一体，这就是 SCI 论文语言（修辞）体系。

什么是修辞呢？修辞是动词"修"加名词"辞"，"修"即修改，操作对象是"辞"，即语句。为何要对"辞"进行"修"呢？当然是为了"辞"被"修"而达到某种语言表达效果。语言表达效果有两个层面：一是基本层面，达到语言基本要求，写出的语句没有语病；二是高级层面，对无语病语句重新调整，使表达效果得到提升，达到语言艺术。"一句话，百样说"，但其中至少有一两句是最好的，如果能从中选出最佳的一句，那么就达到了高级层面。这两个层面的修辞，前者叫消极修辞，后者叫积极修辞。

何为消极和积极呢？所谓消极，就是自觉不自觉地进行，潜移默化地遵守，本能地达到；而积极是没事找事，有意地去做、去操作、去完成，只为一个目标——上档次，提效果，艺术化。消极修辞关注语意的准确传递，达到明确、通顺、平匀、稳密、规范；明确是表意准确而不含混，通顺是符合客观事理和思维规律，平匀是能用一个结构表达清楚的就不混用几个结构，稳密是避免不该重复而重复语句或该重复而未重复语句，规范是遵守写作与出版规范；积极修辞追求语言效果的提升，有超规范、辞格和辞趣三个层面。超规范是出于表达需要而有意突破常规规范，辞格是巧妙使用在人类漫长语用实践中所形成的能够大大提升语言表达效果的各种固定修辞手法，辞趣是通过调整音、形、意的外在感观形式而达到某种意境和情趣。

其中，明确和通顺只与内容有关，辞趣只与形式有关，而其他则既与内容又与形式有关。

什么是内容和形式呢？内容是表意的实质，形式是呈现表意的一种外在感观，语意就是蕴含在形式里面的内容。内容修辞更多关注怎样把意思清楚表达出来，而形式修辞更侧重把意思以何种式样呈现出来，给读者以外观美感。

消极、积极修辞中的内容与形式与语言要素修辞中的内容与形式相映射，组成一个语言修辞综合体系，这就是论文的语言体系。撰写论文只有综合地运用好语言体系的各种要素及其表现方式才能最终获得理想的表达效果。

1.6 SCI 论文质量体系

以上介绍了 SCI 论文的价值、结构和语言三大体系，价值体系侧重论文的内容，结构体系侧重论文的结构，语言体系侧重论文的语言。一篇论文如果在内容、结构和语言上都好，那么就是一篇好文章。这就有文章质量高低的问题，衡量的标准就是论文的内容、结构和语言体系中各要素是否规范和协调，撰写论文就是要"玩"好、关联好这些要素，这样就形成了一个质量体系。笔者根据上述内容建立了 SCI 论文质量体系，如图 1-7 所示。

SCI 论文质量包括选题、成果和写作三个层面。选题质量指课题价值大小，包括期刊类、学科类等；期刊类指与目标期刊的吻合性，即论文选题与目标期刊重点关注方向是否吻合；学科类指论文选题与目标期刊学科方向是否吻合。成果质量指课题的研究水准或成果的先进性，包括研究、案例和学术；研究指研究的水准，包括科学性、原创性等；案例指论文中所举案例的水准；学术指成果的学术贡献。理想情况下，研究和案例质量都要好，难以都好时，研究质量应优于案例质量。写作质量包括文体、语言、法规和伦理四个层面：文体质量包括对论文类型和结构的把握，语言质量是语言表达达到可读性、准确性、简明性和规范性。

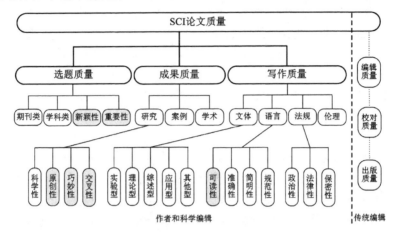

图1-7　SCI论文质量体系

一篇论文只有在选题、成果和写作质量上都过关了，才是高质量的论文，其中写作质量是基础。如果一篇论文选题价值大，研究水准也不低，而用来呈现这二者的论文在写作上很糟糕，那么这个选题价值和研究水准就被这质量低的写作给淹没了，呈现给读者的机会就会丧失掉，那么再好的选题质量、再优秀的成果又如何能有效传承呢？广大作者不仅要做好研究，还要做有意义的研究，最终还要用高质量的语言文本记录下来，即使选题、成果质量不好，但是从为读者、社会负责的角度看，也应该规范表达，将论文写好。

从出版的角度讲，论文的质量还有一个出版质量（编校质量）。出版质量主要由传统编辑来保障，而写作质量主要由作者和科学编辑共同来保障（作者写作是基础，编辑引领是保障）。

1.7　SCI论文过程体系

以上从多个方面描绘了 SCI 论文是什么。作者懂得 SCI 论文，拥有写作材料，接下来就是写作实战了，如果说论文基本知识是理论性的，那么按照理论性知识撰写论文就是实践（实战）性的了。作者只有将这种理论和实践完美结合，才能写出、写成、写好论文。下面就开始这种实战，先剖析论文写作准备、进行阶段分别做些什么工作，描绘 SCI 论文过程体系。以后的章节便从论文各组成部分的内容和结构的角度来讲述如何撰写论文。

1.7.1　论文形成过程

SCI 论文同其他任何文章一样均属语言作品，形成过程总体上大致可以分为准备阶段（写作前）、进行阶段（写作中）、完成阶段（写作后），完成阶段又分为出版阶段（发表前）和传播阶段（发表后），如图1-8所示。

在论文写作前，作者需要进行必要的准备工作，这个过程就是写作的准备阶段，准备阶段的工作做好了，写作才好开始。作者在此阶段的主要工作是，搜集整理写作材料及形成写作内容。搜集整理材料通常有观测、调查、检阅、回忆、体验、想象、整合等方法、途径，写作内容主要有由这些方法、途径而获得的经验、学问、见解、趣味等。常有作者想写或计划、打算写论文,但不知需要准备,不知如何开始,即使开始写也很难下笔,不知写什么、不知怎么写、不知怎么办,常常郁闷、苦恼。其实,这多是由于作者没有做准备工作或没有将准备工作做到位所致。写文章好比盖房子,盖房子是一定需要各种材料的,如果没有将所需材料准备到位,那么水平再高的能工巧匠,恐怕也无从下手;写文章也是需要材料的,如果材料没有到位就开始写作,那么水平再高的写作高手,也只能彷徨郁闷、望洋兴叹了!因此这个准备工作是否有、是否充分、是否到位十分关键,是论文能否写成、写好的基础,可以说写作准备是写作进行的前提条件。

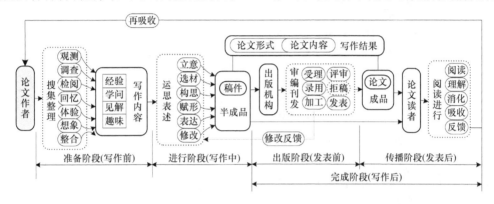

图 1-8　论文形成过程

如果作者在实际写作过程中感到非常困难,那么建议先不要动手,而应思考一下是否做好了准备工作,如果没有,那么就扎扎实实从准备工作开始吧!也许有的读者会问,"我也准备了,资料也查了,文献也读了,可就是没有思路,那又是为什么呢?"笔者的答复是,"你的准备工作还是不够,还是不到位,不信的话,你回头再试试,奇迹一定会出现的!"其实,准备工作也是一个量的积累问题,只要积累够了,那么质变就是必然的。笔者上大学时,班主任杜教授曾这样说过,"博士论文其实不难写,你先读100篇相关文献,就自然好写了!"后来笔者在工作实践中也经常引用这句话,因为他确实说到了要害,当文献阅读达到一定数量时,其实不仅有了写作材料和内容,而且还有了写作框架和思路,甚至还有了写作层次和素养。

在进行阶段即写作阶段,是作者运用获得的写作材料进行内部运思和外部表述。所谓内部运思,就是运用大脑思维,根据写作的目的、内容和要求,对论文的主题、内容、框架、结构等进行全面的思考,大体上包括立意、选材、构思和赋形几个重要环节,这个过程中论文即使还没有开始写,但较为完整的意态文已在作者的脑海里基本形成,相当于设计图样已经出来,等待下一步的实现就可以了。外部表述就是将内部运思出来的意态文用语言文字表达出来而形成初级半成品文稿(初稿),然后不断修改使其规范化,最后形成一篇高级半成品文稿(稿件),再向目标期刊投稿。内部运思中的作者相当于画图员、设计者,外部表述中的作者就是加工员、实现者。(所谓半成品,就是作者所完成论文的初稿,准备向目标期刊投稿;或待定稿,不用来出版,待别人审阅修改后使用,若质量较高,符合使用要求,就无须修改;或定稿,作者直接使用或自己留用。)

完成阶段简单地说就是出版(发表)阶段,主要是目标期刊将作者投来的稿件经过出版过程的评审、修改再制作成论文成品，将其发表而进行传播。"半"指距发表后的成品还有一定距离，需要内容完善、结构调整、文字修改，最终达到出版后的成品的要求。完成阶段大致分为出版和传播两个阶段。

作者投稿成功后，目标期刊启动审编刊发流程。编辑先对稿件进行初审，初审未通过就退稿（拒稿），通过则安排专家评审（同行评议），编辑参照评审意见给出处理意见决定录用与否。有录用意向（拟录用）后，进入编辑修改环节（提升学术水准和写作质量），作者按专家评审意见和编辑处理意见对论文进行修改。此过程可能需要几个来回（质量好的通常一个来回，很少有不经过此环节就直接进入生产环节），持续一定时间，结果就产生了相对于初稿质量上有较大提升的修改稿（学术上没有问题，写作上符合论文写作要求）。修改稿完成后，进入生产环节，即正式出版前的制作过程，涉及论文语言文字加工、润色、排版、校对、数字文件制作、上线、印刷等多个子环节，直到成品论文上线和期刊印制完成，即成品论文发表。这就是完成阶段的出版阶段，发生在论文传播阶段之前。

成品论文发表后，就进入流通环节与读者见面，由大众来阅读、理解、消化和吸收，成为其精神食粮。这就是完成阶段的传播阶段，发生在论文正式发表之后。

读者还可将阅读论文后形成的意见、建议、效果、结果等反馈给或提交给出版商、出版平台、期刊出版部门或作者个人，对作者来说，这是一个写作内容再吸收的过程，对改进论文或相关研究有积极作用，也可能会对作者未来撰写其他文章产生影响。

1.7.2 写作准备阶段

论文写作首先从进入准备阶段开始。作者有了写论文的需求、意向和打算时，就要开始计划启动和完成时间，并着手进行相应的准备，从开始准备写作到开始动手写作往往还有较多时日，这个过程就是准备阶段。此阶段作者的主要工作是搜集整理写作材料及形成写作内容。搜集整理写作材料所做工作通常有观测、调查、检阅、回忆、体验、想象、整合等方法、途径，形成的写作内容有经验、学问、见解、趣味等方面，如图1-9所示。

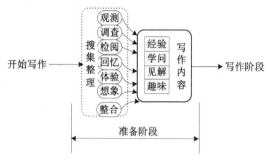

图1-9 论文写作准备阶段

1. 观测

观测包括观察和测量。（一般写作如文学创作，通常不会涉及测量，这时的观测用观察即可；但SCI论文写作通常是少不了测量的，因此这时是观测而不是观察。）观察是仔细察看事物或现象；测量是用仪器确定空间、时间、温度、速度、功能等有关数值。

观察的规模可大可小、可长可短，大的观察可能需要漫长岁月，如几年、几十年；小的则可以在短时间内完成，如几小时、几天、几月。但不论规模如何，都要讲究客观真实、严谨深刻、敏锐细致，避免因观察者的生理、心理、个性、习惯、爱好等个人特点而产生错误，这与探求学问在本质上并无多大差异。细心实时的观察不仅能克服作者修养上的见解僵化、趣味低级，而且还能带来语言表达上的新鲜活泼、生动有力。观察的作用如此之大，可将其看作是一种修养。

观察的结果通常是感观的、定性的，如大小、长短、轻重、深浅、好坏等，如果需要相应的、准确的度量值，那就得借助测量，通过测量达到对客观事物某个层面、某个角度或某个属性等的理性、定量认识。

客观事物和现象、实验过程和结果等的记述和量化通常来自观测，都是写作的重要内容。

2. 调查

观察所得到的材料往往是第一手的，当然是珍贵的，但作者不可能事必躬亲，什么事都跑到现场去观察，有时事已发生，现场已不复存在，或者现场虽然存在，但事已过去，或有的事干脆就没有现场，不可能有现场，或即便有现场也不便、不能或没有必要进入。因此，观察具有一定的局限性，这种不足往往可以通过调查来有效弥补。

调查是为了了解情况而进行的考察（多指到现场）。调查一般是到现场进行，当然也可不到现场而向他人了解情况。调查结果有两个来源：一是作者到现场亲自考察的结果，这与其观察所得结果本质上完全相同；二是作者未到现场而从他人那里获得的结果，这种结果虽然不是作者亲自考察而来的，但很可能是他人亲自观察、考察而来的，因此在某种程度上等同于作者自己的观察、考察结果，而且他人的观察、考察结果实际上也能够延伸作者个人的感知与认识范围。读书就是向别人学习，本质上就是一种调查。

3. 检阅

检阅就是翻检阅读，分为检索和阅读。

检索简单地说就是查询，即按领域、主题和关键词等查检、搜索、寻找各类相关文献，如图书、期刊、会议文集、学位论文、标准、专利、电子资源或其他资料，查询结果应尽量充分、全面而且具有代表性。参考文献一般为出版物，有时也可以是非出版物。

阅读，即查看有关图书、检索到的文献并领会其内容。阅读能学习文化知识，了解相关研究现状，借鉴已有研究成果，丰富写作内容和素材，形成广征博引的写作特色；还能获得文体范本和写作格式范例，向经典文章或文本学习写作技巧；最终还能提升自身的科学素养和文化底蕴，改变精神气质和写作修养。爱阅读的人不一定都会写作，但会写作的人没有不爱阅读、不多阅读的。

参考文献所记述的事物或情况可能经过了他人的剪裁删节或修改完善，可能比不上个人观察、调查的结果那样准确、直接和具体，也可能偏离原始形貌而变成了另一种样子。因此检阅与观察、调查相比，更需用经验、学问来修正，其特点是从字里行间来推求真相，这就如同历史研究者从历史记载中探寻历史正误，法律工作者从众多证据材料中推断案情真假。历史记载可正看，也可反看、侧看，参考文献不见得完全可信，究竟怎么"看"和怎么"用"，要根据现实情况来定，只有这样才会形成和写出作者自己所拥有的独特内容。

4. 回忆

回忆就是回想，挖掘一下过去的事所包含的价值内涵，回顾一下过去所做研究工作的得失、成就与不足，已写作、发表论文的经历与情况，已经历过的值得借鉴的难忘之事，以及值得参考或分享的其他有价值的内容。SCI论文中引入回忆，不仅能增添一点历史素材，更能关联过去，展现作者的阅历与文化素养，活跃论文的表现氛围，最终增加论文的表现力。

总体上说，观测、调查是向"当前"要写作素材，表现为取材的现在时，而回忆则是向"过去"要写作素材，表现为取材的过去时。实用写作偏重于实践（运动记忆）和知识（词汇记忆），文学写作则以感情（情绪记忆）为触发点而引起回忆，并贯穿回忆的全过程，成为回忆的内聚力，同时还必须依靠生活（形象记忆）。

5. 体验

体验就是通过实践来认识周围或相关事

物，或是一种亲身经历，即作者的思想、情感与客观生活（事物客观运行状态）相关联所形成的独特心理感受。无论是记述一个细微事件，还是表现一个壮阔场面，无论是刻画独特的事物，还是描绘讲述形形色色的大自然（自然科学）、复杂多变的人类社会（社会科学）、严密深奥的思维逻辑（逻辑、思维科学）、精巧独特的人体器官（人体科学）、严密抽象的世界观和方法论（哲学）……，只要投射进作者的某种心灵体验，就能见其形、传其神。一般记人、叙事类文章要写得有韵味，就要加进体验，文学写作则更需体验。对 SCI 论文来说，如果能巧妙地加进人的某种情感和体验，则会收到高超的修辞效果，使严谨深奥、平淡无味的科学内容变得简单形象、生动有趣。

6. 想象

想象是指对于不在眼前的事物想出它的具体形象，还指设想，在心理学上是指在知觉材料的基础上，经过新的配合而创造出新形象的心理过程。作者可运用想象来拓宽题材，深化意蕴。一般有象形想象（抽象—具象）、象征想象（具象—抽象）、类比想象（具象—具象）、推测想象（已知—未知）。想象对经验的重组应适度，必须在打破经验秩序的同时来把握事物的内在逻辑关系，特别要符合情感、事理逻辑（即使出乎意料，也合乎情理），例如童话、故事、科幻小说等文体中会大量运用想象。想象属于形象思维，讲究思维的多向与拓展，在丰富写作材料的内涵、发掘写作材料的价值方面相当重要。

SCI 论文讲求表达准确、严谨，内容符合事理、规律，追求客观性、真理性，但人类由于自身或条件所限，对事物的研究、认识总是处于不断深化、接近真理的过程中，再加上事物本身也在不断变化着，所以人们对事物的认识在有的方面较为准确，而在别的方面还可能较为模糊。因此作者对事物的描述、分析、判断和推理，不可能总能基于客观、准确的数据或字字句句都能符合事理，有时加进作者的一点灵感和合乎情理的想象，反而有助于人们对事物从另一种境界来认识，因此想象可以成为论文写作准备的一个环节。

历史上不少科学发现和技术发明，都是在研究者或发明家在最后的苦思冥想中突发灵感的一刹那中做出的，这是想象的极高境界。但天上从来是不会白白掉馅饼的，灵感常从苦思冥想中来，而苦思冥想是要有前期工作基础的，只有在前期巨大付出和深厚积累的基础上苦思冥想，才会获得必然的真理性结果，否则就是空想、白想。

7. 整合

整合是指重新组合，对前面所获得的各类写作材料进行分析和综合。

分析是把一件事物、一种现象、一个概念分成较为简单的组成部分，找出这些部分的本质属性和彼此之间的关系（与综合相对）。它是为了避免笼统的模糊认识而把事物化一为多，再研究其各组成部分、阶段、侧面及各因素间的联系，从而形成对事物的比较鉴别，把握事物的特征，最终认识事物的本质。

综合是把分析过的对象或现象的各部分、各属性联合成一个统一的整体（与分析相对），或是将不同种类、不同性质的事物组合在一起。它是在分析的各层次含义之间寻找聚合点，对各种含义做出深层或本质意义的归纳，产生出"总体大于部分之和"的情形，或"整体意义大于、精于各个部分意义"的状况。

整合属于抽象思维，讲究思维的定向与收缩，在丰富写作材料的内涵、发掘写作材料的价值方面也起着相当重要的作用。论文重在"议""论""推理"，整合在论文写作的整个准备阶段占有相当重要的位置。

1.7.3 写作进行阶段

论文写作准备阶段完成后，接着自然就进入论文写作进行阶段，如图1-10所示。进行阶段主要是运用在准备阶段中获得或搜集到的写作材料（素材）进行内部运思和外部表述。

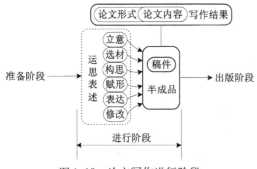

图1-10 论文写作进行阶段

内部运思指作者根据论文的主题和内容，运用大脑思维对写作材料进行思考，在思想层面规划出材料的运用方案，属于写作上的"意化"过程，具体包括立意、选材、构思和赋形。

外部表述指作者对规划出的写作材料运用方案，用语言文字以某种语言形式表达出来并进行修改，以达到写作的基本要求和某些标准、规范，实现写作内容到论文内容的转换，属于写作上的"物化"过程，具体包括表达和修改两大环节。

1. 立意

立意就是命意，即确立主题，形成作者自己的价值判断。主题一般来自感悟、提炼或研究课题。感悟就是有所感触而领悟，是作者对生活（或研究）的感受和体验及生活（或研究）经验（或研究结果）给予的启迪和暗示，是人在认识事物过程中的质的飞跃，它的产生需要一个量的积累过程。

感悟有极大的偶然性，但终究不是天赐的灵感，经常是从苦思冥想开始的。很多作者为写成一篇论文，先不忙于动手，而是不断仔细思考，实时记录心得，或在纸上勾勾画画，或在计算机、手机上录录写写，想不通的情况时有发生，在一段时间里可能吃饭、走路，甚至休息、游玩都在想来想去。一时可能想不通，想不通也没有关系，直到某一时刻灵感突然降临，当然就通了顺了，再继续进行记录、写作，而写作中还会产生新的问题，需要进行新的思考，新的灵感也往往会在不经意之中光顾。

钱学森认为，灵感实际上是一种潜思维，平时想不起某些信息的，并不意味着这些信息的消失，而是这些信息在人脑的另一部分里面加工，只是人没有意识到而已。写作与科学创造不完全相同，但也有相同之处。作者在进行"写"这一行为之前，即使对写作任务很明确，对写作内容很熟悉，但对最终要表现怎样的主题仍然可能确定不下来，需要在所得材料的基础上，一而再、再而三地进行分析、归纳、提升，逐步形成较为深刻的认识，这就是提炼。

2. 选材

选材是对材料或素材的选择与使用，即根据表现主题的需要，作者对已获得的写作材料作进一步的挑选，并对挑选出的材料进行加工。如果将材料比作文章的血肉，那么材料过少，就会形销骨立、苍白无力、空洞无物，这当然不好；而材料堆砌，就会叠床架屋、庞大臃肿、冗长乏味，这当然也不好。

选材不同于搜集材料，常在立意之后，而搜集材料一般在立意之前。

3. 构思

构思是作者运用心思在大脑里勾画草图，从内涵到体式对写作内容进行全面预备、构想，梳理思路、描绘轮廓、构建框架，并策划可操作的程序，设计完整的写作蓝图，勾勒出写作雏形，形成某种意态文。构思过程中还应始终贯穿文体意识，受文体形式规范的制约，避免写出不伦不类的内容。SCI论文有原创论文、综述、研究热点、读者来信等多种文体类别，每类的内容和结构不同，写作要求和侧重当然都不相同，构思时一定要考虑文体之间的差异，避免写出不伦不类的论文来。

立意和选材主要是获取和挖掘材料，解决用什么写、写什么的问题，属于材料准备的物质范畴；而构思则主要是使用和用好所获得和挖掘到的材料，解决怎么写、如何写好的问题，属于材料使用的意识范畴。

4. 赋形

赋形是在心理上为由构思所形成的意态文勾画出具体形态，对写作内容的结构、体式、语言及每个表达细节做出大致安排，或者写提纲（安排层次标题），或者形成腹稿，虚拟写作成品的整体形态。虽然这时的内在语言与将来写作出来的外部语言不可能完全一致，在写作中还要更进一步深入、细化，甚至推翻原来构思的雏形，但如果没有这个雏形做基础，则写作就无法进行了。这是因为赋形为写作设计了线路图，使写作初具形态、规模。

写作内容早已在作者大脑中存在了，但未被赋形时处于离散状态。写作中没有思路，下不了笔，郁闷苦恼常伴，痛苦中煎熬，多是由未对内容赋形好所致。这就需要未雨绸缪，论文虽未写出，雏形却已形成。雏形使用了思维语，而用文字语替代思维语就进入表达环节了。

5. 表达

表达就是表示，基于赋形结果将构思出的目标书面化、外在化，即通过语言文字对构思中形成的写作雏形进行表述和传达，使用词语、句子、标点、体式和语言色彩等诸多语言要素，使作者心目中的意态文最终得以实现，成为实体文，即作品（稿件，半成品）。

表达不仅把意义定型下来，还要对原先的构思有深化、促进和提升作用。表达离不开修辞，通过修辞来调整语言，使语言恰当地、更好地传达所要表达的意义。

6. 修改

修改是从内容到形式对初稿进行全面的加工、调整和修订，尽可能改正所有发现的错误、缺点。即使是名家大家，其初稿完成后也很难做到不改一字一词，更何况是一般的作者。据说曹雪芹以坚韧不拔的毅力，专心致志地从事小说《红楼梦》的写作和修订，披阅十载、增删五次，才写出了这部把中国古典小说创作推向巅峰的文学巨著。实际中，一篇论文的完成，不是只进行一次修改就能完事，而是需要几次、多次甚至"无数次"的反反复复的修改，为的是内容上的准确通顺，形式上的得体美观，表达上的精益求精，最终提升论文的写作质量，提高论文的可读性和可理解性。

1.8 SCI 论文评价体系

1.8.1 SCI 论文

SCI 论文发表后的作用究竟如何，需要评价而确定，这就是 SCI 论文评价。

SCI 论文发表有两个方面作用：一方面，作者现实功用，如毕业答辩、学位申请、职称评审、课题验收、项目结题和业绩考核等；另一方面，增加科技财富，增强科研能力，改变思想认识，提升改造世界水平。论文评价往往是针对后一方面来说的。

仔细考查不难发现，SCI 论文从投稿到发表出来实际上经历了两个评价阶段：一是录用前的同行评议（把握发表价值），二是发表后的绩效评价（评估传播价值）。这里是指后一种。

论文发表后的绩效，从定性层面上来讲，包括获得（下载）、阅读（学习）、改变认识（思想变化）、参考（科研）、引用（写作）。论文阅读需要先行被获得，但被获得了不见得就能被阅读。阅读在于改变认识，如果一篇文章阅读后没有任何作用，那么其发表就没有意义,相反如果能够改变人们的认识,那么就有意义,认识改变程度越高,论文发表意义就越大,被引用(写文章)的可能性就越大。若后来相关研究参考了某篇论文,则该篇论文所承载的科学成果就得到传承,论文被参考得越多(人为因素除外),其传承的价值就越大。

任何科学研究都不是从零开始的,都要在前人已有成果的基础上进行,这就是牛顿所说的:"如果说我看得比别人更远些,那是因为我站在了巨人的肩膀上。"因此从科研大业的角度来说,论文发表的最大功用就是作科研参考(复用)。论文既然要让别人参考,那么首先要能被找到、看到,这在目前的网络和大数据时代是很容易实现的。论文如果有一个好的题目和摘要,再加上有让别人感兴趣的内容,那么被下载、阅读的可能性就大大提高了;如果还有令别人科研参考的高价值内容,那么被别人写文章引用的概率也就提高了。

论文发表后有下载和引用两个非常关键的动作,对应的量化指标就是全文下载量(下载量,Full-Text Downloads)和被引次数(Times Cited),这两个指标可以较为客观地反映单篇论文的水平和影响力。

下载量是基于某数据库或出版商平台的文献数据库所统计出来的某论文的全文在一定时期内(如一年)被下载的总次数。这个指标越高,该论文的现实价值(潜在价值)就越大。

被引次数(被引量)是基于某数据库或出版商平台的文献数据库所统计出来的某论文在一定时期内(通常一年)被已发表的别的文章引用的总次数。这个指标越高,该论文的参考价值就越大,影响就越大。

期刊编辑部常关注其期刊年度下载量、年度被引次数靠前(如前10位)的论文,对它们给予通告和奖励,将其作为办刊绩效的量化证明,作为后续项目申报、年度考核和对外宣传等的重要材料,还可为其期刊未来刊登何种文章能达到高下载量、高被引而提供参考或依据。

1.8.2 SCI 期刊

上一节所述的 SCI 论文评价是从单篇论文来说的,但如果从某 SCI 期刊在一定时期内(通常一年)刊登的全部论文来说,就是 SCI 期刊评价了。期刊评价的内涵是,众多论文共同作用产生一个合力影响,进而形成整个期刊的影响,对论文集合的评价就是对承载这些论文的期刊的评价。SCI 期刊评价有多个量化指标,下面简单介绍几个常见的指标。指标值均是基于某个数据库或出版商平台来统计的,不同的系统或平台,指标值不大可能相同。

1. 周期

周期指论文的出版周期(出版时滞),属论文发表前的范畴。论文从投稿到发表经历了编辑和生产两个过程,编辑是从论文投稿开始到编辑做出最终决定(录用或退稿)的过程,生产是从论文录用到在线发表的过程。前一过程所经历的时间称为录用周期(No. of days from submission to first decision),后一过程所经历的时间称为生产周期(No. of days from acceptance to Online First)。这两个周期的总和即为出版周期。

不同论文的录用周期、生产周期往往不同,对某一期刊来讲,某篇论文出版周期的长短并不具有代表性,出版周期通常是针对某一期刊在一定时间(通常一年)内发表的所有论文的平均出版周期。这个平均出版周期虽是一个平均值,不针对某一具体论文,但能从整体上反映出期刊的出版快慢。此值高,该刊出版快;反之,出版慢。作者一般更愿意将自己的论文投给出版周期较短的期刊。

实际中,追求较短的出版周期是各个期刊共同追求的目标,但除了一些名刊如

Nature、Science、Cell 等的出版周期很短或较短外，大部分期刊特别是中国较多的 SCI 期刊，出版周期往往比较长。产生这一问题的原因是多方面的，如编辑工作模式、审稿专家不可控、稿件数量较多、期刊容量较小、编辑和生产工作量大、编辑管理不到位等，想改变这一现状并不容易。笔者认为，学术论文的出版周期在 8~12 个月还算比较正常，低于 8 个月则可以列为目标，超出 12 个月甚至达到 2 年或以上就不可取了，应采取措施予以解决。

2. 使用

使用（Usage）指论文发表后由读者去检索和浏览、下载和阅读、参考和引用，属于论文发表后的范畴。某期刊刊登的论文被下载越多，从某种程度说，对该期刊的论文感兴趣的人或组织机构就越多，可能对更多的人越有参考价值，其潜在价值就越大，为读者后面撰写文章就能提供更多的帮助，被引用的概率就越大。试想，如果某期刊的论文从未被下载过，或下载很少，那么在正常情况下对其论文的引用能高吗？使用方面的指标常见的有以下几类。

（1）下载量（No. of Downloads）

下载量是某期刊所刊登的论文的全文在一定时期内（通常一年）被下载的总量。这个指标反映了该期刊的整体潜在价值（单篇论文的下载量仅反映该论文的潜在价值）。在期刊年度报告中，关于下载量的指标还有一些，例如：

1）全年下载量（含月度分布）（Successful Full-Text Downloads）；

2）下载量前 10 名论文（Top 10 Article Downloads）；

3）出版年度下载量（Downloads by Content Age），如 Current（2019）、Contemporary（2015–2019）等；

4）下载量地域分布（Visits by Geography），如 Asia-Pacific、Europe、North America、Middle East 等；

5）下载渠道（Visitor Referral），如 Google、Direct、Google Scholar、springer. com、apps. webofknowledge. com 等。

（2）期刊使用因子（Median UFJ（Usage Factor for Journals））

期刊使用因子是某期刊在某一时期内（如 2017/2018）在线发表的论文在相同时期内的下载量的平均值（It is the median value of the number of downloads in a certain period（such as 2017/2018）for all articles published online in that particular journal during the same time period.）

（3）被引频次（Total Cited Frequency）

被引频次是期刊自创刊以来所刊登的全部论文在统计当年被引用的总次数。该指标可显示出期刊被使用和受重视的程度，以及在科技交流中的绝对影响力的大小。

（4）被引频次学科排名（Ranking within Categories in Total Cited Frequency Year）

此指标是指专业排名，是在统计当年某一期刊的被引频次在某一特定学科（专业）中的相对排名位置，也就是该期刊在此学科中的压倒性百分比优势。

3. 影响

影响（Impact）是从论文被引用次数来说的，引用越多，影响就越大；反之，影响就越小；若是零引，则没有影响。论文被引用次数的多少是计算影响引子（Impact Factor）的基础，是整个 SCI 期刊或其他核心期刊评价体系的基础数据。影响方面的指标常见的有以下几类。

（1）收录期刊论文的数据库或索引系统（Coverage in Abstracting & Indexing（A&I）Services）

这是指一个期刊刊登的论文被某数据库或索引系统收录，也就是说该期刊被某数据库或索引系统收录，收录该期刊的数据库或索引系统越多，就从某个角度说明该期刊的影响越大。例如常见的数据库或索引系统有：Science Citation Index Expanded（SciSearch）、Journal Citation Reports/Science Edition、SCOPUS、INSPEC、Zentralblatt Math、Chemical Abstracts Service（CAS）、Google Scholar、CSA、Chinese Science Citation Database、Earthquake Engineering Abstracts、EI-Compendex、OCLC、SCImago、Summon by ProQuest 等。

（2）h5 指数（h5 Index）

h5 指数是 Google 学术使用的一个评价某期刊影响力的指标，意思是最近 5 年内该期刊有 h 篇论文被引用超过 h 次。（This metric is based on the articles published by a journal over the previous 5 calendar years with a minimum of 100 articles in this period. If a journal publishes 100 articles sooner, an h5 Index can be calculated earlier. h is the largest number of articles that have each been cited h times. The h5 Index therefore cannot be dominated by one or several highly cited articles.）h5 指数与影响因子相似，两者都是评估论文被引用情况，但 h5 指数计数的是期刊发表顶尖论文的数量，而影响因子评价的是平均水平的论文引用次数。

（3）SCImago 期刊排名（SCImago Journal Rank，SJR）

该指标是基于引文来源信息对期刊排名的计量指标，旨在突出对期刊的评价，反映期刊的信誉或论文被权威期刊引用的可能性大小。它不只是依赖于引文的数量，而是综合考虑引文的数量和质量。它采用 Google 的 PageRank 算法，赋予高声望期刊的引用以较高权重，并以此规则迭代计算直到收敛。（This metric is a measure of scientific influence of scholarly journals that accounts for both the number of citations received by a journal and the importance or prestige of the journals where such citations come from.）

SJR 是以三年期作为计算时间区间，以某期刊 2018 年的 SJR 值为例，是用其前三年（2015 到 2017 年）发表的论文于 2018 年被引用的次数来进行计算的，比影响因子的两年期时间区间长、数据量大而且趋势更稳定。此外，SJR 将期刊自引的门槛限定在 33%，意即若期刊自引在当年度超过其整体被引比例的 33%，则超出的自引数将不予计算。

（4）源标准化论文影响力指数（Source Normalized Impact per Paper，SNIP）

SNIP 是衡量期刊影响力的新工具，旨在对不同主题领域的期刊影响力进行评价。它给每个学科（甚至每一主题）都增加一个权重，而这个权重是根据这个学科（或主题）发表文章的被引总量计算的，对引用很少或不大可能引用的主题领域发生的单次引用的影响给予较高权重，反之亦然。（This metric measures contextual citation impact by weighting citations based on the total number of citations in a subject field. The impact of a single citation is given higher value in subject areas where citations are less likely, and vice versa.）

（5）期刊影响因子（Journal Impact Factor，JIF）

JIF 是某一期刊的文章在特定年份或时期被引用的频率，是衡量学术期刊影响力的一个重要指标。它是由美国科学情报研究所（ISI）创始人尤金·加菲得（Eugene Garfield）在 1960 年创立的，随后成为汤森路透（Thomson Reuters）⊖自 1975 年以来每年定期

⊖ 全球领先专业智能信息提供商汤森路透（Thomson Reuters）于 2016 年 7 月 11 日宣布，以 35.5 亿美元的价格将旗下知识产权和科学业务卖给了加拿大 Onex 公司（Onex Corp）和霸菱亚洲投资基金（Baring Private Equity Asia），其中知识产权和科学业务包含 Web of Science、Thomson CompuMark、Thomson Innovation、MarkMonitor、Thomson Reuters Cortellis 和 Thomson IP Manager。因此 SCI 现在已换东家了，由汤森路透（Thomson Reuters）易主为科睿唯安（Clarivate Analytics）。

发布、出品的期刊引证报告（Journal Citation Reports，JCR）中的一项数据，是一个相对统计量，现已成为国际上通用的期刊评价指标，不仅是测度期刊有用性和显示度的指标，而且也是测度期刊学术水平乃至论文质量的重要指标。JIF 的初衷在于展示某一期刊相较于其他期刊的影响力，在计算时是使用某期刊在前 2 年（或前 5 年）发表的论文在第 3 年（或第 6 年）的平均被引次数。不同于来自非业内的主观评价，JIF 所具有的优势是直接反映了科学家和学者自己对于最值得关注和有帮助的科学研究的判断。同时，JIF 也为文献计量学的发展带来了一系列重大革新。

影响因子定义中的特定年数或时期是 2 年或 5 年，以 2 年的发文数据作为统计源来计算的影响因子称为 2 年影响因子（第 3 年引用了前 2 年的发文），以 5 年的发文数据来计算的称为 5 年影响因子（第 6 年引用了前 5 年的发文）。

2 年影响因子计算方法：某期刊相对于统计年的前 2 年发表的文章在统计年（JCR 报告年份）的被引用次数除以该期刊在这 2 年内发表的文章（指原创论文和综述）的总数。以 2019 年某期刊影响因子的计算为例：

$$影响因子（2019）= A/B，$$

其中 A 为该期刊在 2017 年和 2018 年发表的所有文章在 2019 年被引用的次数，B 为该期刊在 2017 年和 2018 年发表的文章（指原创论文和综述）的总数。

例如，The International Journal of Advanced Manufacturing Technology（《国际先进制造技术》），2010 年发表文章 70 篇，2011 年发表 79 篇，这两年共发表 70 + 79 = 149 篇；2012 年引用了 2010 年发表的文章 187 次，引用了 2011 年发表的 143 篇，2012 年共引用了 2010 年和 2011 年发表的 187 + 143 = 330 篇文章。这样该刊 2012 年的影响因子为 330/149 = 2.215。

通常，期刊的影响因子越高，其学术影响和作用就越大，学术水平也就越高。每年期刊的影响因子是动态变化的，与期刊的发文量和被引用量直接相关。图书订购机构（如图书馆）可根据期刊的影响因子客观评估期刊质量，制定期刊引进政策；作者可根据影响因子大小决定投稿的目标期刊。对期刊的某一论文来说是没有影响因子这一概念的，而通过对该论文的被引用次数可相对客观地评价该文的作用。

（6）影响因子学科排名（Ranking within Categories in IF Year）

影响因子学科排名也即影响因子专业排名，是统计年某一期刊的影响因子在某一特定学科（专业）的 JIF 中的相对排名位置，即此期刊在此学科中的压倒性百分比优势。根据全球多家学术期刊的测评机构分析数据表明，影响因子虽能较好地反映同一学科内不同期刊的影响水平差别，但是对于相似学科或不同学科间的期刊比较则完全缺乏说服力，而影响因子学科排名这一指标弥补了影响因子自身的这一不足。理解这一指标还要注意以下几点：

1）某些冷门学科期刊的影响因子并不高，学科整体影响因子偏低，因而影响因子相对偏高的期刊，其影响水平应予以更多的肯定；

2）期刊影响因子的波动（上升或下降）往往属正常现象，并不一定说明期刊影响因子学科排名随着影响因子的波动有明显的上升或下降；

3）某一期刊涵盖多个学科领域时，它在不同学科的影响因子学科排名往往是不同的。

4）同一期刊的影响因子在不同学科的排名可能大相径庭，说明某一期刊在不同学科的影响程度有所不同。

4. 新指标

JIF 客观地揭示了期刊之间的引用与被引用关系，可让使用者了解那些影响力较高的、人们较为常用或常说的热门期刊，但不能代表一篇论文或者一项研究的水平。为此，科睿唯安推出了一些新的评价指标进行补充。

（1）期刊规范化的引文影响力（Journal Normalized Citation Impact，JNCI）

JNCI 对论文发表在特定期刊上的被引次数进行规范化，即每篇论文的 JNCI 值为该文实际被引频次与该期刊上发表的同出版年、同文献类型论文的平均被引频次的比值。一组论文的 JNCI 值即为每篇论文 JNCI 值加和后的平均值。JNCI 指标能提供某一（组）论文与其他科研工作者发表在同一（组）期刊上成果的比较信息，它能回答诸如"我的论文在所发表期刊上表现如何？"之类的问题。JNCI 超过 1，说明该科研主体影响力高于平均值；JNCI 低于 1，说明其影响力低于平均值。JNCI 对于出版机构评价论文发表后的影响力水平也十分有用，它揭示出那些超过平均水平并提高了期刊被引频次的研究工作。

（2）学科规范化的引文影响力（Category Normalized Citation Impact，CNCI）

一篇论文的 CNCI 是通过其实际被引次数除以同文献类型、同出版年、同学科领域论文的平均被引次数获得的。CNCI 可与 JNCI 一起使用，进行作者层面的分析。

（3）特征影响因子（Eigenfactor Score）

在影响力较大的期刊中的引用将获得更高的该指标得分，而且该指标消除了自引的影响。

（4）期刊影响因子百分位（JIF Percentile）

这是一个规范化的指标，其价值在于实现不同学科领域期刊的对比分析。

（5）论文影响值（Article Influence Score）

此指标用来评估某一期刊基于每篇文章的相对重要性。

1.8.3 影响因子观

1. 影响因子的影响因素

由影响因子计算式可看出，影响因子只和被引次数（被引频次）和论文数（发文数）直接相关，但实际上还与很多别的潜在因素密切相关。这些因素大体上包括以下方面。

（1）论文因素

论文因素包括论文的出版周期（时滞）、类型（文体）、篇幅（长短）及作者数等。出版周期短的论文更易获得较多的引用，出版周期较长时，会有一部分引文因老化（超过 2 年或 5 年）而未能统计进来，即未参与影响因子的计算，从而影响影响因子的提升。计算影响因子时，刊登量仅统计原创论文和综述，而对评论、来信、通讯及其他类文章则不予统计。原创论文和综述的篇幅较长，其他文章一般较短，短文章多为新闻、消息类的，容易得到引用。有资料表明，热门专业、课题的文章，如果篇幅较短、发表较快，则对其引用会较快达到高峰，进而使影响因子快速上升，然后又迅速下降；完整的原创论文，持续被引用的时间相对较长，影响因子升高较为持久；论文的被引频次还与论文的作者数呈显著的正相关。

（2）期刊因素

期刊因素包括期刊的刊登量（发文量）、类型，以及其他引证指标如即年指标、被引用半衰期、地区分布数、基金论文比、发行范围、发行量等。根据经验，发文量少的期刊更易得到高的影响因子，而且影响因子在年度间的波动会较大；发文量多且创刊年代久的期刊易得到较多的被引，但影响因子不一定因被引增多而增高。期刊的类型通常根据刊登文章的主体类型来说的，如原创类、综述类、专门类、交叉类、评论类、新闻（消息）类等，一般来说，综述类、交叉类、评论类、新闻类期刊相对原创类、专门类会有更多的被引。期刊的规模和结构也会影响影响因子，一般来讲，同类期刊的规模越大，其影响因子总体来说就越高；期刊刊登的热门主题、专业的文章越多，被引就越多，影响因子也就越高。

（3）学科因素

学科因素包括不同学科的期刊数、平均参考文献数、引用半衰期等，这些因素也会对影响因子产生影响。影响因子是以论文的引用与被引用的数量关系为基础来计算的。一个学科的引文数量，总体水平取决于各学科自身的发展特点和该学科期刊在数据库来源期刊中的占比（数量占比）两个主要因素。总体上说，某学科来源期刊越多，该学科期刊的被引频次和影响因子就越大，决定了学科影响因子和被引频次分布的不均衡性。例如，生物学期刊一直是 SCI 期刊中比较引人注目的，它不仅在期刊数量上明显多于其他学科，而且在被引频次和影响因子的数量上也占显著优势，表明了生物科学在当代科学中的重要位置。此外，影响因子还受期刊所涉及的学科在专业意义上的社会覆盖面的影响，如果某个期刊在专业意义上的社会覆盖面非常小，而且同类期刊又很少，那么该期刊的影响因子就不可能很高。

不同学科因其内在科研规律和外在需求不同，在做研究时所需引用他人科研成果的情况就不尽相同。这种区别至少会在两个方面影响到影响因子：一是需要引用他人成果的数量；二是引用他人成果的时间。引用他人成果的数量对应期刊的容量，引用他人成果的时间就是实际引用时间，而期刊的容量对应影响因子（这里针对 2 年影响因子）计算式中的近 2 年（统计年前面的 2 年）期刊的发文数，实际引用时间对应影响因子计算式中的近 2 年（论文发表年的后面 2

年）。这样不难看出，按近 2 年内的引文年限分布情况所做的排序结果和通过用影响因子方法对期刊的排序结果具有一致性，但影响因子不能正确反应出不同学科期刊之间影响力的大小，因为不同学科的论文在近 2 年的引文分布情况可能存在较大差异，例如医药、人体、生物等直接与人的生命和健康相关的学科的论文明显被人们关注较快、较多，短期内见效（被引用）的概率大，而其他学科的则相对较慢、较少，也许在更长时间（如 2 年、5 年或更多年）后才能见效，这是当前影响因子计算方法所不能解决的问题。

由于历史或其他原因，一个国家不同学科、同一学科的不同分支学科的建设和发展是不平衡的。有的学科规模很小，但从事这一学科的科研人员较多，资金投入也很大，相关期刊就较多，这样就会形成一种规模优势。而往往那些规模较小或大一些的学科可能不具备这种优势，从而其期刊的影响因子不会高。就学科规模发展速度而言，不同学科有冷、热之分：热门学科由于时代的需要，其规模发展速度较快，其文章在规模发展期间将产生较多被引；冷门学科正好相反，产生较少被引。但这种冷、热之分往往不是出于科学自身发展的需要，而多是由经济、社会等一些非科学因素的制约所造成的。还有一些学科包含不少热门课题，这些课题的文章虽有较多的被引，但并无多大的科学价值。可以看出，仅仅因为学科规模的大小和发展速度的快慢而造成论文被引用多少的不同，进而引起期刊影响因子大小的不同，从而造成在重要性的排序上的不同，不是科学本身发展造成的，而是一些非科学因素造成的。因此，对规模虽大但受众相对较少的学科或冷门专业的学科进行影响因子评价是极不合理和公平的。

（4）索引系统因素

索引系统因素包括参与统计的期刊来

源、引文条目的统计范围等。对于特定刊物来说，在各国、各种索引系统中，由于其所收录的期刊群体组成的差异较大，因此计算出的影响因子有较大差异，而且同一期刊在不同语种的数据库系统中有明显不同的影响因子及其他指标。

（5）名人效应因素

名人效应因素是作者常引用名人的文章来增加自己文章的权威性，即使在还有别的更适合自己文章引用的文献时也不去用这些文献，而是特意引用不怎么相关的名人文章；署有名人名字的文章或被名人推荐的文章容易在高档次期刊上发表，因而也容易被SCI收录，而且有时文章本没有名人的科研成果，却为了能在目标期刊上发表就署上了无关名人的名字，这样就过分地强调被引或收录情况，给文章被引频次和期刊影响因子带来由人为因素所造成的偏差。

2. 影响因子的先天缺陷

影响因子并非是一个最为客观的评价期刊影响力的标准。一般来说，影响因子越高，期刊的影响力就越大。对综合类或受众较多的大的研究领域来说，因其研究领域广而引用率就比较高，如生物、生命、人体和化学类期刊通常容易有较高的影响力。影响因子虽然可在一定程度上反映期刊学术质量的高低，但影响因子与学术质量并非呈线性正比关系，比如不能说影响因子为8.0的期刊一定优于影响因子为2.0的期刊，因为影响因子不具备对学术质量进行较为准确定量评价的功能。国内不少高校、科研机构在进行科研绩效考评时常以累计影响因子或单篇论文影响因子达到多少作为量化标准，有的研究者可能因影响因子差0.1分而不能晋升职称或评定奖金……，这种做法极不公平，产生的后果较为糟糕。

另外，影响因子因计算方法太过简单，好多相关因素并未考虑进来，这样就会出现漏洞，一些人为因素就容易钻了空子，致使计算结果过于离谱，这就是影响因子的先天缺陷。比如：

（1）不少期刊采用种种技术手法，想方设法让作者在修改文章或其他刊发文时引用较多本刊的文章，并要求作者对其文章在本刊发表后的被引潜力做出承诺，这里的被引潜力不取决于文章的水准和质量，而与文章的主题、热点性以及作者的权威性、研究规模、实力、发文情况、发文被引承诺等密切相关。文章发了，只要有引用、多引用就行，而文章的水准、质量就无所谓了。

（2）不少期刊故意大量缩减期刊的发文量，通过降低影响因子计算式中的发文分母来快速提升影响因子，这样就有大量文章被拒之门外，发文门槛大大抬高，作者积怨颇深，大量优秀论文与期刊失之交臂，结果是办刊与科研成果规模相脱节，违背办刊的科学宗旨。

（3）有的期刊大量增加除原创和综述外的别的文体，致使期刊的影响因子增加较快，但偏离了期刊原来的学术定位，结果是学术刊变得更像科普刊了。

（4）作者在其文章中引用了未参考过的文章，即有的文章未被参考却被有意引用。

（5）作者在其文章中未引用参考过的文章，即有的文章虽被参考却未被引用。

以上列举的这些情况在期刊界较为盛行，类似的情况也不少。过分依靠人为因素来提高影响因子盛行时，这种以人衡量论文、学术不再起重要作用的怪相的后果就出现了，使本来就"不怎么样"的影响因子就变得"更不怎样了"。难怪不少权威机构或个人对影响因子提出异议，甚至倡议停止使用。下面不妨列举几个事例：

（1）2016年7月25日，*Science*、*Springer Nature*等主流出版集团高层人士共同在bioRxiv联名发文，呼吁淡化期刊影响因子的影响，推广引用分布评价方法。如此联名发文实不多见，也许 IF 的改革真是一个时间问题。

（2）2016 年 7 月 12 日，美国微生物学会（ASM）在其官网发布消息，并在旗下 8 本期刊发表相关社论：ASM 期刊总编和 ASM 领导层决定，以后将不在 ASM 期刊网站上公布 IF。IF 评价系统过分强调高 IF，这一决定正是为了避免为这一扭曲的系统"推波助澜"。高 IF 期刊限制刊发论文数量，创造出一种排他性的印象。而且，有些研究人员因为在高 IF 期刊上发表论文而获得不恰当的奖励。这样扭曲的评价系统损害了科学本身，阻碍了科研工作的交流。

（3）2013 年，诺贝尔生理、医学奖得主 Randy Schekman 在英国《卫报》发文，宣称其实验室不再向 *Science*、*Nature*、*Cell* 投稿，这些名刊扭曲了科学进程，鼓励研究人员走捷径，在华而不实而非真正重要的领域进行研究。

（4）2016 年 7 月 11 日，汤森路透（Thomson Reuters）宣布，将以 35.5 亿美金的价格出售旗下包括 SCI 的知识产权与科技业务。重金售出科技业务的汤森路透即将变现，大把钞票"满血复活"。消息传来，SCI 的"接盘侠"令人大跌眼镜，它既不是众人猜测的学术期刊出版商，也不是谷歌学术搜索或政府机构，而是"门外汉"——加拿大 Onex 公司和霸菱亚洲投资基金（Baring Private Equity Asia）。

（5）中国《科学通报》中文版主编、中科院院士高福这样说："（汤森路透出售 SCI 等知识产权和科技业务）属于正常的商业运作，（对国内期刊发展）不会有什么影响。（该事件）倒是让国内科学界明白了 SCI 的本质。"

3. 正确认识并淡化影响因子

在当下唯影响因子评价盛行的制度下，中国英文期刊纷纷压缩发文量，发文量逐年下降。由 SCI 统计数据显示，对 2013—2017 年 SCI 收录期刊，期刊数、总被引频次、影响因子逐年增长，平均增长率分别为 6.16%、30.06%、18.03%，其中中国 SCI 期刊的总被引频次、影响因子平均增长率分别为 52.65%、92.71%，高于世界增长水平，而载文量呈现下降趋势，即为负增长（SCI 收录期刊平均发文量为 2013 年 151 篇，2014 年 154 篇，2015 年 157 篇，2016 年 161 篇，2017 年 164 篇，增幅为 8.68%；而中国 SCI 收录期刊平均发文量为 2013 年 167 篇，2014 年 158 篇，2015 年 146 篇，2016 年 144 篇，2017 年 137 篇，增幅为 -17.96%）。载文量的下降趋势将会对我国科技期刊的稿源竞争力和学术交流地位产生不利影响，从长远看不利于我国科技期刊的国际化进程。可以说，唯 SCI 影响因子的评价是导致我国优质稿源大量外流的重要原因。

因此，要正确认识影响因子的本质，不宜过分扩大其作用。笔者认为，影响因子是量化和半质化指标，是针对期刊的，并非直接针对论文。它只是一个检索工具而非评价工具，只是评估期刊的一个指标，而不适合评价文章。高影响因子的期刊有低水平文章，低影响因子的期刊也有不少高水平文章。日本出现诺奖井喷现象，但有的获奖者多将研究成果发表在不怎么知名的本土期刊上，而发表在国际顶尖期刊的论文并不多，有些还未发表在高影响因子和英文期刊上。可见，论文的价值重在内容，与用何种语言来写及在何种期刊上发表并无多大关联。

此外，还要正确认识影响因子的形成机制。据有关资料表明，期刊历年发表的多数文章（70% 以上）的被引次数小于其影响因子，即某期刊所谓的高影响因子是由其少数高被引文章（30% 以下）拉起的。例如，高影响因子期刊 *Nature*、*Science* 在 2015 年最高引文章达 905、694 次（低引文章占比 74.8%、75.5%）；在低影响因子期刊也有类似现象,如 *PLoS ONE*、*Scientific Reports* 在 2015 年最高引文章为 114 次、141 次(低引文章占比 72.2%、73.2%)。世界上影响因子最高的期刊 *CA：Cancer Journal for Clinicians* 的高影响因子 244.585 实际上是由 Ahmedin Jemal 教授每年主笔的 2 篇文章 "Global cancer statistics" 和 "Cancer statistics" 造就的,若排除这两篇文章,影响因子将缩水 80% 左右。

近日,中共中央办公厅、国务院办公厅印发了《关于深化项目评审、人才评价、机构评估改革的意见》,指出以后人才评价不唯论文、不唯职称、不唯学历、不唯奖项,要求各地区、各部门结合实际认真贯彻落实,这一重要指导思想将对我国科技期刊未来发展产生重要影响。笔者认为,对科技期刊的评价体系应该贯彻"重论文而不唯论文,重职称而不唯职称,重学历不唯学历,重奖项而不唯奖项"的思路,着力构建能体现能力、水平和贡献的科技期刊评价体系,这是一项政策性很强的重要战略性任务,也是科技期刊健康快速发展的重要内容。

第 2 章　SCI 论文主体写作

SCI 论文的价值在于其内容，而内容又必须依附结构通过语言来呈现。虽然论文写作涉及内容确定、材料获取、主题确立、结构安排、论据选择、论证使用、标题拟定、段落划分、选词造句、语法修辞等多个方面，但从质量上讲，不外乎就是内容、结构和语言，高质量的论文就是在内容、结构和语言上都好的论文。论文的结构是其各个组成部分及其之间的顺序，相同文体在结构上相同或相近，不同文体在结构上差别较大；各组成部分在表达上有相同之处，但由于其自身特点，表达差异也往往较大。因此从论文整体看，论文的结构容易理解和把握，但从论文局部看，因研究领域、内容、主题、对象、目的和方法等的不同，论文各部分的结构可能存在较大差异，因此写作中应该根据实际情况分别对待。

本章主要以 SCI 综述和原创论文为对象，较为详细地阐述论文主体部分的写作，涉及内容和结构、写作要求和方法、实例分析和修改等。后续章节对论文辅体（第 3 章）以及论文中内嵌要素（如量和单位、插图、表格、数学式，第 4~7 章）的写作进行讲述。只要按照 SCI 论文写作要求、方法及有关标准、规范认真写作和仔细修改，就能写出符合文体要求，并在主题思想、内容结构、表达手法、写作风格和编辑排版等方面各具特色的高质量论文。

2.1　层次标题

层次标题也称段落标题或小标题，是在论文题名统领下的各级标题，在结构形式上使整个论文层次分明，在内容上对各部分内容高度概括。层次标题是论文内容的划分、归类和关联，构成论文的框架，而论文内容是层次标题的实质、展开和细化，形成标题的实质，标题好比"骨"，内容则是"肉"。

层次标题与文体相关，有些文体如研究热点（Research Highlight）、新闻视角（News and Views）等篇幅很短，不用层次标题；有些文体如读者来信（Letter 或 Letter to the Editor）篇幅长一些，可用层次标题，也可不用，取决于表达的需要；而篇幅较长的文体如综述（Review）和原创论文（Original Article）必须有层次标题。层次标题在形式上有不编码和编码两种，不编码的形式在国际上较为流行，而国内期刊多采用编码的。

（1）不编码。各层次标题都不编码但如同编码，按顺序出现，层级通过字体、字号、大小写、正斜体、是否加粗的一致性来体现。例如：一级标题每个词全大写，字号较大；二级标题每个词或第一个词的首字母大写，字号适中、加粗；三级标题第一个词的首字母大写，字号适中或较小、斜体。

（2）编码。各层次标题一律编码，常用阿拉伯数字分级连续编写，不同层次的两个号码间用下圆点"."分隔，即一级标题的编码为 1，2，…（或从 0 开始）；二级标题的为 1.1，1.2，…；三级标题的为 1.1.1，1.1.2，…；以此类推。通常圆点加在数字的右下角，终止层次的号码之后加不加圆点均可。（编码一般左顶格排写，最后一个数字后加空来接排标题。）

下面给出一些示例。

【1】
Scattering on scattering
……（正文）

【2】

Hunting for the mutant without the MAP（K）

……（正文）

此两例分别属研究热点、新闻视角类文体，内容单一、集中，篇幅短，通常 2 个页码，正文不用任何层次标题。

【3】

Simple β-lactones are potent irreversible antagonists for strigolactone receptors

Dear Editor,

……（正文）

【4】

High-sensitivity infrared vibrational nanospectroscopy in water

……（正文）

METHODS

Experimental setup

Sample preparation

Simulations

此两例属读者来信类文体，内容稍多，篇幅稍长，通常 4 至 5 个页码，正文通常不用层次标题，如例【3】；但有时为了表达需要，在正文后面增加有关实验内容，这部分就要用层次标题，如例【4】。

【5】

Optical manipulation from the microscale to the nanoscale: fundamentals, advances and prospects

INTRODUCTION

FUNDAMENTALS OF OPTICAL FORCES AND COMPUTATIONAL APPROACHES

NON-CONSERVATIVE FORCES AND OPTICAL TORQUE

FORCE ENHANCEMENT BY PLASMONICS AT THE NANOSCALE

APPLICATIONS IN BIOCHEMICAL MANIPULATION

CONCLUSIONS AND FUTURE PROSPECTS

例【5】属综述类文体，对某领域或某问题的研究现状充分回顾、分析和总结，得出指导性结论，指明未来发展方向，篇幅通常比原创类论文还要长，10 多个页码很常见，层次标题是必需的（结尾的 **CONCLUSIONS AND FUTURE PROSPECTS** 或与此同义的其他词语最典型，一篇综述如果没有这一标题则不规范），但通常较为单一，即标题的层级较少。

【6】

Realization of the first sub-shot-noise wide field microscope

INTRODUCTION

MATERIALS AND METHODS

RESULTS AND DISCUSSION

CONCLUSIONS

【7】

H7N9 virulent mutants detected in chickens in China pose an increased threat to humans

Introduction

Results

Surveillance and genetic analysis of H7N9 avian influenza viruses

Replication and virulence of H7N9 HA mutant A/chicken/Guangdong/SD008/2017（CK/SD008）in chickens

Replication and virulence of H7N9 virus CK/SD008 in mice

Replication and transmission of the CK/SD008 virus in ferrets

Replication and virulence of CK/SD008 PB2 mutants in mice

Replication, virulence, and transmission of CK/SD008 PB2 mutants in ferrets

Receptor-binding preference of the CK/SD008 virus

Thermal stability of H7N9 viruses

Discussion

Materials and Methods

Ethics statements

Biosafety statement and facility

Sample collection and virus isolation

Genetic and phylogenetic analysis

Animal studies

Chicken study

Mouse study

Ferret study

Receptor-binding analysis

Heat stability test

Polymerase activity analysis

Statistical analysis

【8】

A fast and automatic full-potential finite volume solver on Cartesian grids for unconventional configurations

1. Introduction

2. Cartesian grid method

2.1. *Geometric model and data structure*

2.2. *Grid initialization and geometric adaption*

2.3. *Cell classifying and smoothing*

3. Full potential finite volume solver

3.1. *Governing equations*

3.2. *Finite volume formulation*

3.2.1 *Spatial discretization*

3.2.2 *Flux computation*

3.3. *Implicit algorithms and GMRES iteration*

3.4. *Solution adaptation*

4. Boundary conditions and viscous drag prediction

4.1. *Wall boundary condition*

4.2. *Kutta condition*

4.3. *Farfield boundary condition*

4.4. *Viscous drag prediction*

5. Validation and results

5.1. *Subsonic flow over DLR-F4*

5.2. *Transonic flow over ONERA M6*

5.3. *Computations on a BWB configuration*

6. Conclusion

例【6】~【8】属原创类文体，篇幅较长，8个页码左右（甚至10多个页码）较常见，层次标题是论文的重要组成部分。实验型论文最具科学价值，其层次标题一般是INTRODUCTION、MATERIALS AND METHODS、RESULTS AND DISCUSSION、CONCLUSIONS（或Introduction、Materials and Methods、Results and Discussion、Conclusions）。

在写作要求方面，层次标题同论文题名一样，应当简短明确，既要概括本层特定内容，又要突出重点或中心，一般用名词、短语。同一层次的标题应只反映同一层次的内容；同一层次的各部分（段）内容是否列标题最好一致，列与不列取决于内容表达的需要。

题名和层次标题基本上体现了论文的结构和组成。下面就论文主体各部分的写作进行较为详细的阐述。

2.2 题名

题名（Title）又称题目、标题、文题或篇名，是简明、确切地反映论文最重要特定内容、研究范围和深度的最恰当的多个词语的逻辑组合。有的题名还包括副题名或引题，一篇论文一般还有若干层次标题。题名相当于论文的"标签"，通常是别人最先浏览的内容，是检索系统首先收录的部分，也是体现论文水平与范围的第一重要信息，具有画龙点睛、启迪思维、激发兴趣等诸多功能。

审稿人和读者一般是先查看题名和作者信息来了解论文内容的。论文内容实际上是围绕题名展开的，题名能否反映论文内容是审稿评估的重要标准。审稿人评审论文时，首先从题名入手，如果感兴趣，再看摘要；如果更感兴趣，接着再看引言、结论和图表；最后才有可能通读全文。一般读者通过上网或查询数据库系统来检索论文，根据查到的题名考虑是否有必要阅读（复制、保存）摘要或全文，这个决定往往是在快速浏览题名的过程中做出的，若题名不吸引人就会失去其应有的作用，使真正需要的读者错过机会，影响论文的引用和交流。另外，图书馆和研究机构大都使用联机检索系统，某种程度上是根据题名中的关键词来查找有关信息的，好的题名直接带来使用上的方便以及查询结果的准确性，而不好的题名可理解性差，没人愿意看就会失去读者，导致论文"丢失"，从而不能被潜在的读者查找到。可见，题名的好坏直接影响人们对论文的第一印象，难怪有"论文的题名是论文的一半"之说。

2.2.1 题名写作要求

题名很重要，但写好较难，再加上作者不重视，题名往往写得不够准确和恰当，影响了论文整体的形象与质量。其实，题名是吸引读者阅读论文的第一步，好题名应能准确反映论文内容，既不空泛，也不繁琐，给人以鲜明的印象。

题名应至少达到准确（accuracy）、简洁（brevity）、清楚（clarity）和吸引人

(attractive) 四点要求：准确是明确充分地反映论文的主要内容，简洁是以最少数量的词语概括尽可能多的内容，清楚是清晰明白地反映论文的具体内容和特色，吸引人是读者看到题名后就想阅读全文。最佳的标题应该是用最少、最合适的词语来准确明白地概括论文的主体内容。

1. 准确

题名要准确表达论文的内容，恰当反映研究的范围和深度，与正文的内容紧密贴切，即题要扣文、文要扣题。题名不要过大或过小，避免题文偏差，要做到让读者和审稿人一看题名就能大概判断论文的研究内容和范围，这是论文写作的基本准则。为确保含义准确，题名不应过于华丽或承诺太多，避免用非定量、含义不明的词。研究型论文的题名应包含由关键词描述的结果。

2. 简洁

题名应简短明了，以最少的词和字符概括尽可能多的内容，即在准确反映、清楚表达最主要特定内容的前提下，词越少越好，坚决去掉冗词。用词要精选，不能太长、繁琐，这样难给人以鲜明的印象，且难记和难引；也不宜太短，使人丈二和尚摸不着头脑，搞不清主题、领域范围。究竟多少词算合适并无硬性规定，一般为 10~12 个词，最好不超过 100 个字符（含空格和标点）。据有关研究报道，SCI 论文题名的长度与其引用率直接相关。

不同机构的期刊对题名的要求不同。例如，AMA（美国医学会）规定题名不超过 2 行，每行不超过 42 个字符和空格；AMS（美国数学学会）要求不超过 12 个词，用词质朴、明确、实事求是，避免用广告式、冗赘夸大式字眼；NCI（美国癌症研究所）要求不超过 14 个单词；英国数学会要求不超过 12 个单词；*Nature* 要求不超过 3 行，每行 30 个字符（含空格），一般不应含有数字、首字母缩略语、缩写或标点符号（必要时可用一个冒号）；*Science* 要求采用描述性短语，不用完整的句子，每行最长 30 个字符，报告和研究型论文的题名不超过 3 行，综述的不超过 100 个字符。

这些规定仅供参考，总体原则是在能够确切反映论文特定内容的前提下，题名用词越少越好，最终达到确切、清晰、简练、醒目即可。

3. 清楚

题名要清晰明白地反映论文的具体内容和特色，明确表明研究工作的独到之处，力求简洁有效、重点突出。为保证表达直接、清楚，引起读者的注意，应尽可能将表达核心内容的关键词（主题词）放在标题的开头。

不宜因一味追求精选词数而影响题名对论文内容的清楚反映，在遇到矛盾需要在两者之间取舍时，宁可多用几个词也要力求表达明确，清楚优于简洁。若题名简短不足以显示论文内容，或反映系列研究内容，或内容层次较多时，可采用主、副标题相结合的方式，来补充说明特定的实验材料、方法、内容等信息，使标题既充实、准确，而又不流于笼统和泛化。

4. 吸引人

题名最终应具有吸引力，即一目了然，使读者看了爱不释手，有继续深入的愿望和冲动。虽然题名居于首先映入审稿人（发表前）或读者（发表后）眼帘的醒目位置，但仍然存在是否吸引人的问题。题名用词及表现内容不同，产生的效果就不同，好的题名既概括了全文，把论文在同类研究中突显出来，又能引人注目，将读者的需求在众多相关研究中定格下来。

吸引人的题名应该是：用词准确、结构合理、详略得当、语序正确、修辞妥当、逻辑通顺，给人以美感。笔者基于多年的工作实践，从以下几个方面阐述题名的写作。

2.2.2 题名内容表达

题名内容表达指题名所述内容准确恰当，与论文正文内容紧密匹配，具体有以下原则。

1. 题文相扣

题名要准确表达论文的内容和主题，恰当反映研究的范围和深度，与论文内容要互相匹配，即题要扣文、文要扣题，这是题名表达的基本准则。实际中常常出现不扣文的过于笼统的题名，多由缺少必要的限定语、题名太短所致。例如：

【1】Research of Reconfigurable Manufacturing System

【2】Research of the Internal Condensation of Water Vapor in Pneumatic System

【3】The Hydraulic Actuators for Automotive Active Safety Control System

以上题名过于笼统，所指研究范围太大而不明确，若针对论文内容或具体研究对象来命名，问题就解决了。题名【1】可改为 Basic Theory and Method of Reconfigurable Manufacturing System；Research Actuality and Development Tendency of Reconfigurable Manufacturing System；Production Path Planning and Method of Reconfigurable Manufacturing System in a Workshop；Computer Aided Process Planning Technology of Reconfigurable Manufacturing System 或 CAPP Technology of Reconfigurable Manufacturing System。还有其他修改方案，取决于论文的最重要特定内容或具体研究对象。题名【2】、【3】可分别改为：Mechanism and Experiment of the Internal Condensation of Water Vapor in Pneumatic System；Performance and Theory of the Hydraulic Actuators for Automotive Active Safety Control System。

【4】Preliminary Observations on the Effect of <u>Certain</u> Antibiotics on <u>Various Species</u> of Bacteria

此题名中 Certain 和 Various Species 不确指，对 Antibiotics 和 Bacteria 的限定作用较宽，因此此题名整体意思较为宽泛，还不如改为非常简短的 Action of Antibiotics on Bacteria，这样修改不仅消除了废词，还提高了表达效果。但从内容上看，修改后的题名因太简短而流于宽泛，再加上使用一般术语（非专门术语），如果论文讨论的不是所有抗生素对所有细菌的作用，那么这种修改使题文更不相扣，就谈不上有什么实质意义了。

如果研究的仅是一种或几种抗生素和细菌，则它们应分别出现在题名中，如果抗生素和细菌的种类数量太多，不便一一列于题名中，则其所属组名或类别应列于题名中。例如：

【5】Action of Streptomycin on Mycobacterium Tuberculosis

【6】Action of Streptomycin, Neomycin, and Tetracycline on Gram-Positive Bacteria

【7】Action of Polyene Antibiotics on Plant-Pathogenic Bacteria

【8】Action of Various Antifungal Antibiotics on Candida Albicans and Aspergillus Fumigatus

这些题名可以接受，但仍不够专门化，因为 Action of 有笼统之感，如果对 Action of 具体化，其含义可能会更清楚，如题名【5】可改为 Inhibition of Growth of Mycobacterium Tuberculosis by Streptomycin。

2. 概念准确

题名中会涉及一些概念，要充分注意并恰当运用概念的外延和内涵，避免写出不恰当的题名。外延指一个概念所反映的每一对象，内涵则指对每一概念对象特有属性的反映。为使题名含义准确，尽量避免使用非定量、含义不明确的词，并力求用词具有专指性。例如：

【9】<u>Particle Swarm Optimization Algo-</u>

rithm Based on Pyramid Model for Satellite Module Layout

【10】Optimal Design Method for Mountain Bike Rear Suspension Mechanism

【11】Kinematic Design and Scale Synthesis of 5-DOF Hybrid Robot with Large Workspace/Limb-stroke Ratio

题名【9】的中心词语是 Particle Swarm Optimization Algorithm，不如将其中的 Algorithm 去掉更加准确。Particle Swarm Optimization，简称 PSO，属于计算机领域的术语，是指通过迭代尝试改进一个给定质量度量标准来优化问题解决方案的一种计算方法，广泛用于技术、工程领域。论文主题内容所着眼的是"优化"和"优化方法"，已暗含"算法"，因此用 Particle Swarm Optimization 比 Particle Swarm Optimization Algorithm 从概念上更准确。同理，题名【10】中的 Method 可以去掉；【11】中的 Kinematic Design 和 Scale Synthesis 形式上为并列关系，但前者可包含后者，因此可以将 and Scale Synthesis 去掉。

3. 表意清楚

题名表意应直接了当、清晰明白，以引起读者的注意，因此应尽可能将表达核心内容的主题词放在题名的开头。例如：

【12】The Effectiveness of Vaccination against Influenza in Healthy, Working Adults

【13】Improved Method for Hilbert Instantaneous Frequency Estimation

题名【12】中，如果用 Vaccination 作题名的开头，读者可能会误认为这是一篇方法性论文，而用 Effectiveness 作为题名的第一个主题词，就直接指明了研究的主题。题名【13】中，用 Method 作为题名的第一个主题词，直接指明了这是一篇方法性论文。

模糊不清的题名往往会给读者和索引工作带来麻烦和不便。例如：

【14】Hybrid Wavelet Packet-Teager Energy Operator Analysis and Its Application for Gearbox Fault Diagnosis

【15】A Complication of Translumbar Aortography

【16】New Hydraulic Actuator's Position Servocontrol Strategy

题名【14】的 Its 指代不明，需费力判断；【15】的 Complication 表意不明，需使劲想象，也难有好的结果。另外，为确保题名含义准确，应尽量避免用非定量、含义不明的词，如 Rapid、New、Good、Important、Advanced 等，并力求用词的专指性，如 A Vanadium-iron Alloy 明显优于 A Magnetic Alloy；【16】的 New 是指作者新提出的，还是别人提出的，表意不大明确。

4. 术语使用

题名用词十分重要，直接关系到读者对论文的取舍态度。要尽量使用通用术语来表达有关概念，以加强概念表达的专业性、准确性、简洁性以及写作的严谨性、细致性、学术性。表达术语时，能用某术语却用了别的词语，或不必要地对其重新给出定义，或给出与其现有公认概念有出入的解释，均是不可取的。例如上述题名【9】中的 Particle Swarm Optimization Algorithm 就是一个计算机术语，简称 PSO，在各领域使用较广。再如：

【17】Intelligent Development Strategy of Process Design Technology Based on Computer

此题名未准确使用术语，其中 Process Design Technology Based on Computer 应改用术语 Computer Aided Process Planning 或其缩写 CAPP。即改为：Intelligent Development Strategy of Computer Aided Process Planning 或 Intelligent Development Strategy of CAPP。

SCI 论文题名强调使用一般的常用术语、通俗化词语，避免用特殊术语、难懂词语，以使领域内专家、同行、非专业人士甚至领域外读者也能看懂，从而有利于交流与传播。

题名中准确的线索（keys）对于文献检索至关重要。目前，大多数索引和摘要服务系统已采取关键词系统，因此题名中的术语应是论文中重要内容的"亮点"（highlight words），且容易被理解和检索。

2.2.3 题名结构表达

题名像一条标签，常由名词性短语构成，习惯上常用以名词或名词性短语为中心的偏正结构，一般不用动宾结构。但当中心动词前有状语时，可用动宾结构；Talk about…, Simple discussion on… 等形式的题名也可用动宾结构。例如：

【1】Study Entrusting-Agent Problem in Vehicle Logistics

此题名是动宾结构（Study + Entrusting-Agent Problem），应改为偏正结构：Study on Entrusting-Agent Problem in Vehicle Logistics，按简洁原则还可将 Study on 去掉而改为 Entrusting-Agent Problem in Vehicle Logistics。

【2】Study Entrusting-Agent Problem in Vehicle Logistics by Using Information Economics

【3】Ameliorate Acoustic Performance of Two-Cylinder Compressors by Using Single-pipe Suction Accumulator

这两题名的中心动词 Study、Ameliorate 分别有状语 by Using Information Economics、by Using Single-pipe Suction Accumulator，用动宾结构合适，但也可改为偏正结构，例如题名【2】可改为 Study on Entrusting-Agent Problem in Vehicle Logistics Using Information Economics，Study on 去掉后更简洁；【3】可改为 Amelioration of Acoustic Performance of Two-Cylinder Compressors by Using Single-pipe Suction Accumulator。

【4】Talk about Entrusting-Agent Problem in Vehicle Logistics

此题名为动宾结构（Talk about + Entrusting-Agent Problem），不用改为偏正结构。

题名常由名词性短语构成，基本上由一个或若干名词加上前置和（或）后置修饰语构成，其中动词多以动名词或分词的形式出现。例如：

【5】Ambient Temperature and Free Stream Turbulence Effects on the Thermal Transient Anemometer

【6】Particle Distribution in Centrifugal Accelerating Fields

【7】Pricing Incentive Strategy of Information Sharing In Supply Chain

【8】Improving the Concept of an Asynchronous Cyclotron

题名【5】【6】画线部分为中心词（名词性短语），后面部分为其后置修饰语；【7】【8】的中心动词分别是其动名词形式 Pricing、分词形式 Improving。

陈述句易使题名具有判断式语意，通常显得不够简洁和醒目，重点也不够突出，况且题名主要应起标示作用，因此题名一般不宜用陈述句（主谓结构）。但为了强调过程性、动态性，有时可使用陈述句，但忌用冗长的主、谓、宾结构的完整语句逐点描述论文内容，少数情况下还可用疑问句，尤其在评论性、综述性和驳斥性论文的题名中，使用探讨性的疑问句型可以有探讨性语气，使题名表达显得较为生动，容易引起读者的兴趣。例如：

【9】The Anthropocene is functionally and stratigraphically distinct from the Holocened

【10】Sorghum Roots Are Inefficient in Uptake of EDTA-chelated Lead

【11】H7N9 virulent mutants detected in chickens in China pose an increased threat to humans

【12】Can Agricultural Mechanization Be

Realized without Petroleum?

【13】A Race for Survival：Can *Bromus Tectorum* Seeds Escape *Pyrenophora Semeniperda*-caused Mortality by Germinating Quickly?

题名【9】~【11】为陈述句，【12】及【13】的副题名为疑问句。

题名比句子简短，且不必主、谓、宾齐全，因此其中词的顺序显得尤为重要，词序不当会导致表达不准确甚至错误。一般来说，表达题名时应首先确定好最能够反映论文核心内容的主题词（中心词），再进行前后修饰扩展，修饰语与相应主题词应紧密相邻。例如：

【14】Cars Blamed for Pollution by Scientists

此题名的 for Pollution 和 by Scientists 的顺序颠倒，使想表达的本意"科学家将污染归罪于汽车"变成"科学家造成的污染归罪于汽车"，原因就在于这两词语的顺序不当。

【15】Nursing of Trans-sphenoid Removal of Pituitary Adenomas

此题名将接受"护理"（Nursing）的对象"病人"（未出现）表达成"手术"（Trans-sphenoid Removal of Pituitary Adenomas），即对"手术"的护理，明显不合逻辑。应改为：Nursing for Patients after Trans-sphenoid Removal of Pituitary Adenomas。修改后，护理的对象就是病人了，即对"病人"的护理（Nursing for Patients），并对手术限定了病人类型。

【16】Neutrons Caused Chain Reaction of Uranium Nuclei

此题名为陈述句（Neutrons 为主语，Caused 为谓语，Chain Reaction of Uranium Nucle 为宾语），若改为短语 Chain Reaction of Uranium Nuclei Caused by Neutrons（Chain Reaction 为中心语，of Uranium Nuclei 和 Caused by Neutrons 为后置修饰语），表达效果会更自然、恰当。

【17】Multi-scale and Multi-phase Nanocomposite Ceramic Tools and Cutting Performance

此题名中 Tools 和 Cutting Performance 并列不妥，因为切削性能仅是刀具的一个属性，不在一个层面上，应在 Cutting Performance 的前面补出必要的词语，如 and it's。如果论文的主题就是 Cutting Performance，则可改为：Cutting Performance of Multi-scale and Multi-phase Nanocomposite Ceramic Tools。（Multi-scale and Multi-phase Nanocomposite Ceramic 是 Tools 的前置修饰语。）

【18】Numerical Simulation by Computational Fluid Dynamics and Experimental Study on Stirred Bioreactor with Punched Impeller

此题名按论文内容，应先介绍 Experimental Study（实验研究），再介绍 Numerical Simulation（数值模拟），因此连词 and 前后部分的顺序颠倒。可改为：Experiment on Stirred Bioreactor with Punched Impeller and Numerical Simulation by Computational Fluid Dynamics。

悬垂分词如 using、causing 等在题名中十分常见，因为其潜在的主语是"人"（研究者）而不是"物"（研究对象），使用时容易出错，因此使用悬垂分词时应十分小心。例如：

【19】Nanoscale Cutting of Monocrystalline Silicon Using Molecular Dynamics Simulation

【20】New Scaling Method for Compressor Maps Using Average Infinitesimal Stage

【21】Characterization of Bacteria Causing Mastitis by Gas-liquid Chromatography

题名【19】容易误解为 Monocrystalline Silicon uses Molecular Dynamics Simulation，因为只能是人（作者）使用分子动态模拟，而非"物"（单晶硅）。可改为：Using Molecular Dynamics Simulation in Nanoscale Cutting of Monocrystalline Silicon。题名【20】错误地表达为 Compressor Maps Use Average Infinitesimal Stage。是人使用 Average Infinitesimal Stage，而不是 Compressor Maps，因此可改为：Using Average Infinitesimal Stage in Scaling Method for Compressor Maps。题名【21】错误地表示成 Bacteria 使用 Gas-liquid Chromatography 而引起 Mastitis。是人使用 Gas-liquid Chromatography，而不是 Bacteria，因此可改为：Using Gas-liquid Chromatography in Characterization of Mastitis Caused by Bacteria。

2.2.4 题名语言表达

题名语言表达指题名的用语和组织要符合语法、逻辑、修辞等方面的规则及结构要求，尽量给读者以清晰和美感，具体有以下原则。

1. 简短精练

题名应确切、具体反映研究的主要内容或对象，用词要简短精练，但不能因一味追求形式上的简短而影响题名对论文内容的准确、恰当反映，为表达需要而适当增加词数是可以的。题名太短常常起不到帮助读者理解论文的作用，但偏长又不利于读者浏览时快速了解信息。例如：

【1】Transition Texture Synthesis

【2】Presence of Triploids among Oak Species

此两题名分别只有 3 个和 6 个单词，词数恰到好处，简洁明确地表达了论文的内容。

【3】Study on Brucella

此题名过短，读者无法知道具体的研究领域，其中的 Brucella 是有关医学、分类学、遗传学、生物化学还是别的什么方面的，不得而知。

【4】Research about Rapid Analysis Method of Chemical Constituents Included in Liquid Steel

【5】Preliminary Observations on the Effect of Zn Element on Anticorrosion of Zinc Plating Layer

题名【4】在语言表达上较为烦琐，存在一些冗词，很明显其中 Research、about、Included in 等在删掉的情况下毫不影响原意的表达。可改为：Rapid Analysis Method of Chemical Constituents of Liquid Steel。修改后词数由 12 个减少为 9 个（Method 也可去掉而只有 8 个词），题名干净利落、简短明了。题名【5】偏长，用词和表意冗余，如 Preliminary Observation、Element，精简后可显著提升效果。可改为：Effect of Zn on Anticorrosion of Zinc Plating Layer。

表达题名时还要避免词意上的重叠，如 Zn Element 中的 Element、Traumatic Injuries 中的 Traumatic、at Temperature 100℃ 中的 Temperature 等都是可以省去的，Experimental Research、Experimental Study 可直接表达为 Experiment。

在短题名不足以显示论文内容（短题名难以简化或语意未尽），或内容层次较多，或系列研究分篇报道时，可以在主题名之后加副题名，副题名补充、说明主题名，使整个题名既充实准确而又不流于笼统和一般化。例如：

【6】Industrial Engineering and Visualisation —A Product Development Perspective

【7】Nano-bearing：The Design of a New Type of Air Bearing with Flexure Structure

【8】Flow in a Pelton Turbine Bucket：Numerical and Experimental Investigations

题名【6】的破折号及【7】、【8】的冒号的前、后部分分别为主、副题名。

简化题名通常可通过删除冠词和说明性冗词来实现。题名中的冠词有简化的趋势，凡可用可不用的均可省去。说明性冗词通常有 Research on、Study of (on)、Investigations on、Analysis of、Development of、Evaluation of、Experimental、On the、Regarding、Report of (on)、Review of、The Nature of、Treatment of、Use of …，这类词语在题名中通常可以省去，但有时不能，如果省略后造成难读难懂甚至会影响原意的表达，就不能省。例如：

【9】The Procedure Sequence of Distribution Center in a Multiple-echelon Supply Chain

【10】Development and Flow Characteristics Study of Novel Combined Inner-Outer Agitator

【11】Experimental Study of the Effect of Spinning on Elastohydrodynamic Lubrication Films

【12】An Efficient Clustering Algorithm for k-Anonymisation

【13】Differential Responses of Lichen Symbionts to Enhanced Nitrogen and Phosphorus Availability：An Experiment with Cladina stellaris

【14】A Comparative Study of Germination Ecology of Four Papaver Taxa

【15】Numerical Study of Flow Resistance Characteristic for Oil Atomized Nozzle at Lower Pressure

【16】Development and Seed Number in Indeterminate Soybean as Affected by Timing and Duration of Exposure to Long Photoperiods after Flowering

题名【9】的定冠词和不定冠词均可省去，【10】的 Study 可删掉，【11】的 Experimental Study of 可删掉或改为 Experiment，【12】~【16】中画线的词语（包括冠词和说明性冗词）就不宜或不能省去（【15】中的 Study 改为 Analysis 效果可能会更好）。

注意：基金（课题）名称主要侧重于研究计划（将研究什么），与 SCI 论文题名主要讲述研究结果（发现了什么）有较大不同，通常含有 The Study of、The Reseach on 之类的语句。

2. 正确使用介词

题名中常见的介词有 with、of、for、in 等，如果不加区分就容易出错。

题名中常用名词做修饰语，如 Radioactive Material Transport，Multizone Moving Mesh Algorithm 等，但有时汉语中起修饰作用的名词译成英语时，用对应的名词直接做前置修饰语可能不合适。比如用名词做修饰语来修饰另一个名词时，如果前者是后者的一部分或所具有的性质、特点，则需要用前置词 with 加名词组成的 "with + 名词" 短语放在所修饰的名词之后来修饰。例如："具有中国特色的新型机器"不能译为 Chinese Characteristics New Types of Machines，而应是 New Types of Machines with Chinese Characteristics；"异形截面工作轮"不能译为 Noncircular Section Rolling Wheel，而应是 Rolling Wheel with Noncircular Section 或 Rolling Wheel with Special Shaped Section。

中文题名中常使用"定语 + 的 + 中心语"的结构，此处"的"在英文中有两个相应的前置词 of、for，其中 of 主要表示所有关系，for 主要表示目的、用途等。题名中还常使用 in 表示位置、包含关系。例如：

【17】Inhibition Mechanism of Na_2MoO_4 for Carbon Steel in 55% LiBr Solution

【18】Nonlinear Estimation Methods for Autonomous Tracked Vehicle with Slip

题名【17】的 Inhibition Mechanism 与 Na_2MoO_4 为所有关系，其间用 of；Na_2MoO_4 与 Carbon Steel 间的 for 表示目的、用途；Carbon Steel 与 LiBr Solution 为包含关系，其间用 in。题名【18】中所指的方法 Nonlinear Estimation Methods 用于车辆 Autonomous Tracked Vehicle，表示方法的用途或使用场

合，所以其间用 for 而不用 of。

3. 语序正确

题名的语序必须正确，语序不当会造成表意混乱，令人费解。另外还要注意题名中"的"字的位置，其位置不同，题名所表达出来的意思就可能不同。关于题名语序方面的内容在前面题名"结构规范表达"一节中已有介绍，这里再举两个例子。

【19】Mediation Method Based on EDM Energy Operator and Its Application in Mechanical Fault Diagnosis

【20】Geometric Accuracy Testing of Computer Aided Machine Tool

题名【19】中 Based on 的对象应是 EDM，而不是 EDM Energy Operator，Its 指 Method，而不是指 Operator，因此存在语序错误。另外 EDM 拼写错误，应改为 EMD（Empirical Mode Decomposition）。可改为：Energy Operator Mediation Method Based on Empirical Mode Decomposition (EMD) and Its Application in Mechanical Fault Diagnosis。题名【20】的语序也不正确。可改为：Computer Aided Testing of Geometric Accuracy of Machine Tool。

4. 正确使用缩略语

题名中可以使用缩略语，但应受到相应读者群的制约，特别当一个缩略语可表示多个意思时，使用时注意其表意明确，不要造成误解，必要时应在其后括号中注明其全称。通常对那些全称较长、已得到科技界或行业公认的缩略语可直接使用。有的缩略语直接用在中文题名中虽然可能不恰当，但用在英文题名中通常是可以的。例如：DNA（Deoxyribonucleic Acid）、AIDS（Acquired Immune Deficiency Syndrome）等已为科技界熟悉和公认，可在各类 SCI 论文的题名中使用；CT（Computerized Tomography）、NMR（Nuclear Magnetic Resonance）等已为医学界熟悉和公认，可在医学类论文的题名中使用；BWR（Boiling Water Reactor）、PWR（Pressurized Water Reactor）等已为核电学界熟悉和公认，可在核电类论文的题名中使用。以下列举几个使用缩略语的题名示例：

【21】CAD/CAM System for Spatial Curved Surface in Wire Cut Electronic Discharge Machining

此题名中直接使用缩略语 CAD/CAM 是可以的，因为 CAD（Computer Aided Design）和 CAM（Computer Aided Manufacturing）已为计算机、工程等领域熟悉和公认，可以在较多领域的论文题名中直接使用。

【22】Forward Displacement Analysis of Generalized 5SPS-1CCS Parallel Robot Mechanism Based on Quaternion

【23】Design of High Resolving Capability STM. IPC-205BJ Type Atomic Force Microscope

【24】Interpreting Module and Coordinate Problem for CNC Based on STEP-NC Interface

题名【22】、【23】直接用缩略语 5SPS-1CCS 和 STM. IPC-205BJ 是可以的，因为二者分别是 Parallel Robot Mechanism Based on Quaternion 和 Atomic Force Microscope 的一种型号，题名中直接使用显得简洁、准确、清楚、醒目和方便。题名【24】中直接使用缩略语 STEP-NC 也是可以的，因为 STEP-NC（ISO 14649）是 CAD/CAM 和 CNC 之间进行数据传递的一个接口标准（兼容 STEP（ISO 10303）），题名中如果不直接使用此缩略语就难以进行表达。

【25】Dynamic Analysis and Motion Control of 6-DOF Underwater Robot

【26】New Method for Rapid Fabricating Masters of PDMS-Based Microfluidic Devices

题名【25】中的 DOF 是 degree of freedom 的缩写，在机械设计和机构学领域使用广泛，题名中可以直接使用⊖。类似的缩略语还有很多，如 MEMS（micro electro-mechanical systems）和 PDM（product data management）等。题名【26】中直接使用缩略语 PDMS 不合适（不排除有时可以），读者看了可能很难明白其含义。这里 PDMS 是一种化学名称 Poly（dimethylsiloxane）（聚二甲基硅氧烷，简称 PDMS）。可改为：New Method for Rapid Fabricating Masters of Poly (dimethylsiloxane)-Based Microfluidic Devices⊖。

【27】Fem Simulation on the 3D Temperature Distribution of Large Area HFCVD System

【28】Simple Tooling with Internal Pressure Source to Evaluate the THF Formability

【29】Method of VMC Formation Based on Similarity Science in RMS

此三题名中的 HFCVD、THF、VMC 和 RMS 使用可能不当。HFCVD 是 Hot Filament Chemical Vapor Deposition 的缩略语，THF 是 Tube Hydro-forming 的缩略语，VMC 是 Virtual Manufacturing Cell 的缩略语，RMS 是 Reconfigurable Manufacturing System 的缩略语，均不是科技界或行业熟悉和公认的缩略语，故不宜在题名中直接使用。题名【27】可改为：Fem Simulation on the 3D Temperature Distribution of Large Area Hot Filament Chemical Vapor Deposition System；【28】可改为：Simple Tooling with Internal Pressure Source to Evaluate the Tube Hydro-forming Formability；【29】可改为：Method of Virtual Manufacturing Cell Formation Based on Similarity Science in Reconfigurable Manufacturing System，或 Method of Virtual Manufacturing Cell（VMC）Formation Based on Similarity Science in Reconfigurable Manufacturing System（RMS），或 Method of VMC（Virtual Manufacturing Cell）Formation Based on Similarity Science in RMS（Reconfigurable Manufacturing System）。

注意：在题名中直接使用非公知公用的缩略语或作者自定义字母词的现象有增多的趋势，在国际名刊如 *Nature*、*Science*、*Cell* 中也有。

5. 索引方便

目前多数索引和摘要服务系统采用 Keyword 系统，因此题名中宜多用论文的主要关键词，所用词语应符合编制题录、索引和检索的有关原则，有助于选定关键词，容易被理解和检索，能为二次文献提供检索的特定实用信息，尽量不要出现式子、上下标、特殊符号、不常用术语、非英语词汇、非公知公用缩略语等不方便查询的语言要素。例如：

【30】Predictability and chaotic nature of daily streamflow（*Australian Journal of Water Resources*，Vol 17，No 1，2013）

【31】Nonmuscle invasive bladder cancer: a primer on immunotherapy（*Cancer Biology & Medicine*，Vol 13，No 2，2016）

【32】Metabolic Alkalosis: A Real Danger of Overdiuresis in Patients with Heart failure（*Journal of International Translational Medicine*，Vol 3，No 2，2015）

例【30】是一篇技术论文的题名，其中 streamflow 是该文的一个主要关键词；【31】是一篇综述论文的题名，其中 bladder cancer 和 immunotherapy 是该文的两个主要关键词；【32】是一篇案例报告的题名，其中 Metabolic Alkalosis、Overdiuresis 和 Heart failure 是该文的三个主要关键词。如果一

⊖ 但笔者不提倡在中文题名中直接使用 DOF。

⊖ 相应的中文题名是：PDMS（聚二甲基硅氧烷）微流控芯片……；或者是：聚二甲基硅氧烷（PDMS）微流控芯片……。

篇论文的题名中没有出现该文的任何关键词，那么该题名就有提升的空间，写作中应注意这个问题，在最终定稿前一定要检查确认题名中是否使用了论文的主要关键词。

2.2.5 题名形式表达

题名在形式上应简洁、醒目，易读、易懂、匀称、协调、美观、大方，常有以下规则：

1）题名既可以是一个名词性词语，也可为一个句子，而且多用现在时。

2）题名常居左或居中排，用一行能排下时就尽量不排为多行（行越多，越有可能会削弱或冲淡读者对论文核心内容的印象），一行排不下时，再排为两行或多行。

3）题名忌用艺术加工式文学语言或口号、命令式语句。

4）题名提倡用公知公认、标准的缩略语，必要时在其后括号中注明其全称。

5）题名开头第一个词尽量不用冠词（包括定冠词 the、不定冠词 a 和 an）。

6）题名不用下画线或斜体，但特别词语可以是斜体。例如：

【1】Fully integrated wearable sensor arrays for multiplexed *in situ* perspiration analysis

7）题名主要讲述研究结果（发现了什么），通常不宜出现 The Study of（on）之类的词语。

8）题名长度无统一硬性规定，一般不超出包括空格、标点在内的 100 个字符。

9）题名大小写无统一规定，主要有实词首字母大写（虚词首字母小写）、第一个词首字母大写（其余小写，特殊词㊀除外）

和全部字母大写三种情况。前一种格式较为标准，类似于专有名词，与正文的区分明显，用得最多；第二种格式占用空间小，简洁、实用，可读性好，有增多的趋势，国际不少名刊也采用这种格式；一般不用全部字母大写。其实题名的大小写只是个形式问题，作者遵循目标期刊的规定和习惯即可，不必考虑过多而分心于形式。例如：

【2】Cryptochromes Interact Directly with PIFs to Control Plant Growth in Limiting Blue Light（引自 *Cell*）

【3】Schizophrenia risk from complex variation of complement component 4（引自 *Nature*）

【4】Active sites of nitrogen-doped carbon materials for oxygen reduction reaction clarified using model catalysts（引自 *Science*）

2.2.6 眉题规范表达

为方便读者阅读，不少期刊发表的论文还提供 running title（眉题）。眉题常由第一作者姓名和论文题名构成，或只由论文题名构成，由于版面限制，眉题常由题名缩减而成（一般不超过 60 个字符），排在论文部分页面（单页码，或双页码，或除首页外的单、双页码）的最上方。例如：

【1】Multi-scale polarisation phenomena *V Kalashnikov et al*

【2】Qi WANG et al. Exploiting write power asymmetry to improve phase change memory system performance

【3】*Max Ent Models for Subjectivity Analysis*

【4】*Effect of Nutrients on the Growth of*

㊀ 专有名词首字母、首字母缩略词、德语名词首字母、句点后单词的首字母等均应大写，而且第一个词应尽量避免使用首字母以"位次"开始的化学名称（如 α-Toluene，其中的 α 表示位次）或以其他类似前缀开始的单词。

Lichen Symbionts

眉题【1】、【2】均由题名和作者姓名构成：前者题名很短，作者姓名在后；后者题名较长，作者姓名在前。【3】、【4】分别由题名 Constructing Maximum Entropy Language Models for Movie Review Subjectivity Analysis 和 Differential Responses of Lichen Symbionts to Enhanced Nitrogen and Phosphorus Availability: An Experiment with *Cladina stellaris* 缩减而成。

眉题无固定格式，不同期刊有不同要求。作者投稿时可以不提供眉题，但为了眉题的准确性，建议作者在投稿时最好提供一个合适的眉题。

2.2.7 系列题名问题

系列题名是指主题名相同但论文系列序号、副题名不同的系列论文的题名。这种题名也无固定格式，主题名与副题名之间通常加论文系列序号，并用破折号或冒号来分隔，破折号或冒号既可位于论文系列序号前，也可位于系列序号后。例如：

【1】Prediction of Right-Side Curves in Forming Limit Diagram of a Sheet Metal —Part Ⅰ: Predicting Fundamentals

【2】Prediction of Right-Side Curves in Forming Limit Diagram of a Sheet Metal —Part Ⅱ: Prediction Method

【3】Over-constraint and a Unified Mobility Method for General Spatial Mechanisms Part 1: Essential Principle

【4】Over-constraint and a Unified Mobility Method for General Spatial Mechanisms Part 2: Application of the Principle

【5】Dynamical Behaviour of a Dislocation Group Containing a Source Ⅰ. Computer Simulation of the Glide Motion of a Dislocation Group Emitted from a Source

【6】Liquid biopsies for liquid tumors: emerging potential of circulating free nucleic acid evaluation for the management of hematologic malignancies

题名【1】~【4】均由主、副题名构成，副题名的前面分别冠以"Part Ⅰ:" "Part Ⅱ:"和"Part 1:" "Part 2:"，属于系列题名。题名【5】中"Ⅰ."的前面部分为主题名，后面部分为副题名，表明还有另一个论文"Ⅱ."，也属于系列题名。题名【6】用冒号分隔为前后两个部分（液体肿瘤的液体活检：用于恶性血液肿瘤管理的循环自由核酸评价新潜力），后一部分补充前一部分，加起来形成一个表义完整的综述文章的题名，虽然没有出现任何如上所述表序号的数字或词语，但属于系列题名。

系列题名有一些问题，如系列论文因主题名重复而使正文内容重复部分（如引言）较多，仅阅读系列论文的部分论文难以了解内容全貌，系列论文不能被同一出版物发表时有失连贯性等，因此除非必要，一般不提倡用系列题名的形式来发表系列论文。对读者来说，每篇论文都应能展示相对独立的内容，这样对作者来说，应尽可能将系列内容合并在一篇论文中写并单独发表，或分别独立成文，分别发表。

2.3 引言

引言（Introduction）又称前言、序言、概述或绪论，属论文的引论部分（开始、开场白），内容涉及研究的领域、目前的研究热点及存在的问题、本论文的研究目的、要解决的问题、主要研究成果及价值意义等，目的是引导读者有序进入论文的主题，对论文的内容有心理和知识准备，进而更加方便、有效、能动地阅读和理解全文。因此，引言有总揽论文全局的重要性，也是论文中非常难写的部分之一，不少论文的缺陷主要在于引言过于简单，没有体现出前人基础和自我创新。然而，一篇好论文对引言的要求非常高，只要引言写好了，论文就差不多成功了一半。因此，必须高度重视引言写作，要付诸行动，下足功夫去完成。

2.3.1 引言内容及结构

引言的内容有较大的伸缩性，但基本差不多，如研究领域（范围、主题）、文献回顾、存在的问题，本文的研究目的、研究内容（目标）、价值意义（创新点）和写作安排等，并基本上按这一顺序来形成引言的结构。

1）研究领域位于引言的开头，陈述领域相关知识（普遍事实、一般认识）或最新研究成果（如某种观点、认识等），涉及面较为宽泛，旨在限定研究领域、说明研究范围、描述研究主题（重要性），整个论文的写作都将围绕此主题在此领域展开。还应有指出相关研究甚少或虽有却不足的表述，凸显本文研究的重要性。

2）文献回顾是对有足够代表性的已有研究成果进行综述（文献全面，新旧结合，最新文献不缺少，时间跨度合适，引文数量适当），阐明前人相关研究的历史、现状，并对同类研究作横向比较，总结前人工作的优势和局限（不足、空白），说明本文研究与过去研究的关系。

文献回顾不是为回顾而回顾，而是为找出现有研究存在的问题，进而确立研究目的。因此在文献回顾时，要有意地将重点逐渐转移到与研究主题相关的内容上，指出有某个问题或现象值得进一步研究，进而将焦点转到本文所要解决的问题上。

3）存在的问题就是发现的问题，即通过文献回顾发现的有待解决的问题，如科学原理解释不清、工程应用有待推广、算法效率和精度需要提高、技术难点有待突破等。

4）研究目的是基于存在的问题而确定的本文将要解决的问题（本文的研究点），阐述问题解决的价值或现实意义，突出本文研究的重要性，即为什么要研究。

5）研究内容是研究目的具体化，是为了实现研究目的而确立的本文的实现目标，可能涉及所用的理论、方法、模型、技术、数据和材料等诸多方面。

6）研究内容的结尾最好还要交待一下本文的价值意义，即贡献或创新之处。研究目标及具体的执行方法常会给研究的工程应用带来意义。

7）写作安排通常在结尾，简要交待论文各部分主体内容出现的先后顺序，涉及内容布局及层次标题安排。这部分并非每篇论文都需要，但对篇幅较长、结构复杂的论文通常是需要的，旨在通过对论文整体构架的介绍来达到对引言的完好收尾，指导、方便读者阅读。

引言在形式上是若干段落，通常不设下级层次标题，各个段落都代表引言基本内容的一类，并按引言结构要求来行文。一般来讲，引言若按内容类别来撰写，并按逻辑顺序来布局，那么从内容的角度看就是合格的，同时若再能遵循引言写作原则，大力提升文字效能，那么就是高质量的。

2.3.2 引言写作要求

引言写作总体要求：内容全面，逐次展开；开门见山，不绕圈子；言简意赅，突出重点；尊重科学，实事求是。引言写作具体要求有多个方面，下面予以总结。

（1）把握总体要求

将引言写作总体要求作为引言写作的大纲，周密计划、合理安排、认真写作，按内容、结构要求逐次展开，不偏离主题、题目，不注释、重复摘要，不涉及、分析和讨论结果（数据），一般不用给出结论，不必铺垫太多、绕大弯子而后进入主题。

（2）考虑读者层次

考虑领域知识适用的读者层次。对研究型论文，其读者往往是领域的研究者、专家和学者们，读者的专业层次较高，他们一般已具备较为广泛的专业基础知识，因此引言中通常不用写一般知识，如果需要写，则用较简短、概括和明了的语言（非叙述性语言）来直接陈述即可。

（3）写清研究背景

较为全面而简练地陈述研究背景，清楚讲述所探讨问题的本质和范围，避免内容过于分散、琐碎而导致的主题不集中，但重要内容的陈述也不宜过于简略，让人感到突兀。陈述作者已有相关工作时，重在交待本文写作的基础和动机，不要写成总结，不必强调过去工作的成就。

（4）充分回顾文献

对相关文献进行充分综述，把领域的研究现状概括总结出来，需要引用充足、有代表性和经典性的文献，要优先引用重要和说服力强的文献，不要刻意回避对一些相关文献尤其是对本文具有某种重要启示性意义的相关文献的引用，也不要引用一些不相关的文献或过多引用作者本人的文献。这部分往往是编辑审稿、同行评议的重要依据，应高度重视。

（5）正确引用文献

正确引用文献中的有关内容，包括结果（如数据）和语句。引用的结果必须正确，引用的数据必须准确，不能与原文有出入，避免片面摘录部分结果而不反映总体结果（以偏概全），对间接引用的数据（即不是从原文献中直接查到而是从原文献引用的其他文献的数据）更应小心。引用文献中的语句也不要完全照搬，而应尽量换用自己的语言来表述。

（6）善于发现问题

在文献回顾过程中努力发现已有研究的局限性，总结出存在的问题，阐明本文的创新点，进而达到整个引言的高潮。阐述局限性时，要客观公正，不要把抬高作者自己的研究价值建立在贬低别人工作之上。阐述创新点时，要紧密围绕过去研究的不足，完整清晰地表述本文的解决方法。涉及面不宜太大，只要解决一两个问题，有所创新，这样的论文才能成为好论文。

对存在的问题要合理分类，类别不同，采用的表述方法就不同。存在的问题至少可分为：

1) 以前的学者尚未研究或处理不够完善的重要课题或研究点；

2) 过去的研究衍生出的有待深入、探讨、优化的新问题；

3) 以前的学者提出的互不相容且需进一步研究才能解决的问题；

4) 可扩充到新的研究课题或领域中的过去的研究成果；

5) 可以扩展到新的应用范围的以前提出的方法、技术。

（7）合理表述创新

慎重而有保留地表述前人工作的欠缺及本文的重要贡献，让读者顺着逻辑顺序来阅读全文。评价论文的价值要恰如其分、实事求是，不要自吹自擂、抬高自己、贬低别人，慎用自我评价式用语，如 discovers … for the first time, presents …for the first time, has (have) very high academic value, fill the gaps at home and abroad⊖, reach(es) interna-

---

⊖ SCI 论文是面向国际读者的，作者应站在国际读者的角度来写，因此 at home and abroad（国内外）在这种语境中出现也不妥当。

tional advanced level 等，因为这些用语只有辅有确切的资料才具说服力。可用相对较委婉的谦虚用语，如 limited to conditions，there are few researches in this area 等；但也不必过谦，如应尽量不用 have little talent and less learning（才疏学浅）、limited to author's level（水平有限）、beg for your advice（恳求指教）和 throw away a brick in order to get a gem（抛砖引玉）等客套用语。

另外，还要适当地使用 We 或 The author 之类的词语，明确指出作者自己所做的工作，以避免难以区分别人和作者所做的工作而引起误解。

（8）正确使用名词

使用规范的名词（名称、术语和缩略语），不要随意、泛滥地使用非公知公用的术语和缩略语。非公知公用的术语、缩略语及作者自定义字母词，首次出现时应对其给予解释、定义或给出全称，以方便有效地阅读和理解。

（9）取舍适宜篇幅

按内容表述的需要来确定引言的合适篇幅，通常为几个段落，但不必为篇幅问题过分纠结。引言篇幅可长可短，与文体类别、研究领域的性质、存在问题的类型、研究主题是否为热点、办刊模式等多方因素有关；若研究主题为许多学者探讨过或还在探讨的问题，则需要引用、讨论较多的文献；相反，若只属近来才兴起的研究方向或只讨论别人最近才提出的问题，研究的人可能很少或较少，则引用、讨论少量的文献就可以了。忌表述空泛，主题不集中，篇幅过长；也忌脱离前人，引文太少，篇幅过短。

（10）提升文字效能

最后提升文字效能，来对引言写作进行收尾。虽然引言初稿完成后写作暂告一个小段落，但从语言表达效果看，往往还会有一定的提升空间。因此初稿写完之后，还要慎之又慎地认真琢磨、仔细修改，检查每一语句表意是否准确、句间关联是否顺畅、语言要素修辞是否妥当，再针对问题进行修改和完善，全面提升文字效能，为引言写作质量提供保障。

2.3.3 引言写作方法

内容决定方法，引言的内容基本决定了其写作方法，这里的写作方法是指写作思路（步骤、过程），后面论文其他组成部分的写作方法同此。引言写作方法大体相同（如下所述），但实际中较为灵活，不同文体、不同内容的引言，其写作方法不大可能相同。

1）陈述领域相关知识（一般认识、普遍事实），或已有最新研究成果（别人或作者自己的认识、观点等，但不一定已上升为知识），指明研究范围、主题；

2）进行全面的文献回顾，阐述以前、现在有谁做过相关研究，有什么经过和结果，存在什么问题，别人给予什么评价等；

3）指出作者自己进行本文研究的目的（有何重要性或意义）、目标（解决何问题）；

4）交待研究中采用了什么方法，有什么新发现和新意义，新发现和新意义即为创新。

高质量的引言内容全面、结构完整、表达合适、详略得当、层次鲜明、条理缜密，基于逻辑性建立起内容上的层层递进关系。

2.3.4 引言写作实例

下面选择若干引言实例，了解其内容、结构和写作方法。

2.3.4.1 实例一

【1】
INTRODUCTION

When the sizes of the devices approach the nanoscale, focusing and manipulating light becomes a great challenge in both scientific research and industrial manufacturing. Nanostructure sustaining surface plasmons (SP) have been demonstrated to be excellent candidates for confining the light field at the nanoscale[1, 2]. The most involved plasmonic materials include metal nanostructures and highly doped semiconducting nanostructures, which exhibit SP resonances ranging from ultraviolet to near-infrared regions[3-7]. For remote, non-destructive and highly sensitive detection and imaging, the operation wavelengths of the SP are preferred to be in the mid-infrared or terahertz regions[8-10]. Graphene with atomic thickness has been shown to support strong SP in these regions[11-15]. The collective oscillations of the Dirac fermions can induce strong graphene SP with long lifetimes, which are able to realize extremely spatial confinement of the electromagnetic field in a broad band. These exceptional characteristics have made graphene an outstanding platform for light focusing and manipulation in the two-dimensional regime[14, 15], which can benefit applications in optical communication[16, 17], sensing and detection[17-20] and imaging[21].

One of the most intriguing merits of graphene is that the plasmon-related characteristics are amenable to wide-range tuning by adjusting the charge carrier density, surrounding dielectric environment and the geometries of the graphene flakes[12, 13, 15, 22-24]. In particular, structuring the graphene monolayer into flakes with nanometer sizes can lead to optical near-fields with specific spatial distributions, whereby the electromagnetic field will experience further confinements[25-27]. However, most of the reported graphene nanostructures are either formed adventitiously during mechanical exfoliation or fabricated with limited geometries[26-30], which limit the tunability of electromagnetic field localizations while preventing elucidation of the relationship between the light field localizations and geometries of the graphene nanostructures. The latter is associated with a more general topic that remains elusive, the electromagnetic field localization behaviors and related mechanisms in two-dimensional nanostructures of atomic thicknesses.

Here, from both the theoretical and experimental perspectives, we explored tailoring of the electromagnetic field localizations in the mid-infrared region using monolayers of graphene two-dimensional nanostructures of different shapes and sizes. We generalized the phenomenological cavity model[31] to visualize the electromagnetic field distributions within the graphene nanostructures. The theoretical predictions were corroborated by mapping the electromagnetic field distributions within the various graphene nanostructures using a nanoimaging technique. We further demonstrated that the localizations of the light field could be modulated with chemical doping of the graphene nanostructures. Our results can provide guidelines for the design of graphene nanostructures with superior light focusing capabilities, and help elucidate the SP mechanisms and therewith the dynamics of the Dirac fermions in the graphene nanostructures.

(Tailoring of electromagnetic field localizations by two-dimensional graphene nanostructures. Light: Science & Application, 2017 Volume 6, Issue 4.)

例【1】是一篇光学领域原创论文的引言。

第一段引用参考文献，陈述对已有研究成果的相关认识（或知识），指明研究范围。首句点出研究领域（设备尺寸接近纳米尺度时聚焦和操纵光）。后面几句缩小领域，逐渐聚焦研究主题：第二至四句陈述SP（表面等离激元）是纳米尺度下限制光场的重要方法及其重要特征（从紫外线到近红外区域的SP共振、更倾向于在中红外或太赫兹区域的SP操作波长）；第五至七句陈述有原子厚度的石墨烯的优异特性及其在二维平面上光聚焦和操纵的应用优势。

第二段前面两句引用参考文献，陈述石墨烯的优点（认识或知识）。接着，第三句话锋一转（However），指出现有石墨烯纳米结构的局限性，即存在的问题（石墨烯纳米结构是在机械剥离过程中偶然形成或在有限几何结构下制造出来的，限制了电磁场定位的可调性，妨碍了对光场定位和石墨烯纳米结构的几何图形之间关系的阐释）。第四句补充说明攻克其中后一问题的不易性，即研究难点，暗示研究的重要性。

第三段前面三句交待本文（Here）所做工作（we explored …，We generalized …，… were corroborated by …），属于研究目标。第四句交待研究结果（We further demonstrated that …）。第五句点出研究结果的创新之处（Our results can provide guidelines …）。

此引言的写作思路：范围、主题、问题、目标、结果、创新。

2.3.4.2 实例二

【2】

Introduction

Influenza viruses are negative-sense RNA viruses, whose genome comprises eight gene segments: basic polymerase 2 (PB2), basic polymerase 1 (PB1), acidic polymerase (PA), hemagglutinin (HA), nucleoprotein (NP), neuraminidase (NA), matrix (M), and nonstructural protein (NS). Each gene segment encodes one or two proteins. Influenza A viruses are categorized into different subtypes on the basis of antigenic differences in their two surface glycoproteins: HA and NA. Currently, 16 different HA and 9 different NA subtypes of influenza viruses have been detected in avian species, but only three subtypes, namely H1N1, H2N2, and H3N2, have caused influenza pandemics in humans [1, 2].

In the last two decades, avian influenza viruses of the H5N1 and H7N9 subtypes have continued to present challenges to the poultry industry and human health. The H5N1 highly pathogenic avian influenza viruses have caused infections and disease outbreaks among poultry and wild birds in over 60 countries around the world [3, 4], and have sporadically jumped to humans and caused severe disease and deaths [5]. Several studies have indicated that the H5N1 influenza viruses will become transmissible in mammals if they acquire more mutations in their HA protein that allow them to recognize human-type receptors and the mutation of lysine (K) at position 627 of their PB2 [6-8], or if they reassort with human influenza viruses [9].

H7N9 subtype viruses have caused severe human infections and deaths every year in China since they emerged in 2013 [10]. Epidemiology studies have shown that humans become infected mainly through exposure to virus-infected poultry or a contaminated environment [11-15]. Biologic studies on H7N9 viruses have revealed several important characters: (i) the viruses can replicate efficiently in chickens but do not cause disease in any avian species [16]; (ii) most of the viruses can bind human-type receptors [16-19], mainly because they bear valine (V) at position 186 and leucine (L) at position 226 in their HA protein [18] (H3 numbering used throughout), which is an important determinant for avian influenza virus to infect humans; and (iii) when the viruses replicate in humans, they can easily obtain the glutamic acid (E) to K mutation at position 627 (E627K) or aspartic acid (D) to asparagine (N) mutation at position 701 (D701N) in their PB2 [10, 11, 16, 20, 21]. These two mutations are known to increase the virulence and transmissibility of avian influenza viruses in mammals [22-27]. Indeed, the human H7N9 viruses are transmissible in ferrets, although their transmissibility varies among different strains [16, 17, 28-30]. The ability to bind to human-type receptors and transmit in mammals is an important indicator of the pandemic potential of the H7N9 viruses. However, because the H7N9 viruses showed low pathogenicity in poultry, strategies to eradicate them in poultry have not been successful in China, with the exception of the temporary closure of live poultry markets in cities where human cases were detected.

The low pathogenic H5 and H7 avian influenza viruses are predisposed to acquire more mutations when they circulate in gallinaceous poultry and subsequently become highly pathogenic for chickens and turkeys, as occurred of the H5N2 outbreak in the United States in

1983［31］, the H5N2 outbreak in Mexico in 1995［32］, and the H7N1 outbreak in Italy in 1999［33］. It is unknown whether the H7N9 viruses can acquire additional mutations during their circulation in nature and become lethal to poultry. Therefore, close monitoring and evaluation of the H7N9 viruses have important implications for both animal and human public health. Here, we characterized H7N9 viruses isolated from avian species in China between 2013 and 2017.

（H7N9 virulent mutants detected in chickens in China pose an increased threat to humans. Cell Research, Vol. 27, No. 12, Dec. 2017：1409-1421.）

例【2】是一篇生物领域原创论文的引言。

第一段指明研究领域，陈述领域知识、范围。第一、二句点出研究领域（流感病毒），并对流感病毒进行解释［一种负链RNA病毒，其基因组由基本聚合酶2（PB2）、基本聚合酶1（PB1）、酸性聚合酶（PA）、血凝素（HA）、核蛋白质（NP）、神经氨酸酶（NA）、基质（M）和非结构蛋白（NS）八个基因片段组成，每个基因片段编码一两种蛋白质］。第三句交待甲型流感病毒的亚型分类（根据两种表面糖蛋白的抗原差异分为HA和NA两种亚型）。第四句引用文献指出禽类中流感病毒亚型的分类、数量及其中三种曾带来危害（禽类中有16种HA和9种NA的流感病毒亚型，但其中仅有H1N1、H2N2和H3N2三种引起过人类流感大流行）。

第二段先指出在过去20年里，两种流感病毒亚型H5N1和H7N9对家禽行业和人类健康带来挑战。接下来对H5N1已有相关研究成果（或认识）进行回顾，主要观点有：

（1）H5N1已在全球60多个国家的家禽和野生鸟类中造成感染和疾病暴发，偶尔会对人类造成严重疾病和死亡。

（2）H5N1如果在其HA蛋白质中获得更多突变，而使其能够识别人类受体及在其PB2的位置627上的赖氨酸（K）的突变，或与人类流感病毒重组，那么将在哺乳动物中传播。

第三段接着对H7N9已有相关研究成果（或认识）进行回顾，最后指出存在的问题。

相关研究成果（或认识）主要包括：

（1）H7N9自2013年出现以来，已每年在中国造成严重的人类感染和死亡。

（2）H7N9的重要特征：①可在鸡体内有效复制，但不会在任何禽类中引起疾病；②多数可与人类受体结合，因为在其HA蛋白质的位置186上有缬氨酸（V）和226上有亮氨酸（L），这是禽流感病毒感染人的一个重要决定因素；③在人体中复制时易在PB2的位置627（E627K）上获得谷氨酸E到K，或位置701（D701N）上获得天冬氨酸（D）到天冬酰胺（N）的突变。

（3）两种突变会增加H7N9在哺乳动物中的毒性和传播性。

（4）人类H7N9病毒在雪貂中可以传播，但传播能力在不同毒株中有所不同。

（5）H7N9与人类受体结合并在哺乳动物中传播的能力是衡量其大流行潜力的重要指标。

（6）由于H7N9病毒在家禽中表现出较低的致病性，家禽中根除H7N9病毒的策略在中国并不成功，除了在发现人类病例的城市中临时关闭活禽市场之外。

第四段先陈述低致病性H5和H7型禽流感病毒传播时容易获得突变而变得高致病性，进而产生严重危害（如1983年美国爆发H5N2，1995年墨西哥爆发H5N2，1999年意大利爆发H7N1）。接着点出当前相关研究的不足，即存在的问题：目前对H7N9在自然循环过程中是否会获得额外突变并对家禽造成致命伤害尚不清楚。第三句指出密切监测和评价 H7N9 对动物和人类的公共卫生具有重要意义，暗示了本文研究工作的意义或重要性。最后一句概括、交待本文所做工作：对从 2013 年到 2017 年在中国从禽类中分离出来的 H7N9 病毒进行研究。

此引言的写作思路：领域、成果（按 H7N1 和 H7N9 病毒分别回顾）、问题、意义、目标。

2.3.4.3 实例三

【3】

Introduction

Plasma membrane is central for homeostatic maintenance in mammalian cells. It is a direct barrier against extracellular environment; it harbors protein sensors and receptors transducing extracellular signals to elicit cellular responses; it contains transporters and channels involved in the trafficking of inorganic ions and small water-soluble organic molecules; and it participates in nutrient and macromolecule transport processes such as endocytosis and exocytosis. The loss of plasma membrane integrity would therefore undoubtedly put an end to cellular life.

Cell death can result from activation of intrinsic cell death programs or passive disruption of membrane integrity by damaging environmental forces. Since all passively disrupted cells present a ruptured plasma membrane, which is a feature of the necrotic phenotype, necrotic cell death has long been defined as a form of uncontrolled passive cell death [1]. However, it is now clear, that besides apoptosis — the best characterized type of programmed cell death with an intact plasma membrane, other intrinsic programs can lead to necrotic cell death [2]. A very recent study has even shown that plasma membrane rupture in apoptotic cells undergoing secondary necrosis is also intrinsically programmed [3].

While apoptosis is generally accepted as a non-inflammatory process, the lytic nature of necrosis leads to the release of intracellular DAMPs (damage-associated molecular patterns) and triggers inflammation [4]. However, distinct programs such as necroptosis and pyroptosis or passive 'mechanical' damages will induce different immunogenic effects [5, 6]. Furthermore, the idea that apoptosis is a non-inflammatory form of cell death may not be accurate since accumulating experimental data indicate that apoptosis can also be immunogenic due to the emission of particular DAMPs [7]. Secondary necrosis might only be partially responsible for DAMPs release during apoptosis since certain DAMPs are preferentially released by apoptotic rather than necrotic cells [6]. Therefore, plasma membrane changes during apoptosis and programmed necrosis are clearly more complicated than previously expected.

Apoptosis was an early focus in the field of cell death study. The mechanisms of nuclear condensation, DNA fragmentation, caspase activation, and phosphatidylserine flipping have been intensively studied [8]. Although plasma membrane blebbing and apoptotic body formation are morphological characteristics of apoptosis, mechanistic information regarding those processes remains limited. Recent advances in necrosis study have drawn our attention to the plasma membrane. Translocation of channel or pore proteins to the plasma membrane increases plasma membrane permeability and causes plasma membrane rupture in programmed necrosis [9-22]. Plasma membrane pore formation is also responsible for the secondary necrosis of apoptotic cells [3]. Due to the significant progress in the recent study of plasma membrane changes in different cell death programs, this article will first review updated information on necroptosis, pyroptosis, and apoptosis with an emphasis on the comparison of the accompanying plasma membrane changes. We will then review and discuss how these plasma membrane changes in dying cells elicit immune responses.

(Plasma membrane changes during programmed cell deaths. *Cell Research*, Vol. 28, No. 1, Jan. 2018: 9-21.)

例【3】是一篇生物细胞领域综述的引言。

第一段陈述哺乳动物细胞中质膜的极其重要性（失去质膜的完整性便会终结细胞的生命），属于一般领域知识，指明了研究领域。

　　第二段陈述细胞死亡的形态及原因，先引用普遍观点（坏死细胞死亡长期以来被定义为一种不可控制的被动细胞死亡形式），接着引用另一不同观点（除了细胞凋亡即最典型的有完整质膜的程序性细胞死亡外，其他内在程序也可能导致坏死细胞死亡），最后引用近期观点（细胞凋亡中发生继发性坏死的质膜破裂也有内在的编程性），逐步引出了研究主题"细胞凋亡"。

　　第三段引用一些参考文献的研究成果，阐述了对细胞凋亡的非炎症性、炎症性的不同认识，并描写作者自己的认识（细胞凋亡和程序性坏死过程中质膜的变化明显比预期的要复杂），进一步阐释了认识上不相统一的研究现状，也暗含着本综述的意义。

　　第四段回顾重要文献，指出早期细胞凋亡研究的局限性及最新研究进展的突破性，接着说明本文将要做何工作，即进行综述（review），并明确交待综述的目标（细胞坏死性、焦亡和凋亡的最新进展；质膜变化；垂死细胞的质膜变化如何引起免疫反应）和方法（回顾、对比、讨论，三个关键词是 review、comparison、discuss）。

　　此引言的写作思路：领域（范围、主题）、现状、问题、目标、方法。

2.3.4.4　实例四

【4】

Introduction

It's hard to recall a revolution that has swept biology more swiftly than CRISPR. Just 3 years ago, scientists reported that the CRISPR system—an adaptive immune system used by microbes to defend themselves against invading viruses by recording and targeting their DNA sequences—could be repurposed into a simple and reliable technique for editing, in living cells, the genomes of mammals and other organisms. CRISPR was soon adapted for a vast range of applications—creating complex animal models of human-inherited diseases and cancers; performing genome-wide screens in human cells to pinpoint the genes underlying biological processes; turning specific genes on or off; and genetically modifying plants—and is being used in thousands of labs worldwide. The prospect that CRISPR might be used to modify the human germline has stimulated international debate.

If there are molecular biologists left who have not heard of CRISPR, I have not met them. Yet, if you ask scientists *how* this revolution came to pass, they often have no idea. The immunologist Sir Peter Medawar observed, "The history of science bores most scientists stiff" (Medawar, 1968). Indeed, scientists focus relentlessly on the future. Once a fact is firmly established, the circuitous path that led to its discovery is seen as a distraction.

Yet, the human stories behind scientific advances can teach us a lot about the miraculous ecosystem that drives biomedical progress—about the roles of serendipity and planning, of pure curiosity and practical application, of hypothesis-free and hypothesis-driven science, of individuals and teams, and of fresh perspectives and deep expertise. Such understanding is important for government agencies and foundations that together invest, in the U.S. alone, more than $40 billion in biomedical research. It is also important for a general public who often imagines scientists as lone geniuses cloistered in laboratories. And, for trainees, it is especially valuable to have a realistic picture of scientific careers, as both guide and inspiration.

Over the past several months, I have sought to understand the 20-year backstory behind CRISPR, including the history of ideas and the stories of individuals. This Perspective is based on published papers, personal interviews, and other materials—including rejection letters from journals. At the end, I try to distill some general lessons. (As background, Figure 1 provides a brief overview of a type II CRISPR system, the variety that has been repurposed for genome engineering.)

Most of all, the Perspective describes an inspiring ensemble of a dozen or so scientists who—with their collaborators and other contributors whose stories are not elaborated here—discovered the CRISPR system, unraveled its molecular mechanisms, and repurposed it as a powerful tool for biological research and biomedicine. Together, they are the Heroes of CRISPR.

(The Heroes of CRISPR. Cell 164, January 14, 2016.)

例【4】是一篇生物医学领域视角（Perspective）的引言。

第一段中，首句给出论点（CRISPR 是生物学领域一场空前的革命），表明作者自己的观点或主张；后面三句给出论据（3 年前科学家报道的 CRISPR 的定义、功用、广泛应用和伦理争论），是作者证明或者支撑其论点的材料、事实。这部分交待了领域范围。

第二段中，第一、二句指出生物学家都知道 CRISPR，但对其产生的历史可能不清楚，指出生物学家对有关科学史掌握不够的现状，这也即作者的观点；第三句引用免疫学家 Peter Medawar 的一句话来支撑作者的观点；最后两句描写科学家们的本质特征（关注未来，注重事实，目标坚定，不折不挠），亮出了与作者前面所提观点相辅相成的另一观点。这部分交待了科学家从事科学研究的一种真实状态（对科学献身但对科学史关注不够），指出存在的问题，即研究现状。

第三段中，第一句提出一种观点（科学背后发生的故事对推动生物医学进步的作用重大）。第二至四句用事实或材料进一步说明这些故事的作用：政府机构、基金会科研项目投资决策参考，改变一般大众心目中的科学家的形象，实习生科学职业远景规划、指导。这部分说明了解和认识科学背后发生的故事的重要意义，指出研究主题。

第四段中，交待本文相关工作（目标）及使用的方法。第一句陈述目标（理解 CRISPR 背后 20 年的故事，包括思想历史和个人故事）；第二句交待方法（查阅、分析

文献，涉及论文、个人访谈及包括期刊退稿信在内的其他材料）；第三句进行总结，但没有给出具体的结果或结论；最后，以括注的形式对整段给予补充性注释（引言中的图 1 概述了一种适于基因组工程多样性的 type II CRISPR 系统）。

第五段中，第一句给出研究结果，即 CRISPR 的科学历史（数十位科学家与其合作者、参与者共同发现了 CRISPR 系统，揭示了其分子机制，将其改造为生物研究和医学领域的强大工具）；第二句进行全文总结，指出这些科学家与其合作者、参与者们是 CRISPR 的英雄，属于结论。

该引言的写作思路：范围、现状（问题）、主题、目标、方法、结果、结论。

引言写作是有规律可循的，只要遵循写作的基本要求，把握好内容和结构，再考虑研究领域、方向的不同，以及表述内容、文体的差别等要素，就能写出合格的引言。当然高质量引言的写作，还需作者具有扎实的研究基本功、优秀的研究内容和基本的写作素养。

2.3.5　不规范引言实例

引言写作中的常见问题有：偏离主题、内容不符，结构层次不清，重复解释摘要，重复给出、分析结果，未考虑读者层次，文献回顾不够，研究背景不明，数据引用不准，问题总结欠佳，名词（术语和缩略语）使用不当，篇幅太短或过长，创新表述不合理，文字效能较差等。以下列举几个不规范的引言（为表述方便，有的后面还附上了所引的参考文献），作简要点评并指出修改方案（对第三个引言还给出了修改后的结果）。

2.3.5.1　实例一

【1】

This paper aims to estimate the residual torque of torsion bar with circular cross section under the predetermined torsion angle for a given period. Generally, such a physical experiment is impossible of achievement due to the long period of given time. Therefore, a method combining damage mechanics theory and experiment is proposed for solving this problem.

Firstly, based on the damage mechanics, establish the functional relationship between torque and time in terms of twist angle and material constant, that is, the theoretical curve of torque versus time and the threshold relational expression between torque and torsion shear stress. This expression indicates that, for some given materials, the bigger the twist angle provides, the faster the attenuation rate of torque with the course of time is.

Then, to shorten the period of the experiment and research, an accelerating experiment scheme is proposed based on the above theoretical analysis. A torsion experiment is performed in the case of large twist angle (far more than the predetermined torsion angle) to determine the torque threshold. After that, the torsion shear strain threshold is determined according to damage mechanics.

Finally, torque threshold under small twist angle is inferred indirectly from the shear strain threshold obtained under large twist angle on basis of damage mechanics.

However, it should be noted that the initial maximum shear stress is close to the yield shear stress of the material under conditions of small twist angle. As a consequence, the bar must be in the elastic-plastic state of the material under large twist angle. Thus, the theoretical and experimental research on traditional solid mechanics and damage mechanics must be carried out in the elastic-plastic zone of the material.

[1] ZHANG Xing, ZHAO Jun. Applied fatigue damage mechanics of metal components [M]. Beijing: National Defence Industry Press, 1998. (in Chinese)

[2] ZHANG Xing, ZHAO Jun, HUANG Kezhi. A method of damage mechanics for the prediction of fatigue life [J]. Key Engineering Materials, 1998, 145-149: 433-442.

[3] ZHANG Xing, ZHAO Jun, ZHENG Xudong. Method of damage mechanics for prediction of structure member fatigue lives [C/CD] //Handbook of Fatigue Crack Propagation in Metallic Structures. CARPINTERI Andrea, editor, Vol. I, Elsevier Science B. V., Amsterdam, the Netherlands, 1994.

[4] LEMAITRE J. A course on damage mechanics [M]. New York: Springer-Verlag, 1992.

此引言共有五段。第一段中，首句指出研究目的，第二句暗示研究现状（问题），第三句指出研究目标及意义；第二至四段主要以"指示性摘要"的形式叙述研究过程或内容，即作者做了哪些工作；最后一段是交待研究结果或结论，还是表述作者的一种认识，未写清楚。

写作上存在的主要问题有：没有陈述研究范围；文献回顾远远不够，没有标引文献，所引文献不具代表性（数量、种类少，发表时间早，近年文献未引），不足以反映研究现状、背景；没有明确指出存在的问题；详写研究过程或内容（引言中不必写研究过程或内容，即使写，也应足够简短，而且不应与摘要重复）；没有交待研究意义和目标；没有写明是结果、结论，还是观点、认识；未明确交待创新点。

2.3.5.2 实例二

【2】

Shipborne electronic equipment serves in poor marine climate conditions. Some unfavorable factors, such as high temperature, high moisture, corrosive substances in the air, salt spray as well as various molds, etc. will have direct influence on the parameters of electronic equipment, for example, inductance, capacitance, electric conductance, magnetic conductance, electronic emission and electromagnetic shielding effectiveness, etc. Most of the time, the influences can be devastating. Moreover, with the increasing development of systematization, comprehensiveness, and intelligence of high-tech electronic equipment, it's required to use under various harsh conditions with high reliability and anti-interference at any time. Therefore the three proofing design including humidity proofing, mold proofing, and salt spray proofing is an important task of the development of shipborne electronic equipment.

The three proofing design involves various aspects of

work, such as materials, components, circuit, structure, machining process and comprehensive technical management, etc. All of the work involved should be carried out simultaneously in the course of development.

[1] Chinese Electronic Research Institute. Three proofing technical manual for electronic equipment [M]. Beijing: Weapon Industry Press, 2000. (in Chinese)

[2] QIU Chengti. Design principle of electronic equipment structure [M]. Nanjing: Southeast University Press, 2001. (in Chinese)

[3] HUA Jing, JIANG Yingtang. Talk about three proofing design for shipborne electronic equipment [J]. Radar & Ecm, 2003, 3: 58-60. (in Chinese)

[4] MA Can. Three proofing design technology [J]. Telecommunication Engineering, 1996, 36 (4): 5-12. (in Chinese)

此引言中，前一段论述三防设计的重要性，属于领域知识；后一段点出三防设计的特点。

在写作上明显存在的问题主要有：完全未按引言内容和结构来写（未交代研究背景、存在的问题和研究目的）；文献回顾远远不够，所引文献不具代表性（未引国际文献，引文数量、种类少，引文发表时间较早，近年文献未引）；没有交待研究意义和目标；没有总结创新之处。

2.3.5.3 实例三

【3】

Virtual manufacturing cell (VMC) is first proposed by C. R. McLean, et al. on the basis of the extension of the traditional manufacturing cell in 1982. The main idea is generating manufacturing cell by choosing appropriate resources from the shared resources database when the production task changes[1-2]. This cell is a whole or fragment entity extracted from the existing physical resources without changing the physical layout of the original resources, and is only a kind of resources reconfiguration in logic. A formation method of VMC is proposed in this paper based on machine pattern and set theory under the following assumptions: (1) Reconfigurable objects are set of manufacturing resources which are composed of equipment with fixed physical locations; (2) Production task is a process of dynamic change; (3) A production task, such as product type, process route and the amount of the product, etc., is fixed; (4) A workpiece can "visit" the same machine repeatedly at various times of the production process; (5) Workpiece is conveyed by AGV; (6) The internal cause of reconfiguration is not covered.

此引言中，首先介绍 VMC（虚拟制造单元）的概念首次由何人在何时提出，并引用两篇文献表述 VMC 的思路；然后阐述 VMC 的原理或含义；最后指出作者在本文中提出的 VMC 生成方法所基于的 6 个假设。

此引言存在未交代研究背景、引用文献太少、未阐述研究意义、未总结创新点等问题，写作上不完整、不规范。以下是修改后的引言：

One of the common features of current manufacturing systems is the lack of reconfigurability. The change in the market demand will create a large number of idle and scraped facilities, resulting in waste of resources and energy. The fundamental way to solve this problem is the implementation of reconfigurable manufacturing system (RMS). Essentially, reconfiguration is to obtain the maximum production flexibility by logical or physical configuration changes in whole life cycle of manufacturing system[1-2]. Related researches have been carried out from the developed countries since the mid-1990s. However, researchers still don't have a complete solution of RMS yet. Therefore, it's of particular importance to further study the implementing method of it.

RMS can be implemented by changing modular components of the reconfigurable machine tool (RMT), or by moving, replacing or adding reconfigurable devices, or by generating a virtual manufacturing cell (VMC) according to logical reconfiguration method. At present, the development of RMT is still in the primary stage, and there are still difficulties in implementation of RMS by changing the physical configuration of it because the equipment used in current manufacturing systems are generally conventional equipment and most of them are permanently fixed. However, the physical reconfiguration can be replaced by the logic reconfiguration using VMC. This is because the equipment in VMC is virtual dynamic entity which can be nonadjacent and fixed at the physical location and interconnected in logic and concepts. The interconnection can be implemented through the path network of logistics systems, such as automated guided vehicle (AGV), without any need to change the existing physical layout of the system. As a particular type of manufacturing cell, VMC is usually generated by using group technology. However, the technology suffers from two crucial shortcomings. One is completely ignoring the sharing behavior among workpieces as well as cells; the other is the pre-setting of some parameters before the formation of cells. For example, BABU, et al[3] proposed a cell formation algorithm to generate multiple cell configuration based on different rank order clustering (ROC), but did not consider the cells sharing in system, and moreover some parameters are needed to pre-set subjectively. SARKER, et al[4] developed a formation method of VMC based on process routes and scheduling rather than cell sharing. The method can be used to find the shortest production route in the scheduling system involving multiple workpieces and multiple machines. RATCHEV[5] proposed a class-ability formation method of manufacturing cell based on "resource cell", which matches up the process requirement with production capability of manufacturing system dynamically. KO, et al[6-7] presented a formation algorithms of VMC to implement the machine sharing based on the concept of "machine pattern". The current researches on manufacturing cell are mainly concentrated on the cell formation and planning, and the practical applications of manufacturing cell on RMS are sparse.

In order to implement the logic reconfiguration of RMS, this paper presents the concept of "machine set pattern" based on similarity theory, and the formation method of VMC under some assumptions is also provided.

此修改后的引言有三段。第一段陈述领域（制造系统）、交待范围（RMS）与主题（RMS 的实现方法）。第二段对现有 RMS 实现方法中的 VMC 生成方法进行文献回顾，指出存在的问题（相关研究主要集中在单元生成及计划上，其中针对 RMS 的应用研究很少）。第三段提出本文的目的或目标（RMS 的逻辑重构）、方法（应用相似性理论）及预期成果（提出设备集合模式和VMC 生成方法）。修改后，增加了文献回顾和引用，清楚地阐明了研究领域（范围、主题）、现状、存在的问题、目的（目标）、方法、成果，写明了作者所做工作与前人工作的不同，暗含了创新之处（提出一种用于 RMS 逻辑重构的 VMC 生成方法）。

2.4 材料与方法

材料与方法（Materials and Methods）是原创型论文的方案部分○，是描述研究是在何种物质条件下怎样展开的。材料是基础，没有充足的材料，研究无从谈起；没有合适的方法，研究便无法实现。材料与方法既是快速判定研究结果能否被重复的重要途径，也为别人对结果的检测和引用提供了便利条件，构成论文科学性、先进性的基础性依据。在论文结构上，材料与方法常位于结果与讨论之前，这符合正常的逻辑，但不同期刊可能有不同的格式体例，如 *Cell Research* 论文中的 Materials and Methods 位于 Discussion 后（Discussion 在 Results 后），而 *Science* 论文（Report 类）中的 Materials and Methods 作为附加材料（Supplementary Materials）不是出现在纸本期刊论文中，而是出现在在线论文中。

2.4.1 材料与方法内容及结构

材料与方法讲述在某种目标支配下，使

○ 广义上讲，综述型论文（综述）中也有材料与方法，只不过综述的材料与方法不是针对作者自己的科学实验的，而是针对作者写此综述所引用的参考文献以及对这些文献进行研究（如统计、分析等）的方法。

用何种材料、施用何种方法、经过何种过程或步骤来进行科学研究（实验或理论研究），旨在交待做了什么、用了什么、怎么做的。科学研究通常较为复杂，具体目标多样，涉及因素繁多，所用方案、方法较广，所走流程、过程各异，因此材料与方法在内容与结构上并无固定的模式，与研究领域、范围、主题及样本复杂程度、表述侧重、论文出版要求等密切相关，这里只能从通用的共性角度来讲述。

材料属于研究的物质层面，即实物条件，指研究用的各种物质资料，涉及研究对象和非研究对象。在研究对象层面，主要描述研究对象的结构、成分（关键成分）、特性（重要特性）、功能（或主要功能）、来源（主要来源、出处）；在非研究对象层面，主要描述研究所用的设施和设备、仪器和仪表、系统和软件、具体的物质资料（特定物质资料）、材料选用的理由或不足等等，涉及功能、参数、构成、特性、数量、环境、条件、优势（或不足）、来源等诸多要素。注意：这里的材料是指广义材料，有的论文将材料限定为狭义材料，不包括设备（如机器、设施、仪器、仪表等），这时可以将"材料"与"设备"并列，即 Material and Equipment。

方法属于研究的解决层面，即实现条件，指研究所用的各种技术、方法及所需的环境、条件，也涉及研究对象和非研究对象两个层面。在研究对象层面，主要描述研究对象的取样、获取、选择、制备的方法及优势，如样本选取方法（样本类型、样本数、样本组成、分组方法等），同时还需明确交待是否随机化分组和盲法实验，明确估计抽样误差，明确实验范围；在非研究对象层面，主要描述研究的具体方案、方法及相应的过程（步骤），如某种工艺、技术、疗程、算法、程序、统计分析方法等，并交待方法选用的理由（或不足），写作的详略程度取决于研究内容的复杂或重要程度。

对于实验方法来说，主要描述有关实验仪器、设备及实验条件、测试方法等事项，并描述主要的实验过程，涉及实验对象，实验材料的名称、来源、性质、数量、选取及处理方法，实验目的，使用的仪器、设备（型号、名称、测量范围及精度等），实验及测定的方法和过程，出现的问题及采取的措施等。

实验方法中要清楚地描述实验设计方案（如随机对照试验、非随机对照试验、交叉对照试验、前后对照试验、双盲等方法），以及研究场所、实验室设施，根据文体要求还可能需要描述干预措施、盲法、测量指标及判断结果的标准等。

在某项复杂的科学实验中，虽然研究的总体目标只有一个，但在具体的实验研究过程中，通常会涉及多个具体的研究目标（子目标），而对于不同的具体目标，所需的材料与方法往往不同，所用的方案和所走的流程当然也不相同。因此，材料与方法的具体分类及事宜并不那么分明，需要按具体目标分别来撰写，不只是写材料和方法，还要点出具体研究目标，即针对各个子目标来描述所需的具体材料与方法。实际写作中，材料与方法可能相当复杂，如果研究对象为动物或人体，则还要交待有关伦理和研究安全方面的道德、规范与法律、法规。

材料与方法的结构并无固定模式，对于简单的实验，可先描述材料，后描述方法；而对于复杂的实验，有多个不同的子目标，则需要不同的研究方案，因而有不同的方法，自然就需不同的材料。因此，这部分在结构上常混合着写，既可先材料后方法，也可先方法后材料。

2.4.2　材料与方法写作要求

材料与方法的内容通常较多，具体内容

也因研究领域、范围、主题等的不同而呈现较大差别，不同期刊的要求也不相同。因此这部分难有统一的规范，下面给出一些通用写作要求：

(1) 确定标题类型

标题因研究类型的不同而略有差别，如实验研究常用"材料与方法"、调查研究常为"对象与方法"、临床试验多用"病例与方法"等，写作上也不完全一样，要确定与研究类型相匹配的标题及相应的写作方法。

(2) 保证内容真实

所述内容必须实事求是、真实可靠，对核心内容还要全面而具体地描述，达到所有数据、资料的准确性和研究（实验）的可靠性。如有不愿写或不方便写的内容，就尽量少写或不写，但只要写出来的，就要保证内容的真实可信，不能含混，也不能缺乏依据。

(3) 清楚描述材料

明白、准确地描述各主要材料的有关参数，涉及技术要求、性质（如试剂的有关物理、化学性质）、数量、来源，以及材料的选取、处理、制备方法等。通常应使用通用、标准的名称和术语，少用商业化或口语化的名称。

(4) 有序描述方法

按研究步骤的先后顺序来描述方法（避免机械地按年、月、日的次序来描述），包括实验环境或条件（如温度、湿度、电压、辐射、隔离措施、特殊光线等），研究对象选择方法，选用特定材料、设备或方法的理由，实验流程、算法与程序，所用统计、分析方法等。无须按时间顺序来描述时，可考虑按重要性程度来描述。有序描述方法有助于研究成果的推广，让有能力的科技工作者按相关内容来复用研究。

(5) 恰当表述创新

采用前人的方法时，对普遍的方法，可直接交待名称，对较新的方法，应注明出处（提供引文）；改进前人的方法时，应交代改进之处及依据；提出自己创新的方法时，应详细说明，必要时可辅以图表式来配合表述，尽可能写明每个所需细节。注意不要将报道新方法（新方法被提出）与使用新方法（新方法被使用）混为一谈（不宜在同一论文中发表）：对于前者，重在详细介绍方法自身内容及实现步骤；对于后者，重在方法使用的情况及相应的操作步骤。

(6) 描述详略得当

不宜将所用材料全盘搬入而写成材料清单，也不宜将自己所做工作一一罗列而写成实验报告，而忽略了对主要、关键和非一般常用内容的描述。不论对材料还是方法进行描述，都应主次分明、重点突出、详略得当，侧重描述"使用了哪些关键材料"和"研究是如何开展的"，而非大杂烩、记流水账，使那些需要让人知道的重要内容湮没在一大堆冗长、无序的文字中。

(7) 了解目标期刊

写作前应先了解目标期刊，知道其论文写作规范，特别是材料与方法的具体要求。例如，有的临床医学类期刊要求作者提供研究对象（志愿者或病人）"授权同意"的声明和作者所在单位的同意函，有的生物科学类期刊要求将有关伦理声明、生物研究安全性声明和设施方面的内容写进材料与方法。

(8) 重视语言效能

材料与方法需要描述的内容往往多而杂，对语言表达质量要求甚高，准确、清楚、简洁且合乎逻辑事理与思维规律是最起码的要求，目的是让科技工作者看得明白，容易理解，减少出错概率，为将来的研究"复用"创造条件。

2.4.3 材料与方法写作方法

(1) 材料的写作

1) 首先制定研究方案，依据研究方案规划各研究子目标及所用材料，按不同的子目标对材料进行归类,并明确其中哪些是研究对象材料,哪些是非研究对象材料;哪些是重点、主要材料,哪些是常规、次要材料。

2)对于研究对象材料,如样品、工件、产品、动物、植物、微生物、病人等,应清楚地介绍其数量、来源、特征、选取或制备方法,还可给出抽样误差估计值,让读者了解研究内容及结果的使用条件或范围。

如果研究对象是动物、植物和微生物,则需要按属、种和世系名来准确标识,并说明其来源和特殊性质(年龄、性别、体重、健康状况、遗传学和生理学状态)、抽样要求或标准等。

如果研究对象是微生物或化合物,则需要描述多种微生物的种属或化合物的来源和特性,可以采用列表的形式,或在正文、表注、图注中给予简单的描述。

如果研究对象是人(志愿者或病人),则需要特别注意目标期刊的具体要求,交代研究对象的选择标准,并根据情况来兼顾一般性的重要统计特征(如年龄、性别和身体状况等)及其他与论文主题相关的统计信息(如体重、身高、种族等)。

3)对于非研究对象材料,先进行概述,接着详细描述其结构、主要成分、重要特性及关键功能等,对采用具有商标名的设备、仪器以及化学试剂、药品时,还应对设备、仪器的规格、功能、技术进行详细的说明,列出试剂、药品的主要化学、物理性质(对常规试剂,只说明名称、生产厂家、规格、批号即可;对新试剂,还要写出分子式和结构式,若需配制,则还要交待配方和制备方法),仪器和样品制造商的名称及所在地通常也要列出。

材料名称应采用国际同行所熟悉的通用名,尽量避免用某国家、某领域或某范围同行才知道或熟悉的专门名称。但当已知有不同特性的产品且其间有重要差别时,就需用商标和制造商名(商标名的首字母应大

写),并将通用的描述紧接在商标名之后,以示与通用名的区别。

下面给出材料写作的几个例句(画单线部分为材料,双线部分为材料来源的标志性词语):

- CLL specimens were obtained from patients at the West Los Angeles VA Hospital Hematology clinic after informed consent and Institutional Review Board approval.

- Rasgrf-1 antibody (Cterminus) was purchased from Proteintech (Chicago, IL), phospho-Rasgrf1 antibody (Serine 929) from Santa Cruz Biotechnology (Dallas, TX), phospho-ERK (Thr202/Tyr204), phospho-Akt (Ser473), phospho-BTK (Tyr223), and actin from Cell Signaling (Beverly, MA). Detection was performed with horseradish peroxidase-conjugated secondary antibodies and chemiluminescence (ECL plus, GE Healthcare and LAS Mini imager, Fuji).

- The 293T cells purchased from ATCC have been tested to be mycoplasma negative by the commonly used PCR method.

此两示例中也有有关方法的描述,如"Detection was performed with …""…by the commonly used PCR method"(画浪纹线部分为标志性词语)。实际中材料与方法不能截然分开,混合着写是一种常态。

(2)方法的写作

1)依据研究方案,为每个研究子目标给出相应的方法,包括标本选择标准、分组方法、制备过程、仪器使用方法、步骤、操作技巧、实验环境、条件、设置、人或动物麻醉、手术、处置方案,各步处理时间、参数设置、注意事项等。

2)清楚介绍设计方案,对各个主要方法尽可能详写,以便让同行能够复用实验,避免混入或尽量不写有关结果或发现方面的内容。通常应完整地描述选择某种特定方法

的理由（优势、不足）。如果方法新颖且未曾发表过，则应提供所有必需的细节；如果方法已经公开报道，则引用相关文献，但如果报道该方法的期刊不怎么知名，则可以稍加详细描述。

3）详细描述统计分析方法，表明作者新设计或使用了什么方法。对普通的统计方法，一般无需评论或解释，但对先进或不常见的，则应适当引用文献。通常需要简要说明在什么条件下使用何种统计学方法及显著性标准，必要时还应说明所用计算手段和软件名称。

4）内容较多时，需要对内容进行层次类别划分，为各个层次类别确立子标题，并尽可能与结论中的内容相"对应"，以保持论文内部的一致呼应，这样有助于让读者快速了解某特定方法及使用该方法而获得的结果。

5）最后还应该有统计分析部分，写出数据处理的盲选法、测量指标及判断差异结果的标准等。

下面给出方法写作的几个例句或几种句式。

- ... activity was detected <u>according to the previous method</u> (Jason et al, the journal of ..., 2016)

- ... activity was detected <u>according to the previous method</u> (Jason et al, the journal of ..., 2016) <u>with slight modification. Briefly, ...</u>.

- In this paper, <u>a modified protocol based on the method</u> reported by Jason et al was used. Briefly, ...

上面例句一，完全采用以前发表过的方法，一笔带过（according to the previous method）；例句二、三部分采用以前发表过的方法，但有适度修改（according to the previous method with slight modification；a modified protocol based on the method），其中Briefly后面省去的部分就是简述作者的方法并写明其中特别之处的语句。

- Lysates <u>were prepared by</u> washing cells with cold PBS and disrupted in lysis buffer (Cell Signaling, MA) supplemented with protease inhibitor cocktail.

- Antibodies specific to A (*name*, *dilution*, *company*) and B (*name*, *dilution*, *company*) <u>were applied in</u> ... according to ... protocol.

- For histological analysis, cells <u>were fixed with</u> ... and <u>stained against</u> ... (dye or antibody, dilution, company).

- Quantitative analysis <u>was performed using</u> × × × test if not otherwise stated. The level of significance <u>was set at</u> $*P < 0.05$. Error bar represent $+/-$ SEM.

以上例句一描述裂解酶的制备方法（在冷的PBS中清洗细胞并溶解在添加有蛋白酶抑制剂混合物的裂解液中），例句二描述使用两种抗体（按照协议将针对A和B的抗体应用于……），例句三描述对细胞进行操作（为病理学分析将细胞和……固定，并对……染色），例句四描述使用某种测试进行定量分析（如果没有另行说明，使用……测试进行了定量分析。重要性级别设定为 $*P < 0.05$。误差条代表 $+/-$ SEM）。这些均属方法范畴，其中括号部分描述了所需的材料（名称、出处）。显然，在方法的描述中又夹杂着材料的描述，当然是以方法描述为主、材料描述为辅。这就是前面所说的，材料与方法通常是混合着写的。

2.4.4 材料与方法写作实例

下面选择若干材料与方法的实例，了解其内容、结构和写作方法。

2.4.4.1 实例一

【1】

MATERIALS AND METHODS

To offer comprehensive comparison of various types of SiNCs, four different materials were studied. Three types of oxide capped SiNCs (O-SiNCs) were used, differing in size, preparation protocol and oxide-capping thickness and quality, and as a reference we studied oxide-free sample of organically capped nanocrystals (C-SiNC). For sample overview, see Table 1 and sketch in Figure 1b.

Table 1　Four types of studied SiNCs samples

Sample	Name	Capping	Diameter [Reference]	Distribution	Preparation [Reference]
1	Por-SiNCs	Naturally grown thin silica oxide	2-3nm[6]	Ensemble	Electrochemical etching[6]
2	Plasma-SiNCs	Naturally grown thin silica oxide	~4nm[41]	Ensemble	Plasma synthesis[41]
3	Litho-SiNCs	Strained thick silica oxide	~4nm[42]	Single NC	Electron beam lithography[42]
4	C-SiNCs	Organic (alkyl)	~2.2 ± 0.5nm[17,40]	Ensemble	Wet-chemical synthesis[17,40]

Additional material and spectroscopic properties of these samples have been extensively studied and reported elsewhere. More details are given in the Experimental section, Supplementary Information (Supplementary Fig. S1) and respective Refs 6, 17, 40 – 42.

First sample, Por-SiNC (Sample 1) consists of small NCs with diameter of 2–3 nm that are made from mechanically pulverized layers of oxidized porous silicon that has been additionally post-etched in hydrogen peroxide solution, leading to increased amounts of-OH surface moieties (see Dohnalová et al.[6] for more information). Second sample, Plasma-SiNCs (Sample 2), contains larger NCs with core diameter of around 4 nm, prepared by plasma synthesis from silane gas. The NC naturally oxidized by exposure to air, which results in a thin, non-thermal oxide layer (more information can be found in Doğan et al.[41]). Finally, third sample, Litho-SiNCs (Sample 3), contains larger Si nanostructures, some of them similarly sized as those of the Plasma-SiNC sample, which we chose for this study. This sample was prepared by electron-beam lithography followed by reactive ion-etching and self-limiting oxidation (more details can be found in Bruhn et al.[42]). This oxidation technique results in SiNCs embedded in a thick strained thermal oxide as indicated in the sketch in Figure 1b. The reference sample C-SiNCs (Sample 4) was prepared by wet-chemical synthesis and have small core diameter of (2.2 ± 0.5) nm and surface passivated by butyl ligands (more details can be found in Refs. 17, 40).

For the microscopic analysis, all colloidal nanocrystals (Por-, Plasma-and C-SiNC samples) were dispersed and sonicated in UV-grade ethanol and drop-casted onto a clean pre-patterned silicon surface. The patterned substrate allowed us to recognize and analyze the same microscopic sample area in the PL and CL measurements. Silicon substrates are covered with a naturally grown thin oxide layer that exhibits negligible PL and CL signals (see Supplementary Information, Supplementary Figs. S5a and S5b), but is sufficiently conductive. For better contrast, the weakly emitting Plasma-SiNCs were deposited onto a glass substrate partially covered by a thin gold sheet. We confirmed that this change of substrates had no influence on the emission spectrum. For more detailed information and analysis of the samples, see Supplementary Fig. S1 and respective Refs. 6, 40 – 42.

For spectral analysis, we used photoluminescence (PL) and cathodoluminescence (CL) micro-spectroscopy setups. Steady-state micro-PL was measured using an inverted wide-field optical microscope (Zeiss AxioVert XY, Zeiss, Oberkochen, Germany) with ×100 air objective (NA 0.7) as shown in Figure 2a. The PL was excited by a ~3.1 eV (405 nm) low power (<5 mW) cw laser diode and detected by a liquid-nitrogen-cooled CCD camera (Pylon 400B, Princeton Instruments, Acton, MA, USA) coupled to a spectrometer (Acton SP2300, Princeton Instruments). PL spectra were measured at room temperature and ambient conditions and corrected for background and spectral response of the detection system. The CL measurements were performed in the vacuum chamber of the scanning electron microscope (SEM; FEI XL-30 SFEG)[43,44] as shown in Figure 2b. Samples were irradiated by a focused e-beam of diameter of ~2–10 nm, electron energies in range of 2–30 keV and beam currents of 0.2–2 nA, to generate color centers and excite the CL emission. In each step, CL is collected from area of approximately 100–200 nm^2 and the beam scanning mode covered an area of approximately 10 μm × 10 μm. This area was large enough to get measurable signal in the follow-up micro-PL measurements to conclude spectral changes after the irradiation. The CL signal is collected by a parabolic mirror and deflected into a liquid-nitrogen-cooled front-illuminated Si CCD camera (Spec-10 100F, Princeton Instruments), coupled to a spectrometer (Acton SP2300, Princeton Instruments). CL has been measured under various exposure times and varying electron energies at room temperature and has been corrected for the spectral response of the detection system.

(Multi-chromatic silicon nanocrystals. *Light: Science & Application*, Volume 6, Issue 3, 2017.)

例【1】是一篇物理学（光学）领域原创论文的材料与方法，共有四段。

第一段直接指出选取四种材料（三类O-SiNCs 和一类 C-SiNC）作为研究样本，指明研究（实验）对象，同时用表格说明四类样本的编号、名称、表面覆盖物、直径、分布性、制备，还用插图对样本给予形象化的呈现。第二段对四类样本的组成、特性、制备进行概括性描述。这两段总体上描述了材料。

第三段描述对样本进行显微分析的主要内容，涉及方法、过程、仪器、设备及具体做法等。第四段描述对样本进行光谱分析（spectral analysis）的主要内容，涉及仪器、设备（型号、参数、厂家、国别），并描述有关步骤、现象、特征和缘由等关键内容。这两段总体上描述了方法，同时也较多涉及具体实验过程中使用的仪器、设备，因此方法中又蕴含着材料。

2.4.4.2 实例二

【2】

Materials and Methods

Ethics statements

This study was carried out in strict accordance with the recommendations in the Guide for the Care and Use of Laboratory Animals of the Ministry of Science and Technology of the People's Republic of China. The protocols were approved by the Committee on the Ethics of Animal Experiments of the Harbin Veterinary Research Institute (HVRI) of the Chinese Academy of Agricultural Sciences (CAAS).

Biosafety statement and facility

All experiments with live H7N9 viruses were conducted within the enhanced animal biosafety level 3 (ABSL3+) facility in the HVRI of the CAAS approved for such use by the Ministry of Agriculture of China. All animal studies were approved by the Review Board of the HVRI, CAAS. The details of the facility and the biosafety and biosecurity measures used have been previously reported [9].

Sample collection and virus isolation

From July 2013 to January 2017, 112 593 samples, including environment, cloacal, and tracheal swab samples of birds (cloacal and tracheal swabs of the same bird were put in the same sample collection tube and counted as one sample) from live poultry markets, poultry farms, poultry slaughterhouses, as well as faeces from wild bird habitats were collected in 24 provinces in China (Supplementary information, Table S1). Each sample was placed in 2 ml of minimal essential medium supplemented with penicillin (2 000 U/ml) and streptomycin (2 000 U/ml). All of the individual samples were inoculated into 10-day-old embryonated chicken eggs for 48 h at 37 ℃. The allantoic fluid was collected and tested for HA activity with 0.5% chicken red blood cells. Where the HA assay was positive, HI assays were performed by using antisera against the 16 HA subtypes of avian influenza viruses and Newcastle disease virus (NDV), another avian virus frequently isolated from avian species. NA subtypes were determined by direct sequencing.

Genetic and phylogenetic analysis

Viral RNA of H7N9 viruses was extracted from virus-infected allantoic fluid with the QIAmp viral RNA mini kit (Qiagen, Hilden, Germany). RT-PCR was performed with a set of gene-specific primers and the products were sequenced on an Applied Biosystems DNA analyzer. Primer sequences are available upon request. The nucleotide sequences were edited using the Seqman module of the DNAStar package. We performed the phylogenetic analysis using the Mega 6.0.6 ClustalW software package, implementing the neighbor-joining method. The tree topology was evaluated by 1 000 bootstrap analyses; 97% sequence identity cut-offs were used to categorize the groups of each gene segment in the phylogenetic trees.

We also created a Bayesian time-resolved phylogenetic tree for the HA gene of the group 1 and group 2 viruses using BEAST 1.8.4. The SRD06 nucleotide substitution model, the uncorrelated relaxed clock with a log-normal distribution, and the skygrid flexible effective population size tree prior were selected for the analysis. A Markov Chain Monte Carlo (MCMC) chain was run. The chain consisted of 30 000 000 steps and was sampled every 3 000 steps; the first 10% of samples were discarded as burn-in. The above MCMC settings were chosen to achieve a post burn-in effective sample size of at least 200 in all parameters, as recommended by the BEAST program [50]. The data were evaluated by using AICM in Tracer 1.6. The tree was viewed in Figtree 1.4.3.

Animal studies

Randomization and blinding were not used for the allocation of animals to experimental groups.

Chicken study

To determine the pathogenicity of the viruses, the IVPI was determined according to the recommendations of the Office International Des Epizooties [38]. Groups of ten 6-week-old SPF White Leghorn chickens housed in isolator cages were inoculated intravenously (i.v.) with 0.1 ml of a 1:10 dilution of bacterium-free allantoic fluid containing virus and were observed for signs of disease or death for 10 days. The organs, including brains, lungs, kidneys, spleens, pancreas, heart, liver, and cecum, of three dead birds inoculated with the index virus CK/SD008 were collected for virus titration in eggs.

Thirteen chickens were also inoculated i.n. with 10^6 EID_{50} of CK/SD008 virus in a 0.1 ml volume, and three chickens were killed on day 3 p.i., and their tracheal and cloacal swabs, organs, including brains, lungs, kidneys, spleens, pancreas, heart, liver, and cecum were collected for virus titration in eggs. The remaining 10 birds and the negative control birds were observed for signs of disease or death for 10 days.

Mouse study

To determine MLD_{50} values, groups of five mice (Vital River Laboratories, Beijing, China) were lightly anesthetized with CO_2 and inoculated intranasally with 10-fold serial dilutions containing 10^1-10^7 50% egg infectious doses (EID_{50}) of CK/SD008 or 10^1-10^6 EID_{50} of CK/SD008-PB2/627K and CK/SD008-PB2/701N in a volume of 50 μl. The mice were monitored for 14 days for weight loss and mortality. To assess virus replication, groups of three mice were lightly anesthetized with CO_2 and inoculated intranasally with 10^6 EID_{50} of the test virus in a volume of 50 μl, and were then euthanized on day 3 p.i.; their nasal turbinates, lungs, spleens, kidneys, and brains were collected and titrated for virus infectivity in eggs.

Ferret study

Four-month-old female ferrets (Wuxi Cay Ferret Farm, Jiangsu, China) that were serologically negative for influenza viruses were used in these studies. The animals were anesthetized via intramuscular injection with ketamine (20 mg/kg) and xylazine (1 mg/kg). To investigate virus replication, groups of two ferrets were anesthetized and inoculated i.n. with 10^6 EID_{50} of test virus in a 500 l volume (250 μl per nostril). The ferrets were killed on day 4 p.i and the nasal turbinates, tonsils, trachea, lung, spleen, kidneys, and brain were collected for virus titration in eggs.

For the respiratory droplet transmission studies, groups of three ferrets were inoculated i.n. with 10^6 EID_{50} of test virus and housed in specially designed cages inside an isolator as reported previously [9, 16]. Twenty-four hours later, three naive animals were placed in an adjacent cage (4 cm away), separated by a double-layered net divider. These cages allow free passage of air. Nasal washes were collected at 2-day intervals, beginning on day 2 p.i. (1 day post exposure) and titrated in eggs. Sera were collected from all animals on day 14 p.i. for HI antibody detection. The ambient conditions for these studies were set at 20-22 ℃ and 30%-40% relative humidity. The airflow in the isolator was horizontal with a speed of 0.1 m/s; the airflow direction was from the inoculated animals to the exposed animals.

Receptor-binding analysis

Receptor specificity was analysed by use of a solid-phase direct binding assay with two different glycopolymers: α-2, 3-siaylglycopolymer [Neu5Acα2-3Galß1-4GlcNAcß1-pAP (para-aminophenyl)-alpha-polyglutamic acid (α-PGA)] (avian-type receptor) and α-2, 6-sialylglycopolymer [Neu5Acα2-6Galß1-4GlcNAcß1-pAP (para-aminophenyl)-alpha-polyglutamic acid (a-PGA)] (human-type receptor) as described previously [9]. Chicken antisera against CK/S1053 virus, A/Sichuan/1/2009 (H1N1) virus, and A/chicken/Hebei/3/2013 (H5N2) virus were generated in SPF chickens in our laboratory, and the horseradish peroxidase (HRP)-conjugated goat anti-chicken antibody was purchased from Sigma-Aldrich (St. Louis, MO, USA).

Heat stability test

Viruses (128 HA units in PBS) were incubated for the times indicated at 50 ℃. Hemagglutination activity was then determined by use of hemagglutination assays using 0.5% chicken red blood cells, and infectivity was determined in 10-day-old chicken embryos.

Polymerase activity analysis

A dual-luciferase reporter assay system (Promega) was used to compare the polymerase activities. Briefly, 0.5 μg of the firefly luciferase reporter plasmid p-Luci and the internal control plasmid Renilla were transfected into 293T cells together with 0.5 μg each of the four protein expression plasmids pCAGGS-PB2 (or pCAGGS-PB2/627K or pCAGGS-PB2/701N), pCAGGS-PB1, pCAGGS-PA, and pCAGGS-NP from the CK/SD008 virus. The assay was performed at 33 and 37 ℃. Cell lysates were analysed 24 h after transfection to measure firefly and Renilla luciferase activities. Luminescence of the firefly luciferase was standardized using a plasmid expressing Renilla luciferase. Values shown are the mean ± SD of three independent experiments and are compared to those obtained with CK/SD008. The 293T cells purchased from ATCC have been tested to be mycoplasma negative by the commonly used PCR method.

Statistical analysis

Virus titres of mice were statistically analysed by one-tailed paired *t*-test. The polymerase activity values were statistically analysed by two-tailed paired *t*-test.

(H7N9 virulent mutants detected in chickens in China pose an increased threat to humans. *Cell Research*, Vol. 27, No. 12, Dec. 2017: 1409-1421.)

例【2】是一篇生物医学领域原创论文的材料与方法，由十二个部分组成，每部分都有一个标题，具体内容如下所述。

（1）第一部分：伦理声明

符合国家实验室动物护理和使用指南。指明所用材料与方法符合伦理要求。

（2）第二部分：生物研究安全性声明和设施

活H7N9病毒试验的安全级别（增强型动物生物研究安全性三级，ABSL3+），选取的样本、使用的设施、生物研究的安全性及采取的安全性措施符合有关规定。

以上两部分属材料与方法的伦理和安全方面，除把人或动物作为研究对象外，一般的原创论文没有这方面的内容。

（3）第三部分：样本收集和病毒隔离

样本制备（实验对象）：样本选取情况，包括时间（201307—201701）、数量（112 593个）、分类（鸟的环境、泄殖腔和气管拭子样本）、涉及省数量（24个）、来源（活禽市场、家禽养殖场、家禽屠宰场、野生鸟类栖息地的粪便)。

病毒隔离方法：放置在最低基本培养基中，接种，收集尿囊液，检测鸡红细胞 HA 活性。

病毒隔离材料：样本收集管、青霉素、链霉素、基本培养基、鸡胚、抗血清、禽流感病毒等，涉及数量、适用范围、具体方法（如接种、收集、检测、直接测序等）以及环境或工作条件（如温度、时间等）。

(4) 第四部分：遗传和系统发育分析

1) 子对象：H7N9 病毒 RNA（子样本）。

目标：提取 H7N9 病毒 RNA。

方法：完成 RT-PCR、对产品测序、使用引物序列、编辑核苷酸序列、分析系统发育、评估树拓扑、对基因片段组分类。

材料（有的还给出来源、数量）：QIAmp viral RNA mini kit（Qiagen, Hilden, Germany）、基因特异性引物、应用生物系统 DNA 分析仪、DNAStar 软件包 Seqman 模块、Mega 6.0.6 ClustalW 软件包等。

2) 子对象：组 1、2 的 H7N9 病毒（子样本）。

目标：创建 HA 基因贝叶斯时间分辨系统树。

方法：优先分析 SRD06 核苷酸替换模型、对数正态分布式不相关松弛时钟、skygrid 灵活有效种群容量树；运行 MCMC 链，每 3 000 步取样，总计 3 000 万步；丢弃前 10% 的老化样本；选择 MCMC 设置来实现至少 200 个参数的岗位老化有效样本容量；评估数据。

材料：Tracer 1.6 的 AICM 模块。

(5) 第五部分：动物研究

专门指出本研究没有使用传统的随机化和盲法对动物实验进行分组。

(6) 第六部分：鸡研究

目标：确定病毒的病原性。

1) 对象：10 个 6 周龄 SPF 白色来亨鸡组和接种 CK/SD008 病毒疫苗的 3 只死鸟的器官。

方法：确定 IVPI、静脉接种、观察疾病或死亡迹象、收集死鸟的器官、病毒滴定。

材料：白色来亨鸡、无细菌含病毒的尿囊液（0.1 ml、1∶10 稀释）、CK/SD008 病毒、鸡胚。

2) 对象：13 只鸡（子样本）。

方法：鸡鼻内接种病毒疫苗，杀死接种后的鸡（3 只、接种 3 日后），收集死鸟的气管、泄殖腔拭子及器官，病毒滴定，观察疾病或死亡迹象。

材料：CK/SD008 的 10^6 EID_{50} 病毒疫苗、鸡胚、阴性对照鸟。

(7) 第七部分：老鼠研究

1) 目标：确定 MLD_{50} 的价值。

对象：5 只老鼠的组（Vital River Laboratories, Beijing, China）。

方法：轻度麻醉、老鼠鼻内接种疫苗、老鼠体重减轻和死亡数监测。

材料：CO_2、10 倍序列稀释剂（包含 50 μl 的 CK/SD008 10^1-10^7 EID_{50} 疫苗或 CK/SD008-PB2/627K、CK/SD008-PB2/701N 10^1-10^6 EID_{50} 疫苗）。

2) 目标：评估病毒的复制。

对象：3 只老鼠的组。

方法：轻度麻醉、老鼠鼻内接种、杀死老鼠、收集老鼠的器官、病毒传染性滴定。

材料：CO_2、测试病毒的 10^6 EID_{50} 疫苗（50μl）、鸡胚。

(8) 第八部分：雪貂研究

1) 目标：病毒的复制。

对象：两只雪貂的组（4 月龄、血清对流感病毒呈阴性的雌性雪貂，Wuxi Cay Ferret Farm, Jiangsu, China）。

方法：对雪貂进行麻醉、雪貂鼻内接种疫苗、杀死雪貂、收集雪貂器官、进行病毒滴定。

材料：氯胺酮（20 mg/kg）、甲苯噻嗪（1 mg/kg），测试病毒的 10^6 EID_{50} 疫苗（500 L），鸡胚。

2）目标：呼吸道飞沫传染；HI 抗体检测。

对象：3 只雪貂的组和 3 只幼龄雪貂。

方法：雪貂组鼻内接种疫苗、放置在隔离器的笼子里；将 3 只幼龄雪貂放置在与隔离器相邻的笼子里（相邻笼子间用双层网分隔物隔开）。收集鼻洗液、病毒传染性滴定。收集所有雪貂的血清。

材料：测试病毒的 10^6 EID_{50} 疫苗、隔离器、笼子、双层网分隔物、鸡胚。

条件：笼子里空气自由流通；接种 1 日后暴露；接种 14 日后收集血清；环境温度 20~22 ℃，相对湿度 30%~40%；气流方向水平，由接种动物流向暴露的动物，气流速度 0.1 m/s。

（9）第九部分：受体结合分析

方法：固相直接结合试验、受体特异性分析。

材料：α-2,3-siaylglycopolymer ［Neu5-Acα2-3Galß1-4GlcNAcß1-pAP（para-aminophenyl）-alpha-polyglutamic acid（α-PGA）］（avian-type receptor）；α-2,6-sialylglycopolymer［Neu5Acα2-6Galß1-4GlcNAcß1-pAP（para-aminophenyl）-alpha-polyglutamic acid（a-PGA）］（human-type receptor）；针对 CK/S1053 病毒、A/Sichuan/1/2009（H1N1）病毒、A/chicken/Hebei/3/2013（H5N2）病毒的鸡抗血清（由 SPF 鸡产生）；辣根过氧化物酶（HRP）-共轭羊抗鸡抗体（Sigma-Aldrich（St. Louis, MO, USA））。

（10）第十部分：热稳定性试验

目标：红血球凝聚的活性及传染性。

方法：孵化病毒、0.5% 鸡红细胞的红血球凝聚试验。

材料：PBS（磷酸盐缓冲液）、10 日龄鸡胚。

（11）第十一部分：聚合酶活性分析

对象：聚合酶。

方法：细胞转染；测定萤火虫和荧光素酶的活性；将测定值与由 CK/SD008 获得的值进行比较；用 PCR 方法对 293T 细胞进行检测。

材料：双荧光素酶报告分析系统（Promega）；荧火虫光素酶报告质体 p-Luci（0.5 μg），内部控制质粒光素酶，四蛋白质表达质粒 pCAGGS-PB2（或 pCAGGS-PB2/627K 或 pCAGGS-PB2/701N），pCAGGS-PB1，pCAGGS-PA，pCAGGS-NP（来自 CK/SD008 病毒，0.5 μg）；293T 细胞（ATCC）。

（12）第十二部分：统计分析

目标：对老鼠的病毒滴定、聚合酶活性值进行统计分析。

方法：单尾配对 t 测试、双尾配对 t 测试。

2.4.4.3 实例三

【3】

Materials and methods

Cell culture and reagents

CLL specimens were obtained from patients at the West Los Angeles VA Hospital Hematology clinic after informed consent and Institutional Review Board approval. CLL specimens for this study were obtained from patients that had not received any prior treatment and had more than 90% CLL cells in the peripheral blood mononuclear cells (PBMC) isolated. Primary CLL cells were isolated by a ficoll gradient and stored in liquid nitrogen. Maver-1 cell line was obtained from ATCC[30]. Activation of BCR was performed by cross linking with a goat F(ab′)2 anti-human IgM antibody (SouthernBiotech, Birmingham, AL) at a concentration of 10 mg/mL for 20 min or as indicated. Cells were also activated by co-culture with stromal cell line HS-5 cells (ATCC) for 24 h[31]. All cell culture experiments were performed with RPMI media with 10% FBS, glutamine 2mM, Pen-Strep, Sodium pyruvate 1mM.

Plasmid constructs and transfection

Full length human Rasgrf-1 cDNA (3822bp, 1273AA) was obtained from Origene, MA. With PCR, a 2004 bp fragment with intact 3′ end of the gene was amplified from the cDNA (nucleotide 2194 to nucleotide 4197, 667AA NM_002891.4). This fragment was cloned in the pCDNA 3.1V5His Topo TA vector (Invitrogen, CA) in frame with the V5 epitope (Rasgrf-1rN605) and lacks 605 AA from the N-terminus region. A control vector with no insert was also constructed. Maver-1 cell line was transfected with Amaxa Nucleofector system using Solution V and program U07. Transfected cells were selected with G418 at 400 mg/mL and pools of selected cells were analyzed for further experiments.

Western blot analysis

Lysates were prepared by washing cells with cold PBS and disrupted in lysis buffer (Cell Signaling, MA) supplemented with protease inhibitor cocktail. Insoluble material was removed by centrifugation (10,000 g, 10 min) and protein concentrations determined by BioRad DC protein assay. Samples were mixed with SDS sample buffer and 20-30 μg aliquots resolved on SDS/PAGE gels. Rasgrf-1 antibody (Cterminus) was purchased from Proteintech (Chicago, IL), phospho-Rasgrf1 antibody (Serine 929) from Santa Cruz Biotechnology (Dallas, TX), phospho-ERK (Thr202/Tyr204), phospho-Akt (Ser473), phospho-BTK (Tyr223), and actin from Cell Signaling (Beverly, MA). Detection was performed with horseradish peroxidase-conjugated secondary antibodies and chemiluminescence (ECL plus, GE Healthcare and LAS Mini imager, Fuji).

Apoptosis and chemotaxis assays

Apoptosis was analyzed by BD Annexin V FITC flow cytometry assay (Becton Dickinson). Briefly, 2×10^5 cells in a 6-well dish were treated with bendamustine at different concentrations and 48 h later stained and analyzed as protocol. Apoptosis was also analyzed in different co-culture conditions, with and without HS-5 co-culture. Cells were then stained and processed by the Annexin flow cytometry protocol. The chemotaxis assay was performed in Transwell culture plates (Costar, Cambridge, MA) with a pore size of 5 μm. Briefly, B-cell lines were suspended in RPMI-1640 with 0.5% BSA. A total of 100 μL, containing 10^5 cells, was added to the top chamber of Transwell culture inserts. Filters then were transferred to wells containing medium with or without SDF-1 (200 ng/mL, R&D systems). The chambers were incubated for 4 h at 37 ℃ in 5% CO_2. After this incubation, the cells in the lower chamber were counted by running through a Accuri flow cytometer at 10 μL/min in triplicates.

(Modulation of B-cell receptor and microenvironment signaling by a guanine exchange factor in B-cell malignancies. *Cancer Biology & Medicine*, Volume 13, Issue 2, June 2016: 277–285.)

例【3】是一篇癌症生物医学领域原创论文的材料与方法。由四部分组成，每部分有一个标题（细胞培养和试剂、质粒结构和转染、蛋白质印迹分析、细胞凋亡和趋化性试验），第一部分描述样本来源及培养（放置），其他部分描述以样本为研究对象的试验方案，涉及过程、方法、材料（如类别、来源、数量、规格）。

第一部分先描述 CLL 标本的来源（西洛杉矶 VA 医院血液学诊所）、构成（未接受过任何先前治疗的患者）；再描述其细胞培养和试剂制作方法，涉及过程（如隔离、储存、BCR 激活、细胞激活）、方法（如聚蔗糖梯度、交联聚合、共培养、激活）和材料（聚蔗糖、液氮、Maver-1 细胞株、山羊 F（ab′）2 抗人免疫球蛋白（IgM）抗体、RPMI 培养基、胎牛血清、谷氨酰胺、链霉素、丙酮酸钠）。对一些材料的来源、数量等也有所交待。

第二部分描述细胞质粒结构和转染方案，涉及过程（如基因片段扩增、克隆、关联、无插入物控制载体构造、细胞珠转染、选择与分析）、方法（如 PCR 技术、程序 U07、细胞核转染）与材料（如人类基因片段 Rasgrf-1 cDNA、溶液 V、G418、Maver-1 细胞珠）。对有的材料还交待了来源，如 Rasgrf-1 cDNA（3822bp，1273AA）（Origene, MA）, pCDNA 3.1V5His Topo TA 载体（Invitrogen, CA）；材料的尺寸规格、浓度等指标也有所交待。

第三部分描述细胞蛋白质印迹分析方案，涉及过程（如裂解液制备、分裂，不溶性材料移去，蛋白质浓度确定，样品与 SDS/PAGE 凝胶上的小份样品混合、检测）、方法（如清洗细胞、离心分离、BioRad DC 蛋白质测定、化学发光）与材料（如 PBS、补充有蛋白酶抑制剂混合物的裂解缓冲液、SDS 样品缓冲液、Rasgrf-1 抗体、phospho-Rasgrf1 抗体），并对一些材料交待来源及定量数据指标。这部分的标题虽然包含中心词 analysis，其正文却不是进行"分析"，而是为了后面"结论与讨论"中的"分析"提前交待的"方案"。

第四部分描述细胞凋亡和趋化性试验方案，涉及过程（如细胞凋亡分析、细胞染色和处理、过滤器迁移到介质池）和方法（如 BD 膜联蛋白 V FITC 流式细胞术、膜联蛋白流式细胞术协议），其中每一过程又包含几个子过程，例如细胞凋亡分析中包括细胞处理、染色并分析、凋亡分析等。本方案还涉及各种层面的材料，如器具类（如一般培养皿、Transwell 培养皿）、仪器类（如 Accuri 流式细胞仪）、流式及其他类（如苯达莫司汀、HS-5、BSA、RPMI-1640 培养液、SDF-1、5% CO_2）。对材料的来源、定量数据或规格也作了清楚交待，典型的表述有：对 6 个培养皿中的 2×10^5 个细胞用不同浓度的苯达莫司汀进行处理，48 h 后按协议对其染色并分析；孔径为 5 μm 的 Transwell 培养皿（Costar, Cambridge, MA）；在 5% CO_2 中 37 ℃下持续培养 4 h；通过 Accuri 流式细胞仪以 10 μL/min 的速度一分为三地来计数等。

2.4.4.4 实例四

【4】

2 Experimental

2.1 Material and equipment

Titanium powder with a average size of 30 μm, titanium hydride powder with a average size of 46 μm, aluminum powder with a average size of 6–8 μm, and toluene were used.

A vibrating mill was used to mix the above powders. An electric tube furnace with high vacuum pump was used to treat the mixed powders. The alloyed powder was characterized by scanning electron microscopy (SEM) and field-emission scanning electron microscope (FESEM) equipped with energy-dispersive spectroscopy (EDS). The particle size of the powders was tested by a laser particle size analyzer.

2.2 Ball milling

High-energy ball milling as a powder preparing technology was applied in preparing the TiAl alloy powders, which can shorten the diffusion distance between titanium and aluminum adequately and refine the grain size. This will increase the speed of diffusion reaction. During ball milling, powder was refined under the control of the fracture and cold welding process. When these two processes achieved a dynamic balance, the particle size of the powders did not change significantly. During high-energy ball milling, it is important to control the breaking process of powder and efficiently obtain ultra-fine powder. Most researchers promote the fracture process by adjusting the technological parameters of high-energy ball milling, such as adding process treating agent or conducting ball milling at low temperature.

Titanium-aluminum powders or titanium hydride-aluminum powders in a mole ratio of 1∶1 were blended and refined, respectively, by high-energy ball milling with toluene as the process control agent. The ball milling tank and balls were made from stainless steel. The vibration frequency was 23.2 Hz, and the mass ratio of the balls to powders was 5∶1. The ball milling time cannot be too long since the oxygen content increased and the process of ball milling was hard to avoid involving impurities with the extension of ball milling time. According to the previous experience, the vibration time was generally set for 1 h. The ball-milled powders were put into the vacuum drying oven under 0.1 Pa at 40 ℃.

Figure 1a, b shows the FESEM images of Ti–Al and TiH_2–Al mixed powders with high-energy ball milling for 1 h, respectively. The "white" area is titanium, the "black" area is aluminum powder as shown in Fig. 1a; the "white" area is titanium hydride, the "black" area is aluminum powder as shown in Fig. 1b. Both mixed powders exist as independent particles of the two powders, not in the form of composite particles of two powders.

2.3 Alloying

The mixed powders were heated by a vacuum tube furnace with the vacuum degree of 4.0×10^{-3} Pa and the heating rate of $5\ ℃ \cdot min^{-1}$. The heat treating regime can be finally determined through the results of the previous experiments. The relatively pure TiAl alloy powders were prepared with Ti and Al powders or TiH_2 and Al powders by ball milling at low temperature. The average content of oxygen in the alloy powders is 0.33 wt%. The ball-milled powder of Ti and Al was heated for 2 h at 500 ℃ and then 3 h at 600 ℃. The ball-milled powder of TiH_2 and Al was heated for 3 h at 750 ℃.

Figure 2 is XRD patterns of the above two kinds of mixed powders after heat treatment in a vacuum environment. As shown in XRD patterns, TiAl and a small amount of Ti_3Al alloy powders were prepared and the grain size of the former is larger than that of the latter due to the fact that the width of the diffraction peak in the pattern (1) is wider than that in the pattern (2) in Fig. 2.

Figure 3 shows that the alloy powder prepared by Ti–Al powders looks relatively "smooth" with irregular shape. The alloy powders prepared with TiH_2–Al powders have a smaller size, and the surface is "soft spiny" with irregular shape.

The particle size distribution of alloy powder prepared by Ti–Al powders is wider, and the average particle size of alloy powder is bigger, about 45 μm (Fig. 4a).

The particle size distribution of alloy powder prepared by TiH_2–Al powders is wider, and the average particle size of alloy powder is smaller, about 20 μm (Fig. 4b). The reason is that the titanium hydride powder has bigger brittleness than titanium powder which is easy to be crushed to smaller size of particles.

(Preparation of TiAl alloy powder by high-energy ball milling and diffusion reaction at low temperature. *RARE METALS*, (2018) 37 (1): 21–25.)

例【4】是一篇材料类原创论文的材料与方法。它的标题不是传统的 Materials and Methods，而是 Experimental，注意这只是形式上的不同，其实表意并无什么差别。总体上描述实验方案，分材料与设备、球磨、合金化处理三个部分（三个主题）：第一部分总体上指广义材料（其中 Material 是狭义上的，不包括实验所用的设备如机器、设施、仪器、仪表等，这些是用 equipment 来指代的）；后两部分为方法或方案（带相应结果显示或描述），方法中又有相应材料的描述。

第一部分有两段。第一段描述实验材料：钛粉（30 μm）、氢化钛粉（46 μm）、铝粉（6~8 μm）、甲苯。第二段描述实验设备：振动磨粉机（混合粉末），配备高真空泵的电动管式炉（处理混合粉末）；扫描电子显微镜（SEM），配备能量分散光谱（EDS）的场发射扫描电子显微镜（FESEM）；激光粒度分析仪（测试粉末颗粒大小）。

第二部分有三段。第一段描述用高能球磨粉末制备技术来制备 TiAl 合金粉末的优势及过程特征。第二段描述以甲苯为工艺控制剂的高能球磨方案，涉及工艺类别（粉末混合、精炼）、工艺参数设置（振动频率、球与粉末质量比、球磨时间、振动时间）和球磨粉末存放环境和条件（真空干燥炉中，0.1 Pa，40 ℃）。第三段显示对 Ti-Al 和 TiH_2-Al 混合粉末高能球磨 1 h 的 FESEM 图像（属结果），点出球磨结果的特征（混合粉末以其独立粒子而非复合粒子存在）。

第三部分有四段。第一段描述对混合粉末热处理的工艺方案，包括过程（混合粉末加热及热处理状态确定、合金粉末低温球磨加工、球磨粉末高温加热）、参数或条件（真空度、加热速度、加热温度及时间、合金粉末平均氧含量）以及实验对象材料（Ti-Al、TiH_2-Al 粉末）和所用设备（真空管炉）。第二段用插图的形式显示真空环境中对 Ti-Al、TiH_2-Al 两种混合粉末热处理后的 XRD 模式，并点出该模式的特征和形成原因。第三段用插图展示由这两种混合粉末制备的合金粉末的形状特征（形状均为不规则，前者相对"光滑"，后者是"软刺"）。第四段用插图展示这两种合金粉末的粒度分布特征均较广泛，但平均粒度相差较大的特征（平均粒度尺寸，前者的约为 45 μm，后者的约为 20 μm），形成鲜明对比，并点出原因。

2.5 结果与讨论

结果与讨论（Results and Discussion）是原创型论文的结果部分（结论也可包括在内），是描述由科学研究（实验）获得的客观结果以及对此结果的评价性认识，旨在交待做出了什么，据此又能得到什么，使有待实践证明的假说、经过科学思维形成的理论认识得到证实，证明作者提出的假说是合理的、科学的，观点是正确的。结果是研究的直接目标，没有结果，研究就失去依据；讨论是研究的最终目标，没有讨论，结果就停留在表象，研究也就失去意义。结果讲求数据、资料的真实性，能否被复用是研究的基本要求；讨论讲求分析、论证的逻辑性，是否合理是研究的价值保障。

2.5.1 结果与讨论内容及结构

结果与讨论常放在一起写，冠以一个总标题（Results and Discussion），也可分开写，有各自独立的标题（Results、Discussion）。撰写初稿时宜将二者分开写，差不多时再按需合并。有时还可将"讨论"与"结论"合并为"讨论与结论"或"结论"，长短没有明确规定。

1. 结果的内容与结构

结果是论文的依据部分，是科学研究探索的答案，直接决定了研究工作能否成功、研究目标能否实现。结果是论文中最关键的部分，是整个论文的立足点及价值所在。全文的一切分析、讨论由结果引发，一切推理、判断由结果导出，一切结论、结语由结果得出。

结果的内容与结构通常为：

（1）结果介绍，指出结果在哪些插图、表格或相关文本表述中列出。

（2）结果描述，描述重要的实验或观测结果。

（3）结果评论，说明、解释结果，并与有关模型或前人结果进行比较。

2. 讨论的内容与结构

讨论是论文的精华部分，是对结果的思考和辩论，阐述意义和作者的见解，说明与前人结果不同的原因。讨论的重点在于对结果解释、推断，说明是否支持某种观点、是否提出新的问题或观点等，以帮助读者更好地理解、消化和吸收结果，助推研究成果的交流和传播。

讨论的内容与结构通常为：

（1）对主要或重要研究结果、发现的

概述。通常先概括交待研究的目的，再概述最重要的结果与发现，但不与结果中已给出的数据和资料简单重复。

（2）对结果内在联系和发展规律的阐释。将实验、观测、研究所获得的资料、数据及科学界公认的理论、原理作为论据，恰当引用参考文献（分量适当，避免成批大段引用），围绕结果全面论证、阐明作者自己的学术观点，从深度和广度（广度指结果分析的角度）达到对结果的进一步认识。

（3）主要研究目的或假设的回顾。充分比较和分析结果，探讨所得结果是否达到预期（是否支持前面的假设甚至获得超出假设的新发现），如未达到，则要说明原因；将自己的结果与前人的进行比较（与国内外相关课题作比较），如果结果相似，则需进一步讨论二者的差别，说明自己结果的新意，但如果相异，也不要断然肯定自己而完全否定他人。

结果没有绝对的错或对，重要的是对主要结果作简要总结和比较，分析自己研究的优劣和局限，找出或解释不同结果产生的原因。SCI论文重视对结果产生机理的解释，尤其对机理性论文，更加强调这种解释，而对一般论文，则可通过引用文献来解释，甚至可能不解释而只作推测，但前提条件是推测一定要合理、可信。

（4）对自己研究结果优势和局限（长处和短处）的说明。要重点阐述优势，尽显研究的科学价值，但对局限也应明确交待，并给予合理解释，二者通常缺一不可。实际上，审稿人对研究的局限可能更加关注，如果作者对局限能如实指出并合理解释，则容易获得审稿人的理解，反之如果刻意掩盖缺陷，则审稿人容易心生疑惑，甚至怀疑是否还有其他未发现的缺陷，进而容易对论文给出否定的评审意见。

（5）对研究结果科学价值和意义的恰当总结。大体有：新的发现及理论意义，能否支持、反驳或修正相应领域中现有的理论，能否证明以前的假设或提出新假设；实用价值，能否将所获的新发现、新方法、新理论用于解决实际问题（有工程价值），或扩展到其他领域，有助于理解更广泛的领域。表述要实事求是，不逾实证界限、夸大其词，应留有余地。（研究结果有无价值不在于做了多少工作，获得了多少数据和漂亮图片，而在于新的发现及科学价值。）

（6）遗留未解决的重要问题及今后的研究方向。指出研究的局限性并加以分析和解释，指出局限性对研究结果的影响，给出相关设想和建议等，指出进一步的研究问题或方向。

以上只是讨论的大体内容和结构，写作时可以作为参考，但注意不要千篇一律，既不要无故缺项，也不要无端增加。因研究领域、内容不同，讨论不可能有固定的内容和顺序，但一定要以论证作者的个人学术观点为主，再引用文献进行比较或辅助说明。应避免喧宾夺主，将讨论变成综述而冲淡了作者对结果的深度剖析，而应有目标、有重点、有条理和分层次地展开。

3. 结果和讨论合写

"结果"和"讨论"可合并为"结果与讨论"，实际中合写更为常见，但这只是一个形式问题，写作时应根据内容及表达需要作相应的内容顺序和格式调整。

2.5.2 结果与讨论写作要求

1. 结果的写作要求

结果中通常包含多个层次、种类的数据，数据的层次、类别不同，其性质也就不同，而其性质往往决定了其在讨论中的重要、详略程度以及描述细节、表述手段（对重要的数据需要作详细讨论），写作前要全面规划结果和讨论的内容。结果的写作要求大体上有以下几个方面。

（1）科学整理、选取、表达数据

对实验或观测的数据进行科学分类、整理以及提炼、取舍，采用合适形式如文本、图表等进行准确、概括表达。避免不分轻重、主次将所有数据和盘托出，应先整理后取舍。整理数据时要善于扬弃，选取必要的部分，但不要只选取符合自己预料的而有意舍去不符的部分。对异常的数据，即使无法解释，也不轻易舍去，而应加以说明，只有找到确凿证据足以说明其确有错误时才可将其剔除。避免数据过多出现，某些数据完全可以以补充部分的形式来呈现；避免数据不充分、不准确、不详实、不一致。准确是指结果必须是真实的，不能伪造和篡改；详实是指将实验所得所有必要结果及分析结果都提供出来，不得有意隐瞒或遗漏某些结果；不一致是指对相同的结果数据在文中不同地方表达时存在相斥和矛盾，从某种意义上说，结果不够详实并不一定导致拒稿，而结果的真实性、一致性被怀疑则肯定导致拒稿。

（2）选用合适的数据类型表达结果

按需选用不同类型的数据来表达结果。对于特别重要的结果，应采用"原始数据"（实际实验、观测数据）的形式来表达；对于一般数据，可采用"总结数据"（如平均值和正负标准偏差）或"转换数据"（如百分数）的形式来表达。这是对繁杂实验数据处理的必要方法。

（3）采用恰当的数据表达呈现形式

采用文字与图表相结合的形式来表达数据，文字优于图表，而图的使用优先于表。数据很少时，如只有一个或很少的测定结果，则用文字描述；数据较多时，应采用图表的形式来描述或记录，通常较为完整、详尽，同时再用文字来指出图表中信息所蕴含的重要特性或趋势。但不宜在文字中简单地重复图表中的数据，而忽略对其趋势、意义及相关推论的叙述。

（4）对原始数据作必要的说明或解释

要对原始数据作必要的说明或解释，帮助读者提前了解研究结果的意义及重要性。结果中可以描述数据的差异，但不宜过多解释，应尽量把解释留在讨论部分（但结果和讨论合写时，结果中可详细描述、解释数据）。

（5）必要时还要提供统计结果

统计结果如方差分析结果应按期刊规定的格式提供，有的要求详细提供分析值、自由度和概率，而有的则只要给出分析值和概率就可以了。

对结果部分的一些常见负面审稿意见包括：①对结果解释太多；②数据不充分、不准确或不一致；③图表质量较差，不符合要求；④图表中的信息不能支撑论题或论点；⑤包含一些无关的数据。

2. 讨论的写作要求

讨论不太好写，因为其中应写的内容往往较难确定，对同样的内容，不同的人会有不同的认识。但不管怎样，也应围绕以下内容展开：①解释所取得的研究成果；②说明成果的意义；③指出自己的成果与前人研究成果或观点的异同；④讨论尚未定论之处和相反的结果；⑤提出研究的问题和方向。最主要的是突出首创性和创新性，说明研究结果的必然性或偶然性。

（1）围绕结果展开讨论，主次分明、层次清楚

将讨论对应的结果按一定层次从多个角度进行讨论，对于长篇讨论，还要区分和确

定子主题。不要在次要问题上大费笔墨，也不要对前面结果中未呈现过的新结果进行讨论。论据要有说服力和逻辑性，除了将本研究的结果作为论据外，还可将从其他角度（如实验设计、理论原理、借鉴别人的分析方法等）获得的结果作为论据来阐述，增强对论题的支撑。

（2）对结果的解释要重点突出，简洁而清楚

将重点集中于作者的主要论点，尽量给出研究结果所能反映的原理、关系和普遍意义。如有意外的重要发现，则应给出适当的解释或建议，但不必对其过于关注。对实验型论文，讨论的内容应基于实验结果，不宜出现超出实验结果的有关数据或发现。为有效回答所研究的问题，可适当简要地回顾研究目的，并概括主要结果，但不宜简单罗列结果。

（3）推论要符合逻辑，避免出现实验数据不足以支持的观点和结论

根据结果进行论证，注意结论和推论的逻辑性。在探讨实验结果或观测事实的相互关系和科学意义时，不要得出试图解释一切的结论。如果把数据外推到一个更大的、不恰当的结论，不仅无益于突出作者的科学贡献，甚至现有数据所支持的结论也会受到质疑。要如实指出实验数据的欠缺或相关推论、结论中的任何例外，绝不可编造或修改数据。

（4）观点或结论的表达要清楚明确

尽可能清楚地阐明作者的观点或结论，并解释其观点或结论是支持还是反对已有的认识，还要大胆地讨论工作的理论意义和可能的实际应用效果或价值，清楚地指出研究的重要性和新颖性。观点或结论的表述要清楚、准确，不能简单地重复实验结果，特别要保持和结果的一致性，即讨论与结果要一一对应、前呼后应、相互衬托。要正确评价分析自己研究的局限性，提出本结果可能推广的假设和今后的研究方向，从而对读者的思路有所启发。

（5）对结果的科学意义和实际应用效果的表述要实事求是，留有余地

除非必要不要使用 For the first time 等词语，应选择适当的词汇来区分推测与事实。例如：用 prove、demonstrate 等表示作者坚信观点的真实性，用 show、indicate、find 等表示只是陈述事实但并不表明作者对问题的答案有确定的回答，用 imply、suggest 等表示推测，用情态动词 can、could、may、probably、possibly、should、will 等表示论点的确定性程度。

（6）总体上用现在时，必要时可用其他时态。讨论是从论文写作适时呈现的时间角度写的，即讨论的是目前、现时的事，故一般用现在时，但不排除需要用过去时表达的情况。

讨论通常离不开分析，分析的主要内容有：以理论为基础，事实为依据，认真、仔细地推敲结果，既肯定结果的可信度和再现性，又进行误差分析，并与理论结果进行比较（如果论题产生的是理论结果，则应由实验结果来验证），说明存在的问题。

分析的写作要求具体来说有以下几点：

1）分析问题要切中要害，不能空泛议论。要压缩或删除对一般性道理的叙述，省略不必要的中间步骤或推导过程，突出精华部分。

2）对实验过程中发现的实验设计、实验方案或执行方法方面的某些不足或错误应加以说明，以供读者借鉴。

3）理论分析应包括论证的理论依据、对所作假设及其合理性的阐述，以及对分析方法的说明，包括假说（假设）、前提条件、分析对象、适用理论、分析方法和计算

过程等。

对讨论部分的一些常见负面审稿意见包括：①未突出强调对结果部分的发现；②分不清结论与推测；③未充分讨论创新性方法；④未充分引用相关文献。

2.5.3 结果与讨论写作方法

1. 结果的写作方法

结果由实验（研究）获得，与引言、材料和方法一样均属说明、描述、汇报类，主要陈述事实和呈现数据，具有不以人的意志为转移的客观性，写作相对容易，总体上以呈现作者的实验结果为主要内容，再辅以相应的研究目的，并作适当的解释、评论。在写作方法上大体有以下几个方面：

（1）概括和提炼实验或观测结果

避免简单地将实验记录数据或观测事实堆积到文字中，要突出有科学意义和具代表性的重要数据，避免重复一般数据而得不到实质性内容。写作时如果囊括所有一切而不遗漏任何细节，并不能表明作者拥有无限的信息，只能说明作者对结果中各个部分的重要程度缺乏甄别的能力。

描述结果的顺序取决于研究目的，可按某种属性或从某一角度来进行：如方法部分中的描写顺序、由老及新的结果呈现顺序（先叙述传统方法的结果，再叙述新方法的结果）、研究过程的时间顺序、研究的重要性程度。

（2）以文图表相结合来表达数据

如果测定结果只有一个或很少，在正文中用文字描述即可；若数据较多，则应采用图表形式完整、详细地表述，文字部分则用来指出图表信息的重要特性。不要简单地描述数据，也不要在文字中简单地重复图表中的数据；避免用插图和表格重复表述同样的数据。

合理使用文字和图表，根据数据具体情况和表达需要来确定采用何种表达方式。表格的优点是可以方便地呈现大量准确的数据或资料，插图则能够形象、直观、有效地表达复杂数据，尤其是对不同组数据间的比较、关联、趋势等。表格和插图本身还具备"自明性"，即图表题名和注释应准确而清楚地表达出数据或资料的含义。

（3）适当解释或说明原始数据

如果论文中有独立的讨论，则应将对于研究结果的详细讨论留到讨论中，但结果中应提及必要的解释或说明，以便让读者在阅读结果部分的内容时能对作者本研究结果的意义或重要性提前了解或认识。对于讨论部分原始数据的说明要适当，不宜将全部原始数据在这里呈现出来。

（4）明确提供相关统计结果

统计结果对实验分析有时十分重要，通常需要提供的统计数据包括：标准偏差（standard deviation）、均值的标准误差（standard error of the mean）、中位数和四分位数的间距（median and interquartile range）、双侧检验（two-sided tests）、置信区间（confidence intervals）等。必要时还要对数据的统计分析方法进行说明或阐述，尤其要注意突出统计的科学意义。

（5）文字表达准确、简洁、清楚

避免使用冗长的语句来介绍或解释图表。为简洁、清楚起见，不宜把图表的序号作为段落主题句的开头（主语），而应在句中指出图表所揭示的结论，并把图表的序号放入括号中。例如：不宜用 Figure 1 shows the relationship between A and B，而用 A is significantly higher than B at all time points checked（Fig. 1）的表达效果要好得多。

2. 讨论的写作方法

讨论旨在体现作者的主观思想和认识，属议论、描写、评价，写作难度较大。讨论总体上以作者的学术观点论证为主要内容，使用正确的论证方法来表明论据和论点之间的必然联系，使论证具有说服力和可信性。

（1）开头重新说明研究的主要发现

讨论的第一段起提纲挈领作用，通常简述研究目的（想做什么）、开展过程（做了什么）、发现的结果（做出了什么）。有关内容在论文的前面部分（如引言、材料与方法、结果）应该讲过了，这里再次写，只是出于写作逻辑性的需要，让人不感到突兀和生硬。因此这部分的写作宜概括，应避免重复前面过多，语句简短为好。

（2）仔细选择需要深入讨论的结果

结果可能由多个部分组成，各部分有轻重之分，有的较为重要，需要详细讨论，而有的可能不怎么重要，无需讨论或仅需简单讨论，一笔带过即可。因此需要选择合适的结果组成部分（分结果）作为深入讨论的对象，通常可根据以下原则来判断：如果结果体现了研究的独特性，是其他研究所没有的，就列为深入讨论对象；如果和前人的研究一致或无显著性差异，就无需深入讨论。讨论的一个重要作用是突出自己研究的创新性，体现出区别于他人的显著特点，区别大还是小是另外一个问题，重要的是有无区别，只要有区别就可能有创新。

（3）对结果要按一定层次多角度讨论

对所得结果特别是数据结果展开讨论时要重在分析，不要重复结果，还应适当引用文献，用以支持相应的结果。对于与别人不同的结果，不要回避，而要深入讨论。鉴于科学研究的复杂性，所选的结果（问题）通常不只一个，两个以上结果很常见。不同结果的层次不同，因此需要按一定的层次来讲述，说理要有根据，问题要讲得清楚、透彻。一般来说，宜把重要的放在中间，次之的放在开头和末尾，这样的顺序前面是铺垫、后面是总结、中间则是核心，这样容易将阅读情绪逐渐带至高潮。

对所选的结果，无论大小、多少和重要程度如何，都应从多个角度展开讨论：

1）对类似的结果进行对比，说明、突出自己结果的独特性；

2）系统阐述某结果产生的原因，可能需要从不同的角度或不同方面来进行，如实验设计、理论原理、分析方法或借鉴别人的观点、手段、方法等，最终将问题阐述清楚。

（4）对讨论所得结果进行有效表述

对讨论所得结果（结论）进行有效表述，解释自己的研究发现，指明本研究表明了什么，对实际问题的解决有什么意义。如果自己的理论观点、研究设计、所用技术和方法等具有不可拟的独特特点，则也要提出来进行讨论。

（5）全面说明本研究的长处和短处

将本研究与前人工作联系起来，通过对照比较优劣，全面总结本研究的长处和短处。指出得出不同于别人结果的原因，不要掩盖自己的缺陷，断言自己正确而别人错误。若有短处而未加讨论，会让读者（包括审者）对论文的可信度产生动摇，进而产生是否还有其他未发现的短处的疑惑。若研究本身的设计、实验手段、实施过程及结果分析等有缺陷，也应进行剖析。

（6）注意保持讨论和结果的一致性

某一讨论要和相应的结果对应，不能出现由讨论的内容可以推出与实验结果相反的结论。若出现了这种情形，则表明作者所进行的讨论、所做的实验是失败的，当然本研究也是失败的。因此"讨论"对语言文字表述准确性和严密性的要求更高。

（7）点明尚待解决的问题及未来方向

要首尾呼应，再次对本研究的发现、意义给予评价，突出科学贡献和创新之处，并指出下一步的研究方向。

（8）选择使用合适的层次结构体例

以上介绍的写作方法仅仅适合一般的研究论文。科学研究往往是复杂的，某研究的总体目的即使只有一个，但研究过程中的目的可能有多个，因此结果有多个方面当属正常，讨论中应将各方面的结果有效串接起来，写作上需要重复以上环节或步骤。因此，讨论部分的写作体例不可能固定，按需可以有灵活的层次结构，有时还需要组织多个下级层次标题。统一写作结构虽然会降低写作篇幅，防止不恰当的推测和重复，减少报道偏差，提高报道的总体质量，但难度较大，现实中也会受到限制。

2.5.4 结果与讨论写作实例

下面选择若干结果与讨论的实例，了解其内容、结构和写作方法。

2.5.4.1 实例一

【1】

RESULTS AND DISCUSSION

To investigate the generation of color centers in the oxide shell of the O-SiNCs, we studied micro-PL and micro-CL emission spectra before, during and after e-beam irradiation. Three different types of O-SiNCs were studied (Figure 1b and Table 1), together with the reference oxide-free C-SiNCs (Supplementary Fig. S4). Samples differ in the NC core size, surface capping and oxide shell strain, allowing us to elucidate the origin and robustness of the induced spectral changes. Essentially, samples 1 and 4 have similar core size, but different capping (oxide vs. organic). Samples 1 and 2 have oxide capping, but different size (~2.5 nm vs. ~4 nm). Samples 2 and 3 have similar sizes, but their silica shells differ in thickness, strain and interface quality (natural thin oxide vs. strained thick thermal oxide). Another difference concerns the measurements where those on samples 1, 2 and 4 were measured on larger numbers of SiNCs at once ('ensemble'), those on sample 3 represent single-nanoparticle measurements due to the extremely low concentration of SiNCs in this sample. These largely different samples allow us to elucidate the generic effect of e-beam irradiation on the emission spectra of the SiNCs and their relation to the oxide shell of O-SiNC.

To study the induced emission changes by the e-beam treatment, we compare the steady-state micro-PL of the O-SiNCs before and after the irradiation (Figure 2c and 2d, respectively), measured under ambient conditions using inverted wide-field optical microscope coupled to a spectrometer (Figure 2a). To generate color centers, samples were irradiated with a focused e-beam in a SEM (Figure 2b). E-beam irradiation also excites the emission in the form of cathodoluminescence (CL), which is analyzed $in\ situ$ by the integrated spectroscopic CL system. To monitor the spectral changes during the irradiation, we alternated short and long e-beam exposures (Figure 2e and 2f, respectively): the short (~few seconds) exposures leaving emission spectra unchanged, the long (~few minutes) exposures introduce defects that act as color centers, continuously changing the emission spectra. After the treatment, samples were removed from the SEM vacuum chamber, and their micro-PL was studied again.

The micro-PL spectra before e-beam irradiation are shown in Figure 2c and reveal the expected spectral properties: absence of green[6] (Por-SiNCs) and the complete absence of green-blue emission (Plasma-SiNCs and Litho-SiNCs). The apparent differences in the spectra reflect the different core size and surface capping of the SiNCs associated with their different preparation. Strikingly, after the e-beam irradiation, very different micro-PL spectra, with much enhanced green-blue emission, are observed for all O-SiNCs (Figure 2d), measured from the same areas as before irradiation. Irrespective of their different initial spectra, all samples feature, in addition to their original PL bands, a new broad PL band that can be fitted with several new emission bands: a bright blue band at around 2.5 eV; a bright green band around 2.2 eV; and a narrow red band at 1.9 eV, broadening the spectrum towards the visible. The choice of the fitting parameters will be explained later.

To investigate the spectral changes in more detail, we look at the development of the CL spectra during the e-beam irradiation. The short exposures were short enough not to generate new defects and only probe the emission spectra of the samples under the higher energy excitation (15 keV), as shown in Figure 2e. Red/NIR emission bands remained unchanged, and only the blue band in Por-SiNCs is blue shifted, with respect to original PL. To emphasize that, we added extra blue band at 2.76 eV. In contrast, the long exposures lead to appearance of new emission bands, eventually resulting in very different spectral characteristics, as shown in Figure 2f. Already after a few minutes of e-beam exposure, the CL spectra show new emission bands—a narrow red band appears at around 1.9 eV, a green emission band at around 2.2 eV, and a blue band appears at around 2.7–2.8 eV (except for the Plasma-SiNCs). The gradual rise of the new bands upon the irradiation is clearly seen in the time evolution of the CL intensity in Supplementary Information, Supplementary Figs. S5 and S6. Where Por-SiNC and Plasma-SiNCs have only very thin silica shells, Litho-SiNC has very thick silica shell and hence spatially resolved CL study was possible, shown in Figure 3. This sample consists of thermally oxidized Si nanowalls (Figure 3a–3d) until the point when the utmost top part of the Si nanowall separates and forms nanocrystal. Near-infrared PL emission around 1.7 eV (Figure 1c) occurs from places in the nanowall where the nanocrystal is formed. Under e-beam irradiation, we found that CL from the sides of the nanowall (Figure 3e, spot 1 and 2) differs from the CL from the center of the nanowall (Figure 3e, spot 3 and 4), i.e. just above the SiNC. In stark contrast to the all O-SiNCs, the reference oxide-free C-SiNCs sample does not show any change upon irradiation, as can be seen in Supplementary Figs. S4a and S4c. Furthermore, signal contribution from the reference silicon substrate with a native silica layer is negligible (Supplementary Fig. S5b). Hence, we conclude that the new spectral features are related to the presence of the silica oxide shell on the O-SiNCs.

To follow the spectral evolution of the emission bands quantitatively, we fit all the PL and CL spectra shown here with a fixed set of peaks with fixed full-width of half maximum and fixed peak position, adjusting only their relative amplitudes between various samples and experimental stages. The peak parameters are retrieved from the best available measurements: for the blue, green and red bands (light blue, green and red lines) we used the time-scans and spatially resolved measurements in the Supplementary Figs. S5 and S6 and Figure 3e, and for the original PL bands (dark blue and violet lines) we used the data of Figure 2c. As shown in Figure 2c–2f, we can describe all the observed PL and CL spectra of any of the three O-SiNCs samples from the superposition of just five major spectral contributions.

The robustness of these spectral features indicates constant underlying mechanisms. In fact, a close look at the characteristic spectral profile shows that we can relate all the emerging spectral features to well-known color centers in bulk and nanostructured silica[19-39]: The very bright narrow red ~1.9 eV band that contributes significantly in all samples is likely related to the silica NBOHC surface variant color center (Figure 1a), as is evident from its characteristic double-peak feature[30, 31]. In the final PL spectra, this band is less intense, which is expected due to its reduced excitation cross-section at 3 eV[45]. The green CL band around 2.2 eV is the most interesting as to the best of our knowledge it does not occur in the native form of the oxide shell of O-SiNCs[1]. From our observation in Figure 3e, we conclude that an Si-rich environment is essential, as well as the presence of strain[38], as the green band consistently shows up only at the Si-rich center of the Si nanowall, but not at all at the silica-rich sides of the wall. Also, it is the brightest in the litho-SiNCs that exhibit the thickest and the most strained silica shell of all the studied samples. It might be possible that green color centers like dioxasilyrane $=Si(O_2)$[23] or $\equiv Si-H$[27] and $=Si=O$[4] (the latter two reported unstable on the surface of the nanostructured silica[19]), are stabilized here within the oxide shell of the SiNCs. Finally, the blue emission band showing in CL at 2.7–2.8 eV and in PL at 2.5 eV is possibly of the same origin and might originate from the oxygen-deficiency centers (silylene in Figure 1a)[20, 35] and/or the defect pair consisting of a dioxasilyrane, $=Si(O_2)$, and a silylene $=Si\bullet\bullet$[37]. To be able to distinguish between the two, more detailed time-resolved PL and CL analysis is needed. Nevertheless, from our spectral analysis it appears likely that both blue bands observed are of the same origin and occur from oxide centers already existing before irradiation, as it appears to be already present in one of the as-grown samples (por-SiNCs). This is supported by the fact that oxygen-deficiency centers can appear as a result of reactions between neighboring silanol $\equiv Si-$

OH groups following the reaction scheme $[\equiv Si-O-H + H-O-Si \equiv \leftrightarrow ODC + H_2]$ and $Si-O-H$ groups are abundant on the surface of our Por-SiNC sample due to a specific post-etch procedure in hydrogen peroxide[6]. By comparing the original PL with the short-exposure CL spectra (por-SiNC in Figure 2e and 2f), we conclude that no new blue-emitting centers are formed. The slight blue-shift of the blue band in the CL compared to the PL can be caused by the different excitation energies, as the blue PL band has been reported to shift under different optical excitation energies[13]. Interpretation of the blue bands as native to O-SiNC shell is consistent with measurements of Plasma-SiNC PL shown in Supplementary Fig. S8, where strong blue PL band develops purely by long term (~1 year) exposure to air.

Considering spectral similarities, time-scans and spatial-analysis of the newly formed emission bands, we suggest that color centers similar to those in silica materials are formed here in the silica-oxide shell of the O-SiNCs. However, unlike in silica, their PL emission can be efficiently excited optically at ~3.1 eV (405 nm) using low power (<5 mW) laser diode, due to the comparably much narrower band gap of our nanocrystals (~1.7–1.8 eV). Besides inherent non-toxicity and abundancy of silicon resources, this is yet another major advantage these materials, opening possibility of optically pumped white phosphors for LEDs.

Spectral changes introduced by the e-beam treatment can be summarized in the color gamut chart in Figure 4a. As a result of the irradiation, all O-SiNCs change their spectral coordinates to very similar end-chromatic coordinates associated with the introduced red, green and blue color centers. The resulting PL emission of all irradiated samples appears warmly white to the eye, with the warmest white obtained for the originally near-infrared emitting Plasma-SiNC. This is different from the reference oxide-free C-SiNC, whose chromatic coordinates do not change by the irradiation, remaining cold blue-white (Figure 4a, red dot and photo in inset Figure 4c). The Por-SiNC sample, as discussed before, shows whitish PL already in its native state (Figure 4a, green dot and inset Figure 4b), but also here the introduction of the missing green emission band results in a better defined white color. The most interesting and pronounced spectral changes from far-red to white color, however, occur for the Plasma-and Litho-SiNC samples. For the latter, the single-nanocrystal measurements indicate that the broad emission spectrum is indeed a single-nanocrystal property, and not an ensemble effect. Importantly, this identifies even a single nanocrystal as a multi-chromatic luminescent emitter with white spectral profile.

Intensity of the induced color center's PL appears to be stable in air for all the samples for several days, which was the typical delay between CL irradiation and subsequent micro-PL measurements. While the spectral shape of emission always changes drastically during e-beam irradiation, the overall integral CL intensity seems to be either stable (Plasma-SiNCs, see Supplementary Figs. S5c and S5d) or slightly enhanced by a factor 2–3 (Por-SiNCs, Supplementary Fig. S6). High resolution of the CL micro-spectroscopy, however, makes it hard to give a definite enhancement factor, due to inhomogeneity of the drop-casted materials in nano-and micro-scales (at every point, signal is collected by focused e-beam of 2–10 nm diameter, from diffraction limited area of 100–200 nm^2). For micro-PL, we found that similar behavior occurs—PL intensity appears to be either similar (Plasma-SiNC) or slightly enhanced by factor ~2 (Supplementary Figs. S7a and S7b). Again, high spatial resolution and nano-/micro-scale inhomogeneity of the drop-casted SiNC samples makes it difficult to give final enhancement factor. Importantly, we have to keep in mind in such evaluations that excitation cross-section for each color center and SiNC core are very different.

(Multi-chromatic silicon nanocrystals. *Light*: Science & Application, Volume 6, Issue 3, 2017.)

例【1】是一篇物理学（光学）领域原创论文的结果与讨论，共有九段。

第一段

第一句交待总体研究目的及工作：探索O-SiNCs氧化壳颜色中心的发生机理；研究

电子束照射前、照射中、照射后的微 PL 和微 CL 发射光谱。

第二句交待首先开展的工作是对四种样本进行研究。第三句指出对样本研究的结果（样本在核心尺寸、表面覆盖物和氧化壳应变方面有差异），并给出对结果的一种认识（诱导光谱变化的起源和鲁棒性与样本间的差异密切相关）。第四至六句对样本研究的结果细化，对共性和差异进行描述和对比。第七句指出样本间的另一差异，即测量方法不同，并给予解释。

第八句提出作者的一种认识，也即本文的主要研究内容：样本的不同有助于揭示电子束照射对 SiNCs 发射光谱的一般影响及其与 O-SiNC 氧化壳的关系。

第二段

第一句交待研究目的、工作及方法：研究电子束处理所引起的诱导发射变化；比较 O-SiNCs 照射前、照射后的稳态微 PL；将反向宽视野光学显微镜与光谱仪耦合而测量。

第二句交待具体研究目的（产生彩色中心）、工作（用聚焦的电子束在 SEM 下照射样本）。

第三句描述对样本的微 CL 研究方案：以 CL 来激发电子束照射发射，再由集成光谱 CL 系统在原位置进行分析。

第四句交待具体研究目的（产生彩色中心；监测照射过程中的光谱变化）、曝光结果（短曝光下发射光谱没有变化；长曝光下产生颜色中心缺陷，不断地改变着发射光谱）及工作（交替使用短、长电子束曝光）。

第五句指出接下来对样本的微 PL 进行研究，以顺畅地引出下文。

还用较多插图显示结果，如图 2a、2b 显示了 PL、CL 的微观设置，图 2c、2d 显示了电子束照射前后所有 O-SiNCs 的 PL 发射光谱，图 2e、2f 显示了短、长电子束曝光的 CL 光谱。

第三段

描述对样本的微 PL 研究方案及结果。

第一句描述电子束照射前的微 PL 光谱（结果显示在图 2c），指出结果与预期的光谱特性一致，光谱存在明显差异（对于 Por-SiNCs，没有绿色发射光谱；对于 Plasma-SiNCs 和 Litho-SiNCs，完全没有绿–蓝色发射光谱）。第二句指出这种差异产生的原因（与样本的核心尺寸、表面覆盖物及制备有关）。

第三句描述电子束照射后的微 PL 光谱（很多增强型绿–蓝色发射光谱，与照射前的微 PL 光谱非常不同，结果显示在图 2d），还交待电子束照射前后的测量位置相同。第四句对结果进行说明，指出新的宽 PL 带与样本的初始光谱、特性及原始 PL 带无关，可用若干新的发射带拟合（2.5 eV 附近的亮蓝色带；2.2 eV 附近的亮绿色带；1.9 eV 的狭窄红色带，光谱向可见方向扩展）。

第五句指出接下来将对拟合参数的选择进行解释，暂时留给读者一个问题。

第四段

描述样本在电子束照射过程中的 CL 光谱的研究方案，将电子束照射分为短曝光和长曝光两种情况进行结果描述和讨论，还专门描述样本 Litho-SiNC 的空间解析 CL 研究。

第一句交待研究目的（详细研究光谱变化）及工作（考察电子束照射中 CL 光谱的发展）。

第二至四句描述短曝光的结果：高能激发下样本的发射光谱（15 keV）（图 2e）；红色/近红外发射带不变；Por-SiNCs 中的蓝色带发生蓝色转移，与原始 PL 有关；在 2.76 eV 上增加了额外的蓝色带。

第五至七句描述长曝光的结果：产生新的发射带和非常不同的光谱特征（图 2f）；几分钟后 CL 光谱显示新发射带——1.9 eV 附近的狭窄红色带，2.2 eV 附近的绿色带，2.7～2.8 eV 的蓝色带（Plasma-SiNCs 除外）；新发射带在照射下的渐升效果（附加材料图 S5、S6）。

第八至十句说明样本 Litho-SiNC 的材料和近红外 PL 发射特性。第八句指出对 Litho-SiNC 进行空间解析 CL 研究的合理性（有很厚的硅壳）。第九句说明 Litho-SiNC 样本的结构组成：热氧化硅纳米墙（图 3a～3d）和顶端的纳米晶体。第十句指出在形成纳米晶体的纳米墙处产生了 1.7 eV 附近的近红外 PL 发射（图 1c）。

第十一至十三句描述电子束照射过程中 CL 光谱的特点：来自纳米墙边缘（图 3e，位置 1、2）和纳米墙中心（图 3e，位置 3、4）的 CL 不同，刚好在 SiNC 之上；无氧 C-SiNCs 没有显示变化（附加材料图 S4a、S4c）；来自带有原生硅层的参考硅衬底的信号可忽略不计（附加材料图 S5b）。

最后一句得出结论：新的光谱特征与 O-SiNCs 硅氧化壳相关。

第五段

本段承接第三段末尾提出的问题。交待目的、工作，描述手段，给出相应结果。

第一句交待研究目的（定量地跟踪发射带的光谱演化）及工作（将 PL 和 CL 光谱用一组固定峰值进行拟合），并描述这组峰值的特性（有半最大的固定全宽和固定的峰值位置），以及作者针对此特性所采取的实验手段（调整峰值在各种样本和实验阶段之间的相对振幅）。

第二句描述重获峰值参数的方式或手段：对于蓝、绿和红色带，使用时间扫描和空间分辨率测量（附加材料图 S5、S6 和 3e）；对于原始 PL 频带，使用电子束照射前所有 O-SiNCs 的发射光谱数据（图 2c）。

第三句交待结果：从五个主要光谱贡献叠加可描述由任何三个 O-SiNCs 样本所观测到的所有 PL 和 CL 光谱。

第六段

本段是讨论的核心部分，旨在揭示光谱特征的潜在常规机制。

第一句指出上述研究结果中蕴含着一种潜在常规机制（论题）。这可由下面讨论得出。

第二至四句描述观察特征光谱图的发现：①新出现的光谱特征与批量彩色中心和纳米结构的硅相关，作用显著、明亮的 ~1.9 eV 狭窄红色带可能与硅 NBOHC 表面变色中心有关；②最终 PL 光谱中波段的强度较低，原因可能是在 3 eV 激发截面的减少；③在 2.2 eV 附近的绿色 CL 带特别有趣，不是以 O-SiNCs 氧化壳的原生态出现的。

第五至八句描述观察图 3e 的推论（论点），并给予解释（论据）。推论：富硅环境中存在应变很重要。解释：①绿色带一直仅出现在硅纳米墙的富硅中心而非富硅侧边；②绿色带在 litho-SiNCs 中最明亮，Litho-SiNCs 在四种样本中有最厚和最张紧的硅壳；③硅基双环氧（dioxasilyrane）=Si(O_2) 或 ≡Si-H 和 =Si=O 类的绿色彩色中心（后两种在纳米结构的硅表面不稳定）有可能在 SiNCs 氧化壳内是稳定的；④显示在 CL 中 2.7～2.8 eV 和 PL 中 2.5 eV 的蓝色带的来源可能相同，均为缺氧中心和（或）由硅基双环氧 = Si（O_2）和硅烯 = Si··组成的缺陷对。

第九句提出另一论点（区分 CL 中 2.7~2.8 eV 和 PL 中 2.5 eV 的蓝色带需要更加详细的 PL 和 CL 时间解析分析）。第十句对这一论点进行反驳论证，描述光谱分析结果（观察到的两个蓝色带的来源可能相同，且发生在照射前就已存在的氧化物中心，似乎出现在已经生长的样本中（Por-SiNCs））。第十一句对此结果产生的机理给予解释（缺氧中心会出现在邻近的硅醇基（≡Si-OH）的反应中，伴随着反应 [≡Si-O-H + H-O-Si≡↔ODC + H_2]，且 Si-O-H 组在 Por-SiNC 样本的表面非常丰富，缘于过氧化氢的一个特定后蚀刻过程）。

第十二句描述对原始的 PL 和短曝光的 CL 光谱（图 2e、2f 中的 Por-SiNC）对比所得出的结果（短曝光的 CL 光谱没有产生新的蓝色发射中心）。第十三句对 CL 蓝色带相对于 PL 的轻微蓝移给予解释，以前人的报道（PL 蓝色带是在不同的光激发能量下发生移动的）作为论据，给出可能的原因（由不同的激发能量引起）。

第十四句指出对 O-SiNC 壳的蓝色带的解释与对 Plasma-SiNC 的 PL 测量的结果一致，其中增强的 PL 蓝色带形成的原因是长期完全暴露在空气中，表明研究正确。

第七段

此段基于光谱相似性、时间扫描及新发射带空间分析的结果，总结 O-SiNCs 与硅材料的相同和差异：O-SiNCs 硅氧化壳中形成类似于硅材料中的颜色中心；O-SiNCs 的 PL 发射能以低功率（<5 mW）激光二极管的方式在 ~3.1 eV（405 nm）上有效地光学激励，还对此差异给出原因（纳米晶体（~1.7－1.8 eV）上有较多可比较的窄带隙）。最后一句总结 O-SiNCs 的优势：无毒性；硅资源丰富；为 LEDs 开启了光学泵浦白色荧光粉的可能性。

第八段

本段主要对电子束处理所引发的光谱变化进行描述和讨论，并进行总结。

第一句用图 4a 所示的色域图来显示由电子束处理所引发的光谱变化。

第二至六句描述或讨论照射结果：①O-SiNCs 光谱坐标转换成很相似的终色坐标，与引发的红、绿、蓝颜色中心相关；②所有样本的 PL 发射产生暖白色，而最初的 Plasma-SiNC 近红外发射产生最暖白色；③Plasma-SiNC 色度坐标未改变，一直保持冷蓝－白色（图 4a 中的红点和图 4c 中的照片），这与无氧的 C-SiNC 参照物不同；④Por-SiNC 样本中显示了原生态中已有的白色 PL（图 4a 中的绿点和图 4b 中的照片），引入缺失的绿色发射带会产生更好定义的白色；⑤Plasma-SiNC、Litho-SiNC 样本中发生

了从远红到白色的最有趣和显著的光谱变化。

最后两句（第七、八句）交待由对 Litho-SiNC 样本进行单纳米晶体测量的结果所揭示的效应、结论：Litho-SiNC 广泛存在的发射光谱具有单纳米晶体性质，不是一个整体效应；单纳米晶体是一种具有白色光谱剖面的多色发光发射器。

第九段

本段阐释诱导色中心的 PL 强度及电子束照射过程中 PL、CL 强度的现象。

第一句阐释对于所有样本都存在的现象：诱导色中心的 PL 的强度在几天内似乎是稳定的，因为在 CL 照射和微 PL 测量之间存在延迟。

第二、三句阐释整体集成 CL 强度（特点及难以确定的原因）：该强度是稳定的（Plasma-SiNCs，附加材料图 S5c、S5d）或轻度增强 2~3 因子（Por-SiNCs，附加材料图 S6），但纳/微尺度上的液滴涂布材料的不均匀性和 CL 显微光谱的高分辨率使得难以给出确定的增强因子。

第四句阐释微 PL 的类似强度：该强度似乎是相似的（Plasma-SiNC）或轻度增强 ~2 因子（附加材料图 S7a、S7b），但液滴涂布 SiNC 样本的高空间分辨率和纳/微尺度的不均匀性使得难以给出最终的增强因子。

最后总结，指出一个重要的共性现象：每个颜色中心和 SiNC 核心的激发截面很不同。

2.5.4.2　实例二

【2】

Results

Surveillance and genetic analysis of H7N9 avian influenza viruses

To monitor the evolution of the H7N9 viruses in poultry, we collected 112 593 samples from poultry markets, farms, wild bird habitats, and slaughterhouses in 24 provinces from July 2013 to January 2017, and inoculated the samples individually into 10-day-old embryonated chicken eggs for virus isolation. In total, 3 664 influenza viruses were detected from these samples, of which 293 strains of H7N9 viruses were isolated across 17 provinces (Supplementary information, Table S1). Six viruses were isolated from samples collected from chicken farms in Fujian, Guangdong, Jiangsu, and Zhejiang provinces; all of the other viruses were isolated from samples collected from live poultry markets (Supplementary information, Table S1).

To detect the key mutations that may significantly affect the biologic properties of the viruses, portions of the HA and PB2 genes of the 293 viruses were sequenced. We found that 280 and 266 of the 293 avian viruses bear 186V and 226L mutations, respectively, in their HA, but none of them bear the 627K or 701N mutations in their PB2 (Table 1). Importantly, 12 extra nucleotides (-aaacggactgcg-) encoding four amino acids (-KRTA-) in the cleavage site of HA were detected in seven viruses isolated from chickens in Guangdong province in 2017 (Table 1).

To investigate the genetic relationships among these viruses, we sequenced 83 representative viruses from different sampling times, places, and species. The HA genes of these viruses shared 88%-100% identity at the nucleotide level and formed four phylogenetic groups (Figure 1A). The HA genes of the group 1 viruses shared over 97% identity and clustered with the HA genes of the 2013/H7N9 viruses, whereas the HA genes of the other three groups belonged to viruses that emerged in China during this time period and were detected only in ducks.

The NA genes of these viruses shared 90%-100% identity at the nucleotide level and formed three phylogenetic groups (Supplementary information, Figure S1A). The six internal genes of these H7N9 viruses showed distinct diversity, with the PB2, PB1, PA, NP, M, and NS genes of the 83 viruses sharing 84.8%-100%, 88.6%-100%, 86.8%-100%, 86.4%-100%, 88.5%-100%, and 87.8%-100% identity, respectively, at the nucleotide level. The PB1 and NP genes each formed eight groups in the phylogenetic trees (Supplementary information, Figure S1C and S1E), and the PB2, PA, M, and NS genes each formed six, nine, five, and four groups, respectively, in their phylogenetic trees (Supplementary information, Figure S1B, S1D, S1F, and S1G).

Given this genomic diversity, we divided these H7N9 viruses into 23 different genotypes (Figure 1B). The predominant viruses were categorized as genotype 1 and 2 viruses because they were detected in eight and nine provinces, respectively; the viruses in the other genotypes were only detected in one to three provinces (Figure 1B; Supplementary information, Figure S3). The seven viruses bearing the four amino acid insertion in their HA belonged to genotypes 1, 2, and 3 (Figure 1B). Of note, the time-scaled phylogenetic analysis suggested that the HA mutants may have arisen from two different H7N9 viruses (Supplementary information, Figure S2), one of which subsequently reassorted with others to form two more genotypes (Figure 1, viruses labeled with two stars).

Replication and virulence of H7N9 HA mutant A/chicken/Guangdong/SD008/2017 (CK/SD008) in chickens

The minimum motif in the HA cleavage site associated with high pathogenicity of H5 and H7 influenza viruses in chickens is -BXBR- (B = basic amino acids arginine or lysine, X = any amino acid, R = arginine) [34] or -RXXR- [35]. The motif in the new H7N9 viruses is "-KRTAR-", which meets the criterion of "-RXXR-" for high pathogenicity. Since not all H5 or H7 viruses that bear these motifs are highly pathogenic to chickens [36, 37], and the H7N9 mutants were all isolated from apparently healthy chickens in live poultry markets, we investigated their virulence by testing the intravenous pathogenicity index (IVPI) of the index strain A/chicken/Guangdong/SD008/2017 (CK/SD008) [38]. Groups of 10 6-week-old specific pathogen-free (SPF) chickens were inoculated intravenously with 0.1 ml of a 1:10 dilution of bacteria-free allantoic fluid containing $10^{7.7}$ 50% egg infectious dose (EID_{50}) of the virus. All of the chickens inoculated with the virus died within 24 h post-inoculation (p.i.) (Figure 2A), yielding an IVPI value of 3 (0 = least pathogenic; 3 = most pathogenic). We collected brains, lungs, spleens, kidneys, pancreases, hearts, livers, and cecum from three chickens that were inoculated with CK/SD008 and determined viral titers in eggs. The virus was detected in all of these organs with mean titers ranging from 5.3 to 7.9 $\log_{10}EID_{50}/g$ (Figure 2B). We also inoculated 13 SPF chickens intranasally (i.n.) with 10^6 EID_{50} of CK/SD008. Three chickens were killed on day 3 p.i. for virus titration and the other 10 were observed for signs of disease and death. The virus replicated systemically in chickens after i.n. inoculation and was detected in both pharyngeal and cloacal swabs (Figure 2B); the observed chickens died within 4 days of infection (Figure 2A). Our results indicate that an H7N9 virus isolated in 2017 that descended from the H7N9 viruses that emerged in China in 2013 has mutated into a highly pathogenic strain for chickens.

Replication and virulence of H7N9 virus CK/SD008 in mice

The multiple basic amino acid motif in the HA cleavage site of H5N1 influenza viruses is a prerequisite for lethality in mammals [25, 39], but not all H5N1 viruses that have this motif are lethal in these animals [40, 41]. To investigate whether the four amino-acid insertion in HA also increases H7N9 virus virulence in mammals, we tested the replication and virulence of virus with this HA insertion in mice and ferrets.

Three 6-week-old BALB/c mice were inoculated i.n. with $10^{6.0}$ EID_{50} of CK/SD008 and then killed 3 days p.i. Their nasal turbinates, lungs, spleens, kidneys, and brains were collected for virus titration. The 50% mouse lethal dose (MLD_{50}) of the virus was determined by inoculating groups of five mice i.n. with $10^{1.0}$-$10^{7.0}$ EID_{50} of the virus, and daily monitoring of body weight, disease signs, and death for 2 weeks. Virus replication was detected in the nasal turbinates and lungs of mice but not in their spleens, kidneys, or brains (Figure 2C). No disease signs or deaths were observed among mice inoculated with any dose of the virus, and all mice gained weight during the observation period (Figure 2D). Therefore, the MLD_{50} of CK/SD008 is >7.5$\log_{10}EID_{50}$ (Figure 2G).

Replication and transmission of the CK/SD008 virus in ferrets

To evaluate viral replication in ferrets, we inoculated two ferrets i.n. with $10^{6.0}$ EID_{50} of CK/SD008. Nasal turbinates, tonsils, trachea, lungs, spleen, kidneys, and brain were collected on day 4 p.i. for virus titration in eggs. Unlike the 2013 H7N9 avian viruses that only replicated in the tonsils and respiratory tracts of ferrets [16], CK/SD008 was detected in the tonsils throughout the lungs, and in the brains of the two ferrets, but not in the spleens or kidneys (Figure 3A).

We then evaluated the transmission of CK/SD008 in ferrets, a commonly used animal model for transmission studies [6, 7, 16, 28]. We used the H7N9 virus CK/S1053, which did not transmit in our previous study [16], as a negative control. Groups of three ferrets were i.n. inoculated with 10^6 EID_{50} of CK/S1053 and CK/SD008, respectively. The ferrets were housed separately in cages within an isolator. Twenty-four hours later, three naive ferrets were placed in adjacent cages. Each pair of animals was separated by a divider as described previously [9, 16, 42, 43]. Nasal washes were collected every 2 days from all of the animals beginning 2 days p.i. (1 day post-exposure (p.e.)) to assess virus shedding. Sera were collected from all animals on day 14 p.i. for hemagglutinin inhibition (HI) antibody detection. Respiratory droplet transmission was confirmed when virus was detected in the nasal washes and by seroconversion of the naive exposed animals at the end of the 2-week observation period.

Virus was detected in all directly infected ferrets (Figure 3D, 3E). A low virus titer was detected on day 9 p.e. from one of the three ferrets that was exposed to the CK/SD008-infected ferrets (Figure 3E); no virus was detected from any ferrets exposed to the CK/S1053-infected ferrets (Figure 3D). Ferrets exposed or infected with CK/SD008 experienced a 1.9%-8.2% weight loss, whereas ferrets directly infected with CK/S1053 showed a 4.0%-4.6% weight loss (Figure 3I, 3J; Table 2). Body temperature increases were detected in two ferrets of each directly infected group (Supplementary information, Figure S5). Seroconversion occurred in all of the animals directly infected with virus, and in one exposed animal in the CK/SD008 group (Table 2). Similar to our findings in 2013 [16], these results indicate that CK/SD008 transmits in ferrets by respiratory droplet with low efficiency.

Replication and virulence of CK/SD008 PB2 mutants in mice

Two amino acids in PB2, 627K, and 701N are important for the virulence and transmission of influenza viruses in mammals [22-27]. We previously showed that some H9N2 viruses, which have similar internal genes to H7N9 viruses, readily acquire the PB2 627K or PB2 701N mutation upon infection of ferrets [42]. The CK/SD008 virus does not contain either of these two PB2 mutations. To investigate whether these mutations occurred in CK/SD008 during its replication in ferrets, we sequenced the PB2 gene of the viruses recovered from the organs of ferrets on day 4 p.i. and from the nasal washes of ferrets that participated in the transmission study. We found viruses bearing PB2 627K and viruses bearing PB2 701N in the organs (Supplementary information, Table S2) and nasal washes of ferrets that were directly infected in the transmission study (Supplementary information, Table S3). The virus in the nasal washes of the exposed animals contained only the PB2 627K mutation (Supplementary information, Table S3).

The PB2 627K and 701N mutations were not detected in any of the H7N9 viruses isolated from poultry (Table 1); however, about 83% of 648 H7N9 viruses isolated from humans contain PB2 627K or PB2 701N (Table 1), indicating that the H7N9 viruses could easily obtain these mutations during their replication in humans. To assess the risk of a CK/SD008-like virus obtaining such mutations after replicating in humans, we purified the mutants from the ferret lung samples by limited dilution in eggs. Two viruses were confirmed by genome sequence analysis to each contain one of the two PB2 mutations (CK/SD008-PB2/627K and CK/SD008-PB2/701N) and were then used for further studies in mice and ferrets.

As observed in other influenza viruses [44], the PB2 627K and 701N mutations also significantly increased the viral polymerase activity of the CK/SD008 virus (Supplementary information, Figure S4). The viral titers of CK/SD008-PB2/627K and CK/SD008-PB2/701N in the nasal turbinates and lungs of mice were significantly higher than those of mice inoculated with CK/SD008. CK/SD008-PB2/627K was also detected in the brains of all three mice, and in the spleen and kidneys of one mouse (Figure 2C). Both viruses caused severe disease and killed mice at low doses (MLD_{50} values of CK/SD008-PB2/627K and CK/SD008-PB2/701N were $1.8\log_{10} EID_{50}$ and $3.4\log_{10} EID_{50}$, respectively) (Figure 2E, 2F, 2H, 2I).

Replication, virulence, and transmission of CK/SD008 PB2 mutants in ferrets

We next evaluated the replication of the two viruses in ferrets. The tissue tropism and viral titers in the organs of ferrets inoculated with CK/SD008-PB2/627K and CK/SD008-PB2/701N were comparable with those of the ferrets inoculated with CK/SD008 (Figure3). We then investigated the respiratory droplet transmission of CK/SD008-PB2/627K and CK/SD008-PB2/701N in ferrets. In the directly infected groups, virus was detected from all animals; in the CK/SD008-PB2/627K-exposed group, virus was detected in one ferret on day 1 p.e. and in all three animals on the other days tested (Figure 3F); in the CK/SD008-PB2/701N-exposed group, virus was detected in one ferret on days 3 and 5 p.e. and in two ferrets on day 7 and 9 p.e. (Figure 3G). One ferret infected with CK/SD008-PB2/627K had a body temperature increase on day 7 p.i., but no marked body temperature change was detected in the CK/SD008-PB2/701N-infected ferrets (Supplementary information, Figure S5). The ferrets directly infected with virus lost 11.3%-28.9% of their body weight (Figure 3K, 3L). One CK/SD008-PB2/627K-inoculated ferret was killed because it showed signs of severe disease, including tremor and torticollis, and became paralyzed on day 10 p.i.; one CK/SD008-PB2/701N-inoculated ferret became very sick and died on day 10 p.i. (Table 2). Seroconversion occurred in all of the inoculated animals and exposed animals (Table 2).

We repeated the ferret transmission study of the CK/

SD008-PB2/627K virus, along with CK/S1053 and A/Anhui/1/2013 (AH/1) as negative and positive controls, respectively. Transmission of CK/S1053 was not detected, but CK/SD008-PB2/627K and AH/1 were transmitted to all three animals. Moreover, one CK/SD008-PB2/627K-inoculated ferret lost 26.9% of its body weight and died on day 8 p.i. (Figure 3D, 3F, 3H; Table 2). These results indicate that the newly emerged chicken-lethal H7N9 virus became highly lethal in mice and efficiently transmissible in ferrets after obtaining the 627K or 701N mutation in its PB2.

Receptor-binding preference of the CK/SD008 virus

Receptor-binding preference is important for influenza virus transmission, and two amino-acid mutations in HA, G186V, and Q226L, which play key roles in H7 avian influenza virus binding to human-type receptors [18], appeared in over 90% of the H7N9 avian influenza field viruses we isolated in this study (Table 1). We tested the receptor-binding properties of the CK/SD008 and two viruses that were isolated in 2013, CK/S1053 and AH/1, which all bear HA 186V and 226L, and found that they all bound to the α2,6-siaylglycopolymer (human-type receptor) with higher affinity than that of their binding with the α2,3-siaylglycopolymer (avian-type receptor) (Figure 4).

Thermal stability of H7N9 viruses

Thermal stability is also reported to be important for the transmissibility of some highly pathogenic H5N1 laboratory-adapted viruses [6]. We therefore compared the thermal stability of seven influenza viruses, including the five H7N9 viruses we used in the transmission study, a 2016 H7N9 avian virus, an H5N1 avian influenza virus, with the 2009 H1N1 human pandemic virus (SC/1), using the method described by Imai et al. [6]. We found that the two 2013 H7N9 viruses CK/S1053 and AH/1 were less stable than the human virus SC/1, but the CK/SD008 virus and its PB2 mutants, as well as the 2016 H7N9 virus and the H5N1 virus, were comparable to or more thermal stable than the human pandemic virus SC/1 (Supplementary information, Figure S6).

Discussion

Influenza viruses mutate; it is their nature. The most undesirable mutations are the ones that convert a low pathogenic avian influenza virus to a highly pathogenic avian influenza virus and the ones that allow a new influenza virus to be transmissible in humans. In this study, we show that these alarming mutations are occurring in the H7N9 viruses. Our findings provide important information for the control of H7N9 influenza. As soon as we detected the highly pathogenic H7N9 mutants in chickens, a series of actions were taken to prevent and minimize the damage they could cause to both poultry and humans, including the establishment of a rapid differential diagnostic test [45], urgent surveillance in poultry, careful analysis of samples from human patients, and evaluation of a poultry vaccine.

Virulence and transmission of influenza viruses are polygenic traits. The MLD_{50} of CK/SD008-PB2/627K was $1.8\log_{10} EID_{50}$, indicating that this virus was > 10^5-fold more lethal than CK/SD008 (MLD_{50}, > $7.5\log_{10} EID_{50}$), and > 10^3-fold more lethal than the 2013 H7N9 human isolates bearing the PB2 627K mutation, whose MLD_{50}s were > $5.4\log_{10} EID_{50}$ [16]. Therefore, the high virulence in mice of CK/SD008-PB2/627K represents genetic changes in both the PB2 and HA genes.

The virulence in mammals of these H7N9 PB2 mutants is similar to that of H5N1 highly pathogenic viruses that caused an ~60% mortality rate in infected humans [46-48], and is over 20% higher than that caused by the current low pathogenic H7N9 viruses in humans. Previous studies suggested that H5N1 mutants that were transmissible in ferrets were attenuated in mammals relative to their wild-type parent viruses, with the loss of virulence being the tradeoff for transmissibility [6, 7]. We previously reported that, after replication in humans, low pathogenic H7N9 viruses could become transmissible in ferrets, but the viruses were not highly lethal in mice or ferrets [16]. In this study, we found that after the new H7N9 chicken-lethal virus acquired the PB2 627K or 701N mutation, it not only became highly transmissible in ferrets, but also became highly lethal in mice and caused severe disease and death in ferrets. Given that over 83% of the low pathogenic H7N9 viruses have obtained the PB2 mutations during their replication in humans (Table 1), it is highly likely that the chicken-lethal H7N9 virus will obtain similar mutations in their PB2 when they replicate in humans. Thus, it is very important to carefully monitor and evaluate the H7N9 human isolates to prevent such a virus from transmitting among humans by aerosol.

After we detected the chicken-lethal H7N9 viruses, we performed vital surveillance, collecting 2 950 samples from chicken farms and live poultry markets in Guangdong province in February, 2017. We isolated 28 H7N9 viruses (Supplementary information, Table S4), and partial sequence analysis of their HA genes revealed that 15 of them had the HA insertion (Supplementary information, Table S5). In addition to this insertion, we detected three additional motifs in the HA cleavage site of these viruses (Supplementary information, Table S5). The viruses with all of the other three different HA cleavage motifs were also lethal in chickens (Supplementary information, Table S5), although their virulence in mammals remains to be investigated. One of the motifs, -PKRKRTAR/G-, was found in isolates from patients in Guangdong province (Supplementary information, Table S5). The PB2 627K mutation was also detected in these human isolates (Supplementary information, Table S5).

We compared the thermal stability of different avian influenza viruses with the 2009 human pandemic H1N1 virus SC/1, and found that the naturally isolated duck H5N1 virus, the recent low and highly pathogenic H7N9 viruses, and the H7N9 PB2 mutants were all more thermally stable than the H1N1 pandemic virus. If thermal stability is important for influenza virus transmission, as reported by Imai et al. [6], our results indicate that some of the H5N1 and H7N9 avian influenza viruses circulating in nature have already acquired this quality. The two H7N9 PB2 mutants are more thermally stable than the parent CK/SD008 virus, suggesting that similar to other properties of influenza virus, thermal stability may be a polygenic trait that is determined by a gene constellation rather than by the HA gene alone.

While this manuscript was in preparation, the H7N9 highly pathogenic virus has spread from Guangdong to several other provinces and caused huge outbreaks, and millions of chickens have been killed in efforts to control the disease [49]. It should be noted that, slaughtering the lethal H7N9 virus-infected poultry alone cannot solve this problem, because the broadly circulating low pathogenic H7N9 viruses can mutate to the highly pathogenic form at any time. Therefore, given the damage the H7N9 lethal virus will cause to poultry and the high risk it poses to human health, control and eradication of both the low and highly pathogenic H7N9 viruses should be the highest priority for animal disease control authorities in China.

(H7N9 virulent mutants detected in chickens in China pose an increased threat to humans. *Cell Research*, Vol. 27, No. 12, Dec. 2017: 1409-1421.)

例【2】是一篇细胞领域原创论文的结果与讨论，其中结果是八大主题（子标题），讨论有六段。

1. 结果

主题一

这部分描述 H7N9 禽流感病毒的监测和遗传分析结果，共有五段。

第一段共三句。第一句交待具体目标㊀（监测家禽中 H7N9 病毒的演变）、样本收集（2013 年 7 月至 2017 年 1 月，24 个省的家禽市场、农场、野生鸟类栖息地和屠宰场，收集 112 593 个样本）及处置（接种到 10 日大的鸡胚中），涉及时间、地点、对

㊀ 具体目标属于目的范畴，可笼统称为目的或直接称为目标。"材料与方法""结果与讨论"中可能有在某"总目的"下的多个"分目的"或某个目标，这里为表述方便，使用术语"具体目标"或"目标"。

象、数量等多个方面。第二、三句描述结果（检测结果）：①检测到3 664种流感病毒；②其中293株H7N9病毒已在17个省被分离出来（见表S1）；③6种病毒是从福建、广东、江苏和浙江省的鸡场采集来的样本中分离出来的；④所有其他病毒都是从活禽市场收集的样本中分离出来的（表S1）。

第二段共三句。首句交待具体目标（检测可能显著影响病毒生物特性的关键突变）及方法（对293种病毒的HA、PB2基因部分进行测序）。第二、三句描述描述结果（发现）：①293种禽流感病毒中，有280、266种在其HA上分别有186V、226L突变，但无一种在其PB2上有627K或701N突变（表1）；②在2017年从广东省的鸡体中分离出的7种病毒中，在其HA裂解位点里有编码了4种氨基酸(-KRTA-)的12种额外核苷酸（-aaacggactgcg-）（表1）。

第三段共三句。第一句交待具体目标（研究病毒间的基因关系）及方法（对来自不同采样时间、地点和物种的83种代表性病毒进行测序）。第二、三句描述结果（病毒HA）：①病毒的HA基因在核苷酸水平上共享88%~100%的一致性，并形成四个系统发育组（图1A）；②第一组病毒的HA基因共享超过97%的一致性，并与2013/H7N9病毒的HA基因聚合在一起；③其他三组的HA基因属于当时（指本文刊发前后）出现在中国的病毒，而且仅在鸭子中检测到了这种病毒。

第四段共三句，接着上一段交待的具体目标，继续描述结果（病毒NA基因）。结果包括：①病毒的NA基因在核苷酸水平上共享90%~100%的一致性，并形成三个系统发育组（附加信息，图S1A）；②这些H7N9病毒的6个内部基因表现出明显的多样性，其中83种病毒的PB2、PB1、PA、NP、M、NS基因分别在核苷酸水平上共享84.8%~100%、88.6%~100%、86.8%~100%、86.4%~100%、88.5~100%的一致性；③PB1、NP基因分别在系统发育树中形成8个组（附加信息，图S1C、S1E），PB2、PA、M、NS基因分别在其系统发育树中形成6、9、5、4个组（附加信息，图S1B、S1D、S1F、S1G）。

第五段共四句，主要描述对H7N9病毒按基因组进行分类的结果，也给出按时间尺度的系统发育分析结果。结果包括：①H7N9病毒分为23种不同基因型；②主要病毒归为基因1、2型，这两类病毒分别是在8、9个省检测到的，其他病毒只是在1~3个省检测到的（图1B；附加信息，图S3）；③携带4种氨基酸插入其HA的7种病毒属于基因1、2、3型（图1B）；④时间尺度的系统发育分析：HA基因突变可能是由两种不同的H7N9病毒引起的（附加信息，图S2），其中一种与其他病毒重组会形成两种以上基因型（图1，标有两个星号的病毒）。

主题二

这部分共一个段落，描述鸡体中H7N9 HA基因突变体A/chicken/Guangdong/SD008/2017（CK/SD008）的复制和毒性，涉及一个具体目标及多个具体方法、结果，表述时方法和结果交替出现。

第一句陈述已有研究结果（与鸡体中高致病性H5、H7流感病毒有关的HA裂解位点里的最小序列是-BXBR-或-RXXR-，引用文献［34，35］）。第二句陈述已有研究结果（新H7N9病毒的序列是-KRTAR-，符合高致病性的-RXXR-的标准）。第三句的从句表原因，由两个分句组成，前一分句陈述已有结果（并非具有这些序列的所有H5或H7病毒都是对鸡高致病性的，引用文献［36，37］），后一分句陈述一个事实（H7N9突变体都是从活禽市场中明显健康的鸡体分离出来的）。以上内容共同成为确立以下具体目标的原因或依据。

第三句的主句交待具体目标（调查指数毒株 CK/SD008 的毒性）及方法（测试指数毒株 CK/SD008 的静脉致病指数 IV-PI），引用文献［38］。

接下来的语句描述方法及结果，即为实现具体目标所做的具体实验及所获得的结果。

第四句描述实验对象、材料、方法。对象：10 个 6 周大的无特定病原体（SPF）鸡群。材料：0.1ml 的 1∶10 稀释无细菌尿囊液，含 CK/SD008 病毒的 $10^{7.7}$ 鸡胚半数感染量（EID_{50}）。方法：静脉注射接种病毒。第五句描述结果：接种病毒的所有鸡在接种 24h 后死亡（图 2A），IVPI 值为 3。

第六句描述方法：收集 3 只接种病毒的鸡的大脑、肺、脾脏、肾脏、胰腺、心脏、肝脏和盲肠，并在鸡胚中做病毒滴度。第七句描述结果：在这些器官中均检测到了接种的病毒，病毒平均滴度值为 5.3 ~ 7.9 $\log_{10}$ EID_{50}/g（图 2B）。

第八、九句描述方法：对 13 只 SPF 鸡鼻内接种 CK/SD008 的 10^6 EID_{50}；将 3 只鸡在接种 3 日后杀死用于病毒滴定，对另外 10 只鸡观察其疾病和死亡迹象。第十句描述结果：鼻内接种后，在咽部和泄殖腔拭子中能检测到病毒在鸡体内有系统的复制（图 2B）；被观察的鸡在感染后 4 日内死亡（图 2A）。

第十一句得出结论：起源于 2013 年在中国出现的并在 2017 年分离出的 H7N9 病毒已突变为鸡高致病性毒株。（注意：本论文没有单独的标题 Conclusions，但这种没有是形式上的，实际上有关结论的内容在 Results 中表述了。）

主题三

这部分共有两段，描述 H7N9 病毒 CK/SD008 在老鼠体内的复制和毒性，涉及原因、目标、方法及结果。

第一段描述原因、目标和方法。第一句陈述已有研究结果（H5N1 流感病毒的 HA 裂解位点上的多重碱性氨基酸序列是对哺乳动物产生致命杀伤力的一个先决条件，引用文献［25，39］；但并不是所有具有这种序列的 H5N1 病毒在这些动物中均是致命的，引用文献［40，41］）。第二句交待具体目标（研究在 HA 中插入四胺基酸是否会增加 H7N9 病毒在哺乳动物中的毒性）及方法（对具有这种 HA 插入的老鼠和雪貂测试了病毒的复制和毒性）。

第二段共六句，描述方法及结果，即为实现具体目标所做的实验及所获得的结果。第一至三句描述方法：①对 3 只 6 周大的 BALB/c 老鼠鼻内接种 CK/SD008 的 $10^{6.0}$ EID_{50}，接种 3 日后杀死这些老鼠；②收集这些老鼠的鼻甲、肺、脾脏、肾脏和大脑用于病毒滴定；③通过对 5 只老鼠组接种 $10^{1.0}$ – $10^{7.0}$ EID_{50} 病毒来确定老鼠半数致死量（MLD_{50}），持续两周每天监测老鼠的体重、疾病体征及死亡情况。第四、五句描述结果：①在老鼠的鼻甲和肺中发现了病毒复制，但在脾脏、肾脏或大脑中没有发现（图 2C）；②在接种过任何剂量病毒的老鼠中均未发现疾病体征或死亡情况，且所有老鼠的体重在观察期间均增加了（图 2D）。第六句得出结论：CK/SD008 的 MLD_{50} 大于 $7.5\log_{10}EID_{50}$（图 2G）。

主题四

这部分有三段，描述 H7N9 病毒 CK/SD008 在雪貂体内的复制和传播，涉及原因、目标、方法及结果。

第一段描述目标、方法及结果。第一句交待目标（评估雪貂体中的病毒复制）、描述方法（对两只雪貂鼻内接种 CK/SD008 的 $10^{6.0}$ EID_{50}）。第二句继续描述方法（在接种 4 日后收集鼻甲、扁桃体、气管、肺、脾脏、肾脏和大脑，用来鸡胚病毒滴定）。第三句描述结果（在两只雪貂的整个肺、扁桃体及大脑中均检测到了 CK/SD008，但在脾脏或肾脏中没有检测到（图3A）），并引用文献［16］来说明这一结果的创新性（与2013年的H7N9禽流感病毒只在扁桃体和呼吸道进行复制不同）。

第二段共九句。前面八句都是描述方法：①对雪貂体内的CK/SD008传播用常规动物模型进行评估；②使用以前研究中没有传播的H7N9病毒CK/S1053作为阴性对照；③对三只雪貂组的鼻内分别接种CK/S1053、CK/SD008的10^6 EID_{50}；④将雪貂分别放置于带有隔离器的不同笼子里；⑤24 h后再将三只幼雪貂放置在相邻的笼子里；⑥每两只雪貂用分隔物分开；⑦接种2日后开始（暴露1日后）每隔2日从雪貂身上收集鼻腔清洗液，用以评估病毒的脱落；⑧接种14日后从所有雪貂身上收集血清，进行血凝抑制（HI）抗体检测。其中句一是总说，句二至句八是分说。最后一句描述结果（在两周观察期结束时，在鼻腔清洗液中发现了病毒，由暴露的幼龄雪貂的血清转化来证实呼吸道的飞沫传播）。

第三段共六句。前面五句描述结果，最后一句得出结论。结果：①在所有直接感染的雪貂体内检测到了病毒（图3D，3E）；②在暴露9日后，从暴露在感染了CK/SD008的3只雪貂中的一只雪貂体内检测到一种低病毒滴度（图3E），暴露在感染了CK/S1053的任一雪貂的体内都没有发现病毒（图3D）；③暴露或感染了CK/SD008的雪貂的体重减少1.9%~8.2%，而直接感染了CK/S1053的雪貂体重下降4.0%~4.6%的（图3I，3J；表2）；④在每一直接感染组的两只雪貂中均检测到体温升高（附加信息，图S5）；⑤血清转化发生在所有直接感染了病毒的雪貂以及暴露在感染了CK/SD008的雪貂组中的一只雪貂（表2）。结论：CK/SD008在雪貂体内以低效的呼吸道飞沫方式传播，与本课题组在2013年的研究成果相类似［16］。

主题五

这部分共有三段，描述H7N9病毒CK/SD008 PB2突变体在老鼠体内的复制和毒性，涉及原因、目标、方法及结果。

第一段描述结果（指已有结果或认识）、目标、方法及结果。前面三句交待已有结果或认识，成为本文研究的原因（PB2、627K和701N中的两种氨基酸对哺乳动物中流感病毒的毒性和传播很重要，本课题以前展示过的一些H9N2病毒具有与H7N9病毒相似的内部基因，由雪貂感染后容易获得PB2 627K或PB2 701N突变；CK/SD008病毒不包含这两种PB2突变）。第四句交待目标（研究这些突变是否发生在CK/SD008在雪貂体内复制的过程中）、描述方法（对从接种4日后的雪貂的器官以及参与传播研究的雪貂的鼻腔清洗液中所发现的病毒的PB2基因进行测序）。第五、六句描述结果（①传播研究中直接感染的雪貂的器官（附加信息，表S2）和鼻腔清洗液（附加信息，表S3）中具有携带PB2 627K或PB2 701N的病毒；②暴露的雪貂的鼻腔清洗液中的病毒只包含PB2 627K突变（附加信息，表S3））。

第二段接着上面描述结果、结论，然后再描述新目标、方法及结果。首句交待结果（在从家禽分离出来的任何H7N9病毒中均未检测到PB2 627K、701N突变，但从人分离出来的648个H7N9病毒中约有83%含有PB2 627K或PB2 701N，并在表1中详细显示）、结论（H7N9病毒在人体复制过程中容易获得这些突变）。第二句交待目标（评估CK/SD008病毒在人体复制后获得突变的风险）、描述方法（通过对鸡胚进行有限稀释而从雪貂肺样本中提纯突变体）。第三句描述结果（两种病毒通过基因组序列分析得到确认，每个病毒都包含PB2/627K、CK/SD008-PB2/701N两个PB2突变之一）及方法（对老鼠和雪貂进一步研究）。

第三段接着上面继续描述结果，即观察发现：①CK/SD008-PB2/627K、CK/SD008-PB2/701N 突变显著提升了 CK/SD008 病毒的病毒聚合酶活性（附加信息，图 S4）；②在老鼠鼻甲和肺中的 CK/SD008-PB2/627K、CK/SD008-PB2/701N 的病毒滴度明显高于用 CK/SD008 接种的老鼠；③在所有三只老鼠的大脑及一只老鼠的脾脏和肾脏（图 2C）中也检测到 CK/SD008-PB2/627K；④两种病毒都造成严重的疾病，并在低剂量下致死老鼠（CK/SD008-PB2/627K、CK/SD008-PB2/701N 的 MLD_{50} 值分别为 $1.8\log_{10} EID_{50}$、$3.4\log_{10} EID_{50}$）（图 2E、2F、2H、2I）。

主题六

这部分共有两段，描述 CK/SD008 PB2 突变体在雪貂体内的复制、毒性及传播，涉及方法、结果，重在展现结果。

第一段描述方法、结果。前三句交待方法及步骤，首句总说（评估两种病毒在雪貂体内的复制），后两句分说，即给出实现步骤（先对接种两种病毒与接种 CK/SD008 的雪貂的器官组织嗜性、病毒滴定进行比较（图 3），后研究两种病毒在雪貂中的呼吸道飞沫传播）。接下来较为详细地按类别描述结果：①直接感染组中，在所有雪貂体内均能检测到病毒；CK/SD008-PB2/627K 暴露组中，在一只暴露 1 日后的雪貂和在另外几日测试的所有三只雪貂体内检测到了病毒（图 3F）；CK/SD008-PB2/701N 暴露组中，在一只暴露 3、5 日后的雪貂和两只暴露 7、9 日后的雪貂体内检测到了病毒（图 3G）。②一只感染了 CK/SD008-PB2/627K 的雪貂在接种 7 日后体温升高，但在感染了 CK/SD008-PB2/701N 的雪貂中到没有检测到明显的体温变化（附加信息，图 S5）。③直接感染病毒的雪貂有 11.3%~28.9% 的体重下降（图 3K，3L）。④一只接种 CK/SD008-PB2/627K 的雪貂显示出有严重疾病的迹象，如震颤和斜颈，并在接种 10 日后开始瘫痪（被杀死）；一只接种 CK/SD008-PB2/701N 的雪貂病得很重，在接种 10 日后死亡（表 2）。⑤在所有接种、暴露的雪貂中均发生血清转化（表 2）。

第二段描述方法与结果。第一句交待方法：重复 CK/SD008-PB2/627K 病毒在雪貂中的传播实验研究，将 CK/S1053、A/Anhui/1/2013（AH/1）分别作为阴性、阳性对照。第二、三句描述结果：没有检测到 CK/S1053 传播，但检测到 CK/SD008-PB2/627K、AH/1 传给了所有三只雪貂。第四句得出结论：新出现的鸡致命性 H7N9 病毒在老鼠中变得高度致命，在其 PB2 获得 627K 或 701N 突变后，在雪貂中的传播更加有效。

主题七

此主题只有一段（两句），描述 CK/SD008 病毒的受体结合偏好，涉及结果（已有结果或认识）、方法及发现。

第一句交待已有结果或认识：受体结合偏好对流感病毒的传播很重要，而且在 HA、G186V 和 Q226L 中的两种氨基酸突变出现在本研究中分离出的 H7N9 禽流感病毒的 90% 以上（表 1），这两种氨基酸在 H7 禽流感病毒与人类受体结合的过程中起着关键作用[18]。第二句描述方法及结果。方法：测试 CK/SD008 以及在 2013 年分离出来的携带 HA 186V 和 226L 的两种病毒 CK/S1053、AH/1 的受体结合特性。结果：CK/SD008、CK/S1053 和 AH/1 与 α2,6-siaylglycopolymer（人类受体）的结合比与 α2,3-siaylglycopolymer（禽类受体）的结合更有亲和力（图 4）。

主题八

该主题只有一段（三句），描述 H7N9 病毒的热稳定性，涉及结果（已有结果或认识）、方法及发现。

第一句交待已有结果或认识：热稳定性

对某些高致病性 H5N1 实验室适应性病毒的传播具有重要意义 [6]。第二句描述方法及结果。方法：对包括本传播研究中使用的五种 H7N9 病毒、一种 2016 年的 H7N9 禽流感病毒和一种 H5N1 禽流感病毒在内的七种流感病毒的热稳定性与 2009 年的 H1N1 大流行性流感病毒（SC/1）进行比较，并使用 Imai 等 [6] 所述的方法。结果（发现）：2013 年的两种 H7N9 禽病毒 CK/S1053 和 AH/1 比人病毒 SC/1 更不稳定，但 CK/SD008 病毒及其 PB2 突变体连同 2016 年的 H7N9、H5N1 病毒，均有与 SC/1 相近或更强的热稳定性（附加信息，图 S6）。

2. 讨论

（1）第一段五句，旨在总结本文研究的价值和意义。

第一、二句陈述一种认识或看法：流感病毒发生突变是常态；最糟糕的突变是从低致病性变成高致病性，并且在人群中传播。第三句指出本研究的重大发现：H7N9 病毒会发生令人惊恐的突变。第四、五句总结该发现的科学价值和意义：为 H7N9 禽流感的控制提供重要信息，指导人们采取行动来预防和减少高致病性 H7N9 突变体对家禽和人造成的危害，包括快速鉴别诊断试验建立、家禽紧急监测、病人样本分析以及家禽疫苗评估。

（2）第二段三句，旨在推断流感病毒的毒性与其基因变化密切相关。

第一句定性陈述一种认识：流感病毒的毒性和传播呈现出多基因特征。第二句定量说明 CK/SD008-PB2/627K 病毒的致命性：它的 MLD_{50} 是 $1.8\log_{10} EID_{50}$，致命性是 CK/SD008 的 10^5 倍（MLD_{50}，$>7.5\log_{10} EID_{50}$），是 2013 年携带 PB2 627K 突变的 H7N9 人类隔离物的 10^3 倍多，其 MLD_{50}s $>5.4\log_{10} EID_{50}$。第三句以上述两句为前提得出一个结论：老鼠中 CK/SD008-PB2/627K 的高毒性代表了 PB2 和 HA 基因的遗传变化。

（3）第三段六句，旨在说明监测和评估 H7N9 病毒的隔离物对防止病毒飞沫传播的重要性。

第一句陈述一种认识：哺乳动物中 H7N9 PB2 突变体的毒性与 H5N1 高致病性病毒相似，导致感染人群约 60% 的死亡率（引用文献 [46-48]），比低致病性 H7N9 病毒导致感染人群的死亡率高 20% 以上。

第二句陈述先前的研究认识：相对于野生型母体病毒而言，雪貂中传播的 H5N1 突变体在哺乳动物中被削弱了，而毒性的丧失是可传播性的平衡（引用文献 [6，7]）。

第三句陈述本课题以前研究的认识：低致病性 H7N9 病毒在人体中复制后，变得能在雪貂中传播，但在老鼠或雪貂中并不是高致病性的（引用文献 [16]）。

第四、五句交待本文研究的新认识：

1）新的鸡致命性 H7N9 病毒在获得 PB2 627K 或 701N 突变后，不仅在雪貂中高度传播，而且对老鼠也变得高致命性，并对雪貂造成严重疾病和死亡。

2）超过 83% 的低致病性 H7N9 病毒在人体复制中获得 PB2 突变（表1），鸡致命性 H7N9 病毒在人体中复制时极有可能在其 PB2 中获得类似的突变。

第六句将以上认识作为前提得出一个结论：仔细监测和评估 H7N9 病毒的人类隔离物非常重要，以防止它通过飞沫在人群中传播。

（4）第四段六句，主要描述本文对 H7N9 病毒监测和检测的一些重要发现。

第一句及第二句中的前面部分交待方法：对 H7N9 病毒进行重要监测；收集来自广东省的鸡场和活禽市场的 2 950 个样本；隔离 28 种 H7N9（附加信息，表 S4），对其 HA 基因部分序列进行分析。

第二句中的后面及第三至六句描述结果（重要发现）。主要内容包括：

1）15种H7N9的HA基因序列有HA插入（附加信息，表S5）；

2）H7N9的HA裂解位点上有3个附加序列（附加信息，表S5）；

3）具有所有其他三种不同HA裂解序列的病毒对鸡同样是致命的（附加信息，表S5），在哺乳动物中的毒性有待进一步研究；

4）一种序列-PKRKRTAR/G-是在广东省病人的隔离物中发现的（附加信息，表S5）；

5）在病人的隔离物中检测到了PB2 627K突变（附加信息，表S5）。

（5）第五段三句，主要描述本文对H7N9病毒热稳定性研究的重要发现。

第一句陈述对不同禽流感病毒的热稳定性与2009年全球流行性H1N1病毒SC/1进行比较的发现：自然隔离的鸭H5N1，最近的低、高致病性H7N9，以及H7N9 PB2突变体都比H1N1具有更好的热稳定性。

第二句以"如果热稳定性对流感病毒的传播很重要"这一假设和文献［6］中Imai等所报道的相关成果作为前提，推出一个结论"一些自然界中传播的H5N1和H7N9禽流感病毒已经获得了热稳定性"。

第三句以"两种H7N9 PB2突变体比母体CK/SD008病毒具有更好的热稳定性"为前提，推出另一结论"与流感病毒的其他特性相似，热稳定性可能是由一个基因群（系）而非仅由HA基因决定的多基因性状"。

（6）第六段三句，旨在强调H7N9的高危害性及控制和根除它的极端重要性。

第一句描述H7N9大规模疫情：本稿撰写阶段，H7N9高致病性病毒已从广东省传播到其他几个省，并引发了大规模疫情，数百万只鸡在这场疾病控制中被杀掉［49］。

第二句提出一个观点：单凭宰杀致命性H7N9病毒感染的家禽并不能解决问题（论点），因为广泛传播的低致病性H7N9在任何时候都可能突变为高致病性H7N9（论据）。

第三句将以上两句为前提，得出结论：H7N9对家禽和人类健康有巨大风险隐患，控制和根除高致病性H7N9应是中国动物疾病控制部门的首要任务。这是全文研究的归宿，研究成果不仅在于认识世界，更在于改造世界，最终造福人类！

2.5.4.3 实例三

【3】

3 Results and discussion

3.1 Diffusion reaction of titanium powder and aluminum powder

The intermetallic compound of Ti and Al elemental powders was synthesized by diffusion control, including the generation of $TiAl_3$, $TiAl_2$, and Ti_3Al intermediate phases. When the temperature is lower than the melting point of Al, Ti and Al particles occur diffusion reaction to form $TiAl_3$ phase on the Ti-Al particle interface, and gradually form $TiAl_2$, Ti_3Al, and other various intermediate phases as the reaction proceeds. $TiAl_2$ and Ti_3Al phases compete for formation at the same time when $TiAl_3$ persists. After $TiAl_3$ consumes up, the amount of Ti_3Al and $TiAl_2$ phases decreases and that of TiAl phase increases. The final reaction product is the mixture of Ti_3Al and TiAl phases, and the respective phase ratio is related to the composition of the material and the specific process.

In short, the synthesis of Ti and Al is divided into three steps: the formation of $TiAl_3$ phase, the formation of intermediate phases $TiAl_2$ and Ti_3Al and a small amount of the TiAl phases, and the formation of TiAl phase, which can be specifically described by the following three reactions [12, 13]:

$$6Ti + 6Al \rightarrow 4Ti + 2TiAl_3 \quad (1)$$
$$4Ti + 2TiAl_3 \rightarrow Ti_3Al + TiAl + 2TiAl_2 \quad (2)$$
$$Ti_3Al + 2TiAl_2 + TiAl \rightarrow 6TiAl \quad (3)$$

Figure 5a shows the internal structure of alloy powders prepared by titanium powder and aluminum powder heated at 500 ℃ for 2 h and 600 ℃ for 1.5 h. As known from the EDS results, the atom ratios of Ti to Al of Points 1–4 in Fig. 5a are 42.88∶57.12, 64.97∶

35.03∶65.09, 34.91, and 99.29∶0.71, respectively. It can be seen that the content of Ti gradually reduces from the inside to the outside, and in the middle part of the powder it is relatively pure Ti. A variety of metaphases which may contain TiAl alloy phase are observed in Points 2 and 3 in Fig. 5a, and the outermost is a compound of Ti and Al which already exists. There is no single aluminum and aluminum spreads to the titanium to form alloy. In the middle of the powder, it still contains some titanium phase due to the fact that the reaction is not complete. It can be inferred that the spread of the diffusion process mainly comes from aluminum atom migration.

Figure 5b shows the internal structure of alloyed powders prepared by titanium powder and aluminum powder heated at 500 ℃ for 2 h and 600 ℃ for 3 h. As known from the EDS results, the atom ratios of Ti to Al of Points 1–3 in Fig. 5b are 47.19∶52.81, 48.21∶51.89, and 47.84∶52.16, respectively. It can be seen that a homogeneous alloy phase finally forms. The above analysis is in accordance with the results of XRD.

3.2 Diffusion reaction of titanium hydride powder and aluminum powder

Titanium hydride dehydrogenates at a certain temperature and time, which vary with the factors of preparing raw material: the particle size and heating rate. The dehydrogenation reaction process is as follows [14, 15]:

$$TiH_2 \rightarrow Ti + H_2 \qquad (4)$$

Figure 6 is the DTA curve of TiH_2 powder (average particle size of 46 μm) under a protective atmosphere of argon at heating rate of 5 ℃·min^{-1}. It is apparent that the dehydrogenation of TiH_2 is an endothermic process which has a small endothermic peak at 443 ℃ and a second larger endothermic peak at 523 ℃, as shown in Fig. 6. The endothermic peak of the two separation description reveals that thermal decomposition of the dehydrogenation reaction of TiH_2 powder is a multi-stage reaction. It can be accounted for the dehydrogenation reaction of TiH_2 powder at heating rate of 5 ℃·min^{-1} and temperature of 440–550 ℃. The TiH_2 and Al powders heated at 500 ℃ for 2 h are the research object, because titanium hydride can be almost dehydrogenated thoroughly and partially alloyed at 500 ℃ for 2 h by the previous studies.

Figure 7a shows the internal structure of alloyed powders prepared by titanium hydride powder and aluminum powder heated at 500 ℃ for 2 h. As known from the EDS results, the atom ratios of Ti to Al of Points 1–4 in Fig. 7a are 43.12∶56.88, 62.26∶37.74, 65.32∶34.68, and 99.16∶0.84, respectively. It can be seen that the reaction of titanium hydride and aluminumpowder is similar to that of titanium powder and aluminum powder, giving priority to the diffusion of aluminum. Aluminum gradually spreads to titanium that comes from dehydrogenation of titanium hydride powder, forming mainly aluminum alloy phase at the surface. And from outside to inside, aluminum content gradually reduces, forming various sorts of metaphases. It is still titanium in the center because the reaction does not come to the end.

Figure 7b shows the internal structure of alloyed powders prepared by titanium hydride powder and aluminum powder heated at 750 ℃ for 3 h. As known from the EDS results, the atom ratios of Ti to Al of Points 1–3 in Fig. 7a are 51.99∶48.01, 52.60∶47.40, and 50.65∶49.35, respectively. It can be seen that a homogeneous alloy phase finally forms. The above analysis is in accordance with the results of XRD.

The TiAl alloy powders were prepared by direct diffusion reaction of Ti and Al using titanium powder and aluminum powder as raw materials, and using titanium hydride powder and aluminum powder as raw materials, respectively. The amount of defects increases in the two kinds of raw materials in the process of ball milling due to mechanical forces, and the defects will gradually release energy at the same time to promote alloying in the following alloying process. The alloy powders can be prepared at a relative lower temperature due to direct diffusion reaction of the titanium powder and aluminum powder. By contrast, TiAl alloy powders cannot be got from titanium hydride and aluminum powders at low temperature since the system energy is low due to the low level of defects and that dehydrogenation reaction is an energy absorbing process. So the heating temperature should be raised to make titanium hydride and aluminum powders change to a pure TiAl alloy powder.

(Preparation of TiAl alloy powder by high-energy ball milling and diffusion reaction at low temperature. RARE METALS, (2018) 37 (1): 21–25.)

例【3】是一篇材料类原创论文的结果与讨论,分两个主题(子标题),分别讲述钛粉和铝粉、氢化钛粉和铝粉的扩散反应,先描述结果,后对结果进行讨论,再提出认识或观点。

主题一(钛粉和铝粉的扩散反应,共四段)

第一段描述结果。第一句描述总体结果:形成 Ti、Al 化合物,包括 $TiAl_3$、$TiAl_2$ 和 Ti_3Al 中间相。第二至五句进行分析,描述具体结果:①温度低于 Al 的熔点时,Ti、Al 粒子发生扩散反应,在 Ti-Al 粒子界面上形成 $TiAl_3$ 相,再逐渐形成 $TiAl_2$、Ti_3Al 和其他中间相。②$TiAl_2$、Ti_3Al 相在 $TiAl_3$ 相持续期间竞相形成。③$TiAl_3$ 消耗完后,Ti_3Al、$TiAl_2$ 相减少,而 TiAl 相数量增加。④最终形成 Ti_3Al、TiAl 相混合物,各自相比与材料组成和具体过程有关。

第二段进行总结,得出一个结论,Ti 和 Al 的合成可分为三步($TiAl_3$ 相的形成、$TiAl_2$ 和 Ti_3Al 中间相和少量 TiAl 相的形成、TiAl 相的形成),并引用文献给出这三步的化学反应式。

第三段描述结果,得出结论。第一句描述图 5a 结果:钛粉和铝粉分别在 500 ℃下加热 2 h 和 600 ℃下加热 1.5 h 所制备的合金粉末的内部结构。第二至六句描述 EDS 结果:①图 5a 中点 1~4 所表示的 Ti 到 Al 的原子比分别是 42.88:57.12、64.97:35.03、65.09:34.91 和 99.29:0.71。②Ti 含量从内到外逐渐减少,在粉末的中间部分是相对纯的 Ti。③从图 5a 中点 2、3 能观察到可能含有 TiAl 合金相的各种中间相,最外层是已经存在的 Ti、Al 的化合物。④没有单一的铝和铝延伸到钛上形成合金。⑤在粉末的中间仍含有一些钛相(由于反应不充分)。第七句推出一个判断即结论:扩散过程中的延伸主要来自铝原子的迁移。

第四段描述结果并得出结论。第一句描述图 5b 结果:钛粉和铝粉分别在 500 ℃下加热 2 h 和 600 ℃下加热 3 h 所制备的合金粉末的内部结构。第二、三句描述 EDS 结果:①图 5b 中点 1~3 所表示的 Ti 到 Al 的原子比分别是 47.19:52.81、48.21:51.89 和 47.84:52.16。②最终形成一个均匀的合金相。第四句推出一个结论:以上分析与 XRD 的结果一致。

主题二(氢化钛粉和铝粉的扩散反应,共五段)

第一段陈述一种观点或认识(在一定的温度和时间氢化钛会脱氢,随原料制备因素"颗粒大小、加热速度"的不同而变化),并引用文献给出氢化钛脱氢的化学反应式。

第二段描述结果、得出结论、提出观点。第一句描述图 6 结果:平均粒径为 $46\mu m$ 的 TiH_2 粉末在氩气保护下加热速度为 $5\ ℃·min^{-1}$ 时的 DTA 曲线。第二句先得出结论(TiH_2 的脱氢是一个吸热过程),再描述结果(吸热过程中有一个在 443 ℃ 的小吸热峰和另一个在 523 ℃ 的较大吸热峰,如图 6 所示)。第三、四句得出结论:两种分离类型的吸热峰揭示了 TiH_2 粉脱氢反应的热分解是一个多阶段的反应,这可以解释 TiH_2 粉末在加热速度为 $5\ ℃·min^{-1}$、温度为 440~550 ℃ 下的脱氢反应。第五句提出一种观点(认识或看法):把 500 ℃ 下加热 2 h 的 TiH_2、Al 粉末作为研究对象的原因是,在以前的研究成果中,氢化钛在 500 ℃ 下加热 2 h 后能彻底脱氢并部分合金化。

第三段主要描述结果并得出一个结论。第一句描述图 7a 结果:氢化钛粉和铝粉在

500 ℃下加热 2 h 所制备的合金粉末的内部结构。第二至五句描述 EDS 结果：①图 7a 中点 1~4 所表示的 Ti 到 Al 的原子比分别是 43.12∶56.88、62.26∶37.74、65.32∶34.68 和 99.16∶0.84。②氢化钛粉和铝粉的反应类似于钛粉和铝粉，且铝优先扩散。③铝逐渐扩散到来自氢化钛粉脱氢反应中的钛，主要在表面形成铝合金相。④从外到内，铝含量逐渐减少，形成各类中间相。第六句推出一个论断即结论，并给予进一步解释：钛仍然是中心，因为反应没有结束。

第四段描述结果并得出一个结论。第一句描述图 7b 结果：氢化钛粉和铝粉在 750 ℃下加热 3 h 所制备的合金粉末的内部结构。第二、三句描述 EDS 结果：①图 7a 中点 1~3 所表示的 Ti 到 Al 的原子比分别是 51.99∶48.01、52.60∶47.40 和 50.65∶49.35。②最终形成一个均匀的合金相。第四句推出一个结论：以上分析与 XRD 的结果一致。

第五段进行总结、分析，再提出认识、推出结论。第一句总结所用方法：分别使用钛粉和铝粉、氢化钛粉和铝粉作为原料，通过 Ti 和 Al 的直接扩散反应来制备 TiAl 合金粉末。第二句分析 TiAl 合金粉末制备机理：球磨过程中，因机械力的作用，两种原料的缺陷量增加，同时缺陷也会逐渐释放能量，从而促进合金化。第三、四句简单讨论，提出相异的观点或认识，形成对比：①因为钛粉和铝粉能直接扩散反应，所以可以在相对较低的温度下制备合金粉末；②因为由低水平的缺陷导致系统能量低，而脱氢反应是一个吸能过程，所以在低温条件下不能从氢化钛和铝粉中获得 TiAl 合金粉末。第五句得出结论：应提高加热温度，使氢化钛和铝粉转化为纯 TiAl 合金粉末。

2.6 结论

结论（Conclusions）又称结语或结束语，位于论文正文的后面部分，是体现作者更深层次认识的整篇论文的全局性总结，是从论文全部材料出发，经过推理、判断、归纳等逻辑分析而得到的新的学术总观念、总见解。结论通常是实验、观测结果和理论分析的逻辑发展，是将实验和观测所得结果经判断、推理、归纳等逻辑分析而得到的对事物本质和规律的总体认识。研究型论文在内容上必须有结论，在形式上既可有单独的结论部分，以"结论"为标题单独列为一段或几段，也可没有单独的结论部分，但至少应有起结论作用的一两个段落，或将有关结论的内容写在"讨论"或"结果与讨论"中。学术论文宜单列"结论"。

读者（包括评审专家）一般习惯于按题名→摘要→结论的顺序来阅读论文，读完结论后有可能形成对论文价值的判断，并决定是否去阅读全文（或是否录用论文）。结论不仅是引起读者阅读兴趣的重要内容，也是文献工作者从事摘要工作的重要依据，写好结论很重要。一篇研究论文应该以一个精心构建的结论来结束，让论文精彩地收尾。

2.6.1 结论内容及结构

结论是作者对研究成果的总体性评价，具有严密的客观性、全局性和科学性，反映研究价值，指导未来研究。结论常与引言遥相呼应，引言既然介绍了研究目的，那么结论就应告知目的是否达到、主要做了何工作、取得了何结果、结果说明了何问题、有何价值和意义、存在或发现了何问题、原因是什么、建议如何解决等，其核心在于回答"研究出什么"。

结论的内容通常包含以下几项，并大体

上按以下顺序形成结构：

1）概括说明研究内容，可先简单交待研究目的，再说明研究内容，重在指出做了什么；

2）简要交待研究成果，证明了何假设、理论，得出了何结果、结论，收获了何成果、见解，解决了何难点、问题等，重在指出做出了什么；

3）总结研究成果揭示的原理、规律，说明和解决的理论与实际问题，具有的理论意义、实用价值，重在指出发现了什么；

4）将研究成果与他人（包括作者自己）已有相关研究成果进行比较，总结优势，交待不足，重在总结异同；

5）指出研究的新意与价值，交待研究的贡献、意义、价值，明确与已有研究的关系，如补充、修改、完善、证实、突破等，重在点出创新；

6）指出研究的局限性，明确遗留未予解决或尚待解决的问题，以及解决这些问题的关键点、方向及基本思路，重在指出问题；

7）展望研究成果可能的应用前景，描述还应做些什么，有什么问题值得进一步研究，对需要进一步深入研究的方向或相关课题给出建议和意见，重在展望前景。

以上各部分是经典研究型论文才全部具备的，而平时看到的很多论文并不具备经典格局。对一篇论文，以上各项内容不见得都要有，实际中应随学科领域、研究内容、学术成果、表达侧重和写作风格等的不同而有所取舍，只写几项或将几项合写是完全可以的。

2.6.2 结论写作要求

结论写作要求大体上有以下几个方面：

1）把由实验、观测所得到的现象、数据以及对它们的阐述、分析作为依据，对每一句都进行准确明白、精练完整、高度概括、直截了当而不含糊其辞、模棱两可地表达；

2）要基于实验、观测结果进行判断、推理，不要作无根据和不合逻辑的推理进而得出无根据和不合逻辑的结论，必要时可根据实验、观测结果进行一些讨论；

3）坚持从整体出发全面考虑的原则，不要将结论写成摘要、标题、正文中有关部分及实验、观测结果的小结，也不能简单地重复这些部分中的语句；

4）恰如其分地评价所得成果并表达创新点，不可夸大其词、自鸣得意，也不要过度谦虚、谨小慎微，证据不足时不要妄下结论，对尚不能完全肯定的内容的叙述要注意留有余地，不要轻率地否定或批评别人的成果，更不能借故贬低别人；

5）措词严谨、逻辑严密、文字具体，内容较多时可分条来写，并给以编号，每条成一段，每段包括几句话或只有一句话，内容较少时写成一段更好；

6）要根据内容和表达需要来确定篇幅，简洁清楚地叙述作者自己研究的最终的重要论点，不涉及论文中不曾指出的事实，不重复论文中其他部分的语句，不叙述其他不重要甚至与本研究无关联的内容；

7）可提出一些开放的问题，为下一项研究预设场景，这也是记录作者对未来可能研究工作的想法的一个好时机，但千万不要在结论中提出任何新的论点；

8）宜从本文、本研究的现时角度来写，多用现在时，但按表述情形，用过去时也可。

2.6.3 结论的句型

结论的语句可分为总结与展望两大类，相应地其句型也分为这两类。

（1）总结类（overall summary）

- The paper concludes by arguing ...
- On this basis, we conclude that ...

- The authors concluded that ... is not confined to ...
- This allows the conclusion that ...
- The findings of this study can be understood as ...
- This may be considered a promising aspect of ...
- This may be considered a further validation of ...
- Remaining issues are subject of ...
- In summary, this paper argues that ...
- This aspect of the research suggested that ...
- In conclusion, ... seems to improve ...
- In conclusion, it would appear that ...
- The analysis leads to the following conclusions: ...
- It is difficult to arrive at any conclusions with regard to ...
- The main conclusion that can be drawn is that ...
- The present findings confirm ...
- As we have argued elsewhere ... may be considered a promising aspect of ...
- Ideally, these findings should be replicated in a study where ...
- By using ... we tested the hypothesis that ...
- Broadly translated our findings indicate that ...
- This is an important finding in the understanding of the ...
- More generally, these basic findings are consistent with research showing that ...
- In addition, these findings provide additional information about ...
- Despite the limitations these are valuable in light of ...
- Overall, our results demonstrate a strong effect of ...
- Nevertheless, we found ...
- To our knowledge, this is the first report of ...
- Our results on ... are broadly consistent with ...
- The broad implication of the present research is that ...
- This conclusion follows from the fact that ...
- Collectively, our results appear consistent with ...
- Importantly, our results provide evidence for ...
- Results provide a basis for ...
- We have shown that ...
- This experiment adds to a growing corpus of research showing ...
- These findings provide a potential mechanism for ...
- Our data indicate that ...; a result that casts a new light on ...
- Our data suggest that we still have a long way to go to ...

（2）展望类（future work）
- Future research should consider the potential effects of ... more carefully, for example ...
- This assumption might be addressed in future studies.
- Future research on ... might extend the explanations of ...
- This is very much the key component in future attempts to overcome ...
- In future work, investigating ... might prove important.
- This is desirable for future work.
- Future investigations are necessary to validate the kinds of conclusions that can be

drawn from this study.

• Future studies could fruitfully explore this issue further by …

• Future research is needed to delimitate …

• It will be important that future research investigate …

• It is a question of future research to investigate …

• We believe that apart from looking for …, future research should look for …

• Regardless, future research could continue to explore …

• This is an issue for future research to explore.

• Future studies could investigate the association between …

• Future studies should aim to replicate results in a larger …

• Future research should be devoted to the development of …

• This may constitute the object of future studies.

• Future research could examine …

• Interesting research questions for future research that can be derived from …

• In future research, more research is needed to apply and test …

• This is an interesting topic for future work.

• Future research should further develop and confirm these initial findings by …

• Future research should certainly further test whether …

• As also recommended above, future research should …

• Future research should examine strategically …

• Future research might apply …

• In addition, … might prove an important area for future research.

• A number of recommendations for future research are given.

• Therefore, future research should be conducted in more realistic settings to …

• Further research on … issue is warranted.

• Further work is certainly required to disentangle these complexities in …

• Looking forward, further attempts could prove quite beneficial to the literature.

• Further research is needed to confirm this novel finding.

• These result warrant further investigation via …

• This provides a good starting point for discussion and further research.

• Further studies should investigate …

• The possibility of … warrants further investigation.

2.6.4 结论写作实例

下面选择若干结论的实例，了解其内容、结构和写作方法。

2.6.4.1 实例一

[1]

CONCLUSIONS

Environmental friendly SiNCs with a spectrally limited emission profile can be turned into a phosphor with a well-balanced visible white emission spectrum upon e-beam irradiation. The spectral changes induced by the e-beam irradiation consist of a considerable spectral shift as well as broadening, irrespective of the initial sample characteristics. We conclude that the irradiation creates new color centers in the oxide shell of the O-SiNC, since the oxide-free organically capped C-SiNCs do not show any change in their emission spectrum upon irradiation and emission from defect centers generated in the native oxide thin film on the Si substrate is negligible. These defects can be related to well-known color centers in bulk and nanostructured silica. Unlike in silica, however, these color sites can be efficiently optically excited in the SiNC systems at 405 nm by a low power laser diode, due to the narrower band gap of the host. From the comparison of the three very different O-SiNC samples, we found this effect to be independent of the preparation protocol and properties of each particular type of O-SiNC, with small variations: whereas the green band emission benefited from thicker and possibly more strained silica shells, red and blue bands appeared in all samples, with the blue band being exceptionally well-developed and stable in air. We thus believe that any oxide-capped SiNC, treated by an e-beam with an energy of around 15 keV for a few minutes can be converted into a brightly warm-white light-emitting material, especially provided a thicker silica shell. This constitutes a novel, robust, and reliable method to convert any environmental friendly and abundant (oxide-capped) SiNCs into a white color phosphor. Further optimization of the material and emission yields is necessary, however, the current study shows that this effect offers many properties sought by white-light applications.

(Multi-chromatic silicon nanocrystals. *Light*: *Science & Application*, Volume 6, Issue 3, 2017.)

例【1】是一篇物理学（光学）领域原创论文的结论，形式上为一大段，内容上包括结果、推论、解释、发现、贡献及局限。

第一、二句描述实验结果：具有光谱限制发射剖面的环境友好型SiNCs可转化为在电子束照射下具有均衡可见白色发射光谱的磷光体；由电子束照射所诱导的光谱变化包括与最初样本特征无关的相当大的光谱变化和扩展。

第三至五句提出推论（结论）并解释。第三句提出由实验结果推断出的新结果（照射在O-SiNC的氧化壳中创建了新的颜色中心），并给予解释（由无氧有机物覆盖的C-SiNCs在照射下，发射光谱没有任何变化，来自由硅基板上原生态氧化物薄膜产生的缺陷中心的发射可以忽略不计）。第四、五句继续解释：缺陷可能与批量彩色中心和纳米结构的硅相关，颜色位点能在405 nm的SiNC系统中由低功率激光二极管高效激活，这是由宿主的窄带隙所致。

第六句描述对三个不同O-SiNC样本进行比较的发现：光谱效应与不同样本的O-SiNC准备协议和属性不甚相关，但有细微的差异（绿色带的发射与硅外壳的厚度、张紧度有关，三个样本中都出现了红色和蓝色带，蓝色带在空气中极其丰富、稳定）。

第七句又提出一个推论：任何氧化物覆盖的SiNC，由电子束以15keV的能量处理时，在短短几分钟内就能转换成一种带有较厚硅壳层的明亮的暖白色发光材料。

第八句鲜明地点出研究的贡献、价值，即科学意义，也即创新点：能为将任何环境友好和氧化物覆盖的SiNCs转换成白色荧光粉提供一种好方法（新颖、鲁棒、可靠）。

第九句指出未来进一步研究的方向（对材料和发射量进一步优化），再次指出本文研究的贡献（也暗含局限）（为白光应用提供了很多特性）。

2.6.4.2 实例二

【2】

4 Conclusion

The relatively pure TiAl alloy powders were prepared through diffusion reaction step at low temperature using Ti-Al powders and TiH_2-Al powders, respectively. The prepared process of alloy powder by titanium powder and titanium hydride powder were heated at 500 ℃ for 2 h and then 600 ℃ for 3 h, and at 750 ℃ for 3 h, respectively, in 4.0×10^{-3} Pa vacuum conditions with heating rate of 5 ℃ · min^{-1}. The average content of oxygen in the alloy powders is 0.33 wt%. The average grain sizes of prepared alloyed powder are 45 and 20 μm with irregular shape, respectively. The forming process of alloy powder contains both the diffusion reaction of Ti and Al, which gives priority to the diffusion of Al.

(Preparation of TiAl alloy powder by high-energy ball milling and diffusion reaction at low temperature. *RARE METALS*, (2018) 37 (1): 21–25.)

例【2】是一篇金属材料领域原创论文的结论，形式上为一段，内容上包括主要工作、所用工艺和重要发现。

第一句与本文题名"由高能球磨粉和低温扩散反应来制备 TiAl 合金粉末"（目标）相对应，稍加展开，交待完成了既定工作，达到了目标：分别使用 Ti-Al 粉末和 TiH_2-Al 粉末，通过低温条件下的扩散反应制备出相对纯的 TiAl 合金粉末。

第二句总结本文提出的基于钛粉和氢化钛粉的合金粉末制备工艺：在 4.0×10^{-3} Pa 的真空环境中以 5℃·min^{-1} 的加热速度，分别在 500℃ 下加热 2 h，600℃ 下加热 3 h，750℃ 下加热 3 h。

第三至五句总结重要发现（贡献）：制备的合金粉末平均氧含量是 0.33%，平均粒度分别为 45μm、20μm 且形状不规则，形成过程包含 Ti、Al 的扩散反应且铝优先扩散。

2.6.4.3 实例三

【3】

5. Conclusions

Enlightened by CSM and CSV, the idea of regional analysis is extended to the moment-independent importance analysis in this work. Two new definitions, RIMPDF and RIMCDF, aiming to evaluate the contributions of specific regions of an input to the output PDF and CDF, are introduced. The properties are discussed, as well as the corresponding computational strategies. By performing the regional moment-independent importance analysis, information concerning how the regions inside the inputs affect the whole output distribution can be obtained. Such information is helpful for analysts to control the output uncertainty, as PDF and CDF are more sufficient to describe the uncertainty than solely depending on the mean or variance. Meanwhile, RIMPDF and RIMCDF can be obtained with the same samples used to estimate δ_i and $S_i^{(CDF)}$, and thus they can be viewed as byproducts of the standard moment-indendent importance analysis, without a need of extra model evaluations. The idea of RIMPDF and RIMCDF provides not a substitution but a viable supplement to sensitivity analysis. Discussions on applying RIMPDF and RIMCDF in two engineering cases demonstrate that the regional moment-independent importance analysis can add more information concerning the contributions of model inputs.⊖（笔者注）

(Regional moment-independent sensitivity analysis with its applications in engineering. *Chinese Journal of Aeronautics*, Vol. 30, No. 3, Jun. 2017: 1031–1042.)

例【3】是一篇航空领域原创论文的结论，形式上为一大段，内容上包括主要工作、所获结果、论文价值和学术贡献。

第一至第四句（指其前面的介词短语）交待本文主要工作：①受 CSM、CSV 的启发，将区域分析的概念扩展到矩独立重要性分析中。②引入 RIMPDF、RIMCDF 两个新定义以评估输入到输出 PDF、CDF 特定区域的贡献。③讨论相关属性及相应计算策略。④进行区域矩独立重要性分析。

第四句（指其后面的主句）描述本文所获结果：获得关于输入里的特定区域如何影响整个输出分布的信息。第五句指出该结果

⊖ CSM—Contribution to Sample Mean（对样本均值的贡献）；CSV—Contribution to Sample Variance（对样本方差的贡献）。PDF—Probability Density Function（概率密度函数）；CDF—Cumulative Distribution Function（累积分布函数）。RIMPDF—Regional Importance Measure based on Probability Density Function（基于概率密度函数的区域重要性测度方法）；RIMCDF—Regional Importance Measure based on Cumulative Distribution Function（基于累积分布函数的区域重要性测度方法）。

的价值或意义（有助于分析人员控制输出的不确定性），并给予解释（PDF、CDF 比单纯依赖均值或方差更能描述不确定性）。

第六句中第一分句描述本文所获的另一结果及意义：可用相同的样本获得 RIMPDF、RIMCDF（结果）；用来估计 δ_i 和 $S_i^{(CDF)}$（意义）。第二分句得出一个结论（获得的 RIMPDF、RIMCDF 可看作标准矩独立重要性分析的副产品，无需额外的模型评估）。

第七句总结本文的学术贡献或创新之处：RIMPDF、RIMCDF 不是用来替代，而是对传统灵敏度分析的一种可行补充，即能弥补传统灵敏度分析的不足。

第八句交待 RIMPDF、RIMCDF 的工程应用实效：引入区域矩独立重要性分析能添加更多有关模型输入贡献的信息。这是用事实（实效）来增强说明本文的贡献或创新之处。

本结论在语言表达上有简化的空间，但在内容布局上还是能够代表工程技术类论文（能改善或解决实际问题，有创新，但学术性不一定高）的结论写作模式。

2.6.4.4 实例四【4】

5 Conclusions

Based on 461 event-based precipitation samples collected from 12 stations in the Qilian Mountains and the Hexi Corridor from May to August of 2013, the effect of sub-cloud evaporation on falling raindrops has been estimated for the months with temperatures above 0 ℃. The raindrops were evaporated by 19%, 13%, 16%, and 18% from the cloud base to the ground in May, June, July, and August, respectively. The spatial pattern showed an obvious decreasing trend from northwest to southeast in the study region, as the lower evaporation values were distributed in the Qilian Mountains while the higher values were in the Hexi Corridor. We also estimated the effect of sub-cloud evaporation on the $\delta^{18}O$ composition of precipitation; the sub-cloud evaporation enrichment rates of $\delta^{18}O$ were 35%, 26%, 39%, and 41% in May, June, July, and August, respectively, and showed an obvious increasing trend from the Qilian Mountains to the Hexi Corridor. Significant positive correlations between E and f indicated that the higher the f is, the higher the E is (more enrichment). The $\delta^{18}O$ composition would be enriched by 1.1‰, 1.3‰, 2.1‰, and 3.1‰ when the raindrops are evaporated by 1.0% in the higher altitudes and lower altitudes of the Qilian Mountains, the Hexi Corridor, and the desert region, respectively. According to our correlation analysis, the influence of temperature on the sub-cloud evaporation enrichment rate of $\delta^{18}O$ was comparatively strong in the Qilian Mountains, whereas relative humidity made a greater contribution to it in the Hexi Corridor. These results provide crucial findings for future study on isotopic hydrology in arid regions.⊖（笔者注）

(Effect of sub-cloud evaporation on the $\delta^{18}O$ of precipitation in Qilian Mountains and Hexi Corridor, China. *Sciences in Cold and Arid Regions*, Volume 8, Issue 5, October 2016: 378-387.)

例【4】是一篇寒旱区领域原创论文的结论，形式上为一大段，内容上包括样本收集、亚云蒸发影响评估、科学发现及论文价值。

第一句前面部分交待样本收集情况：从祁连山和河西走廊 12 个气象站收集了 2013 年 5 月至 8 月期间 461 个基于事件的降水样本。

第一句后面部分和第二、三句交待本文主要工作及发现（结果、结论）。工作：评估气温超过 0 ℃ 的那几个月中亚云蒸发对雨滴降落的影响。发现：①5~8 月的 4 个月里，雨滴从云层底部到地面分别蒸发了 19%、13%、16%、18%。②这种蒸发呈现

⊖ E—The relative effect of sub-cloud evaporation（亚云蒸发相对效率）；f—The evaporation rate（蒸发率）。

出研究区域内从西北到东南的明显下降趋势（低蒸发值分布在祁连山，较高值分布在河西走廊）。

第四至七句交待本文另一主要工作及相关发现（结果、结论）。工作：评估亚云蒸发对降水中 $\delta^{18}O$ 构成的影响。发现：①5月到8月的4个月里，$\delta^{18}O$ 的亚云蒸发浓缩率分别为 35%、26%、39%、41%，呈现出从祁连山到河西走廊的明显上升趋势。②E、f 之间显著正相关，f 越高，E 就越高。③雨滴蒸发 1.0% 时，在祁连山区的高、低海拔地区以及河西走廊、沙漠地区的 $\delta^{18}O$ 的构成分别增加 1.1%、1.3%、2.1%、3.1%。④温度对祁连山区 $\delta^{18}O$ 亚云蒸发浓缩率的影响相对较强，而相对湿度对河西走廊的影响更大。

第八句总结本文的贡献或创新（价值）：研究成果为干旱地区同位素水文学的进一步研究提供了重要发现。

2.6.4.5 实例五

【5】

Conclusions and future directions

The analysis of CFNA clearly offers a potential for diagnostics, prognostics, management and pathologic insights into various hematologic malignancies. Despite longstanding knowledge of the existence of CFNA[1, 2], it is only in the past two decades that research has focused initially on cfDNA[3] and more recently miRNA[4]. The science is nascent but rapidly evolving.

The blood of patients with hematologic malignancy contains higher levels of cfDNA[2] that harbors mutations, chromosomal translocations and epigenetic changes present in the tumor population and as such presents an opportunity for simple, non-invasive, repeatable analysis of these genetic profiles. Furthermore, with increasingly sensitive methods[32-35] of interrogation this source of genetic material may be more sensitive than single biopsies of primary sites of disease or that obtained from circulating tumor cells[33] and this theoretically may be of particular importance in the case of spatially and genetically heterogeneous malignancies[15] whereby CFNA analysis may provide a more 'holistic' description of a tumor's mutational profile. Clearly larger studies are needed to compare mutational profiles identified in CFNA with those found in tissue biopsies from primary sites of disease and identify any correlation with patient outcomes. Current prognostic algorithms[23] have been established for mutations detected in primary tumors, but to date their significance when detected in CFNA is unclear. Simple but important questions such as the significance of differing mutational burdens in the peripheral and the issue of how the identification of a novel mutation in the blood that may otherwise not have been identified in primary tissues should be addressed remain unanswered.

The prospective role of circulating miRNA is less evolved and less clear than that of cfDNA. The source of circulating miRNA remains contentious, with studies frequently finding no correlation between that which is found in the peripheral blood and primary tumor cells[63, 92]. Current micro-array platforms, whilst very sensitive, identify vastly different miRNA signatures with little or no overlap between independent studies of the same diseases (see section regarding miRNA in AML and MM). This raises questions of mere association as opposed to a true signal and a potentially significant role in disease pathogenesis. Further efforts investigating circulating miRNA may best be focused on specific miRNA known to play roles in normal and malignant hemopoiesis[80, 93], as well as those already recurrently identified in more than one disease. For instance miR-150 is elevated in both AML[66] and CLL[78], whilst miR-92a is reduced in both AML[68, 69] and NHL[76].

Many questions have emerged in relation to the possible pathologic effects exerted by dysregulated circulating miRNA. Does the prognostic significance associated with an elevated specific miRNA result from its ability to interfere with tumor suppressor genes, the theoretical possibility that it may act as an inter-cellular messenger potentially inhibiting activity of immune effector cells or is it simply an association? How might reduced levels of specific miRNAs exert a prognostic effect? Is it due to increased cellular uptake influencing tumor and/or the microenvironment or is it representative an associated underlying genetic lesion? To properly understand the significance of dysregulated miRNA, functional studies are required. These would include evaluating mechanisms of cellular release and uptake; 'genetic interference' in tumor cells, the supporting micro-environment and immune effector cells; followed by correlation with clinical outcomes. Albeit complex these would provide insight into the true significance of dysregulated miRNA.

Prospects for clinical application are wide ranging, as novel testing platforms become more sensitive, quicker and more affordable, validation and standardization will be urgently required not only for 'inter-study' comparison but for potential integration into standard pathology practice[64]. Whilst controls for cfDNA analyses have largely been established, little or no agreement exists for controls and standardization of miRNA PCR and is urgently needed. The field of CFNA is rapidly evolving, with the prospects of liquid biopsy either complementing or even replacing BM and/or tissue biopsy a real possibility in the future. However, until platforms and practice are standardized, greater concordance in the data achieved, paired with an understanding of the mechanisms behind the observations, hematologists shouldn't throw out the marrow needle just yet. ⊖（笔者注）

(Liquid biopsies for liquid tumors: emerging potential of circulating free nucleic acid evaluation for the management of hematologic malignancies.
Cancer Biology & Medicine,
Volume. 13, Issue 2, June 2016: 215-225.)

例【5】是一篇生物医学领域的综述的结论。综述一般应有"展望"，常将"结论"与"展望"放在一起写，取一个共同的标题。此综述就是这样的，标题为 Con-clusions and future directions，形式上为五个自然段。

第一段描述对 CFNA 的总结性认识。第一句概括 CFNA 分析的优势：可清楚地为恶性肿瘤提供诊断、预测、管理和病理分析。第二句梳理 CFNA 研究的历程：长期以来对 CFNA 研究、认知较多，但在过去 20 年里，研究开始聚焦 cfDNA，最近更多关注 miRNA。第三句总结 cfDNA 和 miRNA 研究的灿烂前景：科学尚处于萌芽阶段，但正在迅速发展中。

第二段描述对 cfDNA 带来挑战和机遇的总结性认识。第一、二句分析患者血液中含有较多 cfDNA 对传统 CFNA 分析提出要求：①cfDNA 存在肿瘤突变、染色体易位和表观遗传变异，为其基因图谱提供了简单、非侵入式、可重复分析的机会。②敏感的审讯方法越来越多，遗传材料的来源比疾病基本位点上的单一组织活检可能更敏感，或遗传材料来源于游离肿瘤细胞，这在理论上对空间和基因方面的异质恶性肿瘤尤为重要，需要 CFNA 分析为肿瘤突变图谱提供更为全面的描述。第三句基于以上认识得出一个结论：需加强两类突变图谱（分别来自 CFNA 和疾病主要部位组织活检）对比研究，并确定与患者预后的相关性。第四、五句总结 CFNA 当前相关研究的进步和不足。进步：已经建立原发性肿瘤中检测突变的预后算法。不足：①对检测到的突变的重要性认识不清；②一些简单却重要的问题未解决（如外围设备中不同突变负担的重要性、在原生组织中识别可能没有发现的新突变的方法）。

第三段描述对循环 miRNA 现有认知和技术的总结性认识。第一、二句描述认知：①循环 miRNA 的预期作用与 cfDNA 相比，

⊖ CFNA—Cell free nucleic acids（细胞游离核酸）；cfDNA—Circulating free DNA（循环游离 DNA）；
miRNA—MicroRNA（微小核糖核酸）；AML—Acute myelogenous leukemia（急性髓系白血病）；
MM—Multiple myeloma（多发性骨髓瘤）；PCR—Polymerase Chain Reaction（聚合酶链式反应）；
CLL—Chronic lymphocytic leukemia（慢性淋巴细胞白血病）；AML—Multiple myeloma（多发性骨髓瘤）；
NHL—Non-hodgkin's lymphoma（非霍奇金淋巴瘤，淋巴肉瘤与网状细胞肉瘤）；BM—Bone marrow（骨髓）。

进化更少、认知也少。②循环 miRNA 的来源不明,研究经常发现在外围血液中的循环 miRNA 与原发性肿瘤细胞中的无相关性。第三、四句描述技术及问题:①微阵列平台很敏感,在同一疾病的独立研究间少有或无重叠,可发现截然不同的 miRNA。②引出仅是关联而非真正信号的问题,以及在发病机理中的潜在重要作用。第五句建议进一步的研究方向:可能最好集中于为人们熟知的在常规和恶性血细胞生成中扮演角色的特定 miRNA,以及已被反复确认不止在一种疾病中存在的 miRNA。第六句举例说明:miR-150 在 AML 和 CLL 中提升了,miR-92a 在 AML 和 NHL 中下降了,并引用一些文献。

第四段总结失调的循环 miRNA 引发的问题及问题解决的意义。第一句总说问题:已经出现了不少由循环 miRNA 引发的可能病理效应相关问题。接着第二至四句分说(或列举)问题:①与提升的特定循环 miRNA 相关的预后意义是由其干扰肿瘤抑制基因的能力造成,理论上是可能作为细胞信使潜在地抑制免疫效应细胞的活动或仅是一个关联?②如何降低特定 miRNA 产生预后效应的水平?③特定 miRNA 是细胞摄取对肿瘤和/或微环境造成影响,还是代表相关潜在遗传损伤?第五、六句提出未来研究方向和问题:需要功能研究,包括评估细胞释放和摄取机制;肿瘤细胞的基因干扰、支持微环境和免疫效应细胞;临床预后相关性。第七句强调了研究难度及意义:研究虽然复杂,但有助于深入了解失调的 miRNA 的真正意义。

第五段描绘 CFNA 的临床应用前景。第一句指出临床应用前景广阔,描述验证和标准化的迫切性及意义:新的测试平台变得更加敏感、快捷和便宜,迫切需要验证和标准化,不仅是为了"内部研究"比较,而且是为了与潜在的标准病理实践集成。第二句描述现状,总结问题:已较好地建立 cfDNA 分析控制机制,但对 miRNA PCR 控制和标准化协议还很少或没有建立,但又迫切需要。第三、四句提出 CFNA 分析前景看好,但需要较长时间:①CFNA 领域正在快速发展中,在未来液体活检可补充甚至取代 BM 和/或组织活检。②在平台和实践的标准化、数据的更大一致性以及对观测机制理解前,血液学家们还不能扔掉手头的骨髓针。

第 3 章　SCI 论文辅体写作

论文写成后不是为作者自存、自赏的，而是为走向社会让别人来阅读而达到交流、学习和传承的，因此具有明显的社会属性，是一种实实在在的产品。论文既然是一种产品，那么除有记录科研成果的内容属性（论文主体）外，还有其他属性，如著作权人（署名）、内容介绍（摘要）、基金项目（致谢）、分工协作（作者贡献）、研究基础（参考文献）、出版信息（日期信息、利益声明、版权许可等）等，这些方面虽不属科研成果和论文正文，却是成果和正文的重要组成部分（论文辅体）。主体和辅体相对独立、功能分明、侧重不同，但又相互补充、依存和渗透，共同组成论文的有机统一体。缺少主体不能成为论文，而缺少辅体就不能成为用来发表的论文，作者自己保存和查看的未发表论文没有产品属性，可以没有辅体，而要成为产品就需要有辅体加入进来。

辅体不属论文主体的科学研究（科研成果）范畴，却又是科学研究必须依赖的部分。辅体篇幅短小、内容单一、结构简单，其写作虽不像主体那样复杂而有规律，但也有其内容、结构及写作要求，同样需要作者来把握。第 2 章讲述了 SCI 论文主体的写作，这一章讲述辅体的写作，如果说主体写作侧重内容和结构，那么辅体写作则讲求内容和形式并举。

3.1　署名

署名是有关作者姓名、单位、联系方式等方面的信息，主要包括作者姓名、单位（Affiliation），有时还包括通信作者（Correspondence 或 Corresponding author），具有记录作者劳动成果、表明文责自负、辅助文献检索和科技评价系统统计分析，以及便于读者与作者联系等功能。全面、准确地刊登署名信息是对作者著作权及其所属单位权益的保护和尊重。因此，作者必须重视作者信息的真实、准确、正确和合理，以免引起著作权纠纷，给作者及其单位造成不必要的损失。作者姓名、单位和通信作者的信息往往是混在一起表述的。

3.1.1　署名体例格式

署名分单作者和多作者。多作者最为常见，按顺序列为第一作者、第二作者……，常把对研究工作与论文写作实际贡献最大的列为第一作者，贡献次之的列为第二作者，以此类推。

署名体例格式：作者姓名依次列出，置于题名下方，各姓名右上角加序号（作者序号），对需注释的作者（如通信作者），还要在此序号后加标识（如星号"＊""†"，有的期刊不要求加）；作者单位及相关信息另行依次并列书写在题名下方，或置于论文首页左下脚、正下方或其他位置，并在各单位名前加上与作者序号对应的序号。一位作者有几个单位时，在其右上角标注多个序号，序号间用逗号分隔。序号用数字或字母，可与单位名称平排或为上标及其他形式；所有作者的单位相同即只有一个单位时，序号全部为1。另外还要在论文首页适当位置给出与署名标识对应的注释信息，如通信作者字样及相关信息（邮箱、网址等）。

下面列举几个署名体例格式实例，供参考。

【1】

Biology and Applications of CRISPR Systems: Harnessing Nature's Toolbox for Geno-me Engineering

Addison V. Wright,[1] James K. Nuñez,[1] and Jennifer A. Doudna[1,2,3,4,5,6,*]

[1] Department of Molecular and Cell Biology, University of California, Berkeley, Berkeley, CA 94720, USA

[2] Howard Hughes Medical Institute HHMI, University of California, Berkeley, Berkeley, CA 94720, USA

[3] Department of Chemistry, University of California, Berkeley, Berkeley, CA 94720, USA

[4] Center for RNA Systems Biology, University of California, Berkeley, Berkeley, CA 94720, USA

[5] Innovative Genomics Initiative, University of California, Berkeley, Berkeley, CA 94720, USA

[6] Physical Biosciences Division, Lawrence Berkeley National Laboratory, Berkeley, Berkeley, CA 94720, USA

*Correspondence: doudna@berkeley.edu

http://dx.doi.org/10.1016/j.cell.2015.12.035

【2】

Rationally engineered Cas9 nucleases with improved specificity

Ian M. Slaymaker,[1,2,3,4,*] Linyi Gao,[1,4,*] Bernd Zetsche,[1,2,3,4] David A. Scott,[1,2,3,4] Winston X. Yan,[1,5,6] Feng Zhang[1,2,3,4,†]

[1] Broad Institute of MIT and Harvard, Cambridge, MA 02142, USA. [2] McGovern Institute for Brain Research, Massachusetts Institute of Technology, Cambridge, MA 02139, USA. [3] Department of Brain and Cognitive Sciences, Massachusetts Institute of Technology, Cambridge, MA 02139, USA. [4] Department of Biological Engineering, Massachusetts Institute of Technology, Cambridge, MA 02139, USA. [5] Graduate Program in Biophysics, Harvard Medical School, Boston, Massachusetts 02115, USA. [6] Harvard-MIT Division of Health Sciences and Technology, Harvard Medical School, Boston, Massachusetts 02115, USA.

*These authors contributed equally to this work.

†Corresponding author. E-mail: zhang@broadinstitute.org

【3】

Fully integrated wearable sensor arrays for multiplexed in situ perspiration analysis

Wei Gao[1,2,3,*], Sam Emaminejad[1,2,3,4,*], Hnin Yin Yin Nyein[1,2,3], Samyuktha Challa[4], Kevin Chen[1,2,3], Austin Peck[5], Hossain M. Fahad[1,2,3], Hiroki Ota[1,2,3], Hiroshi Shiraki[1,2,3], Daisuke Kiriya[1,2,3], Der-Hsien Lien[1,2,3], George A. Brooks[5], Ronald W. Davis[4] & Ali Javey[1,2,3]

……

[1] Department of Electrical Engineering and Computer Sciences, University of California, Berkeley, California 94720, USA.

[2] Berkeley Sensor and Actuator Center, University of California, Berkeley, California 94720, USA. [3] Materials Sciences Division, Lawrence Berkeley National Laboratory, Berkeley, California 94720, USA. [4] Stanford Genome Technology Center, Stanford School of Medicine, Palo Alto, California 94304, USA. [5] Integrative Biology, University of California, Berkeley, California 94720, USA.

*These authors contributed equally to this work.

【4】

Identification of blood vascular endothelial stem cells by the expression of C receptor

Qing Cissy Yu[1], Wenqian Song[1], Daisong Wang[1], Yi Arial Zeng[1]

[1] *The State Key Laboratroy of Cell Biology, CAS center for Excellence in Molecular Cell Science,*

Institute of Biochemistry and Cell Biology, Shanghai Institute for Biological Science, Chinese Academy of Science, Shanghai 200031, *China*

……

———————

Correspondence：Yi Ari Zeng

Tel：+86-21-5492-1433；Fax：+86-21-5492-1225

E-mail：yzeng@sibcb.ac.cn

例【1】摘自 *Cell*，作者右上角的序号置于分隔姓名的逗号之后，每位作者的单位及相关信息各自另行依次书写，再接着给出通信作者信息。例【2】摘自 *Nature*，作者右上角的序号也置于分隔姓名的逗号之后，每位作者的单位及相关信息依次书写（但没有各自另行）。特别地，作者姓名右上角出现了两种序号"*""†"，分别标识特别注释和通信作者。在单位及相关信息之后再给出特别注释、通信作者信息。例【3】摘自 *Science*，作者右上角的序号置于分隔姓名的逗号之前，每位作者的单位及相关信息依次书写（但没有各自另行），再接着给出特别注释信息，且以脚注的形式统一置于论文首页的正下方。例【4】摘自 *Cell Research*，所有作者的单位相同，序号全部为"1"，作者姓名中未标识通信作者，但以脚注的形式给出了通信作者信息。

作者序号常用数字（多为阿拉伯数字），但用字母及其他符号也是可以的，例如：

【5】

H. Hallevi[a]*, I. Hazan-Halevy[b]* and E. Paran[c]

[a]*Department of Neurology,* [b]*Department of Biochemistry and* [c]*Hypertension Unit, Soroka University Hospital, Beer-Sheva, Israel*

【6】

Fuqun HUANG[a,*]**, Bin LIU**[b]

[a] *Institute for Dependability Engineering, Seattle, WA* 98115, *USA*

[b] *School of Reliability and System Engineering, Beihang University, Beijing* 100083, *China*

例【5】、【6】的作者序号均使用拉丁字母（如 a、b），前者的作者单位依次书写（但没有各自另行），而后者的依次各自另行书写。

不少中国英文期刊因受中国传统习惯的影响，在署名格式上与国际惯例有差异，主要表现在姓名大小写、姓和名先后顺序及单位位置、排版形式等方面。中国传统习惯是单位名称紧接着另行放在作者姓名之后，署名左右居中排，而国外较为灵活，单位可以放在远离作者姓名的任何其他合适位置，而且更热衷于居左排。例如：

【7】

LIU Jing[1,2,3], ZHU Weidong[3], CHARALA-MBIDES Panos G[3], SHAO Yimin[1,*],
XU Yongfeng[3], WU Kai[3], and XIAO Huifang[4]

1 *State Key Laboratory of Mechanical Transmission, Chongqing University, Chongqing* 400030, *China*

2 *College of Mechanical Engineering, Chongqing University, Chongqing* 400030, *China*

3 *Department of Mechanical Engineering, University of Maryland Baltimore County, Baltimore, MD* 21250, *USA*

4 *National Engineering Research Center of Flat Rolling Equipment, University of Science and*

Technology Beijing, Beijing 100083, China

【8】

RONG Hui[1,2], QIAN ChunXiang[1,2]* & WANG RuiXing[1,2]

[1] *School of Materials Science and Engineering, Southeast University, Nanjing 211189, China;*
[2] *Jiangsu Key Laboratory of Construction Material, Nanjing 211189, China*

【9】

Lixin WANG, Youguang GUO, Qi ZHANG, Ting YUE*

School of Aeronautic Science and Engineering, Beihang University, Beijing 100191, China

以上三例摘自中国英文期刊，与前面那些例子在格式上有明显差异，请读者自行体会。

3.1.2 人名惯用写法

人名的国际惯用形式是"名在前，姓在后"，即"first name（首名），middle name（中间名），last name（姓）"。中间名多写成缩写形式（一个或几个首字母加或不加缩写点），也可以写成全写，较多的人名无中间名，有时也会见到首名写成字母而中间名全写的情况。例如：Addison V. Wright, Benjamin P. Kleinstiver, Pedro A. B. Reis, Shao-shan Carol Huang, Joanne Chory, Junji Nakamura, J. Keith Joung, Sheng-Cai Lin, Juliette D Godin, Alexander FG Goldberg, Adi Schejter Bar-Noam, Mark-Alexander Henn 等。人名相当复杂，不太可能有统一的书写规格。

中间名之所以不用全写而用首字母，是为了便于计算机检索和文献引用对作者姓和名的识别，如 Robert Smith Jones 的形式可能会导致难以区分其中的姓是 Jones 还是 Robert Smith，但若用 Robert S. Jones，则很容易就将 Jones 定格为姓，使姓和名的区分简单方便。

为减少因人名相同而导致文献识别方面的混乱，部分期刊（如一些医学类期刊）要求作者将其学位放在其姓名的前或后面，甚至将作者职衔列于其姓名和学位之后（或在论文首页的脚注中说明）。例如：Dr. Joseph Kipnis-Psychiatrist, Dr. Eli Lowitz-Proctologist 等。

汉语人名一般有汉语拼音和韦氏拼音（Wade-Giles System）两种表达方式，后者在我国港澳台地区仍较为普遍使用。引用汉语人名时，要注意区分这两种不同的拼音系统，对用韦氏拼音书写的人名不得强行改用汉语拼音方式，如果对 1950 年以前去世的或姓名以旧式注音而著称的人采用以汉语拼音书写的姓名时，则需用括号附上以韦氏拼音书写的姓名。

按韦氏拼音，姓的首字母大写，双名间用连字符。例如：Chiapyng Lee（李嘉平），Chen Ning Yang（杨振宁），Huang Tso-lin（Huang Zuolin，黄佐林），Tsung-Dao Lee（李政道）等。

按国家标准 GB/T 16159—2012《汉语拼音正词法基本规则》，汉语人名译为英文人名时，应遵守以下规则：姓和名分写，姓在前，名在后；复姓连写，双姓中间加连接号；姓和名的首字母分别大写；笔名、别名等按姓名写法处理。例如：Zhang Xia（张霞），Ning Ruxin（宁汝新），Xi Bojifu（西伯吉父）；Dongfang Shuo（东方朔），Zhuge Kongming（诸葛孔明），Zhang-Wang Shufang（张王淑芳）；Lu Xun（鲁迅），Zhang San（张三），Wang Mazi（王麻子）。

韦氏、汉语拼音人名采用中国式"姓在前，名在后"的形式，与"名在前，姓在后"的国际惯用形式正好相反。那么拼音姓名究竟该用哪种形式呢？对这个问题其实没有必要纠结太多，只要遵循目标期刊的要求即可。不同期刊对人名写法有差异，国外期刊多是"名在前，姓在后"，而中国期刊五花八门，各种形式的都有，而且不少期刊的编辑非常认真，常为这一问题烦恼，但一般不会有什么理想的结果。有人认为，中国人名"姓在前，名在后"天经地义，没有任何理由去变更；而也有人认为，英文期刊是面向全球国际大家庭的，是给老外看的，而且中国英文期刊也刊登老外的论文，人名的写法当然要纳入到国际背景和体系中来。

每一期刊都有其相对统一的人名形式，不同期刊的人名形式有差异，就以"梁福军"的拼音姓名为例，其写法就不尽相同（表3-1）。作者应根据目标期刊的要求来书写人名。

表3-1 不同期刊的论文人名（作者姓名）形式[①]

	期刊名称	人名（作者姓名）形式
国际期刊	*Science*（科学）	Fujun Liang；Fu-Jun Liang；Fu Jun Liang
	Nature（自然）	Fujun Liang；Fu-Jun Liang
	Cell（细胞）	Fujun Liang
	PNAS[②]（美国科学院院刊）	Fujun Liang
	Annals of Botany（植物学报）	FUJUN LIANG
	The Archive of Mechanical Engineering（机械工程档案）	FUJUN LIANG；Fujun LIANG；Fujun Liang
	Learned Publishing（学术出版）	Fujun LIANG
	Journal of Fluids Engineering（ASME）（流体工程学报）	F. J. Liang；Fujun Liang
	Measurement Science and Technology（测量科学与技术）	F J Liang；Fujun Liang
国内期刊	*Cell Research*（细胞研究）	Fujun Liang
	Light | Science & Application（光：科学与应用）	Fujun Liang
	Chinese Medical Journal（中华医学杂志）	LIANG Fu-jun
	Acta Geologica Sinica（地质学报）	LIANG Fujun
	Chinese Journal of Mechanical Engineering（中国机械工程学报）	LIANG Fujun；Fujun Liang；
	Chinese Medical Sciences Journal（中国医学科学杂志）	Fu-jun Liang
	Journal of Computer Science & Tecnology（计算机科学技术学报）	Fu-Jun Liang
	Acta Mathematica Sinica（数学学报）	Fu Jun LIANG
	Acta Metallurgica Sinica（金属学报）	Fujun LIANG
	Journal of Integrative Plant Biology（植物学报）	Fu-Jun Liang
	SCIENCE CHINA Technological sciences（中国科学：技术科学）	LIANG FuJun
国内期刊	*Chinese Journal of Aeronautics*（中国航空学报）	Fujun LIANG；F. LIANG
	Insect Science（昆虫科学）	FU-JUN LIANG
	化学学报（*Acta Chimica Sinica*）（中文刊）	Liang, Fujun

① 此表所列的人名形式是阶段性的，不排除某期刊后期可能发生某种变化，因此仅供参考。
② 该刊的全称是 Proceedings of the National Academy of Sciences of the United States of America.

笔者认为，一本中国英文期刊，如果完全在我国自主的环境和体制下办，那么署名规则由主编、社长来定，选用一种形式即可；但如果在国际的环境和体制下办（如中外合作创刊、办刊，我方负责论文内容，国际出版商负责生产出版），那就按国际的生产要求，遵守其格式体例。笔者曾负责一本英文期刊与 Springer-Nature 合作出版，开始时理直气壮地要求"姓在前，名在后"的人名形式，但对方的一位主管委婉地回复："由于大规模数字化 XML 加工的技术需要，以及网页显示的设计要求，Springer 有一些统一的版式标准，难以做太多的个性化设计！"这就是答案。（外方一般不懂汉语人名和拼音构造规则，对拼音姓名中"姓"和"名"能区分出来，但对二字或多字名中的不同拼音音节就不能区分了，比如对 Fujun Liang（梁福军），国际出版商生产部门常将其改为 F. Liang，如果想得到正确的 F. J. Liang，那么中方提供其的论文中这一姓名就必须为 Fu-Jun Liang 或 Fu-jun Liang 或 Fu Jun Liang。）

我国编辑非常坚持"一致性"，他们觉得对一本纳入国际生产体系的中国英文期刊，如果对中国作者的论文采用"姓在前，名在后"的形式，而对外国作者的论文采用"名在前，姓在后"的形式，那不就不一致了吗？再者，对一篇既有中国作者又有外国作者的合作论文应该采用什么样的人名形式呢？这个问题属于形式问题，形式上的东西无需再争论。

另外，作者应尽量采用其本人相对固定的人名形式，编辑也应尊重其习惯形式，以减少在文献检索和论文引用中被误解、误判的可能性而给作者和期刊带来不必要的损失。

3.1.3 单位名称表达

单位名称相对固定，准确就行，尽量写全称，不要随意省略，简称或缩写宜少用。使用单位简称特别是作者自定义简称（非官方简称），有时会使读者不知所云，造成阅读上的困难，如不要把 Nanjing University of Aeronautics and Astronautics 写为 NUAA 或 Nanhang University。

作者一定要了解单位的官方英文名称，必要时需查证，不可随意自行翻译。例如："机械工业出版社"的官方英文名称是 China Machine Press，不要写为 Mechanical Industrial Publishing House；"科学出版社"是 Science Press，不要写为 Beijing Scientific Publishing House。如果单位还没有官方英文名称，作者应正确翻译，尽可能写出国际通用的名称。有些单位的名称容易写错，如 Tsinghua University，Peking University，Hohai University（河海大学），Soochow University（苏州大学），Shanghai Jiao Tong University，The University of Hong Kong，The Chinese University of Hong Kong 等，写作中应多加注意。另外还要注意导向问题，如 National Taiwan University 应写为 Taiwan University 或 Taiwan University, Taipei, China.

另外，单位英文名称的书写顺序是"由小至大"，与中文名称的"由大至小"正好相反。例如："天津工业大学机械电子工程学院"的英文名称应写为"School of Mechanical and Electric Engineering, Tianjin Polytechnic University"，而不是"Tianjin Polytechnic University, School of Mechanical and Electric Engineering"。但在书写"……大学……教育部重点实验室"之类的英文名称时，不宜将"教育部"置于"大学"的后面，这是因为"教育部重点实验室"是一个整体，不应分开写，如"大连理工大学精密与特种加工教育部重点实验室"的英文名称应该是"Key Laboratory of Precision & Non-traditional Machining of Ministry of Education, Dalian University of Technology"，

而不宜写成"Key Laboratory of Precision & Non-traditional Machining, Dalian University of Technology, Ministry of Education"。

3.1.4 署名细节表达

以上介绍了作者署名的一般情况，实际写作中，作者署名的情况千差万别，各种情况都可能会出现，写作时应灵活，多注重细节的规范表达。下面介绍几种署名细节情况。

1）明确标注通信作者（只有一位作者或第一作者就是通信作者时，也需标注；通信作者可以有多位，有几位就标注几位），并给出其联系方式，如邮箱、电话和网址等。多以星号、脚注的形式标注通信作者。3.1.1 节中已给出一些例子，再如：

【1】

Tatsuya Hirano[1, *]

[1] Chromosome Dynamics Laboratory, RIKEN, 2-1 Hirosawa, Wako, Saitama 351-0198, Japan

[*] Correspondence：hiranot@riken.jp

http：//dx.doi.org/10.1016/j.cell.2016.01.033

【2】

David Silver[1*], Aja Huang[1*], Chris J. Maddison[1], Arthur Guez[1], Laurent Sifre[1], Georgevan den Driessche[1], Julian Schrittwieser[1], Ioannis Antonoglou[1], Veda Panneershelvam[1], Marc Lanctot[1], Sander Dieleman[1], Dominik Grewe[1], John Nham[2], Nal Kalchbrenner[1], Ilya Sutskever[2], Timothy Lillicrap[1], Madeleine Leach[1], Koray Kavukcuoglu[1], Thore Graepel[1] & Demis Hassabis[1]
……

---

[1] Google DeepMind, 5 New Street Square, London EC4A 3TW, UK. [2] Google, 1600 Amphitheatre Parkway, Mountain View, California 94043, USA.

[*] These authors contributed equally to this work.

【3】

Donghui Guo,[1] **Riku Shibuya,**[2] **Chisato Akiba,**[2] **Shunsuke Saji,**[2] **Takahiro Kondo,**[1, *] **Junji Nakamura**[1 *]
……

---

1 Faculty of Pure and Applied Sciences, University of Tsukuba, 1-1-1 Tennodai, Tsukuba, Ibaraki 305-8573, Japan.

2 Graduate School of Pure and Applied Sciences, University of Tsukuba, 1-1-1 Tennodai, Tsukuba, Ibaraki 305-8573, Japan.

[*] Corresponding author. E-mail：takahiro@ims.tsukuba.ac.jp（T.K.）；nakamura@ims.tsukuba.ac.jp（J.N.）

例【1】只有一位作者，当然也是通信作者，只有一个作者序号，通信作者注释信息另行紧随作者单位；【2】有 20 位作者，前两位为给予特别注释的作者（*These authors contributed equally to this work.），而不是通信作者（通信作者的信息放在了文后的作者信息中），有两个作者序号，通信作者注释信息放在了首页的最下方；【3】有 6 位作者，最后两位为通信作者，有两个作者序号，通信作者注释信息以脚注的形式放在了首页的左下方。

有的期刊对通信作者的注释采用致谢的形式。例如：

【4】
* Corresponding author, To whom correspondence should be addressed

【5】
* The person to whom inquiries regarding the paper should be addressed

2) 一位作者需要署名几个单位或需要体现其兼职单位（包括客座研究单位）时，通常应依次写出这些不同的单位，并标识不同的作者序号，如 3.1.1 节中的示例【1】~【3】（其中标有多个作者序号的作者）；但对有某种关系或地址相同的单位，可合并写成一个单位的形式，只标识一个作者序号。例如：

【6】
Molecular Pathology Unit, Center for Cancer Research, and Center for Computational and Integrative Biology, Massachusetts General Hospital, Charlestown, Massachusetts 02129, USA.

【7】
Department of Stem Cell and Regenerative Biology, Harvard University, and Harvard Stem Cell Institute, Cambridge, MA 02138, USA.

例【6】给出一位作者的三个平级单位（Molecular Pathology Unit；Center for Cancer Research；Center for Computational and Integrative Biology），均为同一上级单位（Massachusetts General Hospital）的下级单位；【7】给出一位作者的两个平级单位（Harvard University；Harvard Stem Cell Institute），这两个单位的地址相同，或许也有某种关系。

3) 除写出单位名称外，还要写出单位的附加信息，如所在国家、地区、城市、城区、街道以及有关的牌号、编号、邮政编码等。附加信息的项目可多可少，不一定全面、详细，取决于单位地址特点、目标期刊要求以及作者写作风格等因素。例如：

【8】
Biognosys AG, 8952 Schlieren, Switzerland

【9】
Department of Chemical and Biomolecular Engineering, Hong Kong University of Science and Technology, Clear Water Bay, Hong Kong, China

【10】
Umeå Plant Science Centre, Department of Forest Genetics and Plant Physiology, Swedish University of Agricultural Sciences, SE-90183 Umeå, Sweden

例【8】所列单位的项目很少，形式上很短；【9】、【10】相对多一些，长一些。

4) 几位作者有相同的单位（如大学、研究院所、科学院、工程院），只是部门不同（如学院/系、研究所、实验室、研究中心等）时，为了书写简化，可以将这些单位合并来写，即将各部门依次并列写出，并分别标识不同的作者序号，再将其共同的上级单位紧接着放在这些部门的后面。例如：

【11】
[a]Department of Neurology, [b]Department of Biochemistry and [c]Hypertension Unit, Soroka University Hospital, Beer-Sheva, Israel

【12】
[1]Center for Genome Sciences and Systems Biology

²Center for Gut Microbiome and Nutrition Research
³Division of Comparative Medicine
Washington University School of Medicine, St. Louis, MO 63110, USA

例【11】将三位作者的部门单位（Department of Neurology；Department of Biochemistry；Hypertension Unit）并列依次写出，并分别标识作者序号 a、b、c，再在后面写出这三个单位的共同上级单位（Soroka University Hospital）；【12】将三位作者的部门单位（Center for Genome Sciences and Systems Biology；Center for Gut Microbiome and Nutrition Research；Division of Comparative Medicine）并列依次另行写出，并分别标识作者序号 1、2、3，再在后面另行写出这三个单位的共同上级单位（Washington University School of Medicine）。

5）论文发表前某作者调到了一个新单位而又想变更时，应该在来得及的情况下及时进行变更，或在论文首页的脚注中（或其他位置）补写这个新单位，以方便读者了解作者的新单位及检索系统统计该单位的论文产出情况。

3.2 摘要

摘要（Abstract，Summary）又称文摘、概要或内容提要，是以提供文献内容梗概为目的，不加评论和补充解释，简明、确切地记述文献重要内容的短文。摘要是论文正文的浓缩，能充分反映研究的主要内容及创新点，通过它不阅读全文就能够获得必要的信息，判断论文的价值取向。摘要往往是论文中继题名之后最先呈现的部分（读者对论文的第一印象），是否具有吸引力通常成为读者是否愿意下载进而阅读全文的重要依据。论文的学科专业、研究背景只有作者最了解，也只有作者才能将相关内容讲好写好，因此作者是写好摘要的关键。

摘要有以下基本特点：

1）在内容上，充分总结全文，有与论文同等的主要信息，不超出论文范围；

2）在逻辑上，行文连贯、顺畅和自然，按顺序体现论文中各主体部分的内容；

3）在形式上，有独立性，通常为一段（也可为多段），位于题名下方正文上方；

4）在篇幅上，无固定词数限制，随论文内容和文体而定，但不宜过长或过短；

5）在语言上，有自明性，简洁明了，一般不出现图表、引文、式子及非公知公用的符号、术语、缩略语，可为更加广泛的读者理解；

6）在写作上，格式体例规范，语言简洁精练，蕴含主要内容，用被动态强化信息（如目标、结果）、弱化作者，反之用主动态强化作者、弱化信息。

3.2.1 摘要的作用

摘要是论文的精华部分，某种意义上比论文还重要，因为有可能决定研究成果能否为同行及更广的群体所承认，这是它的重要作用。摘要还有其他作用，大体上有以下几个方面：

1）作为整篇论文的前序，为读者提供研究所要解决的问题、采用的方法、得到的结果和结论以及创新点等方面的简短介绍，让读者尽可能快速地了解论文的主要内容。读者通常先阅读摘要、再判断是否值得花费时间阅读全文，以弥补只阅读题名的不足。现代科技文献信息浩如烟海，摘要担负着介绍论文主要内容和吸引读者的重要任务。

2）作为检索期刊、系统中几乎独立的短文，是检索的重点内容，在其全文还没有被查阅的情况下就可以被参考，可为科技文献检索数据库的建设、运营提供方便。网上查询、检索和下载专业文档和数据已成为当前科技信息搜索、查询的重要方式，网上各类全文、摘要数据库不断丰富，越来越显示出现代社会信息交流的水平和发展趋势。

3）作为文献检索的重要工具，发表后就可为检索期刊或各类数据库直接（或稍加修改）使用，减轻二次出版物的编辑工作，避免他人编写摘要可能产生误解、欠缺或错误的不足。摘要质量的高低直接影响论文的检索率和被引频次，质量高会对出版物和论文增加检索和引用机会、吸引读者、扩大影响起着不可忽视的作用。

4）作为国际检索系统收录论文的基本标准，是国际学术交流与合作、科学知识和成果传播的桥梁和媒介。目前国际上各主要检索系统（如SCI、Ei等）的数据库对摘要写作质量的要求很高，摘要的特殊意义和作用更加显现。

5）作为投稿后被首次审查的未发表论文的介绍，是一次出版物的编辑初审、同行评审快速作出决策的重要依据，编辑和专家先看摘要就能较为准确地估计出该文的深度和创造性，进而缩短审稿选稿流程，提高工作效率。

6）摘要还有其他作用，如图书馆、情报部门采购人员通过摘要对期刊或系列出版物的内容形成一个订购意向判断，一些组织或会议的网站、报纸等为其会员提供有关文章的摘要。

摘要的这些作用，均要求它对论文所报道的科研成果有准确而可靠的描述、归纳、提炼和总结。论文发表的最终目的是要被别人参考，如果摘要写得不好，论文被收录、阅读、引用的机会就会减少甚至丧失，可见摘要的作用是多么重要！

3.2.2 摘要内容及结构

摘要本质上是由一篇"大"论文高度浓缩后所形成的"小"短文，其内容与论文主体内容相同，主要包括研究的目的、方法、过程、结果、结论、创新点和其他信息（如局限）。

1）目的是研究工作的前提、目标、任务、意义（重要性、必要性）、领域（范围、主题）。

2）方法是研究施用的方法，如理论、技术、工具、手段、材料、设备、算法、程序等。

3）过程是研究的过程、步骤，如实验、模拟（仿真）等的具体过程、步骤。

4）结果是实验和理论研究的结果、得到的数据、看到的现象、收获的发现，如观测、实验、模拟、计算、公式推导等的数据和结果，以及得到的效果、性能和结论等。

5）结论是通过对结果的分析、比较、评价和应用而提出的问题、观点和理论等，是结果的价值、用途和意义。假设、启发、建议、预测及今后的课题等也可列入此部分。

6）创新点是本研究解决了什么别人没有解决的问题，既可指提出新的观点、理论、学说，也可指发明新的工艺、技术、方法，还可指研发新的产品、设施、装备，等等。

7）其他信息是有某种重要信息价值的内容，如研究的局限，下一步工作的方向或建议。

摘要类型不同，对以上要素侧重不同，如报道性摘要可以不写、少写或简写要素3）；而指示性摘要侧重要素3），其他要素相对少、简单或没有。

摘要的各项内容是按一定的逻辑顺序来组织排列的。一般来讲，摘要由开头的问题陈述、中间的研究内容和结尾的创新点组成，而中间的研究内容包括研究的方法和过程、结果和结论。这样摘要大体上有以下结构：

1) 开头陈述问题，简明扼要地指出当前相关研究的不足，引出问题，交待研究的目的（原因）和范围，有时还可指出或暗示研究的特点、结果和意义。

2) 然后描述方法、过程，对实验型论文，叙述用何方法经过何过程来进行研究，涉及方案、方法、技术、原理、程序、操作、步骤及数据、计算精度等，或对非实验型论文，描述写作文献资料的来源及对文献资料的处理方法。

3) 接着给出结果、结论，展现或陈述获得的研究结果以及通过对结果进行分析、讨论和综合而得到的结论，明确指出所提问题是否得到解决或改进。注意区分事实和推测，有多个发现时，应首先考虑新的和经过验证的事件、与以前理论不相符或与实际问题相关的发现。

4) 结尾交待创新点，从论文或作者的角度用一句话点明本文的最高价值。

因学科特点及对摘要各部分突显程度的不同，以上内容要素在摘要里的权重或详略程度会有所不同。例如：问题陈述时，为突显问题解决的紧迫性或重要性，可适当多描述问题陈述部分；若所提问题较为普遍，就应一笔带过、简单交待，甚至不交待。描述研究方法时，若旨在凸显方法的创新性，就应着重笔墨，详写方法及有关过程；若方法（如某种技术、工艺、算法）较为成熟，就可简写方法而不写过程。

下面给出实例摘要，从内容的角度给予分析、归类，帮助读者对摘要内容和结构的理解。

【1】

The game of Go has long been viewed as the most challenging of classic games for artificial intelligence owing to its enormous search space and the difficulty of evaluating board positions and moves. Here we introduce a new approach to computer Go that uses 'value networks' to evaluate board positions and 'policy networks' to select moves. These deep neural networks are trained by a novel combination of supervised learning from human expert games, and reinforcement learning from games of self-play. Without any lookahead search, the neural networks play Go at the level of state-of-the-art Monte Carlo tree search programs that simulate thousands of random games of self-play. We also introduce a new search algorithm that combines Monte Carlo simulation with value and policy networks. Using this search algorithm, our program AlphaGo achieved a 99.8% winning rate against other Go programs, and defeated the human European Go champion by 5 games to 0. This is the first time that a computer program has defeated a human professional player in the full-sized game of Go, a feat previously thought to be at least a decade away.

(Mastering the game of Go with deep neural networks and tree search. Nature, Vol 529, 28 January 2016)

例【1】是 Nature 的一篇原创论文的摘要。

第一句交待研究领域、范围：围棋一直是人工智能领域最具挑战性的经典游戏。

第二句提出研究目的和方法：提出一种评估棋局位置和选择落子的新方法——基于价值网络、策略网络。

第三句进一步阐释方法：对围棋高手下过的棋局进行监督学习，对自我对局的棋局进行强化学习，将二者结合起来训练这些深度神经网络（即价值、策略网络）。

第四句陈述使用上述方法的结果，说明方法的先进性：不用任何前向搜索，深度神经网络通过模拟成千上万的随机自我对局，可以达到最先进的蒙特卡洛树搜索程序的水准。

第五句提出另一研究目的和方法：提出一种新的搜索算法，即将蒙特卡罗模拟与价值、策略网络相结合。

第六句陈述使用这一新算法的结果：开发出的围棋比赛程序 AlphaGo 相对其他程序的获胜率达 99.8%，并以 5:0 击败了欧洲围棋冠军。

第七句点出创新点：首次实现了围棋比

赛中计算机程序击败人类职业选手，是一种比常规至少提前 10 年实现的壮举。

【2】

Classically, G protein-coupled receptor (GPCR) stimulation promotes G protein signaling at the plasma membrane, followed by rapid β-arrestin-mediated desensitization and receptor internalization into endosomes. However, it has been demonstrated that some GPCRs activate G proteins from within internalized cellular compartments, resulting in sustained signaling. We have used a variety of biochemical, biophysical, and cell-based methods to demonstrate the existence, functionality, and architecture of internalized receptor complexes composed of a single GPCR, β-arrestin, and G protein. These super-complexes or "megaplexes" more readily form at receptors that interact strongly with β-arrestins via a C-terminal tail containing clusters of serine/threonine phosphorylation sites. Single-particle electron microscopy analysis of negative-stained purified megaplexes reveals that a single receptor simultaneously binds through its core region with G protein and through its phosphorylated C-terminal tail with β-arrestin. The formation of such megaplexes provides a potential physical basis for the newly appreciated sustained G protein signaling from internalized GPCRs.

(GPCR-G Protein-β-Arrestin Super-Complex Mediates Sustained G Protein Signaling. Cell 166, 1–13, August 11, 2016)

例【2】是 Cell 的一篇原创论文的摘要。

第一句交待了研究领域、范围：GPCR 促进了质膜上的 G 蛋白信号，伴随着快速的 β 抑制蛋白介导的脱敏和受体内化进入核内体。

第二句指出存在的问题，暗含研究目的：GPCR 从内化的细胞区室激活 G 蛋白，导致持续的信号传导。

第三句陈述研究方法：用多种生物化学、生物物理和基于细胞的方法来证明内部受体复合物的存在、功能及结构，这些复合物由单一 GPCR、β 抑制蛋白和 G 蛋白组成。

第四句描述看到的现象，属研究结果：超级复合物或巨细胞更容易在受体中形成，受体通过一个包含大量丝氨酸/苏氨酸磷酸化位点的 C 末端尾巴与 β 抑制蛋白相互作用。

第五句交待实验观察及分析结果：用单粒子电子显微镜对负染色纯化巨细胞的分析表明，单一受体同时通过其核心区域与 G 蛋白结合，并通过磷酸化的 C 末端尾巴与 β 抑制蛋白结合。

第六句总结研究结果的重要性，点出了创新点：巨细胞的形成能为新认识的、来自内化 GPCRs 的持续 G 蛋白信号提供潜在的物理基础。

另外，文体不同，摘要的内容要素侧重也不相同。比如综述，其摘要一般不会写研究方法，更多的是较为详细的研究领域、主题的背景信息，重在交待进行综述的意义，如果能写明目前缺少相关综述研究，而行业、领域发展又需要此类研究来引领，那么就更理想了；中间部分还可以写综述的思路、过程及结果、结论，也可以不写；结尾用一句话陈述，总结或点明创新点，即本文主要提出了什么指导性的理论、借鉴或观点，填补了行业、领域或某研究点目前缺少相关综述来引领的空白。例如：

【3】

Human activity is leaving a pervasive and persistent signature on Earth. Vigorous debate continues about whether this warrants recognition as a new geologic time unit known as the Anthropocene. We review anthropogenic markers of functional changes in the Earth system through the stratigraphic record. The appearance of manufactured materials in sediments, including aluminum, plastics, and concrete, coincides with global spikes in fallout radionuclides and particulates from fossil fuel combustion. Carbon, nitrogen, and phosphorus cycles have been substantially modified over the past century. Rates of sea-level rise and the extent of human perturbation of the climate system exceed Late Holocene changes. Biotic changes include species invasions worldwide and accelerating rates of extinction. These combined signals render the Anthropocene stratigraphically distinct from the Holocene and earlier epochs.

(The Anthropocene is functionally and stratigraphically distinct from the Holocene. *Science*, Vol 351, Issue 6269, 8 January 2016)

例【3】是 *Science* 的一篇综述的摘要。

第一、二句交待研究领域、主题：人类活动在地球上留下了普遍而持久的印记，关于这是否可以表明所称作的人类纪是一个新的地质时期的激烈争论一直存在。

第三句指出研究目的（本文工作）：通过地层记录回顾地球系统功能变化的人类起源标记。

第四至七句阐述结果，给出由回顾得出的结论性认识：包括铝、塑料和混凝土在内的沉积物中制造材料的出现，与化石燃料燃烧产生的放射性核素和微粒的全球峰值相吻合；在过去一个世纪里，碳、氮和磷的循环发生了很大改变；海平面上升的速率和人类对气候系统的干扰程度超过了全新世晚期的变化；生物变化包括世界范围的物种入侵和加速灭绝的速度。

第八句进行总结，给出总结性结论：以上各种信息结合起来使人类纪的地层学与全新世和更早期的截然不同。

3.2.3 摘要的类型

按文体内容侧重和写作要求的不同，摘要大体分为报道性、指示性和复合性三类。

3.2.3.1 报道性摘要

报道性摘要（informative abstract）也称信息、资料性摘要，能较为全面而又简要地反映研究目的、对象、范围、方法、过程、条件、性质、结果和结论等，提供较多的定性和定量信息，充分反映创新点。报道性摘要相当于简介，不但包含研究目的和（或）方法，还提供研究结果、结论甚至建议；不但包括论文的基本思想和主要论点，还应包括基本事实和主要论据，通常可部分取代阅读全文。这种摘要涵盖论文的实质内容，能独立存在，只要注明出处，就可供直接使用，实用价值高。原创论文若缺少创新内容以及经得起检验的独特方法或结论，是不大可能引起读者的兴趣的，这类论文和各种专题研究报告常优先使用这种摘要，篇幅相对长一些。

报道性摘要又分为传统型（或非结构式）和结构式两类，包含以下基本内容要素：①主题（main topic）；②目的（purpose）；③方法（methods）；④材料（materials）；⑤结果（results）；⑥结论（conclusions）。

（1）传统型摘要（非结构式摘要）

传统型摘要中，上述要素以一定逻辑关系连续写出，不分段落或以明显标识相区分。比较而言，这种摘要的段落不够分明，给审稿、编辑、阅读及计算机检索带来一些不便。结构式摘要中，上述要素分段或以相关标识词加以区分，段落清晰、明了，便于审稿、编辑、阅读及计算机检索。3.2.2 节中的摘要【1】～【3】属传统型摘要，下面再举几个例子。

【1】

Schizophrenia is a heritable brain illness with unknown pathogenic mechanisms. Schizophrenia's strongest genetic association at a population level involves variation in the major histocompatibility complex (MHC) locus, but the genes and molecular mechanisms accounting for this have been challenging to identify. Here we show that this association arises in part from many structurally diverse alleles of the complement component 4 (*C4*) genes. We found that these alleles generated widely varying levels of *C4A* and *C4B* expression in the brain, with each common *C4* allele associating with schizophrenia in proportion to its tendency to generate greater expression of *C4A*. Human *C4* protein localized to neuronal synapses, dendrites, axons, and cell bodies. In mice, *C4* mediated synapse elimination during postnatal development. These results implicate excessive complement activity in the development of schizophrenia and may help explain the reduced numbers of synapses in the brains of individuals with schizophrenia.

(Schizophrenia risk from complex variation of complement component 4. *Nature*, January 2016. doi: 10.1038/nature16549.)

例【1】是 *Nature* 的一篇原创论文的摘要，共有七句。第一、二句交待研究领域（精神分裂症）、范围（遗传性大脑疾病）与目的（从基因和分子机制的角度来解释精神分裂症的发病机理）。第三至六句交待研究的发现，即结果（精神分裂症与 *C4* 中结构多样化的等位基因及其 *C4A* 表达密切相关；人的 *C4* 蛋白质定位于神经突触、树突、轴突和细胞体中；老鼠的 *C4* 在其出生后的发育过程中调节了突触消除）。第七句对以上结果进行总结，得出结论（精神分裂症在发展过程中存在过量的补充活动），并点出创新点（研究结果解释了精神分裂症患者大脑中突触数量减少的原因）。

【2】

To investigate the control of morphing wings by means of interacting effectors, this article proposes a distributed coordinated control scheme with sampled communication on ths basis of a simple morphing wing model, established with arrayed agents. The control scheme can change the shape of airfoil into an expected one and keep it smooth during morphing. As the interconnection of communication network and the agents would make the behavior of the morphing wing system complicated, a diagrammatic stability analysis method is put forward to ensure the system stability. Two simulations are carried out on the morphing wing system by using MATLAB. The results stand witness to the feasibility of the distributed coordinated control scheme and the effectiveness of the diagrammatic stability analysis method.

摘要【2】共有五句。第一句提出研究目的（提出基于简单变形翼模型的拥有采样通信的分布式协调控制方案）和方法（简单变形翼模型、排列代理）。第二句交待研究结果（用以上控制方案能改变机翼的形状，变形过程中保持平滑）。第三句提出另一研究目的（提出能保证系统稳定性的图解稳定分析方法）。第四句交待研究方法（用 MATLAB 对变形翼系统进行仿真）。第五句交待仿真结果（所提分布式协调控制方案和图解稳定性分析方法是有效性的）。

【3】

Corporal punishment has been the focus of considerable study over the past decade. Some recent research suggesting that the use of corporal punishment may have significant long-term negative effects on children has prompted increasing exploration and interest in the issue. We used tobit regression analysis and data from the 2000 National Longitudinal Survey of Youth to examine both the prevalence and the chronicity of spanking in a nationally representative sample of parents. Mother's characteristics (e. g., age, education) and neighborhood context did not show a relationship with parental use of corporal punishment. Among parents who used corporal punishment, being Protestant had a relatively large relationship with its use. Although children's externalizing behaviors had some association with parent's propensity to spank, findings suggest that use of corporal punishment may be better understood as part of a constellation of behaviors relating to a parenting style. Further, findings indicate that it is easier to predict the incidence of corporal punishment than to predict its frequency of use.

摘要【3】共有七句。前两句点交待研究领域（体罚）、主题（体罚的负面影响）、现状（研究较多）。第三句交待研究方法（采用 2000 年全国青少年纵向调查的 tobit 回归分析和数据，对全国代表性的父母样本进行调查）和目的（调查体罚的普遍性和长期性）。第四至七句陈述调查和研究结果（母亲、邻里关系与体罚不相关；新教徒与使用体罚很相关；体罚与家教方式有关；体罚的发生率比使用率更易预测)。

【4】

Since the emergence of Zika virus (ZIKV), reports of microcephaly have increased considerably in Brazil; however, causality between the viral epidemic and malformations in fetal brains needs further confirmation. We examined the effects of ZIKV infection in human neural stem cells growing as neurospheres and brain organoids. Using immunocytochemistry and electron microscopy, we showed that ZIKV targets human brain cells, reducing their viability and growth as neurospheres and brain organoids. These results suggest that ZIKV abrogates neurogenesis during human brain development.

(Zika virus impairs growth in human neurospheres and brain organoids. *Science*, Vol 352, Issue 6287, 13 May 2016)

例【4】是 *Science* 的一篇报告类论文的摘要,共有四句。首句的第一分句,指出生物学领域的一种现象(巴西出现了越来越多的小头症,可能与 ZIKV 有关);第二分句交待主题,提出问题(需要研究病毒流行与胎儿大脑畸形之间的关系)。第二句给出研究目的(ZIKV 感染在人类神经干细胞和脑细胞类中生长的影响)。第三句交待研究方法(利用免疫细胞化学和电子显微镜),并给出研究结果(ZIKV 在人类大脑细胞中的生长特点)。最后一句给出全局性结论(ZIKV 在人类大脑发育中废除了神经发生)。

(2) 结构式摘要

按包含内容要素的多少,结构式摘要可分为全结构式和半结构式两类。

全结构式摘要包含全部应有的要素。1974 年,加拿大 McMaster 大学医学中心的 R. Brian Haynes 博士首先提出建立临床研究论文的结构式摘要,在 Edward J. Huth 博士的倡导下,美国 *Annuals of Internal Medicine*(《内科学记事》)在国际上率先采用了这种摘要。Haynes 提出的全结构式摘要包含以下八个要素:①目的(objective)——说明要解决的问题;②设计(design)——说明研究的基本设计,包括研究性质;③地点(setting)——说明研究的地点和研究机构的等级;④对象(patients, participants, subjects)——说明参加并完成研究的患者或受试者的性质、数量及挑选方法;⑤处理(interventions)——说明确切的治疗或处理方法;⑥主要测定项目(main outcome measures)——说明为评定研究结果而进行的主要测定项目;⑦结果(results)——说明主要的客观结果;⑧结论(conclusions)——说明主要的结论,包括直接临床应用意义。

全结构式摘要的观点更明确,信息更多,差错更少,同时也更符合数据库的建设和使用要求,但缺点也是明显的,即烦琐、重复、篇幅过长,而且并非所有研究内容都能按以上八个要素来分类。于是,更多的科技期刊扬长避短,采用半结构式摘要。

半结构式摘要也称四要素摘要,包括目的(objective、purpose、aim)、方法(methods)、结果(results)和结论(conclusions),示例如下。

【5】

Objective To investigate the prevalence of nutritional risks, undernutrition, overweight/obesity, and nutritional support in major hospitals in Beijing. **Methods** Adult patients in 6 departments from 3 major hospitals in Beijing were consecutively enrolled from March 2005 to April 2006. Patients with Nutritional Risk Screening 2002 (NRS2002) score ≥ 3 were defined as under nutritional risk. Patients with body mass index (BMI) < 18.5 kg/m^2 were defined as undernutrition. NRS2002 was performed on first morning and nutritional support evaluation on the 14th day of admission or on the discharge day. The relationship between nutritional risk and nutritional support was analyzed. **Results** A total of 1 127 patients were enrolled, and 971 patients (86.2%) underwent NRS2002. Overall prevalence of undernutrition was 8.5% and nutritional risk was

22.9%. If the patients without accurate BMI were excluded from analysis, the prevalence of undernutrition was 7.6% and nutritional risk was 20.1%. Totally 93 patients (36.0%) receiving nutritional support had a NRS2002 ≥ 3. And 122 patients (14.0%) receiving nutritional support when NRS2002 < 3. The average PN：EN ratio was 5.6：1. **Conclusions** A large propotion of inpatients were at nutritional risk or undernutrition in major hospitals in Beijing. The application of PN and EN is inappropriate in these hospitals. Evidence-based guideline is needed to improve this situation.

【6】

Background and aims Mycorrhizal fungi play a vital role in providing a carbon subsidy to support the germination and establishment of orchids from tiny seeds, but their roles in adult orchids have not been adequately characterized. Recent evidence that carbon is supplied by *Goodyera repens* to its fungal partner in return for nitrogen has established the mutualistic nature of the symbiosis in this orchid. In this paper the role of the fungus in the capture and transfer of inorganic phosphorus (P) to the orchid is unequivocally demonstrated for thr first time.
Methods Mycorrhiza-mediated uptake of phosphorus in *G. repens* was investigated using spatially separated, two-dimensional agar-based microcosms.
Results External mycelium growing from this green orchid is shown to be effective in assimilating and transporting the radiotracer ^{33}P orthophosphate into the plant. After 7 d of exposure, over 10% of the P supplied was transported over a diffusion barrier by the fungus and to the plants, more than half of this to the shoots.
Conclusions *Goodyera repens* can obtain significant amounts of P from its mycorrhizal partner. These results provide further support for the view that mycorrhizal associations in some adult green orchids are mutualistic.

摘要【5】、【6】均包含四个要素，分别是目标（Objective/Background and aims）、方法（Methods）、结果（Results）、结论（Conclusions），未达到包含全要素，属于半结构式摘要。

目前不少科技期刊已从原来的非结构式摘要转为半结构式摘要，写文章采用何种摘要形式需要根据文体和目标期刊的要求而定，不可强行统一。

3.2.3.2 指示性摘要

指示性摘要（indicative abstract）也称说明性摘要、描述性摘要或论点摘要，一般用两三句话概括论文的领域和（或）主题、对象，而不涉及论据和结论，多用于综述、观点（视角）、研究简报和图书介绍等。此类摘要不要求一定包含研究目的和方法，此外，研究结果、结论和建议也是不要求提供的，篇幅通常较短。它重在罗列作者研究工作的过程即做了什么，而无具体的实质信息即没有交待做出了什么，因此仅起指导阅读的作用，读者不能从中直接获取所需事实，而只有阅读全文才能了解论文的主要内容，得知具体的方法、结果和结论。它可用于帮助潜在的读者来决定是否有必要阅读全文，适用于重在讲述工作过程、无创新或创新少的论文。下面列举指示性摘要的几个例子。

【7】

Three years ago, scientists reported that CRISPR technology can enable precise and efficient genome editing in living eukaryotic cells. Since then, the method has taken the scientific community by storm, with thousands of labs using it for applications from biomedicine to agriculture. Yet, the preceding 20-year journey—the discovery of a strange microbial repeat sequence; its recognition as an adaptive immune system; its biological characterization; and its repurposing for genome engineering—remains little known. This Perspective aims to fill in this backstory—the history of ideas and the stories of pioneers—and draw lessons about the remarkable ecosystem underlying scientific discovery.

(The Heroes of CRISPR. *Cell* 164, January 14, 2016.)

摘要【7】是一篇生物医学领域视角（Perspective）的摘要，共有四句。前三句陈述研究领域、主题及现状（生物学领域，CRISPR技术的超前性带来了广泛的应用，但与其相关的一些科学现象为人们所不知）。最后一句交待研究目的（填补空白，吸取教训，暗含着对发现CRISPR的前辈们（pioneers）的赞美，与题名CRISPR的英雄们（heroes）相呼应）。

【8】

Condensins are large protein complexes that play a central role in chromosome organization and segregation in the three domains of life. They display highly characteristic, rod-shaped structures with SMC (structural maintenance of chromosomes) ATPases as their core subunits and organize large-scale chromosome structure through active mechanisms. Most eukaryotic species have two distinct condensin complexes whose balanced usage is adapted flexibly to different organisms and cell types. Studies of bacterial condensins provide deep insights into the fundamental mechanisms of chromosome segregation. This Review surveys both conserved features and rich variations of condensin-based chromosome organization and discusses their evolutionary implications.

(Condensin-Based Chromosome Organization from Bacteria to Vertebrates. *Cell* 164, February 25, 2016.)

摘要【8】是一篇生物医学领域综述的摘要，共有五句。前三句陈述生物领域凝缩蛋白的常识，第四句交待对细菌凝缩蛋白研究的作用或意义（为染色体分离的基本机制提供深入见解）。最后一句才指出本文的工作，即对"基于凝缩蛋白的染色体组织的保守特性和丰富的变化"进行综述和讨论，但综述和讨论的结果、结论是什么，并未写出，对未来的展望也未交待，要想知道具体内容，就得阅读全文。可见本摘要属于指示性摘要。

【9】

Recent developments in the methodology of large-eddy simulation applied to turbulent, reacting flows are reviewed, with specific emphasis on mixture-fraction-based approaches to nonpremixed reactions. Some typical results are presented, and the potential use of the methodology in application and the future outlook are discussed.

摘要【9】的三个被动句子的谓语动词，分别指出作者做了什么工作，一是综述（reviewed），二是提出（presented），三是讨论（discussed）。但综述、提出、讨论出了什么，即做出了什么成果，具体结果、结论是什么，丝毫没有交待，因此本摘要是典型的指示性摘要。

有时，指示性摘要的篇幅可以短到只有一句话，相当于论文的题名，只要点出作者所做的核心工作就可以了。

3.2.3.3 复合性摘要

复合性摘要就是指报道-指示性摘要（informative-indicative abstract），以报道性摘要的形式表述论文中价值较高的那部分内容，以指示性摘要的形式表述其余部分，篇幅通常介于报道性摘要和指示性摘要之间。下面给出报道-指示性摘要的几个示例。

【10】

Hydraulic hybrid vehicles with secondary regulation improve fuel economy of vehicles by controlling the engine working at high efficiency zone and recycling the braking energy. Hydrostatic transmission technology with secondary regulation has large power density as well as fully charged and discharged capacity as compared to electric technology. However, the power matching and special control strategies are required to obtain optimal working way of power modules due to its lower energy density. This paper proposes a multi-objective optimization approach for identifying the optimal location of parameters for the key components of hydraulic hybrid vehicles, and designs the hydraulic regenerative braking and energy using strategies for recycling of the braking energy. Research results show that parameters matching of key components and the proposed control strategies can effectively improve system efficiency and fuel economy of vehicles in urban conditions.

摘要【10】共有五句。前两句交待混

合动力汽车采用二次调节静液压传动技术的原理及特点（常识），第三句话锋一转，指出该技术的不足（问题）——需要功率匹配和特殊控制策略来获得功率模块较低能量密度的优化工作方式。这些均属背景内容。第四句使用两个关键谓语动词（proposes 和 designs），陈述本文做了什么工作（成果），但没有交待其具体内容，属指示性摘要的写法。最后一句给出价值较高的结论，点出本文的创新之处（意义），属报道性摘要的写法。

【11】

The aim of the paper is to present the results of investigations conducted on the free surface flow in a Pelton turbine model bucket. Unsteady numerical simulations, based on the two-phase homogeneous model, are performed together with wall pressure measurements and flow visualizations. The results obtained allow defining five distinct zones in the bucket from the flow patterns and the pressure signal shapes. The flow patterns in the buckets are analyzed from the results. An investigation of the momentum transfer between the water particles and the bucket is performed, showing the regions of the bucket surface that contribute the most to the torque. The study is also conducted for the backside of the bucket, evidencing a probable Coanda interaction between the bucket cutout area and the water jet.

摘要【11】共有六句。首句开门见山，交待研究目的（提出调查结果）。第二句陈述第一项工作（进行数值模拟），第三句紧接着给出模拟结果（定义出 5 个不同区域），属报道性摘要的写法。第四句陈述第二项工作（分析桶中的流型），但没有给出分析结果，属指示性摘要的写法。第五句陈述第三项工作（研究水粒与桶间动量转移），第六句陈述第四项工作（研究桶的背面），而且都给出了研究结果，属报道性摘要的写法。

三种摘要大体可这样区别：不仅交待做了什么，还相应地交待做出了什么，属报道性摘要；仅交待做了什么，而没有交待任何做出了什么，属指示性摘要；既交待做了什么，又对其中部分交待做出了什么，属于报道-指示性摘要。一般地，原创论文、大综述、研究报告应选用报道性或报道-指示性摘要，小综述、简报以及创新少或没有创新的论文宜选用指示性摘要。一篇论文价值很高、创新内容很多，若其摘要写成指示性摘要，就可能会减少展现论文学术价值的机会，进而失去较多的读者，希望这点引起广大作者的注意。

3.2.4 摘要的语法

摘要写作涉及很多方面，只有在各个方面都规范了，整个摘要才是高质量的：内容适合、结构恰当、信息准确、文字精练、连贯流畅、逻辑性强、通俗易懂、引人入胜。

3.2.4.1 摘要的时态

摘要的语句常用一般现在时、一般过去时，少用现在完成时、过去完成时，基本不用进行时。描述作者的工作一般用过去时（因为工作是在过去做的），但在陈述由这些工作所得出的结论时宜用现在时。

一般现在时用于说明研究目的、叙述研究方法、描述研究结果、得出研究结论、提出建议或进行讨论等。涉及公认事实、自然规律和永恒真理等时，用一般现在时。例如：In order to study…, …is concluded; As a result, all of paramters satisfy…; The result shows (reveals) …; It is found that…; The conclusions are…; It is suggested that…; The experimental results confirm that…。

一般过去时用于叙述过去某一时刻或时段的发现、某一研究过程，如实验、观测、调查、医疗等的过程。例如：

• The algorithms were developed with Visual C++, and the correctness of these algorithms was verified through examples test.

• The heat pulse technique was applied

to study the stemstaflow（树干液流）of two main deciduous broadleaved tree species in July and August, 1996.

注意：用一般过去时描述的一定范围内的发现、现象往往是尚不能确认为自然规律、永恒真理的，而只是当时的现象、结果等，所描述的研究过程也明显带有过去时间的痕迹。

完成时应尽量少用或不用，但不是不可以用。现在完成时把过去发生的或已发生、已完成的事情与现在联系起来，表示过程的延续性，强调过去发生的某事件（或过程）对现实所产生的影响，而过去完成时表示过去某一时间以前已经完成的事情，或在一个过去的事情完成之前就已完成的另一过去的事情。例如：

- Man has not yet learned to store the solar energy.
- However, subsequent research reports have not been presented.
- The fact is that after the experiments had been repeated like Table 3 for different values of d, we obtained the same conclusion, that the deviation of the value of k is very small.

摘要的语句究竟采用何种时态应视情况而定，应力求表达自然、妥当，大致有以下原则：

1）介绍背景信息时，句子的内容若为不受时间影响的普遍事实，宜用现在时；若是对某种研究趋势的概述，则宜用现在完成时。

2）叙述研究目的或主要研究活动时，若采用"论文导向"，则多用现在时。例如：This paper presents …, This paper investigates …, This paper is to analyzed …。

若采用"研究导向"，则用过去时。例如：This study presented …, This study investigated …, This study was to analyze …。

3）概述实验程序、方法和主要结果时常用现在时。例如：The result shows …, Our results indicate …, We describe …, Extensive experiments show …。

4）叙述结论或建议时可用现在时，也可用臆测动词或 may、should、could 等助动词。

3.2.4.2　摘要的语态

摘要的语句采用何种语态，既要考虑摘要的特点，又要满足表达的需要。摘要较短时，尽量不要随便混用语态，更不宜在一个复句的几个分句里混用不同语态。

科技论文中被动语态的使用在 20 世纪 20 至 70 年代曾经比较流行。现在仍有不少科技期刊强调或要求摘要中的谓语采用被动语态，以减少主观因素，增强客观性。理由是科技论文主要用来说明事实经过，至于事情是谁所为，无须一一证明。例如：

- Energy balance concepts were used to determine the amount of energy lost due to damping in a run-arrest fracture event. Possible sources of damping were identified and experiments were conducted to determine their relative contribution to the overall damping.

现在不少科技期刊的编辑和语言学家，越来越多地主张科技写作（包括摘要）的表达多用主动语态，如 A exceeds B 的表达比 B is exceeded by A 的表达更好。理由是主动语态的表达更为准确、自然，更易阅读、理解，国际名刊如 Nature、Cell 等尤其如此。例如：

- In this Review, we discuss recent advances in understanding the diverse echanisms by which Cas proteins respond to foreign nucleic acids and how these systems have been harnessed for precision genome manipulation in a wide array of organisms.

事实上，指示性摘要中，为强调动作承受者，采用被动语态为好；报道性摘要中，即使有些情况下动作承受者是无关紧要的，也需要用强调的事物做主语，采用被动语态。例如：

● In this case, a greater accuracy in measuring distance might be obtained.

3.2.4.3　摘要的人称

摘要的语句用被动语态时，主语用第三人称；用主动语态时，主语多用第三人称，有时也用第一人称。例如：

● CRISPR-Cas9 nucleases are widely used for genome editing but can induce unwanted off-target mutations.

● This Perspective aims to fill in this backstory—the history of ideas and the stories of pioneers—and draw lessons about the remarkable ecosystem underlying scientific discovery.

● We present models for the analysis of existing star network protocols. We also propose a new access protocol for star networks.

第三人称主语常见的有 This paper、This article、This study、This research、This review、This project、The author(s)、The writer(s)、This project team 等；第一人称主语有 We、Our team（即使论文作者只有一人，也用 We 而不用 I）。

摘要的语句有时可以不用任何人称而直接以动词不定式开头，使表意直截了当。例如：To solve ..., To study ..., To develop ..., To resolve ..., To introduce ..., To describe ..., To investigate ..., To assess ..., To determine ...。

在语义明确时最好不要出现 In this paper、In this research、Here 等状语，这类词是冗词，虽然有了不算错，但去掉后又不影响语义。例如下句中的 In this paper 完全可以去掉：

● In this paper, we have first designed and implemented wide-use algebra on the presentation level.

3.2.4.4　摘要的句式

摘要更追求用词准确、层次清楚，掌握一些特定的表达方式或常用句式很有必要。摘要类型不同，写法也就不同，即使对相同内容的摘要，不同人也有不同的写法，但不论摘要的类型如何，其句式还是有一些规律可以遵循的。摘要各组成部分的内容不同，常用的句式也就不同。

（1）引言部分

1）回顾研究背景的常用句式有：

● We review ...

● We summarize ...

● We present ...

● We describe ...

● This paper outlines ...

2）阐明研究目的的常用句式有：

● We attempt to ...

● For comparison purposes we present ...

● With the aim to ..., we ...

● In addition to ..., this paper aims to ...

● To ..., we ...

● This paper develops a theoretical framework to ...

● This paper presents an approach to ...

● This paper has two main objectives ...

● This research project is devoted to ...

● This paper describes recent ..., aimed at ...

● Our goal has been to develop ...

● The objective (purpose, motivation, etc.) of this paper (report, program, etc.) is ...

● Recent research on ... show that .... A methodology for ... is presented in this paper.

● There are some ... methods for ... at present. However, the effects are unsatisfied.

● This paper (report, thesis, work,

presentation, document, account, etc.) describes (reports, explains, outlines, summarizes, documents, evaluates, surveys, develops, investigates, discusses, focuses on, analyzes, etc.) the results (approach, role, framework, etc.) of ...

3）介绍重点内容或研究范围的常用句式有：

- Here we study ...
- This paper includes ...
- This paper presents ...
- This paper focuses on ...
- This paper synthesizes ...
- The paper lays particular emphasis on ...
- This paper (article, report, etc.) addresses (is concerned with, argues, specifies, covers, etc.) the following questions ...
- The focus of this paper is ...
- The main emphasis of this paper is ...
- We emphasize ...
- We draw attention to the problem ...

（2）方法部分

1）说明研究或实验方法的常用句式有：

- We have developed ...to estimate ...
- This study presents estimates of ...
- We ...to measure ...
- ...to be calculated as ...
- The method of preparation is based on ...

2）介绍研究或实验过程的常用句式有：

- We use ...to investigate ...
- We present an analysis of ...
- We tested ...
- We study ...
- This paper examines how ...
- Numerical experiments indicate also ...
- This paper discusses ...

- This paper considers ...
- ... have been investigated in dryhydrogen sulphide between 25 ℃ and 450 ℃.

3）介绍应用、用途的常用句式有：

- Our program uses ...
- As an application, we ...
- We used ...
- Using ..., we show ...
- We apply ...

（3）结果部分

1）展示研究结果的常用句式有：

- We show ...
- Our results suggest ...
- Recent research has shown ...
- Our results show ...
- The results we obtained demonstrate ...
- We present the results of ...
- We present ...
- It was found that both molecular weight and its distribution affected tensile strength ...
- It has been observed (shown, proved, etc.) that ...
- These experiments indicate (reveal, show, demonstrate, etc.) that ...
- The approach (method, framework, etc.) promises to be very useful for ...
- The (experimental) results show (indicate, suggest, etc.) that ...
- It is shown (concluded, proposed, etc.) that ...

2）介绍结论的常用句式有：

- We introduce ...
- By means of ...we conclude ...
- We give a summary of ...
- This could imply that ...
- These studies are of significance to ...
- These results have direct application to ...
- This strategy appeared to be effective

in …

（4）讨论部分

1）陈述论点和作者认识、观点的常用句式有：

- The results suggest …
- In this study, we describe …
- We report here that …
- We present …
- …important findings that explain mechanisms involved in …
- We expect …

2）阐明论证的常用句式有：

- We showed …
- These results demonstrate …
- Our conclusions are supported by …
- Here we provide evidence from …
- Our studies indicate …
- We find …
- Finally, we demonstrate …
- Here we present records of …
- We clarify how …

3）推荐和建议的常用句式有：

- The authors suggest …
- We suggest …
- The paper suggests …
- We recommend …
- We propose …
- In this paper, …is proposed which …
- I expect that …

目的和范围也常用名词短语前置的句型，把重点内容放在最显著的位置加以强调。例如：

- Procedures for testing atmospheric transport and dispersion models for distances of several hundred to 1 000 km from sources of pollutants are reviewed.
- The first known measurement of the differential cross section for electron capture to the continuum（ECC）from atomic hydrogen is presented.

为使句子平衡而不至于过分头重脚轻，也常使用下列句式：

- New results are presented of studies of the application of inorganic exchangers in the following fields …
- Detailed information is presented about…
- An account is provided of …

3.2.5 摘要的效能

实际中有不少摘要离要求相距甚远：有的摘要虽然很长，但冗余语句较多，效能较低；有的摘要虽很短，但缺少关键内容，冗余语句也不少，效能也不高。因此，提升摘要的效能很具现实意义。所谓效能就是表达效果，涉及语言的各个要素。摘要效能提升的总原则是内容精练、语句简洁，大体上有以下几个方面，这些都是SCI论文摘要的写作要求和目标。

（1）内容精、篇幅短

内容精指摘要内容切题而概括，以有限篇幅陈述较多内容。这样就得区分内容类别，哪些必须写、哪些无须写、哪些可写可不写，对后两类应毫不吝啬地加以舍弃。使摘要内容精减的方法主要有：①背景信息应只包含新情况、新内容且与主题密切相关；②研究成果中应多提炼观点，突出创新内容和技术要点；③摘要内容不能无中生有，在正文中必须出现过，定量、定性信息均要与正文相符；④不引文，但对证实或否定了他人已发表成果的特别文献除外，涉及他人的成果时应明确指出；⑤不对论文作补充和修改，不作诠释和评论，尤其不作自我评价；⑥排除领域知识、常识，少写研究或工作过程，不列举例证；⑦不简单重复题名、前言（除非必要）；⑧除非需要，不用复杂数学式、化学结构式，不用插图、表格。

还要注意：除非事实，摘要中不宜出现

言过其实的表达。例如：
- This paper is complement (improvement, development, validation) of the past research of …
- This paper presents … for the first time.
- This work realizes … for the first time.
- The research similar to this paper has not been found by literaturesearch.
- The similar researches like this paper have not been found by literature search.

篇幅短指摘要用词少而形式短，变短的方法主要有：①多用短句；②不写或少写背景信息；③取消过去研究细节；④不写未来计划；⑤删除多余语句；⑥简化通用词；⑦简化措辞和重复单元；⑧不重复题名，特别是首句不重复题名；⑨不出现图表及对图表、文献的引用。

内容精决定篇幅短，篇幅短呈现内容精，内容精与篇幅短互为因果关系。

（2）表意通俗易懂

摘要表意应通俗易懂、完整清楚，尽量不用标号、记号、代号、特殊字符、图符等难懂的超语言要素以及太专业化的术语，不用文学描述手法，文词要纯朴无华。

提倡使用公知公用的标准的术语和符号、缩略语（简称）、代号等，除了相关专业的读者能清楚理解的以外，在首次出现时应写出其全称。例如：若用缩略语 GERT 代替其全称 graphical evaluation and review technique，则在其首次出现时应表达为 graphical evaluation and review technique (GERT) 或 GERT (graphical evaluation and review technique)，再次出现时才可直接用 GERT。如果首次出现时就直接用了 GERT，恐怕就没有多少人能理解其所指，除非再去论文中查找其全称或通过别的方式来弄懂其意思。

要正确使用量和单位，注意量名称、量符号及单位（包括单位词头）的准确性、大小写、正斜体及字符种类，使表意准确、易懂。

（3）语句简洁至上

摘要语句不宜将整个题名或题名的大部分拿来直接充当关键动词（如 research、study、present、analyze、outline 等）的主语或宾语，避免表达太笼统。例如：若题名是 Step-stress Accelerated Degradation Test Modeling and Statistical Analysis Methods（步进应力加速退化试验建模与统计分析方法），则摘要中就不宜用 <u>Step-stress accelerated degradation test modeling and statistical analysis methods</u> are researched 或 This paper researches <u>step-stress accelerated degradation test modeling and statistical analysis methods</u> 这样的语句，其中画线部分为整个题名。

一些不必要出现的词语有时可以直接省略或通过改变句式来省略。例如：In this paper, It is reported, The author discusses, This paper concerned with, Extensive investigations show 之类的表意通常是明显的，摘要中出现这类词语就是多余的。

尽量简化一些措辞和表意重复的词语。例如：at a temperature of 250 ℃ to 300 ℃ 应改为 at 250 – 300 ℃（temperature 与 ℃ 重复）；at a high pressure of 200 kPa 应改为 at 200 kPa（pressure 与 kPa 重复）；discussed and studied in detail 应直接表示为 discussed 或 studied（discuss、study、in detail 三者都含有仔细、详尽的语义）。

可用动词时尽量避免用动词的名词形式。例如：Thickness of plastic sheets was <u>measured</u> 不写为 <u>Measurement</u> of thickness of plastic sheet was made（measurement 是动词 measure 的名词形式）。

（4）语言妥帖恰当

摘要语句必须正确使用语言文字和标点符号，句子表达应力求简单，语言文字和标点符号成分要搭配，避免用长句（长句容易造成语意不清）；避免单调和重复；避免用长系列形容词或名词来修饰名词，即不要连续使用多个形容词、名词来修饰名词，可用连字符连接名词词组中的名词或使用介词短语形成修饰单元，而将修饰单元置于中心语之后。例如：

• The chlorine containing <u>high melt index propylene based</u> polymer.

此句画线部分由多个词（形容词 high，名词 index 和 propylene 等）组成，一起作 polymer 的修饰语，但连续使用多个名词，太中国化，应改为 The chlorine containing propylene-based polymer of high melt index（含氯高熔融指数丙烯基聚合物）。

严密组织句子，谓语尽量靠近主语，用重要的事实开头，尽量不用辅助从句开头。例如：

• <u>The decolorization</u> in solutions of the pigment in dioxane, which were exposed to 10 h of irradiation, <u>was no longer irreversible</u>.

此句的主语 The decolorization 与谓语 was … irreversible 之间被定语从句 which were … irradiation 分隔，使语义紧密的二者在形式上相距较远，造成表意松散。若改为 When the pigment was dissolved in dioxane, <u>decolorization was irreversible</u> after 10h of irradiation，主语与谓语在形式上紧密相邻，问题就解决了。

此外，还要注意状语的位置。状语（表示时间、方式、条件、原因等）通常置于句末，比置于句首或句中更为妥当。不少作者习惯将状语置于句首，应注意改变这种习惯。例如：

• <u>From data obtained experimentally</u>, power consumption of telephone switching system was determined.

• <u>After CIK transfusion</u>, 6 cases' liver function (ALT and/or BIL) got much better, and the other 6 cases continued normal.

此两句重在表达后面主句的意思，前面画线部分仅为陪衬性的状语成分，不如放在主句后的表达效果好。前一句应改为 Power consumption of telephone switching system was determined from data obtained experimentally，后一句应改为 Six cases' liver function (ALT and/or BIL) got much better, and the other 6 cases continued normal after CIK transfusion.

通常，能用名词作定语的就不要用动名词，能用形容词作定语的不要用名词，即作定语的优先顺序为：形容词→名词→动名词。例如：experimental accuracy 胜过 experiment results，measurement accuracy 胜过 measuring accuracy。

（5）冠词不宜丢失

不要随便省略冠词，尤其是定冠词 the。当定冠词用于表示独一无二的事物、形容词最高级等情况时较为容易掌握，但用于特指时，不小心就易"丢失"。用定冠词时，读者应能确切知道其所指，这是定冠词使用的基本原则。例如：

• <u>The</u> author designed a new machine. <u>The</u> machine is operated with solar energy.

• Molar mass M has long been considered one of <u>the</u> most important factors among various relevant parameters. <u>The</u> parameter Molar mass M was calculated with <u>the</u> following equation.

此两例中的定冠词均不能省略。前一例有两个定冠词，分别加在 author 和 machine 之前，特指"本论文的作者"和"前面提到的那台新设计的机器"。后一例有三个定冠词，第一个用来构成形容词最高级，第二个加在 parameter 前特指"前面提到的参数"，第三个用来构成固定短语 the following equation。

现在固定短语或缩略语使用越来越多，要注意区分其前面的不定冠词是 a 还是 an。例如：an X-ray、an SFC 中的 an 不能写成 a。

（6）单复数不混淆

避免单复数不分。一些名词的单复数形

式不易辨别，不小心就易造成谓语出错。例如：

- The data are shown in Table 2.

此句的 are 不能写为 is（这里 data 是复数形式，其单数形式是 datum，但很少用）。

- Literature does not support the need for removal of all bone and metal fragments.

此句的 Literature does 不能写成 Literatures do（Literature 指文献时是不可数名词，是单数，其复数形式不多用）。

（7）首词数字区分

避免用阿拉伯数字作首词，如果用数字作首词，则用其相应的英文数词。例如：

- Ten algorithms are developed with Visual C++, and the correctness of them is verified through examples test.
- More than 20 mathematical models are built in this test.
- Over 20 mathematical models are built in this test.

前一句的首词 Ten 不写成阿拉伯数字 10，后两句的 More than 20 和 Over 20 不写成 20 more。

（8）使用好关键词

摘要中要多用论文的关键词（主题词），如果用好了能增加论文被搜索出来的概率，从而有助于增加论文的可见度和被引频次。例如：题为 The Heroes of CRISPR 的文章（Cell 164, January 14, 2016），其中一个主题词 CRISPR（Clustered Regularly Interspaced Short Palindromic Repeats 的缩略语）在标题和摘要中都使用了，在正文中出现了 110 多次。

这里再引一个小故事：某作者在 2015 年发表了一篇 SCI 论文 A。论文发表后，发表该文的期刊编辑被告知，有人抱怨论文 A 没有引用论文 B。编辑仔细查看、深入分析后发现，论文 B 的摘要写得不完整，用词不贴近，该用的关键词没有用。由于该作者在研究和写作过程中，根本就没有检索到论文 B，因此就不可能引用论文 B。这个小故事说明，摘要中如果不用、少用合适的关键词，发表后被"淹没"的可能性就增大。

（9）区分英语种类

尽可能使用标准英语，英式、美式均可，但每篇论文应保持一致，不宜两种英语混用。

3.2.6 摘要写作方法

3.2.6.1 摘要写作步骤

摘要写作一般有两种方法，一是从正文中提取主题内容（关键内容、核心内容），二是将题名进行扩展，再按逻辑顺序将各部分内容表述出来，前一种方法较常用。因为研究领域、文体、内容侧重、个人风格、英语水平等的不同，再加上语言之间的差异，摘要写作既需要呈现共性要素，也需要灵活对待个性要素。作者应了解摘要写作的基本思路、步骤，掌握一定的方法、技巧，虽然语言问题可以通过后期的英文润色去解决，但摘要的内容和结构还是需要作者在前期不断推敲。

摘要写作一般分为四个步骤，分别是写前准备、内容规划、语言表述和最后定稿。

（1）写前准备

摘要是正文的浓缩，正文是摘要的母材。摘要写作应在正文写好之后，所谓写好，就是已定稿或基本定稿。正文写好后，论文的内容就固定了，摘要的内容再从中选取而定。如果正文未写好就写摘要，就可能出现日后因正文内容变化而导致重写摘要的情况。

接着再确定论文的文体，文体不同，所需摘要的类别就会不同，进而写法就存在差异，如原创论文、研究报告等的摘要常为报道性摘要；观点（视角）、研究简报等的摘要常为指示性摘要；综述的摘要既可为报道性摘要，也可为指示性摘要；而各种文体的摘要都可写成报道-指示性摘要。摘要类型确定好后，其内容就会进一步明确、精化，但因内容侧重、目标期刊要求及写作风格等要素的不同，同类摘要的内容也会存在差异。

（2）内容规划

摘要类型确定后，就开始规划摘要写作内容了。

1）首先树立文体内容类别主线意识，再顺着这条主线从正文筛选内容，如有出入，例如若主线内容类别不能涵盖论文主题内容，则增加主线内容类别以外的内容，否则若主线内容类别多于论文主题内容，则按论文主题内容类别的范围来写。原创论文的内容类别主线通常是：①目的与范围→②方法与过程→③结果与结论→④创新或独到之处；综述的这个主线通常是：①目的与范围→②结果与结论。

2）通读论文全文，按照主线内容类别在正文中筛选可用作摘要的内容，但不宜将正文所有部分的内容都作为摘要的内容，并作出适当的标记。

① 目的与范围主要交待作者写此文的目的或主要解决的问题，定位读者的视野和注意力。

② 方法与过程重在简述所用的理论、技术、工具、手段、材料、设备、算法或程序等具体方法，重要、特殊的处理方法，以及实现方法的相关过程、步骤，以增加趣味性和可阅读性。

③ 结果与结论呈现客观的研究结果及对结果进行分析所得出的认识性结果、结论。实验、观测、计算等结果是论文最核心、最重要的内容，也是读者最关心、最需了解的资料，筛选时须认真细心地分析比较，选择出最主要、最恰当的，选择得当与否直接影响读者对原文的正确理解，是决定摘要优劣的关键一环。结果太多不能全部选入时，要首先选择那些可信度和价值高的部分，重要或重大的发现、发明，与现有理论相矛盾的结果、结论，或与实际问题密切相关的其他部分。

展现结果与陈述结论要客观真实、有理有据，尽可能显现论文的学术价值和科学意义，体现论文的新颖性和特殊性。同时，要注意不要表现太多，不要留过多悬念，这样有迂腐感，让作者提前产生反感，当然更不要误导读者。

④ 创新或独到之处通常通过对正文的结果和结论部分进行再总结、拔高而得出，通常是总结研究的学术价值和科研意义，点出创新点，还可以提出展望。

以上各部分内容产生后，接着就要考虑其相关性，规划其写作顺序。摘要是一篇完整的短文，其各部分要按逻辑顺序来安排，每句话都要表意明白，句子间应前后连贯、互相呼应。

读者首先是透过摘要对正文有大致了解的，故作者在筛选摘要内容时必须要细心斟酌、好好规划。

（3）语言表述

摘要写作时应重新阅读筛选出的已在原文中做过标记的内容，再对这些内容进行适当的压缩，然后选词造句，用语言叙述出来。最好用英文进行思考，要求作者有扎实的英文基础。

摘要写作应使用恰当的句式、句型，采用一些连接或过渡手法，借助词汇、语法和逻辑等修辞手法，不用空泛、笼统、含混之词，达到语义简明确切、结构严谨严密、过渡顺畅自然、易于阅读理解。谓语动词不宜太多，避免动作行为叠加、主次轻重不分、语句冗长乏味。

通常，作者在写作前、写作中已阅读了相关文献，写作时也可适当模仿部分相似语句。

（4）最后定稿

完成上述步骤，就得到了摘要的初稿，

再对其进行审核性阅读,作质量检查,找出错误、不足或不规范的表达,进行修改而提高。这种检查通常包括:①内容的完整性;②结构的连贯性;③类型的合适性;④语法的正确性;⑤效能的提升性;⑥全局的点题性。

一般来说,原创论文的摘要应包括能回答原文献题名向读者作出许诺的主要结果,以及使读者能正确理解此结果的基本要素,这就是摘要的点题性。

3.2.6.2　各个部分写作

(1) 目的或问题(开头)

摘要开头应明确交代论文的目的或需要解决的问题,简要介绍前人的工作;不谈或少谈背景信息;避免在第一句话重复题目或题目的一部分。开头写法多样,较为普遍的有以下两种:

1) 用陈述目的和范围的主题句开始,定位研究主题(如 This paper describes recent…, aimed at …, 或 In order to …, this paper investigates …, 或 Aming at …, this paper presents …)。

2) 在回顾历史或总结现状的基础上提出问题,引出研究主题(如 There are some … methods for … at present. However, the effects are unsatisfied)。

这两种方法都较为常见:前一种开门见山,直截了当,一下子就切入主题;后一种逻辑性强,丝丝入扣,使读者产生一种只有一口气读完才能找到问题解决方案的冲动或强烈愿望。

(2) 过程与方法(中间前)

过程与方法的阐述起着承前启后的作用。开头交代了要解决的问题,接着自然就要回答如何解决问题,而且后面的结果和结论也往往与过程和方法密切相关。阐述过程与方法,避免泛泛而谈、空洞无物,只作定性描述,使得读者很难清楚了解具体内容。因此,在说明过程与方法时,应结合实验流程、系统框图、边界条件、设备仪器、公式推导以及图表呈现的曲线、数据等内容来进行阐述,给读者一个清晰的思路和一种可信的感觉。

有的摘要没有方法和过程,或将其与目的和范围写在了一起,即合写成一句。

(3) 结果与结论(中间后)

结果与结论代表论文的主要成就和贡献,直接决定着论文的价值以及是否值得被阅读。写作时,应尽量结合实验、仿真或其他结果的图、表和曲线等内容来加以说明,使结果部分客观真实、简洁明了、可信可靠,使结论部分言之有物、有理有据、说服力强;同时,对读者来说,通过图表并结合摘要的介绍,就能比较清楚地了解论文的结果与结论。

(4) 总结语或创新点(结尾)

结尾应给人留下深刻印象,重在点出创新和独到之处,必要时还可与他人最新相关研究进行比较,进一步突出主要贡献及创新、独到之处。结尾的写作方法常用的有以下几种:

1) 对实验型论文,以实验结论结尾,指出实验结果表明了什么(如 The results indicate that …);对非实验型论文,以发现或发明一种新的方法、工艺或装置等结尾,指明其用途或价值(如…promises to be very useful for scientific purposes and applicable to a wide range of experimental research)。

2) 指出文献中的其他内容(如 The consequences of … are also considered 或 This paper also includes a comparison with other … studies performed elsewhere)。

3) 指出创新与独到之处(如 These results provide new proofs of the evolutional process of … in … regions)。

3.2.7 摘要写作实例

摘要写作思路虽然可以总结，但不太可能固定，以上只是给出了一般思路和步骤——普遍性要求。实际写作中，应尽量实现这种要求，再考虑期刊和文体要求、领域特点和表意需要，并发挥个人专长和风格，写出既符合共性要求又蕴涵写作技巧、紧扣内容特点等个性要求的摘要。下面不妨从一些名刊选几个摘要实例（前五个为原创论文的摘要，最后一个为综述的摘要），了解其内容安排和写作思路，供读者参考。

3.2.7.1 实例一

【1】

Synchrotron radiation (SR) sources are <u>immensely useful tools</u> for scientific researches and many practical applications. <u>Currently</u>, the state-of-the-art synchrotrons <u>rely on conventional</u> accelerators, where electrons are accelerated in a straight line and radiate in bending magnets or other insertion devices. <u>However</u>, these facilities are usually large and costly. <u>Here</u>, we <u>study</u> a compact all optical synchrotron-like radiation source <u>based on</u> laser-plasma acceleration either in a straight or a curved plasma channel. <u>With</u> the laser pulse off-axially injected, its centroid oscillates transversely in the plasma channel. <u>This</u> <u>results in</u> a wiggler motion of the whole accelerating structure and the self-trapped electrons behind the laser pulse, <u>leading to</u> strong synchrotron-like radiations with tunable spectra. It <u>is further shown</u> that a palmtop ring-shaped synchrotron is possible with current high power laser technologies. <u>With</u> its potential of high flexibility and tunability, such light sources once realized <u>would find applications</u> in wide areas and <u>make up the shortage</u> of large SR facilities.

(Tunable synchrotron-like radiation from centimeter scale plasma channels. *Light: Science & Applications*, Volume. 5, Issue 1, January 2016.)

此摘要共八句，内容上分为三部分：前三句（第一部分）交待研究领域、范围与问题（目的），接着四句（第二部分）陈述研究对象、方法、结果与结论，最后一句（第三部分）总结创新之处。画线词语为体现逻辑关联性、表明内容特征的关键词，用好这类词对写好摘要很关键。

第一句陈述同步加速器辐射源极其有用（SR sources are immensely useful tools for …）。接着，第二句以 Currently 开始，指出目前最先进的同步加速器依赖于传统加速器，以直线方式加速并在弯曲磁铁或其他插入装置中辐射（the state-of-the-art synchrotrons rely on conventional acceler-ators …），暗含着这种设备的特点与不足（范围），接下来引出问题。第三句话锋一转，以 However 开始，点出存在的问题，即这种设备大而贵（these facilities are usually large and costly），这就是本文要解决或改进的问题（目的）。

第四句以 Here 开头，明确告知接下来的内容就是本文的工作，即摘要的主体内容。这句陈述研究对象"基于激光等离子体加速的直线或弯曲式紧凑全光同步辐射源"（a compact all optical synchrotron-like radiation source based on …）。第五句交待使用的方法"形心在等离子体通道振荡式激光脉冲离轴注入"（the laser pulse off-axially injected, its centroid oscillates …）。第六句的主语 This 指前述方法，谓语 results in 后面即为由 This 产生的结果"加速结构的摇摆运动，激光脉冲的自捕捉电子，带有可调谐光谱的强同步辐射"（a wiggler motion of the whole accelerating structure, the self-trapped electrons behind the laser pulse, strong synchrotron-like radiations with tunable spectra）。第七句中的 is further shown 进一步给出由以上结果得到的结论"使用目前高功率激光技术实现掌上环形同步加速器是有可能的"（a palmtop ring-shaped synchrotron is possible with current high power laser technologies）。

最后一句全局总结，指出创新之处

"所提光源有高度的灵活性和可调谐性,能弥补大型 SR 设备的不足,应用前景看好"(such light sources once realized would find applications in wide areas and make up the shortage of large SR facilities)。

此摘要写作思路:领域→范围→问题(目的)→对象→方法→结果→结论→创新点。

3.2.7.2 实例二

【2】

Cancer cells <u>are known for</u> their capacity to rewire metabolic pathways to support survival and proliferation under various stress conditions. Ketone bodies, <u>though</u> produced in the liver, are not consumed in normal adult liver cells. <u>We find</u> here that ketone catabolism or ketolysis is re-activated in hepatocellular carcinoma (HCC) cells under nutrition deprivation conditions. <u>Mechanistically</u>, 3-oxoacid CoA-transferase 1 (OXCT1), a rate-limiting ketolytic enzyme whose expression is suppressed in normal adult liver tissues, is re-induced by serum starvation-triggered mTORC2-AKT-SP1 signaling in HCC cells. <u>Moreover</u>, we observe that enhanced ketolysis in HCC is critical for repression of AMPK activation and protects HCC cells from excessive autophagy, <u>thereby</u> enhancing tumor growth. <u>Importantly</u>, analysis of clinical HCC samples <u>reveals</u> that increased OXCT1 expression predicts higher patient mortality. <u>Taken together</u>, we <u>uncover</u> here a novel metabolic adaptation by which nutrition-deprived HCC cells employ ketone bodies for energy supply and cancer progression.

(Hepatocellular carcinoma redirects to ketolysis for progression under nutrition deprivation stress. *Cell Research*, Vol. 26, No. 10, October 2016: 1112.)

此摘要共七句,内容上分三大部分:前两句(第一部分)交待领域(范围)、问题,接着四句(即三至六句,第二部分)主要陈述结果(含少量方法),最后一句(第三部分)总结创新之处。画线词语为体现逻辑关联性、表明内容特征的关键词。

第一句陈述癌症细胞的重要特征"通过重新连接代谢途径来支持各种应力状态下的生存和增殖能力"(Cancer cells are known for …),属领域(范围);接着,第二句指出"酮体来源于在肝脏,但在正常成人肝脏细胞中并不消耗"(Ketone bodies are not consumed in …)这一种特别现象,暗示本文要研究的主题(问题)。

第三句以 We find 开头,后面 that 部分即为 find 的结果。第三、四句为并列关系,第五句表示更进一步的结果(Moreover),第六句的过渡词 Importantly 和谓语动词 reveals 表示由结果得出重要发现(结论)。

第三至六句的主要内容:酮体代谢、分解在缺少营养时在肝细胞癌(HCC)细胞中被重新激活(ketone catabolism or ketolysis is re-activated in …);在正常成人肝脏组织中被抑制的一种速率限制酮体转移酶(OXCT1)通过 HCC 细胞中被血清饥饿激发的 mTORC2-AKT-SP1 重新诱导(3-oxoacid CoA-transferase 1 (OXCT1) … is re-induced by …);HCC 的增强酮体分解对于抑制 AMPK 活化和保护 HCC 细胞免过度自体吞噬的作用很重要,从而增强肿瘤的生长(we observe that enhanced ketolysis in HCC is critical for …);对临床 HCC 样本分析表明,增高的 OXCT1 预示着更高的患者死亡率(analysis of clinical HCC samples reveals that …)。其中 analysis of clinical HCC samples 指出得到这一重要结论所用的方法,而前面三句没有交待方法。

第七句以显著的过渡词 Taken together 开头,作全局总结,由谓语动词 uncover 指出创新点——本文揭开一种新的代谢适应机理,即营养缺乏的 HCC 细胞用酮体来进行能量供应并促进癌症发展(we uncover here a novel metabolic adaptation …)。

此摘要写作思路:领域(范围)→问题→结果(含少量方法)→创新点。

3.2.7.3　实例三

【3】

Traditional Global Sensitivity Analysis (GSA) focuses on ranking inputs according to their contributions to the output uncertainty. However, information about how the specific regions inside an input affect the output is beyond the traditional GSA techniques. To fully address this issue, in this work, two regional moment-independent importance measures, Regional Importance Measure based on Probability Density Function (RIMPDF) and Regional Importance Measure based on Cumulative Distribution Function (RIMCDF), are introduced to find out the contributions of specific regions of an input to the whole output distribution. The two regional importance measures prove to be reasonable supplements of the traditional GSA techniques. The ideas of RIMPDF and RIMCDF are applied in two engineering examples to demonstrate that the regional moment-independent importance analysis can add more information concerning the contributions of model inputs.

(Regional moment-independent sensitivity analysis with its applications in engineering. *Chinese Journal of Aeronautics*, Vol. 30, No. 3, Jun. 2017: 1031)

此摘要共五句，内容上分四个部分：前两句（第一部分）交待主题（领域、范围）及存在的问题，第三句（第二部分）交待目的、方法和成果（结果），第四句（第三部分）描述结论，第五句（第四部分）总结创新点。画线词语为体现逻辑关联性、表明内容特征的关键词。

第一句陈述传统全球敏感性分析（GSA）研究领域的关注焦点"根据对输出不确定性的贡献来对输入进行排序"（Traditional Global Sensitivity Analysis (GSA) focuses on …），指出主题（领域、范围）。接着，第二句由 However 开头，指出传统 GSA 未能解决输入里特定区域如何影响输出这一问题（However, … is beyond the traditional GSA techniques），指出问题之所在。第三句以 To fully address this issue 开头，明确地交待本文的方法（基于 RIMPDF、RIMCDF 的两种区域矩独立重要性测度方法）和目的"发现输入的特定区域对整个输出分布的贡献"（Probability Density Function (RIMPDF), Cumulative Distribution Function (RIMCDF); the contributions of specific regions of …），将方法和目的写在了一起。

第四句描述所提出的两个区域重要性测度方法的效能——弥补传统 GSA 的不足，交待合理性、可靠性，属结论（The two regional importance measures prove to be …）。

最后一句以工程应用实例来证明方法的优势——引入区域矩独立的重要性分析，增添更多有关模型输入贡献的信息（The regional moment-independent importance analysis can add more information …）。这实际上较为隐含地点出本文的学术价值，属于创新点，还以实证的口吻交待本文方法的工程应用前景。

此摘要在语言表达上有简化的空间，但在内容布局上还是能够代表工程技术类论文（能改善或解决实际问题，有创新，但学术性不一定高）的摘要写作模式。

此摘要写作思路：主题→问题→目的→方法→成果（结果）→结论→创新点。

3.2.7.4　实例四

【4】

The sub-cloud evaporation effect refers to the evaporation process for raindrops that fall from the cloud base to the ground, which is usually accompanied by depleted light isotopes and enriched heavy isotopes in the precipitation. Based on 461 event-based precipitation samples collected from 12 weather stations in the Qilian Mountains and the Hexi Corridor from May to August of 2013, our results indicated that sub-cloud evaporation has a great influence on the $\delta^{18}O$ of precipitation, especially in small-amount precipitation events. In May, June, July, and August the $\delta^{18}O$ composition was enriched by 35%, 26%, 39%, and 41%, respectively, from the cloud base to the ground. This influence clearly strengthened with temperature rise, from the Qilian Mountains to the Hexi Corridor. When falling raindrops are evaporated by 1.0% in the Qilian Mountains and the Hexi Corridor, the composition of $\delta^{18}O$ would be enriched by 1.2% and 2.6%, respectively. Temperature dominated the sub-cloud evaporation in the Qilian Mountains, whereas relative humidity controlled it in the Hexi Corridor. These results provide new proofs of the evolutional process of stable isotopes in precipitation in arid regions.

(Effect of sub-cloud evaporation on the $\delta^{18}O$ of precipitation in Qilian Mountains and Hexi Corridor, China. *Sciences in Cold and Arid Regions*, Volume 8, Issue 5, October 2016: 378.)

此摘要共七句，内容上分为三个部分：第一部分即第一句交待研究领域或主题；第二部分较长，包括第二至六句，但大体均为结果；第三部分即最后一句，总结创新之处。画线词语为体现逻辑关联性、表明内容特征的关键词。

第一句陈述亚云蒸发效应的概念、特征（雨滴从云层底部坠落到地面的蒸发过程，伴随耗尽的光同位素和降水中丰富的重同位素），领域或主题非常分明，但问题和目的未明确交待。

第二句先指出方法（收集样本，调查分析：从祁连山和河西走廊 12 个气象站收集 2013 年 5 至 8 月期间 461 个基于事件的降水样本），接着给出结果（亚云蒸发影响：亚云蒸发对降水量特别是小降水量的 $\delta^{18}O$ 影响很大）。第三句对此结果定量说明（5 至 8 月从云层底部到地面的 $\delta^{18}O$ 构成分别增加 35%、26%、39% 和 41%）。第四句总结影响规律（这种影响随祁连山区到河西走廊的温度上升而明显加强）。第五句对此规律定量说明（在祁连山区和河西走廊，当降雨量被蒸发 1.0% 时，其 $\delta^{18}O$ 构成将分别增加 1.2% 和 2.6%）。第六句给出结论（祁连山区的亚云蒸发由温度控制，河西走廊的由相对湿度控制）。

第二至六句的布局安排也是有顺序的（给出结果，对结果定量说明；总结规律，对规律定量说明；给出结论），体现了摘要对过程写作的要求。

第七句全局总结，指出论文价值或创新之处（研究结果可为干旱地区降水稳定同位素的演化过程提供新证据）。

此摘要写作思路：领域或主题→方法→结果→结论→创新点。

3.2.7.5 实例五

【5】

Magnetic properties and magnetocaloric effects (MCEs) of the PrSi compound were studied. The PrSi compound undergoes a second-order ferromagnetic-to-paramagnetic transition at the Curie temperature of $T_C = 52$ K. Large MCE with no magnetic hysteresis loss is observed around T_C. The maximum values of magnetic entropy change (ΔS) are found to be -8.6 and -15.3 J·kg^{-1}·K^{-1} for the magnetic field changes of 0–2 T and 0–5 T, respectively. The large ΔS with no hysteresis makes PrSi compound a competitive candidate for magnetic refrigerant.

(Magnetic properties and magnetocaloric effects of PrSi. *RARE METALS*, (2014) 33 (3): 239.)

此摘要相对短一些。第一句开门见山，直接点出研究目的（PrSi 化合物的磁性特性和磁热效应）。剩余几句则为研究结果、结论，并辅以定量说明，提升说服力。

结果：PrSi 在居里温度 $T_C = 52$ K 经历了二阶铁磁 – 顺磁转变；在 T_C 上下观察到无磁滞损失的大 MCE；磁熵变的最大值为 8.6、15.3 J·kg^{-1}·K^{-1}，与磁场变化 0~2 T 和 0~5 T 相对应。

结论：无磁滞的大 ΔS 使 PrSi 化合物成为磁致冷材料的竞争对手。

此摘要写作思路：目的→结果→结论。

3.2.7.6 实例六

【6】

Bacteria and archaea possess a range of defense mechanisms to combat plasmids and viral infections. Uniqueamong these are the CRISPR-Cas (clustered regularly interspaced short palindromic repeats-CRISPR associated) systems, which provide adaptive immunity against foreign nucleic acids. CRISPR systems function by acquiring genetic records of invaders to facilitate robust interference upon reinfection. In this Review, we discuss recent advances in understanding the diverse mechanisms by which Cas proteins respond to foreign nucleic acids and how these systems have been harnessed for precision genome manipulation in a wide array of organisms.

(Biology and Applications of CRISPR Systems: Harnessing Nature's Toolbox for Genome Engineering. *Cell* 164, January 14, 2016)

此例为综述的摘要, 写法上属指示性摘要。前三句以较多篇幅陈述生物领域有关 CRISPR 系统的知识, 点出主题(领域、范围), 但未交待相关综述研究的必要性; 最后一句交待本文做了什么工作(目的), 但没有给出结果及指导性结论、展望。如果补充结果、结论和展望, 按报道性或报道-指标性摘要来写, 则篇幅会长很多, 参见下节中对一个综述摘要的评改。

有关知识(领域、范围、主题): 细菌和古生菌有一系列对抗质粒和病毒感染的防御机制。其中最特别的防御机制是为外来核酸提供适应性免疫的 CRISPR 系统, 该系统通过获取入侵病毒的基因记录来促进对再感染的强力干预。

本文工作(目的): 讨论有关 Cas 蛋白对外来核酸的多样化反应机制认识的新进展; Cas 系统怎样广泛用于对各种生物进行精密基因组操纵。

此摘要写作思路: 有关知识(领域、范围、主题)→本文工作(目的)。

3.2.8 不规范摘要修改

摘要写作中的常见问题有: 摘要类型把握不到位; 内容和结构不完整(如缺少必要的目的、方法、结果、结论或创新点等), 篇幅偏短; 背景信息过多(如重复前言); 照搬层次标题或结论的语句; 内容不浓缩、不概括, 表达冗余, 篇幅过长; 出现了不必要的引文、式子或举例; 无独立性与自明性。以下列举几个不规范的摘要, 进行点评、修改。

3.2.8.1 实例一

【1】

It is well known that various parameters of semiconductor devices, such as $I_s(T)$, $B(T)$, $C_1(T)$, $C_p(T)$, etc., are sensitive to changes in temperature. When the circuit works, the heat is easily generated due to the power consumption of the components integrated on the chip. For the different thermal resistance of the materials used in the semiconductor devices and base, there will be uneven distribution of heat on the chip, especially for the power integrated circuits (PIC).

For the sake of simplicity, the temperature difference is often ignored in the performance analysis of integrated circuits (IC). It's assumed that all components are working at the same temperature. The commercial computer programs, such as Simulation Program with Integrated Circuit Emphasis (SPICE), use this assumption. It's obvious that such an assumption will introduce a certain calculation error in the analysis of IC, which could make matters even worse in the analysis of PIC. This paper aims at determining the temperature distribution of IC chip, calculating the characteristics of circuit when the temperature difference exists, and studying the interaction between heat and electricity on the chip.

This paper introduces the thermal simulation model of integrated circuit, emulates thermal path problem into circuit problem, and solves the chip temperature distribution using circuit simulation program. Doing so can take advantage of sophisticated circuit analysis program and greatly improve the speed and accuracy of the calculation. In addition, a computer program YM-LiN-3 written in FORTRAN is developed based on this method. With the program, temperature distribution and the characteristics of the chip when the temperature difference exists can be determined. Lastly, the program is verified on IBM-PC and satisfied results are obtained.

此摘要有三段，形似结构式摘要，每段都似一个摘要，整体篇幅很长。

第一段以半导体器件工作原理常识为论据进行论证，得出论点"芯片上各点温度不可能相同"和"芯片上存在着不均匀的温度分布"。这些均不属摘要应有的内容，不必写进来，因为摘要不写常识，不作论证。

第二段针对现有计算方法的缺点（计算误差太大）指出本文研究目的，但对现有计算方法描述太细、太多，缺乏提炼、概括，问题不突出。最后一句（画线部分）交待研究目的（确定集成电路芯片的温度分布，计算元件温度不同时的电路特性，研究芯片上热、电的相互作用），但太笼统，与论文主题不扣，而且"芯片上热、电的相互作用"的内容在后面语句中根本没有出现过。

第三段的首句交待三个研究目的（提出集成电路热模拟模型，将热路问题模拟成电路问题，用电路模拟程序求解芯片温度分布），按表意，后面两个目的实现是第一个目的实现的方法与过程，因此这三个目的不能并列。应先单独提出第一个目的（集成电路热模拟模型），然后交待实现此目的用了什么方法，所用方法的效能、效果，以及用此模型开发了一个程序，此程序的结果、优势（创新）。

以下是修改后的摘要：

In order to determine the temperature distribution of the IC chip and the circuit characteristics when the temperature difference exists, this paper proposes a thermal analysis model that resembles the circuit analysis model. The model considering the interaction of heat and electricity on IC chip can be solved by the commercial circuit analysis programs, resulting in efficiency and accuracy improvement. A FORTRAN program based on this model is provided. Lastly, the program is verified on IBM-PC computer and satisfactory results are obtained.

修改说明：

1）删去第一段，以及第二段最后一句前面的所有语句。

2）将第二段最后一句（This paper aims at ... on the chip）写成目的复句的从句：

• In order to determine the temperature distribution of the IC chip and the circuit characteristics when the temperature difference exists,

修改后，将两个分词短语 determining ... 和 calculating ... 合并为一个不定式短语 to determine ...，去掉了第三个分词短语 studying ...。

3）将第三段开头句子（This paper introduces ... program）写成目的复句的主句：

• this paper proposes a thermal analysis model that resembles the circuit analysis model.

修改后，去掉了并列谓语 emulates ... 和 solves ...，谓语 introduces 改为 proposes⊖。另外，将分词短语 using circuit simulation program 改为定语从句 that resembles the circuit analysis model，修饰 a thermal analysis model。

4）进一步提升接下来的语句（Doing so can ... can be determined）的文字效能。

• The model considering the interaction of heat and electricity on IC chip can be solved by the commercial circuit analysis programs, resulting in efficiency and accuracy improvement. A FORTRAN program based on this model is provided.

修改后，对所提出的模型（model）进行限定（considering ... IC chip），给出其实现方法（by ... programs），陈述其功用或效

⊖ propose 重在提出，含创新；而 introduce 重在介绍，创新可能不突出。

能（efficiency ... improvement），并指出此模型的一个应用（A FORTRAN program ... is provided）。

总体上，去掉了冗余语句，内容紧密扣题、扣文，表意更加准确、细腻，结构更加简单、精巧，逻辑更加顺畅、自然，语言文字效能得到提升。

3.2.8.2 实例二

【2】

There are some fault diagnosis methods for gear at present. However, the effects are unsatisfied. Major goal of current research is to find a better new approach with excellent comprehensive performance, such as high accuracy, high sensitivity, good anti-interference and simplicity of calculation, etc. <u>The proposed energy operator separation algorithm</u> (EOSA) is a new demodulation method <u>which is inspired by the phenomena produced from the research process of generating mechanism of voice signal</u>. It's implemented by optimizing the difference equation with given length of unit impulse response of filter and fixed weighting coefficients at key points. This algorithm has been successfully applied to the diagnosis of broken teeth and fatigue cracks of gear, which provides an alternative to the demodulation analysis of mechanical signal.

此摘要开头一句点出主题或领域范围（fault diagnosis methods for gear），属常识，不用专门交待。第二句指出存在的问题（the effects are unsatisfied），但 the effects 指代不明，整句过于简短。第三句将目的降格写成目标（Major goal ... is to find a better new approach ...），目的与目标有语义差异，目的在于解决存在的问题，而目标在于完成具体工作，获得具体成果。第四句以 The proposed ... algorithm 作主语，对其进行介绍，但表述太突然，前文中缺与之对应的语句，应该与目的结合着来写；定语从句 which is inspired by ... 指出算法的机理，应该与第五句（算法的实现方法）结合着来写，即先指出机理，再交待实现方法。最后一句陈述本文算法的应用情况及实用价值，暗含创新之处，但与开头指出的问题相扣

不够。

以下是修改后的摘要：

Aiming at the inefficient fault diagnosis method for gear, an energy operator demodulation approach with high accuracy, high sensitivity, good anti-interference and simplicity of calculation is proposed. It's inspired by the phenomena produced from the research process of generating mechanism of voice signal. By using the nonlinear differential operator, it optimizes the difference equation with given length of unit impulse response of filter and fixed weighting coefficients at key points. This approach has been successfully applied to the diagnosis of broken teeth and fatigue cracks of gear, whose effectiveness is validated by a wide range of practical examples.

修改说明：

1）首句开门见山，直接以问题（Aiming at ... method for gear）和目的（an energy operator demodulation approach with ... is proposed）开头。其中 with 短语（with high accuracy, high sensitivity, good anti-interference and simplicity of calculation）对 approach 有准确的限定。

2）第二句直接陈述机理（It's inspired by the phenomena produced from ...）。

3）第三句交待实现方法，并进一步交待工作机理（By using the nonlinear differential operator, it optimizes the difference equation with ...）。

4）第四句交待应用情况，并与开头的目的相呼应指出应用效果（inefficient 与 effectiveness 直接呼应）。

修改后，问题明确、目的突出，围绕目的有序展开（机理、方法、应用、效果），摘要的概要功能恰到好处，文字效能提高，逻辑条理更加分明，读起来省力、省事、省心。

3.2.8.3 实例三

【3】

PSO is emerging evolutionary computation technology based on swarm intelligence, which has been applied successfully in many fields. <u>To further improve the</u>

global search ability of PSO, a particle swarm optimization based on pyramid model (PPSO for short) is presented to solve optimization problems such as the layout design of an international commercial communication satellite (INTELSAT-Ⅲ) cabin. 3 methods are developed here, 1) Population diversity is maintained by searching synchronously solution space of multi-swarms based on pyramid model; 2) Particles' velocities are adjusted dynamically according to their deformation of collision; 3) Mutation operation is applied to the particles which lost search ability. The performance of PPSO is compared to global version PSO, ring and Neumann PSO of local version in the numerical examples of the layout design of this satellite cabin, demonstrating its feasibility and availability.

此摘要开头一句是常识，可不写。第二句前后均有表示目的的不定式短语（To further improve … 和 to solve …)，目的不太明确。其实，前一个是要实现的目标，后一个是目标（成果）的应用，因此应合写（前后并列或写在一起）或分开写（不在同一句）。第三句用三句话较为详细地陈述所提出的三个方法，有些啰嗦（摘要应侧重成果引导，而非具体过程介绍），应将这三个句子概括为三个短语（每个方法有一个名称）。最后对所提出的 PPSO 与全局版、局部版 PSO 进行对比，后面以分词短语（demonstrating …）的状语形式指出对比结果（PPSO 有较高的可行性和适用性）；从句式看，表意轻重倒置，将主体内容（对比结果）用分词状语的形式不够突出，应专门用一个句子来表达。此摘要还存在核心缩略语 PSO 首次出现时没有写出全称，阿拉伯数字置于句首，用词不准确、不到位，语言不简洁、不精练等问题。

以下是修改后的摘要：

To improve the global search ability of particle swarm optimization (PSO), a multi-population PSO based on pyramid model (PPSO) is presented. Then, it is applied to solve the layout optimization problems against the background of an international commercial communication satellite (INTELSAT-Ⅲ) module. Three improvement methods are developed, including multi-population search based on pyramid model, adaptive collision avoidance among particles, and mutation of degraded particles. In the numerical examples of the layout design of this simplified satellite module, the performance of PPSO is compared to global version PSO and local version PSO (ring and Neumann PSO algorithms). The results show that PPSO has higher computational accuracy, efficiency and success ratio.

修改说明：

1）去掉了背景知识，明确了目的，以不定式开头直接表述（To improve …）。

2）将另一目的（to solve …）单写为一句（Then, it is applied to solve …），属成果应用。

3）去掉过程，将三种方法概括为三个名称（multi-population search based on pyramid model; adaptive collision avoidance among particles; mutation of degraded particles）。

4）将原来的最后一句分成两句，前一句交待对 PPSO 与 PSO 作对比（the performance of PPSO is compared to …），后一句交待对比结果（The results show that …）。

修改后为指示-报道性摘要，目的明确、内容精致、篇幅简短、逻辑顺畅，写作质量有较大提升。

3.2.8.4 实例四

【4】

Five methods for deploying and forming large parabolic membrane antennas are compared and analyzed including inflation, inflation-rigidization, elastic ribs driving, SMP-inflation and electrostatic forming, and membrane material properties for parabolic membrane antennas are presented. Additionally, the development of structure configurations, tensioning system design and dynamic analysis of large planar membrane antenna structures are discussed. Finally, future directions of large space membrane antenna structures are summarized and technical difficulties are proposed based on design and analysis, membrane materials and processes, membrane packing and surface accuracy maintaining.

本例为一篇综述的摘要，每个句子都用被动语态，都是叙述做了什么，而未交待做出了什么，即只有过程，没有结果，属指示性摘要。

综述的摘要提倡写成报道性或报道－指示性摘要，其内容和结构应是这样的：

开头用简短的语句点出写此综述的必要性，如别人少有研究，行业、领域发展需要引领；中间部分陈述本综述的重要成果、结论；结尾点明创新点，即提出（或解决了）何指导性观点（或问题），填补了行业、领域目前缺少此类综述引领的空白。如果可能，还应与正文的 Conclusions and Outlook 或 Outlook 相呼应，站开较高的战略高度，指出未来发展方向，完好收尾。按这种内容和结构写出的摘要，内容较详细，篇幅较长。

目前有些 SCI 期刊的论文的摘要，在内容和结构上通常较为简单，多由开头的背景信息和结尾的指示性语句组成，背景信息陈述行业发展现状，指示性语句叙述本文所做工作。这种摘要多属指示性摘要或报道－指示性摘要，内容较简略，篇幅适中。

下面给出对本例摘要的几种修改方案。

<方案一>

①The demand for large antennas in future space missions has increasingly stimulated the development of deployable membrane antenna structures owing to their light weight and small stowage volume. ②However, there is little literature providing a comprehensive review and comparison of different membrane antenna structures. ③Space-borne membrane antenna structures are mainly classified as either parabolic or planar membrane antenna structures. ④For parabolic membrane antenna structures, there are five deploying and forming methods, including inflation, inflation-rigidization, elastic ribs driven, Shape Memory Polymer (SMP)-inflation, and electrostatic forming. ⑤The development and detailed comparison of these five methods are presented. ⑥Then, properties of membrane materials (including polyester film and polyimide film) for parabolic membrane antennas are compared. ⑦Additionally, for planar membrane antenna structures, frame shapes have changed from circular to rectangular, and different tensioning systems have emerged successively, including single, Miura-Natori, double, and multi-layer tensioning systems. ⑧Recent advances in configurations, tensioning system design, and dynamic analysis for planar membrane antenna structures are investigated. ⑨Finally, future trends for large space membrane antenna structures are pointed out and technical problems are proposed, including design and analysis of membrane structures, materials and processes, membrane packing, surface accuracy stability, and test and verification technology. ⑩Through a review of large deployable membrane antenna structures, guidance for space membrane-antenna research and applications is provided.

修改说明（为表述需要，笔者在每句的开头加了数字编号）：

1）增加了背景信息，陈述航天器大型薄膜可展开天线结构的发展需求，指出写此综述的意义（前面两句），陈述了空间运载、抛物面薄膜天线结构的分类知识（第三、四句）；

2）指示本文所做工作：概述五种方法的研究现状并作比较（comparison of … are presented），对抛物面薄膜天线材料的特性作比较（properties of … are compared）（第五、六句）；

3）增加研究结果，即对于平面薄膜天线结构，框架形状由圆形变成矩形，相继出现不同的张拉系统（第七句）；

4）指示本文所做工作：研究航天器大型平面薄膜天线结构的构型、张拉系统设计及结构动力学分析的最新发展现状（第八句）；

5）陈述重要成果或结论：薄膜结构设计与分析、材料与工艺、天线收拢、形面精度在轨保持、测试与验证是航天器大型薄膜天线结构的发展趋势及需要攻克的关键技术（第九句）；

6）结尾高度总结，点出本综述能对空间薄膜天线的研究和应用提供指导（第十句）。

这是按报道-指示性摘要来写的（第五、六、八句属指示性部分），增加了一些内容，内容全面、丰富，但篇幅过长，语句结构混杂，可读性较差。

<方案二>

Background and aims The demand for large antennas in future space missions has increasingly stimulated the development of deployable membrane antenna structures owing to their light weight and small stowage volume. However, there is little literature providing a comprehensive review and comparison of different membrane antenna structures. Space-borne membrane antenna structures are mainly classified as either parabolic or planar membrane antenna structures. For parabolic membrane antenna structures, there are five deploying and forming methods, including inflation, inflation-rigidization, elastic ribs driven, shape memory polymer (SMP)-inflation, and electrostatic forming.

Objective and Process The development and detailed comparison of these five methods are presented. Then, properties of membrane materials (including polyester film and polyimide film) for parabolic membrane antennas are compared. Additionally, for planar membrane antenna structures, frame shapes have changed from circular to rectangular, and different tensioning systems have emerged successively, including single, Miura-Natori, double, and multi-layer tensioning systems. Recent advances in structural configurations, tensioning system design, and dynamic analysis for planar membrane antenna structures are investigated.

Conclusions and Outlook Finally, future trends for large space membrane antenna structures are pointed out and technical problems are proposed, including design and analysis of membrane structures, materials and proces-

ses, membrane packing, surface accuracy stability, and test and verification technology.

Summary Through a review of large deployable membrane antenna structures, guidance for space membrane-antenna research and applications is provided.

以上是按结构式摘要来修改的，结构层次较为清楚，效果得到提高。

<方案三>

The demand for large antennas in future space missions has increasingly stimulated the development of deployable membrane antenna structures owing to their light weight and small stowage volume. However, there is little literature providing a comprehensive review and comparison of different membrane antenna structures. In this Review, we present the development and detailed comparison of five methods for deploying and forming large parabolic membrane antennas, compare properties of membrane materials for parabolic membrane antennas, and investigate recent advances in configurations, tensioning system design, and dynamic analysis for planar membrane antenna structures. Finally, future trends for large space membrane antenna structures are pointed out and technical problems are proposed.

以上是参照国际主流期刊的综述的摘要写作体例来写的，虽然还属指示性摘要，但与原摘要相比，增加了行业现状、问题描述，作者工作的指示性描述更加简洁、明确，是较好的写作范例。

3.2.9 摘要与结论比较

摘要是读者和论文的"约会、初见"，旨在通过浅显的介绍引导读者进入论文主体；而结论是读者和论文的"相识、相知"，旨在通过高度的总结和升华给读者一个交待，二者在功能、内容和结构上均有差异。⊖

（1）功能

摘要的基本功能是构成论文准入条件：投稿后，编辑初审时通过浏览摘要判断论文

⊖ 这部分的写作引用或参考了文献[60]。

的相关性，之后再安排评审；送审或发表后，专家评审或读者阅读也是先看摘要，判断论文的水准，形成认识和评价意见。摘要的另一重要功能是体现写作能力：摘要是论文的浓缩，妥当的内容、合理的结构、简洁的文字、通畅的逻辑能让编辑、专家和读者在同等条件下给予更多的肯定。

结论的功能在于强调发现，从前文密密麻麻的语言文字中发掘蕴含的价值，让读者在将要结束论文阅读的时刻加强记忆，记得论文讲了什么、解决了什么。

摘要好比"脸"，用来获得人们对论文的第一印象；结论好比"精神"，论文的价值在于"精神"，但前提是看"脸"获得好感。摘要是论文的开始，通俗性强，具有商人般的气质，目的是吸引读者，功利性明显；结论是论文的结束，有一些"酒香不怕巷子深"的学术味道，功利性下降，学术性显著提升。

（2）内容

总体上，摘要体现的是悬念、疑问，结论则体现的是结局、趋势。

摘要的背景是一个过渡接口，是为避免读者看了摘要有唐突感而设，当读者看完摘要继续往下读时，背景便失去价值；结论中直接点出成果，不必再谈背景。

摘要的总结体现从未知到已知的差距，诱惑成分多，旨在引起读者继续阅读论文的兴趣；结论的总结体现从已知到熟知的深入，使读者的认识得到升华。

摘要的外延多在谈可能、潜能、未来，多可编入科学研究转化为应用的分母；结论的外延往往体现更加切实的操作。

（3）结构

摘要涵盖昨天（背景）、今天（结果）和明天（外延）；结论则重述今天（强调发现、问题与改进）和展望明天（下一步工作）。

摘要交待背景的意义在于设定舞台，为整个论文的内容建立空间；描述结果重在实事求是，提供基础、构成核心；规划外延的意义在于预备，描绘远景、给出希望，将假设、启发、建议、预测及今后研究方向点出来。

结论陈述发现、自暴问题、提出改进，重点在于高效传承和发展科学；下一步工作用寥寥数语给出答案，不在于细碎的数据、知识点以及逻辑链条的各个环节，是学术体系之外的价值体现，也是站在现在对未来的勾画。

（4）实例解析

下面以 2015 年 *Nature* 的一篇原创论文 The origins of high hardening and low ductility in magnesium（镁高硬化和低塑性的起因）为例，对其摘要和结论的区别进行说明（为表述方便，笔者在摘要和结论各句开头分别加了数字编号①~⑥和❶~❹）。

<Abstract>

① Magnesium is a lightweight structural metal but it exhibits low ductility—connected with unusual, mechanistically unexplained, dislocation and plasticity phenomena—which makes it difficult to form and use in energy-saving lightweight structures. ② We employ long-time molecular dynamics simulations utilizing a density-functional-theory validated interatomic potential, and reveal the fundamental origins of the previously unexplained phenomena. ③ Here we show that the key <c+a> dislocation (where <c+a> indicates the magnitude and direction of slip) is metastable on easy-glide pyramidal Ⅱ planes; we find that it undergoes a thermally activated, stress-dependent transition to one of three lower-energy, basal-dissociated immobile dislocation structures, which cannot contribute to plastic straining and that serve as strong obstacles to the motion of all other dislocations. ④ This transition is intrinsic to magnesium, driven by reduction in dislocation energy and predicted to occur at very high frequency at room temperature, thus eliminating all major dislocation slip systems able to contribute to c-axis strain and leading to the high hardening and low ductility of magnesium.

⑤Enhanced ductility can thus be achieved by increasing the time and temperature at which the transition from the easy-glide metastable dislocation to the immobile basal-dissociated structures occurs. ⑥Our results provide the underlying insights needed to guide the design of ductile magnesium alloys.

<Conclusions>

❶In summary, use of a new DFT-validated interatomic potential in long-time MD studies reveals a rich set of intrinsic structural transitions of the key <c+a> dislocations in Mg that explain long-standing experimental puzzles and are responsible for low ductility in Mg. ❷The easy-glide pyramidal II <c+a> undergoes thermally activated, stress dependent transitions into various lower-energy products lying on basal planes. ❸ The dislocation structures are in good agreement with experimental observations, the differences between experiments are explained, the temperature range where the transition is operative agrees with experiments, and the product dislocations are immobile and so cause high strain hardening by serving as obstacles for all other dislocations, leading to low ductility. ❹This new overall understanding opens opportunities for design of Mg-based alloys based on the mechanistic concept of energetically stabilizing the easy-glide <c+a> dislocations on pyramidal II planes.

1）摘要。该文的摘要共计六句，承载着摘要的内容和结构。

① 镁是一种轻量化结构金属，但有一些说不清道不明的基本问题导致其塑性差，使得它在节能轻量化结构中很难形成和使用。

此句直接切入背景（is），提出表观问题（exhibits、makes）、low ductility、difficult to form and use 和 energy-saving lightweight 均是相关研究问题与目标，也是材料和工业界常识。用词通俗易懂，读者群体较为宽泛，对材料类在读博士，大多数人无障碍阅读通过是没有问题的。

② 使用能验证原子间相互作用的密度泛函理论来实现长时分子动力学模拟，揭示了那些说不清道不明的现象。

此句进入方法（employ…utilizing）、发现（reveal），涉及难懂的专业知识。核心方法是 molecular dynamics simulations + density-functional-theory，而 reveal origins of unexpained 是其重要成果（但未交待具体所得结果），reveal 可以认为是文章学术质量的定性之词。这里开始涉及难懂的术语，对分子动力学和密度泛函这样的术语，材料物理、材料化学方面的专业人士才可能懂，材料类博士中可能就只有部分人能轻松理解。

③ 这里我们展示了键<c+a>的位错（<c+a>表示滑动的大小和方向）在易滑锥体 II 平面上是亚稳态的；我们发现它经历了一个热激活的，依赖压力变异成三个能量低、基底分裂而不动的位错结构之一，这不能导致塑性应变，对所有其他混乱的运动都形成一个巨大障碍。（意译：有个不稳定的叫位错的高能量原子级别的结构，在温度和力的作用下发生变异，制造出一个变种同类。此变种不喜欢运动，不仅自己不喜欢运动，还横在跑道上挡着别人运动。）

这是表述研究结果的较为细致的理论部分，阐明镁金属微观世界发生的现象，如位错、滑移。想要说明宏观现象，自然要从微观找原因。到此能顺畅理解的人就不多了。

④ 这种变异是镁金属的固有特性，受位错能量减少的驱使，预测在室温下发生的频率高，从而消除所有主要位错滑移系统对c轴应变的贡献，并导致镁的高硬化和低塑性。（意译：在镁金属世界容易产生这种变异，而且在自然条件下就能发生。这样，那些本来能正常履行职能的正常结构被这些变异体抢了岗位，但正常结构愿意出力干活儿，变异体却尸位素餐，结果就是生产变得不顺畅，民怨沸腾，矛盾升级。）

这是接着句③继续表述，由微观升级到宏观，由机理外化到现象，从论文正文回到论文标题。诸如 room temperature、high hardening、low ductility 就是宏观的概念，也是论文所提问题的表象一层。理解的人也不会多。

⑤ 可通过增加从易滑的亚稳态变异到基底分裂而不动的位错结构的时间和温度来达到增强的塑性。（意译：要想恢复常规秩序，就要去除变异，而方法就是剔除利于变异的因素。）

这是给出研究结果所揭示问题的宏观层次解决方案（by increasing）。能理解的人有所回升，即便对同一个专业，深度也不相同，明白宏观概念的人总是多于潜心研究精细问题的人。

⑥ 我们的结果为指导高塑性镁合金的设计提供了基本洞见。

此句冲出专业知识框架，回到最初的表观问题，指出本文的贡献、价值，即创新点（provide、guide）。这里，能理解的人又回到了大多数。

以上对可理解人数的定性描述只是一种大体宏观表述，却能表征知识深度的变化。这就不难理解深入浅出是如何实现的，摘要多是按浅入、深入、浅出的思路来行文的。若要做到浅入浅出，则需要剔除深层概念和专业术语。

此摘要总体撰写思路是提出问题和解决问题。内容和结构为：①背景、问题（宏观问题）；②方法、发现（总括式发现）；③微观讨论；④宏观讨论；⑤问题解决方案；⑥创新点（价值）。

2）结论。该文的结论共计四句，承载着结论的内容和结构。

❶长时分子动力学研究用新的密度泛函理论验证原子间相互作用，揭示镁金属中键$<c+a>$位错的一组丰富的内在结构变异，解释了长期存在的实验难题，也是镁低塑性产生的原因。

此句横贯和概括全文，直接点明使用方法而获得重要发现（reveals）——用一种方法揭示微观世界的某种行为，解释了宏观性能的一个疑团。注意这个总结和摘要句②的总结不同：摘要告诉做了什么，但没有告诉具体所得结果，这是摘要广告性的体现；结论告诉做了什么，并将具体所得结果一起放送，散发着学术风味。结论中有$<c+a>$这种小圈子内的专业术语，也有 long-standing puzzle 这种多数人都会感兴趣的谜底解开时的那种豁然感油然而生的字眼，总结相当完美。

❷易滑锥体 II $<c+a>$承受了热激活、依赖压力而向基底平面上各种低能量产品的变异。

此句重述了镁金属的微观行为，虽与摘要的有关表述重复，却是必要的。

摘要是论文的前面部分，读者读了前面部分，通常还不知道未来会发生什么，即使摘要对未来有所交待，读者接下来经过对较长正文的阅读，往往会遇到不少似懂非懂的词语以及还没有搞清楚的学术内容，此过程中会有较多的内容、观点甚至疑惑涌入读者的脑海，有的原本清晰的内容可能变得模糊起来，清晰与模糊交织、转化，读到后面，读者可能疲惫不堪。如果在论文后面的结论部分能看到贴切的总结语句来结束阅读，那么对读者来说是莫大的需要和关怀。因此结论中重述摘要的一些意思是必要的，但从写作来看，结论的表达应更加直截了当、简洁明快，任何冗余词语都是不用出现的。

❸位错结构与实验观测结果吻合较好，解释了实验间的不同，变异形成的温度范围与实验一致，而产品的位错是不动的，并引起阻挡所有其他变异的高应变硬化，进而导致低塑性。

此句由四个分句组成。前面三句基本上是用实验数据来支撑作者自己的模拟结果，即说明自己的模拟结果是可靠的。最后一句重述了金属镁的宏观行为（位错、高硬化和低塑性），与摘要的有关表述重复，这种重复是必要的，因为其宏观行为易受到更多人的关注。

此句对有关实验验证进行表述。摘要在于点出科学发现，有无创新和吸引力是关键；而结论还要考虑对此新发现的质量提供保证，有无验证和可信度是关键。

❹这种全新的理解为镁合金的设计提供了机会，这是建立在充分稳定锥体Ⅱ平面上的易滑<c+a>位错的一种机械概念基础之上的。

这句鲜明地点出创新点，表明解决了什么问题（发现的意义），与摘要相比，还补充交待了创新所依据的原理或途径（based on the mechanistic concept of ...），为镁合金设计掀开了新篇章。

结论的创新点侧重新发现，通常还应指出新发现的依据（如原理、途径等）的表述，这样会使结论的表述不至于太简短、武断或笼统，而摘要对创新点的表述通常更直接，多侧重结果。发现是结果的结果，结果是发现的前提。

此结论总体撰写思路是问题解决及问题解决得如何。其内容和结构为：❶方法和发现（详说式发现）；❷微观讨论；❸实验验证、宏观讨论；❹创新点。

3.3 参考文献

参考文献（Rederences 或 References and Notes）是指对一个信息资源或其中一部分进行准确和详细著录的数据，位于文末或文中的信息源，简单地说就是论文中引用前人（包括作者自己）已发表的有关文献。引自参考文献中的成果，如原理、观点、方法、数据、图表、式子和结果等，均应对所引文献在文中引用的地方予以标注，并在文后列出、著录这些参考文献。这里所说的著录指作者著录参考文献，而不是指图书馆员、文献目录编制者及索引编辑编制各种文献类型。参考文献标注和著录（合称引用）是论文中不可缺少的重要组成部分，其引用的质量和数量是评价论文质量、水平及其起点、深度、科学依据的重要指标，是进行引文统计分析的重要信息源之一。多数收录机构或索引系统通常除收录论文的题名、摘要外，还收录其参考文献。参考文献已成为通过其 DOI 实现引文全球互联的关键。

3.3.1 参考文献的概念

参考文献分为阅读型参考文献（reading reference）和引文参考文献（cited reference），前者是指著者为撰写或编辑文章而阅读过的信息资源，或供读者进一步阅读的信息资源，后者是指著者为撰写或编辑文章而引用的信息资源。文章写作前或写作过程中，作者需要阅读充足的文献，阅读过的文献即为阅读型参考文献；写作的成品需要从其所阅读过的相关文献中选择出有代表性的、典型的文献，在文中合适的位置进行标注，并在文后以列表的形式按某种顺序和著录格式进行列示，这种被标注、列示的文献即为引文参考文献。这就是说，对某一特定文章的参考文献来说，引文参考文献是阅读型参考文献的子集。

论文中引用参考文献的作用主要有：倡导引领学术诚信，培育伦理道德，保留完整记录；科学继承、发展，尊重知识产权，共享信息资源；反映作者的科学态度及论文的科学依据，评价论文水平；区别作者与前人成果，尊重他人，避免抄袭、剽窃的嫌疑；索引导航，方便读者找到和了解相关资料和文献；省去无用的重复内容，精简语句、缩短篇幅，方便叙述；有助于情报学、文献计量学研究，助推学科、科学发展；引文分析，对出版物水准做出较为客观公正的评价。

3.3.2 参考文献的类型

参考文献有多种类别，如图 3-1 所示，不同类参考文献的著录项目与著录格式不同。

参考文献类别
- 专著：普通图书、学位论文、会议文集、报告、标准、古籍、汇编、多卷书、丛书等
- 连续出版物：期刊、报纸等
- 析出文献：普通图书的析出文献、期刊的析出文献、会议文集的析出文献、报纸的析出文献等
- 专利文献：专利申请书、专利说明书、专利公报、专利年度索引等
- 电子资源：电子公告、电子图书、电子期刊、数据库等

图 3-1 参考文献类别

专著（monograph）是以单行本或多卷册形式出版的印刷型或非印刷型出版物（在限定的期限内出齐），包括普通图书、学位论文、会议文集、报告、标准、汇编等。（档案以出版物的形式出现时，可列为专著，如中国清朝档案汇总、政府公文汇总、法律法规文件汇总等；否则，就不属专著，如一般形式的中国清朝档案、政府公文、法律法规文件等。）

连续出版物（serial）是通常载有年卷期号或年月顺序号，并计划无限期地连续出版发行的印刷或非印刷型出版物，如期刊（杂志）、报纸、年鉴、会刊等。

析出文献（contribution）是从整个信息资源中析出的具有独立篇名的文献，如专著或连续出版物的析出文献。

专利文献（patent）是专利申请文件经国家主管专利的机关依法受理、审查合格后，定期出版的各种官方出版物的总称。

电子资源（electronic resource）也称数字化资源或数字资源，是以数字方式将图、文、声、像等信息存储在磁、光、电介质上，通过计算机、网络或相关设备使用的记录有知识内容或艺术内容的信息资源，包括电子公告、电子图书、电子期刊、数据库等。它是随着计算机、信息及网络技术的发展而产生的一种新型文献产品，是以数字形式发布、存取、利用的信息资源，其出现和迅猛发展使原有的文献载体更加多样化。

3.3.3 参考文献标注法

正文中引用文献的标注方法分为顺序编码制和著者-出版年制两大类。

3.3.3.1 按顺序编码制标注

顺序编码制是引文参考文献的一种标注体系——引文采用序号标注，相应地文后参考文献表中各篇文献按照正文部分标注的序号依次列出。

用顺序编码制标注参考文献有以下原则：

1）按正文中引用的文献首次出现的先后顺序连续编码，将序号置于引用处，是否加括号（如方括号或圆括号），用上标还是平排，取决于目标期刊的要求。

2）引用单篇文献时，引文序号的排列形式大体有以下几种情况。

- Jouglard, et al. studied the relationship between productivity and pallet pool while using horizontal machining centers to manufacture small lot sizes[5]. Ray, et al. studied the benefits of using pallet[6].

此例中引文序号（[5]、[6]）置于上标方括号中。

- Recently, deep convolutional neural networks have achieved unprecedented performance in visual domains: for example, image classification[17], face recognition[18], and playing Atari games[19]. They use many layers of neurons, each arranged in overlapping tiles, to construct increasingly abstract, localized representations of an image[20].

此例中引文序号（17、18、19、20）置于上标，但不加括号。

• The low pathogenic H5 and H7 avian influenza viruses are predisposed to acquire more mutations when they circulate in gallinaceous poultry and subsequently become highly pathogenic for chickens and turkeys, as occurred of the H5N2 outbreak in the United States in 1983 [31], the H5N2 outbreak in Mexico in 1995 [32], and the H7N1 outbreak in Italy in 1999 [33].

此例中引文序号（[31]、[32]、[33]）置于平排方括号中。

• Recent anthropogenic deposits, which are the products of mining, waste disposal (landfill), construction, and urbanization (19), contain the greatest expansion of new minerals since the Great Oxygenation Event at 2400 Ma (20) and are accompanied by many new forms of "rock," in the broad sense of geological materials with the potential for longterm persistence. Over many millennia, humans have manufactured materials previously unknown on Earth, such as pottery, glass, bricks, and copper alloys. Remains of these materials are present as a persistent and wide spread geological signal that is markedly time-transgressive, reflecting the migration of peoples (21).

此例中序号（(19)、(20)、(21)）置于平排圆括号中。

3）同一处引用多篇文献时，应将各篇文献的序号全部列出，各序号间用","分隔，如遇三个及以上连续序号，起讫序号间用短横线连接。例如：

• Several strategies to enhance Cas9 specificity have been reported, including reducing the amount of active Cas9 in the cell (3, 5, 6), using Cas9 nickase mutants to create a pair of juxtaposed single-stranded DNA nicks (7, 8), truncating the guide sequence at the 5′ end (9), and using a pair of catalytically-inactive Cas9 nucleases, each fused to a FokI nuclease domain (10, 11).

此例中非连续序号间（(3, 5, 6)）或两个连续序号间（(7, 8)、(10, 11)）用","分隔，序号置于平排圆括号中。

• Mismatches between the sgRNA and its DNA target in the first 8-12 PAM-proximal nucleotides can eliminate nuclease activity; however, this nuclease activity can be restored by introducing a DNA:DNA mismatch at that location (16-19).

此例中三个以上连续序号间（(16-19)）用短横线连接，序号置于平排圆括号中。

• MA-based perovskites are thermally unstable and suffer from halide segregation instabilities, and are thus likely to be unsuitable (16). FA-based perovskites are the most likely to deliver the best balance between structural and thermal stability (13, 21-25).

此例中非连续序号间（(13, 21)）用","分隔，三个以上连续序号间（(21-25)）用短横线连接，序号置于平排圆括号中。

• Wearable electronics are devices that can be worn or mated with human skin to continuously and closely monitor an individual's activities, without interrupting or limiting the user's motions[1-9]. Thus wearable biosensors could enable real-time continuous monitoring of an individual's physiological biomarkers[10-12].

此例中三个及以上连续序号间（1-9, 10-12）用短横线连接，序号置于上标中，但不加方括号。

• In this paper, a new kind of anti-backlash end face engagement worm gear (EFEWG) is proposed firstly on the basis of the considerable study works for WANG and DENG[10-12].

此例中三个连续序号间用短横线连接，序号置于上标方括号中。

4）引文序号做句子成分（如主语、动宾或介宾）时，不宜单独使用，应在其前面加上表文献的关键词或其缩写（如 Ref., Reference, 或其复数形式 Refs., References）。

• Refs. [20-21, 62-64] demonstrate that the ALT plan obtained by the above method is more robust in terms of the model deviation than the compromise plan.

- From Fig. 8 and Table 1, the result of constraint singularity analysis is consistent with Ref. [34], which turns out that if $\theta = 180°$, that is, the moving platform and the base are parallel and the moving platform is upside down, the manipulator is in its constraint singularity.

此两例中，加有"Refs."和"Ref."的引文号（Refs. [20-21, 62-64]和Ref. [34]）分别做句子的主语和介词with的宾语时必须平排，而且通常加方括号。

5）相同的文献在不同处引用时，其形式取决于它在句子的作用（如标示或做句子成分），可能混用多种形式（如平排、上标等）。例如：

- …TIAN, et al[14-15], discussed the effect of bearing outer clearance on the rotor dynamic characteristics by using the run-up and run-down simulation method…

…As shown in Fig. 2, the model diagram is a modified version of the lumped parameter model described in Ref. [15] to show the turbocharger supported in FRBs, turbocharger rotor is simplified to four stations connected by three uniformly circular beam sections…

- In this respect, although the traditional theories on regression diagnosis are rich [7, 8, 85, 86], few of them are applicable to the censored data and non-normal distribution. In addition to the graphics method in Refs. [7, 8], to meet the need of the ALT for electrical connectors, based on the principle of failure physics, hypothesis testing, and regression theory, Qian, et al. [87, 88] and Liu [89] proposed methods of testing the multivariate stress-life relationship and the assumptions of cumulative damage of a time-censored ALT with Weibull distribution, respectively.

前一例子中，引文序号15在两处出现了：第一处它起标示作用，用了上标的形式；第二处它加上"Ref."一起做介词in的宾语，为平排的形式。这样就出现了同一引文序号多种形式混用的现象。后一例子中，引文序号7、8存在直接引用和其前面加"Refs."两种形式，前一情况用来标示，后一情况用来做介词的宾语。

3.3.3.2 按著者-出版年制标注

著者-出版年制是引文参考文献的另一种标注体系——引文采用著者-出版年标注，参考文献表按著者字母顺序（姓氏首字母的顺序）和出版年排序。

用著者-出版年制标注参考文献有以下原则：

1）引用的文献采用著者-出版年制时，各篇文献的标注内容由著者姓氏与出版年构成，并置于"（）"内。倘若只标注著者姓氏无法识别人名时，可标注著者姓名（全名）。倘若正文中已提及著者姓名，则在其后的括号内只著录出版年。如遇句中已有圆括号，则标注文献的括号可用另一形式的括号如方括号。有时根据表达需要，可以在文献标注部分中著者姓氏前面加相关词语。例如：

- The notion of an invisible college has been explored in the sciences (Crane, 1972). Its absence among historians was noted by Stieg (1981) …

- Finally, Siksnys showed that the system could also be reconstituted in a second way—by combining purified His-tagged Cas9, in-vitro-transcribed tracrRNA and crRNA, and RNase III—and that both RNAs were essential for Cas9 to cut DNA. (They would ultimately drop the second reconstitution from their revised paper, but they reported all of the work in their published U.S. patent application filed in March 2012 [Siksnys et al., 2012]).

- When scientists in the late 1980s devised a way to alter mammalian genomes in living cells, it transformed biomedical research—including making it possible to insert DNA at a specific location in mouse embryonic stem cells and then produce mice carrying the genetic modification (reviewed in Capecchi, 2005).

例一中有两个括号部分,即为两处单篇文献引用:第一处括号内为姓氏 Crane 与出版年 1972,其间用逗号分隔;第二处括号内省去了姓氏 Stieg,仅为出版年 1981,因为在括号前面已提及该姓氏,括号内没有必要再重复著录。例二中标注文献的括号用了方括号"[ ]",以与所在句里的圆括号"( )"相区分。例三中在姓氏 Capecchi 前面增加了词语"reviewed in"。

2)引用多著者文献时,对著者标注第一著者的姓氏(其后附"et al.",姓氏与"et al."之间留空隙,或加逗号","分隔),或标注几位(两位或更多位)著者的姓氏。例如:

● This finding supported earlier suggestions that the palindromic nature of the repeats would lead to secondary structure formation in the crRNA (Sorek et al., 2008).

● They even filed a patent application including the use of CRISPR to cut or correct genomic loci in eukaryotic cells, but it lacked sufficient experimental demonstration and they eventually abandoned it (Sontheimer and Marraffini, 2008).

前一例子中,只标注了第一著者的姓氏 Sorek,其后附"et al.";后一例子中,标注了两位作者的姓氏,分别为 Sontheimer 和 Marraffini。

3)同一处引用多篇文献时,对其著者可采用以上方法分别标注,并用分号分隔。例如:

● Because the school had hardly any start-up funds or lab space, he turned to bioinformatics to investigate the strange repeats, which he dubbed short regularly spaced repeats (SRSRs); the name would later be changed, at his suggestion, to clustered regularly interspaced palindromic repeats (CRISPR) (Jansen et al., 2002; Mojica and Garrett, 2012).

● Nearly two decades after CRISPR loci were first identified in Escherichia coli, spacers were found to derive from viral genomes and conjugative plasmids, serving as records of previous infection (Bolotin et al., 2005; Ishino et al., 1987; Mojica et al., 2005; Pourcel et al., 2005).

● Phylogenetic studies suggested that some *csm* and *cmr* genes are distant homologs of cas genes that compose the Cascade complex of Type I systems, and subsequent structural studies have revealed a striking structural conservation between Cascade and the Csm and Cmr complexes (Hochstrasser et al., 2014; Jackson et al., 2014; Makarova et al., 2013; Mulepati et al., 2014; Osawa et al., 2015; Staals et al., 2014; Taylor et al., 2015; Zhao et al., 2014).

第一个例子中,引用了两篇参考文献,第一篇只标注了第一著者的姓氏 Jansen,后附"et al.",第二篇标注了两位著者的姓氏 Mojica 和 Garrett,加上年份以逗号分隔共同置于括号内。第二个例子中,引用了四篇参考文献,括号内各注录项用分号分隔。第三个例子中,引用了八篇参考文献,括号内各注录项用分号分隔。

4)当引用同一著者在同一年出版的多篇文献时,可在文献标注部分的年份后加小写字母 a,b……,相应地文后参考文献表中著录这些文献时,其出版年后也加这些小写字母。例如:

● Intriguingly, expression of dCas9 results in the acquisition of primarily self-targeting spacers, suggesting that many acquisition events lead to self-targeting and suicide (Wei et al., 2015b).

● In addition, while the trans-activating crRNA (tracrRNA) that forms a complex with Cas9 and the crRNA is necessary for acquisition, it is unclear whether a corresponding crRNA is also required (Heleretal., 2015; Wei et al., 2015b).

● The sequence requirements for protospacer integration in Type II-A systems were recently demonstrated in S. thermophilus (Wei et al., 2015a). Similar to E. coli, the leader and a single repeat were sufficient to direct integration. Furthermore, only the ten nucleotides of the leader proximal to the first repeat are required to license the integration of new spacers, in contrast to the 60 nt minimal requirement in E. coli (Wei et al., 2015a; Yosef et al., 2012). A limited mutational study of the repeat showed that the first two nucleotides are necessary for acquisition, while the final two nucleotides can be mutated without consequence (Wei et al., 2015a).

此三语段摘自同一论文的相邻几段，其中多处引用同一著者（Wei）同年出版的两篇文献，在标注部分的年份后加了小写字母a，b，文后参考文献表中这两篇文献的著录项目中也加了相应的字母。例如：

Wei, Y., Chesne, M. T., Terns, R. M., and Terns, M. P. (2015a). Sequences spanning the leader-repeat junction mediate CRISPR adaptation to phage in Streptococcus thermophilus. Nucleic Acids Res. 43, 1749-1758.

Wei, Y., Terns, R. M., and Terns, M. P. (2015b). Cas9 function and host genome sampling in Type II-A CRISPR-Cas adaptation. Genes Dev. 29, 356-361.

5) 当引用同一著者（常指第一作者）在不同年出版的多篇文献时，可以只对著者姓氏标注一次，而对不同的年份连续标注。例如：

● Depending on the strength of the GPCR-barr interaction, the receptor may either undergo transient internalization, followed by recycling to the plasma membrane for weak interactions (class A GPCRs), or sustained internalization into endosomes for stronger interactions (class B GPCRs) (Oakley et al., 1999, 2000).

● The b2V2R has been rigorously characterized both herein and in previous studies; it displays similar biological properties to the V2R, as well as to other class B GPCRs, and has been routinely used as a robust model class B GPCR (Lee et al., 2016; Oakley et al., 1999, 2000; Tohgo et al., 2003).

此两语段摘自同一论文，均引用了同一著者Oakley在1999年和2000年发表的两篇文献。

6) 多次引用同一著者的同一文献，可在正文中标注著者与出版年，并在"（）"外以角标的形式著录引文页码。例如：（Liang, 2018）[66]；（Liang, 2018）[88]；（Liang, 2018）[196]。

3.3.4 参考文献表组织

参考文献表可按顺序编码制组织，也可按著者-出版年制组织，集中著录在文后。

3.3.4.1 按顺序编码制组织

参考文献表按顺序编码制组织时，各篇文献应按正文部分标注的序号依次列出。例如：

References

1. Allis, L. V. *Searching for Solutions in Games and Artificial Intelligence*. PhD thesis, Univ. Limburg, Maastricht, The Netherlands (1994).
2. van den Herik, H., Uiterwijk, J. W. & van Rijswijck, J. Games solved: now and in the future. *Artif. Intell.* **134**, 277-311 (2002).
3. Schaeffer, J. The games computers (and people) play. *Advances in Computers* **52**, 189-266 (2000).
4. Campbell, M., Hoane, A. & Hsu, F. Deep Blue. *Artif. Intell.* **134**, 57-83 (2002).
5. Schaeffer, J. et al. A world championship caliber checkers program. *Artif. Intell.* **53**, 273-289 (1992).
6. Buro, M. From simple features to sophisticated evaluation functions. In *1st International Conference on Computers and Games*, 126-145 (1999).
7. Müller, M. Computer Go. *Artif. Intell.* **134**, 145-179 (2002).
8. Tesauro, G. & Galperin, G. On-line policy improvement using Monte-Carlo search. In *Advances in Neural Information Processing*, 1068-1074 (1996).
……
35. Browne, C. *et al.* A survey of Monte-Carlo tree search methods. *IEEE Trans. Comput. Intell. AI in Games* **4**, 1-43 (2012).

36. Gelly, S. et al. The grand challenge of computer Go: Monte Carlo tree search and extensions. *Commun. ACM* **55**, 106–113 (2012).

37. Coulom, R. Whole-history rating: A Bayesian rating system for players of time-varying strength. In *International Conference on Computers and Games*, 113–124 (2008).

38. KGS. Rating system math. http://www.gokgs.com/help/rmath.html.

3.3.4.2 按著者-出版年制组织

参考文献表按著者-出版年制组织时，按姓氏首字母的顺序（A→B→…→Z）排列。例如：

References

Audet, N., Charfi, I., Mnie-Filali, O., Amraei, M., Chabot-Doré, A. J., Millecamps, M., Stone, L. S., and Pineyro, G. (2012). Differential association of receptor-Gbg complexes with b-arrestin2 determines recycling bias and potential for tolerance of d opioid receptor agonists. J. Neurosci. *32*, 4827–4840.

Calebiro, D., Nikolaev, V. O., Gagliani, M. C., de Filippis, T., Dees, C., Tacchetti, C., Persani, L., and Lohse, M. J. (2009). Persistent cAMP-signals triggered by internalized G-protein-coupled receptors. PLoS Biol. *7*, e1000172.

Feinstein, T. N., Wehbi, V. L., Ardura, J. A., Wheeler, D. S., Ferrandon, S., Gardella, T. J., and Vilardaga, J. P. (2011). Retromer terminates the generation of cAMP by internalized PTH receptors. Nat. Chem. Biol. *7*, 278–284.

Feinstein, T. N., Yui, N., Webber, M. J., Wehbi, V. L., Stevenson, H. P., King, J. D., Jr., Hallows, K. R., Brown, D., Bouley, R., and Vilardaga, J. P. (2013). Noncanonical control of vasopressin receptor type 2 signaling by retromer and arrestin. J. Biol. Chem. *288*, 27849–27860.

Ferrandon, S., Feinstein, T. N., Castro, M., Wang, B., Bouley, R., Potts, J. T., Gardella, T. J., and Vilardaga, J. P. (2009). Sustained cyclic AMP production by parathyroid hormone receptor endocytosis. Nat. Chem. Biol. *5*, 734–742.

Gale's, C., VanDurm, J. J., Schaak, S., Pontier, S., Percherancier, Y., Audet, M., Paris, H., and Bouvier, M. (2006). Probing the activation-promoted structural rearrangements in preassembled receptor-G protein complexes. Nat. Struct. Mol. Biol. *13*, 778–786.

Gilliland, C. T., Salanga, C. L., Kawamura, T., Trejo, J., and Handel, T. M. (2013). The chemokine receptor CCR1 is constitutively active, which leads to G protein-independent, b-arrestin-mediated internalization. J. Biol. Chem. *288*, 32194–32210.

Gilman, A. G. (1987). G proteins: transducers of receptor-generated signals. Annu. Rev. Biochem. *56*, 615–649.

……

Szczepek, M., Beyrière, F., Hofmann, K. P., Elgeti, M., Kazmin, R., Rose, A., Bartl, F. J., von Stetten, D., Heck, M., Sommer, M. E., et al. (2014). Crystal structure of a common GPCR-binding interface for G protein and arrestin. Nat. Commun. *5*, 4801.

Tohgo, A., Choy, E. W., Gesty-Palmer, D., Pierce, K. L., Laporte, S., Oakley, R. H., Caron, M. G., Lefkowitz, R. J., and Luttrell, L. M. (2003). The stability of the G protein-coupled receptor-beta-arrestin interaction determines the mechanism and functional consequence of ERK activation. J. Biol. Chem. *278*, 6258–6267.

Vilardaga, J. P., Krasel, C., Chauvin, S., Bambino, T., Lohse, M. J., and Nissenson, R. A. (2002). Internalization determinants of the parathyroid hormone receptor differentially regulate beta-arrestin/receptor association. J. Biol. Chem. *277*, 8121–8129.

Violin, J. D., DiPilato, L. M., Yildirim, N., Elston, T. C., Zhang, J., and Lefkowitz, R. J. (2008). beta2-adrenergic receptor signaling and desensitization elucidated by quantitative modeling of real time cAMP dynamics. J. Biol. Chem. *283*, 2949–2961.

Wehbi, V. L., Stevenson, H. P., Feinstein, T. N., Calero, G., Romero, G., and Vilardaga, J. P. (2013). Noncanonical GPCR signaling arising from a PTH receptor-arrestin-Gbg complex. Proc. Natl. Acad. Sci. USA *110*, 1530-1535.

Westfield, G. H., Rasmussen, S. G., Su, M., Dutta, S., DeVree, B. T., Chung, K. Y., Calinski, D., Velez-Ruiz, G., Oleskie, A. N., Pardon, E., et al. (2011). Structural flexibility of the G alpha s alpha-helical domain in the beta2-adrenoceptor Gs complex. Proc. Natl. Acad. Sci. USA **108**, 16086–16091.

3.3.5 参考文献著录项目

参考文献著录应规范，做到著录项目完整、格式规范、与正文引证相符、姓名书写正确、信息项（如年份、卷号/期号/页码）全面或表达正确。不规范的著录将增加退稿概率，或增加返修次数，加长修改周期，推迟论文发表，而且还将影响论文的质量、科学性及可读性。作者应认真研读征稿简则（作者须知）或浏览样刊，对目标期刊的参考文献著录格式体例了解清楚。当然，文献种类、著录项目的多样性，不同类型文献的著录项目、格式的差异性，以及著录形式、细节的复杂性，给参考文献规范著录带来困难。

下面参照名刊（如 *Nature*、*Science*、*Cell*、*Cell Research*、*Light：S&A* 等）的参考文献著录实例，并结合国家标准 GB/T 7714—2015《信息与文献 参考文献著录规则》，对参考文献著录项目与格式进行总结，给出较为典型的著录格式示例。为撰写和表述方便，这里的著录格式示例主要是基于顺序编码制。著者–出版年制和顺序编码制的著录格式差异主要体现在年份的位置上，其他方面大同小异，因此基于顺序编码制的著录格式也可供著者–出版年制的借鉴。例如以下为著者–出版年制的著录示例，其中的年份"（2012）"位于主要责任者的后面：

Mojica, F. J. M., and Garrett, R. A. (2012). Discovery and SeminalDevelopments in the CRISPR Field. In CRISPR-Cas Systems, R. Barrangou and J. van der Oost, eds. (Berlin, Heidelberg: Springer Berlin Heidelberg), pp. 1-31. (from *Sell*)

3.3.5.1 专著

专著著录项目包括：主要责任者[①]、题名项、其他责任者、版本项、出版项、获取和访问路径、DOI[②]。

专著著录格式：主要责任者. 专著名.（:）其他专著名信息. 其他责任者. 版本项.（出版者，出版地，出版年），引文页码[③]（引用年份或日期）. 获取和访问路径. DOI.

不同类别的专著在著录格式上可能有差异，以下给出几种常见专著的著录格式及示例。

（1）普通图书

普通图书著录大体格式：主要责任者. 图书名.（:）其他书名信息. 其他责任者. 版本项.（出版者，出版地，出版年），引文页码（引用年份或日期）. 获取和访问路径. DOI. 例如：

1. Sutton, R. & Barto, A. *Reinforcement Learning：an Introduction* (MIT Press, 1998). (from *Nature*)

例 1 引自 *Nature*，其人名为先姓后名，名为首字母加缩写点，姓和名之间用逗号分隔，括号内为出版者和出版年。

2. C. P. Summerhayes, Earth's Climate Evolution (Wiley-Blackwell, 2015). (from *Science*)

[①] 主要责任者主要是创建信息资源的实体，即对信息资源的知识或艺术内容负主要责任的个人或团体，包括著者、编者、学位论文撰写者、专利申请者或专利权人、报告撰写者、标准提出者、析出文献的著者等。

[②] 获取和访问路径、DOI 是针对电子资源的，如果文献获取是通过网络途径获得的电子资源，那么著录项目就应该有获取和访问路径（即网址）。获取和访问路径和 DOI 可以同时著录，或只著录其中一项，获取和访问路径中也可能包含有 DOI。

[③] 引用整本专著时无引文页码项。

例2引自 Science，与上例不同之处是先名后姓，名和姓之间用空格分隔，括号内为出版者和出版年。

3. Schmidt, R. F. & Thews, G. *Human Physiology*. (Springer, Berlin, Heidelberg, 1989). (from *Light S&A*)

4. Efron, U. *Spatial Light Modulator Technology*: *Materials, Devices, and Applications*. (Marcel Dekker, New York, 1995). (from *Light S&A*)

5. Rogalski, A. *Infrared Detectors*. 2nd edn. (CRC Press, Boca Raton, 2011). (from *Light S&A*)

6. Pacchioni, G., Skuja, L. & Griscom, D. L. *Defects in SiO₂ and Related Dielectrics*: *Science and Technology*. (Springer, The Netherlands, 2000), p 73. (from *Light S&A*)

例3~6引自 *Light S&A*（2018以前版本），人名写法同例1，括号部分为出版项，包括出版者、出版地和出版年。例5多了一个版本项（2nd edn）。例6多了一个引文页码（p 73）。

7. *Manual of diagnostic tests and vaccines for terrestrial animals*. Office International des Epizooties. Paris, 2011. (from *Cell Research*)

例7引自 *Cell Research*。第一项为手册（属于专著）名，第二、三项为手册主要责任者及所在地，最后为年份。

8. Koestler, A. *The Ghost in The Machine*. (Hutchinson & Co (Publishers) Ltd., London, 1967).

9. Tang, X. J. *Newspaper Economy and Management*. (Xinhua Press, Beijing, 1999), pp. 117–121. (in Chinese)

10. Literature Editorial Committee of the Central Committee of the Communist Party of China. *Selected Works of Deng Xiaoping*: *Volume III*. (Beijing: Peoples Publishing House, 1993). (in Chinese)

11. Richard, O. D., Peter, E. H. & David, G. S. *Pattern Classification*. Li, H. D. & Yao, T. X. et al. trans. (China Machine Press, CITIC Press Corporation, Beijing, 2003). (in Chinese)

12. Rood, H. J. *Logic and Structured Design for Computer Programmers*. 3rd ed. (Brooks/Cole-Thomson Learning, 2001).

13. Zhao, Y. D. *Industrial Engineers of the New Era*. (Popular Culture Press, Taipei, 1998) (1998-09-26). http://www.ie.nthu.edu.tw/info/ie.newie.htm (Big5). (in Chinese)

14. Turcotte, D. L. *Fractals and Chaos in Geology and Geophysics*. (Cambridge University Press, New York, 1992) (1998-09-23). http://www.seg.org/reviews//mccorm30.html.

15. Fan, X., Sommers, C. H. *Food Irradiation Research and Technology*. 2nd ed. (Blackwell Publishing, Iowa, Ames, 2013), pp. 25-26 (2014-06-26). http://onlinelibrary.wiley.com/doi/10.1002/9781118422557.ch2/summary.

例8、9为典型的图书，9还多了页码（pp. 117–121）。例10主要责任者为机构（Literature Editorial Committee of the Central Committee of the Communist Party of China），而且有其他书名信息（Volume III）。例11有其他责任者（译者项：Li, H. D. & Yao, T. X. et al. trans），括号内列出两个出版社（China Machine Press, CITIC Press Corporation）。例12有版本项（3rd ed）。例13~15是通过网络获得的图书电子资源，有引用日期和网址（实际中日期可直接用年份代替），15还多了引文页码（pp. 25-26）。

（2）会议文集（论文集、会议录）

这里的会议文集指整本会议文集而非其中的某篇文章，即引用的是整本文集而非其中析出的具体文献，因此其著录属于专著范畴。

会议文集著录大体格式：主要责任者. 会议文集名.（，或:）其他会议文集信息㊀. 其他责任者.（出版者, 出版地, 出版年），引文页码（引用年份或日期）. 获取和访问路径. DOI. 例如：

㊀ 其他会议文集信息可以包括有关会议的一些信息，如会议召开时间、地点和国家。

16. Xin, X. M. *International Symposium on Information Technologies and Information Services*: Set A. (Social Sciences Press, Beijing, 1994). (in Chinese)

17. The Chinese Society of Theoretical and Applied Mechanics. *Proceedings of the 3rd National Conference on Experimental Fluid Mechanics of China*. (Tianjin, 1990). (in Chinese)

18. Rosenthall, E. M. *Proceedings of the Fifth Canadian Mathematical Congress*, University of Montreal, 1961. (University of Toronto Press, Toronto, 1963).

19. Yufin, S. A. *Geoecology and Computers*: *Proceedings of the Third International Conference on Advances of Computer Methods in Geotechnical and Geoenvironmental Engineering*, Moscow, Russian, February 1–4, 2000. (A. A. Balkema, Rotterdam, 2000).

20. Chen, Z. Y. *Study on the Cultural Value of Finance and Taxation in China*: *International Symposium on Finance and Taxation Culture in China*. (Economic Science Press, Beijing, 2011) (2013-10-14). http://apabi.lib.pku.edu.cn/usp/pku/pub.mvc?pid = book.detail & metaid = m.metaid = m.20110628- BPO-889-0135 & cult = CN. (in Chinese)

例 16~20 中，斜体部分为会议文集名，括号（指第一个括号）部分为出版项，包括出版者、出版地和出版年（可能有的不全）。除例 17 的主要责任者为机构外，其他例子均为个人；例 20 是通过网络获得的会议文集电子资源，在后面给出引用日期和网址（日期可用年份代替）。

（3）报告

这里的报告指整个报告而非其中的部分篇章，引用的是整个报告而非其中析出的具体文献，因此其著录属于专著范畴。

报告著录大体格式：主要责任者. (,) 报告名. 其他责任者. (报告单位，报告地，报告年) 或 (出版者，出版地，出版年)，引文页码 (引用年份或日期). (;) 获取和访问路径. DOI. 例如：

21. IPCC, *Climate Change* 2013: *The Physical Science Basis. Contribution of Working Group I to the Fifth Assessment Report of the Intergovernmental Panel on Climate Change*, T. F. Stocker et al., Eds. (Cambridge Univ. Press, 2013). (from *Science*)

22. UNSCEAR-United Nations Scientific Committee on the Effects of Atomic Radiation, *Sources and Effects of Ionizing Radiation* (United Nations, New York, 2000). (from *Science*)

23. Pan American Health Organization (PAHO), World Health Organization (WHO), "*Epidemiological alert*: *Neurological syndrome, congenital malformations, and Zika virus infection. Implications for public health in the Americas*" (PAHO/WHO, 2015). (from *Science*)

24. WHO, "*Assessment of infants with microcephaly in the context of Zika virus*" (WHO Interim Report, 2016); http://apps.who.int/iris/bitstream/10665/204475/1/WHO_ZIKV_MOC_16.3_eng.pdf. (from *Science*)

例 21~24 引自 *Science*。其中斜体部分为报告名，斜体部分之前是主要责任者（报告形成或发布单位，例 23 是 PAHO 和 WHO 两个单位并列），括号部分主要是报告单位、报告年（例 22~24）或出版者、出版年（例 21）。例 21 有其他责任者（编者项：T. F. Stocker et al., Eds）。例 24 有网址，表明是通过网络访问和获取的。

25. U. S. Department of Transportation Federal Highway Administration. *Guidelines for handling excavated acid-producting materials*: PB 91 194001. (U. S. Department of Commerce National Information Service, Springfield, 1990).

26. World Health Organization. *Factors regulating the immune response*: *report of WHO Scientific Group*. (WHO, Geneva, 1970).

27. Calkin, D., Ager, A, Thompson, M. *A comparative risk assessment framework for wildand fire management*: *the* 2010 *cohesive strategy science report*: *RMRS-GTR*-262. (2011), pp. 8–9.

28. Kang, X. M. *Study on machining deformation for large-scale monolithic component*: Post-doctoral report. (Zhejiang University, Hangzhou, 2002. (in Chinese)

29. Tang, W. J., Yang, Y. X., Liu, W. et al. *Final report on the development of important technical standards for human safety*: 7178999 X-2006 BAK04 A10 /10. 2013 (2014-06-24). http://www. nstrs. org. cn/xiangxiBG. aspx? id = 41707.

例 25～29 的著录项目和格式同例 21～24。例 27 的括号里仅有报告年，后面还给出引文页码（pp. 8-9）；例 28 为博士后出站报告；例 29 为电子资源，有引用日期（2014-06-24）。

（4）学位论文

学位论文大体著录格式：主要责任者. 学位论文名. 学位类别，保存单位，地点（城市，国家）（年份），引文页码（引用年份或日期）. 获取和访问路径. DOI. 例如：

30. Allis, L. V. *Searching for Solutions in Games and Artificial Intelligence*. PhD thesis, Univ. Limburg, Maastricht, The Netherlands (1994). (from *Nature*)

31. Son, S. Y. *Design principles and methodologies for reconfigurable machining system*. PhD thesis, University of Michigan, Michigan (2000).

32. Liang, F. J. *Comprehensive Study on Mechanized Agricultural Production Systems*. Master thesis, China Agricultural University, Beijing, China (1996) (2018-09-04). https://www. nstl. gov. cn/facade/search/toFullView. do? checkedSEQNO = 13fc8820 d9903bed2b21bf247452cb8e. (in Chinese)

此三例为学位论文，其中斜体部分为学位论文的名称。例 30、31 为博士论文（PhD thesis）；例 32 为硕士论文（Master thesis），电子资源，引用日期为 2018-09-04。

（5）标准

标准大体著录格式：主要责任者. 标准名：标准编号（标准代号 顺序号—发布年）.（出版者，出版地，出版年），引文页码（引用年份或日期）. 获取和访问路径. DOI. 例如：

33. State Bureau of Technology Supervision of China. *GB 3100～3102—1993 Quantities and Unit.* (China Standard Publishing House, Beijing, 1994). (in Chinese)

34. General Administration of Quality Supervision, Inspection and Quarantine of the People's Republic of China; Standardization Administration of the People's Republic of China. *GB/T 7714—2015 Information and documentation—Rules for bibliographic references and citations to information resources.* (China Standard Publishing House, Beijing, 2015). (in Chinese)

35. *Information and documentation-the Dublin core metadata element set*: ISO 15836; 2009 (2013-03-24). http://www.iso.org/iso/home/store/catalogue_tc/catalogue_detail.htm? csnumber = 52142.

此三例为标准，其中斜体部分为标准的名称。例 33、34 括号内为出版项（出版者、出版地和出版年），而且例 34 有两个主要责任者（以分号相隔）；例 35 没有著录主要责任者和出版项，是电子资源，有网址和引用日期。

（6）汇编

汇编大体著录格式：主要责任者. 汇编名. 版本项.（出版者，出版地，出版年），引文页码（引用年份或日期）. 获取和访问路径. DOI. 例如：

36. China Machinery Industry Information Institute. *Survey of Overseas Machinery Industry.* (China Machine Press, Beijing, 2001). (in Chinese)

37. Technology Development Division of General Administration of Press and Publication of the People's Republic of China; Book Publishing Division of General Administration of Press and Publication of the People's Republic of China; China Standard Publishing House. *Common Standards and Specifications for Authors and Editors.* 2nd ed. (China Standard Publishing House, Beijing,

2005). (in Chinese)

此两例为汇编,其中斜体部分为汇编的名称,括号内为出版项(出版者、出版地和出版年)。例37有三个主要责任者(以分号相隔),并且有版本项(2nd ed)。

3.3.5.2 专著的析出文献

专著的析出文献著录项目包括:析出文献主要责任者、析出文献题名项、析出文献其他责任者、出处项、版本项、出版项、获取和访问路径、DOI。

此类文献大体著录格式:析出文献主要责任者. 析出文献名. 析出文献其他责任者. In 专著名:其他题名信息,版本项,专著主要责任者(出版者,出版地,出版年),引文页码(引用年份或日期). 获取和访问路径. DOI. ("引文页码"也可位于"(出版者,出版地,出版年)"前)。

(1) 普通图书的析出文献

下面给出普通图书的析出文献著录的一些示例。

38. Baudiš, P. & Gailly, J. -L. Pachi: State of the art open source Go program. In *Advances in Computer Games*, 24-38 (Springer, 2012). (from *Nature*)

例38引自 *Nature*。其著录格式为:①析出文献主要责任者(Baudiš, P. & Gailly, J. -L., 先姓后名,名为首字母加缩写点,姓和名之间用逗号分隔);②析出文献名(Pachi: State of the art open source Go program);③In + 图书名(In *Advances in Computer Games*, 图书名用斜体);④引文页码(24-38);⑤出版项,包括出版者和出版年(Springer, 2012)。

39. B. Pillans, P. Gibbard, "The Quaternary Period," in *The Geologic Time Scale*, F. M. Gradstein, J. Ogg, M. Schmitz, G. Ogg, Eds. (Elsevier B. V., 2012), pp. 979-1010. (from *Science*)

40. C. N. Waters, J. A. Zalasiewicz, M. Williams, M. A. Ellis, A. M. Snelling, "A stratigraphical basis for the Anthropocene?," in *A Stratigraphical Basis for the Anthropocene*, C. N. Waters, J. A. Zalasiewicz, M. Williams, M. A. Ellis, A. M. Snelling, Eds. (Geological Society, London, 2014), pp. 1-21. (from *Science*)

41. J. Zalasiewicz, M. Williams, C. N. Waters, A. D. Barnosky, P. Haff, "Anthropocene," in *Origins*, O. Seberg, D. A. Harper, Eds. (Cambridge Univ. Press, in press). (from *Science*)

42. A. G. Smith, T. Barry, P. Bown, J. Cope, A. Gale, P. L. Gibbard, J. Gregory, M. Hounslow, D. Kemp, R. Knox, J. Marshall, M. Oates, P. Rawson, J. Powell, C. Waters, "GSSPs, global stratigraphy and correlation," in *Strata and Time: Probing the Gaps in Our Understanding*, D. G. Smith, R. J. Bailey, P. M. Burgess, A. J. Fraser, Eds. (Special Publication 404, Geological Society, London, 2014), pp. 37-67. (from *Science*)

例39~42引自 *Science*,其著录项目和格式基本同例38,但也有差异,例如析出文献加有引号、有专著主要责任者(标志是 Eds., 即"×编"之意)。例39、40和42有引文页码(标志是 pp.);例39的出版项只有两项(出版者、出版年),例40的出版项有三项(出版者、出版地、出版年),例41的出版项有两项(一项是出版者,另一项是 in press,表明引用时该文献还未正式出版),例42的出版项有四项(比正常的三项多了一项 Special Publication 404,即对文献给予特别注释)。不管责任者有多少位(如例42的析出文献主要责任者有15位,图书主要责任者有4位),都如实全部著录。

43. Delerue C, Allan G, Lannoo M. Theory of silicon nanocrystals. In: Pavesi L, Gaponenko S, Dal Negro L editors. *Towards the First Silicon Laser*. The Netherlands: Springer; 2003, pp 243-260. (from *Light S&A*)

例43引自 *Light S&A*,其著录项目和格式基本同以上示例。但也略有差异:表"×编"的标志是 editors 而不是 Eds.;出版项未加括号,格式为"出版地:出版者;出版年";图书主要责任者位于"In:"之后和图书名之前（例44同此，但例39~42中的图书主要责任者位于图书名后，而图书名位于"In"之后）。

44. Roberson, J. A., Burneson, E. G. Drinking water standards, regulations and goals. In: Ameriacan Water Works Association, Eds. *Water quality & treatment*: *a handbook on drinking water*. 6th ed. (McGraw-Hill, New York, 2011), pp. 1.1-1.36 (2012-12-10). http://lib.myilibrary.com/Open.aspx? id=291430.

例44为电子资源，有引用时间和网址。另外，还有版本项（6th ed），版本项通常位于图书名的后面；图书主要责任者为机构（Ameriacan Water Works Association）而非个人。

（2）会议文集的析出文献

下面给出会议文集的析出文献著录的一些示例。

45. Buro, M. From simple features to sophisticated evaluation functions. In *1st International Conference on Computers and Games*, 126-145 (1999). (from *Nature*)

46. Enzenberger, M. Evaluation in Go by a neural network using soft segmentation. In *10th Advances in Computer Games Conference*, 97-108 (2003). 267. (from *Nature*)

47. Tesauro, G. & Galperin, G. On-line policy improvement using Monte-Carlo search. In *Advances in Neural Information Processing*, 1068-1074 (1996). (from *Nature*)

48. Krizhevsky, A., Sutskever, I. & Hinton, G. ImageNet classification with deep convolutional neural networks. In *Advances in Neural Information Processing Systems*, 1097-1105 (2012). (from *Nature*)

以上四例引自 *Nature*。其著录格式为：①析出文献主要责任者；②析出文献名；③会议（会议文集）名（斜体，标志词是其前面加 In）；④引文页码；⑤年份。例45、46有一位责任者，例46中的引文页码分两部分（97-108、267），分别放在年份的前后；例47有两位责任者，以符号 & 分

隔两个姓名；例48有三位责任者，后两位以 & 分隔。

49. Xiao L. F. et al. Impedance control of a robot needle with a fiber optic force sensor. In *Proceedings of the 13th International Conference on Signal Processing* 1379-11383（IEEE, Chengdu, China, 2016）. (from *Light S&A*)

50. Raghunathan, R. et al. Evaluating changes in brain vasculature of murine embryos in utero due to maternal alcohol consumption using optical coherence tomography. In *Proceedings Volume* 10340, *International Conference on Biophotonics V*; 29 April 2017; Perth, Australia (eds David D. Sampson, Dennis L. Matthews, Jürgen Popp, Halina Rubinsztein-Dunlop, and Brian C. Wilson.) 1-7 (SPIE, Perth, Australia, 2017). (from *Light S&A*)

51. Chen, S. Y. et al. Measuring absolute microvascular blood flow in cortex using visible-light optical coherence tomography. In *Proceedings of the 36th Annual International Conference of the IEEE Engineering in Medicine and Biology Society*; 26-30 August 2014; Chicago, IL, USA (eds Besio, W. et al.) 3881-3884 (IEEE, Chicago, IL, USA, 2014). (from *Light S&A*)

52. Dudley, D., Duncan, W. M., Slaughter, J. Emerging digital micromirror device (DMD) applications. In *Proc. SPIE* 4958, *MOEMS Display and Imaging Systems*, 20 January 2003, ed. Urey H. 14-25 (SPIE, San Jose, CA, USA, 2003). (from *Light S&A*)

以上四例引自 *Light S&A*，其著录格式与以上 *Nature* 的基本相同，不同之处在于括号内的会议信息除了年份外，还增加了主办机构、举办地点及国家、时间之类的会议信息。在著录细节上的差异有：例49无其他责任者，会议名后没有给出会议信息；例50有其他责任者，标志词 eds 后加所有译者姓名（共五位）置于括号中，而且会议名后加分号，再给出会议信息（时间、地点和国家：29 April 2017; Perth, Australia）；例51也有其他责任者，但标

志词是 eds 后仅给出一位译者姓名,其余译者用"et al."代替,而且会议名后加分号,再给出会议信息(时间、地点和国家:26-30 *August* 2014;*Chicago*,*IL*,*USA*);例 52 也有其他责任者,但会议名后加逗号,再给出会议信息(仅时间一项:20 *January* 2003),会议信息后加逗号,再直接给出其他责任者(ed. Urey H.),这样其他责任者就未加括号。

53. Metcalf, S. W. The Tort Hall air emission study. In *The International Congress on Hazardous Waste*,*Atlanta Marriott Marquis Hotel*,*Atlanta*,*Georgia*,*June* 5-8,1995:impact on human and ecological health(1998-09-22). http://atsdrl.atsdr.cdc.gov:8080/cong95.html.

此例为电子资源,由网上获得,给出了网址和引用日期。另外,其会议名中已包含会议地点和日期信息(*Atlanta Marriott Marquis Hotel*,*Atlanta*,*Georgia*,*June* 5-8,1995),即会议信息已属于会议名的一部分,因此无须再另行著录。

(3) 汇编的析出文献

下面给出汇编的析出文献著录的一些示例。

54. Salh R. Defect related luminescence in silicon dioxide network:a review. in *INTECH Open Access Publisher*. (Croatia, EU), 2011. (from *Light S&A*)

55. Han,J. R. Characteristics of staff and workers' education. in *Chinese Staff and Workers' Education Association. Collected Papers of Staff and Workers's Education Research* 90-99(People's Education Press, Beijing, 1985). (in Chinese)

56. Information Classification and Coding Institute of National Bureau of Standards of China. GB/T 2659—1986 Codes for names of countries and regions in the world. in *Compilation of National Standards for Documentation*:3(eds China National Technical Committee of Standardization for Documentation)59-92(China Standard Publishing House, Beijing, 1988). (in Chinese)

以上三例为汇编的析出文献,汇编形同会议文集,其著录项目和格式与会议文集相同,其中 in 后面的斜体部分为汇编名。例 54 著录项目较少,没有其他责任者和引文页码,出版项(Croatia, EU)也较简单;例 55 多了引文页码(90-99)和出版项(People's Education Press, Beijing, 1985);例 56 有其他责任者(eds China National Technical Committee of Standardization for Documentation)、引文页码(59-92)和出版项(China Standard Publishing House, Beijing, 1988),项目较为完整。

(4) 报告的析出文献

下面为报告的析出文献著录示例。

57. U. S. Geological Survey, in *Historical Statistics for Mineral and Material Commodities in the United States*, T. D. Kelly, G. R. Matos, Eds. (U. S. Geological Survey Data Series 140, U. S. Geological Survey, 2010); http://minerals.usgs.gov/minerals/pubs/historical-statistics/cement-use.pdf. (from *Science*)

此例引自 *Science*,属于电子资源,因此给出了网址。其他著录项目同会议文集。此例的著录格式为:析出文献名(U. S. Geological Survey),报告名(前面有标志词 in),其他责任者(后面有标志词 Eds.),报告出版、发布或负责单位及年份(U. S. Geological Survey Data Series 140, U. S. Geological Survey, 2010),网址。

3.3.5.3 连续出版物

连续出版物著录项目包括:主要责任者、题名项、年卷期或其他标志、出版项、获取和访问路径、DOI。

此类文献著录大体格式:主要责任者.(,)连续出版物名:其他题名信息. 年卷(期)页码.(出版者,出版地,出版年),引文页码(引用年份或日期). 获取和访问路径. DOI. 例如:

58. M. A. Lancaster *et al.*, *Nature* 501, 373-379 (2013). (from *Science*)

59. M. A. Lancaster, J. A. Knoblich, *Nat. Protoc.* **9**, 2329–2340（2014）.（from *Science*）

60. G. Calvet *et al.*, *Lancet Infect. Dis.* 10. 1016/ S1473-3099（16）00095-5（2016）.（from *Science*）

61. Chen, J. et al. *Cell Res.* https：//doi. org/10. 1038/ s41422-018-0076-9（2018）.（from *Cell Research*）

例 58～61 引自 *Science*，均只引了作者、期刊而未给出文章名，其中期刊名一律用斜体。前两例的著录项目和格式为"作者，期刊名 卷，引文页码（年）."，后两例为电子资源，著录项目和格式为"作者，期刊名 DOI 或网址（年）."

62. Geological Society of China, *Geological Review*, 1（1）（1936）-（Geological Publishing House, Beijing, 1936 - ）.（in Chinese）

63. American Association for the Advancement of Science, *Science*, 1（1）1883-（American Association for the Advancement of Science, Washington, D. C., 1883- ）.

64. Chinese Mechanical Engineering Society（CMES）, *Mechanical Engineering Trends*,（1）2015-（12）2019（Chinese Mechanical Engineering Society （CMES）, Beijing, 2015-2019）.（in Chinese）

例 62～64 均引用了多本期刊，斜体部分为期刊名，期刊名的前面部分为期刊的主要责任者（即主办单位），后面的括号部分为出版项（出版者、出版地和出版年），期刊名和出版项之间为年卷期信息。例 62 中的"1（1）（1936)-"指从 1936 年第 1 卷第 1 期以来的所有 *Geological Review* 期刊，"1936-"指从 1936 年以来的各年。同理，例 63 中的"1（1）1883-"指从 1883 年第 1 卷第 1 期以来的所有 *Science* 期刊，"1883-"指从 1883 年以来的各年。例 64 中的"（1）2015-（12）2019"指从 2015 年第 1 期到 2019 年第 12 期的所有 *Mechanical Engineering Trends* 期刊，"2015-2019"指从 2015 到 2019 年以来的这五年。

3.3.5.4 连续出版物的析出文献

连续出版物的析出文献著录项目包括：析出文献主要责任者、析出文献题名项、出处项、获取和访问路径、DOI。

此类文献大体著录格式：析出文献主要责任者. 析出文献名. 连续出版物名：其他题名信息，卷（期），页码（年）⊖，引文页码（引用年份或日期）. 获取和访问路径. DOI.

（1）期刊的析出文献

下面给出期刊的析出文献著录的一些示例。

65. Kim, D. H. *et al.* Epidermal electronics. *Science* **333**, 838–843（2011）.（from *Nature*）

66. Takei, K. et al. Nanowire active-matrix circuitry for low-voltage macroscale artificial skin. *Nature Mater.* **9**, 821–826（2010）.（from *Nature*）

67. Sonner, Z. *et al.* The microfluidics of the eccrine sweat gland, including biomarker partitioning, transport, and biosensing implications. *Biomicrofluidics* **9**, 031301（2015）.（from *Nature*）

68. McAlpine, M. C., Ahmad, H., Wang, D. & Heath, J. R. Highly ordered nanowire arrays on plastic substrates for ultrasensitive flexible chemical sensors. *Nature Mater.* **6**, 379–384（2007）.（from *Nature*）

69. Schizophrenia Psychiatric Genome-Wide Association Study Consortium. Genome-wide association study identifies five new schizophrenia loci. *Nature Genet.* **43**, 969–976（2011）.（from *Nature*）

70. International Schizophrenia Consortium et al. Common polygenic variation contributes to risk of schizophrenia and bipolar disorder. *Nature* **460**, 748–752（2009）.（from *Nature*）

71. Howson, J. M., Walker, N. M., Clayton, D. &

⊖ 报纸的"年，卷（期）：页码"改为"出版日期（版次）"，如"2018 - 10 - 01（1）"。

Todd, J. A. Confirmation of HLA class II independent type 1 diabetes associations in the major histocompatibility complex including HLA-B and HLA-A. *Diabetes Obes. Metab.* **11** (Suppl 1), 31–45 (2009). (from *Nature*)

72. Jia, X. et al. Imputing amino acid polymorphisms in human leukocyte antigens. *PLoS ONE* **8**, e64683 (2013). (from *Nature*)

73. Levinovitz, A. The mystery of Go, the ancient game that computers still can't win. *Wired Magazine* (2014). (from *Nature*)

74. Slaymaker, I. M. et al. Rationally engineered Cas9 nucleases with improved specificity. *Science* http://dx.doi.org/10.1126/science.aad5227 (2015). (from *Nature*)

75. Jinek, M. et al. Structures of Cas9 endonucleases reveal RNA-mediated conformational activation. *Science* **343**, http://dx.doi.org/10.1126/science.1247997 (2014). (from *Nature*)

例65~75引自 *Nature*，斜体部分为期刊名，加粗体（黑体）为期刊的卷号，除最后两个电子资源外，其基本著录项目和格式为：作者．文章名．期刊名，卷（期），页码（年）。例65~67中，只著录第一位作者，其余作者用 et al. 代替；65、67的刊名用了全写（*Science* 和 *Biomicrofluidics*），66的刊名用了缩写（*Nature Mater.*），67的页码项为 031301。例68、71给出全部四位作者，后两位之间用 & 分隔。例69的作者项为三个机构，以空格分隔（Schizophrenia Psychiatric Genome-Wide Association Study Consortium）。例70的作者项仅著录了一个机构，其余用 et al. 代替。例71的"期"为增刊信息（Suppl 1）。例72的"卷"为电子卷号（e64683）。例73没有著录卷（期）和页码，只有年（2014）。例74、75为电子资源，加了网址，74只著录了年（位于网址后），75著录了卷和年，卷在正常位置（刊名后），年位于网址后。

76. L. Cong, F. A. Ran, D. Cox, S. Lin, R. Barretto, N. Habib, P. D. Hsu, X. Wu, W. Jiang, L. A. Marraffini, F. Zhang, Multiplex genome engineering using CRISPR/Cas systems. *Science* **339**, 819–823 (2013). Medline doi：10.1126/science.1231143 (from *Science*)

77. W. Steffen, J. Grinevald, P. Crutzen, J. McNeill, The Anthropocene：Conceptual and historical perspectives. *Philos. Trans. R. Soc. London Ser. A* 369, 842–867 (2011). doi：10.1098/rsta.2010.0327；pmid：21282150. (from *Science*)

78. C. H. Vane et al., Chemical signatures of the Anthropocene in the Clyde estuary, UK：Sediment-hosted Pb, $^{207/206}$Pb, total petroleum hydrocarbon, polyaromatic hydrocarbon and polychlorinated biphenyl pollution records. *Philos. Trans. R. Soc. London Ser. A* 369, 1085–1111 (2011). doi：10.1098/rsta.2010.0298；pmid：21282161. (from *Science*)

例76~78引自 *Science*，均为电子资源，都给出了 DOI，后两个还给出了 pmid。总体上著录项目和格式与 *Nature* 相同，只是人名写法有差异，一种是先姓后名（*Nature*），另一种是先名后姓（*Science*）。

79. Perego, A. M., Smirnov, S. V., Staliunas, K., Churkin, D. V. & Wabnitz, S. Self-induced Faraday instability laser. *Phys. Rev. Lett.* **120**, 213902 (2018). (from *Light S&A*)

80. Guo, T. A., Liu, F., Guan, B. O. & Albert, J. [INVITED] Tilted fiber grating mechanical and biochemical sensors. *Opt. Laser Technol.* **78**, 19–33 (2016). (from *Light S&A*)

81. Zhuo, Y. et al. Quantitative analysis of focal adhesion dynamics using photonic resonator outcoupler microscopy (PROM). *Light Sci. Appl.* https://doi.org/10.1038/s41377-018-0027-8 (2018). (from *Light S&A*)

例79~81引自 *Light S&A*，著录项目和格式同 *Nature*，但应注意例80中文章名前面加有"[INVITED]"，表明本文是特约文章。其他这里不再赘述。

82. Shen, H. M., Peters, A., Baron, B., Zhu, X. & Storb, U. Mutation of BCL-6 gene in normal B

cells by the process of somatic hypermutation of Ig genes. *Science* **280**, 1750 – 1752（1998）.（from *Cell Research*）

83. Feng, H. et al. Calumenin-15 facilitates filopodia formation by promoting TGF-beta superfamily cytokine GDF-15 transcription. *Cell Death Dis.* **4**, e870（2013）.（from *Cell Research*）

84. Guo, J. U. & Bartel, D. P. RNA G-quadruplexes are globally unfolded in eukaryotic cells and depleted in bacteria. *Science* 353, https：//doi.org/10.1126/science.aaf5371（2016）.（from *Cell Research*）

85. Yuan, L. et al. Etoposide-induced protein 2.4 functions as a regulator of the calcium ATPase and protects pancreatic beta cell survival. *J. Biol. Chem.* https：//doi.org/10.1074/jbc.RA118.002399（2018）.（from *Cell Research*）

例 82 ~ 85 引自 *Cell Research*，著录项目和格式同 *Nature*，这里不赘述。

（2）报纸的析出文献

下面给出报纸的析出文献著录的一些示例。

86. H7N9 has been classed as the most deadly virus by World Health Organization Whether interpersonal communication is unable to answer. *Reference News* 2013-4-26（7）.（in Chinese）

87. Fu, G., Zhao, C., Li, J. L. Thinking after sandstorm. *Beijing Youth Daily* 2000-04-12（14）（2005-07-12）. http：//www.bjyouth.com.cn/Bqb/20000412/GB/4216%5ED_0412B1401.htm.（in Chinese）

此两例为报纸的析出文献，斜体部分为报纸名，报纸名前面为报纸中的文章名，后面为该报纸的出版日期（版次），例 87 中网址前面括号中的日期"2005-07-12"为引用日期。

3.3.5.5 专利文献

专利文献著录项目包括：专利申请者或所有者、题名项、出版项、获取和访问路径、DOI。

专利文献大体著录格式：专利申请者或所有者（年份）. 专利名. 临时专利申请号, 申请日期；公告或公开的专利号（申请结果）.（引用年份或日期）. 获取和访问路径. DOI. 例如：

88. Siksnys, V., Gasiunas, G., and Karvelis, T. (2012). RNA-directed DNA cleavage by the Cas9-crRNA complex from CRISPR3/Cas immune system of Streptococcus thermophilus. U. S. Provisional Patent Application 61/613, 373, filed March 20, 2012; later published as US2015/0045546 (pending).（from *Cell*）

89. Sontheimer, E., and Marraffini, L. (2008). Target DNA interference with crRNA. U. S. Provisional Patent Application 61/009, 317, filed September 23, 2008; later published as US2010/0076057 (abandoned).（from *Cell*）

90. Zhang, F. (2012). Systems Methods and Compositions for Sequence Manipulation. U. S. Provisional Patent Application 61/736, 527, filed December 12, 2012; later published as US008697359B1 (awarded).（from *Cell*）

91. Koseki, A, Momose, H., Kawahito, M. et al. (2015). Compiler. US828402.（2005-05-28）. http：// FF&p = 1&u = netahtml/PTO/search-bool.html&r = 5&f = G&1 = 50&col = AND&d = PG01&s1 = IBM.AS.&OS = AN/IBM&RS = AN/IBM.（from *cell*）

例 88 ~ 91 引自 *Cell*，为专利文献，采用著者-出版年制的体系来著录（这里前面加编号是为了本章写作体例的一致性，原文并没有此编号），年份位于专利申请者或所有者后面。前三篇文献的著录项目和格式为"专利申请者或所有者（年份）. 专利名. 临时申请号, 申请日期；公告专利号（申请结果）."，申请结果分别为受理中（pending）、未通过（abandoned）、通过（awarded）；最后一篇的著录项目和格式为"专利申请者或所有者（年份）. 专利名. 专利号.（引用日期）. 网址."。

3.3.5.6 普通电子资源

凡属电子专著、电子专著的析出文献、

电子连续出版物、电子连续出版物的析出文献以及电子专利文献的著录项目与格式分别按以上 3.3.5.1～3.3.5.5 节中的有关规则处理。除此而外的电子资源（笔者统称为普通电子资源）根据以下著录项目与格式来著录。

普通电子资源著录项目包括：主要责任者、题名项、出版项、获取和访问路径、DOI。

此类文献大体著录格式：主要责任者. 文献名（其他题名信息）. 出版项（出版者，出版地，出版年）（引用年份或日期）. 获取和访问路径. DOI。

以下给出普通电子资源著录的一些示例。

92. KGS. Rating system math. http://www.gokgs.com/help/rmath.html. (from *Nature*)

例 92 引自 *Nature*，著录项目和格式"文献名. 网址."。

93. European Centre for Disease Prevention and Control (ECDC), "Rapid risk assessment: Microcephaly in Brazil potentially linked to the Zika virus epidemic" (ECDC, 2015); http://ecdc.europa.eu/en/publications/Publications/zika-microcephaly-Brazil-rapid-risk-assessment-Nov-2015.pdf. (from *Science*)

94. Secretaria de Vigilância em Saúde, "Boletim epidemiológico: Monitoramento dos casos de dengue, febre de chikungunya e febre pelo vírus Zika até a semana epidemiológica 4, 2016" (in Portuguese) (Ministério da Saúde do Brasil, 2016); vol. 47, no. 7; http://portalsaude.saude.gov.br/images/pdf/2016/fevereiro/29/2016-005—Dengue-SE4-publica——o.pdf. (from *Science*)

95. "Population," History Database of the Global Environment (Netherlands Environmental Assessment Agency, Bilthoven, Netherlands, 2013); http://themasites.pbl.nl/tridion/en/themasites/hyde/basicdrivingfactors/population/index-2.html. (from *Science*)

96. E. A. Holland, J. Lee-Taylor, C. Nevison, J. Sulzman, *Global N Cycle: Fluxes and N_2O Mixing Ratios Originating from Human Activity. Data Set* (Oak Ridge National Laboratory Distributed Active Archive Center, Oak Ridge, TN, 2005); http://daac.ornl.gov/cgi-bin/dsviewer.pl?ds_id=797. (from *Science*)

97. *Plastics-the Facts* 2013. *An Analysis of European Latest Plastics Production, Demand and Waste Data* (PlasticsEurope, 2013); www.plasticseurope.org/documents/document/20131014095824-final_plastics_the_facts_2013_published_october2013.pdf. (from *Science*)

例 93～97 引自 *Science*，著录项目和格式为"主要责任者，文献名（其他题名信息）（出版项）；网址."，文献名一般加引号。例 93 的主要责任者为机构，文献名后有其他题名信息和年份（ECDC，2015）。例 94 的主要责任者也为机构，文献名后有其他题名信息（in Portuguese）和出版项（Ministério da Saúde do Brasil，2016）。例 95 先著录文献名（"Population,"History Database of the Global Environment），接着著录出版项（Netherlands Environmental Assessment Agency，Bilthoven，Netherlands，2013），其中的机构也可理解为主要责任者。例 96 的主要责任者为个人（四位），文献名未加引号但用了斜体，后有出版项（Oak Ridge National Laboratory Distributed Active Archive Center，Oak Ridge，TN，2005），其中的机构也可理解为主要责任者。例 97 先著录文献名，文献名未加引号但用了斜体，后有出版项（PlasticsEurope，2013）。

98. World Health Organ; zation. Influenza at the human-animal interface. 2017. Available from: URL: http://www.who.int/influenza/human_animal_interface/Influenza_Summary_IRA_HA_interface_07_25_2017.pdf. (from *Cell Research*)

99. World Organ; zation for Animal Health. Available from: URL: http://www.oie.int/wahis_2/public/

wahid. php/Reviewreport/Review? reportid＝23367. 2017. (from *Cell Research*)

100. García, C. H. Introduction To DNA Damage Response (DDR). Brief Posts of Granada University (http://www.radiologyandphysicalmedicine.com/introduction-to-dna-damage-response-ddr/) (2014). (from *Cell Research*)

例 98～100 引自 *Cell Research*，著录项目包括主要责任者、文献名、网址。例 98 的著录格式为"主要责任者．文献名．年份．Available from：网址．"。例 99 的著录格式为"主要责任者．Available from：网址．年份．"。例 100 的著录格式为"主要责任者．文献名（网址）（年份）．"。

101. Ha S. T., et al. Lasing action in active dielectric nanoantenna arrays. Preprint at https://arxiv.org/abs/1803.09993（2018）. (from *Light S&A*)

102. Kusch P., et al. Quantum nature of plasmon-enhanced Raman scattering. https://arxiv.org/abs/1503.03835v3（2015）. (from *Light S&A*)

例 101、102 引自 *Light S&A*，著录项目包括主要责任者、文献名、网址。例 101 的著录格式为"主要责任者．文献名．Preprint at 网址（年份）．"。例 102 的著录格式为"主要责任者．文献名．网址（年份）．"。

103. Pandika, M. (2014) Jennifer Doudna, CRISPR Code Killer, Ozy.com, January 7, 2014. <http://www.ozy.com/rising-stars/jennifer-doudna-crispr-code-killer/4690>. (from *Cell*)

例 103 引自 *Cell*，著录项目包括主要责任者、年份、文献名、日期、网址，著录格式为"主要责任者（年份）文献名，引用日期．<网址>．"。

104. PACS-L: the public-access computer systems forum. Houston, Tex: University of Houston Libraries, 1989 (1995-05-17). http://info.lib.uh.Edu/pacsl.html.

105. Hopkinson, A. UNIMARC and metadata: Dublin Core. (1999-12-08). http//www.ifla.org/IV/ifla64/138-161e.htm.

106. Dublin core metadata element set: version 1.1. (2014-06-14). http://dublincore.org/documents/dces/.

此三例著录项目加起来包括主要责任者、文献名、年份、日期、网址。例 104 的著录格式为"文献名，年份（引用日期）．网址"。例 105 的著录格式为"主要责任者．文献名．（引用日期）．网址．"。例 106 的著录格式为"文献名．（引用日期）．网址．"。

3.3.5.7 特别电子资源

任何事物都有特殊性，参考文献也不例外，也有特殊电子资源。例如：

107. See the supplementary materials on Science Online. (from *Science*)

108. Scitor Corporation. Project scheduler [CP/DK]. Sunnyvale, Calif.: Scitor Corporation, c1983.

例 107 没有著录具体的某篇参考文献，而是提示参见 *Science* 在线的附加材料。例 108 在文献名后加了一个特别符号 [CP/DK]，该符号就是 [文献类型标识/文献载体标识]，其中 CP、DK 分别是 computer program（计算机程序）和 disk（磁盘）的缩写，组合起来便是磁盘计算机程序之意，说明这篇文献是电子资源，不过它不是通过常规的访问网站（网址）来获得，而是通过磁盘计算机程序来获得。此文献著录中如果不加这样的注释，读者就不大可能知道这是一个电子资源而误认为是传统的纸质文献。这种特别电子资源文献、载体类型和标识代码如表 3-2 所示。

表 3-2　特别电子资源文献、载体类型和标识代码示例

标识代码	英 文 名	文献、载体类型
DB/MT	database on magnetic tape	磁带数据库
DB/CD	database on CD-ROM	光盘数据库
M/CD	monograph on CD-ROM	光盘普通图书
C/CD	conference works on CD-ROM	光盘会议文集
CP/DK	computer program on disk	磁盘计算机程序

3.3.6　参考文献引用规则

1. 引用基本原则

参考文献引用通常应遵循以下几个基本原则：

（1）提倡引用必要和新的文献。撰写文章可能会阅读、参考较多文献，但一般不用全部引用，只引用那些重要、相关、合适以及年代较近的文献即可。

（2）提倡引用已公开发表的文献。私人通信、内部讲义以及未发表出来的文章、著作（即使已被录用）一般不宜引用，但必要时也可以引用，也可以用脚注或文内注的方式说明引用的依据。

（3）宜采用与目标期刊一致的标注方法。引文标注方法不是只有一种，不同标注方法的标注格式体例并不相同，应按所选的标注方法对引文进行标注。

（4）宜采用与目标期刊一致的著录格式。引文标注方法不同，文献著录格式也就不同。文献种类多，载体形式也不少，有传统纸介文献，还有现代电子资源等，著录格式有差异。

2. 著录信息源

参考文献的著录信息源是被著录的信息资源本身。专著、会议文集、学位论文、报告、专利文献等可依据题名页、版权页、封面等主要信息源著录各个著录项目；专著、会议文集等的析出篇章与报刊上的文章，应依据参考文献本身著录析出文献的信息，并依据主要信息源著录析出文献的出处；电子资源通常依据特定网址、网站的信息著录。

3. 著录用文字

SCI 论文通常用英文语种著录。著录时有以下事项需要注意：

（1）著录数字，如卷期号、页码、出版年、版次、引用日期、顺序编码制的参考文献序号等，用阿拉伯数字表示。

（2）个人著者，其姓全部著录，首字母或全部字母大写，名可缩写为首字母；用首字母无法识别该人名时，可以用全名。

（3）附在出版地之后或其他处的省名、州名、国名等以及作为限定语的机关团体名称，应按国际公认的方法缩写。

（4）期刊名可用缩写，其缩写可参照 ISO 4 的规定或按常规表达形式。

（5）字母用大写还是小写，宜符合信息源本身文种的习惯用法，或遵循目标期刊的要求。

4. 著录用符号

按著者-出版年制组织的参考文献表中的第一个著录项目，如主要责任者、析出文献主要责任者、专利申请者或所有者等的前面不使用任何标识符号。按顺序编码制组织的参考文献表中的各篇文献序号直接用阿拉伯数字，或用阿拉伯数字加小圆点或加方括号：如 1、2…，1.、2.…，［1］、［2］…，等等。

参考文献使用下列规定的标识符号（不同于标点符号），如表 3-3 所示。

表3-3 参考文献著录用符号

符号	使用场合
.	用于题名项、析出文献题名项、其他责任者、析出文献其他责任者、年卷期之类的标识项、版本项、出版项、析出文献的出处项、网址以及DOI前；用于每一条参考文献的结尾
:	用于其他题名信息前，析出文献标志词in（In）后；用于分隔人名与文献名、doi与pmid、网址标志词（Available from 或 URL）与网址、文献名与版本项等
,	用于年份、页码、地名、Eds、Trans等前；用于分隔不同人名、出版项各项、人名与文献名等
;	用于分隔出版项与网址、不同机构名、出版者与年份、会议名与会议时间、会议时间与会议地点、doi与pmid、专利申请日期与公告专利号、同一责任者的合订题名⊖等
in	用于析出文献的出处项（责任者、题名）前
（ ）	用于期刊期号、报纸版次、电子资源引用年份或日期、其他责任者（如编、译者）、出版项、专利申请结果状态等
[ ]	用于文献序号、文献类型标识、自拟的信息；用于注释；用于代替"（ ）"，以与著录文字中已包含"（ ）"相区分
/	用于连续出版物合期的期号间
-	用于起讫序号和起讫页码间

3.3.7 参考文献著录细则

1. 主要、其他责任者

（1）个人著者姓和名的先后顺序取决于目标期刊的要求。姓通常首字母大写（但也有小写的情况⊜），名可以用缩写字母，缩写字母后是否加缩写点（小圆点）取决于目标期刊。例如：Schmidt，R. F. & Thews，G.；B. Pillans，P. Gibbard 等。GB/T 28039—2011《中国人名汉语拼音字母拼写规则》和 GB/T 16159—2012《汉语拼音正词法基本规则》规定汉语拼音书写的人名，姓全大写，名可缩写、取每个汉字拼音的首字母，其中姓全大写与国际期刊人名写法有出入。

（2）著作方式相同的责任者多于一位时，既可全部著录，也可部分著录，只著录一位或部分著录时，后加"et al."。国内期刊的常规规定"超过三位时，著录前三位，后面加 et al."，与国际期刊人名著录有出入。

（3）无责任者或责任者情况不明时，可以省去责任者。

（4）凡是对文献负责的机关团体名称，通常根据著录信息源著录。机关团体名称应由下至上分级著录，作为限定语的机关团体名称可按照国际公认的方法缩写⊜。

2. 题名

题名包括书名、刊名、报纸名、专利名、报告名、标准名、学位论文名、档案名、舆图名、析出的文献名等，要按著录信息源所载的内容著录。

（1）同一责任者的多个合订题名，著录前三个合订题名。对于不同责任者的多个合订

⊖ 合订题名指由两种或两种以上的著作汇编而成的无总题名的文献中各部著作的题名。

⊜ 例如：van den Herik, H., Uiterwijk, J. W. & van Rijswijck, J. Games solved: now and in the future. Artif. Intell. 134，277-311（2002）。

⊜ 机关团体英文名称的常规表达习惯是由下至上分级著录，如"Department of Civil Engineering, Stanford University"，而不是"Stanford University, Department of Civil Engineering"。

题名，可以只著录第一个或处于显要位置的合订题名。在参考文献中不著录并列题名㊀。

（2）国际期刊不要求著录文献类型标识（含文献载体标识）。如不著录文献类型标识不能清楚表达或容易引起混淆、误解时，可以著录文献类型标识，参见 GB/T 7714—2015《信息与文献　参考文献著录规则》附录 B《文献类型与文献载体标识代码》。

（3）其他题名信息根据信息资源外部特征的具体情况决定取舍。其他题名信息包括副题名，说明题名文字，多卷书的分卷书名、卷次，册次，专利号，报告号，标准号等。

3. 版本

第 1 版不著录，其他版本说明应著录，宜用阿拉伯数字、序数缩写形式或其他标识表示，如 5th ed.、Rev. ed.、2017 ed. 等。

4. 出版项

出版项应按出版者、出版地、出版年的顺序著录（如 Academic Press，New York，2019）。

（1）出版者可按著录信息源所载的形式著录，也可按国际公认的简化形式或缩写形式著录（如 Elsevier Science Publishers；IRRI 或 International Rice Research Institute；Wiley 或 John Wiley and Sons Ltd.）。文献中载有多个出版者时，可全部著录，或只著录第一个或处于显要位置的出版者（如①ALA，Chicago，1978 或 American Library Association，Chicago，1978；②Canadian library Association，Ottawa，1978）。无出版者时，可以省略此项。

（2）出版地著录出版者所在地的城市名。对同名异地或不为人们熟悉的城市名，宜在城市名后附省名、州名或国名等限定语，且按国际公认的方法缩写（如①Cambridge，Eng.；②Cambridge，Mass.）。文献中载有多个出版地时，可全部著录，或只著录第一个或处于显要位置的出版地。例如：① Science Press，Beijing & Shanghai，2013；② Butterworths，London，2000（取代 Butterworths，London，Boston，Durban，Syngapore，Sydney，Toronto，Wellington，2000）。无出版地时，可省略此项（如①MacMillan，1975；②Open University Press，2011）。

（3）出版年采用公元纪年，并用阿拉伯数字著录，如有其他纪年形式，将原有的纪年形式置于"（　）"内。报纸的出版日期按照"YYYY-MM-DD"格式，用阿拉伯数字著录（如 2018-12-08）。出版年无法确定时，可依次选用版权年（如 c2018）、印刷年、估计的出版年，估计的出版年应置于方括号内（如 [1936]）。公告日期、引用日期可按照"YYYY-MM-DD"格式，用阿拉伯数字著录。

5. 页码

专著或期刊的析出文献的页码或引文页码，应采用阿拉伯数字著录。例如：①*Science* **333**，838–843（2011）；②（Xinhua Press，Beijing，1999），pp. 117–121。引自序言或扉页题词的页码，可按实际情况著录。

6. 获取和访问路径

根据电子资源在互联网中的实际情况，著录其获取和访问路径（即网址）。例如：① http：//vip. calis. edu. cn/asp/Detail. asp；②http：//lib. myilibrary. com/Open. aspx？id = 253987。

7. DOI

获取和访问路径中不含 DOI 时，可以依原文如实著录 DOI。否则，可以省略 DOI。例如：①http：//wenku. baidu. com/link？url = GJDJxb4lxBUXnIPmq1XoEGSIr1H8TMLbid W_Lj1Yu33tpt 707u62rKliyp U _FBGUmox7-ovP-NaVIVBALAMd5yfwuKUUOAGYuB7cuZ-BYE-hXa. DOI：10. 7666/d. y351065；② http：// dx. doi. org/ 10. 1126/science. aad5227（2015）。

㊀ 并列题名指在文献著录信息源中出现的对应于正题名的另一种语言文字的题名，包括对应于正题名的外文题名、少数民族文字题名等，但不包括汉语拼音题名。

8. 析出文献

专著的析出文献与源文献的关系用 In 或 in（此标志词后可以加冒号）表示；期刊、报纸的析出文献与源文献的关系用"."表示。例如：

① Tenopir, C. Online databases: quality control. *Library Journal*, **113**（3）: 124–125 (1987).

② H7N9 has been classed as the most deadly virus by World Health Organization Whether interpersonal communication is unable to answer. *Reference News* 2013-4-26 (7).

期刊的析出文献，应在刊名后注明其年卷期和页码（期号也可不著录）。例如：

① **40**, 23–30 (2018); ② **40**（8）, 23–30 (2018); ③ **11**（Suppl 1）, 31–45 (2009)。

对从合期中析出的文献，可在圆括号内注明合期号。例如：(3/4): 23–30 (2016)。凡在同一期刊上连载的文献，其后续部分不必另行著录，可在已著录部分后直接注明后续部分的年卷期和页码等。例如：

① **40**（1）, 88–96 (2018); ② **40**（2）, 100–106 (2018)（或 **40**, 88–96 (2018); **40**, 100–106 (2018)）。

报纸的析出文献应在报纸名后著录出版日期与版次。例如：

① 2008-08-08 (1); ② 2018-12-08 (2)。

3.4 致谢和作者贡献

致谢（Acknowledgements）和作者贡献（Author Contributions）不是论文的必要组成部分，一般位于论文的后面部分，参考文献表的前面或后面。通常分别单独成段，冠以各自独立的标题；或将作者贡献归入致谢，把 Author Contributions 列为 Acknowledgements 下的子标题；或将二者写到一起，冠以一个标题 Acknowledgements，即致谢中包含作者贡献。可见这部分写作形式的多样性，不同期刊、不同表述需求有其较为灵活的格式。

致谢用来对致谢对象表达道义上的感谢，也是尊重致谢对象贡献的标志。致谢对象主要有：研究工作得到资助的基金项目（资助项目、科学基金）；对研究工作有直接和实质帮助的组织或个人；协助完成研究工作、提供某种帮助和便利条件的组织或个人；对论文写作付出较多工夫或对论文写作质量提升做出较多贡献的作者或作者团队以外的个人；给予转载和引用权的资料、图片、文献、思想和设想等的所有者；其他应感谢的组织和个人。

致谢的内容主要有以下两个方面：

1) 感谢全部或部分研究工作得到资助的基金项目，可以附上基金项目、合同书等的编号给予证明。

2) 感谢个人或组织在研究工作或论文写作中给予的帮助或所做的贡献，包括提供仪器、设备或相关实验材料，给予技术、信息、物质或经费等帮助，协助实验方案制定、实验流程执行和实验结果处理，提供有益的启发、建议、指导、审阅，承担某些辅助性工作等。

致谢的写作应遵循以下原则：

1) 具体而恰如其分地表达致谢的内容，明确是对何致谢对象所做的何工作表达感谢，是感谢基金项目、奖学金、合同单位、企业、组织，还是感谢对论文选题、构思、撰写或修改等给予指导的人员，还是感谢对考察、实验、观测、分析等做出的某种贡献，还是别的什么方面，均应表达清楚。

2) 使用恰当的词语和句式表达谢意，避免因疏忽而冒犯本可接受感谢的个人或组织。

3) 表达谢意的主体应该明确，缺省或通常情况下应为本文、本研究、本项目、本团队、我们或全体作者等，具有集合或集体属性，但实际中也可为这些集合或集体中的个体、子集成员，具有个体或部分属性，如全体作者中的某位或某几位作者等。

4) 参照目标期刊对致谢的习惯和规定

的表达形式，如有的期刊要求将基金项目信息单独放在论文首页的脚注中或其他位置，这样在致谢中就不用有这部分内容了。

5）在投稿前应与致谢对象联络、沟通，必要时请其审阅论文。在不特别指出的情况下，致谢某人就意味着他赞同论文的观点或结论，但如果只是感谢他的一个具体的思想、建议、解释或别的具体方面，则应特别指出，明确交待。

6）准确、完整地书写基金项目的名称及其编号，不用不为人们知道的缩写作项目名称。

作者贡献用来对论文的每位作者在本研究中所做的具体工作或对论文所做的主要贡献进行大致分类和概括描述，比如概念构思、实验方案制定、实验装置制作、实验执行和完成、算法设计、代码编写、计算推导、数据分析、论文撰写、语言润色等等。实际上，这部分描绘出一个研究分工图，将每位作者的主体工作或贡献清晰地展现出来。

下面几个致谢和作者贡献实例选自一些名刊，我们来看看其内容安排和写作思路。

【1】

Acknowledgements The sensor design, characterization and testing aspects of this work were supported by the Berkeley Sensor and Actuator Center, and National Institutes of Health grant number P01 HG000205. The sensor fabrication was performed in the Electronic Materials (E-MAT) laboratory funded by the Director, Office of Science, Office of Basic Energy Sciences, Materials Sciences and Engineering Division of the US Department of Energy under contract number DE-AC02-05CH11231. K. C. acknowledges funding from the NSF Nanomanufacturing Systems for mobile Computing and Energy Technologies (NASCENT) Center. H. O. acknowledges support from a Japan Society for the Promotion of Science (JSPS) Fellowship. We thank J. Bullock, C. M. Sutter-Fella, H. W. W. Nyein, Z. Shahpar, M. Zhou, E. Wu and W. Chen for their help.

Author Contributions W. G., S. E. and A. J. conceived the idea and designed the experiments. W. G., S. E., H. Y. Y. N. and S. C. led the experiments (with assistance from K. C., A. P., H. M. F., H. O., H. S., H. O., D. K., D.-H. L.). W. G., S. E., A. P., G. A. B., R. W. D. and A. J. contributed to data analysis and interpretation. W. G., S. E., H. Y. Y. N., G. A. B. and A. J. wrote the paper and all authors provided feedback.

(Fully integrated wearable sensor arrays for multiplexed in situ perspiration analysis. *Nature*, 2016, 529 (7587). doi: https://doi.org/10.1038/nature16521).

此例中致谢和作者贡献各自独立成段，先写致谢，后写作者贡献。表达了五种感谢，不同感谢的致谢对象、内容不同，致谢主体也可能不同：

1）感谢美国伯克利传感器和执行器中心、国立卫生研究院对本项目中传感器设计、特性描述和测试的资助（P01 HG000205）。

2）感谢美国能源部材料科学和工程分部基础能源科学局科学办公室主任对电子材料（E-MAT）实验室完成传感器制造的资助（DE-AC02-05CH11231）。

3）作者之一 K. C.（Kevin Chen）感谢美国国家自然科学基金（NSF）移动计算和能源技术纳米制造系统（NASCENT）中心的资助。

4）另一作者 H. O.（Hiroki Ota）感谢日本科学促进学会（JSPS）Fellowship 奖的资助。

5）感谢 J. Bullock，C. M. Sutter-Fella，H. W. W. Nyein，Z. Shahpar，M. Zhou，E. Wu 和 W. Chen 提供的帮助。

此作者贡献将研究工作分为构思想法和设计实验、领导实验、数据分析与解释、撰写论文与提供反馈四部分，对每部分工作由谁来完成及谁提供了帮助均做了明确描述。具体分工如下：W. G.，S. E. 和 A. J. 构思想法和设计实验；W. G.，S. E.，H. Y. Y. N. 和 S. C. 领导实验（得到 K. C.，A. P.，H. M. F.，H. O.，H. S.，H. O.，D. K.，D.-

H. L. 的帮助);W. G., S. E., A. P., G. A. B., R. W. D. 和 A. J. 进行数据分析与解释;W. G., S. E., H. Y. N., G. A. B. 和 A. J. 撰写论文和所有作者提供反馈。

【2】
ACKNOWLEDGMENTS

This project was funded in part by the Engineering and Physical Sciences Research Council through the Supergen Solar Energy Hub SuperSolar (EP/M024881/1, EP/M014797/1) and the European Research Council through the Stg-2011 Hybrid Photovoltaic Energy Relays and the European Union Seventh Framework Programme (FP7/2007-2013) under grant agreement 604032 of the MESO project, and the U. S. Office of Naval Research. M. H. is funded by Oxford PV Ltd. W. R. is supported by the Hans-Boeckler-Foundation. We thank our colleagues from the Centre For Renewable Energy Technologies Photovoltaic Measurement and Testing Laboratory, Loughborough University, for their contributions to the measurements of the semi-transparent devices. We also thank K. Jacob and M. Wittig [Helmholtz-Zentrum Berlin (HZB), Institute for Silicon Photovoltaics], L. Mazzarella, and S. Kirner (HZB, Institute PVcomB) for their contributions to fabricating the SHJ cell. The University of Oxford has filed a patent related to this work. The project was designed and conceptualized by D. M. and H. J. S. D. M. performed experiments, analyzed data, and wrote the first draft of the paper. G. S. fabricated and measured devices with semi-transparent electrodes. W. R. characterized the material using THz spectroscopy. G. E. helped with the experimental work and provided technical feedback on the writing of the paper. M. S. provided input and technical direction on the FA/Cs cation mixture. M. H. performed simulations for the optical modeling and calculated the maximum achievable V_{OC}. A. H. analyzed XRD data. N. S. provided input on the preparation of thin films using chemical bath depositions. L. K. and B. R. designed and supervised the fabrication of the SHJ-cells. M. J. performed and analyzed EQE measurements. L. H. supervised and analyzed the THz spectroscopy measurements. H. J. S. supervised the overall conception and design of this project. All authors contributed to the writing of the paper.

(A mixed-cation lead mixed-halide perovskite absorber for tandem solar cells. *Science*, 8 January 2016 · Vol 351 Issue 6269:151-155.)

此例前面六句(This project was funded in part … has filed a patent related to this work.)为致谢,后面全部语句(The project was designed and conceptualized by … to the writing of the paper.)为作者贡献,在形式上只有一段,实则将作者贡献放在致谢中一起写,作者贡献成为致谢的一部分,即作者贡献列入致谢范畴。具体内容如下:

1)感谢本项目部分得到英国工程和物理科学研究委员会通过 Supergen(可持续电力生产和供给)太阳能中心 SuperSolar(EP/M024881/1,EP/M014797/1)、欧洲科学研究委员会通过 MESO 项目下的 Stg-2011 混合动力光电继电器和欧盟第七框架计划(FP7/2007-2013)(合同号 604032)以及美国海军研究办公室的资助。

2)作者之一 M. H.(Laura M. Herz)感谢得到牛津光伏公司的资助。

3)另一作者 W. R.(Waqaas Rehman)感谢得到汉斯贝克勒基金会的资助。

4)感谢来自拉夫堡大学可再生能源技术光电测量和测试实验室的同事们对半透明设备测量所做出的贡献。

5)感谢 K. Jacob 和 M. Wittig(HZB⊖硅光伏研究所)、L. Mazzarella 和 S. Kirner(HZB PVcomB⊜)对 Si 异质结电池⊜制作所做出的贡献。

6)感谢牛津大学已经提交了一项与这项工作相关的专利。

7)本项目由 D. M. 和 H. J. S. 设计和概念化。D. M. 完成实验、分析数据,并撰写初稿。G. S. 用半透明电极制造和测量设

⊖ HZB—Helmholtz-Zentrum Berlin(柏林亥姆霍兹中心)。
⊜ PVcomB—Institute Competence Centre Photovoltaics Berlin(柏林光伏能力中心)。
⊜ SHJ cell—Si Heterojunction cell(Si 异质结电池)。

备。W. R. 用 THz 光谱分析材料。G. E. 帮助进行实验，对论文撰写提供技术反馈。M. S. 对 FA/Cs 阳离子混合物提供输入和技术方向。M. H. 对光学模型进行模拟，并计算最大可达到 V_{OC}。A. H 分析 XRD 数据。N. S. 使用化学浴沉积为薄膜制备提供输入。L. K. 和 B. R. 设计并监督 Si 异质结电池的制造。M. J. 完成并分析 EQE 测量。L. H. 监督和分析 THz 光谱测量。H. J. S. 监督本项目的总体构思和设计。所有作者都对论文撰写做出了贡献。

【3】

AUTHOR CONTRIBUTIONS

U. V. P. and J. C. designed the experiments, and U. V. P. performed most of the experiments with the following exceptions: S. C. H. performed RNA-seq and ChIP-seq analyses, P. A. B. R. performed the ChIP-qPCR analysis, J. H. performed the BiFC experiments and phenotypic measurements, B. J. C. contributed qRT-PCR and HyDE analyses, K. L. measured free IAA, P. S. expressed proteins in mammalian cells, M. Z. performed ChIP-seq experiments, J. R. N. performed sequencing and K. N. provided reagents. J. R. E. supervised S. C. H. and M. Z. All authors commented on the manuscript.

ACKNOWLEDGMENTS

We thank Z. Avramova, T. Yamashino, and C. Fankhauser for XTH33ox, ATHB2ox, and pin seeds; C. Lin and A. Nagatani for CRY and PHY antiserum; C. Lagarias for phycocyanobilin; Y. Jaillais, A. Seluzicki, C. Procko, and D. O'Keefe for critical reading of the draft; and R. Granbom for assistance with the IAA measurements. K. L. was funded by the Swedish Governmental Agency for Innovation Systems, the Swedish Research Council, and the Marianne and Marcus Wallenberg Foundation. M. Z. was supported by DFG (Za-730/1-1). J. H. was supported by the NIH (T32GM007240), the Rose Hills Foundation, and the H. A. and Mary K. Chapman Charitable Trust. J. R. E. was supported by DOE (FG02-04ER15517), the NSF (MCB-1024999), and the Gordon and Betty Moore Foundation (GBMF3034). J. C. and J. R. E. are investigators of the Howard Hughes Medical Institute. NIH grant R01-GM52413 to J. C. funded this study.

(Cryptochromes Interact Directly with PIFs to Control Plant Growth in Limiting Blue Light. *Cell* 164, 1–13, January 14, 2016)

此例中致谢和作者贡献各自独立成段（同于示例【1】），但先写作者贡献，后写致谢（又不同于示例【1】）。

作者贡献的内容包括：

U. V. P. 和 J. C. 设计实验，U. V. P. 完成大部分实验，但下列工作除外：S. C. H. 完成 RNA-seq 和 ChIP-seq 分析；P. A. B. R. 完成 ChIP-qPCR 分析；J. H. 完成 BiFC 实验和表型测量；B. J. C. 进行 qRT-PCR 和 HyDE 分析；K. L. 测量自由 IAA；P. S. 表达哺乳动物细胞蛋白；M. Z. 完成 ChIP-seq 实验；J. R. N. 完成测序；K. N. 提供试剂。J. R. E. 监督 S. C. H. 和 M. Z. 所有作者均对文稿进行评价。

致谢的内容如下：

感谢 Z. Avramova、T. Yamashino 和 C. Fankhauser 提供 XTH33ox，ATHB2ox 和针形种子；C. Lin 和 A. Nagatani 提供 CRY 和 PHY 抗血清；C. Lagarias 提供藻蓝素；Y. Jaillais、A. Seluzicki、C. Procko 和 D. O'Keefe 对初稿给予批判性阅读；R. Granbom 对 IAA 测量给予帮助。作者 K. L. 得到瑞典政府创新系统部门、瑞典研究委员会、玛丽安和马库斯·瓦伦堡基金会资助。作者 M. Z. 得到德国科学基金会⊖的资助（Za-730/1-1）。J. H. 得到美国国家卫生研究院（NIH）（T32GM007240）、玫瑰山基金会、H. A. 和 Mary K. 查普曼慈善信托

⊖ DFG——Deutsche Forschungsgemeinschaft（德国科学基金会）。

的资助。J. R. E. 得到美国能源部（FG02-04ER15517）、国家科学基金会（MCB-1024999）、戈登与贝蒂－摩尔基金会（GBMF3034）的资助。J. C. 和 J. R. E. 是霍华德·休斯医学研究所的调查人员。J. C. 得到 NIH 的资助（R01-GM52413）。

【4】

Acknowledgements

We thank Susan Watson for editing the manuscript. This work was supported by the National Natural Science Foundation of China（31521005）, the National Key R&D Program of China（2016YFD0500201 and 2016YFD0500203）, and the China Agriculture Research System（CARS-41-G12）. Virus sequence data from this study were deposited in GenBank with the accession numbers MF629922 to MF630577 and MF988735 to MF988742.

Author Contributions

JS, DG, ZB, and HC designed the study. JS, GD, HK, CG, SM, XY, XZ, PC, YC, HY, XW, XW, LL, PC, YJ, JL, YG, ML, ZQ, LG, JZ, WG, SH, YS, YH, ZW, LG, WY, LL, HB, GT, YL, CQ, and LJ performed the experiments. JS, CL, YS, ZB, and HC analysed the data. HC wrote the paper.

（H7N9 virulent mutants detected in chickens in China pose an increased threat to humans. *Cell Research*, Vol. 27, No. 12, Dec. 2017：1409–1421）

此例中致谢和作者贡献各自独立成段，但作者贡献以低一层次的标题置于致谢的后面。

致谢的内容包括：

感谢 Susan Watson 编辑稿件。本项目得到国家自然科学基金（31521005）、国家科技攻关计划（2016YFD0500201、2016YFD0500203）和中国农业研究系统专项资金（CARS-41-G12）资助。本研究的病毒序列数据存入 GenBank[⊖]，注册登记号是从 MF629922 到 MF630577 和从 MF988735 到 MF988742。致谢对象明确，分别有 Susan Watson、基金项目（国家自然科学基金、国家科技攻关计划、中国农业研究系统专项资金）和 GenBank。

作者贡献的内容包括：

JS、DG、ZB 和 HC 设计项目。JS、GD、HK……LJ 完成实验。JS、CL、YS、ZB 和 HC 分析数据。HC 撰写论文。贡献分类明确，分别有设计项目、完成实验、分析数据和撰写论文。

致谢与作者贡献写作应注意以下几点：

1）实事求是，简短概括，不偏不倚，公平合理。

2）没有固定形式，写作时应先了解目标期刊，即使同一期刊的论文，因表述需要或个人写作风格的差异，其致谢与作者贡献的写作形式也可不一致。例如 *Light*：*S&A*，有的原创论文只有致谢，有的致谢和作者贡献都有，且通常先写作者贡献，后写致谢，二者独立成段。

3）有多个基金项目时，各项目应依次列出，其间用标点符号分隔。例如：

This project is supported by National Natural Science Foundation of China（Grant Nos. 51135003, U1234208, 51205050）, New Teachers' Fund for Doctor Stations, Ministry of Education of China（Grant No. 20110042120020）, Fundamental Research Funds for the Central Universities, China（Grant No. N110303003）, and China Postdoctoral Science Foundation（Grant No. 2011M500564）.

4）篇幅取决于相关内容的多少，如研究的规模，得到资助的基金项目数，研究合作、分工的复杂性与关联程度等，不好说具体多长篇幅合适。既可写得很长，如以上示例【2】，实际中还有更长的；也可写得较短或很短，只对几个或一个对象表示感谢。例如：

【5】

ACKNOWLEDGMENTS

This work was funded by US National Science Founda-

⊖ GenBank 是美国国家生物技术信息中心（National Center for Biotechnology Information，NCBI）建立的 DNA 序列数据库。

tion grant number 1244557 to J. A. D. A. V. W. and J. K. N. are NSF Graduate Research Fellows. Megan Hochstrasser provided valuable input on the manuscript.

【6】
Acknowledgments This study was financially supported by the National High Technology Research and Development Program of China (No. 2013AA031104).

【7】
ACKNOWLEDGMENTS Min Gu thanks the Australian Research Council Laureate Fellowship project (FL100100099).

5) 基金项目的名称应准确、正确书写。宜使用官方公布的正规名称，对不为普通大众熟知的缩写名称（字母词）尽量不用，以避免让读者过于分心去猜测。表3-4列出了我国部分基金项目的名称，供读者参考。

表3-4 我国部分基金项目的名称

英文名称	中文名称
National Hi-tech Research and Development Program of China (863 Program)	国家高技术研究发展计划（863计划）
National Basic Research Program of China (973 Program)	国家重点基础研究发展计划（973计划）
National Plan for Key and Major Programs in State Basic Research of China (Climbing Plan)	国家基础性研究重大关键项目（攀登计划）
National Key Technologies R & D Program of China	国家科技攻关计划
National Key Technology R & D Program of China during the 14th Five-Year Plan Period	"十四五"国家科技支撑计划重大项目
National Natural Science Foundation of China (General Program; Key Program; Major Program)	国家自然科学基金（面上项目；重点项目；重大项目）
National Science Fund for Distinguished Young Scholars of China	国家杰出青年科学基金
Joint Research Fund for Overseas Chinese, Hong Kong and Macao Young Scholars of China	海外及中国香港、澳门青年学者合作研究基金
Knowledge Innovation Programs of Chinese Academy of Sciences	中国科学院知识创新项目
Major Programs of Chinese Academy of Sciences during the 14th Five-Year Plan Period	中国科学院"十四五"重大项目
Key Program of Chinese Academy of Sciences	中国科学院重点资助项目
Advanced Programs of Shanghai Branch, Chinese Academy of Sciences	中国科学院上海分院择优资助项目
Ph. D. Programs Foundation of Ministry of Education of China	教育部博士点基金资助项目
Specialized Research Fund for the Doctoral Program of Higher Education of China	高等学校博士点专项科研基金
National Medical Science and Technique Foundation of China during the 14th Five-Year Plan Period	"十四五"国家医学科技攻关基金资助项目
× Municipal Natural Science Foundation of China	×市自然科学基金
× Provincial Natural Science Foundation of China	×省自然科学基金
National Aerospace Science Foundation of China	国家航空科学基金
Science & Technology Innovation Foundation of Ministry of Science & Technology for Small-Medium Enterprises, China	科技部科技型中小企业创新基金
National Hi-tech Research and Development Program for CIMS, China	国家863/CIMS主题计划

基金项目写作中常出现项目名称不准确、表达不严谨、缩写词随意使用等问题。例如：将National Natural Science Foundation of China 写成 Natural Science Foundation of

China，或 National Science Foundation of China，或 National Science Projection of China，或 National Natural Foundation of China，或 National Natural Projection of China，或 Natural Science Foundation of Our Country 等，或将以上名称中的"of China"漏写，甚至直接写为更不完整、可读性更差的缩写词 SFC 或 SF（完整的应为 NSFC）。这些现象值得引起大家的注意和重视。

3.5 作者介绍

作者介绍（简介）不是论文的必要组成部分，目前多数期刊包括国际名刊的论文中并没有这一项，有关作者信息一般在署名中体现，但有的期刊的论文是有这一项的，比如将这部分内容单列一个标题（Author Information 或 Authors' Information 或 Biographical notes）。

作者介绍一般位于参考文献表的前面或后面，或致谢的前面或后面，或论文首页脚注处，或论文中其他位置。可包括作者个人情况和联系方式：个人情况有姓名、性别、出生时间、文化程度、工作单位、职称、职务（行政职务、技术职务或项目职务等）、所获荣誉和奖励、技术特长、研究方向，以及发表论文、出版著作和发明专利等；联系方式主要有通信地址和 E-mail。这部分可长可短，简单或较简单、详细或较详细均可，取决于具体期刊的要求。

作者介绍写作原则：概括地介绍作者个人有关情况，不必过于仔细、详实，语句应精练简洁，篇幅应简短适中，但也不能过于简单笼统，内容不完整、项目不全就反映不出作者的必要信息，简介的效果就难以体现出来。作者介绍的详略取舍还应考虑文体类别、正文篇幅、版面限制和个人风格等因素，不可一概而论。下面给出作者介绍的一个示例。

Authors' Information

Yi-Min Zhang, born in 1958, is currently a professor and a PhD candidate supervisor at *School of Mechanical Engineering and Automation*, *Northeastern University*, *China*. He is a Cheung Kong scholar of mechanical design and theory and a member of *the Academic Degrees Committee of the State Council of China for Mechanical Engineering*, etc. His main research interests include mechanical dynamic design, mechanical reliability design, and modern design methodology, etc. Tel：+ 86-24-83689169；E-mail：zhangymneu@sohu.com

Qin-Chuan Li, born in 1975, is currently a professor at *Zhejiang Sci-Tech University*, *China*. He received his PhD degree on mechanism design and theory from *Yanshan University*, *China*, in 2003. His research interests include mechanism theory of parallel manipulators and application. Tel：+ 86-571-86843686；E-mail：lqchuan@zstu.edu.cn

3.6 附录

附录（Appendix 或 Appendices）不是论文的必要组成部分。从形式上看，它仅是论文的一个附件，但因占用版面较多，对增加论文被引没有影响，故在学术期刊界越来越以影响因子作为至上办刊目标的当下时代，多数期刊也越来越不喜欢这一项，而逐渐将其"扫地出门"了。

附录主要用来在不增加论文正文篇幅和不影响正文主体内容叙述连贯性的前提下，向读者提供文中有关内容的详尽推导、演算、证明、解释、说明，以及有关数据、曲线、照片、公式或其他辅助资料，如计算机框图、软件算法或程序、详细实验方案或流程步骤等。

附录写作原则：内容恰当、篇幅合适和语言规范。内容恰当是确定需要用附录表述的内容，不宜把适于在正文中表述的内容放在附录中；篇幅合适是既不冗长，占用过多版面，增加作者出版费用，影响他文发表周期（出版物容量一般是有限的），也不过短，过短时应直接放在正文中；语言规范是其行文规范与正文处于同等地位，不要出现表达随意、结构松散、语句不通和标点错误等问题。另外，附录与正文一样，应编入连续页码。

3.7 出版信息

论文中有些内容无需作者来撰写（投稿时不写），而是由出版部门在后期生产环节中来补上（编排时补充），成为发表后的论文的重要组成部分。这些内容虽然不用作者提供或撰写，但作者也应该有所了解，为论文传播或以后撰写论文积淀见识、增长知识。笔者将这部分内容统称为论文的出版信息。这类信息的类别和具体文本内容，对多数期刊来说是共性多于个性，但对一些期刊来说其间差异还是较大的。以下介绍几类常见的出版信息。

3.7.1 论文 DOI

论文 DOI（Digital Object Indentifier，数字对象标识符）是论文信息（About Journal）的一种。它是为便于论文的检索、全文索取、远程传送、参考文献互联及著作权保护、管理等而为论文设置的一种全球唯一的标识符。它由字母和数字组合而成，相当于论文的身份证明，其突出作用是实现全球引文互联。引文互联就是通过 DOI 技术实现所引文献与被引文献在互联网上互相链接，即一篇文章所引用的文献与这些文献的原文链接，以及与引用了此篇文章的别的文献的原文链接。

目前美国 CrossRef 公司是国际 DOI 基金会指定的唯一官方 DOI 注册机构。在 DOI 中心目录中，DOI 与对象（内容）的解析地址（OpenURL）关联。DOI 发表在 OpenURL 的位置上，避免了因对象移动而导致的链接失败，这就意味着对象的存储地点虽可能发生变化，但 DOI 始终不变，对象照常能够被链接上。使用 DOI 的最大优势是，在互联网的任何一个节点，只要用鼠标点击某 DOI 号就可到达用户所需对象的地址并与其全文链接上，使传统模式下的大量对象不再成为"信息孤岛"。

DOI 由前缀和后缀两部分构成，前缀与后缀间以斜线分隔。前缀由识别码管理机构指定（CrossRef 注册中心分配的 DOI 前缀通常从 10 开始）；后缀由出版机构或版权所有者等自行命名或分配。例如：10.3724/SP. J. 1006. 2008. 00619；10.3881/j. issn. 1008-5882. 2008. 06. 015；10. 1086/301055；10. 1126/science. 286. 5445. 1679e 等。下面展现几本名刊的 DOI 的形式（位置）。

【1】
ARTICLE   doi：10. 1038/nature16526

【2】
A mixed-cation lead mixed-halide perovskite absorber for tandem solar cells
David P. McMeekin, Golnaz Sadoughi, Waqaas Rehman, Giles E. Eperon, Michael Saliba,
Maximilian T. Hörantner, Amir Haghighirad, Nobuya Sakai, Lars Korte, Bernd Rech, Michael B. Johnston,
Laura M. Herz and Henry J. Snaith（January 7, 2016）
Science **351**（6269），151-155. ［doi：10. 1126/science. aad5845］

【3】
The Heroes of CRISPR
Eric S. Lander [1,2,3,*]
[1] Broad Institute of MIT and Harvard, 415 Main Street, Cambridge, MA 02142, USA
[2] Department of Biology, Massachusetts Institute of Technology, Cambridge, MA 02139, USA

[3] Department of Systems Biology, Harvard Medical School, Boston, MA 02115, USA

* Correspondence: lander@ broadinstitute. org

http: //dx. doi. org/10. 1016/j. cell. 2015. 12. 041

【4】

Multi-chromatic silicon nanocrystals

Benjamin Bruhn[1,*], Benjamin JM Brenny[2,*], Sidoeri Dekker[1], Ilker Dŏgan[3,4], Peter Schall[1] & Katerina Dohnalová[1]

Silicon nanocrystals (SiNCs) have great potential to become environmental friendly alternatives to heavy-metal containing nanocrystals for applications including medical imaging, lighting and displays. SiNCs exhibit excellent photostability, non-toxicity and abundant resources, but their often reported inefficient and spectrally limited light emission seriously impair their applications. Here we demonstrate a new method that converts SiNCs into an efficient and robust multi-chromatic phosphor. Using ~ 15 keV electron-beam irradiation of oxide-capped SiNCs, we introduce several types of color centers into the nanocrystal's oxide shell with efficient blue, green and red emission bands, together yielding warm-white photoluminescence, even for a single SiNC. Introduced centers are not native to the original system and we relate them to known defects in silica. Unlike in the silica host, however, here the centers are efficiently optically excitable. Provided further optimization and up-scaling of this method, e-beam irradiated SiNCs can be of great interest as white phosphors for applications such as LEDs.

Light: Science & Applications (2017) **6**, e17007; doi: 10. 1038/lsa. 2017. 7; published online 30 June 2017

Keywords: cathodoluminscence; color center; electron beam; multi-chromaticity; silicon nanocrystals

【5】

H7N9 virulent mutants detected in chickens in China pose an increased threat to humans

Jianzhong Shi[1,*], Guohua Deng[1,*], Huihui Kong[1,*], Chunyang Gu[1,*], Shujie Ma[1,*], Xin Yin[1,*], Xianying Zeng[1], Pengfei Cui[1], Yan Chen[1], Huanliang Yang[1], Xiaopeng Wan[1], Xiurong Wang[1], Liling Liu[1], Pucheng Chen[1], Yongping Jiang[1], Jinxiong Liu[1], Yuntao Guan[1], Mei Li[1], Zhiyuan Qu[1], Lizheng Guan[1], Jinkai Zang[1], Wenli Gu[1], Shuyu Han[1], Yangming Song[1], Yuzhen Hu[1], Zeng Wang[1], Linlin Gu[1], Wenyu Yang[1], Libin Liang[1], Hongmei Bao[1], Guobin Tian[1], Yanbing Li[1], Chuanling Qiao[1], Li Jiang[1], Chengjun Li[1], Zhigao Bu[1] & Hualan Chen[1]

[1] *State Key Laboratory of Veterinary Biotechnology, Harbin Veterinary Research Institute, Chinese Academy of Agricultural Sciences, Harbin 150001, China;* [2] *College of Life and Health Sciences, Chubu University, Aichi 487-8501, Japan*

Certain low pathogenic avian influenza viruses can mutate to highly pathogenic viruses when they circulate in domestic poultry, at which point they can cause devastating poultry diseases and severe economic damage. The H7N9 influenza viruses that emerged in 2013 in China had caused severe human infections and deaths. However, these viruses were nonlethal in poultry. It is unknown whether the H7N9 viruses can acquire additional mutations during their circulation in nature and become lethal to poultry and more dangerous for humans. Here, we evaluated the evolution of H7N9 viruses isolated from avian species between 2013 and 2017 in China and found 23 different genotypes, 7 of which were detected only in ducks and were genetically distinct from the other 16 genotypes that evolved from the 2013 H7N9 viruses. Importantly, some H7N9 viruses obtained an insertion of four amino acids in their hemagglutinin (HA) cleavage site and were lethal in chickens. The index strain was not lethal in mice or ferrets, but readily obtained the 627K or 701N mutation in its PB2 segment upon replication in ferrets, causing it to become highly lethal in mice and ferrets and to be transmitted efficiently in ferrets by respiratory droplet. H7N9 viruses bearing the HA insertion and PB2 627K mutation have been detected in humans in China. Our study indicates that the new H7N9 mutants are lethal to chickens and pose an increased threat to human health, and thus highlights the need to control and eradicate the H7N9 viruses to prevent a possible pandemic.

Keywords：influenza virus；H7N9；highly pathogenic；pandemic potential；transmission
Cell Research（2017）27：1409-1421. doi：10. 1038/cr. 2017. 129；published online 24 October 2017

以上示例分别引自名刊 *Nature*、*Science*（电子论文）、*Cell*、*Light：S&A*、*Cell Research*。*Nature* 论文的 DOI 位于论文首页书眉的右端；*Science* 的位于论文信息页作者姓名的下方；*Cell* 的位于署名中作者单位的下方；*Light：S&A* 的位于摘要后、关键词前；*Cell Research* 的位于关键词的下方，关键词位于摘要后面。

3.7.2 日期信息

日期信息是论文信息的另外一种，它是有关论文提交（投稿）、修改、接收（录用）、上线发布等的时间信息。此信息属论文题名的一种注释，位于论文首页脚注处或其他位置，一般以"Received …；revised …；accepted …；published online …"作为标识。不同期刊对日期信息的具体标识项目与格式可能有所不同，下面展现几本名刊的日期信息。

- **Received 19 May；accepted 18 December 2015. Published online 27 January 2016.**
（*Nature*——位于论文正文后面，参考文献表前面。）
- 2 March 2016；accepted 4 April 2016
Published online 14 April 2016
10. 1126/science. aaf6116
（*Science*——位于附加信息后面，全文最后。）
- Received：May 28，2015
Revised：August 26，2015
Accepted：January 15，2016
Published：February 18，2016
（*Cell*——位于致谢后面，参考文献表前面，每类日期另行书写。）
- *Light：Science & Applications*（2017）**6**，e17007；doi：10. 1038/lsa. 2017. 7；published online 30 June 2017
- Received 1 August 2016；revised 1 February 2017；accepted 8 February；accepted article preview online 10 February 2017
（*Light：S&A*——有两处日期信息：一处是上线日期，位于位于论文 DOI 后面；另一处是除上线日期以外的日期，位于论文首页脚注部分的最后。）
- Received 11 July 2017；revised 17 September 2017；accepted 26 September 2017；published online 24 October 2017
（*Cell Research*——位于论文首页脚注部分的最后。）

日期信息是体现研究成果时效（新旧）、统计有关期刊指标（如出版周期）以及反映编辑出版工作效率的重要依据，因此做到日期信息的完整、准确非常重要。

3.7.3 附加信息

附加信息（Supplementary Information 或 Supplemental Information）有时也称附件材料、附加材料（Supplementary Materials 或 Supplemental Materials），是指引读者去点击相关网址查看有关论文支撑材料的包含或指明网址的引导类信息，是支持论文内容而又不便或不能写入正文、随论文在线发表后与正文一起放在网上供点击查看的材料或数据，如插图和表格、程序和算法、实验流程和文档材料、加工过程和模拟（仿真）结果视频等。正文引用附加信息的常见格式是在引用序号中加字母 S，如 Supplementary

Figure S1、Figs. S5c and S5d、Table S1 等。阅读或观看附件信息有助于加深理解论文内容，特别对于视频类附件信息，观看它能取得静态的语言文字永远无法产生的动态、真实甚至如临其境的效果。

下面展现几本名刊的附加信息。

- **Supplementary Information** is available in the online version of the paper.

  （*Nature*——附加信息位于参考文献表后面，致谢前面。）

- **SUPPLEMENTARY MATERIALS**

  www. sciencemag. org/content/351/6269/151/suppl/DC1

  Materials and Methods

  Supplementary Text

  Figs. S1 to S15

  References (38–42)

  （*Science*——附加信息位于致谢后面，全文最后的日期信息的前面。）

- **SUPPLEMENTAL INFORMATION**

  Supplemental Information includes Supplemental Experimental Procedures, four figures, and eight tables and can be found with this article online at http：//dx. doi. org/10. 1016/j. cell. 2016. 01. 024.

  （*Cell*——附加信息位于致谢前面，致谢位于参考文献表前面。）

- Supplementary Information for this article can be found on the *Light*：*Science & Applications*' website（http：//www. nature. com/lsa）.

  （*Light*：*S&A*——附加信息位于全文最后。）

- （**Supplementary Information** is linked to the online version of the paper on the *Cell Research* website.）

  （*Cell Research*——附加信息位于参考文献表后面，版权许可前面。）

注意附加信息与附录的异同。相同之处：二者均是论文正文的附件，都能节省正文篇幅，补充正文功能。但区别也是明显的：附录是随同论文一起存在的，犹如论文的一个有机组成部分，是印刷在纸质期刊论文中的；而附加信息是论文以外的另一个事物，严格意义上说不是论文的有机组成部分，只能看作是论文的一个补充材料，是不会被印刷在纸质期刊论文中的，只能以数字的形式在网上被查看。另外，附录作为论文的一个组成部分，是随论文一起由作者投稿的；而附加信息是在稿件被录用后，由作者撰写、设计、录制、拍摄好提交，再经出版部门审核、修改、加工而放到网上的，这部分内容主要是由作者提供、后经出版部门加工制作。可见，数字时代的论文写作内涵已发生了显著变化，不仅仅是传统意义的"纯写"了，还有现代先进技术意义上的"制作"。

3.7.4 利益声明

利益声明即利益冲突声明（Conflict of Interest），是作者发表论文对不存在金融利益问题所做出的一种公开承诺或保证，相当于论文的作者与期刊出版机构之间默签的一份出版协议。这种声明在 SCI 期刊中较为多见，多位于正文后面、作者贡献前面或后面。它的常见格式和文本通常有以下几种：

- **Conflict of Interest**

  The authors declare no conflict of interest.

- **Conflict of Interest**

  The authors declare that they have no conflict of interest.

- **Competing Financial Interests**

  The authors declare that they have no conflict of interest.

- **Conflict of Interest statement**

  No potential conflicts of interest are disclosed.

这类声明可以不是以上单列标题的形式，还可放在某类出版信息中加以表述。例如：

Author Information Reprints and permissions information is available at www. nature. com/reprints. The authors declare no competing financial interests. Readers are welcome to comment on the online version of the paper. Correspondence and requests for materials should be addressed to S. A. M. （mccarroll@ genetics. med. harvard. edu）.

这是 *Nature* 论文的作者信息：再版和许可信息可从网站 www. nature. com/reprints 获得；作者声明无竞争性金融利益；欢迎读者对在线论文发表评论；通信和材料获取应联系 S. A. M. （mccarroll@ genetics. med. harvard. edu）。利益声明是其中的一项内容。

3.7.5 作者信息

这里的作者信息主要是作者发表论文后对有关论文资源和信息获得方式、对在线论文发表评论等的提示，有时还包括通信作者、利益声明等信息，例如上节中示例的 *Nature* 论文的作者信息。这里的作者信息不同于3.5节中的作者介绍，英文叫法一样（Author Information），但内容完全不同，请注意这一点。

3.7.6 版权许可

OA 论文通常有版权许可声明，一般位于论文的最后。其文本通常如下：

This work is is licensed under a Creative Commons Attribution-NonCommercial-NoDerivs 4.0 Unported License. The images or other third party material in this article are included in the article's Creative Commons license, unless indicated otherwise in the credit line; if the material is not included under the Creative Commons license, users will need to obtain permission from the license holder to reproduce the material. To view a copy of this license, visit http：//creativecommons. org/licenses/by-nc-nd/4.0/.

以上文本的主要内容包括：①本文得到知识共享许可协议（Creative Commons Attribution-NonCommercial-NoDerivs 4.0 Unported License）的许可。②文中的插图或其他第三方材料均受本文知识共享许可的保护，除非在权利许可情况中另有说明。③如果这些材料不包含在知识共享许可协议中，用户需获得许可持有人的许可方可使用这些材料。

该文本通常是纸本期刊论文的印刷文本，稍简单些。期刊网站或在线论文的此文本相对详细些，现摘录如下供参考。

Rights and permissions

Open Access This article is licensed under a Creative Commons Attribution 4.0 International License, which permits use, sharing, adaptation, distribution and reproduction in any medium or format, as long as you give appropriate credit to the original author(s) and the source, provide a link to the Creative Commons license, and indicate if changes were made. The images or other third party material in this article are included in the article's Creative Commons license, unless indicated otherwise in a credit line to the material. If material is not included in the article's Creative Commons license and your intended use is not permitted by statutory regulation or exceeds the permitted use, you will need to obtain permission directly from the copyright holder. To view a copy of this license, visit http：//creativecommons. org/licenses/by/4.0/.

第 4 章　SCI 论文量和单位使用

科技论文往往有量和单位,用来对科学概念进行定义、描述、代替、度量、计算和比较,其使用标准、规范与否直接影响论文水准的高低。世界各国对量和单位的标准化、规范化一般比较重视,对论文中量和单位的使用一般也有明确的要求。我国在这方面要求也很严格,于 1994 年发布了《关于在全国开展"量和单位"系列国家标准宣传贯彻工作的通知》,明确指出:"根据《中华人民共和国计量法》和《中华人民共和国标准化法》,要求所有 1995 年 7 月 1 日以后出版的科技书刊、报纸、新闻稿件、教材、产品铭牌、产品说明书等,在使用量和单位的名称、符号、书写规则时都应符合新标准的规定;所有出版物再版时,都要按新标准规定进行修订。"这个新标准就是 GB 3100~3102—1993《量和单位》。

本章基于国家标准《量和单位》的规定,并参照一些国际名刊论文中有关量和单位使用的范例,阐述 SCI 论文中量和单位使用应遵循的基本原则及常见的问题,以期读者树立和加强量和单位的标准观,在论文写作中规范使用量和单位,进而提升论文的写作质量。

4.1　量和单位使用基本原则

1. 量

由国家标准可以总结出论文中有关量名称使用的以下基本原则:

(1) 一个量一般有一个名称,但有的有几个名称。例如:acceleration of free fall 与 acceleration due to gravity, moment of momentum 与 angular momentum, volumic charge、charge density 与 volume density of charge, time、time interval 与 duration 等为同一量的不同名称。

(2) 有的量名称有全称和简称两种叫法,简称一般为常用叫法,论文中首次出现时宜优先使用全称。例如:viscosity 与 dynamic viscosity, resistance 与 resistance to direct current, resistance 与 resistance to alternating current, mass 与 mechanical mass 等分别为量名称的简称和全称。

(3) 对于有多个名称的量,这些名称未加区别时处同等的地位。例如:rotational frequency 和 rotational speed, linear strain 和 relative elongation, angle 和 plane angle 等为同一量的两个名称;transmission factor 或 transmittance 和 transmission coefficient 为同一量的三个名称,均有同等的地位。

(4) 在国家标准中增加了一些新的量名称,相应地也就废弃(取代)了一些旧名称。例如:specific gravity 改为 density 或 mass density, absolute temperature 和 kelvin temperature 改为 thermodynamic temperature, specific heat 改为 massic heat capacity 或 specific heat capacity, current strength 改为 electric current, weight percentage 改为 mass fraction, volume percentage 改为 volume fraction, atomic weight 改为 relative atomic mass, molecular weight 改为 relative molecular mass。

由国家标准可以总结出论文中有关量符号使用的以下基本原则:

(1) 量符号一般用单个字母或者含有上下标(包括字母、数字、符号)、其他说明性标记的字母(包括拉丁字母或希腊字母)表示,但有的量符号用两个字母或多个符号组合来表示,有的用加有某种符号或记号的单个字母来表示。例如:slowing-down area 的符号 (L_s^2、L_{s1}^2) 用含有上下标的字母表示;Reynolds number (Re)、Mach number (Ma) 等 25 个特征数用两个字母表示;mass energy absorption coefficient (μ_{en}/ρ)、directional dose equivalent($H'(d,\Omega)$)用多个符号组合表示;absorbed dose rate ($\dot{D}$) 用上面加有小圆点的单个字母表示。

(2) 一个量一般有一个符号,但有的量有两个或两个以上符号。一个量同时有几个符号而未加区别时,这些符号处于同等地位,可根据情况进行选择。当量的主符号与其他量的符号发生冲突或按习惯需要使用时可使用备用符号。例如:Celsius temperature 有两个符号 t、θ,它们具有同等地位;weight 有三个符号 W、P、G,其中 P、G 为备用符号。

(3) 不同的量的符号一般是不相同的,但有的量的符号与另外的量的符号是相同的,即同一符号可作不同的量的符号。例如:W 可作为 weight 和 work 这两个量的符号,T 可作为 period、periodic time 和 thermodynamic temperature 的符号,p 可作为 pressure、momentum 和 object distance 的符号。

(4) 名称表面上相近但概念不同的量的符号可能是截然不同的。例如:force 的符号为 F,surface tension 的却为 γ 或 σ;作为 7 个基本量之一的 mass,其符号为 m,在声学中 "(mechanical) mass" 表示惯性力抗除以角频率,其符号为 M;length、wavelength 和 length of path 具有相近的量名称,但其符号是不同的,分别为 l(或 L)、λ 和 s,而在数学中可用小写的拉丁字母(如 a、b 等)或两个连写的字母(如 |AB|、AB 等)表示直线段的长度。

(5) 量符号通常用斜体字符表示,但表示酸碱度的符号 pH 和表示材料硬度的符号 HRC 等可当作量的符号使用,并可用正体字符表示。量符号有下标时,下标的正斜体要根据具体情况而定(参见 4.2.2 节中有关内容),也有的下标是由正、斜体字符复合而成的。例如:表示数的字母 n、坐标轴的字母 x 等作下标时用斜体表示;massic heat capacity at constant volume 的符号为 c_V,其下标 V 用斜体表示(由 volume 的量符号 V 而来);group velocity 的符号为 c_g、v_g,其下标 g 用正体表示(由 group 的首字母 g 而来)。

(6) 量符号应区分字母类别、大小写及字体。例如:表示 coefficient of heat transfer、angular repetency、angular wavenumber 的符号 k 的字母类别为拉丁字母,curvature、compressibility、thermal conductivity、isentropic exponent 的符号 κ 的字母类别为希腊字母;表示 power、particle radiance 等的符号常用大写字母 P,pressure、object distance 或 momentum 等的符号常用小写字母 p;表示矩阵、矢量(向量)和张量的符号要用黑(加粗)斜体字母。

2. 单位

由国家标准可以总结出以下有关单位名称使用的几个基本原则:

(1) 单位名称中不宜出现任何其他多余的字符,组合单位中的 per 不宜出现两次。

(2) 对乘方形式的单位名称,其顺序不受"指数名称在前、单位名称在后"⊖的限制。

(3) 除 angle、plane angle 和 solid angle 这两个量纲一的量的单位名称规定为 radian、steradian 外,其他量纲一的量的单位名称均为 one。

⊖ 中文科技论文中,对乘方形式的单位名称来说,其顺序通常受"指数名称在前、单位名称在后"的限制。

由国家标准可以总结出以下有关单位符号使用的几个基本原则：

（1）单位符号（单位）在国际上通用，属标准化符号，用于一切需要使用单位的场合。

（2）单位符号多用于数学式、数据表、曲线图、刻度盘和产品铭牌等需要明了的地方，也用于叙述性语句中。

（3）单位符号是以一个或若干拉丁字母或希腊字母表示的单一或独立符号，或是由几个字母（包括词头符号）和空格或"·"或（和）"/"及（或）指数组合而成的组合单位。组合单位中的"/"不宜多于一条，对于分子为1的组合单位符号，一律用负数幂的形式。例如：coefficient of heat transfer 的单位符号为 W/（m²·K），不能为 W/m²/K；volumic cross-section 或 macroscopic cross-section 为 m⁻¹，不宜为 1/m。

（4）单位符号多用正体字符表示，除来源于人名的单位符号第一个字母大写外，其余一般为小写。例如：W、V、N、Pa、mol、cd、rad 等。表示因数大于或等于 10^6 的词头符号用大写体，否则用小写体。例如：大写字母 P 表示 10^{15}，小写字母 p 表示 10^{-12}；大写字母 M 表示 10^6，小写 m 表示 10^{-3} 等。除 angle，plane angle 和 solid angle 这两个量的单位外，其他量纲一的量的单位均为数字 1，在实际中并不写出。

（5）词头可加在单位符号前来构成一个新的（十进倍数或分数）单位符号，以避免单位前的数值过大或过小。词头与单位符号之间不留空隙，即作为一个整体不可分割。例如：1 cm³ =（10^{-2} m)³ = 10^{-6} m³；1 μs⁻¹ =（10^{-6} s)⁻¹ = 10^6 s⁻¹；1 kA/m =（10^3 A）/m = 10^3 A/m。

4.2 量和单位规范使用

以下从量名称、量符号、单位名称、单位符号、词头、法定单位、量纲匹配、行文统一多个方面总结 SCI 论文中量和单位的规范使用。

4.2.1 量名称

量名称的使用具体有以下规则：

（1）除非表达需要不宜使用废弃的量名称（表 4-1）。例如：不宜使用 specific gravity、specific heat、molecular weight、current strength 和 volume percentage concentration 等废弃的量名称来作 density、specific heat capacity、relative molecular mass、electric current 和 volume fraction 等标准的量名称。

（2）不要使用含义不确切的词或短语作量名称。例如：不要直接使用 concentration、fraction 和 content 作量名称。

concentration 既可指①mass concentration of B，也可指②concentration of B 或 amount-of-substance concentration of B，还可指③molality of solute B，三者的单位分别为 kg/L、mol/m³（或 mol/L）、mol/kg。

fraction 既可指 mass fraction of B，也可指 volume fraction of B，二者的单位均为 1，但前者是某物质的质量与混合物的质量之比，后者可理解为某物质的体积与混合物的体积之比⊖。

content 不是物理量，商品中的含量指质量或体积，科技中的含量包括有关混合物组成的各个量，如 mass fraction、volume fraction、mass concentration 等。content 用于

⊖ 有关"volume fraction of B"（B 的体积分数）的定义参见国家标准 GB 3100～3102—1993《量和单位》第 222 页。

定性描述时可直接用,如"Starch content of the grain is high, but protein content of it is low"(谷物的淀粉含量高,蛋白质含量低);但定量阐述时,宜用标准名称,如 Volume fraction of O_2 in the air is 21%(空气中 O_2 的体积分数为21%)。

表4-1 常见废弃的量名称与标准量名称

废弃的量名称	标准量名称
specific gravity	volumic mass, mass density, density
specific volume	massic volume
fineness	lineic mass, linear density
absolute temperature, kelvin temperature	thermodynamic temperature
specific heat	massic heat capacity, specific heat capacity
specific heat at constant volume	massic heat capacity at constant volume, specific heat capacity at constant volume
specific heat at constant pressure	massic haet capacity at constant pressure, specific haet capacity at constant pressure
coefficient of heat exchange	coefficient of heat transfer, thermal transmittance
coefficient of convective heat transfer, heat emission coefficient	surface coefficient of heat transfer
adiabatic exponent	isentropic exponent
current strength	electric current
gram equivalent number, molar number, gram molecular number, gram atomic number, gram ion number	amount of substance
gram molecular ratio, mole percentage, gram molecular percentage	mole fraction, mole ratio
gram molecular weight, gram atomic weight, gram ion weight	molar mass
gram molecular concentration, volumic gram molecular concentration, molar concentration, equivalent concentration	amount-of-substance concentration, concentration
weight gram molecular concentration, weight molar concentration	molality
molecular weight	relative molecular mass, mass of molecule
atomic weight	relative atomic mass
concentration, weight percentage, mass percentage concentration	mass fraction
concentration, volume percentage, volume percentage concentration	volume fraction
concentration	mass concentration
gram molecular heat capacity	molar heat capacity
gram molecular gas constant	molar gas constant
light intensity	luminous intensity
luminous emissivity	luminance
particle dose	particle fluence
radiation strength, radioactivity	activity
refractive coefficient	refractive index

（3）不要使用 unit + number 的形式作量名称。例如：用 molar number 表示 amount of substance，tonne number、kilogram number 表示 mass，hour number、second number 表示 time，metre number 表示 length、breadth、height，watt number 表示 power 等均是错误的。

（4）不要为有多个量名称的量过分考虑哪个量名称优先使用。例如：reflection coefficient、reflection factor 和 reflectance 通常没有多大区别，择一即可；同理，thermodynamic energy 与 internal energy，modulus of elasticity 与 Young modulus，electric flux density 与 electric displacement 等基本没有什么区别⊖。

4.2.2 量符号

量符号的使用具体有以下规则：

（1）提倡优先用标准量符号（表4-2）。例如 mass 的标准量符号是 m，而 M、W、P、μ 等则是其非标准量符号。为一个有几个标准符号的量选用符号时，可根据具体情况选择一个恰当的符号。当量的符号与其他量的符号发生冲突或应该按习惯使用时，可考虑使用备用符号。例如：行文中若已用 t 作 time 的符号，就不宜再用 t 作 Celsius temperature 的符号。

表 4-2 常见非标准量符号与标准量符号

量 名 称	非标准量符号	标准量符号
mass	M, W, P, μ	m
force	f, N, T	F
pressure	P	p
power	p	P
Celsius temperature	T	t, θ
electric charge, quantity of electricity	q	Q
magnetic induction	H, F	B
concentration of B	C_B	c_B
mass fraction of B	ω_B	w_B
volume fraction of B	ψ_B	φ_B

（2）不提倡用字符串作量符号。字符串常来自量名称的缩写，有时为整个名称（词或短语），常见字符串与标准量符号见表4-3。例如：用 *WEIGHT* 作 weight 的符号，*CR* 或 *pcritical pressure* 作 critical pressure 的符号均不规范，但不是不可以使用。

表 4-3 常见字符串量符号与标准量符号

量 名 称	字符串量符号	标准量符号
mass	MASS, *MASS*	m
weight	WEIGHT, *WEIGHT*	W, (P, G)
movement velocity	MV, *MV*	v_m
body mass (body weight)	BW, *BW*	M, (m_b)
critical high temperature	CHT, *CHT*	$T_{c,h}$
critical low temperature	CLT, *CLT*	$T_{c,l}$
dry mass (dry weight)	DW, *DW*	m_d
fresh mass (fresh weight)	FW, *FW*	m_f
critical pressure	CRP, *CRP*	p_{cr}
arterial pressure	AP, *AP*	p_a
venous pressure	VP, *VP*	p_v
pressure of oxygen	PO$_2$, *PO*$_2$	$p(O_2)$
sound pressure level	SPL, *SPL*	L_p
sound noise ratio	SNR, *SNR*	R_{SN}, γ_{SN}

（3）表意不明确时不宜用化学名称、元素符号（包括原子式或分子式）作量符号。例如：① "barium fluoride：sodium chloride = 4：6" 表达不规范，因为使用了化学名称作量符号（barium fluoride 为氟化钡的名称，sodium chloride 为氯化钠的名称）；② "CO_2：O_2 = 1：5" 也不规范，因为使用了分子式作量符号。但在表意明确的情况下，以上表达也是可以使用的。对于以上表达②，若指体积比，可改为 $V(CO_2)$：$V(O_2)$ = 1：5；若指浓度比，可改为 $c(CO_2)$：$c(O_2)$ = 1：5。又如：Ca = 20 mg，MnO_2% = 30%，可改为 $m(Ca)$ = 20 mg，

⊖ 这里的表述是针对 SCI 论文来说的，但对中文论文不适用，在中文论文中使用这些量名称通常是有优先级的。

$w(MnO_2) = 30\%$ ⊖。

（4）不宜把量纲不是一的量符号作为纯数。例如：对 velocity 的量符号 v 取对数 $\lg v$ (m·s^{-1}) 不妥，因为 v 的量纲不是一，不能取对数；速度与其单位之比 $v/$(m·s^{-1}) 是一个数，数可以取对数，故正确的表达是 $\lg (v/$(m·s^{-1}))。又如：Neon molecular number equals $0.5L$, in which L is Avogadro constant，此句表意容易理解，但逻辑上不通，因为分子数的单位是 1，而阿伏加德罗常数的单位是 mol^{-1}，二者不能相等。可改为 Neon molecular number equals $0.5L$, in which L is the value of Avogadro constant expressed in the unit mol^{-1}。

（5）量符号常用斜体。除表示酸碱度的符号 pH 和材料硬度的 HRC 等用正体字母外，其他量符号通常用斜体字符表示。也有的期刊如 *Cell*，其论文中各种符号包括量符号均用正体。

（6）矩阵、矢量和张量符号多用黑（加粗）斜体字母。例如：将矩阵 **A** 表示成非黑体 A，或字符加方括号的形式 $[A]$，或字符上方加箭头的形式 $\vec{A}$ 或 $\overrightarrow{A}$，或字符串（如 MA、matrixA）等形式均不规范。

（7）不要对两字符量符号与两个量符号相乘相混淆。为避免把由两个字母组成的量符号误解为两个量相乘，相乘的量符号间应有乘号（如·或×）或加空。例如：表示 radius R 与 eccentricity e 相乘的 Re 与表示 Reynolds number（雷诺数）的 Re 同时出现时容易混淆，应加以区分，可将表示相乘的 Re 表示为 $R·e$ 或 $R×e$ 或 $R\ e$。

当不同量用同一字母表示，或同一量有不同使用特点，或有不同量值要表示时，为相互区别，可用主符号附加下标的形式（必要时可用上标及其他标记）作量符号。表下标时，宜区分下标的字母类别、正斜体、大小写等。下标规范与不规范表示对照示例见表 4-4。

表 4-4　下标规范与不规范表示对照示例

量名称	规范表示	不规范表示	备注
massic heat capacity at constant pressure	c_p	c_P, c_P, c_p	压力的符号 p 用小写斜体
massic heat capacity at constant volume	c_V	c_V, c_v, c_v	体积的符号 V 用大写斜体
electric current	I_i ($i=1,2,\cdots$)	I_i ($i=1,2,\cdots$)	变量 i 用斜体
force of axis y	F_y	F_y	坐标轴 y 用斜体
	$\Sigma a_x b_x$	$\Sigma a_x b_x$	连续数 x 用斜体
area of triangle ABC	$S_{\triangle ABC}$	$S_{\triangle ABC}$	点 A, B, C 用斜体
potential energy	E_p	E_p, E_P	potential 的首字母 p 用小写正体
static friction factor	μ_s, f_s	μ_s, f_s	static 的首字母 s 用小写正体
Fermi temperature	T_F	T_f, T_F	源于人名的缩写 F 用大写正体
energy of 10 hours	E_{10h}	E_{10H}, E_{10hr}	时间的单位 h 用小写正体
maximum resistance	R_{max}	R_{max}, R_{MAX}, R_{MAX}	缩写词 max 用小写正体
half thickness	$d_{1/2}$	$d_{1/2}$	纯数字用正体
mass fraction of CO_2	w_{CO_2}, $w(CO_2)$	w_{CO_2}, $w(CO_2)$	化学元素符号用正体
linear ionization by a particle	N_{il}	N_{il}, N_{il}	ionization 的首字母 i 用正体，长度的符号 l 用斜体
spectral angular cross-section（能谱角截面）	$\sigma_{\Omega, E}$	$\sigma_{\Omega, E}$	立体角、能量的符号 Ω, E 用斜体

⊖　m, w 分别表示 mass 和 mass fraction。也可将 Ca 和 MnO_2 改为下标的形式，如 $m_{Ca} = 20$ mg，$w_{MnO_2} = 30\%$。

下标的规范使用有以下规则：

（1）数字、数学符号、记号（标记）、代表变动性数字的字母（连续性字母）、量符号、单位符号、来源于人名的缩写、关键英文词首字母、英文词缩写等均可作下标。

（2）下标为量符号，表示变动性数字的字母，坐标轴符号和表示几何图形中的点、线、面、体的字母时宜用斜体，其余宜用正体。

（3）下标为量符号、单位符号时，大小写同原符号；缩写作下标时，来源于人名的缩写用大写，其他缩写多用小写。

（4）优先使用国际上和行业中规定或通用的下标写法。

（5）可用同一字母的大小写两种不同写法或在量符号上方加某些记号，来表示下标不足以表示不同量之间区别时的量符号。

（6）一个量符号中出现几个下标或下标所代表的符号比较复杂时，可把这些下标符号加在"（）"中以平排的形式（即与主符号平齐）共同置于量符号之后。

（7）按需可以用复合下标，即下标的下标（二级下标）、二级下标的下标（三级下标）。

（8）按需可以使用上标或其他标记符号。

4.2.3 单位名称

单位名称的使用具体有以下规则：

（1）相除组合单位的名称与其符号的顺序应一致。符号中的乘号无对应的名称，除号对应的名称为 per，不论分母中有几个单位，per 宜出现一次。例如：massic heat capacity 单位 J/(kg·K) 的名称不是 joule per kilogram per kelvin，而是 joule per kilogram kelvin；velocity 单位 m/s 不是 second metre、metre second 或 per second metre，而是 metre per second；dose 单位 mg/(kg·d) 不是 milligram per kilogram per day，而是 milligram per kilogram day。

（2）区分乘方形式的单位名称。乘方形式的单位名称，其顺序通常是单位名称在前，指数名称在后，且指数名称由序数词加 power 构成。例如：second moment of area 单位 m^4 的名称为 metre to the fourth power。但当指数为 2、3 时，单位名称后的限定语常为 squared、cubed；长度的 2、3 次幂分别表面积、体积时，相应的限定语应分别为 square、cubic，并置长度单位之前，否则称这两个限定语为 squared、cubed。例如：volume 单位 dm^3 的名称是 cubic decimetre，非 decimetre cubed；section modulus 单位 m^3 是 metre cubed，非 cubic metre。

（3）组合单位的名称中不得加多余的符号（如表示乘、除的数学符号"·""/"或其他符号），即单位名称中不得加任何符号。例如：pressure 单位 N/m^2 ⊖ 的名称是 newton per square metre，而不是 newton/per square metre、newton/square metre、newton/metre^2 或 newton metre $^{-2}$；resistivity 单位 $\Omega·m$ 的名称是 ohm metre，而不是 ohm·metre。

（4）不提倡使用非法定单位名称（包括单位名称的旧称）。例如：dyne、erg（calorie）、horsepower、foot、inch 等非法定单位名称应少用或不用，而用 newton、joule、watt、metre 或 centimetre、nautical mile、litre、hour 等法定单位名称。

4.2.4 单位符号

单位符号的使用应注意以下几个方面：

1. 规范使用字体

单位符号应严格区分符号的字母类别、大小写及正斜体。一般用小写字母，但来源于人名首字母时用大写字母；无例外均采用正体字母。在字母类别上易混淆的字母有 k

---

⊖ 此单位有专门名称 Pa，1 Pa = 1 N/m^2。

与 κ，v 与 ν，u 与 μ 等（前者为拉丁字母，后者为希腊字母）；在大小写上易混淆的有 c 与 C，k 与 K，v 与 V，u 与 U，o 与 O，p 与 P，w 与 W，s 与 S 等。正确与错误单位符号示例见表 4-5。

表 4-5　正确与错误单位符号示例

量　名　称	正确单位符号		错误单位符号
length，radius of curvature，wavelength	m	m	M，M
time，period，time constant of an exponentially varying quantity	s	s	S，S
mass（质量）	kg，t	Kg，t	Kg，T，Kg，T
thermodynamic temperature	K	K	k，k
pressure，normal stress，modulus of elasticity	Pa	Pa	pa，pa
frequency	Hz	Hz	HZ，H_Z，H_z；HZ，H_Z，H_z
power，heat flow rate	W	W	w，w
electric charge，electric flux，elementary charge	C	C	c，c
conductance，admittance，susceptance	S	S	s，s
electric potential，potential difference，electromotive force	V	V	v，v
neutron separation energy，nuclear binding energy，level width	eV	eV	ev，ev
magnetic flux density，magnetic polarization	T	T	t，t
permeance	H	H	h，h
illuminance	lx	lx	Lx，Lx
luminous flux	lm	lm	Lm，Lm
luminous intensity	cd	cd	CD，CD
sound pressure level，sound intensity level，sound power level	B	B	b，b

2. 规范使用法定单位符号

提倡用法定单位，少用非法定或形似单位符号，在 SCI 论文中可以用非法定或形似单位符号充当单位符号。下列几类就属非法定或形似单位符号：

（1）表示 time 的非标准单位符号，如旧符号 sec、m、hr、y 或 yr（它们的法定单位分别是 s、min、h、a），以及为没有国际单位符号的量给出了自定义单位符号 wk、mo。如果使用的这种单位符号正好是相应某词的缩写，那么就相当于用词来充当单位符号了。

（2）表示单位符号的缩写，如 rpm、bps 或 Bps，其法定单位应分别是 r/min、bit/s 或 B/s。如果用这种缩写作了单位，就相当于赋予这种缩写以单位的地位，可以理解为用缩写来表示单位。

（3）表示数量份额的缩写，如 ppm（parts per million，10^{-6}），pphm（parts per hundred million，10^{-8}），ppb（parts per billion，在中美法表 10^{-9}、英德表 10^{-12}），ppt（parts per trillion，在中美法表 10^{-12}、英德表 10^{-18}）。不宜用这种缩写作单位符号。例如：Mass fraction w/ppm 不规范，因为 Mass fraction 的量纲是一，单位为 1，不是 ppm；chemical shift δ = 5.5 ppm 也不妥，形式上是将 ppm 作为 chemical shift δ 的单位了，应改为 chemical shift δ = 5.5，但不写为

chemical shift $\delta = 5.5 \times 10^{-6}$⊖。用这种数量份额缩写作单位时，虽不科学、不严谨，但从表意上看是没问题的。

3. 规范使用组合单位符号

组合单位符号使用具体有以下规则：

（1）当组合单位符号由几个单位符号相乘构成时，用单位符号间加圆点或留空隙的形式表示。例如：由 N 和 m 相乘构成的单位应表示为 N·m 和 N m 两种形式之一。N m 也可写成中间不留空隙的形式 Nm，但当组合单位符号中某单位的符号又属于词头符号并有可能发生混淆时，则应尽量将其置于右侧，这一点要特别注意。例如：力矩单位符号应写成 N·m、N m 或 Nm，其中 Nm 不要写成 mN，因为 mN 表示 millinewton，而不是 newton metre。

（2）当组合单位符号由两个单位相除构成时，用单位符号分别作分子、分母的分数或单位符号间加斜线或圆点的形式表示（情况复杂时可加括号）。例如：由 m 和 s 相除构成的单位可表示为 $\dfrac{m}{s}$、m/s、m·s^{-1} 三种形式之一。用斜线表相除时，单位符号的分子和分母都应与斜线处于同一行内。分母中包含两个以上单位符号时，整个分母一般应加圆括号。在一个组合单位符号中，同一行内的斜线不宜多于一条，除了加括号避免混淆外，斜线后不宜直接有乘号或除号。情况复杂时宜用负数幂或括号。例如：coefficient of heat transfer 的单位不是 W/m²/K、W/m²·K 或 W/m²·K^{-1}，而是 W/（m²·K）或 W·m^{-2}·K^{-1}。

（3）当表示分子为 1 的单位时，应采用负数幂的形式。例如：Avogadro constant 的单位是 mol^{-1}，一般不写为 1/mol；particle number density 的单位是 m^{-3}，一般不写为 1/m³；repetency 的单位是 m^{-1}，一般不写为 1/m。

（4）当用"°""′""″"构成组合单位时，要给其加圆括号"（）"。例如："25′/min"应表示为"25（′）/min"；"β/°"应表示为"β/（°）"。

（5）非物理量的单位，如 time、piece、person、RMB Yuan 等，可与单位国际符号构成组合形式的单位，也可写成负数幂的形式。例如 RMB Yuan/d、time/s、piece/（h·person）、L/time 或 L·time^{-1}、L/person 或 L·person^{-1}。

4. 无须修饰单位符号

在单位符号上不要附加任何其他标记或符号。单位没有复数形式，在其后加 s 是错误的；在其上附加表示量的特性和测量过程信息的标志也是错误的。具体有以下规则：

（1）不要给单位符号附加上、下标。例如：The maxium tension eauals 220 V 应表达为 $U_{max} = 220$ V，而不是 $U = 220$ V$_{max}$，因为给电压的单位 V 加下标 max 是错误的；The force acted on point A equals 100 N 应表达成 $F_A = 100$ N，而不是 $F = 100$ N$_A$，因为给力的单位 N 加下标 A 是错误的。

（2）不要在单位符号间插入修饰性字符。例如：$\rho = 1\,000$ kg（H$_2$O）/m³ 应为 ρ（H$_2$O）$= 1\,000$ kg/m³；200 kg（nitrogen fertilizer）/hm² 应为 Amount of nitrogen fertilizer 200 kg/hm²。此两例的共同错误是，在组合单位符号间插入了多余的修饰性字符。

（3）不要受中文论文有关要求的影响，认为不能用 m/m、V/V 之类的表达来表示质量分数、体积分数。例如，85%（m/m）和 Mass fraction 85%，68%（V/V）和 Vol-

---

⊖ 按国际纯粹与应用化学联合会（International Union of Pure and Applied Chemistry，IUPAC）为化学位移给出的新定义，化学位移的计算公式为 $\delta = 10^6 (\nu - \nu_0)/\nu_0$，定义中已含有 10^{-6} 之意，因此无须再用 ppm 或 10^{-6} 重复表意。

ume fraction 68% 等均是正确的表达。

（4）不要为单位加习惯性修饰符号（包括前置修饰符号和下标）。例如：用 Nm³ 或 m³ⁿ 表示标准立方米，NL 或 L_n 表示标准升均是错误的，应分别为 m³、L 或 l（升）。

5. 规范表示量值

提倡基于量和单位的关系 $A = \{A\} \cdot [A]$ 及有关规定表示量值，具体有以下规则：

（1）数值与单位符号间留空隙。表示量值时，单位符号应置于数值之后，数值与单位符号间留空隙。必须指出，Celsius temperature 的单位符号℃与其前面的数值间也可留空隙，唯一例外的是，平面角的单位符号"°""′"""与其前面数值间不留空隙。例如：$t = 100℃$ 应为 $t = 100\ ℃$，$α = 68\ °17\ ′20\ ″$ 应为 $α = 68°17′20″$。

（2）不要把单位插在数值中间或把单位符号（或名称）拆开使用。例如：1m73、10s09、20″15 表达错误（因为把单位插在了数值中间），应分别为 1.73 m、10.09 s、20.15″；不要将 34℃ 表示为"34°C"，"0℃–100℃"表示为"0°–100℃"（因为"℃"是一个整体单位符号，不可拆开使用，拆开后相当于用 angle（角）的单位"°"与拉丁字母 C 以并列的形式来表示摄氏温度的单位）；不要将 100 degree Celsius 写为 Celsius 100 degree（因为作为℃的名称 degree Celsius（摄氏度）也是一个整体，不能拆开）。

（3）对量值的和或差规范表示。当所表示的量为量的和或差时，应当加圆括号将数值组合，且置共同的单位符号于全部数值之后，或者写成各个量的和或差的形式，示例见表 4-6。

表 4-6 量值的和或差规范与不规范表示对照示例

量值规范表示	量值不规范表示
$l = 20\ m - 15\ m = (20 - 15)\ m = 5\ m$	$l = 20 - 15\ m = 5\ m$ 或 $l = 20 - 15 = 5\ m$
$t = 28.4\ ℃ ± 0.2\ ℃ = (28.4 ± 0.2)℃$	$t = 28.4\ ℃ ± 0.2\ ℃$
$λ = 220 × (1 ± 0.02)\ W/(m·K)$	$λ = 220 × (1 ± 0.02\ W/(m·K))$

（4）对量值的范围规范表示。表量值范围宜用短横线"-"（或浪纹线连接号"~"）。例如：1.2–2.4 kg·m/s（只在后一数字后加单位）或 1.2 kg·m/s–2.4 kg·m/s（在前后两数字后均加单位）。但有时需要使用后一种形式，是为了避免引起误解。例如：0.2–30%，既可理解为 0.2 到 30%，又可能理解为 0.2% 到 30%。在实际中需要根据具体情况来选用具体形式。

（5）在图表中用特定单位表示量值宜选用合适的形式（表 4-7），大体上有以下几种：①量符号等于量值，如 $λ = 589.6$ nm；②单位符号加括号置于量符号之后，如 $λ$（nm）$= 589.6$；③量符号与单位符号之间用逗号分隔，如 $λ$, nm $= 589.6$；④量符号与单位符号之比，如 $λ/nm = 589.6$；⑤量符号加花括号"{ }"、单位符号作下标，如 $\{λ\}_{nm} = 589.6$。

表 4-7 特定单位量值表示形式示例

$λ(nm)$ 或"$λ, nm$"，$λ/nm$
$v(km/h)$，"$v, km·h^{-1}$"，$v/(km/h)$，$v/(km·h^{-1})$
$\ln p(MPa)$，$\ln(p/MPa)$
$w(10^6)$，$w × 10^6$，$w/10^{-6}$，w/ppm

前两种在 SCI 论文中使用较为普遍。实际中，量名称与量符号可相互替代，如 Velocity（km·h⁻¹）与 v（km·h⁻¹），Velocity/（km·h⁻¹）与 v/（km·h⁻¹），Mass fraction（10⁻⁶）与 w（10⁻⁶），Mass fraction/

10^{-6} 与 $w/10^{-6}$ 表意相同，可选其中一个。

4.2.5 词头

词头的使用应注意以下几个方面：

（1）使用正确字体

使用正确字体指使用词头必须严格区分其字母类别、正斜体及大小写。词头所用字母除 micro（微）（10^{-6}）用希腊字母 μ 表示外，其他均用拉丁字母表示；词头用正体字母表示，大小写需要按其所表示的因数大小来区分。区分词头大小写的规则主要有以下两条：

1）表示的因数等于或大于 10^6 时用大写。这样的词头共 7 个，包括 M（10^6）、G（10^9）、T（10^{12}）、P（10^{15}）、E（10^{18}）、Z（10^{21}）、Y（10^{24}）；

2）表示的因数等于或小于 10^3 时用小写。这样的词头共 13 个，包括 k（10^3）、h（10^2）、da（10^1）、d（10^{-1}）、c（10^{-2}）、m（10^{-3}）、μ（10^{-6}）、n（10^{-9}）、p（10^{-12}）、f（10^{-15}）、a（10^{-18}）、z（10^{-21}）、y（10^{-24}）。

（2）词头与单位连用

词头只有置于单位符号之前与单位符号同时使用才有效，即词头只有与单位符号连用（单位符号之间不留间隙）才有因数意义，也即词头不得独立使用；词头也不能重叠使用。例如：5 km 不写成 5 k，128 Gb 不写成 128 G；nm 不写成 mμm，pF 不写成 μμF，GW 不写成 kMW。

通过相乘构成的组合单位一般只用一个词头，通常加在组合单位中的第一个单位前。例如：moment of force 单位 kN·m 不能写成 N·km。为只通过相除构成的组合单位或通过乘和除构成的组合单位加词头时，词头一般加在分子中的第一个单位之前，分母中一般不用词头，但 mass 单位 kg 不作为有词头的单位对待。例如：molar internal energy 单位 kJ/mol 不写成 J/mmol，而 specific energy 单位可以是 J/kg。当组合单位的分母是 length、area 或 volume 的单位时，按习惯与方便，分母中可以选用词头构成倍数单位或分数单位。例如：mass density 单位可以选用 g/cm。一般不在组合单位的分子、分母中同时采用词头。例如：electric field strength 单位不要用 kV/mm，而应当用 MV/m。

（3）选用合适的词头

使用词头的目的是使量值中的数值变得短小、简洁（国家标准规定最好在 0.1～1 000 范围内），为此要根据量值大小来确定词头因数的大小，进而选用合适的词头符号。例如：5 000×10^6 Pa·s/m 应当表示为 5 GPa·s/m，而不是 5 000 MPa·s/m；0.000 05 m 应当表示为 50 μm，而不是 0.05 mm。

（4）考虑词头使用的限制性

考虑哪些单位不允许加词头，避免对不允许加词头的单位加词头。例如："°" "′" "″" "min" "h" "d" "n mile" "kn" "kg" 等单位不得加词头构成倍数单位或分数单位。由于历史原因，mass 的基本单位名称 kilogram 中含有词头 kilo，其十进倍数和分数单位由词头加在 gram 之前构成，如 milligram 的单位是 mg，而不是 μkg。还要注意，1998 年 SI 第 7 版新规定 "℃" 可以用词头，k℃ 和 m℃ 等均是正确的单位符号。

（5）正确处理词头与单位的幂次关系

将词头符号与其所紧接的单位符号作为一个整体对待且有相同幂次，即倍数或分数单位的指数是包括词头在内的整个单位的幂。例如：1 cm^2 ≠ 10^{-2} m^2 （1 cm^2 = 1 (10^{-2}m)^2 = 1×10^{-4} m^2）；8 500 m^3/d ≠ 8.5 km^3/d （8 500 m^3/d = 8.5×10^3 m^3/d = 8.5×(10 m)^3/d）；10 000 000 m^2 ≠ 10 Mm^2 （10 000 000 m^2 = 10 km^2）；1 000 000 000 m^{-3} ≠ 1 Gm^{-3} （1 000 000 000 m^{-3} = 1×10^9×m^{-3} = 1×(10^{-3}m)$^{-3}$ = 1 mm^{-3}）。

（6）考虑词头的习惯用法

尊重和兼顾我国对一些数词的习惯用法。例如：10^4（万）、10^8（亿）、10^{12}（万亿）等是我国习惯用的数词，可用在单位前，相当于词头，如 ten thousand kilometers 可记为 10^4 km，ten thousand ton kilometers 可记为 10^4 t·km。

4.2.6 法定单位

使用法定单位是单位规范使用的重要方面。非法定与法定单位对照示例见表 4-8。

表 4-8 非法定与法定单位对照示例

非法定单位		法定单位	备注
名 称	符 号		
mile	mile	m	1 mile = 1 609.344 m
yard	yd	m	1 yd = 0.914 4 m
li（[市]里）			1 li = 500 m
foot	ft	m	1 ft = 0.304 8 m
inch	in	m	1 in = 0.025 4 m
mu（亩）	mu	m^2，hm^2	1 mu =（10^4/15）m^2 = 666.6 m^2，1 hm^2 = 15 mu
gong mu（公亩）	a	m^2	1 a = 100 m^2
foot per second	ft/s	m/s	1 ft/s = 0.304 8 m/s
mile per hour	mile/h	m/s	1 mile/h = 0.447 04 m/s
pound	lb	kg	1 lb = 0.453 592 37 kg
kilogram-force	kgf	N	1 kgf = 9.806 65 N
pound-force	lbf	N	1 lbf = 4.448 22 N
dyne	dyn	N	1 dyn = 10^{-5} N
kilogram-force per square centimetre	kgf/cm^2	N/m^2 或 Pa	1 kgf/cm^2 = 0.098 066 5 MPa
millimeter of mercury	mmHg	Pa	1 mmHg = 133.322 Pa（医学中可用 mmHg）
torr（托）	Torr	Pa	1 Torr = 133.322 Pa
technical atmosphere	at	Pa	1 at = 98.066 5 kPa
standard atmosphere	atm	Pa	1 atm = 101.325 kPa
calorie, kilocalorie	cal, kcal	J	1 cal = 4.186 8 J
	erg	J	1 erg = 10^{-7} J
	M	mol/L	1 M = 1 mol/L
	N	(mol/L)/ionic valency	1 N =（1 mol/L）/ionic valency
	cc	cm^3 或 mL	1 cc = 1 cm^3 = 1 mL
Dalton	D, Da	u	1 D = 1 u，1 u ≈（1.660 540 2 ± 0.000 001 0）× 10^{-27} kg
var	var	V·A	1 var = 1 V·A
kilowatt hour		kW·h	1 kilowatt hour = 1 kW·h
metric horsepower		W	1 metric horsepower = 735.499 W
British horsepower	hp	W	1 hp = 745.700 W
calorie per second	cal/s	W	1 cal/s = 4.186 8 W
degree Fahrenheit（华氏度）	°F	K 或 °C	表示温度差和温度间隔时：1 °F =（5/9）K，1 °C = 1 K；表示温度数值时：$T = 5(\theta + 459.67)/9$，$t = 5(\theta - 32)/9$，$t = T - 273.15$

(续)

非法定单位		法定单位	备 注
名 称	符 号		
degree Rankine	°R	K 或℃	表示温度差和温度间隔时：1°R =（5/9）K，1℃ = 1 K；表示温度数值时：$T = 5\Theta/9$，$t = 5(\Theta - 491.67)/9$，$t = T - 273.15$
Gauss	Gs, G	T	$1\ Gs = 10^{-4}\ T$

说明：hm^2 的名称是 hectare，其国际通用符号为 ha；u 的名称是 unified atomic mass unit；T，t，θ，Θ 分别表示 thermodynamic temperature、Celsius temperature、Fahrenheit temperature、Rankine temperature。

4.2.7 量纲匹配

量纲匹配指式中等号或不等号两边的量纲相同，若不相同，两边就不能相等或作大小比较。例如："$t = \lg(1 - Q)$, where t is release time of medicine, Q is release amount of medicine"⊖，等号左边的 t 是一个表示时间的量，有量纲，而右边是对 $1 - Q$ 这个数取对数，取对数的结果只能是一个纯数，因此等号两边的量纲不相同，即不可能相等，说明此式可能有误。再如：$c(O_2) = 0.0347 + 0.06741I$，此式等号左边的 $c(O_2)$ 为氧气的浓度（单位为 $mol·L^{-1}$），而右边的 I（单位为 A）为电流测量值，因此等号两边的量纲不相同，不可能相等，说明此式可能有误。

4.2.8 行文统一

行文统一指同一论文中对同一量宜始终保持用同一名称、符号。同一符号应只表示同一量，而同一量也应只用同一符号表示；若表示不同条件或特定状态下的同一量，则应采用在量符号加上下标的形式加以区别。例如：若用 friction factor，则应在整篇论文中统一用该名称，而不宜再混用其另一名称 coefficient of friction；若已用 t 表示 time，就不宜再用它表示 Celsius temperature，而应选用其他符号如 θ 表示；若已用 θ 表示摄氏温度，就不宜再用 t 加下标的形式表示不同时刻的此温度，而要用 θ 加下标，如 θ_0、θ_1、…、θ_c（critical temperature）表示。

4.3 量和单位使用常见问题

SCI 论文中量和单位常见问题涉及名称是否准确，符号的字母类别、大小写、正斜体、字体、上下标等是否规范，关系表达是否合理等，大体有以下几个方面：

（1）任意使用一些量和单位的名称和符号，导致概念混用、混淆和张冠李戴。例如：笼统用 concentration 一词，混淆了一些名称里含该词的量；thermodynamic temperature 的符号 T 与 Celsius temperature 的符号 t 混用；mass 的单位 kg、t，与 weight、force 的单位 N 混用。

（2）用自造的或国家标准中已经废弃的量名称。例如：用 specific gravity、specific heat、molecular weight、content 或 percentage 等废弃的量名称，而未用与其相应的 mass density、massic heat capacity 或 specific heat capacity、relative molecular mass 和 mass fraction 等标准量名称。

（3）随意用多字符字符串或英文单词、短语表示一个物理量。例如：用 *WEIGHT* 作 weight 的符号；用 *CT* 或 *critical temperature* 作 critical temperature 的符号。

⊖ release time of medicine—释药时间，amount of medicine—药物释放量。

（4）用国家标准中已经废弃的非法定单位。例如：在不必要的情况下使用 kgf、dyn、kgf/cm²、kgf·m、kcal、kcal/h 等非法定单位。

（5）误将形似单位符号作单位，包括表示时间的单词缩写、表示名词的短语、表示数量份额的缩写以及其他非法定单位符号。例如：误将 hr、sec、rpm、ppm、bps 和 joule 等作标准单位。

（6）对有专门名称的 SI 导出单位，仍用原来的旧名称。例如：在表示 pressure 和 stress 的单位时，仍用旧单位 N/m² 而未用专门名称 Pa；表示 energy、work、heat 或 quantity of heat 的单位时，仍用旧单位 N·m 而未用专门名称 J。

（7）用单位名称或单位名称的组合作单位符号。例如：把 pressure 200 Pa 写成 pressure 200 pascal；把 A·m² 写成 ampere·metre² 或 ampere·square metre。

（8）用单位名称和符号的组合形式表示单位符号。例如：velocity 用 m/second，surface density 用 kilogram/m²，magnetic moment 用 ampere·m² 表示。

（9）未区分量符号（含上下标）和单位符号（包括词头）的字母类别、大小写、正斜体等。例如：用大写字母 P 而未优先用小写字母 p 表示 pressure 和 stress；用斜体字母 T 而未用正体字母 T 表示矩阵转置的上标；用大写字母 M 而未用小写字母 m 表示 length 的单位；用 KW 而未用 kW 表示 power 的单位；用拉丁字母 k 或 K 而未用希腊字母 κ 表示 curvature 的符号。

（10）未正确使用词头。例如：将 1.53×10^6 m³ 写成 1.53 Mm³，kN·m 表示成 N·km，kJ/mol 写成 J/mmol。

（11）未用规范的格式表示图表中的量和单位。例如：用不规范的 Rotational speed $n/r \cdot \min^{-1}$ 或 Rotational speed $n/r/\min$，而未用规范的 Rotational speed n (r/min) 或 Rotational speed n，r/min 或 Rotational speed $n/(r \cdot \min^{-1})$ 或 Rotational speed (r/min) 来表示坐标轴的标目或表格中的参数列。

（12）未用单个黑（加粗）斜体字符表示矩阵、矢量和张量。例如：将矩阵 **K** 表示成非黑体（未加粗）字母 K 或 K，或字符加方括号的形式 [K]，或字符上方加箭头的形式 $\vec{K}$ 或 $\overleftrightarrow{K}$，或其他形式的字符串（如 MK 或 matrixK）。

（13）未优先使用单位矩阵的标准符号 E 或 I 表示单位矩阵。

（14）未优先使用单位矢量的标准符号 e 表示单位矢量。例如：用 n 而不是 e_n 表示单位法向矢量；用 t 而不是 e_t 表示单位切向矢量。

（15）在单位名称的后面附以 number 代替量名称。例如：将 Time (h) 表示成 Number of hours (h)，Force (N) 表示成 Number of Newton (N)。

（16）行文中对同一量的表达不统一。例如：混用多个符号 U、V、u 或 v 来表示同一量 potential difference。

4.4 名刊量和单位实例分析

4.4.1 *Nature* 实例

【1】

During the exercise, the heart rate, oxygen consumption (V_{O_2}), and pulmonary minute ventilation were measured using external monitoring instruments, and were found to increase proportionally with increasing power output as shown in Fig. 3c. Figure 3d illustrates the corresponding real-time measurements on the subject's forehead using a FISA. The skin temperature remains constant at 34 ℃ up to perspiration initiation at about 320 s.

例【1】中出现的量名称有：heart rate；oxygen consumption；pulmonary minute ventilation；power output；skin temperature。其中 oxygen consumption 还带量符号 V_{O_2}。出现的单位及数值有：34 ℃ 和 320 s，℃ 和 s 分别为 Celsius temperature 和 time 的单位。

【2】

At the end of simulation, the <u>action values and visit counts of all traversed edges</u> are updated. Each edge accumulates the visit count and <u>mean evaluation of all simulations passing through that edge</u>

$$N(s,a) = \sum_{i=1}^{n} 1(s,a,i)$$

$$Q(s,a) = \frac{1}{N(s,a)} \sum_{i=1}^{n} 1(s,a,i) V(s_L^i)$$

where s_L^i is the leaf node from the ith simulation, and $1(s, a, i)$ indicates whether an edge (s, a) was traversed during the ith simulation. Once the search is complete, the algorithm chooses the most visited move from the root position.

例【2】中含有数学式。式前部分出现的量名称有：action value of traversed edge；visit count of traversed edge；mean evaluation of all simulations passing through that edge。接着给出后面两个量的计算式，$N(s,a)$ 和 $Q(s,a)$ 为后面两个量的符号，又出现了其他量的符号，如 $1(s, a, i)$、s_L^i。式后部分对这两个新出现的量进行解释，相当于给出其量名称：s_L^i is the leaf node from the ith simulation，$1(s, a, i)$ indicates whether an edge (s, a) was traversed during the ith simulation。

【3】

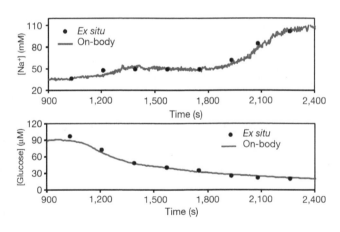

图 4-1 量和单位使用实例一[一]

例【3】（图 4-1）所示为两分图插图，图类为二维坐标图，坐标轴均有标目。横纵坐标轴的标目分别为 Time（s）、[Na⁺]（mM）、[Glucose]（μM），其中括号部分为单位，括号前面为量。量名称有 time、[Na⁺]（concentration of Na⁺）、[Glucose]（concentration of glucose），单位符号有 s、mM（mmol/L）、μM（μmol/L）。

[一] 摘自 Nature 的 RESEARCH ｜ LETTER 类：Fully integrated wearable sensor arrays for multiplexed *in situ* perspiration analysis. Figure 3b. doi：10.1038/nature16521.

【4】

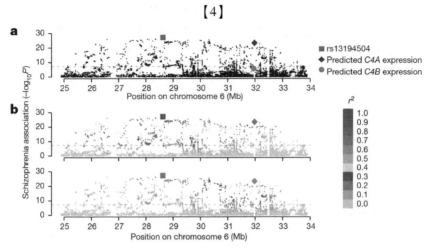

图 4-2 量和单位使用实例二[⊖]

例【4】（图 4-2）所示有两个分图，其中 b 分图又有两个子分图，这三个图均为二维坐标图，坐标轴均有标目，横纵坐标轴分别有相同的标目。横坐标的标目为 Position on chromosome 6（Mb），纵坐标的标目为 Schizophrenia association（$-\log_{10}P$），其中 Mb 为单位，$-\log_{10}P$ 为量的计算式。量名称有 Position on chromosome、Schizophrenia association。另外，图右侧彩条上方的 r^2 为某量符号的平方。

【5】

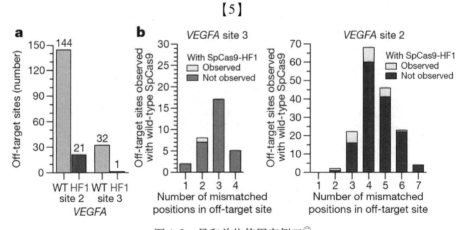

图 4-3 量和单位使用实例三[⊖]

例【5】（图 4-3）为两个分图 a 和 b，其中 b 分图有两个子分图。图类均为二维坐标图，坐标轴均有标目，但均为量纲一的量，故未出现单位。图 a 中的量名称有：VEGFA（vascular endothelial growth factor A）；Off-target sites（number）。图 b 中的量名称有：Number of mismatched positions in off-target site；Off-target sites observed with wild-type SpCas9。

⊖ 摘自 Nature 的 RESEARCH｜ARTICLE 类：Schizophrenia risk from complex variation of complement component 4. Figure 4a, b. doi：10.1038/nature16549.

⊖ 摘自 Nature 的 RESEARCH｜ARTICLE 类：High-fidelity CRISPR-Cas9 nucleases with no detectable genome-wide off-target effects. Figure 4. doi：10.1038/nature16526.

第 4 章　SCI 论文量和单位使用

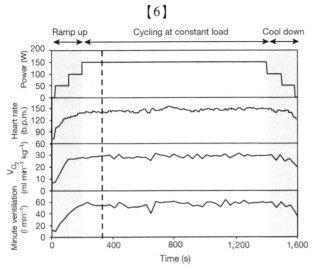

图 4-4　量和单位使用实例四[○1]

例【6】（图 4-4）有四个二维坐标图。横纵坐标的标目有 Time（s）、Power（W）、Heart rate（b.p.m.）、V_{O_2}（ml min^{-1} kg^{-1}）、Minute ventilation（1 min^{-1}），括号部分为单位，括号前为量。量名称有 time、Power、Heart rate、V_{O_2}、Minute ventilation，单位符号有 s、W、b.p.m.（beats per minute）、ml min^{-1} kg^{-1}、1 min^{-1}。V_{O_2} 本是量符号，这里直接用来代替量名称 Oxygen consumption。

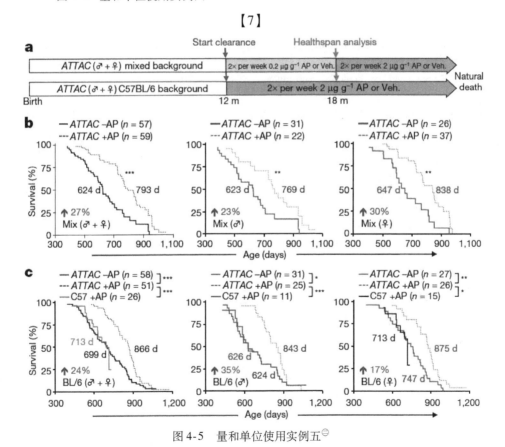

图 4-5　量和单位使用实例五[○2]

[○1] 摘自 Nature 的 RESEARCH | LETTER 类：Fully integrated wearable sensor arrays for multiplexed *in situ* perspiration analysis. Figure 3c. doi：10.1038/nature16521.

[○2] 摘自 Nature 的 RESEARCH | ARTICLE 类：Naturally occurring p16^{Ink4a}-positive cells shorten healthy lifespan. Figure 2. doi：10.1038/nature16932.

例【7】（图 4-5）所示为三组分图 a、b、c，b、c 又各有三个子分图，均为二维坐标图。图 a 中出现了含量值（数值和单位）的表达式，如 2× per week 0.2 μg g^{-1} AP or Veh.，2× per week 2 μg g^{-1} AP or Veh.，还出现了量 Birth（出生时长）及其量值 12 m 和 18 m。图 b、c 的三个子分图的横纵坐标轴分别共用标目 Age（days）和 Survivals（%）。量名称有 Age、Survivals，单位符号有 days 和%。其中 days 是用单词作单位，其标准单位符号应该是 d。图中还出现大量的量值，如表示 Age 的 624 d，793 d，…，747 d 和表示 Survivals 的百分数 27%，23%，…，17%。

4.4.2 Science 实例

【1】
Concerning the more thermally stable FAPbX$_3$ perovskite, an increase in optical band gap has not resulted in an expected increase in <u>opencircuit voltage</u> (V_{OC})（13）. Furthermore, as iodide is substituted with bromide, a crystal phase transition occurs from a trigonal to a cubic structure; in compositions near the transition, the material is unable to crystallize, resulting in an apparently "amorphous" phase with high levels of energetic disorder and unexpectedly low absorption. These compositions additionally have much lower <u>charge-carrier mobilities</u> in the range of 1 cm^2 V^{-1} s^{-1}, in comparison to >20 cm^2 V^{-1} s^{-1} in the neat iodide perovskite（17）. For tandem applications, these problems arise at the Br composition needed to form the desired <u>top-cell band gap</u> of ~1.7 to 1.8 eV.

例【1】语段中出现的量名称有 open-circuit voltage、charge-carrier mobilities 和 top-cell band gap。其中，opencircuit voltage 带量符号 V_{OC}，charge-carrier mobilities 有量值范围 1 cm^2 V^{-1} s^{-1}（另一个量值范围 20 cm^2 V^{-1} s^{-1} 用于比较），top-cell band gap 有量值范围 ~1.7 到 1.8 eV。

【2】
Human iPS-derived NSCs were exposed to ZIKV [multiplicity of infection（MOI），0.25 to 0.002 5]. After 24 hours, ZIKV was detected in NSCs (Fig. 1, A to D); viral envelope protein was evident in 10.10% (MOI, 0.025) and 21.7% (MOI, 0.25) of cells exposed to ZIKV (Fig. 1E).⊖

As a result of ZIKV infection, the <u>average growth area of ZIKV-exposed organoids</u> was reduced by 40% compared with <u>brain organoids under mock conditions</u> [0.624±0.064 mm^2 for ZIKV-exposed organoids versus 1.051±0.108 4 mm^2 for mock-infected organoids (normalized); Fig. 4E].

例【2】段一中，三处出现量名称 multiplicity of infection（MOI），量值为 0.25 到 0.002 5。段二中，量名称有 average growth area of ZIKV-exposed organoids、（average growth area of）brain organoids under mock conditions，二者量值分别为 0.624±0.064 mm^2 和 1.051±0.108 4 mm^2。

【3】

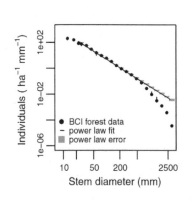 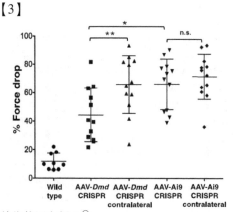

图 4-6 量和单位使用实例六⊖

⊖ iPS—induced pluripotent stem；NSCs—neural stem cells；ZIKV—Zika virus；MOI—multiplicity of infection。

⊖ 左图摘自 Science 的 Dominance of the suppressed：Power-law size structure in tropical forests. Fig. 1. 8 JANUARY 2016 · VOL 351 ISSUE 6269. 右图摘自 Science 的 RESEARCH | REPORTS 类：In vivo gene editing in dystrophic mouse muscle and muscle stem cells. Fig. 2F. 22 JANUARY 2016 · VOL 351 ISSUE 6271.

例【3】（图4-6）所示为两个二维坐标图A和B。图A的两个坐标轴有标目，分别为Stem diameter（mm）和Individuals（ha^{-1} mm^{-1}），其中括号部分为单位，括号前面为量名称。量名称有Stem diameter、Individuals，单位符号有mm、ha^{-1}mm^{-1}。图B的横坐标不是标目的形式，给出了Wild type，AAV-*Dmd* CRISPR，AAV-*Dmd* CRISPR contralateral，AAV-Ai9 CRISPR，AAV-Ai9 CRISPR contralateral 五个类别[一]，而纵坐标为标目的形式，量纲为一，只有量名称% Force drop，其中%相当于Percent of，坐标轴刻度旁的数值即为此量的数值。

【4】

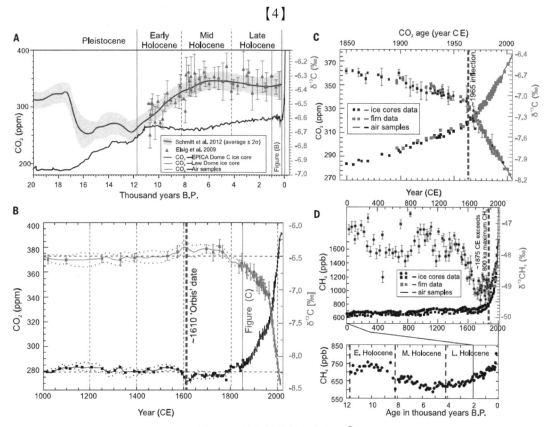

图4-7　量和单位使用实例七[二]

例【4】（图4-7）所示为四组二维坐标图，其中D组又包括上下两个子图[三]。

图A有一横两纵三个坐标轴，坐标轴有标目。横坐标轴的标目为Thousand years B. P.，纵坐标轴的标目为 CO_2（ppm）和 δ^{13}C（‰）；量名称有Thousand years B. P.、CO_2（CO_2含量）、δ^{13}C（δ^{13}C含量）；单位符号有ppm、‰[四]。

图B有两横两纵四个坐标轴，上下横坐标轴共用量和量值，坐标轴有标目。横坐

[一] AAV—adeno-associated virus（腺病毒群）；*Dmd*—Duchenne muscular dystrophy（杜氏肌肉营养不良症）；CRISPR—clustered regularly interspaced short palindromic repeats（规律成簇的间隔短回文重复）。

[二] 摘自*Science*的RESEARCH | REVIEW类：The Anthropocene is functionally and stratigraphically distinct from the Holocenes. Fig. 5. 8 JANUARY 2016 · VOL 351 ISSUE 6269.

[三] B. P.—before the present（距今……以前，现在以前）；CE—Cosmic Era（宇宙纪元）；δ^{13}C—碳同位素比值。

[四] ppm和‰本不是单位符号，这里用作单位符号。

标轴的标目为 Year（CE），纵坐标轴的标目为 CO_2（ppm）和 $\delta^{13}C$ [‰]；量名称有 Year、CO_2（CO_2 含量）、$\delta^{13}C$（$\delta^{13}C$ 含量）；单位符号有 CE、ppm、‰。

图 C 有两横两纵四个坐标轴，上下横坐标共用量和量值，坐标轴有标目。横坐标轴的标目为 CO_2 age（year CE），纵坐标轴的标目为 CO_2（ppm）和 $\delta^{13}C$（‰）；量名称有 CO_2 age、CO_2（CO_2 含量）、$\delta^{13}C$（$\delta^{13}C$ 含量）；单位符号有 year CE、ppm、‰。

图 D 中两个坐标图均有两横两纵四个坐标轴。上图两个横坐标轴共用量和量值，下图两个横坐标轴和两个纵坐标轴分别共用各自的量和量值。上图中，横坐标轴的标目为 Year（CE），纵坐标轴的标目为 CH_4（ppb）和 $\delta^{13}CH_4$（‰）。下图中，横坐标轴的标目为 Age in thousand years B. P.，纵坐标轴的标目为 CH_4（ppb）。量名称有 Year、Age in thousand years B. P.、CH_4（CH_4 含量）、$\delta^{13}CH_4$（$\delta^{13}CH_4$ 含量）；单位符号有 CE、ppb、‰。

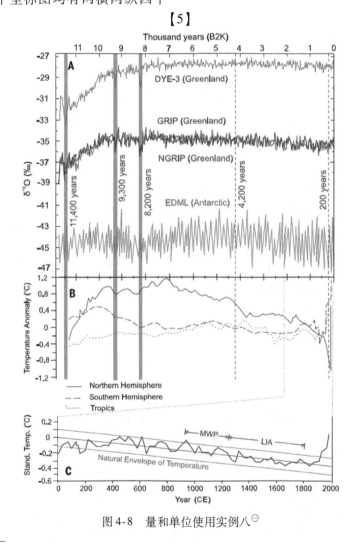

【5】

图 4-8　量和单位使用实例八㊀

㊀ 摘自 Science 的 RESEARCH | REVIEW 类：The Anthropocene is functionally and stratigraphically distinct from the Holocenes. Fig. 6.8 JANUARY 2016 · VOL 351 ISSUE 6269.

例【5】（图 4-8）的三个分图为二维坐标图，坐标轴有标目，图 B、C 横坐标轴共用标目。

图 A 中，横坐标轴的标目为 Thousand years（B2K）⊖，纵坐标轴的标目为 $\delta^{18}O$（‰）。量名称有 Thousand years 和 $\delta^{18}O$（$\delta^{18}O$ 含量）；单位符号有 B2K 和‰。

图 B 中，横坐标轴的标目为 Year（CE），纵坐标轴的标目为 Temperature Anomaly（℃）。量名称有 Year 和 Temperature Anomaly；单位符号有 CE 和℃。

图 C 中，横坐标轴的标目同图 B，纵坐标轴的标目为 Stand. Temp.（℃）⊖。量名称有 Year、Stand. Temp.；单位符号同图 B。

4.4.3　Cell 实例

【1】

Two observations indicate that ATP affects the dynamics of stress granules post-assembly. First, granules in cells treated with $NaAsO_2$ for 60 min were observed to move and fuse in the cytoplasm (Movie S2), while granules in ATP-depleted cells were static and showed no fusion events (Movie S3). Second, FRAP analysis revealed that stress granules in cells treated with 2DG and CCCP showed reduced total recovery of GFP-G3BP signal and increased $t_{1/2}$ of recovery ($t_{1/2}$ = 37.5 s) as compared to cells with normal levels of ATP ($t_{1/2}$ = 22.5 s; p < 0.000 1) (Figure 5B). Thus, ATP is required to fully maintain the exchangeable pool of G3BP in stress granules and to allow for liquid-like behavior of these assemblies.

例【1】中出现的量名称有：total recovery（total time of recovery，总恢复时间）；$t_{1/2}$ of recovery（half time of recovery）。出现的量符号及量值有：$t_{1/2}$ = 37.5 s，$t_{1/2}$ = 22.5 s，p < 0.000 1。其中，$t_{1/2}$ 为量 half time of recovery 的符号，s 为该量的单位符号，s 前面的数字即为该量的数值。但要注意，文中仅给出 p 这个量符号，而没有给出其量名称⊖。还要特别注意的是，Cell 有的文章对量符号一律用了正体，这与多数期刊不一样。

【2】

Analysis of the combined mRNA and protein abundance data were overall in agreement with each other, showing larger abundance changes at 48 and 72 hr compared to 8 and 24 hr but also highlighted the differences of the three cell lines and some discordance for mRNA and protein abundance involved in the cell-cycle response (Figure 6; Table S5).

例【2】中出现了表示 time（时间）的量值 "48 and 72 hr" "8 and 24 hr"，其中 hr 用作单位，但不是国际标准单位符号，而是借用单词 hour 的缩写形式 hr。它的标准单位符号是 h。SCI 论文中表示时间的单位可以用各种形式，如 h、hr、hour（s）。

【3】

We extended our analysis of breast milk HMOs to mothers enrolled in a second birth cohort study conducted in rural Malawi (iLiNS-DYAD-M) (Ashorn et al., 2015). Breast milk samples (n = 215) were selected for HMO analysis based on infant HAZ scores at 6 months postpartum. Similar to LCNI-5 mothers, we found that total and sialylated HMO content was significantly elevated for mothers of healthy infants (HAZ > 0; n = 70) compared to mothers of stunted infants (HAZ < -2; n = 145) (Figure 1B; Table S1B). Fucosylated HMO content was not significantly enriched for mothers of healthy infants in the iLiNSDYAD-M cohort.

例【3】中出现了三处 HAZ，第一处表示一个量的名称（全写应为 height-for-age Z score），后两处用作该量的符号（HAZ > 0；HAZ < -2）。另外，三处出现了同一量符号 n（n = 215；n = 70；n = 145），按语义，此量的名称应是 Number of samples。

⊖ B2K—before 2000 years。它本不是单位符号，这里用作单位符号。

⊖ Stand. Temp.—Standardized global mean temperature（标准化全球平均温度）。

⊖ 此量名应为 level of significance（显著性水平），也称 p 值（P-value）。

【4】

The observed differences in weight and lean body mass gain were not attributable to differences in food consumption, which was not significantly different between treatment groups (2.17 ± 0.44 g/mouse/day [mean ± SD] versus 2.92 ± 0.33 g/mouse/day for control and S-BMO-treated animals, respectively; p = 0.08, Student's t test).

例【4】中出现两处组合单位 g/mouse/day，其中 g 为 mass 的标准单位，mouse、day 是用单词来充当单位（mouse 是名词，不是单位；day 的标准单位符号是 d）。另外，还出现两个量名称，分别是 weight 和 lean body mass gain；还出现了一个量符号 p，同例【1】中的 p。

【5】

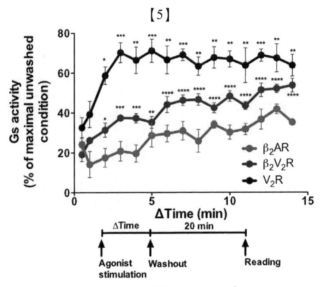

图 4-9 量和单位使用实例九⊖

例【5】（图 4-9）为上下两个分图，上图为二维坐标图，坐标轴有标目，下图为与时间有关的过程示意图。横坐标轴的标目为 ΔTime (min)，纵坐标轴的标目为 Gs activity (% of maximal unwashed condition)。其中 Gs activity⊜ 为量名称，其后括号中的 "% of maximal unwashed condition" 是对 Gs activity 的解释，相当于这一量名称的另一叫法，% 相当于 percent，这里用 % 代替 percent，能达到语言简洁及简化的效果。单位符号有 min。

【6】

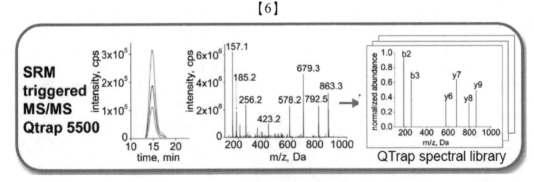

图 4-10 量和单位使用实例十⊜

⊖ 摘自 *Cell* 的 Article 类：GPCR-G Protein-β-Arrestin Super-Complex Mediates Sustained G Protein Signaling. Figure 2C. *Cell* 166, 1–13, August 11, 2016.
⊜ Gs—Glutamine synthetase（谷氨酰氨合成酶）。
⊜ 摘自 *Cell* 的 Resource 类：Human SRMatlas: A Resource of Targeted Assays to Quantify the Complete Human Proteome. Part of Figure 1. *Cell* 166, 1–13, July 28, 2016.

例【6】（图4-10）所示三个分图均为二维坐标图，坐标轴有标目。

第一分图中，横坐标轴的标目为 time, min；纵坐标轴的标目为 intensity, cps㊀。

第二分图中，横坐标轴的标目为 m/z, Da；纵坐标轴的标目为 intensity, cps。

第三分图中，横坐标轴的标目为 m/z, Da；纵坐标轴的标目为 normalized abundance。

量名称有 time、intensity、m/z 和 normalized abundance。其中 m/z 是用两个量 mass 和 charge state 的符号相除来表示一个量，该量的名称应该是 ratio of mass and charge state 或 pair of mass to charge，即质量与电荷态比，简称质荷比。

SCI 论文中表达名称、术语、符号（包括量和单位）等较为灵活随意，重在表意的可理解性，不大关心表达形式如何，而我国科技期刊在这些方面要求通常较为严格。

4.4.4　*Light*：S&A 实例

【1】

If the object is considered as dipolar in the wide sense (the particle size is much smaller than λ/n, where λ is the incident wavelength in the background medium), its electric and magnetic polarizabilities α_e and α_m can be written in terms of the coefficients a_1 and b_1 of the first Mie electric and magnetic partial waves as follows: $\alpha_e = i\frac{3\varepsilon}{2k^3}a_1$ and $\alpha_m = i\frac{3}{2\mu k^3}b_1$ and $k = n\omega/c$. Then, the ith Cartesian component of the averaged force may be expressed in the following form:[14,66]

$$\langle F_i \rangle = \frac{1}{2}\text{Re}(p_j\partial_i E_j^* + m_j\partial_i B_j^*) -$$

$$\frac{k^4}{3}\sqrt{\frac{\mu}{\varepsilon}}\text{Re}((p \times m^*)_i)\ (i,j=1,2,3)$$

例【1】中出现了较多的量名称及符号。例如：particle size; incident wavelength (λ); electric polarizabilitie (α_e), magnetic polarizabilitie (α_m); coefficient a_1 of the first Mie electric partial wave (a_1), coefficient b_1 of the first Mie magnetic partial wave (b_1); the ith Cartesian component of the averaged force ($\langle F_i \rangle$)。最后给出 $\langle F_i \rangle$ 的计算公式，同时也表达出不同量之间的关系。

值得注意的是，在多数科技期刊中，量符号（包括表示点、线、面、体、坐标轴、变动性数字等的字符）用斜体；下标当取自关键词的首字母或词、短语时用正体；矢量、矩阵、张量符号用加粗（黑）斜体；数学符号如实部、虚部符号（Re, Im），微分、增量符号（d, Δ），三角函数符号（sin, tan, arcsin 等），指数函数符号（e, exp），对数函数符号（ln, lg, lb），圆周率符号 π，虚数单位（i, j）等用正体。

例【2】（图4-11）所示为五组分图，a、b 组中出现的量值（5 μm, 400 nm）表示比例标尺大小，e 组包括四个二维坐标图，坐标轴有标目。这四个分坐标图的类别、性质和结构完全相同，只是分别用来表示四个点（Spot 1 ~ Spot 4）的数据，因此其横纵坐标的标目、标值和标值线（小短横）完全相同。横坐标的标目是 Energy (eV)，纵坐标的标目是 Norm. CL intensity (AU)，其中量名称是 Energy、Norm. CL intensity，单位是 eV 和 AU。㊁

㊀ cps—counts per second（每秒计数量）。

㊁ CL—cathodoluminescence（阴极发光）；AU—arbitrary unit（任意单位），表示相对强度，常写为小写的形式 a. u.。

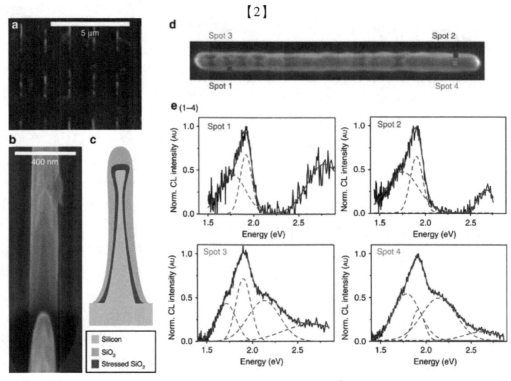

图 4-11 量和单位使用实例十一[⊖]

4.4.5 Cell Research 实例

【1】

All mouse experiments were conducted in accordance with the Guide for the Care and Use of Animals for research purposes, and were approved by the Committee of Animal Ethics, Zhejiang University. Four-week-old female nude mice were bred in a specific pathogen-free environment in the Animal Facility, Zhejiang University. DLD1 cells were infected by lentiviral particles for 3 days, and then treated with 2 μg/ml puromycin for 1 day. The puromycin-resistant cells were trypsinized, washed and resuspended in PBS/Matrigel (1:1) and subcutaneously injected into the left flank of nude mice (4×10^6 cells per mouse). Tumor diameters were serially measured with calipers every 5 days, and tumor volumes were calculated using the formula $V = (L \times W^2)/2$, where V = volume (in mm^3), L = length (in mm), W = width (in mm). The mice were killed and the tumors were isolated at 28 days after inoculation for further analysis.

例【1】中出现了几个量名称和较多的量值（数值+单位）。量名称有：Tumor diameter；tumor volume (volume)、length、width，并给出 V 与 L、W 的关系式 $V = (L \times W^2)/2$。单位符号有：day 或 days（用单词代替标准单位符号 d）、μg/ml、mm、mm^3。注意 PBS/Matrigel (1:1)[⊖]这一表达，是指 PBS 和 Matrigel 两种材料的体积之比，这是直接用事物的名称来作量符号，表达上非常简洁。还要注意 V = volume (in mm^3)、L = length (in mm)、W = width (in mm) 这种表达，这是对量符号进行解释，即给出量符号所代表的量名称，量符号和量名称之间用等号（实际中用破折号或系词的形式更为多见）分隔，表达上较为随意，但表义非常明确。

[⊖] 摘自 Light S&A 的 ORIGINAL ARTICLE 类：Multi-chromatic silicon nanocrystals. Light S&A (2017) 6, e17007. Figure 3. doi: 10.1038/lsa.2017.7.

[⊖] PBS—phosphate buffer saline（磷酸缓冲盐溶液）；Matrigel—人工基底膜；基底膜基质。

【2】

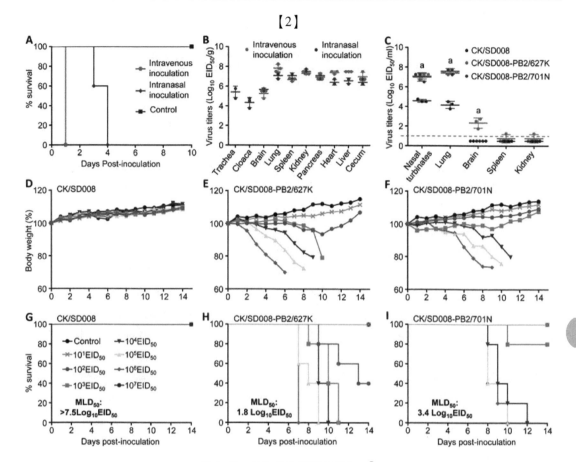

图 4-12　量和单位使用实例十二[一]

例【2】（图 4-12）所示为九个坐标分图，纵坐标（指图 A～I）和有标值的横坐标（指除图 B、C 以外的其余七个分图）均有标目。这些有标值的分图的横坐标轴的标目相同，均为 Days post-inoculation。图 A、G、H、I 的纵坐标轴的标目为 "% survival"（Percent of survival）。图 B 的纵坐标轴的标目为 "Virus titers（$\text{Log}_{10}\ \text{EID}_{50}/\text{g}$）"[二]（$\text{Log}_{10}\ \text{EID}_{50}/\text{g}$）。图 C 的纵坐标轴的标目为 "Virus titers（$\text{Log}_{10}\ \text{EID}_{50}/\text{ml}$）"（$\text{Log}_{10}\ \text{EID}_{50}/\text{ml}$）。图 B、C 这两个标目的差异仅在于单位的不同，前者的是 $\text{Log}_{10}\ \text{EID}_{50}/\text{g}$，后者的是 $\text{Log}_{10}\ \text{EID}_{50}/\text{ml}$。图 D、E、F 的纵坐标轴的标目为 Body weight（%）。

[一] 摘自 *Cell Research* 的 ORIGINAL ARTICLE 类：H7N9 virulent mutants detected in chickens in China pose an increased threat to humans. Figure 2. *Cell Research* (2017) 27：1409-1421.

[二] EID50—鸡胚半数感染量。

第 5 章　SCI 论文插图使用

插图是一种形象化的表达方式，被誉为"形象语言"和"视觉文学"，其突出的特点是形象、直观，具有达到简化、方便地表达用文字难以表达效果的作用，在论文中能代替、辅助、补充文字叙述，集中、概括、简洁、明了地表达客观事物，成为 SCI 论文中不可缺少的重要表达手段。插图的科学性、准确性和规范性直接影响论文的水准和期刊的质量。作者应充分了解和掌握插图的分类、构成、使用原则及设计制作要求，在论文写作中注意规范地选择、设计和安排插图，加强对插图的审查和核对，达到对插图的规范使用。规范使用插图，探索其处理方法和技巧是 SCI 论文写作的重要环节，对高水平论文写作具有重要的现实意义。

5.1　插图的分类

SCI 论文的插图多种多样，可从多个角度来分类。比如，按包含子图成员的数量，可分为单图和组合图；按制版技术，分为线条图、网纹图、黑白图和彩色图等；按构图方式，分为坐标图、结构图、功能图、线路图、透视图等；按表现手法，分为构思图、模拟图和实物图等；还可按领域分，如细胞图、分子图、建筑图、机械图、电路图……。

以下介绍 SCI 论文中较为常见的几种插图。

5.1.1　单图和组合图

单图指一个图序（总图号）、图题下仅有一个图，而组合图指一个图序下含有两个或两个以上图，这些图即为子图，各子图又是相对完整的插图，通常还有相应的分图序和分图题。这些子图即为整个总图的分图，其类别可以相同，也可以不同。组合图在 SCI 论文中较为常见，能更加完整系统地表达科学概念、现象和特性及事物运行状态、过程和关联等。例如图 5-1 为单图，而图 5-2 为组合图。

图 5-1 仅有 1 个完整的插图，属于单图，图序和图题为 "**Fig. 5. Schematic pathway for oxygen reduction reaction on nitrogen-doped carbon materials.**"。

图 5-2 有 5 个完整的子图（图序分别为 a、b、c、d、e），属于组合图，总图序和总图题为 "**Figure 4 | Hydration status analysis during group outdoor running using the FISAs.**"。分图序和分图题分别为：

a, Schematic illustration showing the group outdoor running trial based on wearable FISAs (packaged as 'smart headbands').

b, **c**, Representative real-time sweat sodium (**b**) and potassium (**c**) levels during an endurance run with water intake.

d, **e**, Representative real-time sweat sodium (**d**) and potassium (**e**) levels during an endurance run without water intake.

分图的概念往往是从一个具体图的类别来说的，只要一个图具有相对完整的表意，且大体属于某个图类，那么该图就可作为一个成员而成为一个总图的分图。从形式上看，分图通常标以分图序和分图题，分图题往往有可长可短的说明性语句，但也有不标分图序和分图题的情况。一个分图序和分图题下也可以包括多个子分图，例如图 5-3。

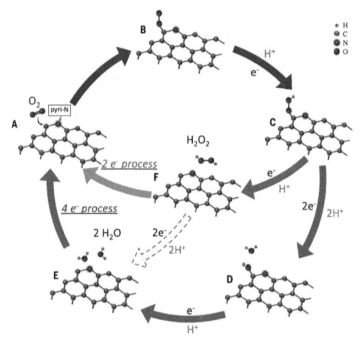

Fig. 5. Schematic pathway for oxygen reduction reaction on nitrogen-doped carbon materials.

图 5-1　单图示例[一]

图 5-3 由四组分图组成：A 组由 8 个子分图组成，子分图类别相同，均为显微照片图；B、C、D 组分别有两组分图，每个第一组分图由 6 个子分图组成，每个子分图类别相同，均为显微照片图；而每个第二组分图均为二维坐标点图，图的结构相同，只是对应的材料不同而已。

组合图中的分图有几个结构相同的坐标图时，有时可以将这几个坐标图连在一起而构成一个完整的图，形式上是一个单图，实质上是一个组合图，只不过各分图共用某些共同要素而分图间不留空隙罢了。例如图 5-4，由 4 个分图组成，各分图共用横坐标的标目"Time（s）"、标值"0，400，800，1,200，1,600"，以及过程阶段标示（最上方的 3 个双向箭头及这些箭头上方的词语 Ramp up、Cycling at constant load 和 Cool down）。

组合图中也可以用表格作分图，如图 5-5 中的分图 C 即为一个表格。

[一] 摘自 Science 的 RESEARCH | REPORTS 类：Active sites of nitrogen-doped carbon materials for oxygen reduction reaction clarified using model catalysts. 22 JANUARY 2016 · VOL 351 ISSUE 6271.

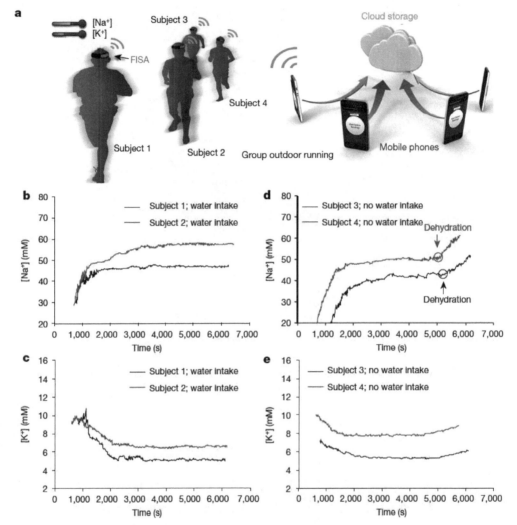

Figure 4 | Hydration status analysis during group outdoor running using the FISAs. a, Schematic illustration showing the group outdoor running trial based on wearable FISAs (packaged as 'smart headbands'). The data are transmitted to the user's cell phone and uploaded to cloud servers. **b, c,** Representative real-time sweat sodium (**b**) and potassium (**c**) levels during an endurance run with water intake. **d, e,** Representative real-time sweat sodium (**d**) and potassium (**e**) levels during an endurance run without water intake.

图 5-2　组合图示例一⊖

⊖　摘自 Nature 的 RESEARCH | LETTER 类:Fully integrated wearable sensor arrays for multiplexed *in situ* perspiration analysis. doi:10.1038/nature16521.

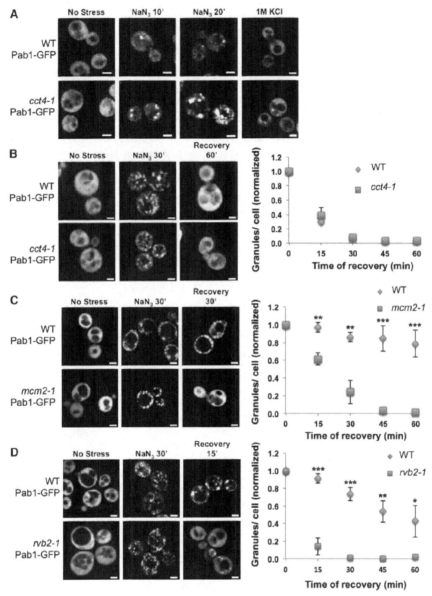

Figure 6. Inhibition of Cct4, Mcm2, or Rvb2 ATPase Activity Affects Stress Granule Assembly/Disassembly
(A) Wild-type or cct4-1 cells carrying Pab1-GFP imaged after shifting to 37℃ (60 min) before NaN_3 stress, after NaN_3 treatment for 10 min, after NaN_3 treatment for 20 min, or with 1 M KCl for 30 min.
(B) Wild-type or cct4-1 cells carrying Pab1-GFP imaged prior to stress, after 30 min of NaN_3, and after 60 min of recovery at 37 ℃. Graph shows mean from three experiments ± SD.
(C) Wild-type and mcm2-1 yeast cells with Pab1-GFP prior to stress, after stress (30 min), and upon recovery from stress. Graph shows mean from three experiments ± SD.
(D) Same as (C) but for rvb2-1 and the corresponding wild-type yeast cells. $^*p < 0.05$; $^{**}p < 0.01$; $^{***}p < 0.0001$. Scale bars, 2 mm.
See also Figure S7.

图 5-3　组合图示例二[一]

[一] 摘自 *Cell* 的 Article 类:ATPase-Modulated Stress Granules Contain a Diverse Proteome and Substructure. *Cell* 164,1-12,January 28,2016.

5.1.2 坐标图

5.1.2.1 线形图

线形图（又称函数曲线图）是用于表示某（几）种因素在一定时间内变化趋势或两（几）个变量（可变因素）之间关系的一种坐标图。仅表示一种因素随时间变化趋势或两个变量之间关系的坐标图为二维线形图，而表示多种因素随时间变化趋势或多个变量之间关系的坐标图为多维线形图。

二维线形图用横、纵两个坐标表示两个可变因素，自变量标在横轴（如 x 轴）上，因变量标在纵轴（如 y 轴）上。计算、数据类线形图通常应给出较为密集的横、纵坐标标值线，以便阅读和查找、比较准确的变量数值（图5-6a）。这种图通常可以简化为简易线形图（又称简易函数曲线图），即省略了长的密集的横、纵坐标标值线，只在坐标轴上留下了部分很短的线段，即刻度或刻度线（图5-6b）。简易线形图具有说明性强、图面简洁、幅面较小、制作容易和使用灵活等诸多优点，较为实用，在能够达到较为方便地阅读和查找、比较准确数值的效果下，提倡使用这种图。

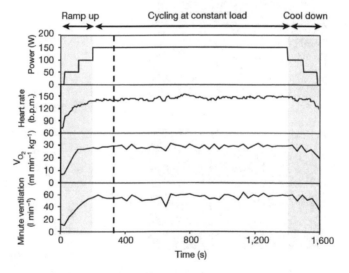

Figure 3c. Constant-load exercise at 150 W: power output, heart rate (in beats per minute, b. p. m.), oxygen consumption (V_{O_2}) and pulmonary minute ventilation, as measured by external monitoring systems

图5-4　组合图示例三㊀

㊀ 摘自 *Nature* 的 RESEARCH | LETTER 类：Fully integrated wearable sensor arrays for multiplexed *in situ* perspiration analysis. doi：10.1038/nature16521.

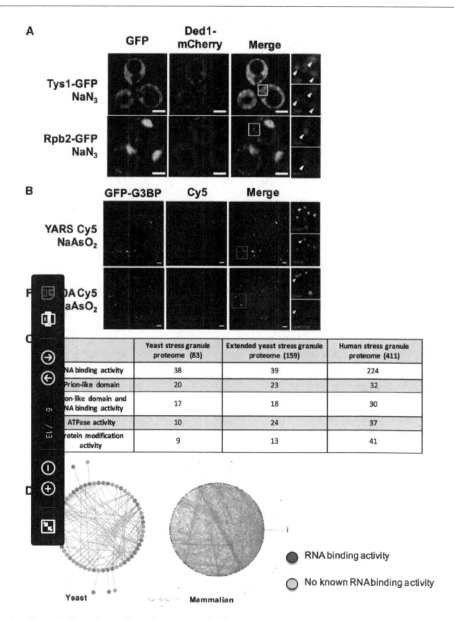

Figure 4. Key Findings from the Stress Granule Proteome
(A) Fluorescence microscopy of cells with Ded1-mCherry and Tys1-GFP or Rpb2-GFP after NaN_3 treatment.
(B) IF in $NaAsO_2$-stressed GFP-G3BP U-2 OS cells using antibodies against YARS or FAM120A detected by a Cy5-labeled secondary antibody. Arrowheads within magnified areas indicate examples of overlap. Scale bars, 2 μm.
(C) Properties of the yeast and mammalian stress granule proteomes.
(D) Yeast and mammalian stress granule "connectomes" showing physical interactions among stress granule proteins. Red nodes represent known RNA-binding proteins.
See also Figure S5 and Tables S1 and S2.

图 5-5　组合图示例四⊖

⊖　摘自 *Cell* 的 Article 类：ATPase-Modulated Stress Granules Contain a Diverse Proteome and Substructure. *Cell* 164, 1-12, January 28, 2016.

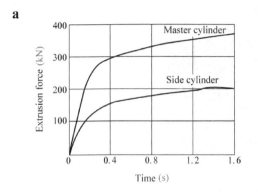 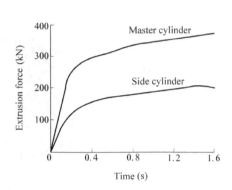

图 5-6 线形图和简易线形图示例

线形图坐标轴上的刻度是测量的尺度，可以是线性的（以相同数量增加或减少，如 50，100，150，…或 150，100，50，…），也可以是对数形式（以相同比例递增或递减，如 1，10，100，…或 100，10，1，…）。图 5-6 所示为二维线形图，当表示多个变量间的关系时需要用多维线形图，图 5-7、图 5-8 即为三维线形图。图 5-7 表示了三个变量之间的关系，图 5-8 表示了变量 Resonance frequency 与参数 α 和 β 的关系。

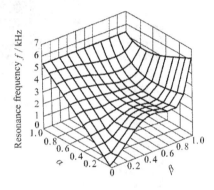

Fig. × Relationship between resonant frequency and α, β

图 5-8 三维线形图示例二

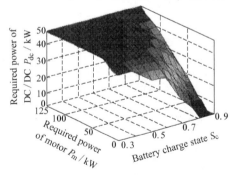

Fig. × 3D diagram of required power control of DC/DC

图 5-7 三维线形图示例一

直方图是函数关系为阶跃形的函数曲线图的一种变种，是用矩形面积来表示某个连续型变量的频率分布的一种图形，如图 5-9 所示。这种图常以横轴表示连续型变量的组段（通常要求等距），纵轴表示频数或频率，尺度常从 0 开始，各直条间不留空隙。

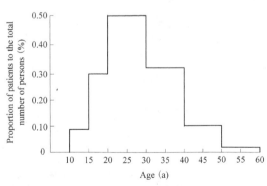

Fig. × Frequency of the age distribution of patients

图 5-9 直方图示例

5.1.2.2 条形图

条形图（直条图）是用宽度相同而长度不同（可部分相同或全部相同）的直条，表示当自变量是分类数据时相互独立的诸参量之间关系的一种坐标图（见图5-10～图5-12）。在这种图中，每个直条代表一类数据，直条的长度表示数据的大小，纵坐标的标值一般从0开始，各个直条或各组直条间的间距应相等。

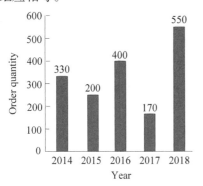

Fig. × Order quantity of a product（2014−2018）
图 5-10　条形图示例一

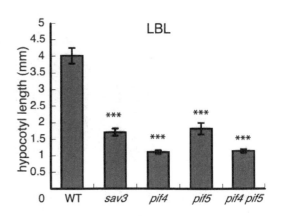

Figure 1C（in part）Hypocotyl length measurements after the indicated treatments（$^{***}p < 0.001$ and $^{**}p < 0.01$；Student's t test）.
图 5-11　条形图示例二

图5-10的横坐标表示5个年份（Year 2014−2018），各年份都有一个直条，直条的长度表示 Order quantity。图5-11的横坐标表示5种植物类别（WT、sav3、pif4、pif5、pif4 pif5），每一类有一个直条，直条的长度表示 hypocotyl length，上方的 LBL 表示这五组数据是在 low blue light 条件下获得的。图5-12的横坐标表示12个研究案例（Study 1−12），每一个研究案例对应一个直条，直条的长度表示 Median survival，直条顶部的数字就是对应的纵坐标值（这是为了阅读、查找数据方便而有意加上的，不加也是完全可以的）；在图的右侧，还给出了与各研究案例对应的图例，指明研究案例的来源，如案例1来自本研究，案例2来自文献24（Sohal et al. 1994），……，案例12来自文献21（Ikeno et al. 2005）。

有时一类变量可分几个水平，这时应该用相应数量的直条来表示，即几个直条组合成一组，这就是复式条形图（图5-13、图5-14），但直条不宜过多。为便于对比，在复式条形图内一般要用诸如横线、竖线、斜线或者小点、小格、空白等图案来对不同对比量加以区别，并相应示出图例。这类图制作要求：直条宽度与长度匹配匀称，线型和图案规矩、大方和美观。

图5-13的横坐标有6组数据，前5组每组均有3类直条，用不同图案（空白、单斜线和双斜线）分别表示 Before springback、After springback 和 CPU time 三种情况，最后一组只有两类直条，同前面各组中的前两类直条。这6组数据中，前两类直条的长度表示 Springback angle，对应左纵坐标；前5组数据中，第三类直条的长度表示 CPU time，对应右纵坐标。

○ WT—wild-type（野生类植株）；sav—shade avoidance（遮荫条件）；pif—phytochrome interacting factor（光敏色素作用因子）。

○ 摘自 Cell 的 Article 类：Cryptochromes Interact Directly with PIFs to Control Plant Growth in Limiting Blue Light. *Cell* 164, 1−13, January 14, 2016.

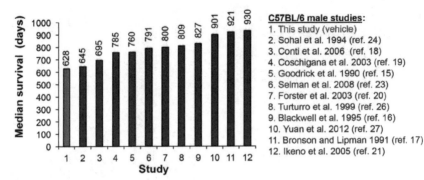

Extended Data Figure 4c Median survival data of unmanipulated C57BL/6 male mice from various laboratories for comparsion to the results obtained from our facility

图 5-12　条形图示例三⊖

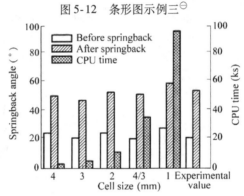

Fig. ×　Effect of cell size on springback angle

图 5-13　复式条形图示例一

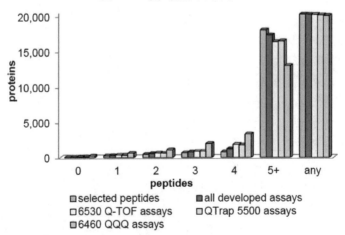

Figure 4. SRM Assay Coverage in the Human SRMAtlas
Assay coverage by peptides per protein and instrument is displayed in green shades; selected peptides are shown in gray. 158 015 successfully developed assays represent 99.7% (20 225 proteins) of the human proteome (dark green). 95.4% of the human proteome is presented by at least three assays. 22 proteins are inaccessible. See also Figure S3 and Table S4.

图 5-14　复式条形图示例二⊖

⊖　摘自 *Nature* 的 RESEARCH | ARTICLE 类：Naturally occurring p16[Ink4a]-positive cells shorten healthy lifespan. doi: 10.1038/nature16932.

⊖　摘自 *Cell* 的 Resource 类：Human SRMAtlas: A Resource of Targeted Assays to Quantify the Complete Human Proteome. Part of Figure 1. *Cell* 166, 1–13, July 28, 2016.

图 5-14 的横坐标有 7 组数据，每组均有 5 个直条，用不同颜色区分，分别表示 selected peptides、all developed assays、6530 QTOF assays、Q-Trap 5500 assays、6460 QQQ assays 五种情况，直条的长度表示 proteins（蛋白质种类）。在图题下对直条及有关结果进行解释：绿色直条代表所有蛋白质和仪器的缩氨酸试验；灰色直条代表所选的缩氨酸。深绿色直条显示 158 015 个成功开发试验，代表人类蛋白质组的 99.7%（20 225 种蛋白质）；至少有三种化验结果代表人类蛋白质组的 95.4%；22 种蛋白质是不可接近的；也可参见 Figure S3 和 Table S4。

以上条形图示例中的直条均是竖向（垂直）的，实际中也可以是横向（水平）的，这种横向条形图即为横式条形图。例如：图 5-15 显示了在 LBL[⊖] 下表达不同 PIF4、PIF5 绑定基因和 PIF4/5、CRY2 共同基因显示出在 pif4pif5 幼苗中的类似错误调节水平，纵坐标表示 PIF4、PIF5 及其和 CRY2 的组合分类（PIF4、PIF5、PIF4 + CRY2、PIF5 + CRY2），直条为水平向，其长度对应横坐标（Percent DE targets misregulated in *pif*4*pif*5）。

另外，甘特图（Gantt Chart，横道图）实际上也是一种横式条形图，由亨利·甘特于 1910 年发明，通过条状图来显示活动（项目）、进度以及其他与时间相关的系统内在关系随时间进展的情况。其中，横轴表示时间，纵轴表示活动，横向条状（横道）表示整个期间内计划和实际活动的完成情况。这种图以图示的方式通过活动列表和时间刻度形象地表示出任何特定活动的顺序与持续时间，可以直观地表明任务计划在什么时段进行以及实际进展与计划要求的对比。

管理者由此可以非常便利地弄清每一项任务还剩下哪些工作要做，并可评估工作是提前、滞后还是正常进行。这种图还具有简单、醒目和便于编制等特点。例如：图 5-16 就属于甘特图，显示了某车间的生产调度情况，其中横坐标表示以 h 为单位的 Time，纵坐标表示 Equipment serial No.，较为形象、直观地将某加工车间内不同设备的调动和使用情况展现出来，让人对车间设备的运行情况一目了然。

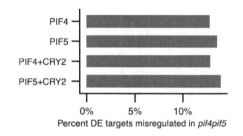

Figure 6E. PIF4, PIF5 bound genes and PIF4/5 and CRY2 common genes that are differentially expressed under LBL show similar level of misregulation in pif4pif5 seedlings.

图 5-15　横式条形图示例一[⊖]

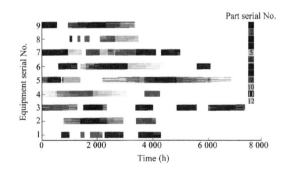

Fig. × Production schedule Gantt chart of a machining shop

图 5-16　横式条形图（甘特图）示例二

⊖ LBL—Limiting Blue Light；CRY—cryptochromes；sav—shade avoidance。
⊖ 摘自 *Cell* 的 Article 类：Cryptochromes Interact Directly with PIFs to Control Plant Growth in Limiting Blue Light. *Cell* 164, 1–13, January 14, 2016.

当自变量是分类数据时，多采用条形图，但也可采用线形图；当自变量是连续数据时，多采用线形图，但也可采用条形图。最终选用哪种图需要根据呈现数据的目的来确定，若强调某一变量随另一变量而连续变化，采用线形图较好；若强调不同类型之间相互比较，则采用条形图比较合适。

5.1.2.3 点图

点图是用点来表示函数关系的一种坐标图。这个点用大小相等的圆点、圆圈或其他图形符号表示，其大小可根据图面实际大小确定。点图分为一般点图和散点图。

一般点图是用点的疏密程度来表示某项指标或参量在特定不同条件下所呈现的频度分布（图 5-17，图 5-18，以及图 5-3B、C、D 中右侧的坐标图），常用于作对比观察或分析。

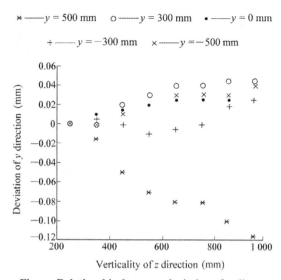

Fig. × Relationship between deviation of *y* direction and verticality of *z* direction before calibration

图 5-18 一般点图示例二

散点图是用坐标图上离散数据点来表述事物中关联参数间的变化规律（图 5-19、图 5-20）。散点图用于表示比较模糊的函数关系，把由若干个点组成的实验、观测结果表示在图中，这些点对应于坐标系中各坐标轴的若干变量，表示某个事件的数值，由其分布可以看出事物运动、变化的趋势和一般规律，若所有的点构成一个条形，则说明存在相关关系。例如：沿着斜线的一组点意味

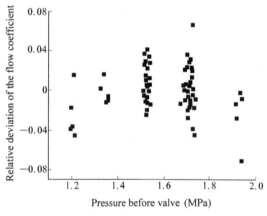

Fig. × Distribution law of relative deviation of the flow coefficient vs. pressure before valve

图 5-17 一般点图示例一

图 5-17 显示了 Relative deviation of the flow coefficient 随 Pressure before valve 的分布情况，图 5-18 显示了标定前 Deviation of *y* direction 与 Verticality of *z* direction 的关系，图 5-3B、C、D 中右侧的坐标图分别显示了在不同材料条件下的 Granules/cell（normalized）与 Time of recovery 的关系。这几个图因其坐标点为离散的点，因此都属于一般点图。

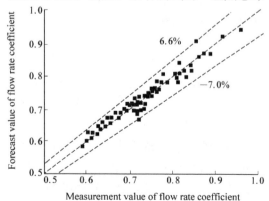

Fig. × Distribution regularities of forecast value of flow rate coefficient

图 5-19 平面散点图示例

着线性相关，一组点离斜线越近越密，说明其相关性越强，即越近越密、越相关；反之，越疏远，其相关性越差，即越远越疏、越不相关。若都落在一条斜线上，则其相关系数为1.0。

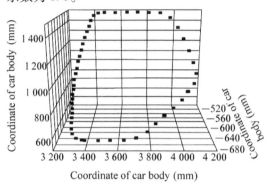

Fig. × Surface outline of left outside the rear gate of a car

图5-20 三维散点图示例

图5-19显示了Forecast value of flow rate coefficient 随 Measurement value of flow rate coefficient 的分布规律，坐标点为离散点，这些离散点较为密集地分布于"斜率"为 −7.0% 和 6.6% 的两条斜线之间近似中间的一条斜线上及其两侧旁边，说明它们之间有很强的相关性，其分布有某种规律性。图5-20为三维坐标图，显示了Coordinate of car body 坐标间的关系，坐标点为离散的点，这些点并不杂乱无章，有序地组成一个"近似圆"的漂亮图形，说明它们之间具有很强的相关性，其分布有某种规律性。因此该图属于散点图，而且是三维散点图。

5.1.3 构成比图

构成比图是用来表示事物构成或物质所含成分比例的一种图形。它多用于对有关数据的统计比较，比较项目不宜过多，分为直条图（图5-21）和圆形图（图5-22）两种。

构成比直条图用直条表示全体中各部分的构成比例。直条多于一条时有较好的对比

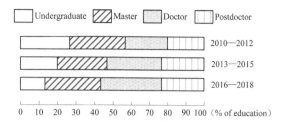

Fig. × Percentage composition of educational background of staffs of a organization

图5-21 构成比直条图示例

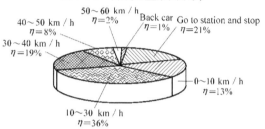

Fig. × Proportion of velocity interval

图5-22 构成比圆形图示例

效果，一般横置，其全长作为100%，用不同的线段或图案按各部分所占比例把直条区分为若干段，在整个直条组的附近给出比例标尺，并在适当位置示出图例。直条长度、宽度要匹配匀称，直条间距大小要适度，线形和图案要规矩、大方、美观。例如：图5-21中，中部的三个横向直条，分别表示某单位员工在三个年段（2010—2012、2013—2015、2016—2018）的教育背景百分比构成，各条均由4种图案组成；在整个图的上方用图例对各个图案进行注释，这4个图例分别表示 Undergraduate、Master、Doctor 和 Postdoctor；在整个图的最下方给出比例标尺。

构成比圆形图（圆形图、圆图或饼图）用圆表示全体中各部分的构成比例。整圆面积为100%，不同线型或图案按各部分占比把圆分割成若干扇形面，各部分标注的字符或说明性词语可直接置于扇面内或用引线拉出圆外，说明性词语可用图注方式放在图的合适位置。为突出各部分的差异，可从明到暗用不同的线或点给各个部分涂上阴影。为

准确、美观,对圆心角的分度要仔细,径向分割线应汇聚于圆心。这种图比较直观,图示整体性很强。例如:图 5-22 中,用整圆表示速度,将圆用不同图案分割成 7 个速度区间,不同区间有不同的速度范围及占整圆的百分比(10-30 km/h,$\eta = 36\%$;30-40 km/h,$\eta = 19\%$;……;0-10 km/h,$\eta = 13\%$)。

5.1.4 示意图

示意图主要用来对事物进行定性描述,若想突出某个方面或想法,可按时间先后、空间顺序或逻辑关系等来安排图的各个部分。这种图具有图形简洁、形式多样、灵活性高、表现力强、制作方便等特点,但制作要求较高,当表意明确时通常宜用较少的线条来表达,即用尽可能少的线条来表达。示意图大体有结构图、原理图、功能图、流程图和网络图等类别。

5.1.4.1 结构图

结构图用线条描述对象外形轮廓及其与周围环境的关系,如图 5-23~图 5-25 所示,用来表达文字难以表述清楚的场合:如机器装备、设备设施、仪器仪表等的零部件或整体结构,地质地貌、山川流域、生物器官组织及解剖、分子和原子、流程、模型、建筑物等的结构,以及声、热、电、力等不可视或无定形的物质的传递系统、装置或零部件结构等,在表达形态变化的细节方面甚至优于照片图。此类图制作要求是形似、合

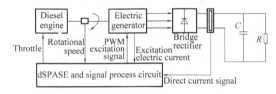

Fig. × Architecture diagram of APU experimental system

图 5-23 结构图示例一

1. Shielding gas output tube;
2. Heating holder;
3. Electric heating rods;
4. Protection block;
5. Tectum;
6. Cooling water tube;
7. Temperature thermocouple;
8. Shielding gas input tube;
9. Probe;
10. Clamping mechanism;
11. Studdle;
12. Fastening screw;
13. Sample;
14. Sample chamber;
15. Pedestal;
16. Relay;
17. PID temperature controller.

Fig. × Self-heating probe instrument

图 5-24 结构图示例二

理简化、突出描述重点。组成元素一般可用引线引出,在引线外端标明其名称或其他说明性词语;也可用阿拉伯数字按顺序编号,并把与编号对应的名称或说明性词语集中置于图中适当位置(图注)。

图 5-23 显示了一种 APU 实验系统的结构组成,如 Diesel engine、Electric generator、Bridge rectifier 等,并用箭头线和一般线段连接各个组成部分,表明其间的空间顺序或某种逻辑关系。这样就较为完整、清晰地以示意图的形式展现出了 APU 实验系统的结构组成。

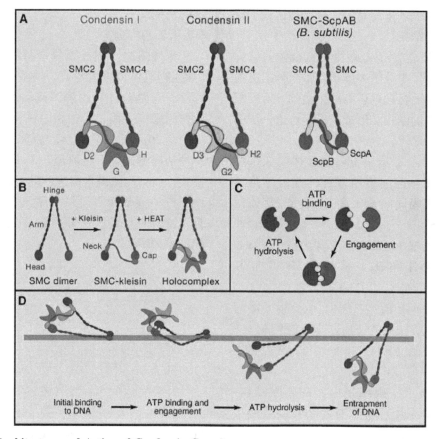

Figure 1. Architecture and Action of Condensin Complexes
(A) Subunit composition. The eukaryotic condensin complexes (condensin I and condensin II) share the same heterodimeric pair of SMC subunits (SMC2 and SMC4). They have distinct sets of non-SMC regulatory subunits, each set composed of a kleisin subunit (CAP-H and -H2) and a pair of HEAT subunits (CAP-D2/G and CAP-D3/G2). SMC-ScpAB is a bacterial condensing from B. subtilis, which is composed of an SMC homodimer, a kleisin subunit (ScpA), and an ScpB dimer.
(B) Assembly of eukaryotic condensin I. The SMC dimer adopts a V-shaped molecule with two coiled-coil arms. The hinge domain is responsible for dimerization, and ATP-binding head domains are located at distal ends of the arms. The kleisin subunit is predicted to bridge the two head domains through an asymmetric binding mode. The two HEAT subunits associate with the central region of the kleisin subunit to form a holocomplex.
(C) The SMC ATPase cycle. Engagement and disengagement of the two head domains regulated by ATP binding and hydrolysis are depicted.
(D) A postulated scheme for DNA entrapment. Initial DNA binding of condensins could occur at the SMC hinge domain. ATP binding would induce head-head engagement, which in turn disrupts an SMC-kleisin interface. ATP hydrolysis then triggers head-head disengagement, thereby opening the otherwise closed ring structure. Re-closing of the ring leads to entrapment of the DNA strand.

图 5-25 结构图示例三㊀

㊀ 摘自 *Cell* 的 Review 类:Condensin-Based Chromosome Organization from Bacteria to Vertebrates. *Cell* 164, February 25, 2016.

图 5-24 显示了一种自热探测仪器的结构组成,以对各组成部件编号、图注的形式展现了该仪器的结构,共由 17 个部件构成,例如:1. Shielding gas output tube,2. Heating holder…17. PID temperature controller。此图就是按仪器实际结构中各组成部分的先后顺序和连接关系来绘制的,真实地再现了该仪器的内部结构。

图 5-25 显示了凝缩蛋白复合体的结构和作用,由 4 组分图来展示,每组分图有独立的标题,图标题后还有较多语句,对凝缩蛋白复合体的结构、形成及作用作进一步的解释。

图 A 显示了凝缩蛋白复合体的亚基结构组成:真核凝缩蛋白复合体(凝缩蛋白 Ⅰ、Ⅱ)有相同的 SMC 亚基异质二聚体对(SMC2、SMC4)⊖;其中有明显不同的非 SMC 调节亚基集,每一亚基集由一个 kleisin 亚基(CAP-H 和-H2)和一对 HEAT 亚基(CAP-D2/G 和 CAP-D3/G2)组成。SMC-ScpAB 是一种由 B. 亚基(B. subtilis)凝缩而成的细菌,由一个 SMC 同型二聚体、一个 kleisin 亚基(ScpA)和一个 ScpB 二聚体组成。

图 B 显示了凝缩蛋白 Ⅰ 的装配结构:SMC 二聚体采用一个带有两个缠绕线圈手臂的 V 形分子;铰链(Hinge)域负责二聚化,而 ATP 绑定头部域位于手臂的末端;kleisin 亚基被预测通过非对称绑定模式来连接两个头部域;两个 HEAT 亚基与 kleisin 亚基的中心区域相关联而形成一个全复合体。

图 C 显示了 SMC 三磷酸腺苷酶循环⊖结构:描述了由 ATP 绑定和水解作用调节的两个头部域的参合和分离。

图 D 显示了 DNA 诱捕过程的结构变化:在 SMC 铰链域中可能发生凝缩蛋白的初始 DNA 绑定;ATP 绑定会导致头-头参合,进而扰乱 SMC-kleisin 接口;然后 ATP 水解作用会触发头-头分离,从而打开另一个闭合的环结构;环重新闭合会导致 DNA 链的诱捕。

5.1.4.2 原理图

原理图用于描述事物或事物组成部分(如生物机体、组织器官、设备装置、机器部件、电路器件等的静态或动态系统)的工作原理、过程、状态和内在运行机制等,如图 5-26、图 5-27 所示。原理图其实也是一种结构图,只不过原理图侧重阐释机制、模式,而结构图侧重构造、组成,在结构图中加进一些表示原理的要素(如运算、逻辑、流向、参数、符号、数学式等)就形成了原理图。

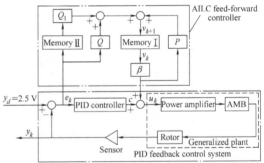

Fig. × AILC compensation principle of AMB system⊖

图 5-26 原理图示例一

图 5-26 显示了 AMB 系统的自适应迭代学习控制(AILC)补偿原理。该图的主体框架是 AMB 系统的结构,包括两大部分:AILC feed-forward controller 和 PID feedback control system。前者包括 Memory Ⅰ 和 Memory Ⅱ,

---

⊖ SMC—structural maintenance of chromosomes(染色体结构维持)。
⊖ ATP—Adenosine Triphosphate(三磷酸腺苷);ATPase—ATP synthase(三磷酸腺苷酶)。
⊖ AILC—Adaptive iterative learning control(自适应迭代学习控制);AMB—Active magnetic bearings(主动磁轴承);PID—Proportion integration differentiation(比例-积分-微分)。

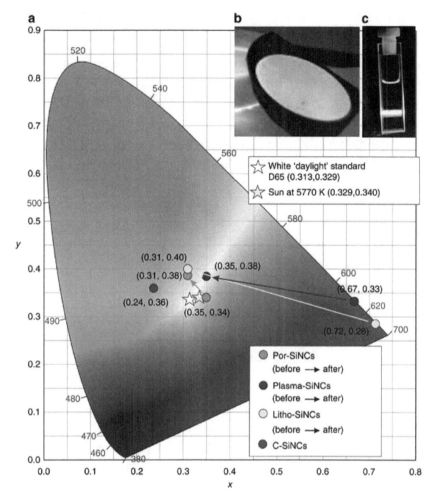

Figure 4 Resulting color changes. (a) Color gamut for PL spectra of all the studied SiNC samples before and after extended e-beam irradiation. CIE coordinates are shown for each sample in the graph and arrows indicate the shift for each sample induced by the e-beam treatment (For the C-SiNCs the position does not change, because irradiation did not lead to any spectral modifications). For comparison, we show also white standard D65 and the Sun's spectrum position. For the color gamut evaluation, CIE 1931 standards were used. Insets: Real-color photos of native Por-SiNC and C-SiNC, both exhibiting whitish color PL that is improved in por-SiNCs by introduction of the green center.

图 5-27　原理图示例二[⊖]

后者包括 PID controller、Power amplifier、AMB、Rotor 和 Sensor。如果图中仅有这些实体部件或装置，那么该图就属于结构图，但因图中加进了较多其他要素，如参数（量符号）、数学式、数学运算符号（加号、减号），这样就侧重表述各部件之间的内在定量关系和工作运行机制，进而就变成原理图了。

图 5-27 是在较大的二维坐标分图 a 的右上方放置了两个较小的照片分图 b 和 c，显示了实验结果中的颜色变化机理。分图 a 有名称，其后面的语句对分图 a 的颜色变化机理进行分析和说明：图中每个样本都显示了 CIE[⊜] 坐标，箭头表示由电子束处理所引

⊖　摘自 *Light S&A* 的 Original Article 类：Multi-chromatic silicon nanocrystals. *Light S&A* (2017) 6, e17007; doi: 10.1038/lsa.2017.7.

⊜　CIE——Commission Internationale de L'Eclairage（国际照明委员会），其前身是 1900 年成立的国际光度委员会（InternationalPhotometric Commission; IPC），1913 年改为现名。总部设在奥地利维也纳。CIE 制订了一系列色度学标准，一直沿用到数字视频时代，其中包括白光标准（D65）和阴极射线管（CRT）内表面红、绿、蓝三种磷光理论上的理想颜色。

起的每个样本的位移（对于 C-SiNCs，此位置不会改变，因为照射不会导致任何光谱变化）。为了比较，还展示了白色标准 D65 和太阳的光谱位置。在色域评估中，使用了 CIE 1931 年标准。图中右上方的小插图（b 和 c）分别为原始 Por-SiNC 和 C-SiNC 的真彩色照片，都表现出带白色的 PL，此 PL 通过引入绿色中心而在 por-SiNCs 中得到了改善。

5.1.4.3 功能图

功能图（系统框图、模型图）是可不涉及事物具体形态和内部结构而将事物抽象为一系列附有文字、符号或算式说明的方框（或其他框），再由这些框相互关联（由直线、箭头线连接）而组成示意图（图 5-28），适于对复杂生物、工程、管理和监控等系统的运行机制、工作过程和特点的动态描述，或用于对事物进行全局或某个层面的建模（模型图，图 5-29）。这种图制作要求是进行合理的抽象，选择对表现主题起关键作用的组成部分，方框的布局要规矩、匀称，其中文字、符号、算式的表达要规范，框间的箭头线按相关规定使用。

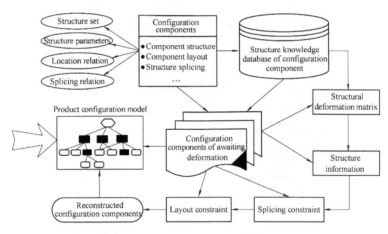

Fig. × Reconstruction process of product structure transformation
图 5-28 系统功能图示例

图 5-28 显示了产品结构转换的重构过程。图中各类框及其文字就是抽象出来的产品结构转换过程中产生或涉及的部件、形态、数据库、约束条件及有关信息等，有的还有子要素、子子要素，再用箭头线将各部分关联起来，以表示其间关系，进而表达出产品结构转换重构这一系统的功能，但不涉及系统的实体结构和具体形态，有较强的概念性、想象性和创意性。

图 5-29 显示应力颗粒组装和动力模型，属模型图，由 4 组分图组成。前三组描述减少的翻译产生单体和低聚 mRNPs 池⊖、初相分离应力颗粒、成熟压力颗粒组装过程及动力特性进行，形成模型图。三组图间用加有文字说明的箭头线，示出其间运行机制与过程。第四组是对第三组中所标示方框部分的局部放大，对模型图局部进行特写与细化，可理解为一种局部模型图。图题下方给出注释语，mRNPs 间的虚线表示相分离壳层中的弱物理相互作用，红色的波浪线代表朊病毒类领域间的强相互作用。用缩略语 RVB、MCM、CCT 表示组间的关系。

⊖ mRNPs—mRNA ribonucleoprotein complexes（mRNA 核糖核蛋白复合体）。

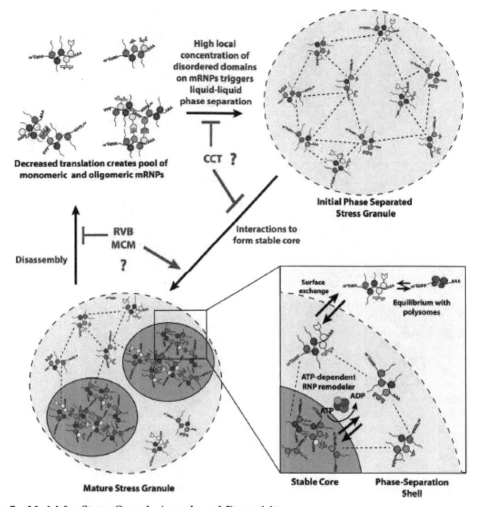

Figure 7. Model for Stress Granule Assembly and Dynamicity
Dashed lines between mRNPs represent weak physical interactions in the phase-separated shell. Red wavy lines represent strong interactions between prion-like domains. Possible sites of activity of the CCT, RVB, and MCM complexes are also shown.

图 5-29　模型图示例[⊖]

5.1.4.4　流程图

流程图记述事物状态关联、运行过程和走向流向，是系统框图的一种特殊类型，按被记述事物的类别是人还是计算机，分为工作流程图和计算机流程图：前者记述工作事项的活动流向顺序，涉及工作过程中的工作环节、步骤和程序，如图 5-30 所示；后者表述计算机系统或软件所反映的运算、监控、管理等的逻辑思维、步骤以及操作运行的程序，如图 5-31 所示。

图 5-30 用 8 个分图记述了柔性传感器阵列的制造过程。上方的词语简明说明柔性传感器阵列的各个制造工艺，按先后顺序排列，便形成整个过程：a，PET[⊖] cleaning→b，Au patterning→c，Parylene deposition→d，O_2 plasma etching→e，Ag patterning→f，Ag etching & chloridation→g，Flexible electrodes array→h，Sensors modification。

⊖　摘自 *Cell* 的 Article 类：ATPase-Modulated Stress Granules Contain a Diverse Proteome and Substructure. *Cell* 164, 1-12, January 28, 2016.
⊖　PET—Flexible polyethylene terephthalate（柔性聚对苯二甲酸乙二醇酯）。

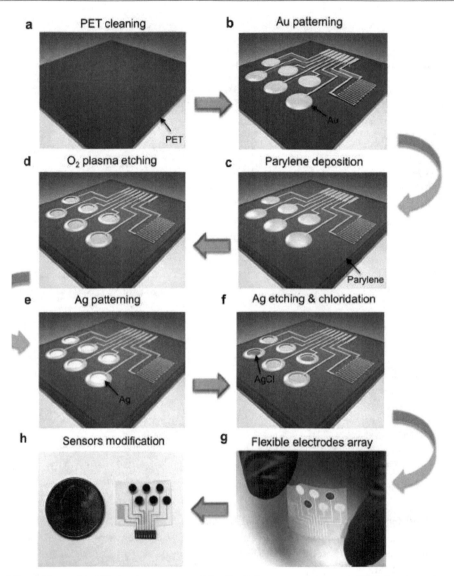

Extended Data Figure 1 | Fabrication process of the flexible sensor array. a, PET cleaning using acetone, isopropanol and O_2 plasma etching. **b**, Patterning of Cr/Au electrodes using photolithography, electron-beam evaporation and lift-off in acetone. **c**, Parylene insulating layer deposition. **d**, Photolithography and O_2 plasma etching of parylene in the electrode areas. **e**, Electron-beam deposition of the Ag layer followed by lift-off in acetone. **f**, Ag etching on the Au working electrode area and Ag chloridation on the reference electrode area. **g**, Optical image of the flexible electrode array. **h**, Photograph of the multiplexed sensor array after surface modification.

图 5-30　工作流程图示例[○]

　　在图题后补充交待了材料、方法或操作对象等，过程表述更加详细：**a**，使用丙酮、异丙醇和 O_2 等离子体蚀刻进行 PET 清洁；**b**，使用光蚀刻法、电子束蒸发和丙酮剥离进行 Cr/Au 图案制作；**c**，聚对二甲苯绝缘层沉积；**d**，对电极区的聚对二甲苯进行光蚀刻法和 O_2 等离子体蚀刻；**e**，由丙酮剥离对 Ag 层进行电子束沉积；**f**，在 Au 工作电极区上进行 Ag 蚀刻，在参考电极区作 Ag 氯化处理；**g**，柔性电极阵列光学成像；**h**，表面修改后的多路传感器阵列照片。

[○] 摘自 *Nature* 的 RESEARCH | LETTER 类：Fully integrated wearable sensor arrays for multiplexed in situ perspiration analysis. doi：10.1038/nature16521.

5.1.4.5 网络图

网络图是把事物进行简化，将其分割成若干单元（或环节），变分布参数为集中参数，然后按单元的性质与顺序组成一个逻辑网络，以供进一步分析或数值计算之用的一种示意图（图 5-32～图 5-34）。这种图常用于表述互联网中的节点分布、电工学中的电路网络、力学中的有限元网络和自动控制中的网络系统等等。

图 5-32 显示了一种多层前馈神经网络的拓扑结构[一]，它由表示节点的小圆圈及连接各节点的箭头线组成，形式上是一个"千丝"交错的网络结构图。

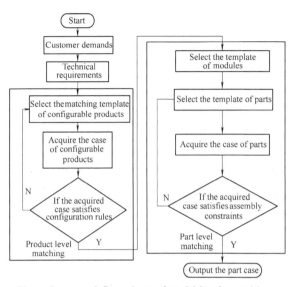

Fig. × Improved flow chart of multi-level matching
图 5-31　计算机流程图示例

图 5-31 是典型的计算机流程图，由开头和结尾的圆角框、表示陈述或动作行为的多个矩形框、表示判断的菱形框（回答 Y 和 N）以及连接各框的箭头线组成，框中的陈述表示"事"，而箭头线表示"事"间的关联和走向，因为这些"事"是由计算机完成的，故称计算机流程图。

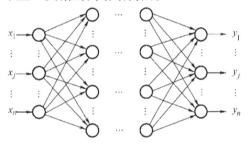

Fig. × Topology structure of MFNN
图 5-32　网络图示例一

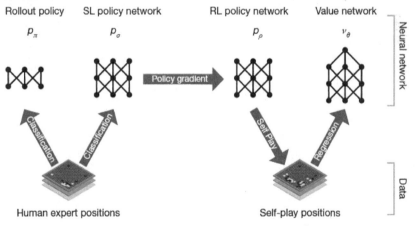

Figure 1 Neural network training pipeline and architecture[三]
图 5-33　网络图示例二[三]

[一] MFNN—multilayer feedforward neural networks（多层前馈神经网络）。
[二] SL—Supervised learning；RL—Reinforcement learning。
[三] 摘自 *Nature* 的 RESEARCH｜ARTICLE 类：Mastering the game of Go with deep neural networks and tree search. doi：10.1038/nature16961.（Figure1 包括两个分图，这里只引了分图 a）

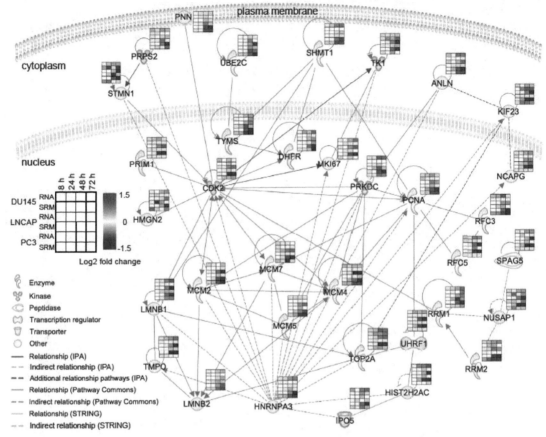

Figure 6 Network of Proteins Associated with Docetaxel Perturbation of the Cell Cycle
SRM-based quantification of a protein network in three prostate cancer cell lines, DU145, LNCaP, and PC-3, at four time points post-treatment with docetaxel and in untreated controls in comparison to mRNA abundance changes. The microarray-derived functional network was visualized with ingenuity pathway analysis (IPA). The structure of the network is based on the IPA Core Analysis-, STRING-, and Pathway Commons-derived direct interactions and indirect relationships. Each heatmap visualizes the log2 abundance change of treated versus control cells for each time in each cell line at the transcript (mRNA) and protein (SRM) level. The signal represents the mean result from two technical replicates at the transcript level and three SRM analyses per sample. See also Figure S4 and Table S5.

图 5-34 网络图示例三[①]

图 5-33 显示了一个神经网络训练管道及结构，它由 4 个网络分图组成，分别是 Rollout policy、SL policy network、RL policy network、Value network，并分别给出量符号 ρ_π、ρ_σ、ρ_ρ、ν_θ，均处于 Neural network 层面。其中前两个网络属于 Human expert positions，后两个网络属于 Self-play positions，这两个位置处于 data 层面。

图 5-34 为细胞周期内与多西他赛（Docetaxel）扰动相关的蛋白质网络图。网络边界为质膜（plasma membrane），网络环境为细胞质（cytoplasm）和细胞核（nucleus），网络节点为各类蛋白质，由不同颜色的不同类图案来表示，蛋白质间相互作用，由不同颜色的不同类线条来连接，参与生物信号传递、基因表达调节、能量和物质代谢及细胞周期调控等生命过程各环节。此网络的结构是基于 IPA（ingenuity pathway analysis，独创性路径分析）核心分析、STRING 和公开获取通路的直接交互和间接关系的。

[①] 摘自 *Cell* 的 Resource 类：Human SRMAtlas: A Resource of Targeted Assays to Quantify the Complete Human Proteome. *Cell* 166, 1-13, July 28, 2016.

图 5-34 左侧中部的图例，显示三个前列腺癌细胞株 DU145、LNCaP 和 PC-3 中基于 SRM[一] 的蛋白质网络量化，与使用多西他赛治疗和未治疗的细胞株与 mRNA 的充裕度变化在 4 个时间点上进行比较。利用 IPA 对微阵列衍生功能网络可视化。每一热图都能在每一细胞株的转录（mRNA）和蛋白质（SRM）水平上，在每一时间段内对治疗和控制细胞的 log2 的充裕度变化可视化，代表了转录水平上的两个技术复制和每个样本的三个 SRM 分析的平均结果。

图 5-34 左侧中下方的图例用不同颜色的不同类图案、线条来表示以下不同的含义：

1）Enzyme、Kinase、Peptidase、Transcription regulator、Transporter、Other。

2）Relationship（IPA），Indirect relationship（IPA），Additional relationship pathways（IPA）；Relationship（Pathway Commons），Indirect relationship（Pathway Commons）；Relationship（STRING），Indirect relationship（STRING）。

5.1.5 记录谱图

记录谱图是由仪器设备直接记录下来的一种线形数据图，如电子能谱图、射线衍射图、热分析曲线图等（图 5-35、图 5-36）。医疗领域由专用医疗设备对人某身体部位或组织器官进行相关操作而记录的输出曲线均属于记录谱图，如利用脑电仪对脑自身微弱的生物电放大记录生成的曲线即脑电图、利用心电仪从体表记录心脏每一心动周期所产生电活动变化的曲线图形即心电图等，用来作为参考依据帮助诊断疾病，但对被检查者没有任何伤害。

制作这种图时，除了线形符合制版要求

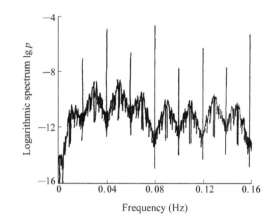

Fig. × Spectrum structure of 8I（$f_0 = 0.159\ 2$ Hz）

图 5-35 记录谱图示例一

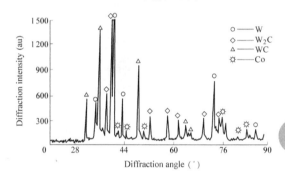

Fig. × Structure of XRD phase analysis of alloy wear surface

图 5-36 记录谱图示例二

或者确有必要利用原记录曲线直接制版（可按需添加数字、符号或文字）外，一般均应对原图重新制作，必要时进行标示和说明，如波峰、波谷或其他特征点有时应有数字及标目（量名称、符号及单位）、标值（数值和单位）和文字说明等，同时还应力求保持原记录的波形特色，达到逼真不走样。

图 5-35、图 5-36 形式上为二维坐标图，横、纵坐标均有标目，但其中的曲线不是一般曲线，而是记录谱图，分别表示 8I 频谱结构和合金磨损表面的 XRD[二] 相位分析

[一] SRM—selected reaction monitoring, also named multiple reaction monitoring［MRM］instead。

[二] XRD—X-Ray Diffraction（X 射线衍射）。

结构，二者分别是 Logarithmic spectrum 随 Frequency、Diffraction intensity 随 Diffraction angel 的输出曲线。注意：图 5-36 中的曲线有四组，对应四组材料（W、W_2C、WC、Co），分别用不同的图例来表示。

5.1.6 等值线图

等值线图是用线条来反映某种物理量在被研究对象（如平面、曲面或切割面等）上分布的一种图形（图 5-37、图 5-38）。其中，每一条等值线代表某一级（值）物理量的点的集合，用这样一组等值线即可描述出整个面域内该量的分布情况。常见的等高线图、等势线图、等电位线图、等压力线图、等浓度线图、等雨量线图等均属这种图。例如：图 5-37 为根据原始数据绘制的等势线图；图 5-38 为护环热成形后内部温度分布与变形分布，分为 Tangential strain、equivalent strain 和 temperature field 三个分图。

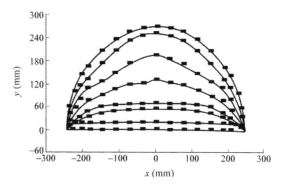

Fig. × Equipotential lines drawn from the original data

图 5-37　等值线图示例一

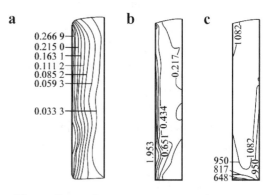

Fig. × Internal temperature and deformation distribution after the hot forming of shroud ring.

(a) Tangential strain, (b) equivalent strain, and (c) temperature field.

图 5-38　等值线图示例二

5.1.7 计算机输出图

计算机输出图是由计算机按某软件和程序经过运行、处理后输出的一种结果图，包括数值计算结果输出图、模拟（仿真）结果图、屏幕图（界面图）等（图 5-39 ~ 图 5-41）。

图 5-39 为曲面计算图，按曲面形状有半球面、车身外形三角域曲面及四边域曲面三种。

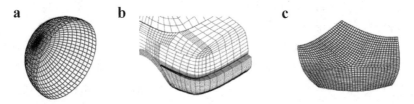

Fig. × Surface computing legend. (a) Semi-spherical, (b) triangular field surface outside the car body, and (c) four-sided field surface

图 5-39　计算机输出图示例一

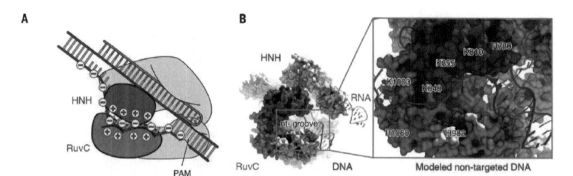

Fig. 1 Structure-guided mutagenesis improves specificity of SpCas9. (**A**) A model of Cas9 unwinding highlighting locations of charge on DNA and the nt-groove. The nt-groove between the RuvC (teal) and HNH (magenta) domains stabilize DNA unwinding through non-specific DNA interactions with the non-complementary strand. RNA：cDNA and Cas9：ncDNA interactions drive DNA unwinding (top arrow) in competition against cDNA：ncDNA rehybridization (bottom arrow). (**B**) A crystal structure of SpCas9 (PDB ID 4UN3) showing the nt-groove situated between the HNH (magenta) and RuvC (teal) domains. The non-target DNA strand (red) was manually modeled into the nt-groove (inset) ...[二]

图 5-40　计算机输出图示例二[二]

Fig. ×. Results of reconfiguration of HMC 125 NC machining center

图 5-41　计算机输出图示例三

图 5-40 中的两个分图为模拟（仿真）结果图。图 A 显示在 DNA 和 nt 凹槽中解旋突出显示电荷位置的 Cas9 仿真模型。RuvC（墨绿色）和 HNH（洋红色）域间的 nt 凹槽通过非特异性 DNA 与非互补链的交互来稳定 DNA 解旋。RNA：cDNA 和 Cas9：ncDNA 交互作用驱动 DNA 解旋（上箭头）与 cDNA：ncDNA 重杂化（下箭头）相竞争。图 **B** 是 SpCas9[三]（PDB ID 4UN3）的一种晶体结构，能显示出位于 HNH（品红色）和 RuvC（墨绿色）域之间的 nt-凹槽。非目标 DNA 链（红色）由手工模仿融入到 nt 凹槽中（插入）。

图 5-41 为 HMC 125 数控加工中心配置结果（软件运行结果）的计算机屏幕截图，可看作一种特殊的照片图。

[一] 原图中还有 **C**、**D**、**E** 分图，这里因表达不需要，省去了这些分图。
[二] 摘自 *Science* 的 Reports 类：Rationally engineered Cas9 nucleases with improved specificity. http://sciencemag.org/content/early/recent/1 December 2015/Page 1/10. 1126/science. aad5227.
[三] SpCas9—Streptococcus pyogenes Cas9（酿脓链球菌 Cas9）。Cas9 (CRISPR associated protein 9) is an RNA-guided DNA endonuclease enzyme associated with the CRISPR (Clustered Regularly Interspersed Palindromic Repeats) adaptive immunity system in Streptococcus pyogenes, among other bacteria。

5.1.8 照片图

照片图通常是原实物照片的翻版，形象逼真、立体感强、视觉效果好，多用作需要分清深浅、层次多变的图形，在显示某种实物、动作以及反映身体器官成像、细胞和材料内部结构变化等方面是最有效的表达手段。照片图可通过照相设备、器材或其他工具拍摄直接获取，也可通过计算机软件或其他技术、工具、方法来生成。常见的照片图有实物照片图（图 5-42 ~ 图 5-44）和显微照片图（图 5-45 ~ 图 5-47）两类，后者是指用显微镜摄影所记录的物像，有细胞图、金相图、分子图、病理切片组织图、细菌图等等。

若不采用这种放大方式而仅用原来的照片，因图的幅面太小，这两块结构的细节根本显示不出来，达不到图示的效果。这三个图的共同特征是用实物照片图来显示事物的外表或外貌（外观形象）或外在结构。

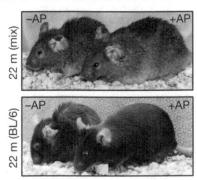

Fig. × Representative images of aged mice with and without senescent cell clearance

图 5-43　实物照片图示例二

Fig. × Appearance of a lunar rover with planetary wheel

图 5-42　实物照片图示例一

图 5-42 显示了行星轮式月球车外观。图 5-43 显示了清除和未清除衰老细胞的老龄小鼠。图 5-44 有三幅照片，显示了在骑固定式脚踏车过程中佩戴智能头带和智能腕带的情形，左上和右上两幅照片是下方照片图中的局部（两处，即一个红框和一个黑框，分别显示智能头带和智能腕带）放大，以清楚地显示智能头带和智能腕带的结构。

图 5-45 显示了一种实验材料的显微结构。图 5-46 显示老龄小鼠的硬化（左）和正常（右）的肾小球，其中 H&E 表示苏木素-伊红、PAS 表示碘酸雪夫氏。图 5-47 有 4 个分图，显示凝缩蛋白的间期染色体组织：图 A 显示凝缩蛋白Ⅱ促成在黑腹果蝇⊖体内二倍体细胞中同源染色体的不配对；图 B 显示凝缩蛋白Ⅱ促成在黑腹果蝇体内多倍体营养细胞中形成染色体区域；图 C 显示凝缩蛋白Ⅱ可在老鼠的神经元干细胞（NSCs）中防止染色体的过度聚类；图 D 显示一个类似于凝缩蛋白Ⅰ的复合体（凝缩蛋白Ⅰ DCC），通过改变雌雄同体的秀丽隐杆线虫⊖X 中的染色体的构造来调节剂量补偿。这三个图的共同特征是用照片图来显示事物的显微结构（指内部结构），既可以是硬体事物（如金属材料），也可以是软体事物（如生物机体、组织）。

⊖ D. melanogaster—Drosophila melanogaster（黑腹果蝇）。

⊖ C. elegans—Caenorhabditis elegans（秀丽隐杆线虫），一种常见的、自由生活的小型土壤线虫，在世界有雌雄同体（Hermaphrodites）和一种雄虫（males）两种性形式。

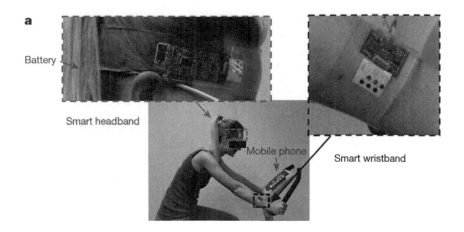

Figure 3a Photographs of a subject wearing a 'smart headband' and a 'smart wristband' during stationary cycling

图 5-44　实物照片图示例三①

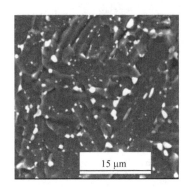

Fig. × Microscopic structure of experimental materials

图 5-45　显微照片图示例一

使用照片图特别是材料显微结构图，常需要标示比例标尺或标注放大倍数，如 Metallograph of 45 steel (×500)，其中"(×500)"指图形是原实物的 500 倍。若需要根据论文版式将照片图缩小或放大，就同时需要对原来标注的放大倍数进行换算。

例如：原来标注的放大倍数是 500，若将其缩小 2/10 使用，则缩小后标注的放大倍数应为 500 (1 − 2/10) = 400，图题应相应地改为 Metallograph of 45 steel (×400)。

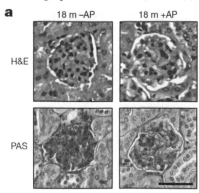

Figure 4a Images of sclerotic (left) and normal (right) glomeruli from the indicated mice. H&E, haematoxylin and eosin; PAS, periodic acid-Schiff.

图 5-46　显微照片图示例二②

---

① 摘自 *Nature* 的 RESEARCH│LETTER 类：Fully integrated wearable sensor arrays for multiplexed *in situ* perspiration analysis. doi：10.1038/nature16521.

② 摘自 *Nature* 的 RESEARCH│ARTICLE 类：Naturally occurring p16[Ink4a]-positive cells shorten healthy lifespan. doi：10.1038/nature16932.

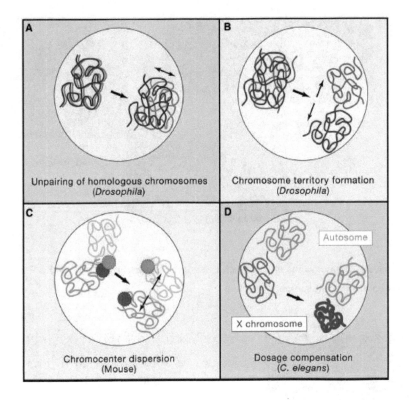

Figure 4. Interphase Chromosome Organization by Condensins
(A) Condensin II contributes to unpairing of homologous chromosomes in somatic diploid cells in D. melanogaster.
(B) Condensin II contributes to the formation of chromosome territories in polyploid nurse cells in D. melanogaster.
(C) Condensin II prevents hyperclustering of chromocenters in neuronal stem cells (NSCs) in mice.
(D) A condensin I-like complex (condensin I DCC) regulates dosage compensation by altering the conformation of the X chromosome in C. elegans hermaphrodites.

图 5-47　显微照片图示例三㊀

5.2　插图的构成及表达

插图类别不同,其构成也不同。下面讲述插图的常规构成,如图序、图题、图例、图注和主图等,线形图的主图通常包括坐标轴、标目、标值线、标值等,如图 5-48、图 5-49 所示。

图 5-48 中,横纵坐标的标目分别为 Time (min) 和 Voltage (V),结构为"量名称(单位)",这是 SCI 论文典型的标目结构。按量和单位国家标准,标目的结构是"量名称 量符号/单位",按此结构,此图的标目就应该是 Time t/min 和 Voltage U/V,但多数 SCI 期刊不用这种结构。

㊀ 摘自 Cell 的 Review 类:Condensin-Based Chromosome Organization from Bacteria to Vertebrates. Cell 164,February 25,2016.

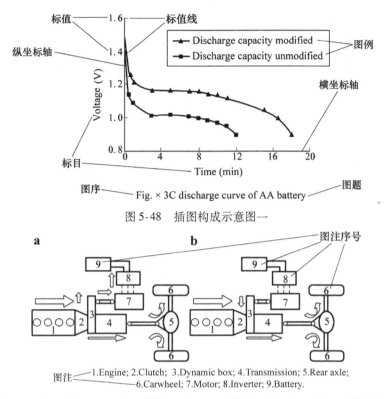

图 5-48　插图构成示意图一

图 5-49　插图构成示意图二

5.2.1　图序和图题

（1）总图序和总图题

总图序和总图题是针对组合图来说的，对于单图，就不必冠以"总"字而直接称图序和图题就好了。图序指插图的序号即图号。根据插图在论文中被提及的顺序，用阿拉伯数字对插图排序，如 **Fig. 1** 或 **Figure 1**、**Fig. 2** 或 **Figure 2** 等，并把插图安排在合适位置（按中国习惯，此位置通常是指第一次提及该插图的段落的后面；但按国外习惯，位置较为随意，没有特别限制，多在页面下部或上部）。另外，一篇论文中只有一个插图时，也应有图序，不应省略数字而用"Fig."。提及插图时，除非表意清楚，不宜写成诸如 see the above figure、see figure below 之类的表达，这种表达有时令人费解，当插图较多时更易造成误解，因为 above 和 below 有时并不容易确指；也不要写成诸如 see the figure in page × 之类的表达，此写法也可能会造成错误，因为论文重新排版时某图所在页码（或位置）可能发生变化，而文中相应的引用表达也要跟随发生变化，但常常被忽略而未作适时修改。

图题指插图的名称或标题，确切反映插图的特定内容，简短精练，常用以名词或名词性词组为中心词的偏正词组，要求有较好的说明性和专指性。避免追求形式上的简洁而用过于泛指的图题，如 Structure diagram、Block diagram、Principle diagram 等，在其前面加上限定词就好了，如 Structure diagram of computer、Block diagram of design of hierarchical intelligent digital control system、Principle diagram of product data management platform；图题中不宜出现 diagram 和 figure 之类的词，如图题 Relationship curve diagram of stress and strain 应改为 Relationship curve of stress and strain 或 Relationship between stress and strain。

（2）分图序和分图题

当几幅插图共用一个图序和图题（总图序和总图题），即同一图序有几个分图时，各分图均应有分图序，按 a、b……或 A、B……（通常置于各分图的左上角），再在总图题后给出分图序、分图题或对分图的解释、说明性语句，各分图序、分图题不一定单独出现，有时可以各自充当某种句法成分而共同组合成全句或局部句子（图 5-2、图 5-3）。在正文中提及某分图时，应当提及分图序而不是总图序，例如提及图 3 中的 d 图时，应写成 Fig. 3d，而不是 Fig. 3。

总图序和总图题间一般不加标点，总图题末常加句点。图序和图题可置于插图下方、左方、右方或别的位置，国际期刊多见居左排，中国期刊多见居中排。图题较长时，可多行排。

5.2.2 图例

图中需要用不同图形或符号来代表不同变量、曲线或其他类别时，例如对辐射方式、发光颜色、处理前后、实验方法、学历级别、速度区间、样本类别、药剂组成或道路类型等进行分类区别或作特别说明，就应使用图例来说明图形或符号的意义。图例常放置于图内（图题下方也可以）。坐标图的图例位于图内时，宜放置于坐标轴所覆盖的区域之内，例如图 5-48，分别用黑色小三角加短线、黑色小方块加短线两个图例表示 Discharge capacity modified 和 Discharge capacity unmodified 两条不同的曲线。

图例通常加外框图，但也可以不加，如果图例周边空白较多或与周边的图的其他要素区别非常明显，那么从图的表达简洁性来说，不给此图例加外框是完全合适的。给图例加外框图的最大优势是形成图例的独特标志，与其周边的区分性非常明显，不易混淆。

5.2.3 图注

图注是简洁地按顺序表达图中所标注符号、标记、代码及所需说明的事项的一种简短文字。未能表达又需表达的信息（如事物结构组成、实验或算式条件、曲线类别或特征、全称或缩略语、引文出处等）均应在图注中说明。线形图中，常用图注给出实验条件，参变量的符号、数值、单位，曲线的代号、名称、注释，以及其他说明语句。图注常放置于图中（上、下方，左、右侧均可）成为图的一部分，也可处于图外（图题下方）成为图的补充部分。

图注处于图中时（图 5-49 ~ 图 5-51），图面集中，读起来方便，不必看了图注序号再将视线移到图外看注释。图注处于图外时（图 5-52），图面简化了，它可直接随正文录排，即不随插图同时制作，修改方便，但读起来可能不方便，看了图注序号后需将视线移到图外看注释。

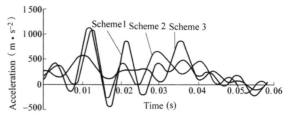

Fig. × Collision acceleration time history curves at the firewall of vehicle under three kinds of scheme

图 5-50　图注处于图中示例

图注安排在图外还是图中，要根据图面空余空间、图注文字所占空间及实际的简洁、美观效果来确定。例如，对于图 5-49 ~ 图 5-51，将图注安排在图中显然是合适的，但对于图 5-52，将图注安排在图外更好，尽管将其放在图题的上方而安排在图中也是正常的。

5.2.4 标目

标目用来说明坐标轴的含义，通常由量名称和单位符号组成（单位符号加括号），如 Liquid density（kg/m^3）（kg/m^3 也可排为 $kg \cdot m^{-3}$ 或 $kg\ m^{-3}$）、Critical pressure（MPa）、Maximum current（A）等；按量和

第 5 章　SCI 论文插图使用

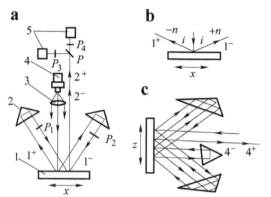

1. Holographic grating;
2. Optical prism;
3. Collimation lens;
4. Semiconductor laser;
5. Photo detector.

Fig. × Holographic grating displacement measurement optical path

图 5-51　图注处于图中和图外均可行示例

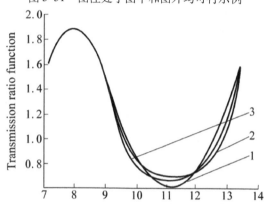

Fig. × Comparison of the transmission ratio function image of a cycle

1. $i_{12} = 0.188\,022\,8\varphi_1^2 - 1.826\,475\,9\varphi_1 + 5.047\,006\,0$;
2. $i_{12} = 1/(-0.173\,039\,2\varphi_1^2 + 1.714\,333\,4\varphi_1 - 2.783\,759\,6)$;
3. $i_{12} = 1/(0.002\,521\,0\varphi_1^4 + 0.030\,403\,7\varphi_1^3 - 0.112\,147\,1\varphi_1^2 + 2.306\,547\,9\varphi_1 - 3.670\,726\,0)$.

图 5-52　图注处于图外示例

单位国家标准，标目应由量名称、量符号及单位符号组成，量符号与单位符号间用"/"分隔，如 Liquid density $\rho/(kg \cdot m^{-3})$、Critical pressure p_c/MPa、Maximum current I_{max}/A 等，这种形式国际期刊很少见；将标目中的量符号及单位符号写成其他形式如"Critical pressure, MPa""p_c（MPa）"或"p_c, MPa"也是可以的。标目是百分率时，可将%看作单位，如 Production efficiency（%）中的%虽不是单位符号，但可将其与单位作同样的处理。

标目应与被标注的坐标轴平行，以坐标轴为准居中排在坐标轴和标值的外侧。标目居中排常见的有以下几种情况：①被标注的坐标轴为下横坐标时，标目排在标值的下方；②被标注的坐标轴为上横坐标时，标目排在标值的上方；③被标注的坐标轴为左纵坐标时，标目排在标值的左方，并且逆时针转 90°，标目顶部朝左，底部朝右，即"顶左底右"；④被标注的坐标轴为右纵坐标时，标目排在标值的右方，也是逆时针转 90° 和"顶左底右"。对于非定量的、只有量符号的简单标目如 x、y、z 等，可排在坐标轴尾部的外侧。

5.2.5 标值线和标值

标值线就是与坐标轴平行的刻度线，可以简化为小短横留在坐标轴上，即长的标值线的残余线段（称为刻度或刻度线）。标值为标值线对应的数字，是坐标轴定量表达的尺度，排在坐标轴外侧紧靠标值线的地方。

设计坐标图时应避免标值线和标值过度密集而出现数码前后重叠连接、辨识不清的现象。标值的数字不宜超过 3 位数，通常为 "0.1n, 0.2n, …" "1n, 2n, …" "10n, 20n, …" ($n=1, 2, …$) 等，同时还要认真选取标目中的单位，如用"3 kg"代替"3 000 g"，用"5 μg"代替"0.005 mg"等。为避免选用不规则的标值，实际中可将不规则的标值改成较为规则的标值。例如：可将"0.385, 0.770, 1.151, …"改为"0.4, 0.8, 1.2, …"，"62.5, 78.3, 101.4, …"改为"60, 80, 100, …"，并相应平移标值线，但不要变动图面内的数据点或曲线。

按量和单位国家标准，标值的数字一般宜处在 0.1~1 000 之间，这可以通过将标目中的单位改用词头形式或在量符号前增加非"1"的因数来实现。例如：某坐标轴的标值是"1 000, 1 200, …, 2 000"，标目为 Normal pressure (N)，则宜将标目改为 Normal pressure (kN)，相应地其标值就须改为"1.0, 1.2, …, 2.0"；某坐标轴的标值是"0.015, 0.020, …, 0.050"，标目为 Slip ratio，则可将标目改为 "(10^3) Slip ratio"，相应地其标值就须改为"15, 20, …, 50"。

5.2.6 坐标轴

平面直角坐标图的横、纵坐标轴是相互垂直的直线，并交于坐标原点。如果坐标轴表达的是定性的变量，即未给出标值线和标值，则在坐标轴的尾端按变量增大的方向画出箭头，并标注变量如 x、y 及原点如 O，如图 5-53 所示；如果坐标轴上已给出标值线和标值，即坐标轴上变量增大的方向已清楚表明，则不必再画箭头，如图 5-50、图 5-52 所示。

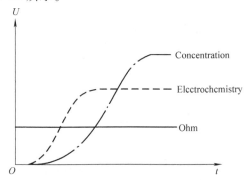

Fig. ×　Cell polarization process

图 5-53　坐标轴带箭头的坐标图示例

5.3　插图使用一般原则

插图使用的原则有所述内容适于用插图表达及插图类型恰当、内容表达贴切、布局结构合理、设计制作规范、幅面尺寸合适等多个方面，是否用及用何种类型的插图需要从内容和读者对象的需求、层次来考虑，其他方面则要服从制图标准、规范以及国际科技期刊对插图的常规要求。插图使用有以下一般原则：

（1）严格精选插图

严格精选插图指坚持"少而精"的插图精选原则。"精选"有两方面含义：一是根据所表达的对象及插图本身的功能决定是否采用插图；二是在初步确定采用插图的基础上对可以使用的同类插图进行分析比较，确定可否将同类插图进行排除（删减）或合并。凡不用插图就能表达清楚的，就不宜用插图；可用文字清楚、方便表达的，也不用插图，坚决不用可有可无的插图；可用较小幅面的插图表达清楚的就不用较大幅面的插图；可用简单插图表达清楚的就不用复杂插图，尽量采用简化图或示意图，必要时可加局部详图；能用黑白图表达清楚的就不宜用彩色图；能用线条图表达清楚的就不宜用照片图。

（2）恰当选择插图类型

恰当选择插图类型指先确定图类，再设计制作插图。不同图类有其各自的特点，用来分别表达同一事物时，可能会有不同甚至差别较大的表达效果。因此，应根据表达对象的性质、论述的目的和内容等来选择图类。例如：线条图含义清晰、线条简明，适于表达说理性和假设性较强的内容以及表达事物间的定性或定量关系，制作也较为方便；照片图层次变化分明、立体感较强，适于反映物体外形或内部显微结构要求较高的原始资料，而彩色照片图色彩丰富、形象逼真，适于只有用色彩才能清楚表达的场合。彩色图在计算机屏幕上看起来清楚、美观，但在纸质黑白稿中通常达不到计算机屏幕的显示效果，因此使用彩色插图时要注意区分实际黑白效果与计算机屏幕彩色效果之间的差别。平面图简洁明快，立体图立体感强。对于一个或一组物体，是用平面图、三维投影图还是立体图表达，要认真比较、合理选择。一般来说，用写真方式来反映一种实验系统或描述一组动态过程时，应优先使用某种框图或单线条示意图，因为框图和示意图形式多样、图形简单、使用灵活、幅面较小、制作方便。对于一组参数的函数曲线，用立体曲面图还是一组离散平面图表达，对于某一事物的成分，用条形图还是圆形图表达，都应仔细斟酌、合理选定。

（3）简化和提炼插图

插图不仅要求表达内容正确，还要求表达形式简化。简化和提炼插图指通过简化、提炼和抽象的方式、过程，将原始图或实际图等一般图设计制作成具有高度表达效果的图。当插图用来说明原理、结构、流程，或实验结果的原理、结构、抽象、流程之类的图时，就不宜把未经简化、提炼的原始图或实际图（如显微组织图、电路图、施工图、装配图、创意构想图等）原封不动地搬到论文中来，而应该在原图的基础上加以简化、提炼、提高和抽象，尽可能突出所要表达、说明的主题，最终提高实际的表达效果。

（4）有效表达插图

有效表达插图指根据表达内容和目的，用最合适的幅面和最恰当的内容来表达插图。插图表达效果所强调的是表达的目的性，而不是图面的完整性，因此应该根据论文的表述要求决定采用整幅画面还是整幅画面中的一部分。例如：当表达某一设备中某部位的某一零件的外形结构时，就可从简化或虚拟的整体设备图上给定部位通过标引编号拉出该零件，给以放大特写即可，而不必给出表达整台设备的全部图，以免造成图面复杂、喧宾夺主，甚至无法突出所要表达的核心内容，最终削弱或失去插图的辅助作用的反面效果。

（5）合理确定插图幅面

合理确定插图幅面指要根据论文字数、版式、插图中文字的字体字号以及允许插图的最大版面空间（双栏排版时，插图的宽度不宜超过栏宽；通栏排版时，插图的宽度不宜超过版心⊖）等因素，来确定使插图达到最佳表达效果而所需采用的最适宜的幅面。插图幅面必须大小协调、比例恰当，太小了容易引起文字密集、字迹模糊而看不清楚，太大了容易引起插图自身表达不美观、与周围文字和别的插图安排不协调以及不必要地多占版面。对于幅面特别大，或较大但又不宜缩小的插图，最好不要使用，必要时可画出局部图。在规划和确定一幅插图时还应考虑：除特殊要求外，插图幅面必须限定在所要求的版心之内；同类型或同等重要的插图幅面应尽可能保持一致；为方便比较，可以把结构类似的图（如纵或横坐标轴相同）合并起来；图例宜放置于图形区内。

⊖ 版心是指书刊幅面内除去四周的白边而剩余的排版范围，用来排文字和图表。

（6）合理布局插图

合理布局插图指按照插图幅面及其内容来合理安排和布置插图中各组成部分和要素的位置、大小及其关系而达到最佳表达效果。除考虑插图内容表达外，还要注意插图布置匀称、疏密适中、不留大的空白、高宽比例协调，这不仅能增强表达效果，而且还能美化版面、节省篇幅，特别对于流程图、功能图、电路图之类的插图更要注重其布局的合理性。

（7）统一插图文种

统一插图文种指插图的文字与正文的文字属于同一语言系统，SCI 论文多是英文。除照片图或其他特殊情况外，一种语言的论文中不宜混用其他语言。例如，有的作者直接照搬中文参考文献的原图或将其稍加修改就使用，或将很多未加翻译的中文词句直接用在插图中，结果使得英文论文的插图中出现了部分甚至全部中文语句。

（8）规范设计制作插图

规范设计制作插图指要按照目标期刊对插图的制作要求来设计制作插图。这一环节包括作者初期设计、编辑中期加工、作者中期修改、制图人员后期制作、编辑后期核对等多个环节。插图的规范性体现在多个方面：构成要素全面、不缺项；图面布置合理、清晰美观；图序、图题、幅面尺寸、文字、量和单位、线型、线距、标目、标值线、标值，以及设计方法等均应符合有关规定和惯例；照片图真实、清晰，主题鲜明、重点突出、反差适中；同一论文中所有或同类插图的风格和体例应当一致。

（9）正确配合文字表达

插图应有自明性，即一幅完整的插图有必要的准确信息，使得读者只看插图而不读正文就能获得其所表达的内容，对插图已清楚表达的，就不必再用文字重复叙述。正确配合文字表达指插图与文字的表达恰当配合，涉及插图位置合理安排与图文表达一致两个方面：前者通常有插图随文排、先见文后见图；后者通常有插图与正文对同一内容的表达要一致且相互配合，文中关于图的叙述在图中能够对应等原则。

按国际习惯，插图一般放在某个页面的上端或下端（左栏上端、右栏上端、左栏下端、右栏下端、通栏上端、通栏下端），而按国内习惯，通常将插图放在引用它的那个段落的后面，当此段后面的空间不足时，再将插图后移到能够排得下的与此段最近的某个段落的后面。

图文紧密结合是按文字表述来配图，再按图的内容来周密设计图，图文相辅相成、互为补充。应先立足全局、通盘考虑、梳理内容，厘清论文主题及内容、结构，接着再决定哪些内容、段落和小节需要配图，进而对插图如何定类、布局、设计等一一做出缜密的考虑与安排。

5.4 插图规范设计制作

5.4.1 设计制作细节

SCI 论文插图规范设计制作细节一般包括以下几个方面：

1）遵守国家、行业有关制图标准、规范，可对引自别的文献中的插图作适当处理；

2）字号以目标期刊要求为准，为突出层次、类属，可对相关文字增大或减小字号；

3）指引线长短和方向适当，线条利落，排列有序，不交叉，不从细微结构处穿过；

4）箭头类型统一，其大小及尖端和燕尾宽窄适当，同一、同类图中的类型应一致；

5）线条粗细应分明，同类线型粗细应一致；曲线过渡应光滑，圆弧连接应准确；

6）无充足空间放置图注时，可考虑精减图注文字或减小图中全部或部分字符字号；

7）善于利用不同的图案来区分性质不同的部分，如条形图中，用有明显区别的线条图案来区分不同的条，若使用灰度来区分，则不同条的灰度应有较为明显的差别；

8）条形图、圆形图的构成部分不宜太多，当构成部分较多时，可以考虑使用表格；

9）以可辨性原则来确定线形图内放置曲线的数量，曲线不宜太多，布置也不宜太密；

10）尽量用简单几何图形（如空心或实心圆圈、三角形、正方形等）表示不同数据类型；

11）树立、加强美学设计思想，比如设计二维坐标图时，除特殊情况外，若将纵坐标轴的长度设计为横坐标轴的 2/3 ~ 3/4，则能达到较高的美学视觉效果。

5.4.2 图中线型选取

线型指线条的不同形状或类别，其中一个较为重要的方面是线条的粗细。线条的形状或类别宜参照有关制图的标准、规范及目标期刊对制图的要求来选取。线条的粗细还要根据插图的幅面、使用场合和图面内线条的疏密程度来确定。线条过粗，会使图面难看，甚至导致线条密集处形成模糊一片；而过细，不仅会使图面美观度下降，而且制版时容易造成断线。

粗线一般用于线形图中的曲线（直线）、工程图中的各种实线（主线）；其他地方多用细线（辅线），如坐标轴线、示意图中的线条、工程图中的点画线和虚线，以及各种插图的指引线等。还可考虑用线条的粗细和线条间的疏密程度来突出某些重要元素，例如：线形图上的曲线和条形图上的条的轮廓通常要比坐标轴的标值线（刻度）更清楚、醒目，而坐标轴的标值线（刻度）又要比坐标轴更清楚、醒目。

5.4.3 图形符号使用

图形符号是把具体事物经过简化但又能保持其特点而简明、直观、形象地表现事物特征的一种图形语言，其基本构成是符号的名称、形态、含义及画法。这种符号的使用给插图设计制作带来极大方便，也使插图的可读性大大提高。

各学科领域中用的图形符号在相应国家、行业标准中均有了规定（某些即使尚未列入标准，但有行业或系统内的一些习惯或约定俗成的画法），使用时应遵守习惯、查阅有关资料。图形符号的规定、习惯画法不是始终不变的，一些习惯画法因其合理性、可行性和创新性可能将被吸收到国家标准中而成为规定画法，而有些已作为国家标准中的规定画法，因其不适应性又可能被取消而成为非规定画法。

5.4.4 图形布局设计

图形布局有图间和图内两个层面，分为图间布局设计和图内布局设计两类。

（1）图间布局设计

图间布局设计指通过调整不同插图的某些共性部分或要素的内容、幅面及其之间的排列顺序而达到这些部分或要素的优化组合排列和得体显示。比如对横纵坐标的标目和标值均相同的一组坐标图，可考虑将其组合在一起共用一个图名；对标值相同的一组坐标图，若每幅图的线条单一，也可将这组图合并成一幅图；对横纵坐标中一个坐标轴的标值相同而另一个不同的一组坐标图，可用双（多）坐标轴表示。图中的曲线过多、过密而难以区分时，可以将插图分解成几个分图，即设计为组合图。这样调整后的插图，既能够节约版面、扩大容量，又便于在同一变量条件下对曲线所对应的数据和形态进行对比。例如：图 5-54 是由三个坐标图合并成的，共用一个横坐标轴，标目为 Time (s)，三图分立纵坐标轴，而后两个共用一个纵坐标轴，即右侧纵坐标是两个标值相同的纵坐标轴的合并，纵坐标的标目分别为 Rotational speed（r·min^{-1}）、Car speed（km·h^{-1}）、Throttle aperture（%）。

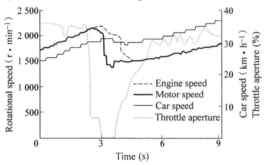

Fig. × Process of gear shift rising from 2 to 3 without motor torque control

图 5-54　共用横、纵坐标轴的双纵坐标图示例

（2）图内布局设计

图内布局设计指通过调整某插图的各组成部分或要素的内容、幅面及其之间的排列顺序而达到这些部分或要素的优化组合排列和得体显示。为使插图布局合理均衡，有稳定的视觉效果，应对插图的各个组成部分进行合理布局，如采取并排、叠排、交叉排、三角形排等多种形式，既要考虑论文段落、插图形态、幅面大小，又要考虑排版要求、美观协调、节约版面等因素。对布局不合理或存在较大空白的插图，在不影响插图内容表达的情况下，要对其进行适当调整，使其布局合适、大小恰当、比例协调、匀称美观。

1）示例一：布局调整前的某一原图（图 5-55）。

图 5-55 在布局上存在的不足主要有：矩形框和其他框内的空白相对较多，即文字虽不少，但相对框内两边的空白多来说就不多了，框内文字的排列、转行不规范（相对完整的词语宜同行排，修饰语与其中心词

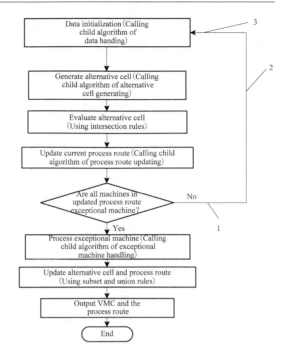

图 5-55　布局调整前的原图示例一

不宜分开转行排）；连接各框的流程箭头线有长有短，且有的明显偏长，很不协调；流程线 1、2 和箭头线 3 与其他要素所围空白偏多；图中文字的字号相对偏小；菱形框内语句末尾的问号可以省去，而且还有文字压线。

针对这些不足对图作布局调整：将多数框内的文字改为两行排，使框的大小与其中文字的幅面协调、一致；缩短长的箭头线，使所有同类箭头线的长度尽可能一致；缩小流程线 1、2 和箭头线 3 与其他要素所围空白；按目标期刊的要求增大字号。调整后如图 5-56 所示，表达效果明显提高。

为进一步降低整个图的高度，以缩小图的幅面，还可通过对若干矩形框的内容合并而对图 5-56 的布局重新调整为如图 5-57 所示。为进一步简化图形，还可通过简化和提炼矩形框内的文字表达而对图 5-57 的布局重新调整为如图 5-58 所示。在图形布局设计中，还可通过将并（竖）式布局改为串（横）式布局而调整（必要时还可用其他调

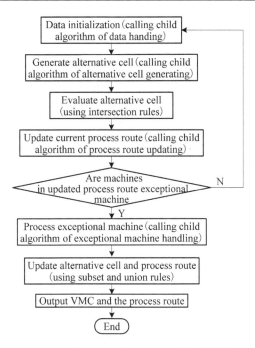

图 5-56　对图 5-55 布局调整后的图形示例

足，对此图的布局重新调整为如图 5-61 所示。重新布局后的表达效果明显好于原图：紧凑，在半栏内能排得下，达到既美观又省版面的效果。

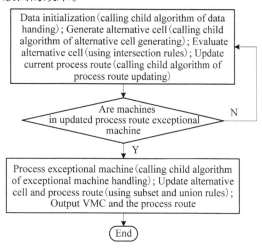

图 5-57　对图 5-56 布局调整后的图形示例

整方式），如可将图 5-56 或图 5-58 的布局重新调整为如图 5-59 所示。

2）示例二：布局调整前的某一原图（图 5-60）。

图 5-60 在布局上明显存在一些不足：矩形框之间的排列较为松散，不紧凑，欠整齐；图内各要素间不必要的空白较多，使得图的幅面整体偏大（特别是偏宽）；此图在半栏内排不下，但将其通栏排版时会浪费版面，还与周围的文字不大协调。针对以上不

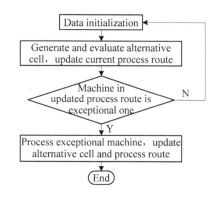

图 5-58　对图 5-57 布局调整后的图形示例

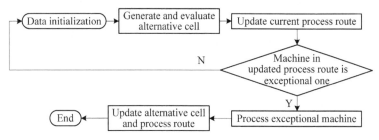

图 5-59　对图 5-56 或图 5-58 布局重新调整后的图形示例

总之，插图的设计应富于变化，版面上美观协调，达到多样的统一；幅面适中，线条密集时幅面可大些，稀疏时幅面可小些，这样的布局给人以舒适感。插图中线条的粗细要搭配，如线形图的坐标轴线和标值线用细线表示，而主图的线条用粗线表示，这样

的布局有层次感。

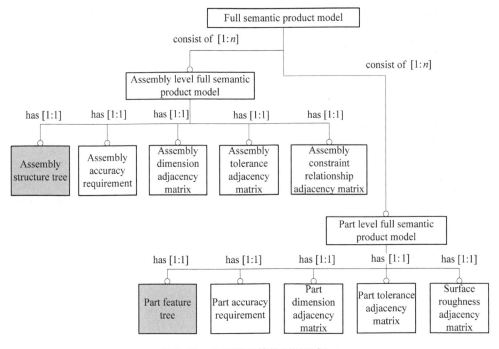

图 5-60　布局调整前的原图示例二

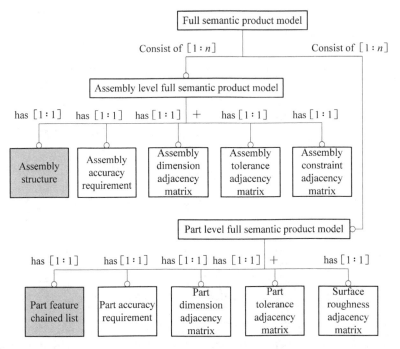

图 5-61　对图 5-60 布局调整后的图形示例

5.4.5 插图幅面确定

插图幅面是其左右边界所在假想垂直线与其上下边界所在假想水平线所围的区域，其大小涉及较多的因素，主要应把握以下两个方面：

（1）论文版心尺寸

插图幅面不宜超过版心，双栏排版时不宜超过栏宽。不同期刊的幅面、版心、栏宽不尽相同，即使对于相同幅面的期刊，其版心尺寸也可能会有差异，因此确定插图幅面应考虑目标期刊的具体规格。

（2）插图自身情况

插图幅面确定还应考虑其复杂程度、是否由多幅分图组成等自身情况。插图简单时，幅面就不宜太大，否则图形会显得空旷、不匀称，浪费版面；较复杂且（或）包含较多文字时，幅面就不宜太小，否则图形会显得拥挤、臃肿，不易看清。对于单幅图，图形较为简单、图线较为稀疏、图内文字较少时，图面宽度可小些，排版后若图旁还有足够的空间，还可考虑在其旁边串排文字；相反，当图形较为复杂、图线较为密集、图内文字较多时，图面宽度应大一些，半栏排不下时需改为通栏，排版后若图旁还有足够的空间，也可考虑在其旁边串排文字。对于组合图，可根据空间富余情况在一（几）行排列多个分图。图内文字太多而按正常字号制图，文字过于密集甚至重叠难以清晰辨认时，可考虑将图内文字排小或排紧凑一些。

5.5 线形图规范设计制作

设计制作线形图时，除要对图序与图题、坐标轴、标目、标值线与标值规范地设计制作外，还要对其重要组成部分"曲线"（包括直线）规范地设计制作，同时要注意一些技巧。

5.5.1 曲线设计制作基本方法

曲线用来表达变量关系及实验、观测结果，不仅形象直观、简洁易懂，而且将函数关系及变化趋势表达得非常直观、清楚，是进行理论和实验分析的强有力工具。其设计制作基本方法有以下几点：

1）选择确定实验点。根据具体情况选择坐标值，将实验点标注在图中。

2）根据要求制点。若不考虑误差及数据分散度就较为简单；若必须考虑误差或明确表示出数据分散度等因素，则可将误差或实验范围表示来。

3）确定曲线制作方式。如果函数变化（趋势）是跳跃式的，则可用折线将数值点连接起来；如果是光滑连续的，则可将所要表示的结果制作成光滑曲线。

4）区分点的标注方式。如果同一图中有种类或参变量不同的多条曲线，则需要对点的标注方式有所区别，可以使用不同的图案（如■、▲、△、▼、▽、◆、◇、○、◎、●、◢、◣、◤、◥、★、☆、＊、⊙、#、×等）来标记。

5.5.2 线形图设计制作技巧

线形图规范设计制作技巧涉及很多方面，以下从四个方面进行讲述：

（1）选取合适的纵横坐标尺寸比例

在纵横坐标尺寸比例不同的情况下，同一曲线的形状肯定不会相同，同一直线的斜率也不会相同。例如：图 5-62 表示了在三种不同纵横坐标尺寸比例下，同一线形图的不同表达效果，左图的纵横坐标尺寸比例较为合适，中图的偏大，右图的则偏小。

纵横坐标尺寸比例的选取与坐标轴上的标值范围、标值间距等因素有关。标值范围要根据图形的数据来确定，标值间距则可以是任选的，不同的选择会使同一曲线有不同的形状，选择不当将会扭曲数据的显示。标值的确定应主要考虑：①选择适当的标值范围使所设计的曲线处于整个数据区域内；②选择适当的标值间距使所设计的曲线能正确反映数据。

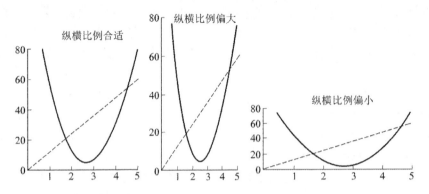

图 5-62　同一线形图在不同纵横坐标尺寸比例下的不同效果示意图

（2）采用表现力强的对数坐标

直线是各种线条中最容易画的，使用很方便，因此当函数本身呈对数关系或自变量的数值跨度很大时，应采用对数坐标使函数曲线变为直线。

在工程实验中，常会遇到 $y = ax + b$ 和 $y = ax^n$ 的函数关系，笛卡尔坐标中前者可绘成一条直线，而后者为一条曲线（抛物线）。若对等式 $y = ax^n$ 两边取对数，则可得

$$\lg y = n\lg x + \lg a,$$

记 $Y = \lg y$，$X = \lg x$，则上式变为 $Y = nX + \lg a$，相当于 $y = ax + b$，为一典型的直线方程，若将 $Y = \lg y$ 和 $X = \lg x$ 绘制在笛卡尔坐标上，就可以得到一条直线。

（3）恰当安排曲线与坐标面的相对位置

这是指把图形的主要部分（曲线）安排在坐标平面内恰当的位置，从而节省版面、增强美感。安排不当常有以下情况：①图面中有多余部分（不必要的空白），曲线相对不够突出，浪费版面，不美观；②曲线超出了坐标轴末端所确定的坐标轴平面。这两个问题可以通过平移坐标轴并同时改变坐标原点，以使坐标平面完全包含整个曲线的方式来解决，必要时还可以延长坐标轴并增加标值线。例如：图 5-63 左图中，通过平移其横纵坐标轴，使原点的坐标由原来的（0，0）变为（1，20），再将横纵坐标轴分别延长，各增加一个标值线（6，100），整个坐标面就能完全包容整个曲线（图 5-63 右图），这样处理后的图形显然是规范的。

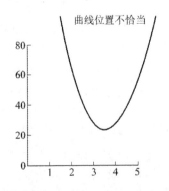
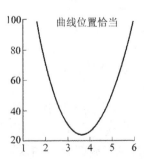

图 5-63　曲线与坐标面的相对位置安排优劣示意图

（4）适当运用同类曲线叠置或分立坐标轴方式

在线形图设计制作中，常会遇到以下情况：某些参变量间的关系在另外一些不同的参变量或条件下呈现出不同的规律和特点，故得到一簇不同的函数曲线，有多少条曲线就设计制作多少个插图，并分别标明各自的图序和图题（图 5-64），这样做显然不规范。

正确做法是把这些曲线放置到同一图上（图 5-65）。一簇曲线的形状比较接近或曲线的条数较多时，将其安排在同一图上会因挤在一起而难以区分，则可考虑用同类曲线分立坐标轴（共用标目）的方法（图 5-66）；或把这些图分设为几个分图，共用一个总图题，必要时加分图序、分图题。运用曲线叠置或分立坐标轴方式能节省或活跃版面，增强对比或显示效果。

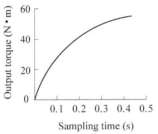

Fig. × Output torque curve of method 1

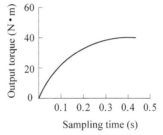

Fig. × Output torque curve of method 2

图 5-64　同类曲线未运用叠置方式示意图

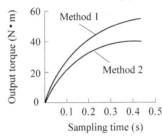

Fig. × Output torque curve of different methods

图 5-65　同类曲线运用叠置方式示意图

线形图中的线条一般不宜过多，但无论有多少条，都应以能清晰分辨为原则，如果无法分辨，也可考虑用表格来呈现有关数据和信息。

5.5.3　线形图设计制作要点

线形图设计制作要点：①线条简洁清晰；②文字、标值易于辨认；③刻度线朝里朝外均可；④标目中的单位不宜省略（量纲一的量除外）；⑤可用缩写或单词代替单位；⑥图例置于合适位置；⑦可用量符号代替量名称；⑧不同变量的符号易于区分；⑨标目的文字方向最好与相应坐标轴平行。

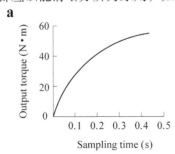

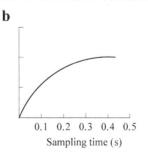

Fig. × Output torque curve of different methods. (**a**) Method 1, and (**b**) method 2

图 5-66　同类曲线分立纵坐标轴（共用标目）示意图

第 6 章　SCI 论文表格使用

表格如同插图一样，也被誉为"形象语言""视觉文学"。科技论文中常有实验结果、统计数据和其他参考资料要反映，采用表格的形式，对作者来说统一集中、便于表达；对读者来说，简洁清晰、便于查找；对期刊来说，活跃形式、美化版面。表格具有简明、清晰、准确、集中及逻辑性、对比性强的特点，在 SCI 论文中得到广泛使用，成为记录论文中数据或事物分类等的一种有效表达方式。设计合理的表格，不仅会使论文表述更加有效，还可起到节省与美化版面的效果。表格的科学性、准确性和规范性也直接影响论文的水准和期刊的质量。写作中应科学地选择、设计和安排表格，仔细地审查、修改和核对表格。科学使用表格，探索其处理方法和技巧也是 SCI 论文写作的重要环节，对高水平论文写作也有重要的现实意义。

6.1　表格的基本名称

以卡线表为例，表格的基本名称如图 6-1 所示。卡线表包括项目栏和说明栏两大部分，项目栏又包括项目头、横表头和竖表头三部分，说明栏即为整个表文。

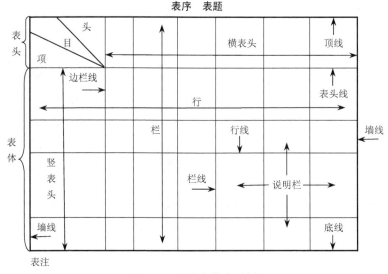

图 6-1　卡线表构成示例

1) 表框线。指表格的四条边线，包括一条顶线、一条底线和两条墙线。顶线位于表格的顶端，即表框线中上边的那条横线；底线位于表格的底部，即表框线中下边的那条横线；墙线位于表格的左右两边，即表框线中左右两边的竖线。表框线一般用粗线条（也可用细线条），而其他线一般用细线条（也可用粗线条）。

2) 行线、栏线及行、栏。表格里的横线即行与行间的线称为行线；竖线即栏与栏间的线称为栏线；行线间称为行；栏线间称为栏。边栏与第二栏的交界线称为边栏线，头行与第二行的交界线称为表头线。

3) 项目栏。指项目头、横表头和竖表头所占的部分。表中左上角有时排一条或一条以上斜角线，有斜角线时称此左上角为项目头（俗称斜角）；横表头（又称横项目栏）位于表格的正上方；竖表头（又称竖项目栏、边栏或名称栏）位于表格的左方。

4) 行头和栏头。表格中每行最左边的一格称为行头，每栏最上方的一格称为栏头。行头是竖表头的组成部分，其所在的栏即表格的第一栏即为竖表头；栏头是横表头的组成部分，其所在的行即表格的第一行称为头行即横表头。

5) 双正线。一个表格左、右侧（或上、下方）的栏目名称完全相同而同时都排表头时，中间相隔的两条正线即为双正线（一般双细线）。这种形式的表格能充分利用版面。

对于三线表，表格的有关名称如图 6-2 所示。其中，与顶线相邻的行线称为栏目线，顶线与栏目线构成的行称为项目栏。三线表的项目栏为横项目栏。

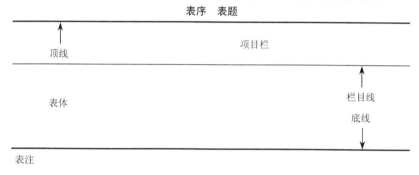

图 6-2　三线表构成示例

项目栏中通常放置多个栏目。栏目是标识表体中该栏信息的特征或属性的词语。例如：表 6-1 的项目头中有 Model、Index 两个栏目，Model 和 Index 分别标识竖项目栏内的各个栏目（Statistical model、Mixed model Ⅰ、Mixed model Ⅱ）和横项目栏内的各个栏目（Multiple correlation coefficient、Residual standard deviation、F-test value）的共同属性；Statistical model 也是栏目，标识数字"0.988 5，0.285 6，1 542.85"的共同属性；Multiple correlation coefficient 也是栏目，标识数字"0.988 5，0.984 3，0.990 7"的共同属性；其他以此类推。

栏目有时相当于插图中的标目，如 Stiffness（MN·m^{-1}）（按量和单位国家标准，此标目的结构应为 Stiffness k/（MN·m^{-1}），但很少有国际期刊使用这种全结构），在本质上也是一种"词语"。卡线表的项目头通常有两个栏目，当然有的有两个以上的栏目，而三线表取消斜线后就只有栏目而无项目头了，此时的栏目无法同时对横、竖项目栏及表体中的信息特征、属性加以标识，而只能标识其所指栏的信息的特征、属性。

6.2　表格的结构分类

SCI 论文的表格按结构一般分为卡线表、三线表、二线表、无线表、系统表等。

（1）卡线表

卡线表是一种用栏线、行线将表格分隔为格并在格内填写表文的表格，见表 6-2。

表 6-1　卡线表示例表格 1
Table ×　Precision of the regression equation

Model \ Index	Multiple correlation coefficient	Residual standard deviation	F-test value
Statistical model	0.988 5	0.285 6	1 542.85
Mixed model Ⅰ	0.984 3	0.305 2	1 084.27
Mixed model Ⅱ	0.990 7	0.307 4	1 496.14

表6-2 卡线表示例表格2

Table × Overall comparison of RMS and traditional manufacturing system

Characteristic	Type	Dedicated manufacturing system (DMS)	Flexible manufacturing system (FMS)	Reconfigurable manufacturing system (RMS)
Basic manufacturing characteristic	Production characteristic	Single or few varieties Mass production	Single family of workpieces Batch production	Multiple families of workpieces Scalable batch production
	Production flexibility	None or very low	Medium	High (variable)
	Process variability	None or minimal	Medium	Large
	Fuction variability	None	None or small	Large
	Scalability	None	Medium	Large
	Cost efficiency	Highest	Medium	High or higher
	Return on investment	Higher or medium	Highest or low	Medium or low or high
System feature	Reconfigurability	Unreconfigurable	Unreconfigurable	Reconfigurable
	Device structure	Fixed (for special use)	Fixed (for common use)	Reconfigurable
	Component structure	Fixed	Fixed	Reconfigurable
	Process operation	Multiple-tool	Single-tool	Variable

卡线表中，横向栏之间用栏线隔开，竖向栏间用行线隔开，在表体中形成很多格，各种数据和事项分别填写在相应的格内。不少卡线表中还有项目头，项目头中有一条斜线，在斜线的右上方用最简单的词语标明横表头的属性和特征，左下方则标明竖表头的属性和特征。

卡线表的优点是数据项分隔清楚，隶属关系一一对应，读起来不易串行，因功能较为齐全，故得到较为广泛的应用；缺点是横竖线多，项目头中还有斜线，不够简练，显得有些复杂，排版较为烦琐，占用版面较多，故科技界多推荐用三线表。无论卡线表有多么复杂，只要精心安排、设计，一般能将其转化为三线表。

（2）三线表

三线表是一种经过简化和改造的特殊类型的卡线表，在SCI论文中使用普遍，其形式见表6-3。它以卡线表为基础，项目头中取消了斜线，省略了行线、栏线，通常只有三条线，即顶线、栏目线和底线，三线表便由此而得名，其中顶线和底线通常为粗线，栏目线通常为细线（也有顶线和底线为细线、栏目线为粗线的三线表，如 *Springer* 期刊论文）。注意三线表并不一定只有三条线，必要时可加上辅助线。辅助线起着和栏目线相呼应并与有关数据相分隔的作用，但一个三线表无论加了多少条辅助线都仍然属于三线表。

随着人们对表格审美要求的提高以及现代科学技术复杂内容表述的需要，目前三线表的形式有所发展，呈现出现代色彩，其使用显出灵活性，实际写作中不宜局限于传统三线表。下面不防看几个现代三线表的实例，见表6-4～表6-6。

表6-3 三线表示例表格

Table × Comparison of design result and enterprise requirement

Parameter	Design value or optimisation result	Enterprise requirement
Rotational speed (r·min^{-1})	985	Yes
Blade number	14	Yes
Internal diameter (radius) (mm)	475	Yes
External diameter (radius) (mm)	1 000	Yes
Maximum camber (%)	2.4	No

表 6-4　现代三线表示例表格一[一]

Table 1. Classification and Examples of CRISPR Systems

Class	Type	Subtype	Hallmarks	Example effector	Example organism	Studies Cited
Class 1	Type I		multisubunit effector complex; Cas3	Cascade	*E. coli*	Brouns et al., 2008
	Type III	III-A	multisubunit effector complex; Csm effector module; DNA targeting	Cas10-Csm	*S. epidermidis*	Marraffini and Sontheimer, 2008
		III-B	multisubunit effector complex; Cmr effector module; RNA targeting	Cmr	*P. furiosus*	Hale et al., 2009
Class 2	Type II		single protein effector; tracrRNA	Cas9	*S. thermophilus*	Bolotin et al., 2005; Barrangou et al., 2007; Sapranauskas et al., 2011; Gasiunas et al., 2012
					S. pyogenes	Deltcheva et al., 2011; Jinek et al., 2012; Cong et al., 2013; Mali et al., 2013
	Type V		single protein effector; single-RNA guided	Cpf1	*F. novicida*	Zetsche et al., 2015

CRISPR systems are currently organized into two overarching classes: Class 1, which contain multi-subunit effectors, and Class 2, which contain single protein effectors. These classes are subdivided into five types (Makarova et al., 2015), with type IV remaining a putative type within Class 1. Although only Class 2 systems have been adapted for genome engineering, the results described in this review emerged from studying a diversity of CRISPR-Cas systems. (Type III-B systems are not discussed but represent an unusual system that targets RNA rather than DNA [Hale et al., 2009]).

表 6-4 所示的表格由水平边框线及辅助线组成，属于三线表，但又有所发展，呈现出现代色彩。主要发展有：①在横项目栏的上方增加了一行，用来放表序和表题，即把表序和表题放在表格内，而且表序和表题所在行与项目栏之间用同边框线一样的粗线；②表体使用了浅灰色的背景，而且表体中各行之间按需使用不同长短的细白线分隔，如大类（Class 1 和 Class 2）之间用全长白线，较小类或小类（如 Type I 和 Type III，Type II 和 Type V，III-A 和 III-B，*S. thermophilus* 和 *S. pyogenes*）之间用非全长白线；③最后一列（Studies Cited）的文字用了蓝色字体；④在表体的下方增加了一行，用来放表注，即把表注也放在了表格内。

表 6-5 所示的表格同表 6-4，也把表序和表题及表注放在表格内，但表序和表题与项目栏之间，表体与表注之间均用空行来分隔；顶线使用了特别粗的线条，取消了底线，而且整个表体用了浅紫色背景；项目栏线用了较粗的线，辅助线用了很细的虚线，而且除了顶线外，其他水平线均左右缩进了一些。此表在传统三线表的基础上创意求新，不仅在展现科学内容，还在展现美感形式，内容与形式完美结合，现代色彩浓厚。

表 6-6 所示的表格虽然发展并不明显，现代色彩不怎么浓厚，但与最常见的三线表相比还是有一些变化，如顶线和底线均未用粗线而用了细线，这样整个表格的线条统一成了相同的细线；另外，项目栏目内的文字即各列的名称（栏目名称）均用了斜体，以与表体相区别。此表格既然有变化，有创新，那么就可以将其列为现代三线表范畴。

[一] 摘自 *Cell* 的 Leading Edge | Perspective 类：The Heroes of CRISPR. *Cell* 164, January 14, 2016.

表 6-5 现代三线表示例表格二[①]

Table 1. Comparison of specific activity per pyridinic N of HOPG model catalysts (in Fig. 2) and N-GNS powder catalysts (in Fig. 4).

Sample	Nitrogen concentration (at. %)*	Pyridinic N concentration (at. %)*	$\|j\|$ at 0.5 V (mA cm^{-2})†	Specific activity per pyridinic N at 0.5 V (e$^-$ s^{-1} pyri-N^{-1})‡
Model HOPG-4	0.60	0.57	0.00041	0.12
Model HOPG-5	4.9	2.2	0.00090	0.066
Model HOPG-6	5.5	3.1	0.0016	0.082
Model HOPG-7	13	3.9	0.0026	0.11
Model HOPG-8	11	6.5	0.0055	0.14
N-GNS-1	1.7	0.72	0.085	0.07
N-GNS-2	2.4	1.9	0.37	0.11
N-GNS-3	8.1	6.3	1.4	0.13

*Nitrogen concentration evaluated by XPS. †ORR current density obtained from current divided by geometric area of electrode surface. ‡Activity derived from ORR current density ($\|j\|$), i.e., number of electrons converted by oxygen reduction per pyridinic N per second (e$^-$ s^{-1} pyri-N), as follows:

$$\text{Activity per pyridinic N} = \frac{\text{number of electrons per sec per cm}^2 \text{ of electrode surface}}{\text{number of pyridinic N per cm}^2 \text{ of electrode surface}}$$

表 6-6 现代三线表示例表格三[②]

Table × Four types of studied SiNCs samples

Sample	Name	Capping	Diameter [Reference]	Distribution	Preparation [Reference]
1	Por-SiNCs	Naturally grown thin silica oxide	2–3 nm[6]	Ensemble	Electrochemical etching[6]
2	Plasma-SiNCs	Naturally grown thin silica oxide	~4 nm[41]	Ensemble	Plasma synthesis[41]
3	Litho-SiNCs	Strained thick silica oxide	~4 nm[42]	Single NC	Electron beam lithography[42]
4	C-SiNCs	Organic (alkyl)	~2.2 ± 0.5 nm[17,40]	Ensemble	Wet-chemical synthesis[17,40]

Additional material and spectroscopic properties of these samples have been extensively studied and reported elsewhere. More details are given in the Experimental section, Supplementary Information (Supplementary Fig. S1) and respective Refs 6, 17, 40–42.

三线表几乎保留了传统卡线表的全部功能，又克服了卡线表的缺点，还增强了表格的简洁性，减少了制表排版的困难，这是SCI论文中普遍使用三线表的重要原因。但它也有缺点，当内容复杂时，读起来容易串行（或串列），甚至引起内容上的混淆。

（3）二线表

二线表是一种只保留顶线和底线的特殊类型的表，适用于较为简单、没有横表头的情况，其形式见表6-7。

[①] 摘自 Science 的 RESEARCH | REPORTS 类：Active sites of nitrogen-doped carbon materials for oxygen reduction reaction clarified using model catalyst. 22 January 2016 · Vol 351 Issue 6271.

[②] 摘自 Light: Science & Application 的 Original Article 类：Multi-chromatic silicon nanocrystals. Light: Science & Application, Volume 6, Issue 4, 2017.

表6-7 二线表示例表格

Table × Static test data of the electromagnet sample developed (relationship between electromagnetic force and current)

Current I/A	2.61	2.63	2.66	2.73	2.78	2.87	2.88	2.90	2.91	2.92
Electromagnetic force F/N	736	808	839	842	845	865	870	871	872	875

（4）无线表

无线表是一种整个表中无任何线条即以空间来隔开的表格，常用于项目和数据较少、表文内容简单的场合，其形式见表6-8。

表6-8 无线表示例表格

Table × Impact factor of an academic journal in 2005−2018

2005	2006	2007	2008	2009	2010	2011	2012	2013	2014	2015	2016	2017	2018
2.127	2.045	2.301	2.384	2.326	2.274	2.352	2.476	2.370	3.262	3.999	4.888	4.665	5.448

（5）系统表

系统表是一种只用横线、竖线或括号、线条把文字连接起来的表格，多用于表述隶属关系的多层次事项，其形式见表6-9。这种表在内容上，结构层次直观、分明，一目了然；在形式上，左小右大或上小下大。它又称分类表，因为适用于分门别类地表示；也称挂线表（也有人将这种表看作图），因为用挂线或大括号联系起来。

表格还可从其他角度来分类，比如，按内容分为数据表、文字表，按用途分为对比表、研究表、计算表等，按文字方向或排式分为横排表、竖排表、侧排表、跨页表（接排表）、对页表（合页表）、插页表等，按位置与上下文关系分为串文表和非串文表……。

有时表文内容实在太多，而省略部分内容又能表述清楚时，则可以使用简易表，见表6-10，在表中用双浪纹线或省略号来表示省略掉的重复部分。

表6-9 系统表示例表格

Table × Classification of the reconfiguration of manufacturing system

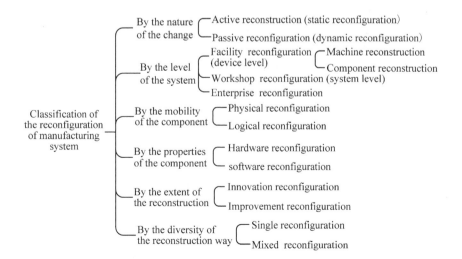

表 6-10 简易表示例表格
Table × Sample table of distance matrix file

Node	1	2	3	4	5	6	7	8	9	29	30
1	−	∞	∞	∞	∞	∞	∞	∞	∞	∞	∞
2	∞	−	∞	∞	∞	∞	∞	∞	∞	∞	∞
3	∞	∞	−	∞	∞	∞	∞	∞	∞	∞	∞
4	∞	∞	∞	−	∞	∞	∞	∞	∞	∞	∞
5	∞	∞	∞	∞	−	∞	∞	∞	∞	∞	∞
6	∞	∞	∞	∞	∞	−	∞	∞	∞	∞	∞
7	∞	∞	∞	∞	∞	∞	−	∞	∞	∞	∞
8	∞	∞	∞	∞	∞	∞	∞	−	∞	∞	∞
29	∞	∞	∞	∞	∞	∞	∞	∞	∞	−	∞
30	∞	∞	∞	∞	∞	∞	∞	∞	∞	∞	−

6.3 表格的构成及表达

SCI 论文的表格通常由表序和表题、表头、表体、表注等部分构成。卡线表的构成如图 6-1 和表 6-1、表 6-2 所示，三线表的构成如图 6-2 和表 6-3 所示。

6.3.1 表序和表题

表格在多数情况下有表序和表题，二者一般与表格同时出现，是表格的重要部分，表序在正文中还要被引用。

（1）表序

表序是表格的编号即序号。给表格编号是为了与正文呼应，通常做法是按表格在文中出现的顺序对其用阿拉伯数字连续编号，如 Table 1、Table 2 等，有分图时，可采用数字加字母的形式，如 Table 1a、Table 1b 等，并置于文中合适的位置（按国内习惯，表格宜放在文中首次提及它的段落的后面，国外无此习惯，表格位置较为灵活，多在页面的下部、上部）。一篇论文只有一个表格时，通常仍应命名为 Table 1（但有的期刊要求用 Table）。

有时按表达需要可以对表格进行分类，论文中会出现不同类别的表格，为区分表格的类型，需要在表序中增加有某种含义的字母，即表序可采用字母加数字的形式，如 Table A1、Table A2（A 表示 Appendix 或 Appendices）、Table S1、Table S2（S 表示 Supplementary information）；有时还可直接在表序前增加有某种含义的词语，如 Extended Data Table 1、Supplementary Table 1、"Supplementary information, Table S1" "Supplementary information, Table S2"。不管以上哪种类别，均可在表序中增加表分图的字母，如 Table S2A、Table S2B、Table S4C 等。（注意：附加信息、扩展数据表一般不出现在印刷版论文中，而是出现在数字版论文中，但对其的引用，不管在哪种版本中，均是需要出现的。）

正文中引用表格一般有两种形式：一种是让表序充当句子的某种成分，如主语（Table 1 shows …；Table 1 summarizes …）、宾语（see Table 1；… in Table 1）；另一种是以表序加括号的形式置于引用处，如（Table 1）、（Extended Data Table 1）、（Supplementary Table 1）。同一论文的正文或附录中不允许出现一号两表或一表两号的交叉、重叠问题，即要保证表序的唯一性。

示例【1】~【7】摘自名刊 *Nature*、*Science* 等，画线部分均为对表格（表序）的引用。

【1】

Within 2 years, researchers had doubled the census and cataloged key features of loci—including the presence of specific CRISPR-associated (cas) genes in the immediate vicinity, which were presumably related to their function (Jansen et al., 2002). (Table 1 summarizes the modern classification of CRISPR systems.) (*Cell*)

【2】

We tested three atovaquone-resistant strains of the rodent malaria parasite *Plasmodium berghei*, each with different mutations in their mitochondrial DNA-encoded *cytB* gene (14, 15), for transmissibility from mouse to mosquito and back to mouse (Table 1). Anopheles stephensi mosquitoes were fed on mice infected with either the parental PbANKA strain or one of the three atovaquone-resistant mutants, and sexual development of parasites in mosquitoes was assayed (Table 1). All three atovaquone-resistant parasite lines produced wild-type numbers of active male gametes (exflagellation) (Table 1) (Science)

【3】

Recently, wearable sweat sensors have been developed, with which a variety of biosensors have been used to measure analytes of interest (Supplementary Table 1) 14–18. (Nature)

【4】

After we detected the chicken-lethal H7N9 viruses, we performed vital surveillance, collecting 2 950 samples from chicken farms and live poultry markets in Guangdong province in February, 2017. We isolated 28 H7N9 viruses (Supplementary information, Table S4), and partial sequence analysis of their HA genes revealed that 15 of them had the HA insertion (Supplementary information, Table S5). In addition to this insertion, we detected three additional motifs in the HA cleavage site of these viruses (Supplementary information, Table S5). The viruses with all of the other three different HA cleavage motifs were also lethal in chickens (Supplementary information, Table S5), although their virulence in mammals remains to be investigated. One of the motifs, -PKRKRTAR/G-, was found in isolates from patients in Guangdong province (Supplementary information, Table S5). The PB2 627K mutation was also detected in these human isolates (Supplementary information, Table S5). (Cell Research)

【5】

Finally, to determine whether the effects of S-BMO on weight gain in piglets were robust to the presence of an opportunistic enteropathogen, 3-day-old animals were colonized with the 17-member bacterial community (Figure 6A; Table S2A) plus two strains of Enterococcus faecalis that were present in the Malawian infant's 25-member culture collection. The genomes of these two strains, E. faecalis MC1 and MC2, contain homologs to 20 and 22 genes, respectively, present in the Virulence Factor Database for the pathogenic E. faecalis strain V583 (Table S2B). Gnotobiotic piglets were weaned onto the M8 diet by experimental day 12. On day 15, animals were split into experimental and control groups (n = 3 and 4, respectively), and for a period of 5 days, piglets in the experimental group were fed the M8 diet supplemented with S-BMO. Control animals were fed unsupplemented M8. COPRO-seq of fecal samples collected on day 18 disclosed that 14/19 (74%) of the input strains, including both strains of E. faecalis, colonized the recipient piglets (Table S4C). (Cell)

【6】

The sequences targeted by these sgRNAs have variable numbers of predicted mismatched sites in the reference human genome (Extended Data Table 1). (Nature)

【7】

The net-work predicted expert moves on a held out test set with an accuracy of 57.0% using all input features, and 55.7% using only raw board position and move history as inputs, compared to the state-of-the-art from other research groups of 44.4% at date of submission 24 (full results in Extended Data Table 3). (Nature)

（2）表题

表题是表格的名称，属于标题性文字，拟定表题的要求与论文题名类似，即表题应当简短精练、准确得体，能确切反映表格的特定内容，通常是以名词或名词性短语为中心词语的偏正短语，表意复杂时中心词语通常需要加上或长或短的前置和（或）后置修饰语（限定语）。

表题应体现专指性，避免单纯用泛指性公用词语，如 Data table、Comparison table、Computation result、Table of parameter changes 等表题显得过于泛指，缺少必要的修饰语，不便于理解，而且一般不宜用 table 结尾或开头，而改用 Initial input data of scheduled process route、Calculation accuracy comparison of new method and traditional method、Results calculated by the finite element method、Parameter changes after setting the supercharger 之类表题就合适了。

表序与表题间通常应留空,其间一般不用加任何标点符号。二者应作为一个整体排在表格顶线的上方,居左排或对整个表格左右居中排,也可排在表格左侧空白的上方,其上边缘与右侧表格的顶线齐平。词数过多的表题应转行排,两行排不下时,可排为三行或三行以上,转行宜在一个完整的词或词组的末尾处进行。表题上方与正文之间、下方与表格顶线之间,在版式上应分别加适当的空行,空行的大小由目标期刊自行确定。

表序与表题间加别的符号的情况也是存在的,这取决于目标期刊对表格格式的设计要求。例如,见表 6-11,其表序 Extended Data Table × 与表题目 Details of match between AlphaGo and Fan Hui 间用符号"｜"分隔,突破了常规格式,现代色彩浓厚。

表 6-11　表序与表题间加符号示例表格

Extended Data Table × ｜ Details of match between AlphaGo and Fan Hui

Date	Black	White	Category	Result
5/10/15	Fan Hui	AlphaGo	Formal	AlphaGo wins by 2.5 points
5/10/15	Fan Hui	AlphaGo	Informal	Fan Hui wins by resignation
6/10/15	AlphaGo	Fan Hui	Formal	AlphaGo wins by resignation
6/10/15	AlphaGo	Fan Hui	Informal	AlphaGo wins by resignation
7/10/15	Fan Hui	AlphaGo	Formal	AlphaGo wins by resignation
7/10/15	Fan Hui	AlphaGo	Informal	AlphaGo wins by resignation
8/10/15	AlphaGo	Fan Hui	Formal	AlphaGo wins by resignation
8/10/15	AlphaGo	Fan Hui	Informal	AlphaGo wins by resignation
9/10/15	Fan Hui	AlphaGo	Formal	AlphaGo wins by resignation
9/10/15	AlphaGo	Fan Hui	Informal	Fan Hui wins by resignation

The match consisted of five formal games with longer time controls, and five informal games with shorter time controls. Time controls and playing conditions were chosen by Fan Hui in advance of the match.

6.3.2　表头

表头也称项目栏,由多个项目栏组成。栏目就是栏的名称,即标识栏目信息的特征或属性的词语,有的相当于坐标图的标目,如 Length of the rod (m)、Velocity of movement (m·s^{-1}) (m·s^{-1}、m s^{-1}、m/s 三种形式应统一)。按量和单位国家标准,标目应由量名称、量符号及单位符号组成,量符号与单位符号间用"/"分隔,如 Length of the rod l / m、Velocity of movement v / (m·s^{-1}) 等,但多数期刊不用这种形式。栏目确立了表格中数据组织的逻辑以及栏目下数据栏的性质,与标题一样应简单明了,忌冗长、烦琐。还应尽量减少栏目中再分栏目的数目,能紧缩的尽量紧缩,这样可以减少栏目,便于理解,还可简化排版工作。

（1）横表头。分单层和双层两种:前者的项目只有单一含义;后者的有几个含义,复分为几个栏。文字通常横排,不适合横排时可改为竖排;转行宜在一个完整词语的末尾处进行。当横表头的栏目较多,甚至左右方向超版心,或格内出现较多长的文字时,可考虑将表格转换为侧排,即将表格按逆时针方向转 90°来排版,不论表格所在页面是双页码还是单页码,但不能超过版心。

（2）竖表头。是表格中最左侧的部分,对右方表文有指引性质,它若本身也属于表文内容就不应视为竖表头。其中文字横排、竖排均可,取一种排法为好,在特殊情况下,如竖表头的文字存在复分情况时,两种排法可以混用。

(3) 项目头。可视为表头的一个组成部分，简单的表格通常不用项目头。项目头中的斜线以不多于一条为宜，而且斜角内的文字越少越好；斜线超过一条时，不容易排，还容易出现文字压线的情况，在不得已出现两条或多条的情况下，必须做到斜线的位置及不同斜线相交的标示正确。项目头中不排斜线时，其内不宜空白，最好加上适当的文字（该文字可视为横表头的组成部分——管下而不管右）。

6.3.3 表体

表体（表身、表文）指表格底线以上、栏目线以下的部分，容纳了表格的大部分信息，是表格的主体。一个表格只有对相关内容正确归类，在表文排式、标目处理、数值表达等多个方面达到规范，才能有助于对其内容清楚理解和正确比较，有关内容参见 6.5 节。

6.3.4 表注

表格的内容即使比较丰富，但由于对其表达简洁性、排版格式的要求较高，往往需要对表格的整体或共性要素及个性要素（如符号、标记、代码以及需要说明的事项等）用简练的语句进行说明、解释或给予补充，这种注释性语句即为表注。表注的作用是减少表体中的重复内容，使表达更加简洁、清楚和有效。

表注按其针对的对象是整体、共性要素还是局部、个性要素，可分为整体表注（表 6-11、表 6-6、表 6-4）和部分表注（表 6-5）。

(1) 整体表注

整体表注属综合性注释，是对表格整体或其中某些共性信息做统一解释、补充、说明和交代，一般不加注释符号，位于表底线下或上方：位于底线下方时，其上方与底线间行距一般较小，下方与正文间行距则相对

大一些；位于底线上方时，它就相当于表体中的最后一行。

表 6-11 中，注文"The match consisted of …the match."位于表格底线的下方，对比赛分类、特征及有关比赛规则进行总体说明——比赛分时间控制长的五场正式比赛和时间控制短的五场非正式比赛，时间控制和比赛条件均由人选手（Fan Hui）在赛前选定。

表 6-6 同表 6-11，注文"Additional … Refs 6，17，40-42."位于表格底线的下方，对各样本的附加材料及光谱特性的研究情况进行总体说明（已有广泛研究和报道），并指出在哪里能够获得有关详情，包括实验部分（本文）、附加信息（Fig. S1）和参考文献（Refs 6，17，40-42）。

表 6-4 不同于前面两个表格，注文"CRISPR systems are … [Hale et al., 2009]）."位于表格底线的上方，形式上是表体的最后部分，对 CRISPR 系统的分类及部分类别的特征统一说明，并就本文有关研究情况或结果给予补充：CRISPR 系统分为两类，类 1 含多亚基蛋白质效应器，类 2 含单蛋白效应器；这两类又可分为 5 个子类（I～V），子类 IV 在类 1 中仍是假定类；仅类 2 系统已用于基因组工程，但在这篇综述中所描述的结果来自于研究 CRISPR-Cas 系统的多样性；子类 III-B 系统未被讨论，但它代表一个以 RNA 而非 DNA 为目标的不同寻常系统。

(2) 部分表注

部分表注是一种与表内某要素或文字相呼应的专指性注释，被注释要素或文字的右上角及表格下方的注文处都用某种字符，如特别符号 *、†、‡……，阿拉伯数字 1)、2)……，阳码①、②……，或字母 a)、b)……。注文处引出注释文字，注文有多条时，可分项接排，项间用标点（如分号）分隔，最后一项末尾用句号；也可编号齐肩，每条注文排为一段，除最后一项末尾用

句号外，其他每项之后常用分号或句号。

表 6-5 中，有 4 处注释位置，分别在表格第二至五列的名称（量名称和单位符号），其中第二、三列的注释符号为＊，第四、五列的分别为†、‡。注文全部列于表格下方（此表为现代三线表，取消了底线，但可以想像其底线的位置），对应＊、†、‡这三个符号的注文排在了一个段落（若考虑最下方的公式，则为两个段落），其间用句点分隔，而且此句点后留有较多的空白，以明显区分这三条注文。这几处注释均是针对表格某列的，因此属于部分表注。

表注通常位于表格下方（底线下方或上方），这种情况的表注又可称为表脚，而整体表注也可位于表题下方，位于表题下方时常用括号括起）。如果表格同时有这两种表注，则部分表注应排于整体表注之后。表注的字号通常比表格中文字的字号小一些。

表注的规范性也是表格规范表达的重要方面，表注处理有以下原则：

1）表注宜简短，尽量避免长表注，对于长表注，应该审时度势加以简化，或将其改作在正文中直接表述，在正文中表述时，对文本长度的限制通常就没那么严格了；

2）对既可在表体又可在表注中表述的内容，应该考虑选用更加清楚有效的组织方式，一般应优先采用表体中表述的方式；

3）对表格中某栏目（横或竖栏）的内容单独注释或说明时，可考虑在表体内加备注（Remark）栏的形式，这样可以避免使用表注的形式。

6.4 表格使用一般原则

表格的使用原则有适于用表格表达及表格类型合适、内容表达贴切、布局结构合理、设计制作规范、幅面尺寸恰当等多个方面，是否选用表格及选用何种类型的表格需要从论文内容和读者对象的需求来考虑，同时还应遵循有关表格的标准、规范及目标期刊对表格的常规要求。表格使用有以下一般原则。

(1) 严格精选表格

这是指按表述对象和表格自身功能确定是否采用表格。下列情况宜用表格：①描述的重点是对比事项的隶属关系或对比数值的准确程度；②按研究和论文写作要求，需要给出能定量反映事物运行过程和结果的系列数据；③避免烦琐的重复性语言文字叙述。

对同一结果，不宜共用插图和表格，但实验、观测结果很重要时，可以共用。有时宜用插图而不用表格；能用简短、概括文字叙述清楚的，就不用篇幅大的表格或对表格作删繁就简的大幅度修改。内容复杂、非单一主题或又派生出子表格时，应以简化原则作分解处理；当用多个数据表说明同一现象而造成表格之间重复时，应选择一个最准确、最有说服力的表格而将重复的表格删除。当文字叙述与插图、表格重复时，应从中选择最合适的一种。

(2) 恰当选择表格类型

这是指在合理选用表格的类型后再去设计相应的表格。之所以强调选择表格类型的重要性，是因为不同类型的表格有各自不同的特点，用其分别表述同一事物时，可能会有不同甚至差别较大的效果。因此，应根据表述对象性质、论述目的、表达内容及排版方便性等因素来选择恰当的表格类型。例如：无线表中没有一根线，适于内容特别简单的场合；系统表可免去水平线（横线）和垂直线（竖线），而只用很短的横线、竖线或括号就可以把文字连接起来；三线表可以克服传统卡线表的横、竖线较多，栏头有斜线，表达不简练，排版较麻烦的缺点，用少量几根线就可清楚地表达，而用现代三线表还能增添表格的现代、美观色彩。

(3) 科学设计表格

这是指对表格从内容到形式作有理、有

序的设计，使其层次清楚、简洁明了、直观易懂、形式合理。在内容方面，表中数据可以是原始或经过整理、处理的数据；栏目、内容的可读性较好，能容易看出或得出有关结论；数据精度不能超出由实际数据所能得到的精度。在形式方面，表中各行、列的排列顺序合理，逻辑性强；表格幅面合理，不宜超出版心；表格布局合理，按需恰当、合理、巧妙和正确运用设计技巧。一个表格宜围绕一个主题来设计，围绕多个主题设计可能会造成表格内容较多、层次叠加、幅面偏大等问题；表格已有正常的横、竖表头，而在表头中又出现新的表头时，表格会复杂化，变得不规范，排版也不方便，这时应考虑将表格分解为主题不同的几个表格。还要恰当处理表中图，不宜过大或过于复杂。

（4）正确配合文字表达

表格结构和信息应完整，使读者只看表格而不看其他部分就能获得必要的内容；表格已清楚表述的内容，就不必再用文字和插图重复表述。除附加类表格（如 Supplementary Information、Extended Data）外，其他表格均应在正文中给出。表格不能只给出表序而无表题，或只给出表题而无表序，或虽给出表序和表题但无表格等。使用表格时通常是先见文后见表（表格与正文呼应），在正文中以 Table × lists、as shown in Table ×、see Table × 之类的表述加以引导；按国际习惯，表格一般放在某个页面的上方或下方，而按国内习惯，通常将表格放在引用它的那个段落的后面，当此段后面的空间不足时，再将表格后移到能够排得下的与此段最近的某个段落的后面。一般不宜先出现表格后提及表序，避免根本不提及表序的情况。

（5）优先使用三线表

SCI 论文中应优先使用三线表，并注意以下原则：

1）不要遗漏项目栏而使表体内容无栏目或标目，没有项目栏的三线表常是不规范的；

2）如果项目或者层次较少，设计时应该合理安排项目栏，必要时可以采用竖项目栏；

3）为便于对比，版面允许时，宜将同一栏目下的信息（主要指数值）作竖向上下排；

4）注意为安排好的项目栏恰当地取名，对于有量纲的量，量名称和单位符号应齐全；

5）对于比较复杂的三线表，要注意科学、合理地安排结构，细致地确定栏目或标目；

6）提倡表格设计创新，基于传统三线表而设计出内容和形式完美呈现的现代三线表。

6.5 表格规范处理

6.5.1 表格幅面确定

表格幅面是其左右边界所在假想垂直线与其上下边界所在假想水平线所围的区域。它的规范处理同插图幅面，即受到版心或栏宽的限制，参见"5.4.5 插图幅面确定"的内容。对于项目、内容较少的表格，一般无须精确确定其宽度，而对于横向栏目较多、宽度较大的表格，就应较为精确地确定其宽度，以实现顺利排版。

表格过宽时可采用以下方法减小表宽：①适当删减表格中可有可无的项目；②对表格标目或栏内文字合理转行；③按实际情况对表格排式合理转换；④按需不妨尝试巧妙地采用侧排表；⑤必要时可考虑采用不常用的表格，如对页表、插页表等。

注意：不同期刊的幅面、版心、栏宽可能不相同，即使对于采用相同幅面的期刊，其版心或其他尺寸也可能会有差异，因此确定表格幅面最终还应考虑具体期刊的实际尺寸规格。

6.5.2 表格拆分、合并、增设和删除

恰当、巧妙地对表格进行拆分、合并、增设或删除，是表格规范使用中十分重要的一项。

（1）表格拆分

当表格中有两个或两个以上中心主题，或包含没有上下关系的两种或两种以上不同表头和表文时，可将此表格拆分为几个表格。拆分表格需重新设计表格，表序、表题也要发生相应变化。例如：表 6-12 包含两种表头和表文，可拆分为表 6-13 和表 6-14。

表 6-12　拆分前示例表格
Table × Process planning and production requirement of the 2nd workshop

Product No.	Procedure No.	Production time per single product of the 2nd workshop (min)	Production time per single product of the 3rd workshop (min)	Product family
1	1	9.00		
	2	7.00	6.00	2
	3	9.00		
2	1	9.00		
	2	8.00	6.00	2
	3	9.00		

Product No.	Period T		
	1	2	3
1	18	18	17
2	13	12	12

表 6-13　表格 6-12 拆分后示例表格 1
Table × Process planning of the 2nd workshop

Product No.	Procedure No.	Production time per single product of the 2nd workshop (min)	Production time per single product of the 3rd workshop (min)	Product family
1	1	9.00		
	2	7.00	6.00	2
	3	9.00		
2	1	9.00		
	2	8.00	6.00	2
	3	9.00		

表 6-14　表格 6-13 拆分后示例表格 2
Table × Production requirement of the 2nd workshop

Product No.	Period T		
	1	2	3
1	18	18	17
2	13	12	12

（2）表格合并

当存在主题相近、位置相邻的两个或两个以上表格时，可以考虑将这几个表格合并为一个表格。合并表格需要更改其后续表格的序号。例如：表 6-15 和表 6-16 的主题相近，位置相邻，可以考虑将它们合并，合并后见表 6-17。

表 6-15 合并前示例表格 1

Table × Comparison of friction power loss while rotational speed is 18 000 r/min

Vacuum pressure (Pa)	Power measurement (W)	Power calculation (W)	
		$A=1$	$A=1.5$
1.70	11.62	14.85	11.96
0.43	4.28	6.42	4.65
0.28	2.58	4.59	3.26

表 6-16 合并前示例表格 2

Table × Comparison of friction power loss while rotational speed is 24 000 r/min

Vacuum pressure (Pa)	Power measurement (W)	Power calculation (W)	
		$A=1$	$A=1.5$
0.61	8.86	14.58	10.90
0.37	6.14	10.14	7.35
0.33	5.64	9.28	6.68
0.32	5.45	9.05	6.50

表 6-17 表 6-15、6-16 合并后示例表格

Table × Comparison of friction power loss at different rotational speed

Rotational speed (r·min^{-1})	Vacuum pressure (Pa)	Power measurement (W)	Power calculation (W)	
			$A=1$	$A=1.5$
18 000	1.70	11.62	14.85	11.96
	0.43	4.28	6.42	4.65
	0.28	2.58	4.59	3.26
24 000	0.61	8.86	14.58	10.90
	0.37	6.14	10.14	7.35
	0.33	5.64	9.28	6.68
	0.32	5.45	9.05	6.50

（3）表格增设

对用文字表述的内容（数据、信息），当其罗列性较强且有对比或统计意义时，可改用（增设）表格来表述，这样既直观清晰又便于比较，可获得用文字表述难以达到的效果。例如以下这段文字叙述就较为啰唆，也不大容易理解，若改成用表 6-18 表述，效果就大大提升。

The gene code generation method of a complex mechanical system layout is generated as follows：Layout parameter is basic mechanism 1 （β_1，d_1），basic mechanism 2 （β_2，d_2），basic mechanism 3 （β_3，d_3），…，basic mechanism N （β_N，d_N）；gene generation method is $\beta_1 = 3$，$d_1 = 23$；$\beta_2 = 1$，$d_2 = 41$；$\beta_3 = 4$，$d_3 = 12$；…；$\beta_N = 2$，$d_N = 33$，code generation method is （3，23，1，41，4，12，…，2，33）.

表 6-18 表格增设示例

Table × Gene code generation method of a complex mechanical system layout

Layout parameter	Basic mechanism							
	1		2		3		…	N	
	β_1	d_1	β_2	d_2	β_3	d_3		β_N	d_N
Gene code	3	23	1	41	4	12	…	2	33

（4）表格删除

对表述过于简单的表格，用文字同样能表述清楚时，可考虑对其改用文字表述而将表格删除。例如：表 6-19 改用文字可表述为：

The actual slot breadth under different line breadth compensation conditions are $b_1 = 0.061\ 1$ mm，$b_2 = 0.082\ 9$ mm，and $b_3 = 0.040\ 8$ mm respectively.

表 6-19 简单表格示例

Table × Actual slot breadth under different line breadth compensation conditions

b_1 (mm)	b_2 (mm)	b_3 (mm)
0.061 1	0.082 9	0.040 8

对表格进行拆分、合并、增设和删除操作后，要注意保证表序的唯一性，即同一论文中不能出现一号两表或一表两号的交叉、重叠，以及表序不连续等问题。

6.5.3 表格排式转换

受到表格幅面及排版空间等因素的限制，有时需要对表格排式进行恰当、灵活的转换。常见的表格排式有以下几种。

（1）表格分段排

当表格的横表头项目较多，全表呈左右宽、上下窄的状态，且一个表行排不下时，应将表格回行转排,即表格分段排(俗称折栏)。表格分段排后,其横表头不同而竖表头相同,上下部分表文间以双横细线相隔(表6-20)。

表 6-20 分段排示例表格
Table × Statistical results of inclusions characteristic parameters

Test sample No.	Number of inclusions	Average diameter of inclusions (μm)	Degree of soiling (%)	Surface density (number · mm^{-2})
1	607	1.431 98	0.056	232.879
2	641	1.185 37	0.048	245.924

Test sample No.	Percentage of inclusion size distribution (%)			
	<0.6 μm	0.6–1.0 μm	1.0–2.0 μm	>2 μm
1	45.5	30.8	13.0	10.7
2	64.7	21.1	5.9	8.3

(2)表格转栏排

当表格的竖表头项目较多,全表呈上下高、左右窄的状态,且单栏(或通栏)有充足的排版空间时,应将表格转栏排。表格转栏排后,其横表头相同而竖表头不同,排式上取左右并列方式,即一表双栏排,两并列部分中间(两栏之间)以双竖细线相隔(表6-21)。

表 6-21 转栏排示例表格
Table × Precise positioning results of the viscous target

Code	x	y	Code	x	y
334	90.69	106.58	313	289.68	437.80
333	281.41	101.08	324	94.97	273.46
332	474.97	95.93	323	285.39	268.86
331	669.30	90.69	322	478.79	264.48
314	99.58	441.52	321	673.38	259.74

(3)表格通栏排

对于正文双栏排版的论文,当一个表格用单栏难以排下,或即使能够排得下但排后其内容要素、形式和布局过于拥挤而表达效果不佳时,可将此表格改用通栏排。

(4)表格单栏排

对于正文双栏排的论文,当一个表格用通栏排版后,其周边还有很充足的富余空间,且其内容、形式和布局可调整为用单栏排版也有好的表达效果时,可考虑将此表格改用单栏排。

(5)无(或有)线表排

表格构成项目及表文较为简单时,可考虑排为无线表,如可以将简单有线表6-22排为表6-23的无线表;相反,当表格构成项目及表文均较为复杂且用无线表难以表述清楚时,可考虑将无线表排为有线表。

表 6-22 简单有线表示例表格
Table × Mass fraction of chemical composition of 400 MPa ultra-fine grain steel

C	Si	Mn	P	S	Cr, Ni	Cu
0.18	0.19	0.60	0.015	0.009	≤0.30	0.17

表 6-23 将表6-22有线表改排为无线表示例表格
Table × Mass fraction of chemical composition of 400 MPa ultra-fine grain steel

C	Si	Mn	P	S	Cr, Ni	Cu
0.18	0.19	0.60	0.015	0.009	≤0.30	0.17

(6)表头互换

有时为了充分利用版面,或受表文限制,或出于视觉美观考虑,在不影响内容正确表述的情况下,可考虑将横、竖表头作互换处理,见表6-24、表6-25。

表 6-24 表头互换前示例表格

	a	b	c
A			
B			
C			
D			
E			
F			

表 6-25　对表 6-24 表头互换后示例表格

	A	B	C	D	E	F
a						
b						
c						

（7）采用顶天立地式表格

当正文用双栏排时，如果表格幅面大而复杂，宜将表格排成"顶天（本页最上方）"或"立地（本页最下方）"的通栏形式，而一般不宜排成处于不同页面的"拦腰截断"形式。

（8）其他形式

表格排式还有跨页表、竖排表、侧排表、对页表、插页表等，实际中要根据具体情况灵活地采用恰当的排式。以跨页表为例，它既可能双跨单，也可能单跨双，或者继续往下跨，要采用最合适的形式。除单页码上的侧排续表外，续表宜重排表头，而且一般不排表序和表题，但应该加 Continued（续表）字样。对于顶线、底线为粗线、栏目线（或辅助线）为细线的表格，当它在某一页未排完时，其底线宜用细线，以表示此表格未排完，而续表的顶线既可用粗线以统一表头的线型类型，也可用细线以表示此表格是续表而非新表。

表旁串文也属于排式问题。双栏排时，表格左或右边通常不会有多余的空白，因此一般不能在表旁串文（表格较小情况除外），但通栏排时，表格左或右边出现多余空白的情况还是有的，这时可以在表旁（表左侧或表右侧）串文。

6.5.4　表格项目头设置

表格项目头位于横表头和竖表头的交叉处，横排表格的项目头应位于表格的左上角，项目头内被斜线分割为若干区域，区域内的文字用来表示表头、表文的共性名称。例如：表 6-26，其项目头内有两条斜线，分为三个区域，其中 Shaft orbit 为竖表头的共性名称，Freq. 为横表头的共性名称，Amplitude 为表文的共性名称。项目头内斜线的数量取决于表达需要，多为一条斜线，但三线表是没有斜线的。

表 6-26　项目头内有两条斜线示例表格
Table × Half power frequency of double spectrum and amplitude at the frequency of power frequency sliced parts

Amplitude (mm) \ Freq. (Hz) \ Shaft orbit	$\omega_r/2$	ω_r	$2\omega_r$
	0.75	0	0
	0	0.331 0	0.010 0
	0	0.500 0	0

实际中常出现项目头不规范的表格。例如：表 6-27 的项目头不规范，处理时应将项目头内的横表头 "Temperature（℃）"（其 8 个数值完全相同）提炼成共性文字置于表题中的合适位置，而且对项目头内的斜线分割、共性名称作规范处理，处理结果见表 6-28。

表 6-27　项目头不规范示例表格
Table × Proportion of each stage under different strain and different duration

Temperature（℃）	565	565	565	565	565	565	565	565
Strain（%）	Duration 10 s				Duration 20 s			
Proportion（%）	0.6	0.8	1.0	1.2	0.6	0.8	1.0	1.2
The 1st stage	0.128	0.155	0.180	0.196	0.120	0.127	0.205	0.221
The 2nd stage	0.712	0.675	0.644	0.601	0.709	0.683	0.557	0.529
The 3rd stage	0.161	0.170	0.175	0.203	0.171	0.189	0.238	0.250

表 6-28　对表 6-27 处理后的项目头规范示例表格
Table × Proportion of each stage under different strain and different duration at 565 ℃

Prop. (%) \ Duration (s) \ Stage	10				20			
Strain (%)	0.6	0.8	1.0	1.2	0.6	0.8	1.0	1.2
1	0.128	0.155	0.180	0.196	0.120	0.127	0.205	0.221
2	0.712	0.675	0.644	0.601	0.709	0.683	0.557	0.529
3	0.161	0.170	0.175	0.203	0.171	0.189	0.238	0.250

项目头内的栏目应有文字，即不宜空白，当项目头不以斜线相隔而只有一种标识时，其内文字宜"管下不管右"（按照需要，"管"右也可以）。栏目文字应能准确、全面、概括地表达出所"管"内容，范围较宽、难以提炼出确指文字时，可选用具有覆盖性的泛指类文字，如 Item、Name、Parameter 等公共性词语。

6.5.5　复式表头使用

一般情况下表头多为单式表头，有时按表达需要，可将单式表头处理为复式表头，或对复式表头进行改造，例如，可将表 6-29、表 6-30 处理为表 6-31，表 6-32、表 6-33 处理为表 6-34。

表 6-29　单式表头示例表格 1
Table × Test parameters of the glass tube and the cast tube in level condition

Test parameter	Glass tube	Cast tube
Velocity (mm·s^{-1})	40	40
Tractive force (N)	230	400
Current (mA)	600	900

表 6-30　单式表头示例表格 2
Table × Test parameters of the glass tube and the cast tube in bending condition

Test parameter	Glass tube	Cast tube
Velocity (mm·s^{-1})	40	40
Tractive force (N)	200	370
Current (mA)	550	860

表 6-31　将表 6-29、6-30 单式表头处理为复式横表头示例表格
Table × Test parameters of the glass tube and the cast tube in different test conditions

Test parameter	Level		Bending	
	Glass tube	Cast tube	Glass tube	Cast tube
Velocity (mm·s^{-1})	40	40	40	40
Tractive force (N)	230	400	200	370
Current (mA)	600	900	550	860

表 6-32　复式横表头示例表格 1
Table × Dispersion zone factor F using different forecasting methods

Temperature (℃)	Forecasting methods				
	Linear cumulative damage law	Strain range partitioning method	Strain energy partitioning method	Frequency correction method	Equivalent strain method
540	1.9	1.67	2.12	3.13	1.21
565	1.3	1.70	1.73	2.17	1.40

表6-33 复式横表头示例表格2
Table × Standard deviation S using different forecasting methods

Temperature (℃)	Forecasting methods				
	Linear cumulative damage law	Strain range partitioning method	Strain energy partitioning method	Frequency correction method	Equivalent strain method
540	0.106	0.104	0.120 0	0.248	0.007 70
565	0.063	0.090	0.091 1	0.099	0.003 16

表6-34 对表6-32、表6-33复式横表头进行改造示例表格
Table × Dispersion zone factor and standard deviation using different forecasting methods at different temperature

Parameter	Temperature (℃)	Linear cumulative damage law	Strain range partitioning method	Strain energy partitioning method	Frequency correction method	Equivalent strain method
Dispersion zone factor F	540	1.9	1.67	2.12	3.13	1.21
	565	1.3	1.70	1.73	2.17	1.40
Standard deviation S	540	0.106	0.104	0.120 0	0.248	0.007 70
	565	0.063	0.090	0.091 1	0.099	0.003 16

6.5.6 栏目取名

栏目用来标识栏内内容的特征和属性，当栏内内容表述事物的名称、行为或状态时，栏目名称一般是名词性的；当表述事物的数量时，栏目相当于标目，可用标目作栏目名称。栏目取名比较困难时，应避免不取名而在栏目内留下空白，或随意取一个泛指、笼统且不能表述相应特征、属性的词（如项目、参数、指标等）作栏目名称。栏目取名大体有以下几个方面的原则。

（1）正确归类、同栏同类

将所述内容正确归类，并尽可能将类别相同的内容放于表格的同一栏（横栏或竖栏）内。归类有误时，自然就难以或不便、不能给栏目正确命名。遇到这种情况时，需要对有关内容的位置进一步调整，必要时采用栏内加辅助线、栏名使用联合词组等变通的方法加以解决。

1）栏内加辅助线。见表6-35，第1栏内大部分信息的特征是Operating point，但概括不了Average value，因此在Average value所在行上方加一条贯穿表格左右的辅助线，问题就迎刃而解了。Pump test、Impeller calculation与其分项栏目间也分别用了辅助线。

2）相同属性栏目组合。见表6-36，第3栏与5~7栏的属性相同，应组合为相同栏目，位置上相邻连续（表6-37），组合后类属更加分明，表意更加清楚。

3）栏目使用联合词组。见表6-38，第1栏的内容明显分为两类，对应两个名词短语Straw types of straw in the rumen 和 disappearance increase of straw in the rumen，如果仅用其中一个作栏目名称就不能概括其共同特征，而表中用其名词性联合词组 Straw types and … in the rumen 就是恰当的。

表 6-35　栏内加辅助线示例表格
Table × Result comparision of impeller calculation and pump test ($n = 1450$ r/min)

Operating point	Flow rate ($L \cdot s^{-1}$)	Pump test		Impeller calculation		
		Lift (m)	Efficiency (%)	Axial force (N)	Lift (m)	Efficiency (%)
1	224	6.269	63.0	2 309	7.233	81.0
2	294	4.830	77.3	1 702	5.285	88.6
3	332	3.956	82.2	1 239	4.129	88.7
4	364	3.135	83.7	769	3.054	86.1
5	380	2.650	83.0	528	2.528	83.4
6	390	2.346	81.7	328	2.104	80.2
7	415	1.586	75.0	−60.5	1.299	69.1
8	431	1.070	64.4	−350	0.717	52.6
Average value	354	3.230	76.3	808	3.294	78.7

表 6-36　相同属性栏目组合前示例表格
Table × Relevant parameters of the snake

Number	Species	Mass (g)	Gender	Total length (mm)	Tail length (mm)	Abdominal width (mm)
Snake-A	Coluber spinalis	120	Female	870	160	15
Snake-B	Coluber spinalis	195	Male	910	150	18

表 6-37　相同属性栏目组合后示例表格
Table × Relevant parameters of the snake

Number	Species	Gender	Body parameter			
			Mass (g)	Total length (mm)	Tail length (mm)	Abdominal width (mm)
Snake-A	Coluber spinalis	Female	120	870	160	15
Snake-B	Coluber spinalis	Male	195	910	150	18

表 6-38　栏目使用联合词组示例表格
Table × Dry matter disappearance of straw (%)

Straw types and disappearance increase of straw in the rumen	Digestion time (h)		
	24	48	72
No ammoniated corn straw	38.21	48.88	63.89
Ammoniated corn straw	53.95	66.95	71.61
Percent of disappearance increase	15.74	18.07	7.72

(2) 分析归纳、抓住本质

栏目取名是通过抽取事物本质属性而进行逻辑上的归纳，选取贴切的栏目名称。例如：某栏内有 Taiwan、Hong Kong、Macao 三项，若此栏目取名 Country，绝对不容许，因为它们不是国家，可取名 Region。又如：某栏内有一组仿真参数 Natural frequency of servo valve (rad·s^{-1})、Bulk modulus of hydraulic oil (MPa)、Stiffness of vertical roll frame (MN·m^{-1})，若栏目取名 Quantity，就太一般化了，不如叫 Simulation parameter 更具体。再如：若把 Movement radius (mm)、Stroke volume ratio、Coefficient of volume utilization 这三个栏目取名为 Radius (mm)、Volume ratio、Coefficient，就不规范，栏目名称中必要的限定语不宜随意省略。

要善于思考，恰当用限定语，避免栏目归类不正确、取名不恰当。例如：见表 6-39，第 1 栏的名称 Diameter (mm) 未确切表示出其下数据的属性，这组数据表示加工孔直径，应取名 Diameter of machining hole；2~4 栏的名称从其下相应数据属性的角度来说是正确的，但其名称的共性部分较多，若不处理就显得啰唆。应将共性部分 Rotational speed（r·min^{-1}）抽取出来置于其上方作这三者的总栏目名称，其间再加一条辅助线，见表6-40。

表6-39 栏目名称修改前示例表格

Table × Production data in a machinery factory

Diameter (mm)	Rotational speed of BTA drilling hole (r·min^{-1})	Rotational speed of BTA trepanning (r·min^{-1})	Rotational speed of BTA boring hole (r·min^{-1})
50	<219	—	—
70	<160	<160	<170
85	—	191	191

表6-40 将表6-39栏目名称修改后示例表格

Table × Production data in a machinery factory

Diameter of machining hole (mm)	Rotational speed (r·min^{-1})		
	BTA drilling hole	BTA trepanning	BTA boring hole
50	<219	—	—
70	<160	<160	<170
85	—	191	191

（3）正确使用标目

量名称很长或不便在表格中列出时，在标目中可用其量符号代替量名称。

表格中量值的单位符号尽量表示在项目栏内，即排在量名称后面（表6-41），将单位排在说明栏内（数值后面）不规范（表6-42）。也不要混淆数值（Value）与量值表达式（Expression），而将量值表达式作为数值，见表6-43，在列名Value下列出了三个量值表达式（$r_p = 195$ mm，$P_i = 3.7$ kW，$F_{max} = 333\ 9$ N）是不规范的。要么改为表6-41所示的标目形式；要么修改列名，将Value改为Expression或Parameter expression之类的名称，见表6-44；也可以将量名称、量符号和量值（数值+单位）分别以列的形式单独列出，见表6-45～表6-47。

表6-41 单位符号位置规范示例表格

Parameter	Value
Radius of circle center (mm)	195
Input power (kW)	3.7
Max. contact force (N)	333 9

表6-42 单位符号位置不规范示例表格

Parameter	Value
Radius of circle center	195 mm
Input power	3.7 kW
Max. contact force	333 9 N

表6-43 量值表达不规范示例表格

Parameter	Value
Radius of circle center	$r_p = 195$ mm
Input power	$P_i = 3.7$ kW
Max. contact force	$F_{max} = 333\ 9$ N

表6-44 量值表达规范示例表格

Parameter	Expression
Radius of circle center	$r_p = 195$ mm
Input power	$P_i = 3.7$ kW
Max. contact force	$F_{max} = 333\ 9$ N

表6-45 量名称、量符号和量值单列示例表格

Parameter	Symbol	Value
Radius of circle center	r_p	195 mm
Input power	P_i	3.7 kW
Max. contact force	F_{max}	333 9 N

表6-46 量名称、量符号、数值、单位单列示例表格

Parameter	Symbol	Value	Unit
Radius of circle center	r_p	195	mm
Input power	P_i	3.7	kW
Max. contact force	F_{max}	333 9	N

表 6-47 量符号、量名称和数值单列示例表格
Extended Data Table × | Parameters used by AlphaGo

Symbol	Parameter	Value
β	Softmax temperature	0.67
λ	Mixing parameter	0.5
n_{vl}	Virtual loss	3
n_{thr}	Expansion threshold	40
c_{puct}	Exploration constant	5

表格中所有标目的单位相同时，可把共同的单位（限一个）提出来置于其共同的总名称（总标目）、各分量名称（可用量符号代替）、表题后面或表格顶线右上方，并加括号（表6-48～表6-51）；多数标目的单位（包括词头）相同时（表6-52），可把共性单位置于表格顶线右上方，其余单位仍留在标目内（表6-53）。

表 6-48 整表共性单位排在各量总名称（总标目）后面示例表格
Table × Relations between line breadth and worktable position

Worktable position S	Line breadth（mm）			Mean value b_{av}
	b_{w1}	b_{w2}	b_{w3}	
2	0.108 00	0.121 00	0.135 00	0.121 00
1	0.025 00	0.022 00	0.027 00	0.024 00
0	0.009 50	0.008 12	0.008 09	0.008 60
−1	0.032 00	0.029 00	0.028 00	0.029 60
−2	0.138 00	0.125 00	0.102 00	0.122 00

表 6-49 整表共性单位排在各分量名称后面示例表格
Table × Relations between line breadth and worktable position

Worktable position S	Line breadth			
	b_{w1}（mm）	b_{w2}（mm）	b_{w3}（mm）	Mean value b_{av}（mm）
2	0.108 00	0.121 00	0.135 00	0.121 00
1	0.025 00	0.022 00	0.027 00	0.024 00
0	0.009 50	0.008 12	0.008 09	0.008 60
−1	0.032 00	0.029 00	0.028 00	0.029 60
−2	0.138 00	0.125 00	0.102 00	0.122 00

表 6-50 整表共性单位排在表题后面示例表格
Table × Relations between line breadth and worktable position（mm）

Worktable position S	Line breadth			
	b_{w1}	b_{w2}	b_{w3}	Mean value b_{av}
2	0.108 00	0.121 00	0.135 00	0.121 00
1	0.025 00	0.022 00	0.027 00	0.024 00
0	0.009 50	0.008 12	0.008 09	0.008 60
−1	0.032 00	0.029 00	0.028 00	0.029 60
−2	0.138 00	0.125 00	0.102 00	0.122 00

表 6-51 整表共性单位排在表格顶线右上方示例表格
Table × Relations between line breadth and worktable position（mm）

Worktable position S	Line breadth			
	b_{w1}	b_{w2}	b_{w3}	Mean value b_{av}
2	0.108 00	0.121 00	0.135 00	0.121 00
1	0.025 00	0.022 00	0.027 00	0.024 00
0	0.009 50	0.008 12	0.008 09	0.008 60
−1	0.032 00	0.029 00	0.028 00	0.029 60
−2	0.138 00	0.125 00	0.102 00	0.122 00

表6-52　整表多数共性单位常规排式示例表格
Table × Comparison of the experimental data of high-speed shear and common shear

Shear mode	Section obliquity (°)		Section roundness (mm)		Section flatness (mm)	
	Rod end	Feed end	Rod end	Feed end	Rod end	Feed end
High-speed shear	0.50	1.28	1.14	1.35	0.67	0.86
Common shear	7.83	9.17	1.33	1.42	2.60	3.10

表6-53　整表多数共性单位排在表格顶线右上方示例表格
Table × Comparison of the experimental data of high-speed shear and common shear　　mm

Shear mode	Section obliquity (°)		Section roundness a		Section flatness b	
	Rod end	Feed end	Rod end	Feed end	Rod end	Feed end
High-speed shear	0.50	1.28	1.14	1.35	0.67	0.86
Common shear	7.83	9.17	1.33	1.42	2.60	3.10

6.5.7　表格数值表达

表格标目中量名称（可用量符号代替）和单位符号间的关系（量名称/单位符号=数值）与坐标图标目中量名称和单位符号间的关系（量名称/单位符号=标值）相同，其中"数值"是指表体中相应栏内的数字。根据这一道理，可以总结出表格中数值表达有以下原则：

1）可通过单位符号前加词头（或换作另一词头）或改变量名称前的因数的方法，使得表体中的数值变得简短（如处在0.1～1 000之间）。例如：表中某栏内的数值是"800，1 000，1 200，…"，相应的标目为Working pressure（Pa），则可将标目改为Working pressure（kPa），数值改为"0.8，1.0，1.2，…"；表中某栏内的数值是"0.008，0.012，0.016，…"，相应的标目为R，则可将标目改为$10^3 R$，数值改为"8，12，16，…"。

2）使用"量符号/单位符号=数值"这一原则，当量纲为一时，此原则可表示为"量符号（包含其前面的因数）=表体中相应栏内的数值"，若不按此原则，就容易出错。例如：在上例中，若不小心就容易错改为"$10^{-3} R$"，数值改为"8，12，16，…"，此时表示的数值就不是"0.008，0.012，0.016，…"而是"8 000，12 000，

16 000，…"了，后者是前者的10^6倍。

3）数值通常不宜带单位，如果遇到百分数，最好不直接用带百分号（%）的数字形式，而应将单位符号、百分号等归并在相应栏目的标目中。例如：见表6-54，将Hz和%放在表体中，显得不规范，应将它们放在标目内表达，见表6-55。

4）数值常用阿拉伯数字，居左或居中排。当同一栏各行的数值按同一标目处理时，其有效位数应相同（表6-54、表6-55）；但按不同标目处理时，则不要求其有效位数相同。例如：对于表6-56，若要求Min. value、Max. value、Mean value各自栏中的数值有效位数相同，则是多余的，而要求同一行中Min. value、Max. value、Mean value的有效位数相同则合理。可通过末位加0或按数的修约原则、四舍五入法来减少位数的办法对数值进行规范化处理。

5）上下或左右相邻栏内文字相同时，应重复写出，不要使用诸如Same as above、Same as left、""""/"之类的词语或符号代替，如表6-57使用Same above和""""来代替0.041，很不规范。正确的处理方法应该是这样的：要么不嫌麻烦，不管重复与否，直接将0.041写出即可，见表6-58；要么采用共用栏的方式，见表6-59，第3栏内的0.041本应重复写9次，按共用栏的方式处理后只写了3次，该数字在共用栏处

于上下居中位置。

表 6-54 表体内数值带单位符号和百分号示例表格

Table × Comparison of identification results

Modality order	Theory modeling		Fourier transform method		GH method	
	Frequency f	Damping ratio A	Frequency f	Damping ratio B	Frequency f	Damping ratio C
1	2.517 Hz	0.019 3%	2.218 Hz	0.015 9%	2.504 Hz	0.018 5%
2	7.648 Hz	0.015 5%	—	—	7.539 Hz	0.014 9%
3	12.135 Hz	0.013 8%	11.874 Hz	0.012 8%	12.064 Hz	0.013 3%
4	29.749 Hz	0.016 4%	29.632 Hz	0.013 6%	29.631 Hz	0.016 1%

表 6-55 表体内数值不带单位符号和百分号示例表格

Table × Comparison of identification results

Modality order	Theory modeling		Fourier transform method		GH method	
	Frequency f/Hz	Damping ratio A/%	Frequency f/Hz	Damping ratio B/%	Frequency f/Hz	Damping ratio C/%
1	2.517	0.019 3	2.218	0.015 9	2.504	0.018 5
2	7.648	0.015 5	—	—	7.539	0.014 9
3	12.135	0.013 8	11.874	0.012 8	12.064	0.013 3
4	29.749	0.016 4	29.632	0.013 6	29.631	0.016 1

表 6-56 表体内数值有效位数不同或相同示例表格

Table × Parameter measurement results

Parameter	Min. value	Max. value	Mean value	Relative error e/%
Mass (kg)	6.1	6.5	6.3	2.1
Length (mm)	117.325	118.640	117.983	1.0
Breadth (mm)	8.62	8.90	8.76	1.5
Volume (m^3)	0.092	0.121	0.107	0.6

表 6-57 表体内重复数字处理不当示例表格

Table × Wet peak and migration time of the export

Variable	Value	Wet peak of export (kg·kg^{-1})	Migration time (s)
Recycled air velocity (m·s^{-1})	1.5	0.041	87.3
	2.0	Same as above	63.3
	3.0	0.039	40.4
Recycled air inlet temperature (℃)	80	0.034	100.1
	100	0.041	87.3
	120	0.048	76.8
Disposal air velocity (m·s^{-1})	1.5	0.041	87.1
	2.0	Same as above	87.3
	3.0	〃	86.9
Rotational speed (r·min^{-1})	0.07	〃	84.1
	0.10	〃	86.3
	0.13	〃	87.3

表 6-58　表体内重复数字常规处理示例表格
Table × Wet peak and migration time of the export

Variable	Value	Wet peak of export ($kg \cdot kg^{-1}$)	Migration time (s)
Recycled air velocity ($m \cdot s^{-1}$)	1.5	0.041	87.3
	2.0	0.041	63.3
	3.0	0.039	40.4
Recycled air inlet temperature (℃)	80	0.034	100.1
	100	0.041	87.3
	120	0.048	76.8
Disposal air velocity ($m \cdot s^{-1}$)	1.5	0.041	87.1
	2.0	0.041	87.3
	3.0	0.041	86.9
Rotational speed ($r \cdot min^{-1}$)	0.07	0.041	84.1
	0.10	0.041	86.3
	0.13	0.041	87.3

表 6-59　表体内重复数字以共用栏方式处理示例表格
Table × Wet peak and migration time of the export

Variable	Value	Wet peak of export ($kg \cdot kg^{-1}$)	Migration time (s)
Recycled air velocity ($m \cdot s^{-1}$)	1.5		87.3
	2.0	**0.041**	63.3
	3.0	0.039	40.4
Recycled air inlet temperature (℃)	80	0.034	100.1
	100	**0.041**	87.3
	120	0.048	76.8
Disposal air velocity ($m \cdot s^{-1}$)	1.5		87.1
	2.0		87.3
	3.0	0.041	86.9
Rotational speed ($r \cdot min^{-1}$)	0.07		84.1
	0.10		86.3
	0.13		87.3

6.5.8　表文排式及标点符号使用

表文较长时回行排。叙述性表文可像正文一样正常使用各种标点符号，末尾是否加标点取决于表达需要。有时需使用短破折号、省略号（表示无此项）和数字 0（实际数值），或空白（表示数据或资料暂未查、测到或还未曾发现）。例如：表 6-60 中，B 乡 Wheat 栏的空白，表示未获得数据（种了小麦而未测定或未将数据报告给制表者）；C 乡 Corn 栏的 0，表示单产测定结果为零（如遭受自然灾害或其他原因而颗粒未收）；A 乡 Rice 栏的"-"，表示无此项即未种植水稻。

表 6-60　表格中格内短破折号、数字、空白适用场合示例表格

Table × Crop yield statistics of three townships

Township code	Wheat	Corn	Rice
A	4.20	4.65	—
B		4.35	4.95
C	4.05	0	4.70

表体中信息量较大、行数或列数较多时，为便于阅读、查找数据，可以适当归类、有规律地每隔数行或数列加辅助线隔开或留出较大的空行。

6.5.9　表中图及式子处理

表格中有时含有插图，即表中图，图具有系列性、完整性、对比性和列示性等特点，与表文具有互补性，组成一个统一整体，通常幅面较小，而且不应特别复杂。其幅面与表格的结构应匹配，若幅面较大，过宽或过高，表中相应位置区间上就难以容纳下该图，或将原本大小合适的位置区间过度撑大，导致表格局部变得凌乱，最终影响表格的整体效果。这时，可采用脚注的形式作规范化处理，如可将表 6-61 处理为表 6-62（其他方面也有一些处理）。

表 6-61　表中插图示例表格

Table × Comparison of experimental results

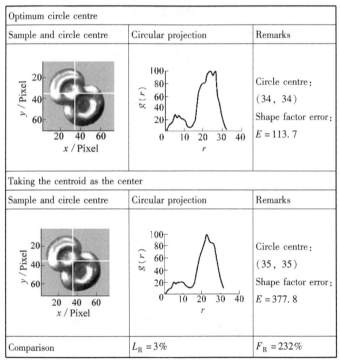

表 6-62　对表 6-61 中插图处理为脚注形式示例表格

Table × Comparison of experimental results

Type of circle centre	Coordinate of circle centre	Shape factor error E	Graphic of sample and circle centre	Graphic of circular projection
Optimum circle centre	(34, 34)	113.7	①	②
Centroid	(35, 35)	377.8	③	④
Relative error	$L_R = 3\%$	$F_R = 232\%$	—	

① ② ③ ④

6.5.10　表格与文字配合

表格应随文排，先引用，再出现，表文合理配合。表文配合不合理的几种常见情况：

1）正文中出现了某表格，但没有提及该表格，结果不知该表格是从哪里冒出来的；

2）正文中虽提及某表格，但没有出现该表格，即使费"九牛二虎之力"也找不到该表格；

3）正文中首次提及的表格的表序不连续，如根本就没有提及表格 3，就提及表格 4；

4）正文中出现的表格未按表序依次连续放置，如在表格 3 后紧接着出现了表格 8；

5）将可在同一页面内排为一个整表的表格拆分而排在不同页面，即一身分处异地；

6）将表格排在距离提及它的文字所在页面较远的另外页面，而实际上完全可以做到排在提及它的文字所在的页面或较近的页面；

7）正文中所述表格内容与相应表格中内容不对应，如正文表述了 calculation results as shown in Table 5，中心语是 calculation results，而 Table 5 表题的中心语是 working process，而且表格内根本就没有有关计算结果的内容，严重对不上。

6.5.11　卡线表转换为三线表

三线表是 SCI 论文广泛使用的表格形式，能用三线表清楚表述的就优先用三线表，但在有些情况下用三线表也未必妥当，例如对于复杂的数据表、统计表、计划表、日程表和工具表等，若用三线表，不一定方便表达。因此，写作时对于用表格呈现的内容应按实际情况来确定是否用三线表，还要掌握卡线表转换为三线表的方法与技巧。

卡线表转换为三线表时，项目头中的斜线消失了，项目头成为栏目，这时的此栏目无法同时标识横、竖项目栏及表体信息特征、属性，而只能标识其所指栏的信息特征、属性。为弥补三线表的这种缺陷，在转换过程中可采用以下两种方法：

（1）栏目选优去次

对转换前的卡线表项目头中的栏目作对比分析，选取其中最有保留价值的一个栏目，而将其他可有可无、次要的栏目去掉。例如：在卡线表 6-63 中，项目头的栏目 Performance 的含义不仅已蕴含在表题中，而且由其所标识的 Moving radius、Stroke volume ratio、Coefficient of volume utilization 的属性已非常明显，完全可以不用栏目 Performance 来标识，但应保留栏目 Line type（型线类型），因此可以进行栏目选优去次处理，处理后见表 6-64。

表 6-63　项目头内有两条斜线的卡线表示例表格
Table × Comparison of line performances

Line type	Moving radius (mm)	Stroke volume ratio	Coefficient of volume utilization
$s_1(\varphi)$	8.670	5.406	0.165
$s_2(\varphi)$	8.670	4.120	0.165
$s_3(\varphi)$	3.345	4.240	0.136
$\Delta(s_1 \text{ vs. } s_2)$		0.312	0
$\Delta(s_1 \text{ vs. } s_3)$		0.275	0.213

表 6-64　对表 6-63 按栏目选优去次转换成的三线表示例表格
Table × Comparison of line performances

Line type	Moving radius (mm)	Stroke volume ratio	Coefficient of volume utilization
$s_1(\varphi)$	8.670	5.406	0.165
$s_2(\varphi)$	8.670	4.120	0.165
$s_3(\varphi)$	3.345	4.240	0.136
$\Delta(s_1 \text{ vs. } s_2)$		0.312	0
$\Delta(s_1 \text{ vs. } s_3)$		0.275	0.213

（2）栏目选优移位

对转换前的卡线表项目头中的栏目作对比分析，选取其中有保留价值的若干栏目，再通过变换位置的方式将其中合适的栏目挪到横项目栏中。例如：在表 6-26 中，项目头中的 Amplitude、"Freq."应去掉（与表题的中心词重复），Shaft orbit 需保留，Freq.（空余较多，Freq. 可全写）所管的三类频率量应移到横项目栏，这样转换成的三线表见表 6-65。

表 6-65　对表 6-26 通过栏目选优移位转换成的三线表示例表格
Table × Half power frequency of double spectrum and amplitude at the frequency of power frequency sliced parts

Shaft orbit	Frequency (Hz)		
	$\omega_r/2$	ω_r	$2\omega_r$
◌	0.75	0	0
◌	0	0.331 0	0.010 0
◌	0	0.500 0	0

卡线表无论多么复杂，只要精心设计和安排均能将其向三线表合理转换。例如：表 6-66 项目头的斜线太多，不美观，排版易出错。按栏目选优去次、移位，表 6-66 可转换成三线表 6-67，转换后简洁、直观，内容和形式均很规范。表 6-66 项目头的栏目 Slip ratio（%）移到表 6-67 的横项目栏，栏目 Adhesion（N）的位置未改变，但不再是项目头中的一项，而是成为表 6-67 的一个栏目；表 6-66 横项目栏的 Maximum radial stress（kPa）与表题重复，不必再作表 6-67 横项目栏的栏目，表中省略的数字属 Maximum radial stress，单位 kPa 可统一标示在表题中。

表 6-66　较为复杂的卡线表示例表格
Table × Relationship between the maximum radial stress and slip ratio

④	③	②	① M&F	Maximum radial stress (kPa)									
				5		14		19		24		27	
				M	F	M	F	M	F	M	F	M	F
1 500		1	1	…	…	…	…	…	…	…	…	…	…
		2	2	…	…	…	…	…	…	…	…	…	…
		3	4	…	…	…	…	…	…	…	…	…	…
2 500		4	1	…	…	…	…	…	…	…	…	…	…
		5	2	…	…	…	…	…	…	…	…	…	…
		6	4	…	…	…	…	…	…	…	…	…	…

①Slip ratio（%）；②Sensor No.；③Measuring point；④Adhesion（N）；M—Measured value；F—Forecast value.

表 6-67　对表 6-66 通过栏目选优去次和选优移位转换成的三线表示例表格
Table × Relationship between maximum radial stress（kPa）and slip ratio

Adhesion (kN)	Measuring point	Sensor No.	Slip ratio（%）									
			5		14		19		24		27	
			M	F	M	F	M	F	M	F	M	F
1.5	1	1	…	…	…	…	…	…	…	…	…	…
	2	2	…	…	…	…	…	…	…	…	…	…
	3	4	…	…	…	…	…	…	…	…	…	…
2.5	4	1	…	…	…	…	…	…	…	…	…	…
	5	2	…	…	…	…	…	…	…	…	…	…
	6	4	…	…	…	…	…	…	…	…	…	…

M—Measured value；F—Forecast value

6.5.12　三线表项目栏配置

三线表中常出现项目栏配置不合理的情况，如缺少栏目、项目栏类型不恰当、栏目名称不正确等，项目栏配置不合理时，均应对其作处理。以下介绍三线表项目栏配置的几种方法：

（1）增设栏目

三线表无栏目时显得不规范。例如：表 6-68 无栏目，形式上是二线表，表意不明确，应该在表格上方从左向右加上相应的栏目 Fault time、Fault cause、Fault degree，见表 6-69。

表 6-68　可设计为三线表而设计成二线表的示例表格
Table × Fault occurrence

2018-10-13 16:55:26	Leakage of superheater side A	Serious	0.75
2018-10-13 16:55:28	Leakage of superheater side A	Very serious	0.97
2018-10-13 16:55:30	Leakage of superheater side A	Very serious	0.99

表 6-69　对表 6-68 增设栏目的三线表示例表格
Table × Fault occurrence

Fault time	Fault cause	Fault degree	
2018-10-13 16:55:26	Leakage of superheater side A	Serious	0.75
2018-10-13 16:55:28		Very serious	0.97
2018-10-13 16:55:30		Very serious	0.99

（2）确定项目栏类型

对于项目及层次较少的三线表，注意合理安排栏目，确定项目栏的合适类型（如横向或竖向），类型不当易导致表中内容无栏目或标目。例如：表 6-70 缺横向栏目，将其改为有横向栏目的表 6-71 后，不仅突出了 Pressure ratio 的地位，而且表体第 1 栏有了栏目 Contrast item。

表 6-70　缺少横向栏目的三线表示例表格
Table × Comparison of measured and calculated values of indicated power (kW) under different pressure ratios

Pressure ratio p_d/p_s	8	7	6	5	4
Measured value	1.700	1.670	1.610	1.500	1.340
Calculated value	1.724	1.670	1.576	1.464	1.130
Relative error (%)	1.160	0	-2.170	-2.640	-2.290

表 6-71　将表 6-70 处理为增加横向栏目的三线表示例表格
Table × Comparison of measured and calculated values of indicated power under different pressure ratios

Contrast item	Pressure ratio p_d/p_s				
	8	7	6	5	4
Measured value (kW)	1.700	1.670	1.610	1.500	1.340
Calculated value (kW)	1.724	1.670	1.576	1.464	1.130
Relative error $e/\%$	1.160	0	-2.170	-2.640	-2.290

(3) 栏目优先竖向排

安排三线表的项目栏时，为便于比较，版面允许时，一般宜将同一栏目下的内容（特别是数值）作竖向上下排列。例如：将三线表 6-72 的竖项目栏改为横项目栏后（表 6-73），同一量的数值处于同一竖栏内，自动取消了原来的表格分段排，表达效果大大提升。

表 6-72　应配置为横项目栏而配置成竖项目栏的三线表示例表格
Table × Minimum relative value of the geometry center distance

Eccentricity	0.05	0.10	0.15
Minimum relative value of the geometry center distance	0.000 018 40	0.000 165 11	0.000 629 83
Eccentricity	0.20	0.25	0.30
Minimum relative value of the geometry center distance	0.001 705 40	0.003 964 81	0.008 122 97

表 6-73　将表 6-72 竖项目栏改为横项目栏的三线表示例表格
Table × Minimum relative value of the geometry center distance

Eccentricity	Min. relative value
0.05	0.000 018 40
0.10	0.000 165 11
0.15	0.000 629 83
0.20	0.001 705 40
0.25	0.003 964 81
0.30	0.008 122 97

(4) 栏目合理归类、取名

栏目归类、取名是三线表项目栏合理配置的重要方面。表 6-74 以 CK/SD008 系列病毒的毒力与转化及其在雪豹体中的突变体为中心思想，设置 6 个栏目：栏 1 列示病毒的类型，栏 2 列示病毒导致雪豹体温的最大增加值，栏 3 列示病毒导致雪豹体重的最大减少值，栏 4 列示雪豹的存活数和总数，栏 5 列示通过 HI 抗体检测而所得血清转化的雪豹数量和总数（与第 4 栏数据相对应，产生显明对比），栏 6 列示呼吸道飞沫传染的效力。栏 2~5 涉及的实验对象（雪豹）又分为 Inoculated 和 Exposed 两类，接种是将病毒注射到雪豹体中，而暴露是将雪豹暴露在有病毒感染的自然环境中（观察飞沫传染），因此这些栏目下又分设 Inoculated 和 Exposed 两个子栏目。此表格栏目设计合理，归类全面，取名准确。

表 6-74　栏目归类正确的三线表示例表格[一]
Table × Virulence and transmission of CK/SD008 and its mutants in ferrets

Virus	Maximum body temperature increase (℃)		Maximum body weight loss (%)		Survival/Total		Seroconversion (HI antibody titers)		Respiratory droplet transmission
	Inoculated	Exposed	Inoculated	Exposed	Inoculated	Exposed	Inoculated	Exposed	
CK/S1053[a]	2.6	0.5	4.6	4.0	6/6	6/6	6/6(320–640)	0/6	None
CK/SD008	3.2	0.4	8.2	1.9	3/3	3/3	3/3(160–640)	1/3 (80)	Inefficient
CK/SD008-PB2/627K[a]	2.0	0.8	26.9	7.6	4/6	6/6	4/4(640–1280)	6/6(160–1280)	Highly efficient
CK/SD008-PB2/701N	0.7	0.7	28.9	12.6	2/3	3/3	2/2(320–640)	3/3(160–640)	Highly efficient
AH/1	1.7	1.6	4.9	3.2	3/3	3/3	3/3(320–640)	3/3(160–640)	Highly efficient

Data shown are from the animal in that group with the maximum body temperature increase or maximum body weight loss. Seroconversion was confirmed from the sera of ferrets collected on day 14 post-infection. [a]Each transmission test was conducted twice; the combined data from both experiments are shown.

再如表 6-75，误将最后两个栏目 Formation 和 Surface roughness 归属 Tool angle，因为表面成形和表面粗糙度属于表面形貌或表面质量，而根本不属于刀具角度范畴。因此，需要重作归类、取名处理，处理后见表 6-76，将最后两个栏目归于 Surface quality of products，并在相应辅助线的相应位置处断开，以与刀具角度类相区分。对于复杂的三线表，更要注意栏目的合理安排。

表 6-75　栏目归类错误的三线表示例表格
Table × Experimental relationship between tool angle and surface quality of products

No.	Tool angle (°)				Formation	Surface roughness Ra
	Tool orthogonal rake γ_0	Tool orthogonal clearance α_0	Tool cutting edge angle κ_r	Tool minor cutting edge angle κ'_r		
01	0	3	75	5	No	
02	0	3	75	15	No	
03	0	3	75	30	No	
04	0	5	90	5	No	
05	0	5	90	15	Yes	0.15
06	0	5	90	30	Yes	0.08

[一] 摘自 *Cell Research* 的 Original Article 类：H7N9 virulent mutants detected in chickens in China pose an increased threat to humans. *Cell Research* (2017) 27：1409–1421.

表 6-76 对表 6-75 规范处理后的三线表示例表格

Table × Experimental relationship between tool angle and surface quality of products

No.	Tool angle (°)				Surface quality of products	
	Orthogonal rake γ_0	Orthogonal clearance α_0	Cutting edge angle κ_r	Minor cutting edge angle κ_r'	Formation	Surface roughness Ra (μm)
01	0	3	75	5	No	
02	0	3	75	15	No	
03	0	3	75	30	No	
04	0	5	90	5	No	
05	0	5	90	15	Yes	0.15
06	0	5	90	30	Yes	0.08

第 7 章 SCI 论文数学式使用

科技论文特别是理论型论文通常不能没有数学式。数学式用来表达量与量之间的逻辑和运算关系，通常蕴涵或涉及较多、复杂的推导过程；是数字、字符的逻辑组合，常常需要使用较多的字符，字符还有字符类别及字体、字号、大小写、正斜体、上下标之分；数学式自身还有转行、接排等情况，在形式上应遵循有关标准、规范。这些均给论文写作带来不便。为实现数学式编排的标准化、规范化，提升论文组成要素间的协调与和谐，避免不必要的版面浪费，作者需要熟悉数学式的表达要求，掌握其编排技巧，做到其规范使用。

对 SCI 论文数学式使用，目前尚无专门的国际、国家标准可循，但就数学符号的规范使用来说，目前可以参照国家标准 GB 3102.11—1993《物理科学和技术中使用的数学符号》，该标准对常用数学符号的使用有明确的规定，对数学式的编排也有所涉及。本章参照一些国际名刊论文中有关数学式的写作范例，再基于上述标准，综合散见在有关标准、规范中的一些相关规定，并根据一些约定俗成及科技期刊编辑界的普遍做法，加上笔者的一些工作实践经验，对 SCI 论文数学式使用进行较为系统的阐述和总结。

7.1 数学式的特点

数学式具有以下特点。

(1) 所用字符种类多

数学式中可能有多种字符，如英文字母（拉丁字母）、希腊字母等，字符还有字体、字号、大小写、正斜体、黑明体、上下标之分；符号包括运算符号、关系符号、逻辑符号、函数符号等，这些符号均有各自的含义和用途。数学式中还可能包括缩写词语，可以说构成数学式的字符是五花八门的。

(2) 所用字符易混淆

很多字符在形体上相似，但表意和适用场合往往不同，式中选用的字符不合适时，容易引起误解。例如：a 与 α，r 与 γ，u 与 μ，v（英文字母）与 ν（希腊字母），w 与 ω，B 与 β，0 与 o，o 与 O，c 与 C，P 与 p 和 ρ，s 与 S，Z 与 z 和 2，x 与 X 和 χ，X 与 ×，1（字母）与 1（数字），s 与 5，Δ（Δ）与 $\triangle$，"《》"与"< <> >"和"≤ ≥"，"⟨ ⟩"与"< >"等，易混淆。

(3) 层次重叠多

字符在数学式中的上下、左右排列位置不同，其含义往往就会不同。例如：数学式中常含有上、下标，上、下标中可能还会含有上、下标（即复式上、下标）；有的数学式中含有繁分式（叠排式）、行列式、矩阵，排版较为复杂。

(4) 变化形式多

同一个数学式可以有不同的形式。例如：分数式可写成 $\frac{a}{b}$ 或 a/b 或 ab^{-1}。正斜体相同的同一符号在不同式中的含义可能不同，而正斜体不同的同一符号在相同或不同式中的含义不同。例如：Δ 可以表示有限增量、拉普拉斯算子，而 $\mathit{\Delta}$ 可以表示某一量的符号；π、e、d 分别表示圆周率、自然对数的底、微分符号，而 π、e、d 可分别表示某一量。

(5) 占用版面多

重要的数学式（一般需要对其编号）

应单独占一行或多行排，有的式子的前边或式与式之间的连词（包括关联词语）等通常要求单独占行排；含有分式、繁分式、行列式、矩阵等的数学式必然会占用更多的版面。

7.2 数学式表达要求

7.2.1 正文排式

数学式在正文中的排式分为串文排和另行排两种。前者是把数学式看作一个词语排在文字行中，即与文字混排在同一行，后者是把数学式另行排，即占独立的行，如以下示例中的 $k' \approx k$，$\omega'_0 \approx \omega_0$，$\partial A_b(\omega, F'(z))/\partial \omega$ 为串文排，而式（1）则为另行排（居左、居中均可）。

When the force differential $F'(z)$ is small enough, $k' \approx k$, $\omega'_0 \approx \omega_0$, in this case optimum working frequency ω_1 can be obtained at the frequency when $\partial A_b(\omega, F'(z))/\partial \omega$ reaches the maximum value. One can obtain the following equation：

$$\delta(A_b(\omega_1, F'(z))) \approx \frac{2}{3\sqrt{3}} \frac{Q}{k} A_b(\omega_0, 0) \delta F'(z). \quad (1)$$

实际中常将另行排作为重要原则，但无须对不必另行排的另行排。一般地，对于重要或较为复杂或需要编码的式子采用另行排，而其他式子采用串文排。式子另行排后，较为醒目，容易引起注意；较为复杂的式子要么较长，要么含有积分号、连加号或连乘号等数学运算符号，要么结构与形式较为复杂（如含有繁分式），虽不一定重要，但采用串文排有可能使同行的文字与上下行间的行距加大很多，造成版面凌乱，舒适感下降，甚至出现需要转行而又难以进行操作；对需编码的式子若不另行排，就无法将其编号排在其同行右端的位置上。

另行排的数学式既可居中排，也可居左排，取决于目标期刊的要求。

7.2.2 符号注释

数学式符号的注释（简称式注）是指对数学式中需要注释的量的符号及其他符号给出名称或进行解释、说明，必要时还要为量给出计量单位。通常是按符号在式中出现的顺序，用准确、简洁的语句、术语对其逐一解释，但对前文中已作过解释的符号则不必重复解释。对于数值方程式中的量还应接着注释语给出计量或计数单位。式注常见的有以下三类。

（1）行文式

将式注看作叙述性文字处理，Where 或 where、Here 或 here 之类的词语另行起，接排要注释的符号（注释对象）及注释语，符号与注释语间用 is（are）、express、represent 之类的词语相连。这种注释的突出优点是结构较为紧凑、节省版面，在 SCI 论文中较为普遍。例如：

Air supply flow rate of air compressor can be obtained by the following formula：

$$q_{ma} = 1.285 \lambda_a \frac{P_s}{U_c}. \quad (2)$$

Where q_{ma} is air supply flow rate（kg/h），λ_a is excess air coefficient，U_c is average working voltage of each battery（V），and P_s is output power of fuel cell stack（kW）.

（2）列示式

数学式列出后，另起行左顶格写出 Where 或 where、Here 或 here 之类的词语，其后接着依次写出注释对象、破折号及注释语。同一行注释对象为单一符号或多个符号，符号间用逗号分隔；一行排不下时转行排，行末一般加标点（如分号）；每个符号的式注单独起行宜应遵循以破折号对齐的原则；最后一个式注的行末加句号。例如：

From the largest gap, taking angle θ for the circumferential coordinate along the drill pipe, considering the changes of cutting fluid thickness caused by the changes of center position e, φ of drill pipe, according to the same type of problem treatment method in rotor dynamics and the lubrication theory, one can describe the problem as follows by using Reynolds equation:

$$\frac{1}{R^2}\frac{\partial}{\partial\theta}\left(\frac{\delta^3}{12\mu}\frac{\partial p}{\partial\theta}\right) + \frac{\partial}{\partial z}\left(\frac{\delta^3}{12\mu}\frac{\partial p}{\partial z}\right) =$$
$$\frac{1}{2}\left(\omega - 2\frac{d\varphi}{dt}\right)\frac{\partial\delta}{\partial\theta} + \frac{de}{dt}\cos\theta. \qquad (3)$$

Where δ—Cutting fluid thickness between the drill pipe and the inner hole wall of the workpiece, $\delta = C(1+\varepsilon\cos\theta)$;

R—Radius of the drill pipe;

ω—Rotational frequency of the drill pipe.

再如：

Multivariate quality loss function of components and parts is

$$L(y_1, y_2, \cdots, y_n) = \sum_{i=1}^{n}\lambda_i L(y_i), \qquad (4)$$

where λ_i—Weight loss of quality characteristic value y_i;

$L(y_i)$—Loss function of y_i.

量方程式用量符号表示量值（即数值×单位），与所选单位无关，式（3）、式（4）是量方程式，故无须对其中的量给出单位注释。数值方程式与所选单位有关，如式（2），应对其中的量给出单位注释，注释时单位符号是否加括号取决于目标期刊的规定。例如式（2）也可表达为列示式：

Air supply flow rate of air compressor can be obtained by the following formula:

$$q_{ma} = 1.285\lambda_a\frac{P_s}{U_c}. \qquad (5)$$

Where q_{ma}—Air supply flow rate (kg/h);

λ_a—Excess air coefficient;

U_c—Average working voltage of each battery (V);

P_s—Output power of fuel cell stack (kW).

以上式注部分中的单位也可以不加括号而直接放在注释语的后面，其前面用逗号，如 q_{ma}—Air supply flow rate, kg/h。

量符号与注释语间的破折号的意思为is、expresses、represents 或其复数形式，因此注释语前不必再出现这类词语。每一注释行中的量符号、破折号与注释语均可看作共同构成一个完整的单句（主谓宾句），各注释行则组成一个并列复句，其间多用分号（有时也可用逗号），最后一行的末尾用句号。式中还会出现量符号以外的其他符号，对其注释的形式同量符号。

（3）子母式

式注中的某一（些）项派生出的新的式子为子式，原式则为母式，排式如下所述。

1）子式与式注同行排，且子式排在式注后面，二者之间用逗号分隔，子式末尾加分号（若处于最后一行则加句号）。例如：式（3）第一个式注中的 $\delta = C(1+\varepsilon\cos\theta)$ 即为此排式。

2）子式单独起行排在式注下方，子式中的符号及注释语与母式中的应被一视同仁地按顺序统一列出。子式一行排不下时可转行排，末尾加分号，若处于最后一行则加句号。例如：

Equation of oil film thickness is shown as follows:
$$\delta = \delta_0 + \Delta\delta, \qquad (6)$$

where δ_0—Thickness of oil film regardless of bearing surface deformation,
$$\delta_0 = c + e_0\cos(\theta - \psi_0) + \tan\left(y - \frac{L}{2}\right) \times$$
$$\cos(\theta - \beta - \psi_0);$$

c—Radius clearance of the bearing;

e_0—Eccentricity of central section of the bearing;

$\Delta\delta$—Oil film thickness changes due to the generated elastic deformation by the effect of oil film pressure in the bearing surface.

3）子式与母式并列排，且排在母式下方，必要时还要为子式编号，子式中的符号及注释语与母式中的应被一视同仁地按顺序统一列出。对式（6）的这种排式是：

Equations of oil film thickness are shown as follows:
$$\delta = \delta_0 + \Delta\delta, \qquad (7)$$
$$\delta_0 = c + e_0\cos(\theta - \psi_0) + \tan\left(y - \frac{L}{2}\right) \times$$
$$\cos(\theta - \beta - \psi_0),$$

where　δ_0——Thickness of oil film regardless of bearing surface deformation；

　　c——Radius clearance of the bearing；

　　e_0——Eccentricity of central section of the bearing；

　　$\Delta\delta$——Oil film thickness changes due to the generated elastic deformation by ... bearing surface.

4）若对子式编号，则最好将子式与母式并列排，再编号；或将子式视作新的母式重新处理，即将子式、母式视作两个不同式子分别进行处理。对式（6）按前一种排式是：

Equations of oil film thickness are shown as follows：
$$\delta = \delta_0 + \Delta\delta, \quad (8)$$
$$\delta_0 = c + e_0\cos(\theta - \psi_0) + \tan\left(y - \frac{L}{2}\right) \times$$
$$\cos(\theta - \beta - \psi_0), \quad (9)$$

where δ_0 is thickness of oil film regardless of bearing surface deformation, c is radius clearance of the bearing, e_0 is eccentricity of central section of the bearing, and $\Delta\delta$ is oil film thickness changes due to the generated elastic deformation by the effect of oil film pressure in the bearing surface.

按后一种排式是：

$$C_k = \frac{\partial g(i_k, x_k)}{\partial x_k}\bigg|_{x_k = x_{k/k-1}} = \frac{K_1}{(x_{k/k-1})^2} - K_2 + \frac{K_3}{x_{k/k-1}} - \frac{K_4}{1 - x_{k/k-1}} - \frac{K_5}{(1 - x_{k/k-1})^2}.$$
(12)

4）编号的式子不太多时，常用自然数表示式号，如（1）、（2）等，但对性质相同的一组式子，则可以采用在同一式号后面加字母的形式，如（13a）、（13b）。例如：

$$v_1^n = C_d\left[F_{min} + (F_{max} - F_{min}) \times \frac{2R_P - H}{2R_P}\frac{f_1}{f_1 + f_2}\right] \times v_1^p, \quad (13a)$$

$$v_2^n = -C_d\left[F_{min} + (F_{max} - F_{min}) \times \frac{2R_P - H}{2R_P}\frac{f_2}{f_1 + f_2}\right] \times v_2^p. \quad (13b)$$

5）对一组不太长的式子，可排在同一行，而且可以共用一个式号。例如：
$$x_C = x_D + h_3\cos\psi, \; y_C = y_D + h_1\sin\psi, \; z_C = z_D. \quad (14)$$

6）同一式子分几种情况而上下几行并排时，应共用一个式号，各行的左端可加一个大括号且左端排齐，式号排在各行整体的上下居中位置，如式（15）。但是，对于一行排不下而排为几行的同一式子，式号宜排在最后一行的末端，如式（16）。

Equation of oil film thickness is shown as follows：
$$\delta = \delta_0 + \Delta\delta, \quad (10)$$

where δ_0 is thickness of oil film regardless of bearing surface deformation, $\Delta\delta$ represents oil film thickness changes due to the generated elastic deformation by the effect of oil film pressure in the bearing surface, and δ_0 is

$$\delta_0 = c + e_0\cos(\theta - \psi_0) + \tan\left(y - \frac{L}{2}\right) \times$$
$$\cos(\theta - \beta - \psi_0), \quad (11)$$

where c is radius clearance of the bearing, and e_0 is eccentricity of central section of the bearing.

7.2.3　式子编号

对再（或多）次被引用的数学式或重要的数学式，应按其在文中出现的顺序给予编号，以便查找、检索和前后呼应。为数学式编号有以下原则：

1）式号均用阿拉伯数字（自然数），置于圆括号内，并右顶格排。

2）各式子的编号应连续，不能重复，不能遗漏。

3）式后无空位或空余少不便排式号，或为排版需要，可将式号排在式下。例如：

$$\sigma_z = \begin{cases} H_{min} = \dfrac{b}{2}\tan\phi - (d + d'), \\ H_{max} = \dfrac{b}{2}\tan(\phi + \theta) - (d + d'). \end{cases} \quad (15)$$

$$f(z) = \| \boldsymbol{\Phi}(z,s) - \boldsymbol{a} \|^2 = (s+1)^2 K(z,z) -$$
$$2(s+1)\sum_{i=1}^{n} \alpha_i(s_i+1)K(z,\boldsymbol{x}_i) +$$
$$\sum_{i=1,j=1}^{n} \alpha_i \alpha_j (s_i+1)(s_j+1) K(\boldsymbol{x}_i, \boldsymbol{x}_j). \tag{16}$$

几个式子上下排,组成一组且共用一个式号时,各行式子的左端应排齐,式号排在该组式子整体的上下居中位置,必要时可在该组式子左端或右端加一个大括号,如式(17)所示。

$$\begin{cases} C_0 = c_d v_d + C_{\min}, \\ C_{\mathrm{op}}^{T_{\mathrm{le}}} = c_c T_{\mathrm{le}}, \\ C_i = (1-\alpha_i) C_0 (1+\sigma)^{-t_i}, \\ C_{\mathrm{op}}^{T_{\mathrm{rci}}} = \beta_{\mathrm{rci}} C_{\mathrm{op}}^{t_{\mathrm{pi}}} (1+\sigma)^{-t_i}, \\ C_{\mathrm{op}}^{t_{\mathrm{pi}}} = t_{\mathrm{pi}}^2 c_{\mathrm{pi}} v_{\mathrm{ri}} (1+\sigma)^{-t_i}, \\ R = \left(\lambda_0 C_0 + \sum_{i=1}^{n} \lambda_i C_i \right)(1+\sigma)^{-t_{n+1}}. \end{cases} \tag{17}$$

一组式子无须编式号但需要加大括号时,大括号通常加在这组式子的左端,尤其对于联立方程更应如此,如式(18)所示。

$$\begin{cases} x = x_b \cos(\beta+\gamma+\theta) + r_b \gamma \sin(\beta+\gamma+\theta), \\ y = x_b \sin(\beta+\gamma+\theta) - r_b \gamma \cos(\beta+\gamma+\theta), \\ z = p\theta. \end{cases} \tag{18}$$

7)正文中应先引用式子,再列出式子,正文中引用的式子编号与式后的编号宜采用相同的形式。避免 The above equation is the calculation formula of …; From comparison of the above equation and equation (3), it is shown that …; as shown in the following equation 之类的叙述,因为作者可能清楚 the above equation 和 the following equation 的具体所指,但对读者来说并不一定清楚,容易造成误解,若将这类叙述改用含有式号的表述,问题就迎刃而解了。

8)对文中未提及或不重要、无须编号的式子,即使采用了另行排,也不用对其编号。

7.2.4　式前用语

式前用语即数学式前的特别用语,是指数学式前面另行起排的短词语(一个词或一个短语)⊖,用来表示式间提示、过渡或逻辑关系,常见的有 if, let, suppose, assume, when, but, however, so, therefore, for example, here, where, from this, hence, the solution is, the result is, in generally speaking, from equation (×) it is known that 等⊖。例如:

Because the electromagnetic force $F = \dfrac{B^2}{2\mu} A$, the medial and lateral friction surfaces are symmetrical, so

$$\frac{F_o}{F_i} = \frac{B_o^2}{B_i^2} = \frac{\phi_o^2}{\phi_i^2} = \frac{R_2}{R_1}, \tag{19}$$

where　B—Magnetic flux density, accordingly

$$\frac{\phi_o}{\phi_i} = \sqrt{\frac{R_2}{R_1}}.$$

⊖　汉语中也称镶字,通常是6个字及以内的词语。

⊖　汉语中镶字分为单字、双字、三字及以上类:单字类有"解、证、设、令、若、当、但、而、和、或、及、故、则、如、即、有";双字类有"式中、其中、此处、这里、假设、由于、因为、所以、故此、于是、因而、由此、为此、因之、再者、亦即、代入、使得、便得、可得、求得";三字及以上类有"由此得、因而有、其解为、其结果为、一般来说、由式(×)可得"。

Combining equations (2) and (5) yields

$$\frac{\frac{a}{b_3}+\frac{h}{b_2}+\frac{a}{b_1}}{\frac{a}{b_3}+\frac{h+a}{b_1}} = \sqrt{\frac{R_2}{R_1}},$$

that is

$$b_2 = \frac{h}{\sqrt{\frac{R_2}{R_1}}\left(\frac{a}{b_3}+\frac{h+a}{b_1}\right)-\left(\frac{a}{b_3}+\frac{a}{b_1}\right)}$$

or

$$\frac{h}{b_2} = \frac{1}{b_1}\left[(h+a)\sqrt{\frac{R_2}{R_1}}-a\right]+\frac{a}{b_3}\left(\sqrt{\frac{R_2}{R_1}}-1\right).$$

此例中几个式子前面的 accordingly、that is、or 均为特别用语。用好式前特别用语是论文中式子使用的重要方面，有以下原则：

1）选择最恰当的词语（语义准确、形式简短）作特别用语，准确反映一个式子与上下文或上下式之间的逻辑关系。

2）特别用语通常左顶格排，并与式子起始端留出一定空位。为节省版面，只要不影响式子正常排，可考虑将特别用语与式子排在同一行。式子超过两行时，特别用语应另行排。

3）式子有编号时，其前特别用语应另行排，不宜与式子、式号排在同一行。

4）式子叠排时，其前特别用语宜另行排，若有必要排在同一行，则其应与式子主体对齐。

7.2.5 自身排式

对数学式特别是复杂的数学式，除实现其在正文中的排式外，还有其自身的排式。数学式自身的排式有很多方法和技巧，以下从几个方面来阐述：

（1）数学式主体对齐

主体对齐是指式子无论单行还是叠排式，无论是否有根号、积分号、连加号、连乘号，无论各符号是否有上下标，凡属式子主体的部分都应在同一水平位置上。属式子主体部分的符号有 =，≡，≈，≠，≤，≥，<，>，∉，⊄ 及分数线等。例如以下括号中的排式不妥当：

$$a = \sqrt{3} \quad (a\ =\ \sqrt{3})$$

$$\varphi = \sum_{i=1}^{n} N_i \varphi_i \quad (\varphi\ =\ \sum_{i=1}^{n} N_i \varphi_i)$$

$$\lim_{x\to\infty} f(x) = 0 \quad (\lim_{x\to\infty} f(x)\ =\ 0)$$

$$s = \frac{\frac{1}{2}\tan(\phi+\theta)-(d+d')}{\frac{1}{2}\tan\phi-(d+d')}$$

$$\left(s\ =\ \frac{\frac{1}{2}\tan(\phi+\theta)-(d+d')}{\frac{1}{2}\tan\phi-(d+d')}\right)$$

（2）数学式主辅线分清

叠排式中有主、辅线之分，主线比辅线要稍长一些，而且主线与式中的主体符号应齐平。同时，式号应放在式中主体符号或主线的水平位置上。例如下式

$$\frac{\frac{R_\mathrm{b}}{\sin\alpha}}{\frac{R_\mathrm{t}}{\cos\beta}} = \frac{R_\mathrm{b}\cos\beta}{R_\mathrm{t}\sin\alpha} \qquad (20)$$

不能排为

$$\frac{\frac{R_\mathrm{b}}{\sin\alpha}}{\frac{R_\mathrm{t}}{\cos\beta}} = \frac{R_\mathrm{b}\cos\beta}{R_\mathrm{t}\sin\alpha} \qquad (20\mathrm{a})$$

或

$$\frac{\frac{R_\mathrm{b}}{\sin\alpha}}{\frac{R_\mathrm{t}}{\cos\beta}} = \frac{R_\mathrm{b}\cos\beta}{R_\mathrm{t}\sin\alpha} \qquad (20\mathrm{b})$$

（3）数学式各单元排列层次分明

数学式中的一些符号，如积分号、连加号、连乘号、缩写词等，应与其两侧的另一单元的符号、数字分开，不能将其左右重叠、交叉混排在一起，但如果还有与其构成一体的其他字符，则不得与这些字符分开、错位排，以达到层次、关系分明。例如以下括号中的不妥当：

$$F = \int_{-\arccos\theta}^{\arccos\theta} f(x)\,\mathrm{d}x \left(F = \int_{-\arccos\theta}^{\arccos\theta} f(x)\,\mathrm{d}x\right)$$

$$\varphi = \sum_{i=r+s+t}^{n} x_1^r x_2^s x_3^t N_i \varphi_i \left(\varphi = \sum_{i=r+s+t}^{n} x_1^r x_2^s x_3^t N_i \varphi_i\right)$$

$$N = \sup_{0<\theta<2\pi} |f(re^{\mathrm{i}\theta})| \left(N = \sup_{0<\theta<2\pi} |f(re^{\mathrm{i}\theta})|\right)$$

(4) 数学式与其约束条件式左对齐排列

数学式（下称主式）如果还有一个或多个约束条件式，则应将主式与约束条件式作为一个整体左对齐排列，约束条件式排在主式的下方。例如：

The system level optimization model can be expressed as

$$\min\ f(z) = z_1^2 + z_2^2, \tag{21}$$
$$\mathrm{s.t.}\ \ J^* = (z_1 - x_1)^2 + (z_2 - x_2)^2 = 0.$$

Where z_1, z_2 are system level design variables, and J^* is system level consistency equality constraints.

(5) 函数排式严格

除指数函数外，函数的自变量通常排在函数符号的后面：有的加圆括号，函数符号与圆括号之间不留空隙，如 $f(x)$、$\cos(\omega t + \varphi)$ 等；有的不加圆括号，函数符号与自变量之间留空隙，如 $\exp x$、$\ln x$、$\sin x$ 等。对于特殊函数，其自变量有的排在函数符号后的圆括号中，如超几何函数（hypergeometric functions）$F(a,b;c;x)$，伽马函数（gamma function）$\Gamma(x)$，柱汉克尔函数（cylindrical Hankel functions）、第三类柱贝塞尔函数（cylindrical Bessel functions of the third kind）$H_l^{(1)}(x)$、$H_l^{(2)}(x)$ 等；有的直接排在函数符号后而不加括号，如误差函数（error function）$\mathrm{erf}\,x$、指数积分（exponential integral）$\mathrm{Ei}\,x$。函数变量与函数符号间应留空隙，如 $\lg x$、$\ln x$、$\sin x$、$\tan x$ 等。如果函数符号由两个或更多的字母组成，且自变量不含"+""-""×""·""/"等运算符号，则自变量外的圆括号可以省略，但函数符号与自变量之间需留一空隙，如 $\mathrm{ent}\,2.4$、$\sin n\pi$、$\cos 2\omega t$、$\mathrm{arcosh}\,2A$、$\mathrm{Ei}\,x$ 等。为了避免混淆，表达函数时应注意合理使用圆括号，如表示"$x+y$"的正弦函数时，应表示为 $\sin(x+y)$，而不是 $\sin x + y$，因为 $\sin x + y$ 是表示 $\sin(x) + y$ 或 $(\sin x) + y$ 之意。

复式函数中的括号都用圆括号或分别用各个层次的括号（如圆括号、方括号、花括号），如 $g(f(x))$ 和 $g[f(x)]$，$h(g(f(x)))$ 和 $h\{g[f(x)]\}$ 等。

在表达分段函数时，函数值、函数式与函数条件式之间留空或加标点；各函数值、函数式一般上下左对齐或左右居中对齐；各函数条件式上下左对齐或自然排在函数值、函数式的后面。例如以下分段函数，前两种排式较为规范，最后一种差一些：

$$F(x,y,z) = \begin{cases} -1 & (x \pm 1)^2 + y^2 < 0.1 \ \mathrm{or}\ x^2 + (y \pm 1)^2 < 0.1 \\ 0 & x^2 + z^2 < 0.1 \ \mathrm{or}\ y^2 + z^2 < 0.1 \\ 1 & x^2 + y^2 < 0.1 \ \mathrm{or}\ x^2 + y^2 > 4 \\ x^2 + y^2 & \mathrm{other} \end{cases} \tag{22}$$

或

$$F(x,y,z) = \begin{cases} -1, (x \pm 1)^2 + y^2 < 0.1 \ \mathrm{or}\ x^2 + (y \pm 1)^2 < 0.1 \\ 0, x^2 + z^2 < 0.1 \ \mathrm{or}\ y^2 + z^2 < 0.1 \\ 1, x^2 + y^2 < 0.1 \ \mathrm{or}\ x^2 + y^2 > 4 \\ x^2 + y^2, \mathrm{other} \end{cases}$$

不宜排为

$$F(x,y,z) = \begin{cases} -1, & (x \pm 1)^2 + y^2 < 0.1 \text{ or } x^2 + (y \pm 1)^2 < 0.1 \\ 0, & x^2 + z^2 < 0.1 \text{ or } y^2 + z^2 < 0.1 \\ 1, & x^2 + y^2 < 0.1 \text{ or } x^2 + y^2 > 4 \\ x^2 + y^2, & \text{other} \end{cases}$$

7.2.6 排式转换

排式转换是指变换式子的排法，即只改变形式而不改变表达内容，从而获得节省版面、提高排版效率和便于阅读的效果。例如：繁分式占用版面较多；长的根式转行较为困难甚至无法转行；指数函数 e^x 中，如果 x 为含有分式的多项式，其中还有多层次的上、下标问题，则字号较小，效果也不好，甚至给阅读带来困难。这些问题均可通过排式转换加以解决。

（1）竖排分式转换为横排分式

1）对于简单的分式（或分数）可直接转换为平排形式，即把横分数线（叠排式）改为斜分数线（平排式）。例如：可以将 $\frac{1}{8}$, $\frac{\pi}{4}$, $\frac{RT}{p}$, $\frac{dx}{dt}$ 直接改写为 $1/8$, $\pi/4$, RT/p, dx/dt。

2）对于分子和分母均为多项式的分式也可转换为平排形式，即把横分数线改为斜分数线，但转换时分子、分母都需加括号。例如：不能将 $\frac{x+y}{x-y}$ 简单地改写为 $x + y/x - y$，因为后者表示 x 与 y/x 相加再减去 y，改变了原意，正确的应是 $(x+y)/(x-y)$。对于分子和分母均为多项式的复杂分式，还要考虑转换后的实际效果。例如：若将

$$\frac{\dfrac{a_1}{a_2} + \left(\dfrac{a}{b} + m\dfrac{h}{2R}\right)}{\dfrac{b_1}{b_2} - \left(\dfrac{c}{d} + n\dfrac{h}{2R}\right)}$$

转换为

$$\{a_1/a_2 + [a/b + mh/(2R)]\}/\{b_1/b_2 - [c/d + nh/(2R)]\},$$

则转换结果很不直观，增加了阅读难度。因此，对于较为复杂的分式是否进行转换，还要看转换后的实际效果。

3）对于分子为单项式、分母为多项式的分式，可将横分数线改为斜分数线，分母加括号。例如：可将

$$\frac{ABC}{ax + by + cz + dr + es + ft + gu + hv + iw}$$

转换为

$$ABC/(ax + by + cz + dr + es + ft + gu + hv + iw)$$

4）对于分母为单项式、分子为多项式的分式，可将分母变为简单分式，分子加括号置于该分式后，并与其分数线对齐。例如：可将

$$\frac{ax + by + cz + dr + es + ft + gu + hv + iw}{ABC}$$

转换为

$$\frac{1}{ABC}(ax + by + cz + dr + es + ft + gu + hv + iw)$$

（2）根式转换为指数形式

根据表达需要，根式可转换为指数形式。例如：可将

$$y = \sqrt[n]{(a_1x_1 + a_2x_2 + a_3x_3 + \cdots + a_nx_n)^m}$$

转换为

$$y = (a_1x_1 + a_2x_2 + a_3x_3 + \cdots + a_nx_n)^{m/n}$$

或

$$y = (a_1x_1 + a_2x_2 + a_3x_3 + \cdots + a_nx_n)^{\frac{m}{n}}$$

（3）指数函数 e^x 转换为 $\exp(x)$ 形式

当指数函数 e^x 中的上标 x 较为复杂时，宜转换为 $\exp(x)$ 的形式。例如：可将

$$e^{\frac{l_1 + l_2}{\arcsin\frac{x_1}{y_1} + \arccos\frac{x_2}{y_2}}}$$

转换为

$$\exp\left(\frac{l_1+l_2}{\arcsin(x_1/y_1)+\arccos(x_2/y_2)}\right)$$

或

$$\exp\left(\frac{l_1+l_2}{\arcsin\dfrac{x_1}{y_1}+\arccos\dfrac{x_2}{y_2}}\right)$$

或

$$\exp((l_1+l_2)/(\arcsin(x_1/y_1)+\arccos(x_2/y_2)))$$

或

$$\exp\left((l_1+l_2)\Big/\left(\arcsin\frac{x_1}{y_1}+\arccos\frac{x_2}{y_2}\right)\right)$$

7.2.7 矩阵和行列式

矩阵与行列式的排式基本相同，不同的只是其元素外面的符号，矩阵用圆括号或方括号表示，而行列式用符号"｜｜"表示。以下以矩阵为例叙述其排式。

（1）矩阵元素行列适当留空

编排矩阵应在其行、列元素间留出适当宽度的空白，各元素的主体（主符号）上下左对齐或左右居中对齐，或各单元以其左侧或居中对称轴线分别对齐。对角矩阵中，对角元素所在的列应该明显加以区分，不能上下重叠。例如：

$$\begin{pmatrix}a_{11} & a_{12} & a_{13}\\ a_{21} & a_{22} & a_{23}\\ a_{31} & a_{32} & a_{33}\end{pmatrix}\text{不能或不宜排成}\begin{pmatrix}a_{11}a_{12}a_{13}\\ a_{21}a_{22}a_{23}\\ a_{31}a_{32}a_{33}\end{pmatrix}$$

$$\begin{pmatrix}a-b & b-c & c-a\\ r_1 & s_1 & t_1\\ r_2 & s_2 & t_2\end{pmatrix}\text{或}\begin{pmatrix}a-b & b-c & c-a\\ r_1 & s_1 & t_1\\ r_2 & s_2 & t_2\end{pmatrix}\text{不宜排成}\begin{pmatrix}a-b & b-c & c-a\\ r_1 & s_1 & t_1\\ r_2 & s_2 & t_2\end{pmatrix}$$

$$\begin{pmatrix}(a+b+3c)x & & \\ & (2a+3b+c)y & \\ & & (4a+b+2c)z\end{pmatrix}\text{不能排成}\begin{pmatrix}(a+b+3c)x & & \\ & (2a+3b+c)y & \\ & & (4a+b+2c)z\end{pmatrix}$$

（2）矩阵元素位置合理排列

编排矩阵应尽可能合理排列其元素的位置。矩阵元素的类别、位数可能全部或部分一致，或全部不一致，既可以是位数可长可短的数字，也可以是简单或复杂的数学式，还可以是阶数或大或小的模块矩阵。因此，矩阵元素位置的排列没有统一原则。以下为一般原则。

1）矩阵元素一般应优先考虑按列居左（或左右居中）位置排列。例如：

$$\begin{pmatrix}fN_x & 0 & u_0 & 0\\ 0 & fN_y & v_0 & 0\\ 0 & 0 & 1 & 0\end{pmatrix}\text{或}\begin{pmatrix}fN_x & 0 & u_0 & 0\\ 0 & fN_y & v_0 & 0\\ 0 & 0 & 1 & 0\end{pmatrix}$$

2）矩阵元素前面有正号（+）、负号（-）时，除常规的左对齐外，还可考虑以这些符号上下对齐；元素若为数字，还应考虑以数字的个位数或小数点等上下对齐。例如：

$$\begin{pmatrix}2\,800 & -1\,400 & 0\\ -1\,400 & 2\,800 & -1\,400\\ 0 & -1\,400 & 1\,400\end{pmatrix},$$

$$\begin{pmatrix}1.96 & -9.80 & 0\\ -9.80 & 1.96 & -9.80\\ 0 & -9.80 & 9.80\end{pmatrix}$$

3）矩阵元素有上下标或为式子时，除常规的左对齐外，还可考虑左右居中排列。例如：

$$Y_{i,M} = \begin{pmatrix} y_i & y_{i+1} & \cdots & y_{i+M-1} \\ y_{i+1} & y_{i+2} & \cdots & y_{i+M} \\ \vdots & \vdots & & \vdots \\ y_{i+N} & y_{i+N+1} & \cdots & y_{i+M+N-1} \end{pmatrix}$$

$$m(t) = \begin{pmatrix} a_1 + \mu_2 l^2 + \mu_1 r_1^2 & (a_2 + \mu_2 l r_r)\cos\Delta\varphi_0 \\ (a_2 + \mu_2 l r_r)\cos\Delta\varphi_0 & a_3 + \mu_2 r_2^2 \end{pmatrix}$$

（3）矩阵中省略号的正确使用

编排含有省略号的矩阵应注意，省略号有横排和竖排之分，最好区分。例如：

$$A = \begin{pmatrix} a_{11} & a_{12} & \cdots & a_{1n} \\ a_{21} & a_{22} & \cdots & a_{2n} \\ \vdots & \vdots & & \vdots \\ a_{m1} & a_{m2} & \cdots & a_{mn} \end{pmatrix} \text{不宜排成}$$

$$A = \begin{pmatrix} a_{11} & a_{12} & \cdots & a_{1n} \\ a_{21} & a_{22} & \cdots & a_{2n} \\ \cdots & \cdots & & \cdots \\ a_{m1} & a_{m2} & \cdots & a_{mn} \end{pmatrix}$$

（4）对角矩阵和单位矩阵简化编排

对角矩阵和单位矩阵有其独特的简化编排形式，要注意使用。例如：对角矩阵

$$\begin{pmatrix} \lambda_1 & 0 & \cdots & 0 \\ 0 & \lambda_2 & \cdots & 0 \\ \vdots & \vdots & & \vdots \\ 0 & 0 & \cdots & \lambda_n \end{pmatrix} \text{可排为}$$

$$\begin{pmatrix} \lambda_1 & & & 0 \\ & \lambda_2 & & \\ & & \ddots & \\ 0 & & & \lambda_n \end{pmatrix} \text{或} \begin{pmatrix} \lambda_1 & & & \\ & \lambda_2 & & \\ & & \ddots & \\ & & & \lambda_n \end{pmatrix}$$

或直接简记为 $\mathbf{diag}(\lambda_1 \quad \lambda_2 \quad \cdots \quad \lambda_n)$。单位矩阵

$$\begin{pmatrix} 1 & 0 & \cdots & 0 \\ 0 & 1 & \cdots & 0 \\ \vdots & \vdots & & \vdots \\ 0 & 0 & \cdots & 1 \end{pmatrix} \text{可排为}$$

$$\begin{pmatrix} 1 & & & 0 \\ & 1 & & \\ & & \ddots & \\ 0 & & & 1 \end{pmatrix} \text{或} \begin{pmatrix} 1 & & & \\ & 1 & & \\ & & \ddots & \\ & & & 1 \end{pmatrix}$$

也可直接记为 $\mathbf{E}$ 或 $\mathbf{I}$。

（5）零矩阵的编排

有时矩阵中的元素为零矩阵（即元素全为数字0的矩阵），笔者认为零矩阵最好用黑（加粗）斜体数字 $\mathbf{0}$ 表示（注意：有的期刊要求用正体）。例如：下式等号后右侧矩阵中的 $\mathbf{0}$ 即为零矩阵元素，而左侧矩阵中的0则全部是数字元素：

$$G = \begin{pmatrix} fN_x & 0 & u_0 & 0 \\ 0 & fN_y & v_0 & 0 \\ 0 & 0 & 1 & 0 \end{pmatrix} \begin{pmatrix} \mathbf{R} & \mathbf{T} + \Delta \mathbf{T} \\ \mathbf{0} & \mathbf{I} \end{pmatrix}$$

（6）矩阵符号的字体选用

矩阵的主符号用单个的黑（加粗）斜体字母表示（必要时可加上下标，上下标为矩阵符号时也宜用黑（加粗）斜体字母表示）。例如：将矩阵 $\mathbf{A}$ 表示成 A、$[A]$、$\vec{A}$、$(\vec{A})$ 或字符串如 matrix、MA、matrixA 之类的形式均不规范。矩阵元素也可为矩阵或包含矩阵的表达式，只要是矩阵，其主符号就宜用单个的黑（加粗）斜体字母表示。

7.2.8 合理转行

一个长的数学式若一行（通栏一行或双栏一行）排不下，或一行虽能排下但排版效果不好而又有充足的版面，就应该转行排。转行有一定规则，不提倡随意转行。

（1）数学式转行基本规则

数学式转行应以转行后不致引起误解为原则（这里的误解是指将转行下来的式子部分误解为新的式子，即本来对一个式子转行，但转行后便在形式上成为几个上下排列的"不同"式子，使读者误以为是不同的式子，而不是一个式子分成几个部分）。转行时应避免这一问题，否则就容易出错。针

对这一问题，GB 3102.11—1993 对数学式转行有明确规定："当一个表示式或方程式需断开、用两行或多行来表示时，最好在紧靠其中记号 =，+，-，±，∓，×，·或/后断开，而在下一行开头不应重复这一记号。"例如：

$$F(x) = P_1(x) + P_2(x) + \int_a^b f_1(x)\mathrm{d}x + \int_b^c f_2(x)\mathrm{d}x + \int_c^d f_3(x)\mathrm{d}x - \int_d^\infty f_4(x)\mathrm{d}x = 0 \tag{23}$$

以上规定是数学式转行的基本规则（以下称转行新规则），与过去约定俗成的数学式转行规则（以下称转行旧规则）有很大差别。转行旧规则有两种：一种是在 =，+，-，±，∓，×，·或/等符号前转行，并把这类符号放在下一行开头，例如式（24）；另一种是在上一行末尾和下一行开头同时写出这类符号，例如式（25）。

$$F(x) = P_1(x) + P_2(x) + \int_a^b f_1(x)\mathrm{d}x + \int_b^c f_2(x)\mathrm{d}x + \int_c^d f_3(x)\mathrm{d}x \\ - \int_d^\infty f_4(x)\mathrm{d}x = 0 \tag{24}$$

$$F(x) = P_1(x) + P_2(x) + \int_a^b f_1(x)\mathrm{d}x + + \int_b^c f_2(x)\mathrm{d}x + \int_c^d f_3(x)\mathrm{d}x - \\ - \int_d^\infty f_4(x)\mathrm{d}x = 0 \tag{25}$$

对式（23），读者看到第二行末尾的"-"就知道式子没有结束，第三行是由第二行转来的，这时的"-"既是运算符，又起连字符的作用，因此不会产生误解；式（24），看到第二行既可以理解为式子没有结束，第三行是由第二行转来的，又可以理解为第一、二行和第三行是两个不同的式子，因此容易产生误解；式（25），虽然不易产生误解，但显得有些啰唆。转行新规则与旧规则相比明显有不易引起歧义的优点，这是新规则的科学之处。国际期刊对式子转行较为随意（更多是以旧规则来转行的）。笔者认为，在不致引起误解时，用旧规则对式子转行没有问题，这也是 SCI 论文的普遍做法，但用旧规则转行确实容易引起误解时，还是提倡用新规则来转行。

使用转行新规则转行时应特别注意：应优先在 =，≡，≈，≠，>，<，≥，≤ 等关系符号之后转行，其次在 +，-，×（·），/（÷）等运算符号之后转行，不得已时才在 Σ，Π，$\int$，$\dfrac{\mathrm{d}y}{\mathrm{d}x}$ 等运算符号或 lim, exp, sin, cos 等缩写符号之前转行，且不得将 Σ，Π，$\int$，lim, exp 等符号与其对象拆开转行。例如：不可将式（23）转行排为

$$F(x) = P_1(x) + P_2(x) + \int_a^b f_1(x)\mathrm{d}x + \int_b^c f_2(x)\mathrm{d}x + \int_c^d f_3(x)\mathrm{d}x - \int_d^\infty f_4(x)\mathrm{d}x = 0$$

又如，不可将

$$L = \sum_{i=1}^n \left[\alpha_i (s_i+1)^2 K(\boldsymbol{x}_i, \boldsymbol{x}_j)\right] - \sum_{i=1}^n \sum_{j=1}^n \left[\alpha_i \alpha_j (s_i+1)(s_j+1) K(\boldsymbol{x}_i, \boldsymbol{x}_j)\right] \tag{26}$$

转行排为

$$L = \sum_{i=1}^{n} \left[\alpha_i (s_i + 1)^2 K(\boldsymbol{x}_i, \boldsymbol{x}_j) \right] - \sum_{i=1}^{n}$$

$$\sum_{j=1}^{n} \left[\alpha_i \alpha_j (s_i + 1)(s_j + 1) K(\boldsymbol{x}_i, \boldsymbol{x}_j) \right]$$

数学式转行后不得改变其原义,不得令人费解或容易产生歧义、误解,在省略的乘号后转行时,最好在上一行末尾补写乘号(如×或·)。例如:不可将

$$W = -\frac{t_1^2}{2d^2} - d^2 c^2 t_2^2 + 4\pi d^2 c(t_1 - t_c)(t_2 - t_c)(f - f_c) = 0 \quad (27)$$

转行排为

$$W = -\frac{t_1^2}{2d^2} - d^2 c^2 t_2^2 + 4\pi d^2 c$$

$$(t_1 - t_c)(t_2 - t_c)(f - f_c) = 0$$

这样转行排后,非常容易将转行后的两行式子误解为两个不同的式子,即使能判断、猜测出这两行式子为同一式子,也需一番推敲、验证,既费时又费力。这种错误在于,在省略的乘号后转行时没有在上行末补写乘号,故式(27)的正确转行排法是

$$W = -\frac{t_1^2}{2d^2} - d^2 c^2 t_2^2 + 4\pi d^2 c \times$$

$$(t_1 - t_c)(t_2 - t_c)(f - f_c) = 0$$

(2)数学式转行的排式

数学式转行的排式需要根据排版空间、表达效果、式间一致性等多种因素来确定,不可生搬硬套地将一篇论文所有数学式的转行只按一种形式来进行。下面介绍数学式转行的几种常见排式,并给出基于转行新规则转行的实例。

1)居左(居中)排式。这是指式中首行及转下来的各行均以所在行(或栏)的左右边界为基准而居左(居中)排版。此排式中,首行和其他行均居左(居中)排版。例如:

$$C_{km} v_k + \int_\Gamma p_{km}^* v_k \mathrm{d}\Gamma = \int_\Gamma U_{km}^* \dot{p}_k \mathrm{d}\Gamma + \int_\Omega U_{km}^* \dot{F}_k \mathrm{d}\Omega +$$

$$\int_\Omega U_{km,j}^* \dot{\sigma}_{kj}^\mathrm{p} \mathrm{d}\Omega + \int_\Gamma U_{km}^* G_{kjpq}^\mathrm{i} v_{p,q}^\mathrm{g} n_j \mathrm{d}\Gamma$$

再如:

$$\rho \left(\frac{\partial v}{\partial t} + u \frac{\partial v}{\partial x} + v \frac{\partial v}{\partial y} + w \frac{\partial v}{\partial z^*} \right) =$$

$$-\left(\frac{\partial p}{\partial y} + \frac{\partial p}{\partial z^*} \frac{\partial z^*}{\partial y} \right) + \mu \left(\frac{\partial^2 v}{\partial x^2} + \frac{\partial^2 v}{\partial y^2} + S \frac{\partial^2 v}{\partial z^{*2}} \right) + C_v + F_y$$

2)错开排式。这是指式中首行一般居左(居中)排,转下的各行向右缩进适当距离,以首行中的主要关系符号(如等号)右侧所在位置或其他位置为准,而左端对齐排版。例如:

$$\sigma_z = -\frac{\lambda(\lambda + G)}{\lambda^* + G} \delta_\mathrm{h} (\varepsilon_{x\mathrm{n}} + \varepsilon_{y\mathrm{n}}) \times$$

$$(D_7 \kappa_1 \cosh \kappa_1 z + D_8 \kappa_2 \cosh \kappa_2 z + D_9) +$$

$$\lambda \varepsilon_{x\mathrm{n}} (D_1 \cosh \kappa_1 z + D_2 \cosh \kappa_2 z + D_3) +$$

$$\lambda \varepsilon_{y\mathrm{n}} (D_4 \cosh \kappa_1 z + D_5 \cosh \kappa_2 z + D_6)$$

再如：

$$\begin{cases} c_1[\sin\lambda + K_1(\cosh\lambda - \cos\lambda)/(2\lambda)] + \\ c_3[\sinh\lambda + K_1(\cosh\lambda - \cos\lambda)/(2\lambda)] = 0 \\ c_1\{[K_1K_2/(2\lambda) - \lambda]\sin\lambda + (K_1/2 + K_2)\cos\lambda + \\ K_1K_2\sinh\lambda/(2\lambda) + K_1\cosh\lambda/2\} + \\ c_3\{K_1K_2\sin\lambda/(2\lambda) + K_1\cos\lambda/2 + [\lambda + \\ K_1K_2/(2\lambda)]\sinh\lambda + (K_1/2 + K_2)\cosh\lambda\} = 0 \end{cases}$$

3) 等号对齐排式。这是指以各行中的等号对齐排版。例如：

$$\begin{aligned} \dot{e} &= \dot{x}_M - \dot{x} = A_M x_M + B_M u - (Ax + Bu) \\ &= (A_M x_M - A_M x) + A_M x - Ax + B_M u - Bu \\ &= A_M e + (A_M - A)x + (B_M - B)u \end{aligned}$$

（3）长分式的转行

分式原则上不能转行，但其分子或分母过长而需要转行时，可采用以下方式转行。

1) 先把长分式的分母写成负数幂形式，再按转行规则转行。例如：可将

$$F(x) = \frac{f_n(x)f_{n+1}(x) + f_{n+2}(x)f_{n+3}(x) + f_{n+4}(x)f_{n+5}(x) + f_{n+6}(x)f_{n+7}(x)}{\sum_i a_i + \sum_j b_j + \sum_k c_k - (a_n + b_n + c_n)} \tag{28}$$

转行排为

$$F(x) = [f_n(x)f_{n+1}(x) + f_{n+2}(x)f_{n+3}(x) + f_{n+4}(x)f_{n+5}(x) + \\ f_{n+6}(x)f_{n+7}(x)] \times \left[\sum_i a_i + \sum_j b_j + \sum_k c_k - (a_n + b_n + c_n)\right]^{-1}$$

2) 若长分式的分子、分母均由相乘因式构成，则可在适当的相乘因式处转行，并在上一行末尾加上乘号。例如：可将

$$\frac{(a_1 + a_2 + a_3 + a_4)(b_1 + b_2 + b_3 + b_4)(c_1 + c_2 + c_3 + c_4)(d_1 + d_2 + d_3 + d_4)}{(X_1^2 + X_2^2 + X_3^2 + X_4^2)(Y_1^2 + Y_2^2 + Y_3^2 + Y_4^2)}$$

转行排为

$$\frac{(a_1 + a_2 + a_3 + a_4)(b_1 + b_2 + b_3 + b_4)}{X_1^2 + X_2^2 + X_3^2 + X_4^2} \times \\ \frac{(c_1 + c_2 + c_3 + c_4)(d_1 + d_2 + d_3 + d_4)}{Y_1^2 + Y_2^2 + Y_3^2 + Y_4^2}$$

3) 若长分式的分子、分母均为多项式，则可在运算符号"＋""－"后断开并转行，在上一行末尾和下一行开头分别加上符号"→""←"。例如：可将式（28）排为

$$F(x) = \frac{f_n(x)f_{n+1}(x) + f_{n+2}(x)f_{n+3}(x) + }{\sum_i a_i + \sum_j b_j + \sum_k c_k -} \rightarrow \\ \leftarrow \frac{f_{n+4}(x)f_{n+5}(x) + f_{n+6}(x)f_{n+7}(x)}{(a_n + b_n + c_n)}$$

4) 若长分式的分子为较长的多项式，分母（不论是否为多项式）却较短，则可

以按照转行规则在分子的适当位置转行,并将该长分式分为上下两个分式,这两个分式的分母相同(均为原长分式的分母)。例如:

$$\frac{\sum_{i=1}^{m}\sum_{j=1}^{n}\left[\frac{q}{2}+\frac{1}{2}\Delta x\frac{\partial f(\xi_i,y_{j-1})}{\partial x}+\frac{1}{2}\Delta y\frac{\partial f(x_{i-1},\eta_j)}{\partial y}+\frac{1}{4}\Delta x\Delta y\frac{\partial f(\xi_i,\zeta_j)}{\partial x\partial y}\right]}{mn}$$

可转行排为

$$\frac{\sum_{i=1}^{m}\sum_{j=1}^{n}\left[\frac{q}{2}+\frac{1}{2}\Delta x\frac{\partial f(\xi_i,y_{j-1})}{\partial x}\right.}{mn}+$$

$$\frac{\left.\frac{1}{2}\Delta y\frac{\partial f(x_{i-1},\eta_j)}{\partial y}+\frac{1}{4}\Delta x\Delta y\frac{\partial f(\xi_i,\zeta_j)}{\partial x\partial y}\right]}{mn}$$

(4) 根式的转行

较长或复杂的根式转行时,可先改写成分数指数的形式,然后按转行规则转行。例如:

$$\sqrt[3]{\frac{a_1}{3}\left(\frac{13\pi}{6}\right)^3+\frac{b_1}{2}\left(\frac{13\pi}{6}\right)^2+c_1\left(\frac{13\pi}{6}\right)-\frac{a_2}{3}\left(\frac{25\pi}{8}\right)^3-\frac{b_2}{2}\left(\frac{25\pi}{8}\right)^2-c_2\left(\frac{25\pi}{8}\right)}$$

可转行排为

$$\left[\frac{a_1}{3}\left(\frac{13\pi}{6}\right)^3+\frac{b_1}{2}\left(\frac{13\pi}{6}\right)^2+c_1\left(\frac{13\pi}{6}\right)-\right.$$

$$\left.\frac{a_2}{3}\left(\frac{25\pi}{8}\right)^3-\frac{b_2}{2}\left(\frac{25\pi}{8}\right)^2-c_2\left(\frac{25\pi}{8}\right)\right]^{\frac{1}{3}}$$

(5) 矩阵、行列式的转行

矩阵、行列式一般不宜转行,但在一行或一栏(半栏或通栏)内排不下时,可采用灵活的变换方式将其排为一行,在不得已的情况下当然可以转行排。具体有以下几种情况。

1) 如果矩阵或行列式的元素为较长的数学式而难以在一行内排下,则可以使用字符来代替这一(些)较长的元素,同时在矩阵或行列式的下方对所用的每个字符加以解释说明,以使矩阵或行列式得以简化而将其整体宽度减小到合适的宽度。例如:

$$A=\begin{pmatrix}0&0&1&0\\0&0&0&1\\a_1&a_2&a_3&a_4\\b_1&b_2&b_3&b_4\end{pmatrix}$$

$a_1=-[(u^2-F)c_{11}+\lambda_1^4+\bar{g}e_{11}]$; $a_2=-[(u^2-F)c_{12}+\bar{g}e_{12}]$; $a_3=-(2M_rub_{11}+\alpha\lambda_1^4)$; $a_4=-2M_rub_{12}$; $b_1=-[(u^2-F)c_{21}+\bar{g}e_{21}]$; $b_2=-[(u^2-F)c_{22}+\lambda_2^4+\bar{g}e_{22}]$; $b_3=-2M_rub_{21}$; $b_4=-(2M_rub_{22}+\alpha\lambda_2^4)$。

2) 如果矩阵或行列式的元素为较长的数学式而难以在一行内排下,也可以考虑将这一(些)较长的元素在适当位置转行,以使矩阵或行列式整体宽度减小而在一行内排下。例如:

$$\begin{vmatrix} \sin\lambda + K_1(\cosh\lambda - \cos\lambda)/(2\lambda) & \sinh\lambda + K_1(\cosh\lambda - \cos\lambda)/(2\lambda) \\ [K_1K_2/(2\lambda) - \lambda]\sin\lambda + (K_1/2 + K_2)\cos\lambda + K_1K_2\sinh\lambda/(2\lambda) + K_1\cosh\lambda/2 & K_1K_2\sin\lambda/(2\lambda) + K_1\cos\lambda/2 + [\lambda + K_1K_2/(2\lambda)]\sinh\lambda + (K_1/2 + K_2)\cosh\lambda \end{vmatrix} \quad (29)$$

用这种方式转行时，提倡遵循转行新规则，并注意在不同列元素间留出适当空白，不同元素及同一元素内部各组成部分的层次要清晰分明。

当然，按照上述 1）的方法，也可将行列式（29）排为

$$\begin{vmatrix} A & B \\ C & D \end{vmatrix}$$

$A = \sin\lambda + K_1(\cosh\lambda - \cos\lambda)/(2\lambda)$；

$B = \sinh\lambda + K_1(\cosh\lambda - \cos\lambda)/(2\lambda)$；

$C = [K_1K_2/(2\lambda) - \lambda]\sin\lambda + (K_1/2 + K_2)\cos\lambda + K_1K_2\sinh\lambda/(2\lambda) + K_1\cosh\lambda/2$；

$D = K_1K_2\sin\lambda/(2\lambda) + K_1\cos\lambda/2 + [\lambda + K_1K_2/(2\lambda)]\sinh\lambda + (K_1/2 + K_2)\cosh\lambda$

3）如果矩阵或行列式的元素为可在一行内排下的数学式，但整个矩阵或行列式无法在一行内排下，则可以考虑将其整体转行排，但必须保证转行后不能改变或影响原意的表达。例如：可考虑将行列式（29）排为

$$\begin{vmatrix} \sin\lambda + \dfrac{K_1(\cosh\lambda - \cos\lambda)}{2\lambda} \\ \left(\dfrac{K_1K_2}{2\lambda} - \lambda\right)\sin\lambda + \left(\dfrac{K_1}{2} + K_2\right)\cos\lambda + \dfrac{K_1K_2\sinh\lambda}{2\lambda} + \dfrac{K_1\cosh\lambda}{2} \\ \sinh\lambda + \dfrac{K_1(\cosh\lambda - \cos\lambda)}{2\lambda} \\ \dfrac{K_1K_2\sin\lambda}{2\lambda} + \dfrac{K_1\cos\lambda}{2} + \left(\lambda + \dfrac{K_1K_2}{2\lambda}\right)\sinh\lambda + \left(\dfrac{K_1}{2} + K_2\right)\cosh\lambda \end{vmatrix}$$

4）如果矩阵或行列式的元素为数字，但由于列数较多，整个矩阵或行列式无法在一行内排下，则可以考虑按上述方法 3）转行。例如：

$$A = \begin{pmatrix} 1.00 & 3.39 & 2.27 & -0.66 & 0.10 & 5.45 & 0.90 \\ -2.39 & 2.68 & 3.57 & 2.82 & -2.52 & 2.92 & -0.52 \\ 8.28 & 3.57 & 5.39 & -3.65 & 6.10 & -2.05 & 0.90 \\ -0.89 & 1.63 & 4.77 & 2.82 & -0.50 & 4.04 & -2.21 \\ -2.00 & 4.39 & 3.27 & 0.76 & 6.10 & 5.86 & 0.99 \\ 3.39 & -3.68 & 4.57 & -2.42 & 2.52 & -2.42 & 2.05 \\ -3.28 & 6.57 & -7.39 & 3.95 & 8.50 & -2.09 & 0.99 \\ 1.89 & 0.63 & 9.77 & 2.02 & -1.58 & 9.08 & -9.02 \end{pmatrix}$$

（6）变通方法的使用

SCI 论文数学式中字符的字号与正文中

字符的字号通常是相同的，但将超版心的"大"数学式改为用小号字来排版，会取得不错的排版效果，同时也能节省版面。另外，在双栏排版中，遇到"大"或复杂的数学式时，可考虑将其改为通栏排式，也可能会获得很好的效果。

7.2.9　式中乘除号

数学式中当两个量之间为相乘关系时，其组合可表示为下列形式之一：ab，$a\ b$，$a\cdot b$，$a\times b$（在矢量运算中，$\boldsymbol{a}\cdot\boldsymbol{b}$ 与 $\boldsymbol{a}\times\boldsymbol{b}$ 是两种不同的运算）。如果一个量被另一个量除，则可表示为下列形式之一：$\dfrac{a}{b}$，a/b，$a\cdot b^{-1}$（有时也可用 $a\div b$，$a:b$ 的形式）。

分子或分母或两者都是相乘或相除时，除加括号能避免混淆外，同一层次的行内表示相除的"/"的后面一般不宜再有乘和除号。例如：$\dfrac{ab}{c}$ 可写为 ab/c 或 abc^{-1}；$\dfrac{a/b}{c/d}$ 可写为 $\dfrac{ad}{bc}$；$\dfrac{a/b}{c}$ 可写为 $(a/b)/c$、$ab^{-1}c^{-1}$，但不写成 $a/b/c$；$\dfrac{a}{bc}$ 可写为 $a/(b\cdot c)$、$a/(bc)$，但不能写成 $a/b\cdot c$。

在分子和分母包含相加或相减的情况下，在使用了圆括号（方括号、花括号）的情况下，也可用"/"表示除号。例如：

$$\frac{a+b}{c+d}=(a+b)/(c+d)$$

（不得写成 $\dfrac{a+b}{c+d}=a+b/c+d$，因为等号右边表示 $a+\dfrac{b}{c}+d$ 即 $a+(b/c)+d$）。

数学式中表示相乘的符号一般是乘号 × 或 ·。乘号有时可省略，有时不能：①量符号间、量符号与其前面的数字间、括号间是相乘关系时，可直接连写即省略乘号；②数字间、分式间是相乘关系时，不能省略乘号；③量符号与其前面的数字作为一个整体再与前面的数字发生相乘关系时，该整体与其前面的数字间不能省略乘号。

7.2.10　式后标点

串文排的式子相当于词语，可看作句子成分，其后该加标点就加，不该加就不加，这个容易理解。但对于另行排的式子，现在没有统一规则，有人认为要么一律加标点，要么一律不加，统一即可。笔者认为，式子与文字表述具有同样的功能，无论串文排还是另行居中排，在式子间、式子与文字间、式子内部要素间，都应按需加合适的标点；但鉴于数学式的超级完整性和分明性，特别是幅面较大的复杂数学式，它与周边语言要素的区分作用极其明显，其后不加标点也丝毫不影响它的完整性和分明性，其后语顿性质非常容易判定。换句话说，对于一个式子，其后语顿性质非常明显时，若再加上标点，则纯粹就是多余的。

目前国际期刊界对式后是否加标点并未统一，即使同一期刊，其不同论文，甚至同一论文的不同式子，其后标点用法也不统一。因此笔者不强调式后是否一定加标点，而是提倡按照语境和表达需要来确定。在不致引起混淆时，式后不加标点完全可行，但当不加标点会引起不能准确表达式子间、式子与文字间、式子内部要素间的关系，进而容易产生歧义时，就要在式后加上合适的标点（如逗号、分号和句号），这样同一论文中的不同式子就有不同"待遇"了，有的加了标点，有的没有加，这种不统一反而是正常的。

还需注意的是，式后使用标点时，标点与式子的主体部分宜排在同一水平位置上。例如：

$$f_1(x)=\sqrt{\frac{\sum_{i=1}^{M-1}\delta_i^{\ 2}}{M}};\ n=\frac{\sigma_{-1}}{\dfrac{k_\sigma}{\varepsilon\beta}\sigma_{\mathrm{da}}+\psi_\sigma\sigma_{\mathrm{dm}}};$$

$$M = \begin{pmatrix} 2 & -3 & 0 \\ 1 & 0 & 8 \\ 4 & 3 & -6 \end{pmatrix}$$

7.2.11 式中字体

变量（如 x，y 等）、变动的上下标（如 x_i 中的下标 i，质量定压热容符号 c_p 中的下标 p 等）、函数（如 f，g，F 等）、点（如 A，B 等）、线段（如 AB，BC 等）、弧（如 $\overset{\frown}{cd}$，$\overset{\frown}{FG}$ 等）以及在特定场合中视为常数的参数（如 a，b 等），用斜体字母表示。

有定义的已知函数（包括特殊函数在内）（如 sin，exp，ln，Γ，Ei，erf 等）、其值不变的数学常数（如 e = 2.718 281 8⋯，π = 3.141 592 6⋯，i² = -1 等）、已定义的算子（如 div，δx 中的变分符号 δ，以及 df/dx 中的微分符号 d 等）及数字，用正体表示。

集合一般用斜体字母表示，但有定义的集合用黑（加粗）体或特殊的正体字母，如非负整数集（自然数集）用 **N** 或 $\mathbb{N}$，整数集用 **Z** 或 $\mathbb{Z}$，有理数集用 **Q** 或 $\mathbb{Q}$，实数集用 **R** 或 $\mathbb{R}$，复数集用 **C** 或 $\mathbb{C}$ 表示，空集用 $\varnothing$ 表示。

矩阵、矢量和张量的符号用黑（加粗）斜体字母表示。

7.2.12 式子完整性

数学式是一个表达整体，其间不得插入多余的成分，如单词、短语。例如：

$$\beta = \{\text{load}_j\} =$$
$$\begin{cases} \text{Let } n \geq m: \sum_{j=1}^{n} x(i,j) \geq 1 \text{ and } \sum_{i=1}^{m} x(i,j) = 1 \\ \text{Let } n < m: \sum_{j=1}^{n} x(i,j) \leq 1 \text{ and } \sum_{i=1}^{m} x(i,j) = 1 \end{cases}$$

此式中，无端插入了表示条件的词语和不等式（Let⋯），破坏了式子的完整性，其实条件类语句（含式子）应置于式子的后面。该式应修改为

$$\beta = \{\text{load}_j\} =$$
$$\left\{\left[\sum_{j=1}^{n} x(i,j) \geq 1 \cap \sum_{i=1}^{m} x(i,j) = 1 \Big| n \geq m\right],\right.$$
$$\left.\left[\sum_{j=1}^{n} x(i,j) \leq 1 \cap \sum_{i=1}^{m} x(i,j) = 1 \Big| n < m\right]\right\}$$

7.3 数学式表达的严谨性

数学式表达讲究严谨性，要求认真地书写和编排式中的每个字符，涉及字符类别、字体、正斜体、是否黑（加粗）体、大小写、字号、上下标等多个方面，稍有疏忽就会出错。不少人对数学式表达很随意，将一些数学符号写错、用错、改错，对数学用语表达也不规范。

以下列举有关数学式表达中的几类常见问题，以说明数学式表达的严谨性：

1）将集合中的 ∉（不属于）、≠（不等于）、⊄（不包含于）或 ∅（空集）等符号中的斜线"/"的方向搞反了，即写排成"\"。

2）将 a divides b 即 b/a（a 除 b）表达为 a divided by b 即 a/b（a 除以 b 或 a 被 b 除），将 a divided by b 表达为 b/a。

3）将表述充分必要条件的 if and only if 或 when and only when（当且仅当）写成表述充分条件的 if 或 when（当）。

4）将正弦函数符号 sin 写成 SIN，余弦函数符号 cos 写成 COS。

5）将远小于符号"≪"写排成两个连写的小于号"<<"，远大于符号"≫"

写排成两个连写的大于号">>"。

6) 将空集符号∅写排成希腊字母 Φ 或 φ。

7) 矩阵表达中不必要地转行。例如：

$$\Delta F_{Mt} = \begin{pmatrix} I_R\omega^2\left[\sum_{m=1}^{\infty}\left(\dfrac{(-1)^2 \times \sin(2m\omega t) \times B_{2m}\sin(\phi_a+\phi_p)}{\cos(\theta)}\right)\right], \\ I_R\omega^2\left[\sum_{m=1}^{\infty}\left(\dfrac{(-1)^2 \times \sin(2m\omega t) \times B_{2m}\sin(\phi_a+\phi_p)}{\cos(\theta)l_c}\right)\right], \\ -I_R\omega^2\left[\sum_{m=1}^{\infty}\left(\dfrac{(-1)^2 \times \sin(2m\omega t) \times B_{2m}\sin(\theta_a+\theta_p)}{\cos(\theta)}\right)\right], \\ -I_R\omega^2\left[\sum_{m=1}^{\infty}\left(\dfrac{(-1)^2 \times \sin(2m\omega t) \times B_{2m}\sin(\theta_a+\theta_p)}{\cos(\theta)l_c}\right)\right], \\ 0,\ 0,\ \cdots,\ 0,\ 0 \end{pmatrix}^T$$

此式等号右边的部分表示一个矩阵的转置，存在的问题主要有：元素间用","分隔不妥；元素虽为较长的数学式，但不必转行排；前面式子部分（第 1～4 行）为列形式，后面数字部分（第 5 行即最后一行）为行形式，是表达一个只有一列的列矩阵还是一个只有一行的行矩阵，不易分清，容易造成误解；三角函数中的括号多余。改为以下形式就清楚了：

$$\Delta F_{Mt} = \begin{pmatrix} I_R\omega^2\sum_{m=1}^{\infty}\left[(-1)^2 \times \sin 2m\omega t \times \dfrac{B_{2m}\sin(\phi_a+\phi_p)}{\cos\theta}\right] \\ I_R\omega^2\sum_{m=1}^{\infty}\left[(-1)^2 \times \sin 2m\omega t \times \dfrac{B_{2m}\sin(\phi_a+\phi_p)}{l_c\cos\theta}\right] \\ -I_R\omega^2\sum_{m=1}^{\infty}\left[(-1)^2 \times \sin 2m\omega t \times \dfrac{B_{2m}\sin(\theta_a+\theta_p)}{\cos\theta}\right] \\ -I_R\omega^2\sum_{m=1}^{\infty}\left[(-1)^2 \times \sin 2m\omega t \times \dfrac{B_{2m}\sin(\theta_a+\theta_p)}{l_c\cos\theta}\right] \\ 0 \\ \vdots \\ 0 \end{pmatrix}$$

8) 将标量积（数量积或内积）运算表达式 (a,b) 写排成 $\langle a,b \rangle$，两矢量夹角表达式 $\langle a,b \rangle$ 写排成 (a,b)。若其中的 a，b 不用黑（加粗）体，则更加错误，因为 (a,b)、$\langle a,b \rangle$ 是 "ordered pair a, b"（有序偶 a, b）或 "couple a, b"（偶 a, b）的标准表达形式。

9) 矩阵表达中加了不必要的省略号。例如：

$$\widetilde{B} = \widetilde{W} \cdot \widetilde{R} = (\widetilde{\omega}_1, \widetilde{\omega}_2, \cdots, \widetilde{\omega}_k) \cdot \begin{pmatrix} \widetilde{r}_{11} & \widetilde{r}_{12} & \cdots & \widetilde{r}_{1n} \\ \widetilde{r}_{21} & \widetilde{r}_{22} & \cdots & \widetilde{r}_{2n} \\ \vdots & \vdots & & \vdots \\ \widetilde{r}_{k1} & \widetilde{r}_{k2} & \cdots & \widetilde{r}_{kn} \end{pmatrix} =$$

$$\begin{pmatrix} \widetilde{\omega}_1 \otimes \widetilde{r}_{11} \oplus \widetilde{\omega}_2 \otimes \widetilde{r}_{21} \oplus \cdots \oplus \widetilde{\omega}_k \otimes \widetilde{r}_{k1} \\ \widetilde{\omega}_1 \otimes \widetilde{r}_{12} \oplus \widetilde{\omega}_2 \otimes \widetilde{r}_{22} \oplus \cdots \oplus \widetilde{\omega}_k \otimes \widetilde{r}_{k2} \\ \vdots \\ \widetilde{\omega}_1 \otimes \widetilde{r}_{1n} \oplus \widetilde{\omega}_2 \otimes \widetilde{r}_{2n} \oplus \cdots \oplus \widetilde{\omega}_k \otimes \widetilde{r}_{kn} \end{pmatrix}^T$$

表示一个 $1 \times k$ 阶矩阵与另一个 $k \times n$ 阶矩阵相乘，按矩阵相乘原理可知，此两矩阵相乘的结果只能为一个 $1 \times n$ 阶矩阵，即 1 行 n 列矩阵，转置后为 n 行 1 列。因此，上式相乘结果的矩阵中放两个竖排省略号是错误的，应去掉一个，且留下的竖排省略号在括号中应居左或居中排，如何把上式等号下方的矩阵排为以下形式：

$$\begin{pmatrix} \widetilde{\omega}_1 \otimes \widetilde{r}_{11} \oplus \widetilde{\omega}_2 \otimes \widetilde{r}_{21} \oplus \cdots \oplus \widetilde{\omega}_k \otimes \widetilde{r}_{k1} \\ \widetilde{\omega}_1 \otimes \widetilde{r}_{12} \oplus \widetilde{\omega}_2 \otimes \widetilde{r}_{22} \oplus \cdots \oplus \widetilde{\omega}_k \otimes \widetilde{r}_{k2} \\ \vdots \\ \widetilde{\omega}_1 \otimes \widetilde{r}_{1n} \oplus \widetilde{\omega}_2 \otimes \widetilde{r}_{2n} \oplus \cdots \oplus \widetilde{\omega}_k \otimes \widetilde{r}_{kn} \end{pmatrix}^T$$

10) 在包含 "/" "Σ" "Π" 以及三角函数、双曲函数符号（如 sin，arctan，coth）等的式子中缺必要的括号。例如：

① $\widetilde{r}_{u1} = \sum_{i=1}^{p} \widetilde{r}_i - 1$ 中，累加的对象是 $\widetilde{r}_i$ 还

是 $\tilde{r}_i - 1$？②$S_b(x, t) = \frac{1}{2}A_b\left[1 + \cos\frac{\pi}{l_b}(x - x_0)\right]$ 中，cos 的作用范围是 $\frac{\pi}{l_b}$ 还是 $\frac{\pi}{l_b}(x - x_0)$？③$n + m \times n + m$ 中，按常规是 n，$m \times n$，m 三项相加，但常有作者用此式表达 $n + m$ 与 $n + m$ 两项相乘，而没有加必要的括号，这些均不容易分清。

11）式中用词语来表示量符号，文字与符号混用，如 "$v = \frac{displacement}{t}$" "$velocity = \frac{s}{t}$" 等。通常，同一式子不宜混用文字和符号，提倡要么都用符号，要么都用文字。文字式在经济、管理类等社科类文章中使用较多，而在自然科学类学术论文中不提倡用。

7.4 数学式使用实例

SCI 论文中式子的使用较为灵活，没有固定的格式体例，不同期刊的要求也不相同，即使同一期刊的不同论文甚至同一论文的不同式子，其格式体例也不尽相同。作者应以内容表述需要为出发点，灵活巧妙地使用、用好式子。下面从几本 SCI 期刊论文中摘取一些数学式使用实例，给予点评，以期对作者撰写论文提供指导。

7.4.1 实例一

此例引自论文 Mastering the game of Go with deep neural networks and tree search (*Nature*, Vol 529, 28 January 2016, p486)。

【1】

AlphaGo combines the policy and value networks in an MCTS algorithm (Fig. 3) that selects actions by lookahead search. Each edge (s, a) of the search tree stores an action value $Q(s, a)$, visit count $N(s, a)$, and prior probability $P(s, a)$. The tree is traversed by simulation (that is, descending the tree in complete games without backup), starting from the root state. At each time step t of each simulation, an action a_t is selected from state s_t

$$a_t = \underset{a}{\mathrm{argmax}}(Q(s_t, a) + u(s_t, a))$$

so as to maximize action value plus a bonus

$$u(s, a) \propto \frac{P(s, a)}{1 + P(s, a)}$$

that is proportional to the prior probability but decays with repeated visits to encourage exploration. When the traversal reaches a leaf node s_L at step L, the leaf node may be expanded. The leaf position s_L is processed just once by the SL policy network p_σ. The output probabilities are stored as prior probabilities P for each legal action a, $P(s, a) = p_\sigma(a|s)$. The leaf node is evaluated in two very different ways: first, by the value network $v_\theta(s_L)$; and second, by the outcome z_L of a random rollout played out until terminal step T using the fast rollout policy $p\pi$; these evaluations are combined, using a mixing parameter λ, into a leaf evaluation $V(s_L)$

$$V(s_L) = (1 - \lambda)v_\theta(s_L) + \lambda z_L$$

此例在形式上有三个部分（三段），每部分后有一个式子（共三个式子）。

第一部分先总体交待棋手 AlphaGo 的下棋策略（在 MCTS⊖ 算法中结合策略和价值网络，由前向搜索来选择动作）。接着描述过程与原理（搜索树的边 (s, a) 储存行动价值 $Q(s, a)$、访问量 $N(s, a)$ 和先验概率 $P(s,a)$，从根状态开始来模拟遍历树）。末尾主句指出行动 a_t 由状态 s_t 来选择（action a_t is selected from state s_t），接着便给出计算式 $a_t = \underset{a}{\mathrm{argmax}}(Q(s_t, a) + u(s_t, a))$。

第二部分是上述末尾主句的目的状语，并给出行动值最大化的关系式 $u(s, a) \propto \frac{P(s,a)}{1 + P(s,a)}$。

⊖ MCTS—Monte Carlo tree search（蒙特卡罗树搜索）。

第三部分开头的句子是定语从句,修饰第二个式子,指出 $u(s,a)$ 与先验概率成正比,但随激励探索重复访问衰减。接着用三句话(画线部分)描述遍历过程,涉及多个量及其之间关系。最后指出由价值网络 $v_\theta(s_L)$ 和终点周期内的随机展示结局 z_L 两种方法来评估叶节点,并引入混合参数 λ 将这两种方法相结合来作叶子评估 $V(s_L)$,给出计算式 $V(s_L) = (1-\lambda)v_\theta(s_L) + \lambda z_L$。

此例行文及式子使用特点:描述 Alpha-Go 下棋的过程和原理,涉及多个不同量及其之间的定性和定量关系,对核心量按先后顺序依次给出计算式;将式子看作词语,作句子成分(这里均作同位语),自然有序行文;在形式上是三个自然段加三个式子,但从语法结构上看,第二、三部分的开头语句均与第一部分末尾的句子共同组成一个完整的句子,因此这三个部分(包括三个数学式)在内容上是一个句法结构完整、表述严密的整体自然段落;式子出现前就已交待了式中有关量,因此在式下就不用再对量作解释了,这与传统式下注释格式体例不同。

7.4.2 实例二

此例引自论文 Value-driven river management:A Murray River case study (*Australian Journal of Water Resources*, Vol 17, No 1, 2013, p53)。

【2】

The hydrological value of each scenario is maximised via the optimisation equation:

$$\max v(V,F) = \sum_{i=1}^{n} a_i \sum_{j=1}^{m} \mu_{ij} V_{ij} + \sum_{i=1}^{n} b_i \sum_{j=1}^{m} \beta_{ij} F_{i,i+1} \quad (1)$$

subject to the water-balance constraints

$$V_{ij} - V_{i-1,j} = F_{i,j+1} - F_{ij} + P_{ij} - Q_{ij} - X_{ij} \quad (2)$$

and the capacity constraints

$$V_{ij}^{\min} \leq V_{i,j} \leq V_{ij}^{\max};\ F_{ij}^{\min} \leq F \leq F_{ij}^{\max} \quad (3)$$

where all quantities are defined in the Notation list at the commencement of the present paper.

此例除式子外,只有四行,式子使用较为简洁,三个式子分别编号(1)、(2)、(3)。第一文字行指出每个场景的水文价值通过最优化方程式(1)得到最大化,其后用冒号引出方程式(1);接着在方程式(1)下面给出约束条件式(2)、(3),标志词是 subject to,这两个方程式上面的语句(即第二、三文字行)与这两个式子间没有停顿,因此其间未用冒号分隔,注意式(2)、(3)分别作 the water-balance constraints 和 the capacity constraints 的同位语。最后一行(第四文字行)对以上各式中的符号作统一解释(论文首页的符号表对所有符号作了定义)。

此例在行文及式子使用上,也将式子作为普通词语来自然行文,形式上虽是几个小段加几个式子,实际上则是一个完整的段落,表出每个场景的水文价值最优化方程。

此例若按方程式(函数式)常规(传统)排式也可排为以下形式:

The hydrological value of each scenario is maximised via the optimisation equation:

$$\max v(V,F) = \sum_{i=1}^{n} a_i \sum_{j=1}^{m} \mu_{ij} V_{ij} + \sum_{i=1}^{n} b_i \sum_{j=1}^{m} \beta_{ij} F_{i,i+1} \quad (1)$$

$$\text{s. t.}\ V_{ij} - V_{i-1,j} = F_{i,j+1} - F_{ij} + P_{ij} - Q_{ij} - X_{ij} \quad (2)$$

$$V_{ij}^{\min} \leq V_{i,j} \leq V_{ij}^{\max};\ F_{ij}^{\min} \leq F \leq F_{ij}^{\max} \quad (3)$$

where equations (2) and (3) are the water-balance constraints and the capacity constraints of equation (1). All quantities are defined in the Notation list at the commencement of the present paper.

7.4.3 实例三

此例引自论文 Discussion on "Design flood estimation in Western Austrilia" by D Flavell (*Australian Journal of Water Resources*, Vol 17, No 1, 2013, p106)。

【3】

As the author points out in the last paragraph of his section 3, highly correlated factors should not be included in multiple linear regression analysis. The Leinster formula, for example,

$$Q_{20} = 1.45(AS_e^{0.5})^{0.85}(L^2/A)^{-0.33} \quad (2)$$

(where Q_{20} = peak discharge (m³/s) of ARI = 20 years; A = catchment area (km²); S_e = mainstream equal-area slope (m/km); and L = mainstream length (km))

shows A in two places, and A is perfectly correlated with itself. Algebra allows this to be re-cast as:

$$Q_{20} = 1.45 A^{1.18} S_e^{0.41} L^{-0.66}$$

此例也是将式子作为普通词语自然行文,式(2)与The Leinster formula 为同位语,一起作句子的主语(The Leinster formula, for example, formula (2) shows A in two places, and A is … itself.)。在式(2)下方和谓语动词 shows 前面已有几行对式中符号的解释语,那么这个式(2)怎么还会做主语呢?请仔细看,这些解释语是用括号括起的,相当于在 formula (2)和 shows A in two places 间插入一个不作句子成分的独立语,即插入语。式下符号解释本是一种常规表达方式,这里采用将式下全体注释语加括号的形式,却很有趣,也很奇特,值得参考;另外,在量符号与注释语(量名称)间未用常规的破折号而用了等号,也是一个特点。

此例若按式下符号解释的常规传统排式,则可排为以下形式:

As the author points out in the last paragraph of his section 3, highly correlated factors should not be included in multiple linear regression analysis. For example, the Leinster formula is

$$Q_{20} = 1.45(AS_e^{0.5})^{0.85}(L^2/A)^{-0.33} \quad (2)$$

where Q_{20} is peak discharge (m³/s) of ARI (20 years), A is catchment area (km²), S_e is mainstream equal-area slope (m/km), and L is mainstream length (km).

This formula shows A in two places, and A is perfectly correlated with itself. Algebra allows this to be re-cast as

$$Q_{20} = 1.45 A^{1.18} S_e^{0.41} L^{-0.66}$$

其中式(2)上方语句末尾的 is 和最后一段末尾的 as 的后面加不加冒号均可(取决于作者写作风格和目标期刊要求),如果加了,冒号起提示和引出式子的作用,如果不加,则是直接将式子作为词语而作句子成分(这里在 is 后作表语,在 as 后作介词宾语)。

此例还以可排为以下形式:

As the author points out in the last paragraph of his section 3, highly correlated factors should not be included in multiple linear regression analysis. The Leinster formula, for example, formula (2) shows A in two places, and A is perfectly correlated with itself.

$$Q_{20} = 1.45(AS_e^{0.5})^{0.85}(L^2/A)^{-0.33} \quad (2)$$

where Q_{20} is peak discharge (m³/s) of ARI (20 years), A is catchment area (km²), S_e is mainstream equal-area slope (m/km), and L is mainstream length (km).

Algebra allows this to be re-cast as

$$Q_{20} = 1.45 A^{1.18} S_e^{0.41} L^{-0.66}$$

以上各种表达中,式中符号解释部分也可表达为符号和注释语间加破折号的形式:

where Q_{20}—Peak discharge (m³/s) of ARI (20 years);
  A—Catchment area (km²);
  S_e—Mainstream equal-area slope (m/km);
  L—Mainstream length (km)

7.4.4 实例四

此例引自论文 Automated design of free-form imaging systems (*Light Science & Application*, 2017 Volume 6, issue 4)。

【4】

The ideal target points (the ideal image points in the general case) $\mathbf{T}_{i,ideal}$ for each feature ray $\mathbf{R}_i$ ($i = 1, 2 \cdots, K$) on the ideal image plane can be calculated on the basis of the given object-image relationships and image plane position. Here, we consider the conventional case whereby the optical system has plane symmetry about the meridional plane. As shown in Figure 1, for a feature ray from a specific sample field (ω_x, ω_y), the global coordinates of $\mathbf{T}_{i,ideal}$ can be written as

$$\begin{aligned}\mathbf{T}_{i,ideal} &= \begin{bmatrix} T_{i,ideal,x} \\ T_{i,ideal,y} \\ T_{i,ideal,z} \end{bmatrix} \\ &= \begin{bmatrix} 1 & 0 & 0 \\ 0 & \cos(\alpha_o) & \sin(\alpha_o) \\ 0 & -\sin(\alpha_o) & \cos(\alpha_o) \end{bmatrix} \begin{bmatrix} f\tan(\omega_x - \omega_{x,central}) \\ f\tan(\omega_y - \omega_{y,central}) \\ 0 \end{bmatrix} \\ &+ \begin{bmatrix} x_o \\ y_o \\ z_o \end{bmatrix} \end{aligned} \quad (1)$$

where f represents the focal length for the system; (x_o, y_o, z_o) are the global coordinates of the center of the image plane (the ideal image point of the central field $(\omega_{x,central}, \omega_{y,central})$ among the full FOV); α_o is the tilt angle of image plane relative to the global x-axis. When the image plane position changes during the design process, $\mathbf{T}_{i,ideal}$ has to be recalculated. Sometimes $\mathbf{T}_i \neq \mathbf{T}_{i,ideal}$ in a special case, which will be discussed later.

后面部分对参数 $\mathbf{T}_{i,ideal}$ 进行讨论（设计过程中当图像平面位置发生变化时，必须对 $\mathbf{T}_{i,ideal}$ 重新计算），并指出在特殊情况下 $\mathbf{T}_i \neq \mathbf{T}_{i,ideal}$，详情将在后面讨论。

此例是一个中间插入式子的段落，此式即式（1）充当介词 as 的宾语。式下前面部分是对式中符号 f、(x_o, y_o, z_o)、α_o 的解释，这三个符号的解释语之间用分号分隔，注意其中的关键词 represents、are、is。式下

注意式（1）的排法，论文是半栏排版，此式需要转行排，而且转行两次，排为了三行；还要注意转行处的数学符号（等号和加号）的位置，它们排在转下来的式子部分的开始。因为此式的整体性很强，不论转行处的数学符号排在上行末尾还是下行开始，效果是相同的，因此无所谓哪种排法更好。按 7.2.8 节中介绍的转行新规则，式（1）也可排为：

$$\mathbf{T}_{i,ideal} = \begin{bmatrix} T_{i,ideal,x} \\ T_{i,ideal,y} \\ T_{i,ideal,z} \end{bmatrix} =$$

$$\begin{bmatrix} 1 & 0 & 0 \\ 0 & \cos(\alpha_o) & \sin(\alpha_o) \\ 0 & -\sin(\alpha_o) & \cos(\alpha_o) \end{bmatrix} \begin{bmatrix} f\tan(\omega_x - \omega_{x,central}) \\ f\tan(\omega_y - \omega_{y,central}) \\ 0 \end{bmatrix} +$$

$$\begin{bmatrix} x_o \\ y_o \\ z_o \end{bmatrix} \quad (1)$$

7.4.5 实例五

此例引自论文 Revealing true coupling strengths in two-dimensional spectroscopy with sparsity-based signal recovery (*Light Science & Application*, 2017 Volume 6, issue 4)。

【5】

As seen from Equation (1) …Once BOMP has removed all of the signal components associated with the stronger peaks, represented in Equation (1), the residual data are fitted to a matrix that describes coupling between modes, with entries of the following form:

$$\begin{aligned}S_{ij}^{\text{coup}}(\omega_\alpha,\omega_\beta;t_i^{(1)},t_j^{(2)}) =& A_0 D(\omega_\alpha,\varphi_\alpha,\sigma_\alpha,\gamma_\alpha;t_i^{(1)}) \\ & \times D(\omega_\beta,\varphi_\beta,\sigma_\beta,\gamma_\beta;t_j^{(2)}) \\ & + D(\omega_\alpha,\varphi_\alpha,\sigma_\alpha,\gamma_\alpha;|t_i^{(1)}-t_j^{(2)}|) \quad (2)\\ & \times \left[\begin{array}{l} B_0 D(\omega_\beta,\varphi_\beta,\sigma_\beta,\gamma_\beta;t_i^{(1)}) \\ + C_0 D(\omega_\beta,\varphi_\beta,\sigma_\beta,\gamma_\beta;t_j^{(2)}) \end{array}\right]\end{aligned}$$

according to the retrieved molecular frequencies. Here, ω_α and ω_β represent two different energy levels of the sample, and A_0, B_0 and C_0 are constants. This step recovers the cross peak values and concludes the analysis.

此例是一个含式子的段落，中间的式（2）充当 the following form 的同位语，其后介词短语（according to …）作状语。式下 Here 部分对式中符号进行解释，最后一句对这一步（This step …）进行总结（此步恢复了交叉峰值并通过分析进行推断）。式（2）上面的语句中，先引用在论文中这一部分的前面已给出的式（1），再引出式（2）。

特别要注意式（2）的排法，总体上转行四次，第四次转行部分（即方括号部分）内部又转行一次，这就形成转行嵌套转行的形式。式（2）本来可以不转这么多行，排为三行是没有问题的（见下面的排式，但效果有所下降），但这里显然考虑了式中相同或相似部分的对称（对齐）排式效果，旨在增强式中要素间的对比性和式子结构的匀称美，给读者以舒适美感。

$$\begin{aligned}S_{ij}^{\text{coup}}(\omega_\alpha,\omega_\beta;t_i^{(1)},t_j^{(2)}) =& A_0 D(\omega_\alpha,\varphi_\alpha,\sigma_\alpha,\gamma_\alpha;t_i^{(1)}) \\ \times D(\omega_\beta,\varphi_\beta,\sigma_\beta,\gamma_\beta;t_j^{(2)}) & + D(\omega_\alpha,\varphi_\alpha,\sigma_\alpha,\gamma_\alpha;|t_i^{(1)}-t_j^{(2)}|) \\ \times [B_0 D(\omega_\beta,\varphi_\beta,\sigma_\beta,\gamma_\beta;t_i^{(1)}) & + C_0 D(\omega_\beta,\varphi_\beta,\sigma_\beta,\gamma_\beta;t_j^{(2)})]\end{aligned}$$

另外，还要注意式（2）中方括号部分的嵌套转行排式，除了 $\left[\begin{array}{l}B_0 D(\omega_\beta,\varphi_\beta,\sigma_\beta,\gamma_\beta;t_i^{(1)}) \\ + C_0 D(\omega_\beta,\varphi_\beta,\sigma_\beta,\gamma_\beta;t_j^{(2)})\end{array}\right]$ 这种形式外，还可排为另一种形式 $[B_0 D(\omega_\beta,\varphi_\beta,\sigma_\beta,\gamma_\beta;t_i^{(1)}) + C_0 D(\omega_\beta,\varphi_\beta,\sigma_\beta,\gamma_\beta;t_j^{(2)})]$，若采用后一种形式，式（2）可排为：

$$\begin{aligned}S_{ij}^{\text{coup}}(\omega_\alpha,\omega_\beta;t_i^{(1)},t_j^{(2)}) =& \\ A_0 D(\omega_\alpha,\varphi_\alpha,\sigma_\alpha,\gamma_\alpha;t_i^{(1)}) & \\ \times D(\omega_\beta,\varphi_\beta,\sigma_\beta,\gamma_\beta;t_j^{(2)}) & \\ + D(\omega_\alpha,\varphi_\alpha,\sigma_\alpha,\gamma_\alpha;|t_i^{(1)}-t_j^{(2)}|) & \quad (2)\\ \times [B_0 D(\omega_\beta,\varphi_\beta,\sigma_\beta,\gamma_\beta;t_i^{(1)}) & \\ + C_0 D(\omega_\beta,\varphi_\beta,\sigma_\beta,\gamma_\beta;t_j^{(2)})] &\end{aligned}$$

显然后一种排式更规范，但当其中的方括号为表矩阵的括号时，倒是用前一种排式也不错，这样可以做到表示矩阵的左右括号排在同一行，当然，排在不同行也是可以的。

第 8 章 SCI 论文投稿与发表

论文在撰写完成后准备提交（投稿）的版本还是半成品，投稿后经过编辑、专家和作者的协同审查、修改和完善，再通过生产发表出来，半成品才成为成品、产品，走向社会与读者见面。论文写作与修改是产品制作的过程，投稿与发表是产品出售获得回报和产值的过程。不论是"高大上"的科学研究，还是一般的职称评定、课题申报、项目验收、学位申请等实际需要，论文写作的直接目标是"出售"，即发表成果，供别人阅读和学习，同时作者自身也获得收益。同实物产品一样，论文质量高、价值大，销售就快。因此作者在投稿前，需要把握论文（产品）的定位、出版物（买家，目标期刊）的水准及投稿与发表（销售）的流程与技巧。

论文投稿和发表，在某种程度上激发着作者的科研兴趣：通过投稿，作者经历了论文撰写后的再修改体验，提高了对论文、期刊的理解深度，锻炼了高质量论文的撰写能力；通过发表，作者与大众分享了自己的研究过程、成果，传播了科学知识、文化，更新了知识体系，还接受同行评议，提高了知名度。论文投稿过程既是作者所写论文的推出，又是论文走向社会的前奏；发表过程既是作者对前一段研究工作的总结，又是其未来开展新工作的指导性文献。因此，论文投稿和发表是科学研究中非常重要的环节。

本章讲述 SCI 论文投稿与发表流程，涉及目标期刊选择、投稿技巧和注意事项、按审稿意见修改论文等，并分享名刊 *Nature* 和国际投审稿系统 EM（Editorial Manager）的有关内容。

8.1 投稿与发表流程

8.1.1 写作完成阶段

第 1 章中已讲过，论文形成过程分为准备、进行和完成三大阶段，完成阶段又包括出版和传播两个阶段，如图 8-1 所示。

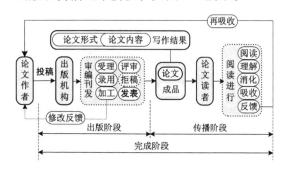

图 8-1 论文写作完成阶段

出版阶段的起点是投稿，终点是发表，而发表又是传播阶段的起点。作者撰写论文是为了发表，就必须投稿，如果不投稿，发表便无从谈起。投稿后存在录用与退稿两种相反的结果。稿件能否被录用，虽然主要取决于其基础质量（投稿质量），但也与其流程运转密切相关，流程中有多个环节，在每个环节都有一些工作要做，使论文的质量在前面环节的基础上得到提升，前面环节的工作相对后面的来说，就是一种准备。因此，投稿固然很重要，但投稿前的准备工作也不容忽视。如果准备工作不到位，要么投稿质量不高，其质量会失去进一步提升的机会；要么投稿质量虽高，但可惜因为投稿流程不合要求而遭遇退稿的命运。

8.1.2 整体流程示意

投稿时，作者不仅首先要按照科技论文写作要求写出规范的论文，还要遵循投稿与发表流程，按目标期刊的要求进一步完善论文，按要求投稿，投稿后走好流程，配合编辑做好出版阶段的各项工作，不断提高论文的质量，增加论文被录用的机会。下面基于采用科学编辑制的国际名刊 *Nature* 的工作流程，给出论文投稿发表整体流程示意图，如图 8-2 所示。

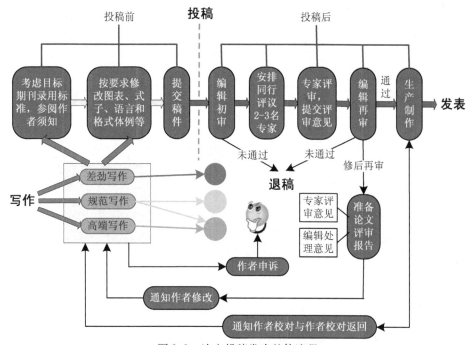

图 8-2　论文投稿发表整体流程

作者撰写论文完成后，不宜急于投稿，而应做好相关准备工作：确定目标期刊，了解录用标准，按标准修改论文，涉及论文图表、式子、语言和格式体例等各个方面。准备工作很关键，准备充分了，对论文录用大有助益；有的作者不重视准备工作，不是写作艰难，郁闷常伴，就是写作随意，写出的文章错误随处可见，格式凌乱，与写作和投稿要求相差甚远。

准备工作到位后，接下来才是正式投稿。投稿相对简单，通常登陆目标期刊的投稿系统，按投稿步骤和要求填写作者和论文信息，再上传论文全文即可完成。

投稿成功后，编辑对稿件进行处理，首先编辑初审，未通过的退稿，通过的安排同行评议，由专家填写评审意见。编辑根据专家评审意见进行再审，做出处理决定。处理结果通常有三种：退稿（严重不达标）；准备论文评审报告，提交作者修改（有修改潜力）；直接提交生产部门加工制作（达到刊登要求）。

在生产制作环节，作者会收到有关通知，并对制作好的论文进行校对。

8.1.3 详细流程概述

论文投稿与发表流程如图 8-3 所示，包括期刊选择、投稿准备、投稿、审稿、修稿、录用和发表，其中每个节点又包括子节点，如期刊选择包括客观评估论文、综合考虑期刊，……，录用和发表包括制图、生产（排版）、校对、发表和版权转让。

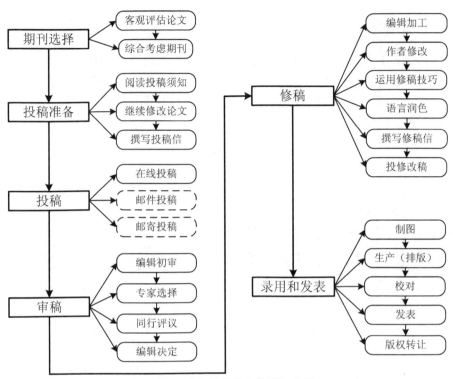

图 8-3　论文投稿发表较详细流程

8.2　期刊选择

论文写成后就要投出去，作者需要选择合适的期刊，有的作者甚至在研究进行中或论文撰写之前，就已心中有数，确定了目标期刊，可以说作者是为了在某一期刊发表论文才开始撰写论文的，将论文投在水准相当或期望的某一期刊上。向不合适的期刊投稿后，通常会遭遇在编辑初审环节就以"不合本刊要求""与本刊刊登方向不符"等理由而被快速退稿，这样还会延误论文的及时发表。因此，为了增加投稿的命中率，作者在选择期刊时，应该花费较多的工夫，正确评估自己论文的学术水平，大体了解目标期刊的档次。

8.2.1　客观评估论文

评估论文应该实事求是、客观准确，既不能太过自信而估计过高，也不能缺少自信而估计过低。有的作者容易高估自己的论文，将论文投到水平较高的期刊，但如果相差太大，论文一般很难通过编辑初审而遭遇直接拒稿；但有时，作者有职称、职务和业绩评定，项目申请、考核和验收，奖学金、毕业和学位申请答辩等实际需要，急需发表论文，或对自己的论文没有什么把握，非常不希望退稿之事发生，就会选择档次较低的期刊投稿。由于低档次期刊的影响力较差，同行认同度不高，论文发表后达不到预期效果。因此选择目标期刊时，对论文的水平进行客观评估是非常重要的，这种评估应该从以下几个方面来展开。

（1）对比同类文献（把握先进性）

作者虽然在论文撰写前或撰写中查阅过大量相关文献，对文献的内容已非常熟悉和了解，但在投稿前仍应查阅一些相关文献及目标期刊近期（最近几年）刊登的论文，获得与自己同类、相关、相近或相似的文献，并作对比分析。（也许论文撰写经历了较长的时间，待论文撰写完成后又有一些新的文献发表出来，这样就更加需要在投稿前再查查有无最新的文章刚刚发表出来而还未来得及去查阅，如有合适的，还可以增加引用，更新论文的内容。）只有在对与自己研究内容相近、结构体例类似的文章有充分的了解和认识后，才能对论文进行客观、公正和全面的对比分析和比较，进而把握论文的学术先进性。对论文撰写当前研究现状的充分了解和掌握是评估论文水平的基础。

(2) 了解同行水准（把握内容）

作者查阅相关文献及目标期刊近期刊登的论文，除了把握、了解这些文献的内容与水准外，还要看看这些文献的作者是谁，有哪些人、团队和相关人士在做相同或类似的研究，看看他们过去发表论文的情况，包括发文数量、内容、所属项目以及发表在哪些期刊和其他出版物上，了解其科研成果、业绩与现状，做到知己知彼，再比较一下作者自己及其团队与这些人、团队的学术水准与科研实力的差距，以及各自的优势和不足，判断一下自己的论文是否达到了他们的水准。（作者虽然在研究进行、论文撰写过程中已对同行研究水准有一定的了解，但在论文撰写完成后投稿前同样需要进行这样的工作，只是出发点不同，前者是为了撰写论文，后者是为了发表论文而选择目标期刊来投稿。）这样也就基本反映出所选目标期刊是否合适，若不合适，就要调整进而选择另一期刊，重复以上步骤，直到选出合适的期刊为止。

(3) 检查论文体裁（把握文体）

选择目标期刊还需考虑论文的体裁类型，把握好文体。论文的体裁有多种多样，不同体裁的论文发表难度是不同的。每种期刊都有其文体定位，有的期刊只刊登原创论文，有的只刊登综述，而有的以刊登原创论文为主、综述为辅。总体而言，原创论文是多数学术期刊的定位，可供选择的目标范围较大；但对综述而言，有的期刊刊登，有的不愿刊登或少量刊登，或只刊登特约综述（邀请专家撰写的综述），可供选择的范围较小；研究热点、读者来信等选择的范围则更小得多。

(4) 总结论文特点（把握创新性）

创新性是论文的灵魂，高水平论文的重要特点就是创新性，论文有无创新的内容或发现、发明是评估其价值的根本出发点。如果论文创新性较高，发表的意义就大，可以考虑向高档次期刊投稿，反之就应向较低档次期刊投稿。作者根据自己论文内容和当时领域研究现状，客观、公正地评估（把握）其科学意义和创新性是十分重要的。当然，投稿前对论文的其他特点也要考虑，从多个方面（如科学性、规范性等）进行考查，大概判断是否达到了要求，差距有多少，能否弥补，若能弥补，就要动手对论文进行修改、完善。

(5) 认识论文缺点（把握不足）

一篇论文同其他任何事物一样，都不可能完美无缺。任何科学研究、实验都是阶段性的，都有承上启下的特点。因此在看到自己论文成就的同时，也要总结存在的问题和不足，如研究问题的提出是否必要、妥当，机理研究是否充分、完善，条理表述是否清晰、通顺，实验或数据是否欠缺、不准，分析与归纳是否合理、到位，综述是否有结论、展望，结论是否全面、高度概括，创新点是否有或突出等等，这样不仅有助于作者客观评价论文水平，规划下一步的研究思路、方案或技术路线，还有助于作者在投稿后、录用前能准确回复审稿人和编辑对论文所提出的类似问题。

由以上这几个方面的分析和总结，相信作者对自己的论文能有一个客观的评估，这个过程也许不那么简单容易，作者需要付出一定的劳动，但付出了就会有回报。

8.2.2 综合考虑期刊

对论文进行客观评估后，接着就要选择合适的期刊。目标期刊可能有多个，需要先了解一下这些期刊，然后从中选出一个最合适的。因此需要阅览、收集期刊的信息。当前是互联网、大数据时代，查找期刊的信息非常容易，往往可以通过一些知名度高的网站，如百度、Google、Web of Science、Pubmed、CNKI、WANFANG DATA 等等，按照学科、期刊名称或其他相关信息，查到某个期刊，了解其基本情况（期刊介绍）、数据指标（如被引频次、影响因子、即年指标等），以及投稿须知（作者须知、稿约、征稿简则、致作者）、投稿注意事项等内容。还可通过参加学术会议或发邮件、打电话等多种方式，与领域同行、专家、学者或单位同事，如研究人员、老师、学生、图书馆员或有关领导、导师等，进行沟通而获得期刊的一些信息。具体来说，选择期刊应该从以下几个方面来展开。

（1）期刊办刊宗旨和报道范围

每个期刊都有其办刊宗旨和报道范围，通常刊登在期刊的封面（如封二、封三、封底）或内文的首页、末页，或者在期刊、出版商的官网及其他有关渠道发布。这种内容有时也可在投稿须知中提到，甚至有较为详细的讲述。办刊宗旨和报道范围主要指期刊的报道领域和侧重点，如 Nature 的办刊宗旨是"将科学发现的重要结果介绍给公众，让公众尽早知道世界每一学科分支取得的所有进展"（Nature's mission: To communicate the world's best and most important science to scientists across the world and to the wider community interested in science），报道范围是"科学所有领域"（Across the full range of scientific disciplines）。

作者首先要确定论文与期刊所属专业是否对口，这是选择目标期刊最基本的要求；其次要重点关注论文的主题与期刊的办刊宗旨是否相符，论文的内容是否符合期刊的报道范围，不符合办刊宗旨、报道范围的，就可以剔除相应不相符的期刊。但在同一领域几个水平相近的期刊中，有时会出现侧重点不同的现象，比如有的倾向于工程技术、临床，有的侧重于理论、基础研究，具体细节均可从作者须知或相关资料中获得。

（2）期刊影响因子及知名度

期刊影响因子是评价期刊水准的重要指标，通常，期刊影响因子高，其学术水平和知名度就高。一篇论文若能被知名期刊录用，其水平在某种程度上就显现出来了，产生较多的被引是有可能的。建议作者根据自己的研究领域，先将国内外的相关期刊进行分级；再根据自己论文的学科方向，找出专业对口的权威期刊，看看这些期刊发表了些什么论文，水准如何，与自己论文水平的差异。

另外作者可能还有现实需求需要考虑，作者单位对发表论文有具体要求，比如有的高校规定，博士学位申请者至少需要在 SCI 期刊发表一篇或几篇文章，甚至还对期刊的 SCI 分区、影响因子学科排名等有要求；如果把在 Q2 区期刊发表论文作为博士学位申请的硬性条件，而作者将论文发表在 Q3、Q4 区的期刊，则对博士学位申请不起作用。

还有一个问题应该引起注意，影响因子只是评价期刊的一种评价体系中的一个指标而已，与期刊的领域地位是两回事，这样就会出现这种情形：有的期刊的影响因子并不算高，却是领域内公认的权威期刊；有的期刊的影响因子暂时可能很高，却未必是大家心目中的权威期刊。因此，期刊的影响因子固然重要，但不宜片面追求，而应全盘考虑。

不同水平的期刊对论文的写作要求并不

相同，作者应多层面、多角度对期刊和论文进行定位后，再选择目标期刊。选择目标期刊有以下基本原则需要考虑：

1）在对论文的水平进行客观而现实评估的基础上，选择出与论文水平档次相同或接近的目标期刊，力求在较高水平的期刊上发表自己的论文。

2）尽可能在客观评估期刊水平的基础上，选择出合适的、理想的期刊，再按所选期刊对论文的要求来仔细修改论文，待修改质量达到要求时再投稿。

3）在向高水平的期刊投稿时，遭遇退稿或退修属于正常现象，应淡然面对，根据退稿或退修意见（同行评审意见、编辑初审或修改意见）来认真修改论文，提升论文水平，改进研究水平及工作思路。这样，即使遭遇退稿，却可能有较大收获。

4）遭遇退修时，必须注重修改质量，不要草率行事，不要马虎和应付，退修次数多，发表周期就长，甚至还会因修改不达标而最终遭遇退稿。

（3）论文处理时间和发表速度

论文从投稿到被编辑部接收再到给出最终决策，需要经过一段时间。其中，论文从接收到发表所经历的时间就是发表周期。发表周期能确切反映论文处理快慢和发表速度。有的期刊发表周期短，有的则长。选择目标期刊时，不要忽视这个指标，因为论文发表往往有实际需求，例如学生毕业、学位申请通常需要有一定的发表论文数来支持，达不到规定的数量，就不能毕业或获得学位证书；再比如，项目验收或结题、职称或级位评定、报奖评奖、业绩考核等也需要一定的发文量。因此作者在投稿前一定要考虑周全，如果论文有发表时间要求，那么就应该估算一下允许该文的最长发表周期，目标期刊的发表速度能否满足这一要求，若不能，就得考虑选用另一期刊。当然，作者也可与期刊编辑部联络，提出期望的发表周期、加急加快处理等特殊要求，但编辑部是否答应、能否做到，还可能是个未知数。因此，作者须考虑周全，不要因选错期刊而导致自己的重要事情被耽搁。

大部分期刊发表的论文会在其某个位置标注出有关论文的一些日期信息，如收稿日期（received）、修回日期（revised）、录用日期（accepted）、上线日期（online，网络发表日期）等，很容易估算出论文的发表周期，再算算其他论文的发表周期，由这些论文的发表周期总和除以论文数，便可计算出论文的平均发表周期。

（4）退稿率

退稿率也称淘汰率，是期刊编辑部在一段时间（通常为一年）内收到的全部稿件中被作退稿处理的稿件占全部所投稿件的百分率。高水平期刊的退稿率较高，如 *Nature*、*Cell Research* 的退稿率为 92%（学术期刊的退稿率宜在 80% 左右）。作者如果急需发表论文，那么就不要向退稿率高的期刊投稿。值得注意的是，这类退稿率高的期刊，往往并不是"孤军奋战"，也就是说它并没有那么"傻"，只刊登了少量的论文，而将大量的其他论文抛入大海；这些被退稿的论文中也不乏好论文，而退稿率高的期刊往往有系列化的兄弟期刊（姐妹刊）来互相配合、取长补短。例如：在 *Nature* 发不了的论文，可以推荐至其期刊家族中档次低一些的期刊如 *Scientific Reports*（科学报告）来发表；由 *Cell Research* 退稿的论文，多数会被推荐至它的姐妹刊 *Cell Discovery* 来发表。

作者是否愿意接受这种降低档次的安排，也需要综合考量。例如：*Cell Discovery* 创办于 2015 年，刚创办的那几年没有 SCI 数据。作者如果发表论文有对期刊影响因子、分区的要求，那么就不要接受在其上发表；但如果没有数据方面的要求，而更看中它与 *Cell Research* 的关系以及 *Cell Research*

的超高影响力（2015 年的影响因子是 14.812，在中国所有期刊中排名第一，在 *Cell Biology* 领域排名是 9/187），进而也相信 *Cell Discovery* 会有很好的发展前景，那么就应该欣然接受这种降档次安排。果然，从 2018 年，*Cell Discovery* 开始有了自己的 SCI 数据，而且出手不凡，其第一个影响因子是 4.462，在 *Cell Biology* 领域排名是 60/190（同期的 *Cell Research* 的影响因子是 15.393，排名是 10/190）。

（5）参考文献发表在哪些期刊

撰写论文必然引用参考文献，所引文献与论文的内容、主题有很强的相关性，因此应该看看这些文献发表在什么期刊，据此可以大概判别自己的论文是否适于发表在这些期刊。如果其中有跟作者的论文在内容上接近或研究主题上相似、相同的文章，那么刊载这种文章的期刊也比较适合刊登作者自己的论文。这样，根据参考文献发表在什么期刊，就可以初步判定哪些期刊适合刊登作者自己的论文。

由参考文献确定的这些期刊可能属于不同的国家和出版商，数量可能较多，期刊间的差异也可能较大，建议作者通过多种途径了解一下这些期刊，最好下载一些这些期刊刊登的代表性论文，大概了解一下这些论文的体裁、内容及格式体例，再与自己的论文进行对比，发现其间的相似和不足，再回过头来处理、修改、完善自己的论文。

（6）投稿与发表是否收费

期刊多是独立运营、自负盈亏的，有的期刊可能隶属于一个统一运营的出版商或出版集团，但不同期刊的业务流程往往是独立的，期刊的发展需要一支稳定、优秀的团队，以及一个可持续发展的网络工作系统，运营成本较高，经济压力往往很大。因此，很多期刊在不同的阶段会向作者收取不同的费用。例如：作者投稿，需要交论文评审费，用于支付安排同行评议所发生的成本；论文在线发表，需交纳 OA（open access）费⊖。有的期刊还收彩图费，按彩图数量来计算费用；有的甚至收加急费，收取后，为论文安排优先发表，比按正常发表的周期缩短一些；有的收单行本（抽印本）费（分纸质和电子两种：offprints、e-offprints of paper）和广告、海报费（poster）。

作者在选择目标期刊投稿前，需要搞清楚该刊是否收费及费用类别、数量，看看自己能否承担，如果费用类别不合适或价格超出自己的能力，就得想办法，如缩短论文篇幅或改投他刊。不少科研项目得到基金项目的资助，基金使用中往往会拿出或预留一部分作为发表论文的专项费用，即作者发表论文的正常费用如评审费、版面费一般是可以报销的，但国际期刊以及与国际出版商合作的中国英文科技期刊的 OA 费一般是不低的，特别是国际名刊，OA 费非常昂贵，如 NPG 旗下的 *Nature Communication* 的 OA 费是每篇 5 200 USD，*Scientific Reports* 是 1 495 USD，*Light*：*S&A* 是 2 600 英镑（这些是某年的数据）。OA 费作者是否愿意交、能否走课题报销，各个单位的政策不同，因此需要作者自己来决定是否交纳这笔费用。

（7）认真鉴别期刊的合法性

期刊种类非常多，每年都会有大量新刊涌现出来，再加上互联网和大数据环境，期刊种类、数量令人眼花缭乱，经常会有一些冒牌刊、假刊，打着真刊的牌子来向作者收取费用，作者没有多想或由于缺少经验，没有鉴别期刊的合法性，结果就上当了。笔者在工作实践中，经常会收到作者这样的电话，"前几天将评审费转给过去了，收到了吧？""我的论文发表在贵刊 2016 年 15 期，版面费刚办理，款是否已收到？"对前一种

⊖ 对于订阅刊，作者可选，一般不强制；对于 OA 刊，是强制的，由作者或期刊社（编辑部）交纳。

情况,需要查证能确认;而对后者,一听就知作者受骗了,因为我刊一直是双月刊,一年只有6本,何来15期啊!这位作者根本就没有向我刊投过稿,更谈不上交什么费用了。这可能是钓鱼网站捣的鬼啊!

请广大作者一定要提高警惕,认真鉴别期刊的合法性,可以通过各种途径,如上官网、打电话、发邮件、投稿前咨询、判别交费通知真伪等方式来进行查证。

8.3 投稿准备

作者选出目标期刊后,下一步就要准备投稿了。投稿是一件非常严肃的事,投稿前作者应仔细阅读期刊的投稿须知,最好能获得样刊或下载该刊已发表的论文(作为范文),按其写作要求及格式体例进一步修改论文,并撰写投稿信。

8.3.1 阅读投稿须知

(1) 投稿须知的作用

投稿须知也称作者须知、稿约、征稿简则、致作者,也可看作投稿指南,不同期刊有不同的叫法,如 *Instructions for Authors*,*Guide for Authors*,*Guide to Authors*,*General Information for Authors*,*Advice to Contributors* 等,是作者在投稿前对目标期刊必须知道和掌握的事项。SCI 论文的基本格式体例可能相差不大,对论文的框架要求大同小异,但各个期刊都有其自身的特色、风格,对不同的期刊没有完全相同的投稿须知,因此也就没有完全相同的论文写作要求。因此,作者在选定目标期刊后,都应严格按照投稿须知同时参照范文来修改论文。可以说,投稿须知是一位不会说话的第一位审稿专家,也是作者投稿前对论文进行修改的助手、参谋。作者按照期刊的投稿须知对论文进行修改,论文就会形成适合该期刊的格式体例和语言风格,论文的内在质量和外观形象得到进一

步的提升,这种结果至少说明作者为投稿下了一定工夫,投稿后被退稿的可能性就会降低,退修次数就会减少,稿件处理进程就会加快,论文发表过程就更加简捷有效,稿件处理效率得到提高。

作者在投稿前认真阅读、理解投稿须知,并按要求全面、仔细修改论文非常重要。这一点须引起广大作者的高度注意,千万不要认为论文还没有被录用,最终能否录用和发表是个未知数,因此就没有多大必要对论文进行仔细修改。作者如果马马虎虎,懒得好好准备,将存在诸多问题的论文草率地投稿,那么对作者只能有百害而无一利,本来应该是经过精心准备可以被录用的论文,就是因为投稿准备工作不到位而被作了退稿处理,多么可惜啊!

(2) 投稿须知的内容

投稿须知主要介绍期刊基本信息、论文写作要求及投稿、发表的流程,包含写稿、投稿、修稿和发表的具体要求及注意事项,大体有以下几个方面。

1) 期刊办刊宗旨。主要强调什么领域、内容的论文适合在本刊刊登,大体规定了论文的水平和基本内容。例如 *Nature* 的办刊宗旨规定了报道和评论科技领域中最重要的突破,将科学发现的重要结果介绍给公众,让公众尽早知道世界每一学科分支取得的所有进展,要求内容具有突出的科学贡献(科学研究需要),还必须令交叉学科的读者感兴趣。

2) 稿件处理速度。主要告知编辑初审、同行评议、作者修回、论文录用和发表的时间间隔和周期,以利于作者评估论文的发表速度。作者也可以根据目标期刊已发表论文的收稿日期、修回日期、录用日期、上线日期信息大概推算和估计。*Nature* 是稿件处理速度最快的期刊,通常是 4~6 周的审稿周期,重要的论文可 2 周发表。

3) 期刊编辑职责。公布期刊编委会的

组成、责任及义务,编辑的职责,出版商的工作任务。编辑是联络作者与同行评审专家的中间人,主要职责之一是对稿件进行编辑初审,初步审核稿件内容和格式体例是否符合要求,检查投稿材料是否齐备,确定是否存在一稿多投、抄袭以及伦理道德等问题,并将同行评议的审稿意见连同编辑处理意见及时反馈给作者,告知作者稿件的处理进程。

4)投稿方式。明确指出投稿方式,包括稿件的投递方式、需要投递的材料、投稿的操作流程。通常,先告知作者通过在线投稿系统进行投稿,给出在线投稿系统的具体网址;接着讲述投稿需要准备、提交的材料,如投稿信、稿件的电子版(Word、RTF、PDF版本等)、图片规格、作者签名信等。

5)稿件格式和排版。规定论文格式体例和排版要求,涉及论文各个组成部分的写作与规范表达。例如:标题的词数、字体、字号、间距、符号及简洁性;作者署名方式和单位地址,通信作者的联系方式(通信地址、邮箱、电话等),如有共同通信作者和共同第一作者,也应明确说明;正文的结构与词数,是否有摘要,各部分如摘要、前言、材料与方法、结果与讨论、结论等的写作要求,还会涉及层次标题、图表、公式、致谢、参考文献、作者简介、附录等诸多方面。有的期刊的投稿须知还会要求作者下载、参考该刊的最新论文写作模板。

6)收费情况。有的期刊的投稿须知还会写明投稿是否交审稿费,论文网络(在线)发表是否收OA费,印刷版发表是否收版面费,若有彩图是否还需要交彩图费等,以及各种费用的收费标准。有的期刊可能没有这方面的内容,或虽有收费类别方面的内容,但不一定公开收费的标准。这往往是期刊编辑部出于某种隐情考虑而有意为之,作者若遇到这样的期刊,必要时可打电话或发邮件向编辑部咨询。

7)作者利益冲突。明确要求作者投稿(或提交修改稿)时明确作者排名次序,提交一份由所有作者签名的信函,避免发生作者利益冲突,并作为将来作者利益冲突处理的依据。论文往往由多位作者署名,署名的先后顺序反映作者对论文的贡献大小,排名越靠前,贡献程度越大,分量就越重,反之,就越轻。通信作者可以排在最后,但分量并不轻。

8)其他内容。还可能包括一些其他方面的内容,如若是邮寄投稿,当遇到撤稿、退稿时,原稿是给作者寄回,还是一律不退回,由编辑部自行处理。另外,还可能有保密、政治、伦理、道德、抄袭、一稿多投、创新、创造性等方面的内容规定。

(3) Nature 投稿须知

为了方便读者借鉴,下面给出 Nature 投稿须知的结构组成和目录清单,详细内容见其官网(http://www.nature.com/nature/authors/index.html)。

FOR AUTHORS
GUIDELINES TO PREPARING AND SUBMITTING A MANUSCRIPT

Each of the sections below provides essential information for authors. We recommend that you take the time to read them before submitting a contribution to Nature. A site map of our guide to authors may help you navigate to the appropriate section. A series of short (1-2 page) information sheets is also available for downloading, which can be accessed in full via the panel to the right or in separate parts throughout the guide to authors.

Getting published in Nature: The Editorial Process

This document provides an outline of the editorial process involved in publishing a scientific paper (Article or Letter) in Nature, and describes how manuscripts are handled by editors between submission and publication.

Table of contents

1. At submission

1.1 Criteria for publication

1.2 Who decides which papers to publish?

1.3 How to submit an Article or Letter

2. After submission

2.1 What happens to a submitted Article or Letter?

2.2 Referees' reports

2.3 Competitors

2.4 Speed

2.5 What the decision letter means

2.6 Appeals

3. After acceptance

3.1 Formats and lengths of papers

3.2 Subediting of accepted papers

3.3 Proofs and reprints

3.4 Publication and the media

Parts of this document are summarized in a downloadable information sheet.

Manuscript formatting guide

This guide describes how to prepare contributions for submission. We recommend you read this in full if you have not previously submitted a contribution to Nature. We also recommend that, before submission, you familiarize yourself with Nature's style and content by reading the journal, either in print or online, particularly if you have not submitted to the journal recently.

Table of contents

1. Formats for Nature contributions

1.1 Articles

1.2 Letters

1.3 Brief Communications Arising and Corrections

1.4 Other types of submission

2. The editorial process

3. Presubmission enquiries

4. Readability

5. Format of Articles and Letters

5.1 Titles

5.2 Text

5.3 Methods

5.4 References

5.5 End notes

5.6 Life sciences reporting guidelines

5.7 Tables

5.8 Figure legends

5.9 Figures

5.10 Production quality figures

5.11 Extended Data

5.12 Supplementary information

5.13 Chemical structures and characterization of chemical materials

6. Submission

7. Publishing in other Nature and Nature Research journals

Parts of this document are summarized in a downloadable information sheet.

Submissions

This section contains information about submitting your article to Nature.

The instructions on this page refer to Articles, Letters, Reviews and Perspectives. Separate guidelines are available for Brief Communications Arising and for other types of submission.

We strongly advise you to read through Nature's manuscript formatting guide before submitting your manuscript. If you are ready to submit, please proceed directly to our online submission system.

Table of contents

1. Presubmission enquiries

2. Initial submissions

3. Final submissions (after acceptance)

4. Supplementary information

Forms and declarations

On this page are links to the various forms you will need to fill in before your paper can be published.

Table of contents

1. Author checklist

2. Competing interests

3. AOP declaration

4. Licence to publish

5. Structures

6. Reprints

8.3.2 继续修改论文

作者看完投稿须知或通过别的途径对目标期刊进行充分或大体了解后,感觉一下自己的论文有无差距、差距是什么,然后确定修改方案，接下来就要对论文进行修改了。论文修改应重点从以下多个方面来展开：

(1) 按格式体例排版

论文典型格式体例为：标题、摘要、关键词、引言、材料与方法、结果与讨论、结论（结论与展望）、致谢、参考文献和作者简介，还有内嵌的图、表、式以及数字、符号、标点等，有时材料与方法位于结果与讨论之后，致谢位于参考文献之后，作者简介列于首页脚注处，有的论文在最后部分还有附录。论文排版较为简单，依据 SCI 论文写作要求以及目标期刊投稿须知、写作样式、已发表论文格式体例排版即可，相对于投稿前的论文写作容易多了。

(2) 按字体、字号等参数排版

每种期刊对论文字体、字号、正斜体和行间距等参数都有具体要求，而且对不同场合的这些参数的要求不相同。论文标题的字号通常较大而且用黑体（加粗体），各级层次标题的字号通常随层次逐渐变小，小标题有的要求用正体，有的用斜体，有的用黑体，至于是全部字母大写、实词首字母大写，还是除第一个字母、缩写和专有名词外全部小写，依具体期刊的要求而定；量符号基本都用斜体（矩阵、矢量符号用黑体），单位基本都用正体；上下标表示变量时用斜体，表示词首字母或词语的缩写时用正体。

(3) 正确书写署名和单位

作者有不同的身份及署名顺序，如第一作者、通信作者、共同第一作者等，而且作者的姓名特别是中国人的汉语拼音姓名可能有不同的书写形式。建议作者检索该刊已发表的文章，借鉴前人已有的人名写法。对作者人数，一般无严格规定。书写单位名称及有关地址信息时，建议作者逐人核对，与官方名称一致，以确保准确无误。

(4) 核对参考文献引用与著录

核对参考文献十分重要。首先，检查引文数量是否达到要求（SCI 期刊通常要求原创论文的引文不少于 30 篇，小综述的不少于 60 篇，大综述的不少于 120 篇），以及引文是否有代表性（文献种类、内容先进性、时间跨度等），不宜缺少近年的文献；接着，检查正文中所引文献的编号首次出现（包括暗引）时，是否按顺序依次引用，不得出现断号（跳号）或反序（先引大号后引小号）引用；其次，确定正文中引用参考文献的编号与文后参考文献表中的相应文献的编号是否匹配（对应）；最后，核对参考文献是否按目标期刊所用的参考文献体系来标注与著录，著录项目是否齐全，著录格式是否正确，涉及姓名的写法与数量，文章名、期刊名、会议文集名，出版信息（如出版时间、出版地点、出版社名），期刊出版信息（如年、卷、期、起止页码），文献获取路径（网址）及引用日期、网页更新日期等。随着科学技术的发展，各种参考文献格式化软件不断出现，如 EndNote 就是一款较为有名的文献管理软件，作者使用这种软件，非常便利、省时，可大大提高文献引用与著录的效率。

(5) 正确使用与标注缩写

论文中可能出现缩写词，有的是大众或行业熟知的，如 CAD、CT、AIDS 等；有的是不为大众或行业熟知的，如 VMC（Virtual Manufcturing Cell）；有的甚至是作者自定义的字母词（非常规缩写词），如 ST（Similarity Theroy）。对于后两类特别是其中的第二类，应该检查它们在文中首次出现时，是否给出了全称或是否给予解释，以及解释是否恰当。在缩写词全称给出或解释完毕后，当后面再次出现这一术语时，就应该直接用该缩写，不得随意混用同一术语的全称与缩写（一会用全称，一会用缩写，非常混乱），更不能先直接使用一个术语的缩写，后面再次出现时才用其全称或给出解释。

(6) 逐一检查层次标题

论文修改完毕即将投稿时，建议再检查

一下全文的层次标题编号是否齐全、连续（是否有漏号、断号），层次标题是否按逻辑顺序展开，结构层次是否清楚。还要看看各个标题是否简短，子标题的中心语及修饰语是否与父标题重复，因为子标题具有继承父标题的特性，因此不宜重复出现父标题中已有的中心语及修饰语。同时还要看看各个标题的结构，优先用定中或偏正结构（名词或名词性词语），必要时还可用动宾或其他结构。最好还要看看各个标题中的词语的大小写是否符合目标期刊的格式体例要求。

（7）确认结论完备性

SCI 论文中结论通常是必不可少的。一篇论文，不管正文的内容如何如何好，如果没有结论，就不完整，将使论文的水准大打折扣。因为作者研究了半天，究竟解决了什么问题，得出了什么全局性、宏观性、指导性的结论是论文必须交待的。论文是否有结论以及结论是否撰写合格也是投稿后编辑初审、同行评议要重点查看的内容，而且不少情况下审稿时先不看正文，而是直接看结论，如果结论这一关没有通过，正文写得再好恐怕也难有机会了。可见结论的写作是多么重要。

（8）增补作者简介

作者的署名和单位信息中可能未给出作者职称、领域、研究方向、联系方式等信息，这些信息非常重要，特别是其中的领域、研究方向非常重要，对编辑和读者了解作者从事研究工作的状况，进一步了解其研究专长、水平以及与其他研究人员的关系很有帮助。很多作者的投稿没有作者简介，给编辑工作带来不便，稿件被作退稿处理的可能性就加大了。因此在投稿前，作者一定要检查论文是否写了作者简介，如果没有，就应该补上。有的访者（特别是通信作者）简介没有写上联系方式（主要是 E-mail），也是不可取的。

（9）全文语言润色

从以上各方面对论文检查、修改和确认后，仍不宜急于投稿，建议再做一件事，就是对全文进行语言润色，即通读全文，从语法、标点、拼写甚至逻辑等多个方面对论文进行润色，消除错词、错句，达到语言表达的地道性、流畅性和优美性，保证用词准确、标点恰当、语句通顺、前后照应，无单词拼写错误或其他低级错误。例如：将语义为中国的 China 写成语义为瓷器的 china；出现了诸如 at home and abroad 之类的狭隘式表达。有条件的，建议作者请润色公司或专业英语老师及其他擅长英语的高水平专家、学者进行润色。难免要花费一些钱，但这个钱值得花，因为前期所有的努力，都为后期论文的录用与发表贡献了正能量。

也许不少作者觉得，语言润色应该在论文录用后、作者再次修改过程中进行更合适，目前很多期刊也是这样做的。但笔者认为，这是一种态度，也是一种信心，既然要投稿，为的是被录用，那么为何不去准备得更好呢！为了成功，也为了论文的质量，投稿前进行润色是必要的。投稿后论文可能有较多的修改，那就再来一次润色。

8.3.3 撰写投稿信

投稿时应同时附上一封投稿信（Cover Letter, Submission Letter 或 Author Comments），信中包含论文、作者的重要信息及作者的某种承诺，为编辑提供有助于对稿件安排同行评议及进行决策的信息。投稿信一般应包括以下内容：

1）论文题目及所有作者的姓名、单位；

2）论文内容及适合在该刊发表的理由；

3）论文的主要发现及创新点、重要性（一两句话）；

4）论文无一稿多投等伦理问题的承诺；

5）论文内容真实性、无伪造的承诺；

6）作者对论文的确切贡献；

7）所有作者均已看过论文，并同意以该版本投稿；

8）推荐适合本论文的审稿人（同行专家）；

9）提出因竞争或其他原因不适合本论文的审稿人；

10）写明通信作者、通信地址和联系方式（如 E-mail）；

11）第一作者或通信作者署名或签名。

下面给出投稿信的几个范例，供参考。

范例 8-1

Dear Editor,

I am an associate professor of the School of Electrical Engineering and Information, Anhui University of Technology, Anhui Province, China. I graduated from Southeast University in 2011 with Doctor Degree. The research area in the manuscript is about propeller cavitation.

The manuscript has not been previously published, is not currently submitted for review to any other journal, and will not be submitted elsewhere before a decision is made by this journal.

Thank you for your help to my manuscript.

Very sincerely,

×××, Ph. D.

School of Electrical Engineering & Information, ××× University of ××× 243032, P. R. China

Tel：008613××××××

范例 8-2

Dear Editor,

We would like to submit an original article entitled "Effect of structure parameters on meshing stiffness of ZN-type dual-lead worm gear pair", which we wish to be considered for publication in this Journal.

Meshing stiffness of the ZN-type dual-lead worm gear pair plays an important role in the transmission error and dynamic characteristics. Based on its time-varying structure and loads, this study aims to establish a finite element model by using the substructure method and analyze its loaded contact status and the meshing stiffness. The effects of structure parameters on the meshing stiffness are fully investigated.

This article has not been submitted and published elsewhere in whole or in part, and all the authors listed have read it and approved to submit to your journal. There are no any ethical/legal conflicts involved in the article.

We would suggest any of the following individuals as potential reviewers：××× （name, address, and email, etc）, ××× （name, address, and email, etc）, ××× （name, address, and email, etc）.

Correspondence about the paper can be directed to ××× at the following address, phone, and e-mail address：

Address：A319, Building West 5, 99 Yanxiang Road, Qujiang Campus, ××× University, Xi'an 710054, China.

Tel：+86-29-×××; E-mail：×××.

Many thanks for your attention and looking forward to your decision.

Sincerely yours,

×××

Dec. 18, 2016

范例 8-3

Dear Editor,

I would like to submit a research paper for publication in this Journal, titled "Effective iterated greedy algorithm for flow-shop scheduling problems with time lags". The paper is co-authored by ×××, ×××, and ×××.

Although various algorithms have been proposed to solve flow-shop problems with time lags, algorithms specifically designed for non-permutation and permutation flowshop problems that consider time lags have not been reported. Therefore, to minimize the makespan and satisfy time lag constraints, we applied the iterated greedy algorithm to non-permutation and permutation flow-shop problems with time lag considerations and developed novel meta-heuristic algorithms for solving scheduling problems. The proposed algorithms were compared with well-known simple and complex instances with various time lag ranges and were found to be superior to conventional algorithms in terms of both solution quality and computational expense.

Because of their easy implementation, the proposed algorithms are suitable for various industrial applications. We believe that this contribution is theoretically and practically relevant. We believe that the findings of this study are relevant to the scope of your journal and will be of interest to its readership.

This manuscript has not been published or presented elsewhere in part or in entirety and is not under consideration by another journal. We have read and understood your journal's policies, and we believe that neither the manuscript nor the study violates any of these. There are no conflicts of interest to declare.

Thank you for your consideration. We hope our manuscript is suitable for publication in your journal.

Sincerely,

×××

School of Mechanical Engineering, University of ×××, Beijing 100083, China

Tel：+86-11-×××××；+86-11-×××××

E-mail：×××@sina.com

8.3.4 *Nature* 投稿准备

向 *Nature* 投稿，准备工作大体是将符合投稿要求的论文、对审稿有正面意义的辅助材料、对投稿所需填写的有关文本信息等准备好，并对投稿所需做出的决定提前想好，这些工作准备越到位，投稿过程就越顺畅，论文录用的可能性就越大。这些准备工作主要包括：

1）进一步修改论文，使其结构体例与投稿要求基本一致；

2）再次确认论文有一个明确、原始的结论，重在总结研究成果的创新性；

3）再次确认论文写作达到简洁、明了，没有使用难懂的专业术语；

4）给编辑提前写好一封短信，解释论文内容对领域内外读者的重要性；

5）大体估计一下论文的篇幅，即论文的词数、占用的版面多少；

6）再次确定有无通信作者，若有就将其联系方式如 email、电话提前准备好；

7）确定论文发表的体裁，是原创论文还是读者来信，前者录用难度很大，可转为后者；

8）了解论文的编辑处理模式，知道投稿后论文将由不同学科的编辑们互相阅读，责任编辑在综合每位编辑的意见后给出意见，每位编辑的意见都很重要；

9）投稿前可以向编辑部发一封询问信，解释论文的重要性，附上摘要、参考文献。

Nature 对论文写作有非常严格的要求，例如有以下基本规定：

1) Explain, don't hype. Show, don't tell.

2) Results should speak for themselves.

3) CONTEXT—Not every reader will understand the details but every reader should appreciate your work's significance.

4) Descriptive not superlative—femtosecond spectroscopy not ultrafast spectroscopy.

5) Format isn't critical. RevTeX is fine.

6) Titles in references are extremely helpful.

8.4 投稿

作者选定目标期刊后，需要仔细阅读投稿须知，多种途径了解期刊情况，根据投稿要求来进行、完成投稿。投稿方式有多种，如在线投稿、邮件投稿、邮寄投稿，其中在线投稿是当前最为普遍的投稿方式，最为传统的是邮寄投稿，而邮件投稿介于二者之间。

8.4.1 在线投稿

互联网和数字化技术的普及和发展，使越来越多的期刊采用在线投稿作为主体投稿方式，有时辅以邮件投稿。所谓在线投稿，就是作者上网登陆目标期刊的投稿系统来进行相关操作，将自己稿件的信息和全文提交给期刊编辑部。不同投稿系统在功能设置、操作步骤、内容细节上有差异，但总体上差别并不大。在线投稿通常由以下四步组成：

（1）用户注册

投稿时找到目标期刊官网，进入在线投稿系统。首次向某期刊投稿时，需要先注册成为其投稿系统的用户，这样就需要进入注册界面，填写注册人（作者之一）的有关信息，如作者姓名、单位、联系方式（主要是 E-mail）等，注册成功后，注册人邮箱会收到注册成功的回执，并告知注册人的用户名和密码。用户名和密码是作者以后登陆投稿系统，查看稿件处理状态、修改论文和以后继续投稿都会用到的密钥，需要牢记或妥善保管。通常注册的多为通信作者或第一作者的信息和邮箱。注册完成后，进入下一步登陆投稿系统进行操作。

（2）登陆系统进行操作

凭用户名和密码登陆进投稿系统后，开始填写有关投稿的一些信息，大体包括选择文章类型（Article Type）、文章题目（Full Title）、作者信息（Given/First Name、Middle Name、Family/Last Name、Academic Degree（s）、E-mail Address、Institution，选择是否 corresponding author）、资助（基金）项目信息（Funding Information）、摘要（Abstract）、投稿信内容（Comments）、推荐审稿人（Suggest Reviews）等，然后上传正文和图表（Attach files）。

（3）确认提交的文档是否符合要求

在上传投稿信息及正文、图表之前，点击某一按钮，系统会自动检查所填写的信息和上传的文档是否符合设定的要求，作者在投稿操作前，需要仔细阅读具体投稿要求，看明白具体要求和操作细节，如词数或字符数是否超出限制、必填项是否未填、文件格式是否正确、插图（格式和分辨率）是否符达标、文件格式和大小是否符合规定，即使各文档已成功上传，在最终正式提交前还应再次确认上传的文档是否符合要求，所填写的信息是否准确完整，如发现有任何问题，都要返回上一步甚至上上步进行修正，修正后再点击下一步继续操作。

（4）完成投稿

完成上述操作后，点击提交新稿按钮（Submit New Manuscript），正常情况下系统会提示投稿成功，这时投稿才算完成。投稿成功后，编辑部会收到稿件，进入编辑处理流程，作者会收到投稿成功的邮件回执。以后作者可随时登陆系统，查看稿件的处理状态。

8.4.2 邮件投稿

邮件投稿即电子邮件投稿，是作者上网登陆某个邮件系统，将投稿的有关信息作为邮件正文和电子版本的论文文档作为邮件附件发送到目标期刊编辑部的投稿邮箱。在传统的邮寄投稿行将退出历史舞台之前，邮件投稿可以说是一种非常快速、先进和令人激动的投稿方式。那时邮件投稿还不算普遍，如果某个期刊编辑部提供邮件投稿功能，那么就可以说该编辑部非常时髦、主流和超前。随着互联网技术的飞速发展，邮件投稿越来越不多见了，但并未销声匿迹，在主体在线投稿不尽人意的时候（如系统升级、运行出现故障或论文文档太大等），它还能派上用场，成为"强大"在线投稿的"小儿科"弥补。

编辑部的投稿邮箱通常在期刊的投稿须知、网站、封面、宣传海报、征稿通知或其他地方给予广而告之，对稿件格式常有电子文件类型如 Word、PDF 版本等的具体要求。邮件投稿同样需要作者提交电子版的投稿信、扫描或拍照版的版权转让声明等相关材料。使用邮件投稿方式时，建议作者选择国际大型网站或其他较为好用的邮箱（QQ 邮箱一般很好用，支持大容量的附件传送），将电子邮件的主题明确写为投稿，并随时关注收件箱内的邮件，及时关注邮件投稿是否成功，如果成功，通常会收到投稿成功的反馈邮件。

8.4.3 邮寄投稿

邮寄投稿就是将纸质稿件邮寄给期刊编辑部，具体一点说就是投稿者将投稿所需要的所有相关资料（主体是论文，还包括图表及其他相关资料）通过快递、挂号信或普通邮递等方式寄送至编辑部的收稿地址，其中快递又包括国际快递和国内快递，国际快递分航运和水运，国内快递分航运和普通快递，不同邮递方式在邮寄速度上不同，投稿人可根据需要并结合自己的实际情况来选择最为合适的一种。

邮寄投稿曾经是期刊投稿的唯一方式，在邮件投稿来临之前，它一直存在着，而且不知道已经存在了多久，大概在我们出生时的很久以前就存在了，当时的人们也许不会想到，以后还会有电子邮件这类"高大上"的、似乎没有物理空间限制的先进方式会在后来的互联网时代迅速取代了邮寄投稿。目前采用邮寄投稿来接收投稿的期刊恐怕已经很少了。

邮寄投稿时，需要投稿人了解期刊编辑部对文稿份数、所需材料等的具体要求，并确定准确的邮寄地址和收稿人（或收稿部门）。通常需要准备以下资料：

（1）投稿信

作者应撰写投稿信，写明投稿需求，对论文内容也应简单介绍，最好交待一下论文的创新点。有条件的可以将投稿信打印在作者（通信作者）单位的公用信笺上；对于学生，就没有必要这么做了，通常用 A4 纸打印就可以了。

（2）论文原稿

论文是整个投稿的核心，作者需要准备好论文的全部内容，包括图表及其他相关资料，通常需要准备若干份，建议作者自己保留一份，以备以后与编辑交流用。

（3）版权转让声明

邮寄投稿时最好同时附上一份版权转让声明，这样就能一次搞定投稿，免得以后编辑部收到作者所投的文稿时再另行通知作者邮寄这种声明。有的期刊可能是在论文录用（Accept）后才通知作者签署版权转让声明。

部分期刊还可能需要与稿件有关的其他资料，如稿件对照检查表、实验数据、佐证材料、原始照片等。邮寄投稿材料时，最好用曲别针将各种资料按类别固定，建议不用订书钉装订，因为订书钉装订容易弄破材料。邮寄照片、光盘时，宜用硬纸板加以保护，并选用大号、结实的信封。邮寄投稿较为麻烦，手续繁琐，还得到邮局排队，最大的问题是邮寄周期较长，邮件对象在邮寄过程中弄不好还可能会丢失，因此它被快速、先进的在线投稿、邮件投稿方式所取代甚至被彻底淘汰将是一种历史的必然。

8.4.4 注意事项

投稿是一种极为严肃的事情，须认真对待，有以下事项需要注意：

（1）投稿前准备好所有所需材料

目前网上报名、网上申请、网上交费、网上报奖之类的在线操作非常普遍，大家对网上操作恐怕早已熟悉，操作经验也很丰富，其实在线投稿也是同样的道理。建议作者在正式投稿前充分做好各项准备工作，将所有必填的内容提前写好电子文本，准备好所有所需提交的附件的电子版，并注意电子版的文件格式，同时还得写好投稿信。投稿时只需从写好的文本中直接复制文字，从存放在电脑里某目录下的文件选上直接上传，即可顺利完成投稿，除非投稿过程中出现网络、机器故障或人为误操作。

（2）避免一稿多投和重复发表

投稿时需要向期刊编辑部保证，不存在一稿多投、重复发表以及其他伦理道德问题，有关内容需要在投稿信里列出，这是投稿的基本要求。既不要明知故犯，同时向几个期刊投稿，而在投稿信里丝毫不会提及有关实情；也不要因为稿件处理周期超出预期，等不到稿件的最终处理结果而又向别的期刊重复投稿。

（3）明白可以接受二次发表的情况

有些类型的文章在某种情况下允许二次发表，如专业机构发布的诊疗指南，但要求比较严格。首先，在二次发表前，作者需要征得各目标期刊编辑部的许可，而且需要向二次发表期刊的编辑部提供首次发表的稿件（电子文件或纸质复印件均可）；其次，允许二次发表的论文是面向不同的读者群的，或二次发表使用另一种语言；最后，需要作者在二次发表的论文中标注该文已全文或部分发表过，并指出首次发表的文献出处。

（4）随时查阅稿件状态，多联络编辑部

对于在线投稿，投稿成功后投稿系统会自动给作者发送投稿成功回执；对邮件、邮寄投稿，多数期刊编辑部会给作者发送投稿成功回执，但有的期刊可能不发送这样的回执。当遇到后一种情况，或者不确认投稿是否成功，或对编辑部的处理过程不放心，或有这样那样的疑问时，建议作者先发送电子邮件询问，必要时打电话提出问题，目前有的编辑部还开设了相关的 QQ 群、微信群，作者也可以通过进入有关群向相关人员进行在线咨询。在线投稿的一个好处是提供在线跟踪功能，作者可以随时登陆系统，查阅稿件处理情况，以及下一步需要做的事项，助推论文处理进展，为论文及时发表添砖加瓦。

8.4.5 *Nature* 投稿

向 *Nature* 投稿，准备工作做好后，接下来就可以投稿了，大体流程及主要事项如下：

1）投稿时务请充分掂量，*Nature* 只有 5%~10% 的中稿率，竞争非常激烈。

2）进入 *Nature* 官网，注册用户，以作者身份登录投稿系统。

3）按投稿步骤和操作要求，在线填写投稿信息，上传论文全文及其他材料，并提交。

4）投稿成功后，系统将为所投稿件分配稿号，同时会用明信片或 email 通知稿号。

5）编辑部对稿件分类，常归为自然科学和生命科学两组，有些学科如海洋属于交叉学科，介于自然科学和生命科学之间，不大好准确归类，最终将这类稿件分到其中一个小组。

6）各小组根据稿件的专业类别，将稿件分给相应专业的编辑，即该稿件的责任编辑。

7）责任编辑对稿件进行初审，即编辑初审，决定稿件是否送同行评议，作出决定前还要安排编辑同事们进行讨论，充分听取他们的意见。此环节重在判断稿件是否有广泛的科学意义和读者群体，领域外的读者是否也适用。

8）*Nature* 不设编委会，避免因编委个人喜好、偏向或歧视而产生审稿的不公正现象，同时还能减少对稿件的决策时间。

9）*Nature* 实行科学编辑制，编辑对稿件完全自主决策，编辑标准趋于统一，将审稿延误时间减少到最小程度。

向 *Nature* 投稿还有一些细节值得大家注意，如果做得充分、到位，将有助于稿件的录用：

1）Cover letters useful but not mandatory.

2）SHORT cover letters are best—if significance can be summarized uniquely in a single concise paragraph, it might be for us! If you need two pages, it probably isn't!

3）Referee suggestions-Can be helpful. -Please don't suggest former supervisor, former students, friends, parents.

4）Try to honour referee exclusion requests, as long as they are reasonable (3-4 individuals).

5）Identify all related papers submitted

elsewhere.

注意已投别处的文章与这次投稿文章的关系,确定是否存在重复发表或一稿多投的问题,如果存在,则坚决杜绝或想办法解决。

8.5 审稿

投稿后,作者往往着急,想尽早有结果,心情可以理解,但着急没有用,静候可能会更好。建议作者暂时忘掉这件事而去做别的事,这样反而感觉就没那么着急了。审稿过程通常是这样的:编辑初审、同行评议(领域专家评审)、编辑再审做出决定(录用、退修、拒稿),必要时再走上数个轮回。虽然审稿不是作者的事,但作者应了解审稿流程及有关细节,避免因稿子状态不合预期而产生不必要的急躁或不满情绪,这样反而无助于稿件的录用。

8.5.1 编辑初审

编辑部收到投稿后,首先进行编辑初审(有的期刊交其编委或客座编辑来完成),除了对论文主题与出版物刊登方向是否相符、有无政治错误、伦理道德(如一稿多投、抄袭等)问题、语言文字重复率是否超过规定值(通常不超过30%)等方面进行审查外,还要审查论文的写作质量、格式体例是否达到目标期刊的基本投稿要求。每种期刊的办刊宗旨、报道范围、领域及优先报道条件,开设的栏目,论文写作格式要求(包括篇幅、图表、公式等),稿件受理、审稿和退修的规定,语言表达是否合适,以及与作者的其他约定等,都体现在投稿须知中。不符合投稿须知或写作很不到位的论文在编辑初审时会被淘汰掉(不经同行评议直接退稿),这就是所谓的 Reject without review(退稿,即直接拒稿),从而失去专家评审机会,低质量的论文即使没有失去专家评审机会,专家评审通过的概率也很低;退一步说,写作质量差的论文即使通过了专家评审,也需要返给作者大修,修改工作量很大,甚至经过多轮返修才能达标,这样论文的发表周期必然会很长。

编辑初审的标准相对较低,但对稿件的淘汰率是不低的,如 Nature、Cell Research 等高影响期刊,其编辑初审的退稿率通常达到90%以上。当然,普通期刊的退稿率一般没有这么高,但有一个有趣的现象,不少期刊逐渐懂得这其中蕴含的成本得失机理。一个期刊的收稿量随着发展的推移,可能有逐年增多的趋势,但其中高质量的占比并不高,如果将过多的差稿送给专家评审,专家可能不乐意审,认为审这种稿子是一种浪费,甚至埋怨编辑部;另外,现在专家可能事务较多,有的并没有将审稿作为一项"正业"来做,这样就会出现审稿拖延甚至审稿石沉大海的现象,审稿效率极低,给编辑部和作者带来较大的损失,这样的稿子不会是一篇或两篇,在一定时间跨度内可能就是一个较大的量。因此,提高编辑对专业研究背景现状的了解深度和范围,提高编辑初审的能力和水平,加强对稿子录用与否的决定权,都是自然而然的事情了。这样,对编辑初审的退稿率有逐渐增多的趋势就并不难理解了。

有的论文可能存在较大的问题,如篇幅过多或过少、图片格式不对、语言表达错误较多,但考虑其有较高的学术价值或创新的内容,修改后容易达标,因此在编辑初审环节没有作退稿处理,而是给予 Revise before review(审前修,即修改后再送同行评议)。

这样，编辑就将稿件返回作者进行修改，作者按要求修改后，需要重新上传修改稿，同时提交修改稿的投稿信（以下称投修改稿信），与最初的投稿过程相似。

有的论文也许在内容、体裁、方向或其他方面与所投期刊的要求不大相符，而适合在另外的期刊上刊登。对于这种稿件，编辑初审也可作 Decline and transfer to transfer desk（转投他刊）的处理。这种处理多发生在同一期刊群间的转投，通过系统来操作，简便容易。注意：一篇稿子如果遭到一个期刊的退稿，转到另一期刊时不见得也会遭到退稿，也就是说，对于一篇稿子，一个期刊可能给出负面的意见，而另一个期刊也许会给出正面的意见。因此，请广大作者一定要有信心，暂时的失败并不可怕，可怕的是轻易放弃。笔者认为，一篇文章只要能写出来，就没有发表不了的，50%的可能性至少是有了。因此，"写"就是"机会"，就是"成功"，如果不写，则就是"零"，永无成功！

论文写作质量差，不论对作者还是对编辑，均是有害而无利的。作者在投稿前必须认真研读投稿须知或浏览样刊，准确领会和掌握论文写作的要求和原则，避免因盲目投稿和写作不规范而影响论文的发表。规范写作是SCI论文发表的前提和基础。

8.5.2 专家选择

稿件通过编辑初审后，责任编辑首先要做的就是为稿件评审选择合适的专家，把符合基本投稿要求的论文送给所选的专家去评审。领域专家有如此之多，其层次、级别及研究方向、学术专长不尽相同，要从有如此众多相异专家的审稿队伍中选择出几位适合评审某篇稿子研究内容的专家来，确实不是一件易事，况且这只是从稿件内容与专家专业研究方向是否适合的角度来说的，如果再考虑一下专家的身体、年龄、忙闲、审稿意愿等实际状况（或状态）因素，那么这个专家选择工作就更难做了。

虽然专家选择需要考虑的因素较多，但不同期刊的做法相差不大。*Nature* 的专家选择较具代表性，下面给出其专家选择大体上考虑的十几个因素：

1）除本篇稿件外，是否还有其他相关稿件也需要考虑送审；

2）如果选择出合适的审稿专家（目标审稿人），那么最近是否给其送审过稿件；

3）目标审稿人在下个月的活动情况是怎样的，是否适合给其安排审稿任务；

4）目标审稿人过去审稿工作情况是怎样的，是否胜任将要安排给的审稿任务；

5）鉴于目标审稿人可能拒审或不能按时审回等意外情况，需要选择备选审稿人，备选审稿人与目标审稿人之间以及备选审稿人之间的专业是否吻合；

6）所选审稿人可能来自不同的国家，应从多种途径（多个方面）来接触、了解审稿人；

7）直接联系审稿人或者通过别的什么途径，落实一下审稿人是否能联系上；

8）直接联系审稿人或者通过别的什么途径，落实一下审稿人是否愿意审稿；

9）安排审稿任务时，首先要求审稿人作出承诺，与稿件的作者无竞争或利害关系；

10）作者可以推荐审稿人，编辑可以参考、判断和选择，当然不一定采纳；

11）作者可以要求回避一些审稿人，编辑一般尊重作者的这种合理诉求。

8.5.3 同行评议

稿件通过编辑初审后，会送给若干专家（通常2~4名）评审，这就是同行评议，这是目前学术期刊界一种较为普遍的有效审稿方式。专家主要审查论文的学术水平，如是否具有发表价值，是否达到先进水平，也可如同编辑初审，对论文内容的相符性以及是否存在一稿多投、抄袭、剽窃或重复他人工作等方面进行审查，并提出修改意见和建议。

审稿意见没有固定的写作格式，写法上较为自由，不过其关注点还是有的：

1）论文是否进行了全面的文献综述，是否清楚交待了研究现状并指出现有研究的不足；

2）论文的原创性、创新性，这是论文的灵魂和根本；

3）论文的水平、内容是否符合期刊的要求；

4）论文的主题是否具有研究价值和意义；

5）研究方法是否合理，立题依据是否充分，实验方法评价是否可靠，技术含量怎样；

6）论文有无结果、结论，且与主题是否相关，是否正确且有意义；

7）论文的语言表达是否地道，图、表、式、参考文献是否规范；

8）对论文不足之处的描述是否实事求是。

Nature 的审稿人选稿标准主要包括以下方面：

1）哪些人会对新的结果感兴趣，感兴趣的原因是什么；

2）是否有相关研究结果，结果成立前需要解决哪些学术问题；

3）是否有创新或贡献，如何看待论文的贡献及其重要性；

4）审稿人只需进行客观评价，不需给出是否适合刊登的意见；

5）审稿意见仅供编辑决策参考，不一定被编辑采纳。

另外还要注意，审稿意见分为给编辑的和给作者的两类，通常两类意见完全相同，或主体内容相同（不方便对作者说的话，就需要在给编辑的审稿意见中写出来）。

审稿人会按期刊的审稿要求逐一写出审稿意见。有的编辑部在安排同行评议时，会给审稿人发送一个文件，列出详细的审稿要点，如期刊重点刊登方向、稿件录用率、论文刊出后被引前景、相关研究的可持续性等等，从而使审稿人有重点地评审，增加审稿的客观性、导向性。国际上并没有公认而统一的审稿标准，再加上审稿人可能来自不同的国家和地区，有不同的专业背景，尽管编辑部要求审稿人在审稿时本着为科研服务、为作者负责、客观准确审稿的态度，但不同审稿人的审稿视角和观点往往存在差别。

值得注意的是，专家审查的重点虽然不是论文的写作水平，但通常也会对写作方面存在的问题提出意见，对写作不规范和语言表达差的论文，不论其学术水平如何，通常难以过关。笔者记得某专家曾对一篇写作非常糟糕的论文给出这样的意见："这是我审稿以来遇到的写作最差的一篇论文！"对有如此评审意见的论文的最终处理结果是可想而知的。这进一步说明了规范的重要性，写作水平而不是学术水平使论文未能通过专家评审，对作者来说是很可惜的。专家在论文写作方面提出的修改意见对作者以后修改论文也有一定的影响。

高水平期刊的审稿人一般为领域权威专家、学者和学术带头人，编辑一般会综合考虑多方因素来选择最合适的审稿专家，有时会要求作者推荐合适的审稿人，作者也可提出需要回避的审稿人。多数专家的态度是认真、严谨的，虽然对论文的最终录用没有决定权，但其意见会影响编辑做出决定，从而决定论文的命运。

下面给出某篇稿件的两个审稿意见范例。其中，审稿意见一对稿件的最终意见是

Minor Revisions（小修），给编辑和作者的具体意见不完全相同；审稿意见二对稿件的最终意见是 Major Revisions（大修），给编辑和作者的具体意见完全相同。可见，对同一稿件，不同审稿人的审稿意见可能不大相同，甚至完全相反，最终处理意见还得由编辑来决定。

范例 8-4
某稿件的审稿意见一

Reviewer Recommendation Term：	Minor Revisions

Comments to Editor：

Comments on paper "Determination of surface roughness in wire and arc additive manufacturing based on laser vision sensing" ×××

1. Innovation
The study reported in the paper is systematic, detailed and innovative. Similar method was used for the same purpose by other researchers but with different light source. The work may provide an effective method for industry of additive manufacturing to measure and therefore to improve the surface roughness of the built parts.
2. Literature and references
The paper reviewed sufficient relevant research results and references.
3. Scientific and academic contribution
The idea of this research is good and creativity. To verify the measurement it is suggested that another alternative method be used to confirm or compare the accuracy of the proposed technique. Also the timing of this method for a measurement should be mentioned as a reference.
4. Writing
The writing of the paper is, in general, good but there are some words used inadequate and in need of checking. In addition, the Section of Calibration looks lengthy and could be shortened if the calibration procedure is a one-go for the setup.
5. Suggestion
This paper should be accepted for publication in this Journal after revision. The content of the research fits the scope of the journal.
6. Actions requested
* Checking English (suggestions attached)
* Shorten some of the basics of ideal pin-hole model calculations, if possible
* Adding labels in the photograph (Figure 2)
* Including one additional Reference which can help further assess the machined surface in 3D and surface functionality：
- K. Cheng and N. Aris, Characterization of the surface functionality on precision machined engineering surfaces, International Journal of Advanced Manufacturing Technology, Vol. 38, No. 3-4, 2008, pp. 402-409.
* See comments on the file

Comments to Author：

The idea of this research is good and creativity. To verify the measurement it is suggested that another alternative method be used to confirm or compare the accuracy of the proposed technique. Also the timing of this method for a measurement should be mentioned as a reference.
The writing of the paper is, in general, good but there are some words used inadequate and in need of checking. In addition, the Section of Calibration looks lengthy and could be shortened if the calibration procedure is a one-go for the setup.
Actions requested：
* Checking English (suggestions attached)
* Shorten some of the basics of ideal pin-hole model calculations, if possible
* Adding labels in the photograph (Figure 2)
* Including one additional Reference which can help further assess the machined surface in 3D and surface functionality：
- K. Cheng and N. Aris, Characterization of the surface functionality on precision machined engineering surfaces, International Journal of Advanced Manufacturing Technology, Vol. 38, No. 3-4, 2008, pp. 402-409.
* See comments on the file

范例 8-5
某稿件的审稿意见二

Reviewer Recommendation Term：	Major Revisions

Comments to Editor：

This paper studies the determination method to quantify the surface roughness based on laser vision sensing. It is useful in additive manufacturing. And I have several questions and suggestions：
1. The word "an idea plane …" in second paragraph of section 3.1 should be "an ideal plane …".
2. There is not enough experiments to prove the methods in this paper.
3. It is better to compare the method mentioned in this paper with the other methods.
4. It is better to add the discussion about the result of this paper.
5. There should be a size expressing in Fig. 5 and Fig. 8(a).

Comments to Author：

This paper studies the determination method to quantify the surface roughness based on laser vision sensing. It is useful in additive manufacturing. And I have several questions and suggestions：
1. The word "an idea plane …" in second paragraph of section 3.1 should be "an ideal plane …".
2. There is not enough experiments to prove the methods in this paper.
3. It is better to compare the method mentioned in this paper with the other methods.
4. It is better to add the discussion about the result of this paper.
5. There should be a size expressing in Fig. 5 and Fig. 8(a).

8.5.4 编辑决定

同行评议的周期一般是 2～4 周，有的可能长一些。专家审稿意见返回后，编辑就应着手处理，汇总审稿人意见，做出决定，必要时应综合其他意见及相关因素，再撰写一封审稿结果处理短信，也称编辑决定意见或编辑决定信（修稿信或退稿信），最后将审稿意见与这封短信反馈给作者（大约在投稿后 2 至 3 月完成）。这个过程即为编辑决定。

1. 稿件最终处理结果

（1）直接录用（Accept）

直接录用是稿件不需修改而录用，但很少出现，一般发生在国际顶尖的科学家、专家学者身上。当然，如果作者在论文写作准备、进行和投稿前肯下工夫，按照 SCI 论文要求及目标期刊的规定来精心准备，达到直接录用也是可能的，只是多数作者缺乏这种认识，进而没有这样做罢了。直接录用的论文一般包含重大研究发现、创新理论和技术，有重大的理论意义或工程应用价值，写作水准极高，已达到目标期刊的要求，录用后直接提交生产部门制作。

（2）编辑后录用（Accept but needs final editing）

编辑后录用是指稿件经过编辑加工而录用，这也是投稿作者期望的事情，平常出现较少。这类论文在内容上具有发表意义和价值，写作上也符合期刊的要求，但仍会有一些地方需要编辑按照刊登要求进行修改，修改合格后录用，提交生产部门制作。

（3）小修（Minor revisions）

小修是稿件存在一些小的问题，需要作者小改，修改后再由编辑决定是否录用。这种情况较多，多数发表过论文的作者，都有根据专家审稿和编辑意见修改论文的经历，有时还可能需要走上几个轮回进行多次修改才能合格。有时作者可以根据编辑意见描述的语气，猜出稿件录用的可能性。小修一般修改较少、较小，比如实验结果解释不够详细，图表质量不合要求、量符号大小写和正斜体处理不当，公式、引文、插图或表格的编号不连续，结论写作不到位，创新点没有明确写出或写作不到位等，通常不需补充实验，但有时可能需要补充一些文献，要针对专家和编辑提出的每个问题认真修改、补充和完善。

（4）大修（Major revisions）

大修就是平常所说的修后再审，指稿件存在较大、较多的问题，需要作者大改，修改后由编辑重新安排同行评议，再来决定稿件录用与否。大修较深、较难或需要修改的地方较多：如研究背景没有写或写清楚（文献引用不足、不具有代表性，综述不够，存在的问题没有交待或交待不充分），结论没有写出来或写成了摘要，实验存在问题而需要完善，实验数据不充分而需要补充，理论支持或总结不够，研究结果缺少分析或分析不足，图、表、式中的字符不清楚，创新点没有任何交待等。条件许可时，作者一定要按照要求补充实验，如果做不到，则应向编辑说明情况；还可能需要补充理论、分析或进行对比说明。修改稿提交后，编辑通常还要送给上次给予大修意见的专家，当然也可以安排别的专家来审稿。

（5）退稿（Reject after review）

退稿（拒稿）有编辑初审和同行评议两种退稿，后一种也称审后退稿，有以下三种情况：

1）未能通过专家评审，编辑部将不再接受该论文的再投稿，即使作者进行了大修，再投稿通常也是没有实际意义的。这种情况下，稿件虽被退了，但作者会收到一个附加物——退稿信，信中会附有专家审稿意见，这样作者就可以按照审稿意见对论文进行修改完善，审稿意见也可为作者以后科研计划制订、论文撰写提供参考。

2）审稿专家意见存在严重分歧或论文写作存在缺陷，如论文研究主题不明确、研究价值未体现、文不扣题、缺少实验结果分析或语言表达错误较多等。作者可以重新撰写、修改后再投，尽管不能保证一定能发表，但通常能得到优先处理。

3）转投其他刊（Decline and transfer to transfer desk）

退稿是 SCI 期刊的一种常态，作者应保持良好的心态，不必为此过分难过，其实完全可以树立信心，再接再厉，准备好了再次尝试，只要有信心就应重新投稿，最终才能收获胜利。当然，作者也可考虑将修改稿改投他刊。

2. Nature 编辑决定

Nature 编辑决定流程及要点主要包括：

1）追求的目标是尽快为所投来的稿件做出所有决定；

2）编辑初审一周内完成，并通知作者初审结果；

3）尽最大可能最快提供审稿报告（审稿意见）；

4）电话或邮件催促未按时审回的审稿人；

5）整理审稿意见和论文内容，撰写编辑决定信；

6）将编辑决定信分享给同事，在同事间传阅；

7）将编辑决定信提交其他科学编辑、主编阅读；

8）坚持公平、公正，确保不同论文之间标准的统一；

9）达成一致时，给作者发信，提交编辑决定信；

10）要求同行评议先返回审稿意见，后返回其他资料如稿件和图表。

从以上流程及要点可以总结出 Nature 编辑决定的内涵：

1）**YES**："Accept in Principle"。

● Minor revisions—we will publish your paper.

2）**NO**："Closed door"。

● Rejection—the paper is not for us.

3）**MAYBE**："Pending + Quotes" or

"Open door".

- We may publish your paper ... or we still might not.
- Important revisions needed.
- No decision until reviewers concerns are addressed.
- Your paper will go back to referees!

3. 编辑决定信范例

以下给出针对上节示例中的那篇稿件的编辑决定信的范例，供参考。

此编辑决定信由三部分组成。前面是正文，告知作者其稿子已被录用，但发表前需要按专家意见进行修改（稿件状态是 Minor revisions），同时告知投稿系统网址及投稿人用户名和密码；后面两部分是两位专家的审稿意见。值得注意的是，编辑决定信是由编辑选择、填写有关内容由系统自动生成的，其中所附专家审稿意见就是给作者的审稿意见，当然编辑可以进行修改，必要时也可把专家给编辑的审稿意见复制过来，补充一下给作者的审稿意见。

范例 8-6
View Letter

Dear Mr ×××,

We have received the reports from our advisors on your manuscript, "Determination of surface roughness in wire and arc additive manufacturing based on laser vision sensing", submitted to this Journal.

Based on the advice received, I have decided that your manuscript can be accepted for publication after you have carried out the corrections as suggested by the reviewer(s).

Below, please find the reviewers' comments for your perusal.

You are kindly requested to also check the website for possible reviewer attachment(s).

Please submit your revised manuscript online by using the Editorial Manager system which can be accessed at:

http://×××.edmgr.com/

Your username is: ********
Your password is: ********

I am looking forward to receiving your revised manuscript before 09 Apr 2017.

With kind regards,

×××, PhD
Associate Editor
Comments for the Author:

Reviewer #1:
1. Innovation

The study reported in the paper is systematic, detailed and innovative. Similar method was used for the same purpose by other researchers but with different light source. The work may provide an effective method for industry of additive manufacturing to measure and therefore to improve the surface roughness of the built parts.

2. Literature and references

The paper reviewed sufficient relevant research results and references.

3. Scientific and academic contribution

The idea of this research is good and creativity. To verify the measurement it is suggested that another alternative method be used to confirm or compare the accuracy of the proposed technique. Also the timing of this method for a measurement should be mentioned as a reference.

4. Writing

The writing of the paper is, in general, good but there are some words used inadequate and in need of checking. In addition, the Section of Calibration looks lengthy and could be shortened if the calibration procedure is a one-go for the setup.

5. Suggestion

This paper should be accepted for publication in this Journal after revision. The content of the research fits the scope of the journal.

6. Actions requested

* Checking English (suggestions attached)
* Shorten some of the basics of ideal pin-hole model calculations, if possible
* Adding labels in the photograph (Figure 2)
* Including one additional Reference which can help further assess the machined surface in 3D and surface functionality:
  - K. Cheng and N. Aris, Characterization of the surface functionality on precision machined engineering surfaces, International Journal of Advanced Manufacturing Technology, Vol. 38, No. 3-4, 2008, pp. 402-409.

* See comments on the file attached.

Reviewer #2:

This paper studies the determination method to quantify the surface roughness based on laser vision sensing. It is useful in additive manufacturing. And I have several questions and suggestions:

1. The word "an idea plane …" in second paragraph of section 3.1 should be "an ideal plane …".

2. There is not enough experiments to prove the methods in this paper.

3. It is better to compare the method mentioned in this paper with the other methods.

4. It is better to add the discussion about the result of this paper.

5. There should be a size expressing in Fig. 5 and Fig. 8a.

8.5.5　*Nature* 审稿模式

Nature 具有独特的审稿模式，其核心是它的科学编辑审稿制度，这也是它的独到之处：

1）Editors make decision based on the substance our referees' comments—**Advice** not **Votes**.

2）The decision is for the editors—not the referees—to make.

3）Most papers require two rounds of review before publication.

8.6　修稿

作者收到论文修改通知后，不论是审前修、小修还是大修，都需认真对待，仔细阅读编辑修稿信及专家审稿意见，按要求仔细修改论文，并撰写作者修稿信，及时将修改稿连同投修改稿信提交至编辑部。

8.6.1　编辑加工

编辑是写作和专家评审的后续。在此环节，编辑在认真通读论文原文的基础上，根据论文写作要求以及有关出版标准、规范和编辑规章、制度等，总结和归纳论文中需要补充、完善、修正、删减的问题，提出具体修改意见，对论文进行恰当、必要的修改，并将修改后的论文版本以及专家评审意见、编辑处理意见等文档和材料返给作者。作者收到修改通知后开始对论文进行修改，修改完成后再将修改后的论文以及其他需要返回的材料进行提交。编辑再检查作者是否按照要求进行了修改。若修改后的论文仍存在问题，有提高、完善的空间，则可根据实际情况重复以上过程，直到论文符合要求。

通过编辑加工过程修改合格的稿件，称为编辑定稿，此时稿件的状态才是最终的录用。

8.6.2　作者修改

作者收到修稿通知后，就要对论文进行修改，相当于进行发表前准备，如同初稿完成后进行投稿前准备一样，作者修稿是论文投稿及发表的必要环节。

审稿专家一般以严格的审视角度来寻找论文的不足之处，显示其学术水平和地位；同时期刊为了保证论文质量、实现近期刊登计划，也要求审稿专家按有关标准和要求来审稿。通常审稿专家审稿会提出较为详细、中肯的意见，作者有责任、义务根据审稿和编辑处理意见全面修改论文，并撰写修稿信，对修改情况给予说明，对审稿意见进行回复。修稿在论文投稿及发表过程中占据相当重要的位置，SCI 期刊的论文在录用前会经过多次甚至几轮的修改。

通知作者修稿并不代表论文已被录用，最终录用与否取决于论文修改质量。因此作者在收到修稿通知后，一定要高度重视，并付诸行动。作者必须抱着对读者和社会高度负责的态度，对论文进行全面修改；作者也可能因受到某种启发、认识水平提高或根据后续研究进展而对论文做一些其他修改，还可能会纠正专家和编辑提出的一些错误或不恰当的意见。实际中，有的作者并未按要求修改论文，或未做实质性修改，甚至未做任何修改就将论文返回编辑部，这种做法显然不可取，因为这样做最终受到负面影响的必然是论文的发表，并有可能遭到退稿处理，最终由作者来承担这一责任。

写作本质上是一个认识过程，包括由客观事物到人的主观认识的意化过程及从主观认识到书面表现的物化过程，意化过程中常出现"意不符物"，即主观认识未能完全、正确地反映客观事物，而物化过程中又容易发生"言不达意"，即不能完整、准确地反映作者的观点。因此，写作中多一次修改，就多一次认识，就前进一步，就向高质量更接近一步，修改贯穿从投稿到发表的整个过程。编辑将论文返给作者修改实质上是写作的延续，是写作的进一步提高。正如名作家老舍所说："文章必须修改，谁也不能一下子就写成一大篇，又快又好。"作者在编辑指导下对论文修改是写作的最后一道工序，是论文的完善和提高阶段。

8.6.3 运用修稿技巧

审稿人是领域的专家、学者，但不一定能保证所给出的审稿意见一定正确；编辑经常接触论文，对论文有一定的认识深度，但也未必能保证所提出的修改意见一定合理。作者在修改论文和回答审稿、编辑意见时应该明白，对论文写作内容和结构安排理解最清楚的是作者自己，而并非专家和编辑。因此作者不能为了发表论文而无原则、无条件地接受所有修改意见，而应该恰当、合理地修改论文，使之既准确地反映研究内容，又符合编辑出版要求，把握好修稿原则，并注重运用修稿技巧。修稿技巧大致有以下几个方面：

（1）仔细阅读理解修稿信

修稿信及审稿意见包含了编辑、专家提出的具体修改意见，可能涉及论文中多个方面的问题：如题文是否相扣，结论总结是否到位，立题依据是否合理，实验是否欠缺或存在不足及如何弥补，实验数据是否完整及如何补充，理论是否欠缺及如何引用、归纳和总结，是否有工程应用或案例支撑，创新点是否明确交待等。

（2）对修稿意见合理分类

修稿意见通常有以下三类：

1）不涉及实质性内容，如插图布局、格式不规范，公式编号不合理、不连续，参考文献引用不合理、著录结构缺项，多种标题（论文、插图、表格等的名称）太长、不简洁，作者署名、单位与作者简介中的不对应等。没有商量余地，作者必须全面修改。

2）涉及关键内容和语句结构调整，如补充实验和实验数据、增加理论分析与对比、删减常识性知识的多余表述，站在国际的角度重写引言并归纳出现有研究的不足，补充近年有代表性的引文并突出本文研究的重要性，将过程式结论改为结果式结论等。要求做重大修改，如果意见合理，作者应无条件接受，全力修改。

3）所提意见不合实际情况，作者不可能做到，如增加定量数据对比，只有仿真而没有实验和实际应用，实验结果不能很好地证明结论，对计算型论文要求增加实验，对设计型论文要求增加理论等。作者如果认为意见不合理，实际不可能做到或条件所限无法做到，就应在修稿信中详加解释、说明，必要时可与编辑电话、邮件沟通。

（3）按正确意见积极修改

作者应虚心接受所有合理的审稿意见和编辑修改要求，认真推敲、细心修改。在写修稿信时，应仔细说明修改情况，对已改的和未改的都要明确说明，对不能修改的要委婉说明理由，不要回避、不要含糊，必要时附加有关文献及其他材料加以支撑。

（4）对不合理意见恰当沟通

对欠妥或有明显错误的审稿意见或修稿要求，作者应该以完全理解的态度，婉转而有技巧性地给予回答，礼貌性地提出自己的观点，明确指出其不合理或实质性错误之处，客观公正地阐明自己的观点，做到有理有据，最好提供文献、材料或数据支持，态度要好，忌用词生硬、强词夺理，避免不必要的冲突。

(5) 认真对待多轮修稿

论文有时需要多轮修改。作者应该明白，之所以让修改，是因为论文有发表价值，只是需要在发表前进行必要的修改，意味着只要修改好了，论文就能录用。因此论文修改不论走上几个轮回，修改几次，均无多大关系，只要认真对待、仔细修改并逐条认真回答就够了。这样做，首先表明作者对编辑和专家的尊敬，更反映出作者谦虚谨慎的态度。对问题不要回避，不能解决的意见更要认真对待，以期获得编辑和专家的理解和支持。

有的作者可能会使用下列语句来询问编辑，"论文能发表吗，如果不能发表，就不修改了"或"论文修改后能发表吧"或"论文是否录用了，还让修改，修改挺麻烦的"。这几类询问均不可取，实在没有什么必要。另外还要注意，编辑对修稿通常有明确的时间要求（1~2个月较为常见），作者应在规定的时间内修改回，否则可能会遭遇自动撤稿或退稿的后果。

8.6.4 语言润色

有的期刊还要求作者对修后的论文进行语言润色。语言润色通常由作者自己来找相关人士，如专业英语老师、外教或其他英语水平较高的人员（如有国外生活、工作经历或正在国外工作的专家、学者或朋友），也可找语言润色公司，但不管找谁来做，这个过程是不宜省略的，尽管作者需要支付一些费用。有的作者可能英文水平很高，甚至在国外长期工作过，英文写作上也游刃有余，对修改稿可能就没有必要进行语言润色

了。最终是否进行语言润色，需要由作者自己来把握，语言润色的目的无非是消除错词错句错标点，提升语言修辞效果，改进语言表达质量，论文达到较高的语言表达水准才是最终的目标，如果作者已将论文修改得在语言上没有什么问题了，那么再找人来润色也就是多余的了。

不管是找个人还是公司来进行语言润色，润色的水准是有差异的，特别是SCI论文，会有较多专业术语和复杂长句，润色还是有相当的难度。因此，作者对润色回的修改稿，一定要仔细察看，感觉一下润色的水准，对不合适或错误的修改一定要修正，对遗漏之处一定要补正，对多余的修改一定要删除。总之，作者对润色结果一定要再次把关，必要时还得找有关人士帮忙推敲、商定。

目前不少SCI期刊加盟了国际出版商（如Springer-Nature、Elsevier、Taylor、WILEY等）的后期生产流程，出版商在生产过程中，也通常会通知作者进行语言润色，并提供一些级别不同的语言润色机构供作者选择（机构级别不同，润色价位也自然不同），作者必然要支付一笔价格可能不菲的费用了。实际中究竟在哪个环节进行语言润色，取决于具体的期刊，不同期刊的工作流程是不同的。

8.6.5 撰写修稿信

提交修改稿的同时最好附上一封修稿信（Resubmission Cover Letter 或 Author Comments 或 Response to Reviewers）。此信不同于投新稿的投稿信，主要包括以下几个方面的内容：

1) 向编辑和审稿专家表示诚挚的谢意。这是十分必要的，需要作者发自内心，并写在修稿信的开头，因为此时编辑和审稿专家已为稿件提供了服务和指导，况且对于审稿专家，其审稿报酬相对较低，特别对于

国际审稿专家，常常是无偿审稿的。专家同意审稿并写出详细的审稿意见，在一定程度上也代表着对论文价值和意义的认同，作者按审稿意见来修稿就是一种对专家的尊重。

2）写明稿号、论文题目以及所有作者姓名。向编辑部提供这些信息后，编辑就能容易地找到该稿的档案（稿袋），便于查找、核对及安排审稿，与只写上作者姓名相比，编辑工作减轻了不少，这样反而会促进论文及早录用、发表。

3）对修稿情况作较为详尽的、重点突出的说明。着重强调论文已按要求作了全部或基本修改，并重点说明主要修改的部分，对于未做修改或改动不多的部分也应详细说明理由，最好有文献、数据或实例支持，理由要充分，起码能自圆其说。

4）在修稿信中可以逐条列出审稿意见，并给予说明或回复。既可以在左侧写出审稿意见，右侧说明修改情况，也可以列出一条修改意见后，紧接着表述修改情况。有几份审稿意见时，应按不同审稿人的意见单独说明，也可以考虑用几个表格的形式分别列出审稿意见及对审稿意见的说明或回复。

以下给出修稿信的两个范例，供参考。

范例8-7

Dear Editor,

Thanks for the comments of all the reviewers! I benefits from these comments in the process of correcting the manuscript. Thanks the editors of this Journal for posting these comments. According to the comments of the reviewers, the corresponding sections of the manuscript have been corrected. The comments of the reviewer and the corresponding modifications for the comment are presented one by one in the next section.

×××, Ph. D.
School of Electrical Engineering & Information, ××× University of Technology, Maanshan 243032, P. R. China
Tel：0086××××××××××

Replies to Reviewer #1
Reviewer #1：

This paper investigates an S-shape acceleration/deceleration interaction problem control method for the real-time look-ahead NURBS interpolation. A new algorithm is proposed to solve the interaction among consecutive speed changed points. The simulations and experiments proves the theories analysis well. In this sense, the research is of great and valuable interest. But a few minor revisions are list below：

— Some new references after 2010 should be referenced to verify it is still a hot area of research.

Replies：

Three references after 2010 have been added in the paper, which can be seen in the paper and marked as red color.

— There are some mistakes in grammar, which should be carefully read and corrected. For example, in page of Fig. 6, line 6, 7 and 8：'As shown in the figure, the federate value of the new point is below zero. In practice, all the values of the velocity should be maintained above zero.' The words of 'below' and 'above'are not accurate.

Replies：

The paper has been carefully checked and corrected. And the mistakes mentioned above are modified.

— In page of computation about the length of the NURBS curve part, line 41：'The approximate value of S (u1, u2) can be expressed as follow：', however, the expression calculate the approximate value of S (um, un). Please correct it right.

Replies：

The mistake has been modified and the paper are carefully read to avoid the similar mistakes.

Replies to Reviewer #2
Reviewer #2：
Thank you for your kind comments.

范例8-8

Dear Editor, ×××, Ph. D：

Thank you for your letter and for the reviewers'comments concerning our manuscript entitled "Research on abrasive-assisted nickel electroforming process with moving cathode" (ID：No. ×××-D-16-×××). Those comments are all valuable and very helpful for revising and improving our paper, as well as the important guiding significance to our researches. We have studied the comments carefully and have made correction which we hope to meet with approval. Revised portion are marked in red in the paper. The main corrections in the paper and the responds to the reviewer's comments are as flowings:

Responds to the reviewer's comments:

Reviewer #1:

1. The text " Temperature unit" outside the borders beyond in figure 1.

Response: We are very sorry for our negligence of the word 'Temperature unit' outside the borders and it was corrected.

2. The graph scale is not clear in figure 8 (a) and (b).

Response: We have made amendments in the graph scale in figure 8 according to the reviewer's comments. Now the graph scale is clear.

Reviewer #2:

To improve the thickness distribution uniformity of relatively complex parts to be electroformed, this paper introduced a combined movement of cathode by integrating rotation with translation during abrasive-assisted electroforming. The measure taken is innovative and seems effective. This paper could be of greater significance to the engineering field and read well if the following suggestions are taken into considerations.

1. More studies including theoretical analysis and experimentation are expected to carry out to prove that improved thickness uniformity can actually be obtained. Little information concerned was provided in the present paper.

2. Macro-scale thickness distribution characteristics are supposed to be the key issue to discuss for the proposed measure, which generally involve mass transfer and current distribution. More data are needed. Additionally, the part electroformed seems too simple to support the conclusion that the combined movement of the cathode is effective to improve uniformity during electroforming complex articles.

3. Expressions are expected to further improve.

Response: Thanks for the reviewers' comments, and we have studied the comments carefully, but maybe there is no research concerning about thickness distribution uniformity in the paper, so it is difficult to response the questions.

Reviewer #3:

A novel method of abrasive-assisted electroforming has been developed for processing the cylindrical parts with complicated profiles in this study. Some results might be in benefit to the researchers in the field of electro-machining and the paper appears to have information of value but requires some clarification and modification.

Further comments are listed as following:

1. In this paper, it is mentioned that cathode's translational movement is carried out by a planar worktable as charged object by stepper motor in X/Y axis linkage (Line18 page 2), but it is not found out any planar worktable in Fig. 1 and not clear for the direction of translation speed V to be shown.

Response: It is really true as reviewer suggested that there is no planar worktable in Fig. 1. Well, firstly, we are very sorry for the schematic diagram not showing the whole electroforming device, because there is not enough space for the movement mechanism in Fig. 1. Secondly, the planar worktable is settled under the electrolyte tank. Translational motion of cathode is transmitted by the rigid support from the bottom up. Thirdly, no planar worktable and the rigid support shown in Fig. 1 will make the schematic diagram look concise and clear. Translation speed V in Fig. 1 shows that the cathode translates anticlockwise in the horizontal plane.

2. A technology of abrasive-assisted electroforming has been used, and the ceramic bead plays an important role in the experimental study. How to choose the size of the ceramic bead?

Response: Free ceramic beads in 0.8-1.2mm diameter were chosen as the abrasive medium in the experiment. According to a great deal of fundamental experiments, there are a lot of research papers [15] about abrasive-polishing-assisted electroformed nickel from our team. They have studied effect of the size of free particles to the abrasion-assisted electroforming technique, neither too big, nor too small.

[15] LI Xuelei., ZHU Di, ZHU Zengwei, Effect of Free Particles to the Abrasion-assisted Electroforming Technique [J]. Electromachining & Mould, 2010: 35-39.

3. The effects of the translation speed (cathode) on the surface morphology and the micro hardness have been studied in this paper. How about the rotational speed? Has it impact on the surface quality and the hardness?

Response: It is really true as reviewer said, the rotational speed also has great effect on the surface quality and the hardness. Our earlier experiments of abrasive polishing assisted electroformed nickel were purely by rotational cathode motion. The surface quality and the hardness value improve with the increase of rotational speed [7]. So we believe that will also impact when the cathode translates as well as rotates. The rotational speed of our electroforming machine is limited, and the rotational speed was set much lower, about 0 ~ 2r/min. Rotation is aimed at keeping the intensity of electric field of cathode surface in uniformity. So the equipment limitation is a big influence factor.

[7] ZHU Di, ZHU Zengwei and QU Ningsong: Abrasive Polishing Assisted Nickel Electroforming Process [J]. CIRP Annals Manufacturing Technology, 2006, 55 (7): 193-196.

4. In Fig.6, when current density is $3A/dm^2$, the micro hardness rises with the increase of translation speed (range from 11-30mm/s). The authors could explain better the graph if the translation speed continues to increase and an optimum speed could be determined.

Response: It is really true as reviewer suggested. Well, it's the first time we proposed the complicated moving cathode in the abrasive-assisted electroforming process. The experiment parameters were all chosen by earlier experience of pure rotation or single translation cathode motion. Wide variation of process parameter will take more time and effort, we can't make it in time. Moreover, the translational speed of our electroforming machine is not in very large scale, about 0-70mm/s. The equipment is a limitation. The subsequent optimal experiments on process parameters are being carried out in the future.

5. Please check the references: the utilization of the page numbers must be uniform (see references 1, 2, 8, 9, 10 ...).

Response: We are very sorry for our negligence of the format of the page numbers and it was corrected in the references. We tried our best to improve the manuscript and made some changes in the manuscript. These changes will not influence the content and framework of the paper.

We appreciate for Editors and Reviewers' warm work earnestly, and hope that the correction will meet with approval. Once again, thank you very much for your comments and suggestions. Looking forward to hearing from you!

Detailed response to editor's annotates:
According to the editor's annotate,
1. We have revised the problem of signature format.
2. We have revised the abstract as requested.
3. We have rewritten the introduction and added some representative references in recent years.
4. We have redesigned the figures as requested in the article.
5. We have revised the formulations' entire format as is requested.
6. We have checked and revised all of the article's symbols.
7. We have redesigned the tables' entire format in the article.
8. We have revised the scale values' format in the coordinate figures.
9. We have modified article's conclusions as it is requested.

Thank you and best regards.
Yours
sincerely,
×××
E-mail: ×××@×××
Corresponding author:
Name: ×××
E-mail: ×××@×××

8.6.6 投修改稿

修改稿完成后要如同投新稿那样,登录系统向编辑部提交,如果有修稿信,则还需一并提交。这其实也是一个投稿过程,只不过所投稿件是修改稿而不是开始的新稿罢了。

8.7 录用和发表

论文录用后,对作者来说,就是等待发表了,这是作者最期待的结果了,也是辛苦劳动回报的体现。对录用的论文,编辑通常会给作者发一封短信,告知作者一些注意事项和有关出版信息,如论文发表费(包括OA费、纸质版面费)、论文在线发表时间、给作者寄送纸刊时间、版权转让事宜等,作者只要按要求完成操作即可。不同期刊的运营模式不尽相同,论文录用和发表的流程也有一定差异。下面介绍论文录用和发表的一般流程。

8.7.1 制图

论文中往往包含插图，插图成为论文的有机组成部分。每个期刊都有插图的标准，对其质量有具体的要求。作者投稿中的插图，通常除质量较好的照片图外，一般达不到发表的要求，如幅面不合适、要素不齐全、布局不合理、线型不标准、字符看不清、符号不妥当、层次不清晰、同类要素不统一等，这就需要对插图重新进行制作和修改。在通知作者修改论文的过程中，编辑通常也会交待作者对插图进行修改或重新制作，但作者制图一般较难达到刊登要求，这多是由于作者对制图标准不是很清楚，或不擅长制图或对制图不重视所致。

多数编辑部会对不合刊登要求的插图交由专业制图公司来重新制作。由公司制作的插图，符合国家或出版行业的制图标准，各种线型达到标准，同类要素达到统一，字体字号相符，……，均称、清晰、美观。当然制图如同修改论文，也要校对，编辑部的插图校对人员和制图公司的插图制作员需要走上"校对→修改→校对→修改"几个来回，最终才能获得合格的制图。

论文录用后，编辑部将编辑定稿及稿中所有制图一起发给生产部门，进入生产环节。

8.7.2 生产

生产在国内也叫排版（typeset），是对编辑定稿进行规定格式和体例的最终实现，是论文发表的实现环节，没有此环节就不能保证编写好的论文最终得以发表。生产人员根据版面编排格式、排版要求和编辑加工的修改、批注、标注进行生产修改，并将所有制图插入到文中相应位置，制作出符合排版要求的高质量论文。

生产是写作、编辑和修改的后续和终结，是论文发表的必要但非本质环节。若没有前期的写作、编辑和修改几个重要环节，生产对论文的发表是起不了多大作用的；但如果没有生产这一环节，论文是走不到发表这一步的，从而就进入不了流通环节与读者见面。

生产多由与期刊合作的出版商、排版公司来进行，而有的期刊由自己的专门人员来完成。

8.7.3 校对

论文排版后的结果怎样，是否达到最终发表要求，还需编辑和作者来校对（proofread），作者一般校对一次，而编辑或校对人员可能校对若干次（通常 2 至 3 次，不同期刊有差异）。

作者对自己行将发表的论文进行最后一次校对是至关重要的，由校对能发现原稿中可能存在的一些或大或小的应该改掉的问题。这是编辑所不及的，因为作者发现的问题往往是内容上的，编辑修改的问题多是形式上的，而且作者是最了解其整个论文的人。因此看校样，对自己的论文做最后一次核对，是作者的天责！作者在收到校样版本后，一定予以高度重视，认真、仔细核对，并在规定时间内校对完毕，在线修改提交或将校对批注版本或校对说明文本即时返回编辑部。

编辑部或合作出版商会明确告知作者具体校对方法及注意事项。校样一般为 PDF 或 Word 版本，或在线校对，作者可以在样稿上进行标注，但标注一定要明确，使编辑一看就清楚需要修改的地方，或在线直接修改，或撰写校对报告写明需要修改之处。作者校对重点关注的主要包括：确认排版后语句内容没有发生变化；摘要、正文、图表所表述出来的实验或观测结果应一致；排版中是否产生了错误；单词拼写是否有错误；段落、式子、表格转行是否恰当；图表的位置是否妥当；以前各个版本所做的修改是否落实等。

实际中，不少作者返回了未做任何修改、批注的校样文档，还声明校对没有发现任何问题。实际上作者应付了之的情况也是存在的，觉得论文反正能发表了，校对不校对无所谓，也不想拿出多少时间来做这项工作。另外，广大作者要注意，校对发生在正式发表（在线发表）的前沿，距正式发表几乎没有多少空余的时间，因此作者必须及时完成校对，如果拖延了，就失去了这最后一次的唯一机会，如果确有重要修改之处，如作者署名、单位变动或名称写错，通信作者邮箱更正等，那么就会成为永久的遗憾。更有甚者，有的作者在论文发表后才提出修改要求，当得知已绝对不可修改后，还非常生气，多么不可取啊！因此，作者一定要树立及时校对返回、不耽误论文发表整体流程这一意识。

另外，作者在校对版本上修改或标记有困难或修改工作量较大时，可以不在校样上操作，最简便有效的做法是直接将修改意图写成说明性文本，以邮件或附件发给编辑或生产部门，由编辑或生产人员代为修改。当然这种文本一定要将修改之处、方法写清楚。有的期刊可能会对作者的校对版本直接进行修改并以此版本来发表，因此作者须认真对待自己的校对版本，对每一处修改都要格外小心，而且还要注意由某处修改可能会引起别的地方的连动变化，如串行、背题、移位、跑图、叠加、参差不齐、整体分开、版式变化、页面增多或减少等。

以下以 Springer 使用 EM 生产系统为例，给出由其作者校对通知邮件正文所给出的链接所下载的校对通知附件文本，供大家了解、学习。

范例 8-9

Dear Author,

Here are the proofs of your article.

- You can submit your corrections **online**, via **e-mail** or by **fax**.
- For **online** submission please insert your corrections in the online correction form. Always indicate the line number to which the correction refers.
- You can also insert your corrections in the proof PDF and **email** the annotated PDF.
- For fax submission, please ensure that your corrections are clearly legible. Use a fine black pen and write the correction in the margin, not too close to the edge of the page.
- Remember to note the **journal title**, **article number**, and **your name** when sending your response via e-mail or fax.
- **Check** the metadata sheet to make sure that the header information, especially author names and the corresponding affiliations are correctly shown.
- **Check** the questions that may have arisen during copy editing and insert your answers/ corrections.
- **Check** that the text is complete and that all figures, tables and their legends are included. Also check the accuracy of special characters, equations, and electronic supplementary material if applicable. If necessary refer to the *Edited manuscript*.
- The publication of inaccurate data such as dosages and units can have serious consequences. Please take particular care that all such details are correct.
- Please **do not** make changes that involve only matters of style. We have generally introduced forms that follow the journal's style.
  Substantial changes in content, e.g., new results, corrected values, title and authorship are not allowed without the approval of the responsible editor. In such a case, please contact the Editorial Office and return his/her consent together with the proof.
- If we do not receive your corrections **within 48 hours**, we will send you a reminder.
- Your article will be published **Online First** approximately one week after receipt of your corrected proofs. This is the **official first publication** citable with the DOI. **Further changes are, therefore, not possible.**
- The **printed version** will follow in a forthcoming issue.

Please note
After online publication, subscribers (personal/institutional) to this journal will have access to the complete article via the DOI using the URL: http://dx.doi.org/ [DOI].
If you would like to know when your article has been

published online, take advantage of our free alert service. For registration and further information go to: http://www.link.springer.com.

Due to the electronic nature of the procedure, the manuscript and the original figures will only be returned to you on special request. When you return your corrections, please inform us if you would like to have these documents returned.

8.7.4 发表

一篇论文首次由生产部门制作好后，生成校对文档（电子或纸质），分别发给作者和编辑。作者、编辑各自校对后提交生产部门，生产部门按校对文档进行修改。这个过程可以走上几个来回（一校、二校或更多校）。论文生产最终完成后，就可安排其上线发表（数字优先发表）。然后到某一既定时间，对已上线发表的论文结集成期，确定刊登期次，更新上线数据，汇总某期文章，生成印制文档，提交印刷部门，最终文章在纸质期刊上发表出来。

多数期刊除出版印刷本外，还有在线版、电子刊等多种数字发表形式（目前新创办的期刊多为纯网刊），这样在生产前后或进行过程中，还会由专人来制作相应的各种版本的数字版产品，完成后即可入库、上线或定点销售、推送。

8.7.5 版权转让

版权（copyright）即著作权，一般是指作者对其作品享有的权利（包括财产权、人身权），是知识产权的一种类型，由自然科学、社会科学以及文学、音乐、戏剧、绘画、雕刻和电影、摄影等方面的作品组成。版权转让就是版权所有者通过买卖、交易、赠与或遗赠等方式把版权中的全部或部分财产权有偿或无偿地交给他人（或其他单位）享有的法律行为。

SCI 论文是一种知识载体，同样具有版权。在 1976 年以前，根据美国 1909 年《版权转让法案》的规定，作者向期刊编辑部投稿的同时自动将作者对论文的版权转让给期刊编辑部（期刊出版商）。1976 年后该法案规定，版权转让必须签署书面文件才具有法律效力。目前多数期刊编辑部执行该法案的规定，要求作者填写版权转让表格，作者收到表格后须照章办事，认真填写，根据要求及时将填好的表格返回编辑部。各期刊的版权转让表格类似，在细节方面可能稍有差别。编辑部收到作者填好的表格后，通常会通知作者其论文的在线、纸质出版时间及其他有关信息，作者耐心等待论文的发表就可以了。

以下为 Springer 期刊提供论文作者签署的某时期或某版本的版权转让协议文本，仅供读者学习或了解，不要对号入座。

范例 8-10
Author's Copyright Transfer of Springer

The copyright to this article, including any graphic elements therein (e.g. illustrations, charts, moving images), is hereby assigned for good and valuable consideration to ××× and Springer-Verlag Berlin Heidelberg effective if and when the article is accepted for publication and to the extent assignable if assignability is restricted for by applicable law or regulations (e.g. for U.S. government or crown employees). Author warrants (i) that he/she is the sole owner or has been authorized by any additional copyright owner to assign the right, (ii) that the article does not infringe any third party rights and no license from or payments to a third party is required to publish the article and (iii) that the article has not been previously published or licensed.

The copyright assignment includes without limitation the exclusive, assignable and sublicensable right, unlimited in time and territory, to reproduce, publish, distribute, transmit, make available and store the article, including abstracts thereof, in all forms of media of expression now known or developed in the future, including pre-and reprints, translations, photographic reproductions and microform. Springer may use the article in whole or in part in electronic form, such as use in databases or data networks for display, print or download to stationary or portable devices. This includes interactive and multimedia use and the right to alter the article to the extent necessary for such use.

Authors may self-archive the Author's accepted manuscript of their articles on their own websites. Authors may also deposit this version of the article in any repository, provided it is only made publicly available 12 months after official publication or later. He/she may not use the publisher's version (the final article), which is posted on SpringerLink and other Springer websites, for the purpose of self-archiving or deposit. Furthermore, the Author may only post his/her version provided acknowledgement is given to the original source of publication and a link is inserted to the published article on Springer's website. The link must be provided by inserting the DOI number of the article in the following sentence: "The final publication is available at Springer via http://dx.doi.org/[insert DOI]".

Prior versions of the article published on non-commercial pre-print servers like arXiv.org can remain on these servers and/or can be updated with Author's accepted version. The final published version (in pdf or html/xml format) cannot be used for this purpose. Acknowledgement needs to be given to the final publication and a link must be inserted to the published article on Springer's website, by inserting the DOI number of the article in the following sentence: "The final publication is available at Springer via http://dx.doi.org/[insert DOI]". Author retains the right to use his/her article for his/her further scientific career by including the final published journal article in other publications such as dissertations and postdoctoral qualifications provided acknowledgement is given to the original source of publication.

Articles disseminated via http://link.springer.com are indexed, abstracted and referenced by many abstracting and information services, bibliographic networks, subscription agencies, library networks, and consortia.

After submission of the agreement signed by the corresponding author, changes of authorship or in the order of the authors listed will not be accepted by Springer.

8.8 论文处理绩效

8.8.1 时间机制

作者投稿后关注的是论文被录用,希望尽快刊登出来;编辑收到论文后关注的是论文的发表价值及写作质量,希望在达标的情况下尽早刊登出来。从发表角度看,作者和编辑的目标是一致的,都希望尽快将论文刊登出来;但从时间看,两者常发生矛盾,作者总对编辑的处理进展感到疑惑或流露不满,认为编辑工作效率太低,但编辑一直按工作流程来进行,并未拖延。产生这一矛盾的原因是多方面的,涉及论文初审、评审、加工、修改等多种时间要素。

(1) 编辑初审时间

论文初审时间是从主编(或其他编辑,或系统管理员)将论文提交给责任编辑到责任编辑完成对该文的初审之间的时间。除特殊情况(如编辑出差、生病、休假或忙于别的工作),专职编辑一般能在较短时间内完成初审。

(2) 论文评审时间

论文评审时间是从责任编辑将论文提交给专家到专家审毕提交评审意见之间的时间。除特殊情况(如专家出差或没有充足时间,专家不熟悉期刊工作系统,系统存在缺陷、故障,论文发送未成功等),专家一般能在预期时间内完成评审。出版部门还建有催审制度(系统自动提醒),对预期内未审回的专家,编辑适时与其联系,督促、提醒其尽快审稿,必要时安排备选专家来审稿。论文评审时间一般不会很久⊖,通常不应成为制约论文处理速度的主要因素。

(3) 论文加工时间

论文加工时间是从论文可以开始加工到完成加工之间的时间。编辑通常不仅处理论文,做期刊(纸质、数字期刊)责任编辑⊖,还做很多日常工作,如选题、组稿、参会、办会、新媒体建设等,工作量较大,因此一篇论文的加工完成速度一般不像作者

⊖ 目前专家越来越忙,审稿有拖延的趋势。

⊖ 主要职责是论文结集,包括选择论文、确定期次、生产制作、校对修改、在线发表、纸质付印等。

想像的那样快。然而，造成加工不够快的另一个因素——论文写作质量较差——往往为作者所忽略。加工本来就是一个需要非常仔细推敲的过程，需要逐字逐句地阅读、推敲和检查，涉及专业、技术、语言、文字、术语、量和单位、插图、表格、式子、各种符号等诸多方面的知识、标准和规范，工作量之大行外人是难以理解的，而对于一篇写作质量差的论文来说，加工将付出成倍的工作量。因此，论文写作质量是决定论文有效、快速编辑加工的重要因素。

（4）论文修改时间

论文修改时间是从论文加工完成后提交给作者进行修改，再到作者修改完成后将论文返回的各次累加时间。其主要因素是作者的修改效率（修改速度＋修改质量）：如果作者以较快的速度修改了论文，但修改质量欠缺，编辑必将论文再次返给作者修改，这样就延长了论文修改时间；如果作者花费了较多时间修改了论文，修改质量很好，编辑对论文的后续处理就会快得多，论文修改时间从整体上有可能大大缩短。

写作质量是影响论文发表周期的最重要因素，一篇写作质量过关的论文，不会因为写作问题而退稿，而且一经录用，编辑、作者花费较少的时间就能加工、修改完毕，甚至不用返作者修改，发表周期会大大缩短。论文写得越差，被退稿的可能性越大，加工、修改时间就越长，即写作质量欠缺所带来的损失由编辑来弥补。从质量的角度看，作者与编辑有统一性和转换性，但转换有限度，超限即论文质量不能通过编辑来做到时，就只能退稿处理了。

因此，作者在投稿前就将论文进行最彻底的高质量写作是超值的，也是必须提倡的。

8.8.2 质量机制

没有一篇文章不经修改就能完成，高质量论文的完成需要反反复复的修改。在投稿前按目标期刊修改的准备阶段，投稿后按专家评审、编辑处理意见修改的退修阶段，以及生产时按出版要求修改的校对和制作阶段，无处不存在着对论文继续修改的环节。*Nature* 可贵的是，当科学编辑发现有发表价值的论文时，若经过"编辑初审→同行评议→编辑审议→准备评审报告→退回修改"一个轮回，论文修改质量未达到预期，那么就再来一个或几个轮回，每经过一个轮回，论文质量就提升一个层次，一轮接着一轮，论文质量步步提升，直到最终达到发表要求，其中蕴含着一种如图 8-4 所示的论文修改质量提升机制。原来，论文写作、投稿流程是为论文质量保驾护航的。难怪 *Nature* 有句名言：论文是修改出来的，而非撰写出来的！

Nature 采用科学编辑制，其编辑有科学研究背景，在世界最好的实验室从事过博士后研究工作，生命科学组和自然科学组的主编还是免疫学家和材料学家，因此其编辑团队很强大，不设编委会，论文是否录用取决于编辑。编辑依据"意见"而不是"投票"来决策，是"编辑"而非"审稿人"做出决策，大部分稿件在发表前要经过两轮审稿。（The decision is for the editors—not the referees—to make. Most papers require two rounds of review before publication.）

Nature 与设立编委会的期刊如 *Science*、*Cell* 的模式不同。后者的流程通常是：投稿后，先编辑初审；初审通过的，送编委（或客座编辑）复审，主要审核论文的价值，即有无发表意义；复审通过的，送多位同行评议，主要审查论文的可行性（技术性），即能否实现。这种模式下，论文能否录用主要决定于编委和专家的意见，编辑在很大程度上只是审稿意见的处理者，而非决策者。

第 8 章 SCI 论文投稿与发表

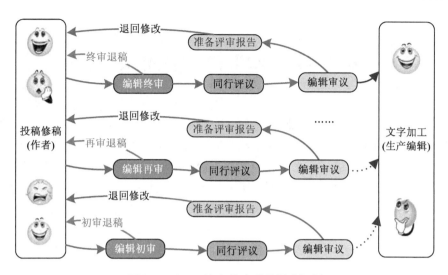

图 8-4 *Nature* 论文修改质量提升机制

第 9 章　EM 投稿流程示例

本章以目标期刊（Springer 出版商）使用国际投审稿系统 EM（Editorial Manager）为例，给出作者从开始投稿到论文发表的操作流程。注意所给出的界面仅用来示例，不可对号入座。

9.1　投稿

作者撰写、准备好论文后，就开始投稿了，下面给出一般流程：

1）进入目标期刊官网，找到作者登录入口界面。如果直接通过有关网址进入目标期刊的 EM 作者登录界面，则没有此步。

2）进入目标期刊的作者登录界面（图9-1）。如果作者已注册过，则直接在 Username 和 Password 框分别输入账号和密码，再单击 Author Login 按钮进行登录；如果还未注册，则单击 Registor Now 进入 Pre-registration Page（注册界面，图9-2）。

图 9-1　作者登录界面

3）成功登录后，进入 Author Main Menu（作者主界面，图9-3）。此界面右边有三栏：第一栏为 New Submissions（新投稿），第二栏为 Revisions（修改稿），第三栏为 Completed（已投稿）。如果投稿，则单击第一栏首行 Submit New Manuscript（提交新稿，投初稿）。

4）进入 New Submission（图9-4）。左侧 New Submission 下面有两行按钮 Select Article Type、Enter Title。先选择 Select Article Type，在 Choose Article Type 框中有可供选择的文章类型（选择文章类型界面，图9-5），如 Review articles、Research 等。选择文章类型（如 Research），单击 Next 按钮进入下一步。（每个期刊的文章类型设置有差异，作者可根据自己文章的类型来选择。）

5）进入 Enter Title（填写文章题名界面，图9-6）。界面右侧的"Please Enter The Full Title of Your Submission""Entering a Full Title is Required for Submission""Enter the title of your manuscript. You cannot submit a manuscript without a title"为提示信息。在下方的题名框内输入文章的题名，单

第 9 章 EM 投稿流程示例

击 Next 按钮进入下一步。

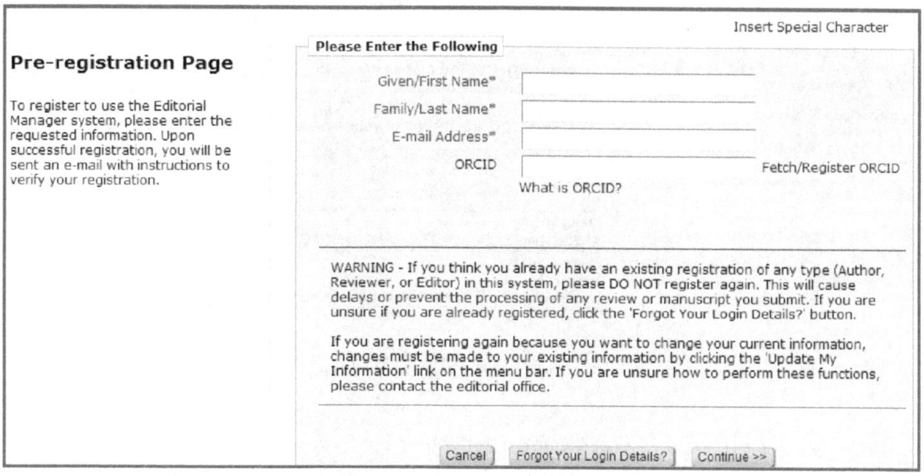

图 9-2　作者注册界面

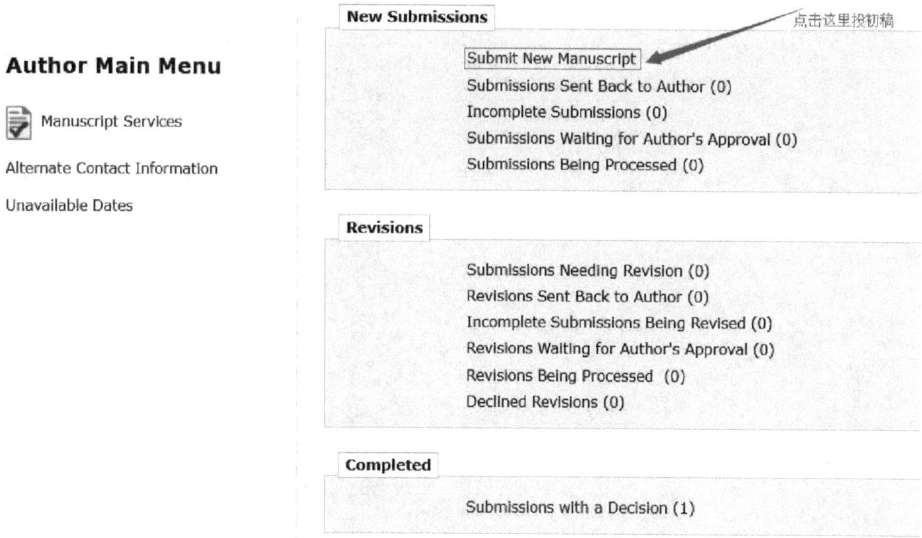

图 9-3　作者主界面（投稿前）

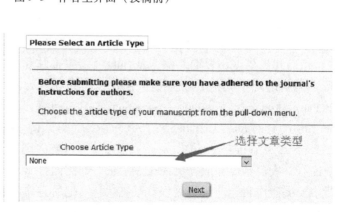

图 9-4　新投稿界面

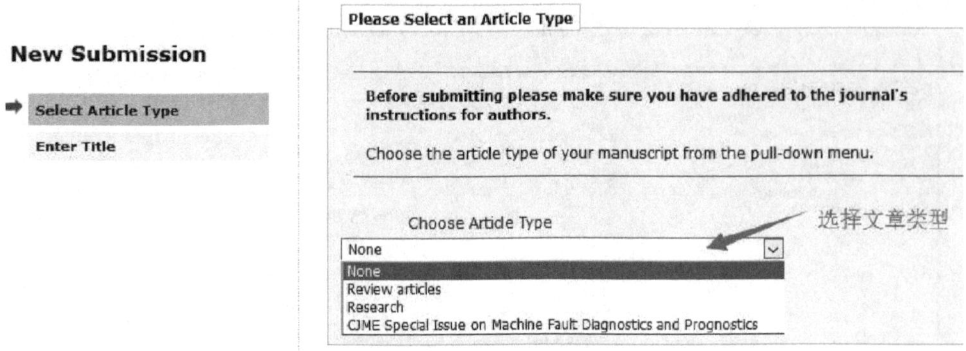

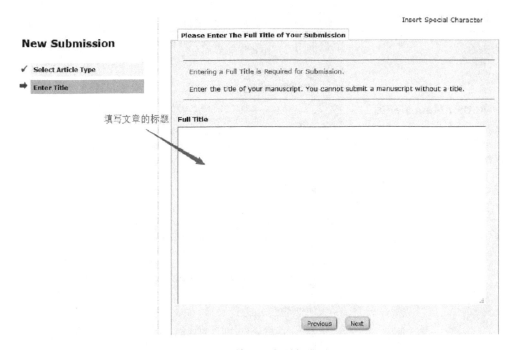

图 9-5　选择文章类型界面

图 9-6　填写文章题名界面

6）文章题名填好后，进入 Add/Edit/Remove Authors（填写作者信息界面，图 9-7）填写作者信息，界面左侧 New Submission 下面新出现了其他 6 行按钮（Add/Edit/Remove Authors；Funding Information；Submit Abstract；Enter Comments；Suggest Reviewers；Attach Files），共有 8 行按钮，按钮前面有√表示已经完成，有箭头表示正在进行中，提醒作者当前投稿进程。系统默认投稿作者为通讯作者。

7）如果没有其他作者，则单击 Next 按钮进入下一步；如果还有其他作者，则必须完善其相关信息，单击 Add Another Author 按钮，弹出 Enter Author Details（作者信息对话框，图 9-8），标有红色字体和星号（*）的为必填项，如果新加的成员为通信作者，则在 This is the corresponding author 前面打√，然后保存。重复这个步骤，直到把所有作者按顺序填毕，再单击 Next 按钮进入下一步。

第 9 章　EM 投稿流程示例

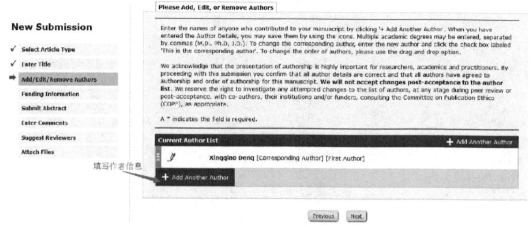

图 9-7　填写作者信息界面

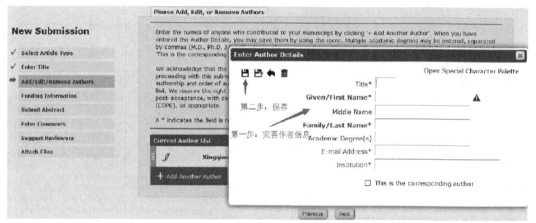

图 9-8　作者信息对话框

8）进入 Funding Information（填写资助信息界面，图 9-9），填写文章资助（基金项目）信息。如果没有资助，则在 Funding information is not applicable/No funding was received 前打√，并单击 Next 按钮；如果有资助，则单击 Add a Funding Source。

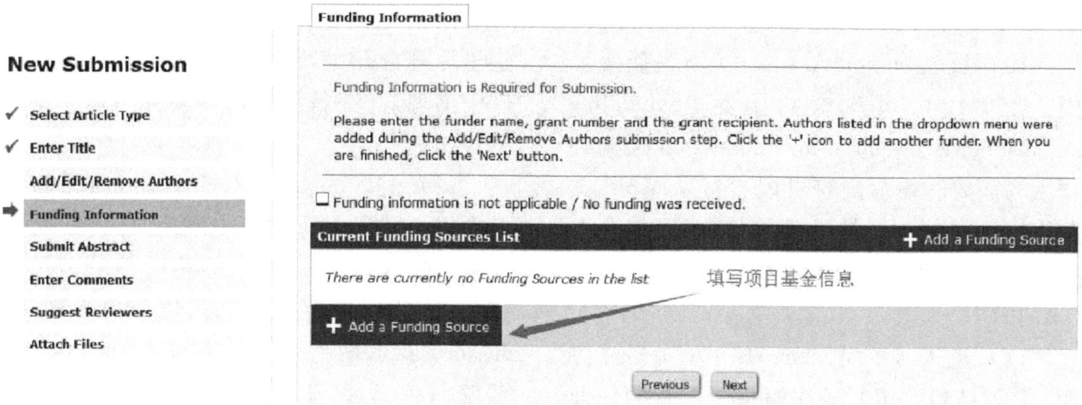

图 9-9　填写资助信息界面

9）单击 Add a Funding Source 后，弹出 Enter Funding Source Details（填写资助信息对话框，图9-10），在 Find a Funder 框里直接输入项目信息或关键词如 National，就会在对话框右侧列示与所填信息相关的基金项目（图9-11）。然后在 Award Number 框里填写项目编号，并在 Grant Recipient 框里填入项目负责人，填完后单击保存图标。

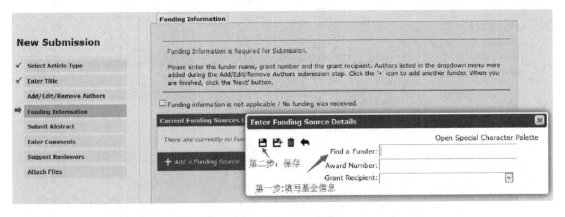

图9-10　填写资助信息对话框

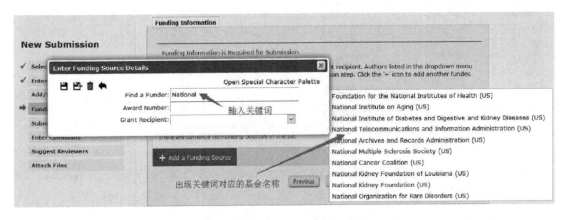

图9-11　相关基金项目列示界面

10）进入 Submit Abstract（填写摘要界面，图9-12），填写文章摘要。Submitting an Abstract is Required for Submission 强调必须填写摘要。填写内容可以直接从 Word 文件里拷贝（复制、粘贴），但格式可能会发生改变。在摘要框内填写完成后，单击 Next 按钮。

11）进入 Enter Commnets（填写备注界面，图9-13），填写备注信息。作者的任何特殊要求，包括文章的亮点、创新点均可在这里填写告知编辑部（所填信息不会在稿件中出现）。在备注框内填写完成后，单击 Next 按钮。

12）进入 Suggest Reviewers（推荐审稿人界面，图9-14），填写审稿人信息。标有红色字体和星号（*）的为必填项。填写完一位审稿人的信息时，可以单击 Add Reviewer，接着填写另一位审稿人的信息，全部填写完成或没有审稿人推荐时，单击 Next 按钮进入下一步。

第 9 章 EM 投稿流程示例

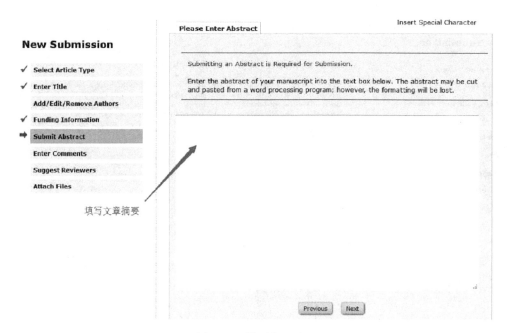

图 9-12 填写摘要界面

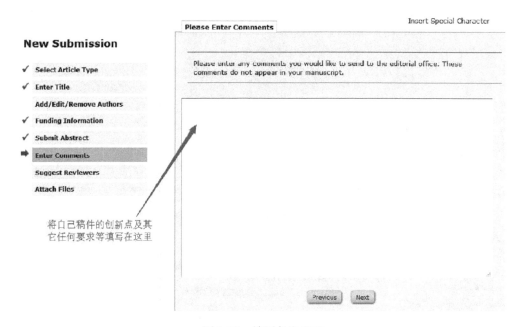

图 9-13 填写备注界面

13) 进入 Attach Files（上传附件界面，图 9-15）上传附件。单击 Item 选择上传文档的类型，其中第一个是 Manuscript，前有 * 号，表示必须上传，其后还有 Table、Figure、Supplementary Material，分别为文章里面的表、图、补充材料，后三类如果没有，则可以不上传。选定上传文档的类型后，在 Description 框内会出现相应文档类型的词语，也可以在这里自行输入别的词语来描述。

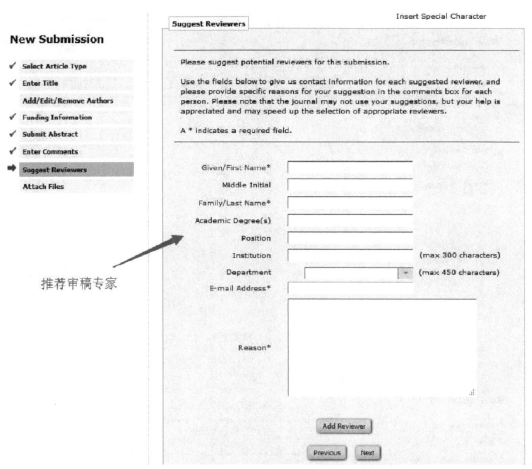

图 9-14　推荐审稿人界面

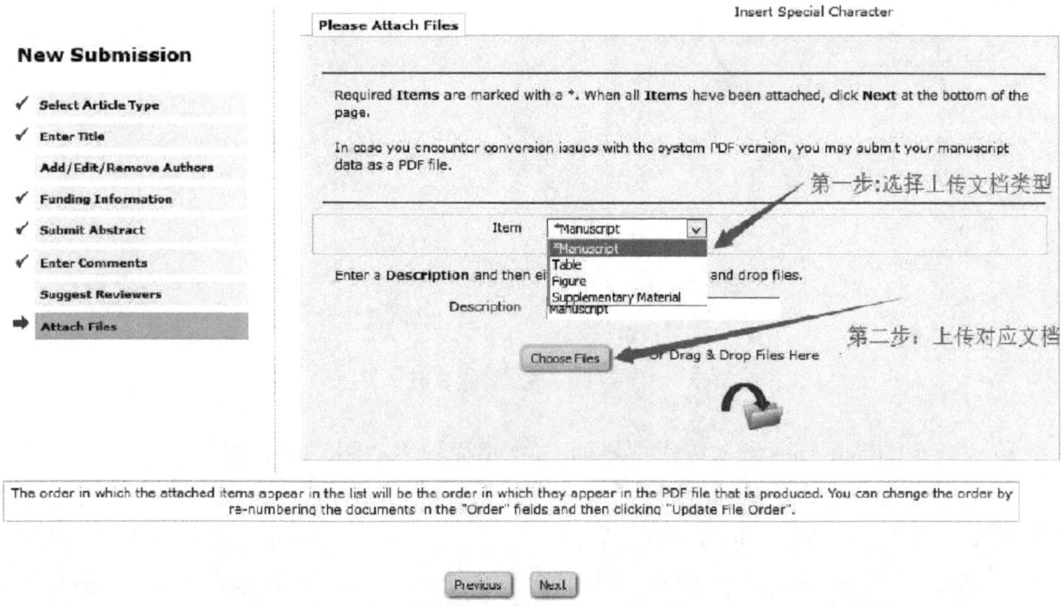

图 9-15　上传附件界面

14）上传完对应的文档后，在界面下方会按上述上传顺序列示对应文档的信息（图9-16）。单击 Download（或 Check All），可检查上传文档是否正确，如果不正确，则单击 Select 复选框，再单击 Remove 按钮，即可完成卸载。可以重填上传文档记录前面的 Order 中的序号，并单击 Update File Order 按钮，来改变上传文档的顺序。上传文档全部正确后，单击 Next 按钮进入下一步。

15）进入上传文档清单界面（图9-17），再次检查上传操作是否正确。确认无误后，单击 Build PDF for my Approval 按钮生成 PDF 文档；如有错误，则单击 Previous 重新操作。

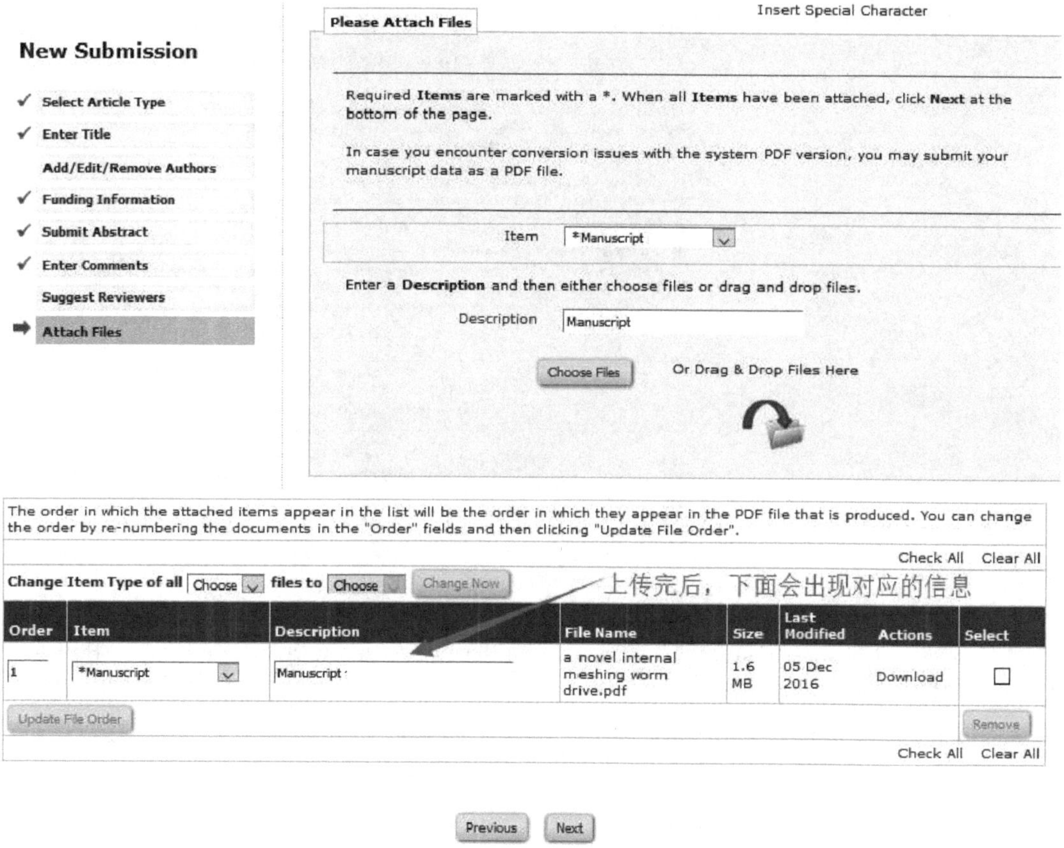

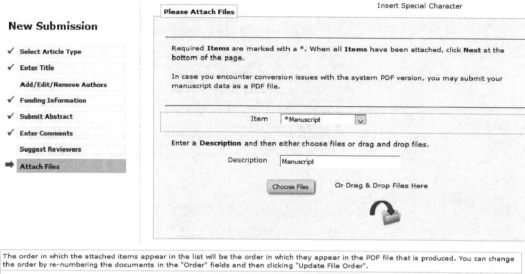

图 9-16　上传附件信息列示界面

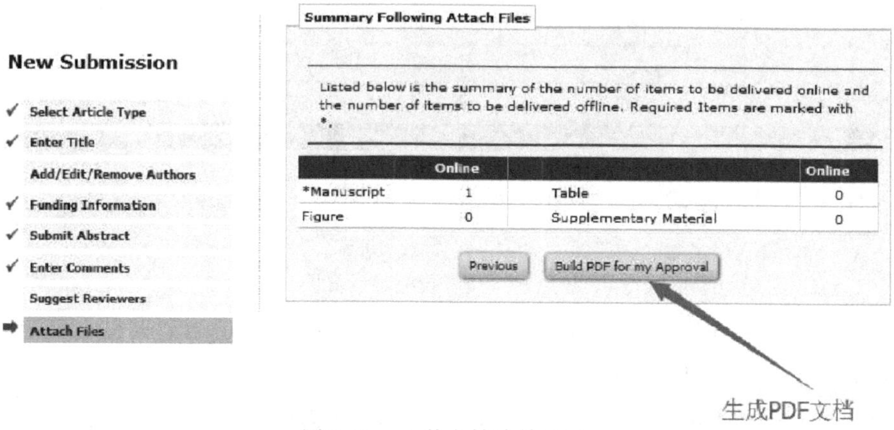

图 9-17　上传文档清单界面

16）进入投稿提示说明界面（图9-18）。标题是 PLEASE NOTE：Your submissions …，大体上告知：所提交的稿件正在生成 PDF 文档，此过程需要耐心等候，不要单击返回作者主界面；在 Submissions Waiting for Author's Approval 页面，可以查看、编辑、确认或移除所创建的 PDF 文档，一旦确认，该文档就会被提交到编辑部；如果投稿过程中指定了别人为通信作者，这时确认 PDF 文档无效，应当由通讯作者注册、登录系统来进行相关操作才可以。

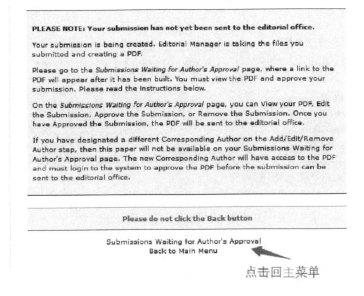

图 9-18　投稿提示说明界面

17）等待 PDF 文档生成的时间根据网速略有差别，大约需要几分钟，单击 Submissions Waiting for Author's Approval 进入作者投稿确认界面界面（图9-19），可看到 Manuscript Number、Title、Data Submission Began、Current Status 等信息，在 Current Status 栏，若显示 Needs Approval，则提示作者做进一步的确认操作，单击最左边的蓝色 Action Links 即可完成。

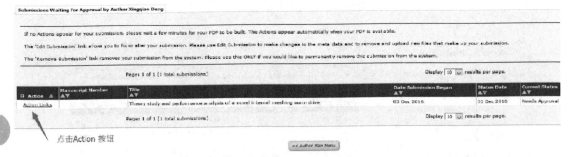

图 9-19　作者投稿确认界面

18）单击 Action Links 后，会弹出一组按钮（图9-20），分别是 View Submission、Edit submission、Approve Submission、Remove Submission、Correspondence、Send E-mail。单击不同的按钮，可完成不同的任务，如显示、编辑、确认（同意）、移除稿

件等。

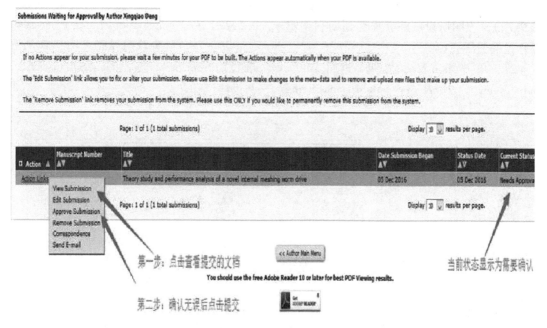

图 9-20　作者投稿确认的 Action Links 操作界面

19）按要求完成全部操作后，系统会自动生成一个 PDF 文档，先单击 View Submission 按钮查看生成的文档（图 9-21），确认无误后再单击 Approve Submission 按钮提交。

图 9-21　作者投稿确认的 View Submission 操作界面

20）单击 Approve Submission 按钮后，会出现 Author's Decision（作者确定界面，图9-22），表明所投稿件已提交到期刊编辑部，投稿最终完成。

21）单击 Main Menu 按钮，返回 Author Main Menu（图9-23），Submissions Being Processed 的状态从 0 变为 1，表明投稿成功。

22）单击 Submissions Being Processed 按钮，进入稿件处理状态界面（图9-24），文章的 Current Status 显示 New Submission，表明投稿成功。

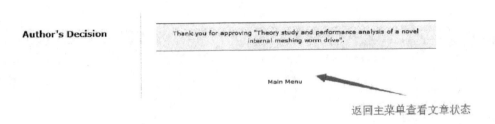

图 9-22　作者确认投稿的 Approve Submission 操作界面（作者确定界面）

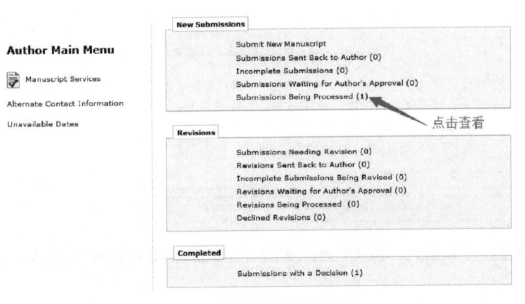

图 9-23　作者主界面投稿状态显示

图 9-24　稿件处理状态界面

9.2 查稿

作者投稿后，关注稿件能否录用，会适时查询稿件状态，下面介绍查稿流程及稿件状态：

1）凭作者（通信作者）的账号和密码，登录 Author Main Menu（图 9-25）。如果查稿，则单击第一栏最后一行 Submissions Being Processed 按钮（稿件处理中）。

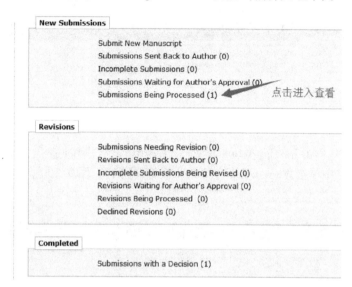

图 9-25 作者主界面（投稿后）

2）投稿成功后，稿件状态是 Editor Assigned（编辑分配、编辑处理中，图 9-26），显示在 Current Status 栏中，通常需要一周左右的时间待编辑处理。所谓编辑处理，就是编辑初审，即编辑对稿件进行审查，未通过的给予退稿，通过的安排同行评议（有的编辑部还会在这期间通知作者交纳论文评审费）。

图 9-26 投稿成功稿件状态界面

3）稿件安排同行评议后，Current Status 栏显示 Under Review（专家审稿中，图 9-27），Status Date 显示安排同行评议的具体时间。整个审稿期内，Current Status 的状态都会保持为 Under Review。

图 9-27 安排同行评议后稿件状态界面

4) 稿件同行评议完成后，编辑会根据专家评审意见对稿件进行处理，并做出决定。这一决定通常有以下几种结果：①直接拒稿，Final Disposition 显示为 Reject（图9-28）；②需要修改，Current Status 显示为 Need Revision；③直接发表，这种情况很少见。

图9-28　退稿状态界面

5) 单击左边的 Action Links，在弹出的对话框中单击 View Decision Letter 按钮，可随时查看审稿（处理）意见（图9-29、图9-30）。

图9-29　查看稿件处理意见

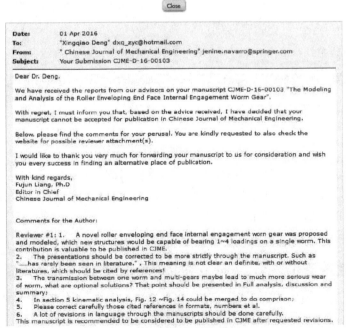

图9-30　稿件处理意见信

9.3 修稿

作者修稿完成后，就要着手投修改稿了，下面给出这一流程：

1）凭作者（通信作者）的账号和密码，登录 Author Main Menu。有修稿任务时，第二栏首行 Submissions Needing Revision 按钮的字体会变为蓝色，其后括号里会显示出待修稿数（图 9-31）。单击 Submissions Needing Revision 按钮，进入下一步。

2）进入稿件修改状态界面，此时 Current Status 显示 Revise，View Decision 显示修改类别（如 Minor revisons、Major revisons 等）（图 9-32）。单击左边的 Action Links 按钮，进入下一步。

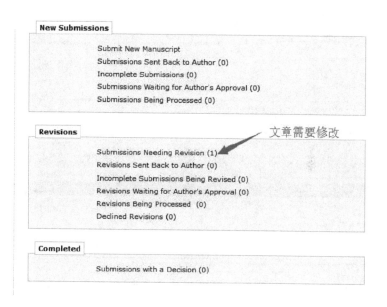

图 9-31　作者主界面（待修稿）

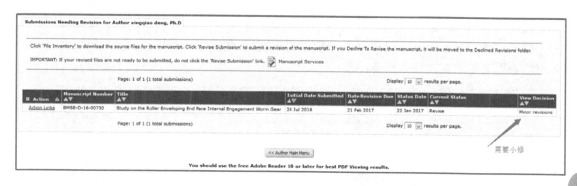

图 9-32　稿件修改状态界面

3）弹出对话框，列示出当前可以执行的各项操作，如 View Submission（浏览稿件）、File Inventory（修改资料）、View Reference Checking Results（浏览参考文献检查结果）、Revise Submission（修改稿件）、Decline to Revise（拒绝修稿）等（图 9-33），单击这些操作按钮，可以阅读或下载相关信息、文档。单击 Revise Submission 按钮，进入下一步。

4）进入投修改稿界面，上传已准备就绪的修改稿和其他文档（与投新稿几乎相同），上传后会持续一段时间生成一个新的 PDF 文档（图 9-34）。

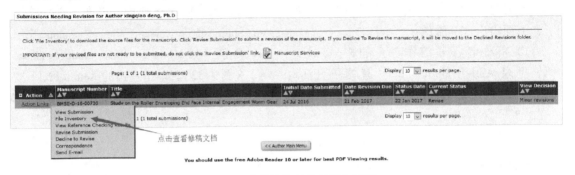

图 9-33　稿件待修可执行操作界面

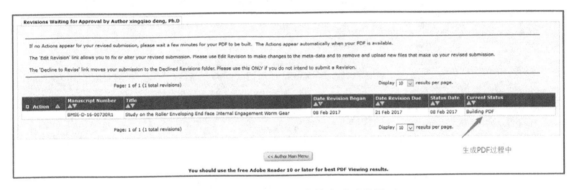

图 9-34　修改稿的 PDF 文档生成过程界面

5）修改稿的新的 PDF 文档生成后，再次单击 Action Links 按钮，在弹出的对话框中单击 View Revision 按钮（图 9-35），出现已上传稿件参数显示界面（图 9-36），据此可以检查所上传的文档是否正确。

6）修改稿文档上传成功后，Current Status 显示 Revision Needs Approval（图 9-37），表示还需作者进行确认，只有确认操作完成后，投修改稿才能最终完成。

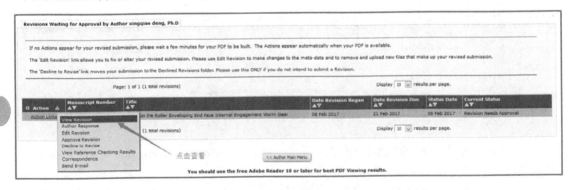

图 9-35　修改稿上传后可执行操作界面（View Revision）

第9章 EM投稿流程示例

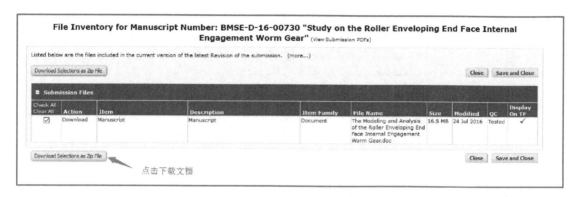

图9-36 修改稿上传后稿件参数显示界面

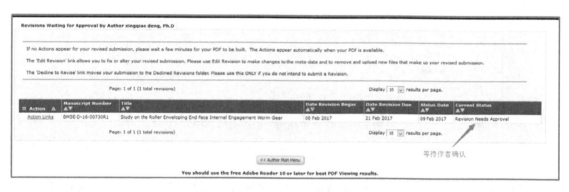

图9-37 修改稿上传后稿件状态界面

7）作者核对修改稿上传情况，确认无误后，再次单击Action Links按钮，在弹出的对话框中单击Approve Revision按钮（图9-38），即最终完成投修改稿。

8）当投修改稿成功后，作者主界面第二栏第五行Revisions Being Processed变为蓝色，表示新投修改稿正在处理中，其后括号中的数字表示处理中的修改稿数（图9-39）。

9）单击Revision Being Processed按钮，进入稿件状态显示界面，此时Current Status显示Revison Submitted（图9-40），表明成功完成了投修改稿。

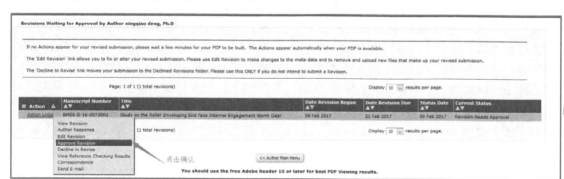

图9-38 修改稿上传后可执行操作界面（Approve Revision）

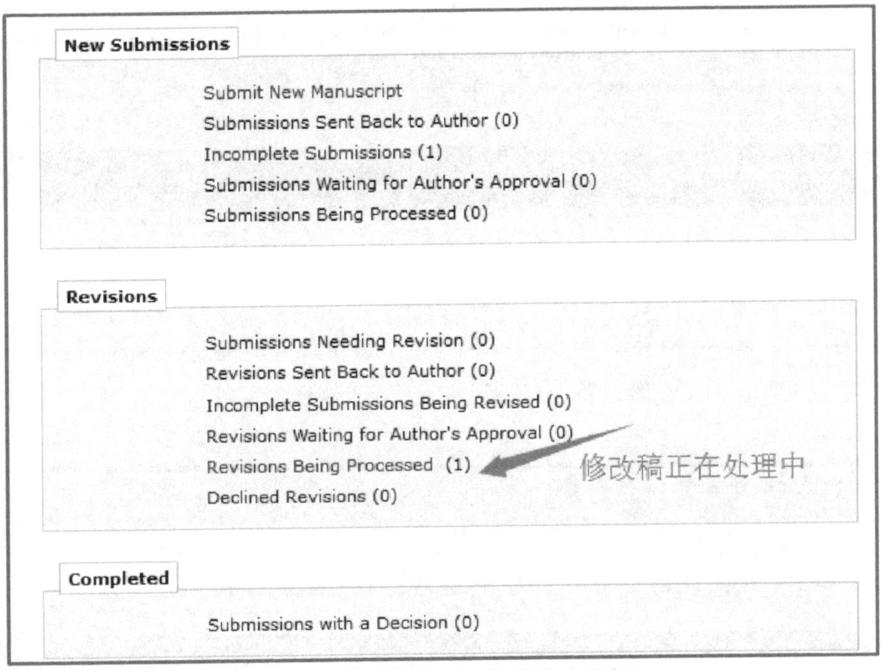

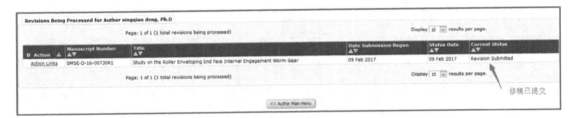

图 9-39 作者主界面（修改稿处理中）

图 9-40 修改稿已提交状态界面

9.4 生产

论文修改合格后进入生产环节，加工制作成产品，这是论文发表前的最后一个环节，虽然主体工作由生产部门来完成，但也与作者、编辑密切相关。论文进入生产环节后，作者首先收到一封告知邮件，如图 9-41 所示。然后进入生产过程，EM 生产流程大体如图 9-42 所示。

EM 生产包括 Article（文章）和 Issue（期刊）两大块，相应地其整体流程分为 Article workflow（文章加工流程）和 Issue workflow（期刊制作流程）前后两个部分。

Article workflow 如图 9-42 上半部分所示，主要包括以下环节：

1）Journal set-up：期刊设置，编辑部和出版商共同确定校对流程、文字加工层级、文章布局、是否彩印、校对安排等；

2）Accepting articles：发送文章，编辑部通过 EM 系统或邮件（FTP）发送需要生产加工的文章及有关信息；

3）Author's choice：发表选项选择，作者收到生产部门通知，选择是否同意版权转让或将论文 OA 出版，是否订阅单行本，是否制作宣传海报，可能还有插图是否彩印的选项；

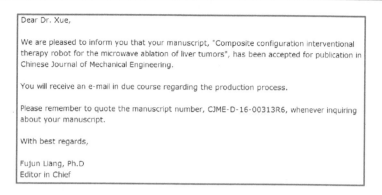

图 9-41　EM 生产收稿告知作者邮件

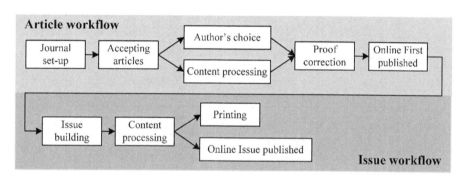

图 9-42　EM 大体生产流程

4）Content processing：内容制作，生产部门对文章创建 XML 数字资源、校对版 PDF 文档、分配 DOI；

5）Proof correction：校样更正，生产部门发给作者（编辑部）校对文本，作者（编辑部）进行校对并将校对结果返回生产部门，生产部门修改校对错误并创建最终版文本；

6）Online First published：数字优先出版，生产部门将最终版论文在出版商有关网站或平台上发布。

Issue workflow 如图 9-42 下半部分所示，主要包括以下环节：

7）Issue building：期刊创建，编辑部确定某期文章的清单，并发给出版商（在线论文中按年、卷、期次集结）；

8）Content processing：内容制作，生产部门对期刊创建 XML 数字资源、为 PDF 文档增加年、卷、期、页码信息，创建 A-pa-ges；

9）Printing：纸版印刷，生产部门制作印刷文件，印刷部分纸本期刊，将印刷文件返给编辑部，编辑部印刷部分纸本期刊；

10）Online Issue published：期刊在线出版，生产部门将期刊在线出版。

以上各环节及其中具体业务，由出版商、生产部门、编辑部、作者一方单独完成或几方协作共同完成，由作者完成的工作主要是论文发表选项选择及校对。

9.5　订购

论文生产成后将进入校对环节，在校对前作者会收到论文订购和版权转让（Copyright Transfer Statement（CTS））通知邮件，如图 9-43、图 9-44 所示。邮件中会给出论文的题目、DOI 及各个订购项目。

> Dear Author,
>
> Thank you for publishing with Springer. This message is to let you know that your article
>
> - Article title: New Family of RPR-Equivalent Parallel Mechanisms: Design and Application
> - DOI: 10.1007/s10033-017-0112-6
>
> has gone into production. Before we can send you your proofs, we have to ask you to provide some additional information. Please go to the following website (you may need to copy and paste the URL into your browser): https://www.springer.com/home?SGWID=0-0-1003-0-0&aqId=3257694&checkval=dc41931d463dc9e40dcbb2915a628bd5
>
> Please indicate if you would like to:
>
> - order Open Choice, i.e. publish the article as open access. The published version will then become freely available for anyone worldwide in exchange for payment of an open access charge.
> - order paper offprints or e-offprints of your article upon issue publication
> - order poster of your article with issue cover page, article title and the authorship
> - order printing of figures in color in the journal

> and to
>
> - transfer the copyright of your article (if you do not order Open Choice)
>
> In order for the publication of your article to proceed you must go to the above website and complete the request. The entire process should take about 10 minutes.
>
> You can help us facilitate rapid publication by returning your answers within 2 working days.
>
> PLEASE NOTE: This link expires WITHIN 5 DAYS after this e-mail has been sent to you so please make sure you complete the request before this date.

图 9-43　论文订购通知邮件

> Authors may self-archive the Author's accepted manuscript of their articles on their own websites. Authors may also deposit this version of the article in any repository, provided it is only made publicly available 12 months after official publication or later. He/she may not use the publisher's version (the final article), which is posted on SpringerLink and other Springer websites, for the purpose of self-archiving or deposit. Furthermore, the Author may only post his/her version provided acknowledgement is given to the original source of publication and a link is inserted to the published article on Springer's website. The link must be provided by inserting the DOI number of the article in the following sentence: "The final publication is available at Springer via http://dx.doi.org/[insert DOI]".
>
> Prior versions of the article published on non-commercial pre-print servers like arXiv.org can remain on these servers and/or can be updated with Author's accepted version. The final published version (in pdf or html/xml format) cannot be used for this purpose. Acknowledgement needs to be given to the final publication and a link must be inserted to the published article on Springer's website, by inserting the DOI number of the article in the following sentence: "The final publication is available at Springer via http://dx.doi.org/[insert DOI]". Author retains the right to use his/her article for his/her further scientific career by including the final published journal article in other publications such as dissertations and postdoctoral qualifications provided acknowledgement is given to the original source of publication.
>
> Articles disseminated via http://link.springer.com are indexed, abstracted and referenced by many abstracting and information services, bibliographic networks, subscription agencies, library networks, and consortia.
>
> After submission of the agreement signed by the corresponding author, changes of authorship or in the order of the authors listed will not be accepted by Springer.

图 9-44　版权转让通知邮件

```
Dear Author,

Please note: This e-mail is a confirmation of your copyright transfer and was sent to you only for your own records.

The copyright to this article, including any graphic elements therein (e.g. illustrations, charts, moving images), is hereby assigned for good and valuable consideration to Chinese Mechanical Engineering Society and Springer-Verlag Berlin Heidelberg effective if and when the article is accepted for publication and to the extent assignable if assignability is restricted for by applicable law or regulations (e.g. for U.S. government or crown employees). Author warrants (i) that he/she is the sole owner or has been authorized by any additional copyright owner to assign the right, (ii) that the article does not infringe any third party rights and no license from or payments to a third party is required to publish the article and (iii) that the article has not been previously published or licensed.

The copyright assignment includes without limitation the exclusive, assignable and sublicensable right, unlimited in time and territory, to reproduce, publish, distribute, transmit, make available and store the article, including abstracts thereof, in all forms of media of expression now known or developed in the future, including pre- and reprints, translations, photographic reproductions and microform. Springer may use the article in whole or in part in electronic form, such as use in databases or data networks for display, print or download to stationary or portable devices. This includes interactive and multimedia use and the right to alter the article to the extent necessary for such use.
```

图 9-44 版权转让通知邮件（续）

订购项目包括以下几个方面：

1）选择论文以 OA 模式发表，发表后可由全球用户免费获取，但需要作者交纳 OA 发表费（如果论文以 OA 模式发表，在后期的论文校对文档上会列示有关论文 OA 的信息）；

2）订购集结成期论文的印刷版单行本和电子版单行本；

3）订购带有期刊封面、文章题目和版权标志的文章宣传海报；

4）订购期刊中插图彩印；

5）文章版权转让（如果不选择 OA）。

填写、提交订单应在 2 个工作日内完成，操作过程大约需要 10 分钟。单击图 9-43 进入该页面中的网址（该链接自邮件通知 5 日内有效），出现 Send Order（发送订单）页面，如图 9-45 所示，在此可以进行各项订购操作，一步一步按操作提示、步骤完成即可。

在发送订单页面，有一个醒目的支付信息提示 "PLEASE NOTE：payment information"（作者如果已订购了产品，则过后将收到一封邮件，该邮件包含一个引导作者完成支付的链接。但请注意，纸本和在线产品的支付是分开进行的。）。"货运信息" 下面有两个表格，分别是 Your printed materials order（印刷产品订单）和 Your online services order（在线产品订单）。如果填写印刷产品订单，则单击右侧的 CHANGE，进入

图 9-45 发送订单页面

Color and Offprints（彩印和单行本）订购页面，如图 9-46 所示（这本是一个完整的界面，因截图空间所限，分为两个子界面展示）。

通信作者（corresponding author）将自动收到其论文的免费电子版单行本（PDF 文件），还可额外订购该电子版单行本的付费印刷版单行本。作者还可订购自己文章的海报，每份海报的价格是€50，海报主要展示刊登作者这篇文章的期刊封面以及文章题

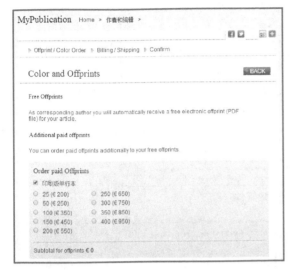

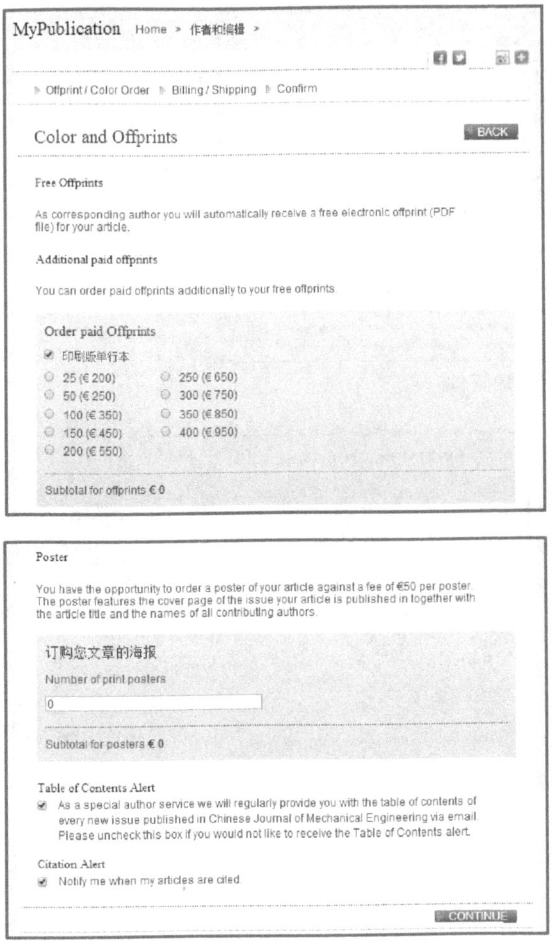

图 9-46　彩印和单行本订购页面

目和所有作者的姓名。

还有 Table of Contents Alert（新文章提示）和 Citation Alert（引用提示）两个复选框，在系统默认情况下，这两个复选框处于选中状态。前者是一个特殊服务，将为作者提供刊登其论文的期刊以后每期所发表的文章的清单；后者也是一个服务，当作者的论文有被引时，告知作者。如果不需要这样的服务，则将复选框的选中状态变为不选中状态，即把勾（✓）去掉。

在线产品订单涉及 OA 选择和版权转让两个方面，一旦选定提交，就不能再更改了。

9.6　校对

校对也是生产中的重要环节。排版后的 pdf 文档由生产部门完成后，将发送给该文的作者、编辑进行校对。以下给出两种模式下的 EM 校对流程：模式一为作者和编辑单独校对，互不干涉；模式二为作者和编辑协同校对，先由作者对首次排版后的文档进行校对，后由编辑进行校对，编辑可以看到作者校对所做的任何修改，还可以纠正作者错改之处。

1. 模式一

（1）论文由生产部门排版后，作者（编辑）收到论文校对通知邮件（图9-47）。

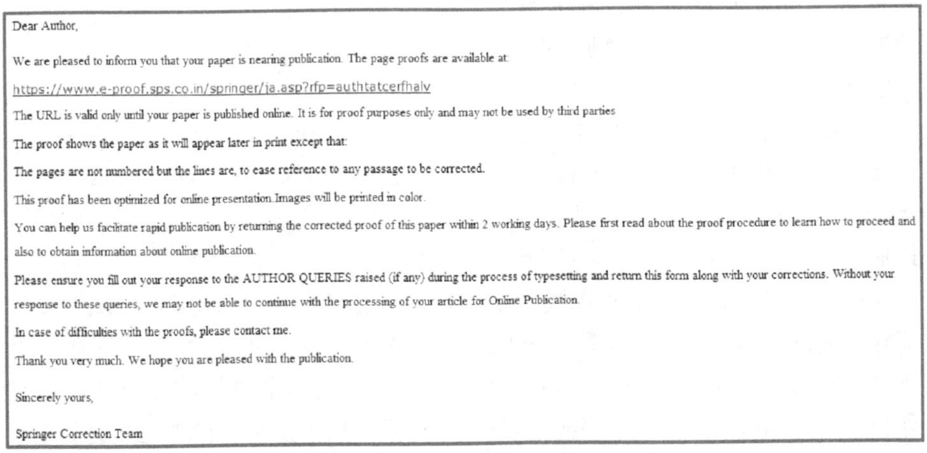

图 9-47　模式一作者论文校对通知邮件

第 9 章　EM 投稿流程示例

（2）单击上一步界面中的网址，进入在线校对操作准备界面。在此界面即可下载本论文排版后的 pdf 版全文，还可以进入在线校对操作使用说明界面。

（3）单击上一步界面中 Online Correction 后面的 Using correction Grid，进入在线校对操作界面（图 9-48）。该界面由左右两部分组成：左面为排版后的 pdf 全文，是需要校对的对象；右边为在线校对修正工作区，对校对中发现的问题进行指正操作，还可上传附件（如图片）、填写修改说明文字，标注字符参数，如是否加粗、斜体、加下划线、上下标。

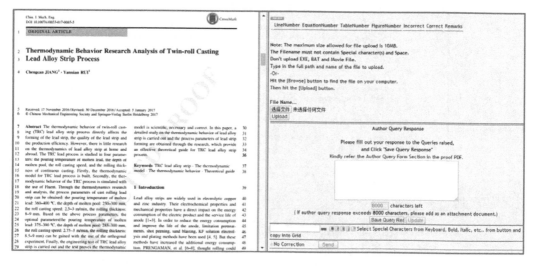

图 9-48　在线校对操作界面

（4）填写过程中可随时进行保存、编辑、删除操作，当全部填写完毕并确认无误后，单击 Send 按钮即可提交完成本次校对。如果校对没有发现任何问题，则勾选 Send 按钮前面的复选框 No Correction，再单击 Send 按钮即可。

（5）校对可以不止一个轮回，具体几个轮回取决于期刊编辑部与出版商的协定。

2. 模式二

（1）论文由生产部门排版后，作者收到论文校对通知邮件；作者校对完成提交后，编辑也会收到相同的邮件（图 9-49）。

（2）单击上一步界面中的网址，进入在线校对操作准备界面。

（3）单击在线校对操作准备界面中右下方的 Start Proofing 按钮，即进入在线校对首界面（Home），与 Home 标签并列的还有 Online Correction、Attachments、Author Query 等标签（图 9-50）。在 Home 页面有 Download File、Online Correction、Supporting Document 三个按钮，单击分别用来下载论文排版后的 pdf 全文、进入在线校对操作界面、校对所需的其他相关文档。

（4）单击上一步界面中的 Online Correction 标签或 Article 下方框中的 Online Correction 按钮，即进入在线校对修正界面（Online Correction，图 9-51）。在此界面中可以完成校对的所有操作，如 Insert（插入）、Change（改正）、Delete（删除）、Comments（批注）及 Bold（斜体）设置等。修正过程中可随时单击 Save 按钮进行保存。待完成所有修正工作并确认无误后，再单击 Submit 按钮在线提交，本次校对即最终完成。

SPRINGER NATURE

Article Title : Dynamic Stability Analysis of Linear Time-varying Systems via an Extended Modal Identification Approach
DOI : 10.1007/s10033-017-0075-7
CJME-D-15-00589MA Zhisai_new

Dear Editor,

We are pleased to inform you that the above-mentioned article is nearing publication. Your article proofs are available at:

http://eproofing.springer.com/journals/index.php?token=RBJv2Qgkp_uBbrAd2BlY9KYpsERS7nNir3z4hw1ka6s

The URL is valid only until the paper is published online. It is for proof purposes only and may not be used by third parties.

We hope you are pleased with the publication. You can help us facilitate quick and accurate publication by using our e.Proofing system. The system will show you an HTML version of the article with the author's proof corrections highlighted. You can view and correct the article online. In addition, you can view/download a PDF version for your reference.

As you are reviewing the proofs, please keep in mind the following:

- This is the only set of proofs you will see prior to publication.
- Only errors introduced during production process or that directly compromise the scientific integrity of the paper may be corrected.
- Any changes that contradict journal style will not be made.

Please submit your corrections within 2 working days. Should you encounter difficulties with the proofs, please contact me.

Thank you very much.

Sincerely yours,

Springer Nature Corrections Team

图 9-49　模式二作者（编辑）论文校对通知邮件

e.Proofing

Home　Online Correction　Attachments　Author Query　Help

Article

Title
Dynamic Stability Analysis of Linear Time-varying Systems via an Extended Modal Identification Approach

Journal
Chinese Journal of Mechanical Engineering

DOI
10.1007/s10033-017-0075-7

Download File
10033_2017_75_Author.pdf

Online Correction
Online Correction

Supporting Document
No Document Found

In case of any queries, please contact the Production Editor: Spr_corrections@sps.co.in
Please note: to read a PDF document online you need Adobe Acrobat Reader
Steps to enable JavaScript in different browsers

图 9-50　在线校对首界面（Home）

第 9 章　EM 投稿流程示例

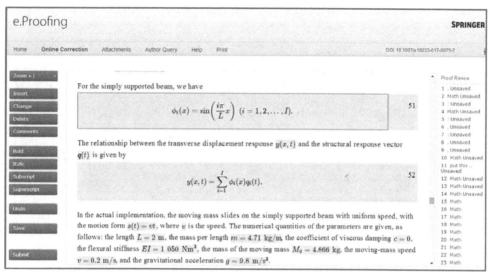

图 9-51　在线校对修正界面（Online Correction）

（5）单击 Attachments 标签，进入在线校对附件上传界面（Attachments，图 9-52），可以上传有关附件，如校对版 pdf 全文、图片或其他文档。

（6）单击 Author Query 标签，进入在线校对问题回复界面（Author Query，图 9-53），可以回复排版制作人员提出的各种问题，涉及作者姓名、单位写法是否正确，插图、表格、式子、参考文献是否按顺序引用等。

（7）在线校对修正界面的标签行中还有一个 Print 标签（图 9-54），单击该标签按钮，即可打印校对文本。

（8）作者（编辑）校对提交后，作者（编辑）会立即收到一个在线校对提交反馈邮件，确认校对提交成功，标志校对工作结束。

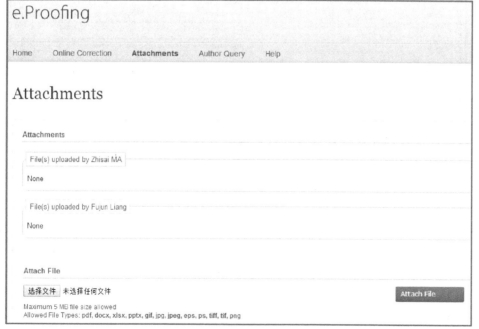

图 9-52　在线校对附件上传界面（Attachments）

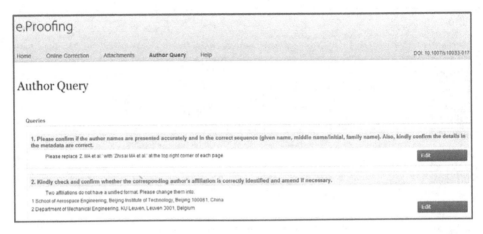

图 9-53　在线校对问题回复界面（Author Query）

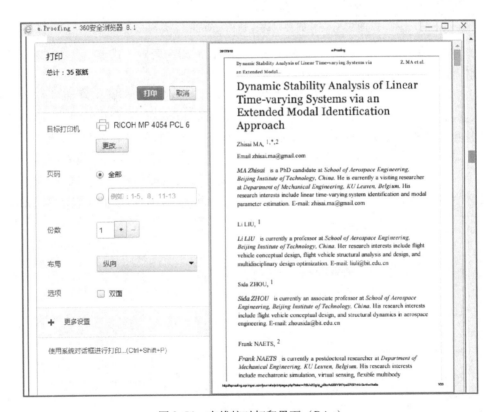

图 9-54　在线校对打印界面（Print）

如果论文以 OA 模式发表，则在校对版本论文的合适位置（如 Conclusions 后面，References 前面）上会出现论文的 OA 信息。例如：

Open Access This article is distributed under the terms of the Creative Commons Attribution 4.0 International License（http：//creativecommons. org/licenses/by/4.0/），which permits unrestricted use, distribution, and reproduction in any medium, provided you give appropriate credit to the original author(s) and the source, provide a link to the Creative Commons license, and indicate if changes were made.

9.7 订购确认

论文校对完成后、发表前,作者会收到论文订购确认(Order confirmation)邮件。单击邮件页面中的网址,出现 Send Order(发送订单)页面,如图9-45、图9-46所示,在此可以检查、确认作者在订购环节所填写的订购信息,如果作者以前没有订购单行本,而现在又打算订购(如增加订购数量),则可以在此填写或更改有关信息。选择OA和版权转让在前面"订购"环节已确定了,在此环节不可更改。

9.8 发表

论文发表分在线发表(Online First)和纸质发表。

1)在线发表后,作者会收到一封告知邮件。邮件内容分为 Congratulations、Announce Your Publication、Citation Information 三个部分。

在 Congratulations 部分,通知作者其论文已在线发表及发表的网址,给出论文的重要信息(如题名、期刊名、DOI),并告知作者该论文将为所有图书馆、科研机构订户获取(下载)。单击页面中的网址,出现论文获取页面(主要包括期刊名、论文及出版信息、References、Copyright information、About this article)。如果论文以 OA 模式发表,则可以被免费自由下载;否则,需要付费后才可以下载(见页面右侧的购买和下载界面)。单击下方的 Re 点 prints and Permissions,可以进入版权页面。

在 Announce Your Publication 部分,告知作者可以将此邮件转发给论文的其他作者,并建议作者在自己的网站或其他社交媒体上提及(增加)论文的出版和 DOI 信息。还告知作者,论文的 SpringerLink 页面设有操作简便的 share 按钮,用来与社交媒体方便地链接并实时了解论文的引用、共享情况。进入 Download Your e-Offprint(PDF file)下方的网址,出现了论文在线下载操作界面。作者须注意这个下载链接是有时效的,必须在四周内完成,否则就失去了这个机会。

在 Citation Information 部分,告知作者论文的引用格式(包括 Author、Journal Title、Year、DOI),论文一旦集结成期,生产便终结,带有某期封面的可随意翻阅的新的电子单行本(e-offprint)文件将生成,而且其 PDF 全文可以自由下载。作者所订购的任何单行本(offprint)、海报(posters)都将由出版商免费邮寄(海运)过来。

2)论文修改合格后进入印刷文档生产环节,加工制作成印刷版电子文档,这是论文发表前的最后一个环节,主体工作由生产部门(出版商)来完成。印刷版电子文档生成发给编辑部进行校对确认,无误后便进行印刷,纸质发表。

9.9 查询

单击某刊论文发表平台网址,进入论文发表查询页面(单击时间2017-03-26)。该页面显示出,该刊2017年第1期以后的论文已在线发表(Online First)的数量(44篇),但还未集结成期(View articles not assigned to an issue)。单击 View articles not assigned to an issue,即可进入该刊当前(截至2017-03-26)所有已在线发表论文的清单。

# 参 考 文 献

REFERENCES

[1] 梁福军. 英文科技论文规范写作与编辑[M]. 北京：清华大学出版社，2014.

[2] 梁福军. 科技论文规范写作与编辑[M]. 3 版. 北京：清华大学出版社，2017.

[3] 梁福军. 科技论文规范写作与编辑[M]. 2 版. 北京：清华大学出版社，2014.

[4] 梁福军. 科技论文规范写作与编辑[M]. 北京：清华大学出版社，2010.

[5] 梁福军. 科技语体语法与修辞[M]. 北京：清华大学出版社，2018.

[6] 梁福军. 科技语体标准与规范[M]. 北京：清华大学出版社，2018.

[7] 梁福军. 科技语体语法、规范与修辞：上、下册[M]. 北京：清华大学出版社，2016.

[8] 复旦教授谈日本诺奖"井喷"现象[OL]. (2015-02-16)[2018-11-14]. http://www.kepu.dicp.ac.cn/doshow6.php?id=111.

[9] WANG Renzhi, RU Jilai. Overall Evaluation of the Effect of Residual Stress Induced by Shot Peening in the Improvement of Fatigue Fracture Resistance for Metallic Materials[J]. CJME, 2015, 28(2)：416−421.

[10] KONG Xianwen. Standing on the Shoulders of Giants：A Brief Note from the Perspective of Kinematics[J]. CJME, 2017, 30(1)：1−2.

[11] 梁福军，宁汝新. RMS 中工件路径网络生成方法[J]. 工业工程与管理，2004(6)：8−14.

[12] GAO Wei, EMAMINEJAD Sam, NYEIN Hnin Yin Yin, et al. Fully integrated wearable sensor arrays for multiplexed in situ perspiration analysis[J]. Nature, 2016, 529(7587)：1586027. https://doi.org/10.1038/nature16521.

[13] KLEINSTIVER Benjamin P, PATTANAYAK Vikram, PREW Michelle S, et al. High-fidelity CRISPR-Cas9 nucleases with no detectable genome-wide off-target effects[J]. Nature, 2016, doi：10.1038/nature16526.

[14] SEKAR Aswin, BIALAS Allison R, RIVERA Heather de, et al. Schizophrenia risk from complex variation of complement component 4[J]. Nature, 2016, doi：10.1038/nature16549.

[15] BAKER Darren J, CHILDS Bennett G, DURIK Matej, et al. Naturally occurring p16Ink4a-positive cells shorten healthy lifespan[J]. Nature, 2016, 530(February). doi：10.1038/nature16932.

[16] SILVER David, HUANG Aja, MADDISON Chris J, et al. Mastering the game of Go with deep neural networks and tree search[J]. Nature, 2016, 529(January). doi：10.1038/nature16961.

[17] SLAYMAKER Ian M, GAO Linyi, ZETSCHE Bernd, et al. Rationally engineered Cas9 nucleases with improved specificity[J]. Science, 2015[2015-12-01]. www/sciencemag.org/content/early/recent/1December2015/Page 1/10.1126/science.aad5227.

[18] FARIA Nuno Rodrigues, AZEVEDO Raimunda do Socorro da Silva, KRAEMER Moritz U G, et al. Zika virus in the Americas：Early epidemiological and genetic findings[J/OL]. Science, 2016, 352(6283)：345−349

[2016-12-14]. http://science.sciencemag.org/. doi：10.1126/science.aaf503.

[19] GUO Donghui, SHIBUYA Riku, AKIBA Chisato, et al. Active sites of nitrogen-doped carbon materials for oxygen reduction reaction clarified using model catalysts[J/OL]. Science, 2016, 351(6271)：361−365 [2016-12-15]. http://science.sciencemag.org/. doi：10.1126/science.aad0832.

[20] WATERS Colin N, ZALASIEWICZ Jan, SUMMERHAYES Colin, et al. The Anthropocene is functionally and stratigraphically distinct from the Holocene [J/OL]. *Science*, 2016, 351 (6269): 137, aad2622-1-aad2622-10 [2016-10-18]. http://science.sciencemag.org/. doi: 10.1126/science.aad2622.

[21] GARCEZ Patricia P, LOIOLA Erick Correia, COSTA Rodrigo Madeiro da, et al. Zika virus impairs growth in human neurospheres and brain organoids [J/OL]. *Science*, 2016, 352 (6287): 816-818 [2016-12-14]. http://science.sciencemag.org/. doi: 10.1126/science.aaf6116.

[22] MCMEEKIN David P, SADOUGHI Golnaz, REHMAN Waqaas, et al. A mixed-cation lead mixed-halide perovskite absorber for tandem solar cells [J/OL]. *Science*, 2016, 351 (6269): 151-155 [2016-11-19]. http://science.sciencemag.org/. doi: 10.1126/science.aad5845.

[23] TABEBORDBAR Mohammadsharif, ZHU Kexian, CHENG Jason K W, et al. In vivo gene editing in dystrophic mouse muscle and muscle stem cells [J/OL]. *Science*, 2016, 351 (6271): 407-411 [2016-12-19]. http://science.sciencemag.org/. doi: 10.1126/science.aad5177.

[24] JAIN Saumya, WHEELER Joshua R, WALTERS Robert W, et al. ATPase-Modulated Stress Granules Contain a Diverse Proteome and Substructure [J/OL]. *Cell*, 2016, 164 (January 28): 1-12. http://dx.doi.org/10.1016/j.cell.2015.12.038.

[25] HIRANO Tatsuya. Condensin-Based Chromosome Organization from Bacteria to Vertebrates [J/OL]. *Cell*, 2016, 164 (February 25): 847-857. http://dx.doi.org/10.1016/j.cell.2016.01.033.

[26] THOMSEN Alex R B, PLOUFFE Bianca, CAHILL III Thomas J, et al. GPCR-G Protein-β-Arrestin Super-Complex Mediates Sustained G Protein Signaling [J/OL]. *Cell*, 2016, 166 (August 11): 1-13. http://dx.doi.org/10.1016/j.cell.2016.07.004.

[27] KUSEBAUCH Ulrike, CAMPBELL David S, DEUTSCH Eric W, et al. Human SRMAtlas: A Resource of Targeted Assays to Quantify the Complete Human Proteome [J/OL]. *Cell*, 2016, 166 (July 28): 1-13. http://dx.doi.org/10.1016/j.cell.2016.06.041.

[28] CHARBONNEAU Mark R, O'DONNELL David, BLANTON Laura V, et al. Sialylated Milk Oligosaccharides Promote Microbiota-Dependent Growth in Models of Infant Undernutrition [J/OL]. *Cell*, 2016, 164 (February 25): 1-13. http://dx.doi.org/10.1016/j.cell.2016.01.024.

[29] PEDMALE Ullas V, HUANG Shao-shan Carol, ZANDER Mark, et al. Cryptochromes Interact Directly with PIFs to Control Plant Growth in Limiting Blue Light [J/OL]. *Cell*, 2016, 164 (January 14): 1-13. http://dx.doi.org/10.1016/j.cell.2015.12.018.

[30] STROOPER Bart De, KARRA Eric. The Cellular Phase of Alzheimer's Disease [J/OL]. *Cell*, 2016, 164 (February 11): 603-615. http://dx.doi.org/10.1016/j.cell.2015.12.056.

[31] LANDER Eric S. The Heroes of CRISPR [J/OL]. *Cell*, 2016, 164 (January 14): 18-28. http://dx.doi.org/10.1016/j.cell.2015.12.041.

[32] WRIGHT Addison V, NÚÑEZ James K, DOUDNA Jennifer A. Biology and Applications of CRISPR Systems: Harnessing Nature's Toolbox for Genome Engineering [J/OL]. *Cell*, 2016, 164 (January 14): 29-44. http://dx.doi.org/10.1016/j.cell.2015.12.035.

[33] SHI Jianzhong, DENG Guohua, KONG Huihui, et al. H7N9 virulent mutants detected in chickens in China pose an increased threat to humans [J]. *Cell Research*, 2017, 27 (12): 1409-1421. doi: 10.1038/cr.2017.129.

[34] BRUHN Benjamin, BRENNY Benjamin JM, DEKKER Sidoeri, et al. Multi-chromatic silicon nanocrystals [J]. Light Science & Application, 2017, 6, e17007. doi: 10.1038/lsa.2017.7.

[35] WU Xu, GUO Zhi-Meng, WANG Hai-Bin, et al. Mechanical properties of WC-Co coatings with different decarburization levels [J/OL]. *Rare Met.*, 2014, 33 (3): 313–317. https://doi.org/10.1007/s12598-014-0257-8.

[36] SHAO Hui-Ping, WANG Zhi, LIN Tao, et al. Preparation of TiAl alloy powder by high-energy ball milling and diffusion reaction at low temperature [J/OL]. *Rare Met.*, 2018, 37 (1): 21–25. https://doi.org/10.1007/s12598-015-0466-9.

[37] ZHOU Changcong, TANG Chenghu, LIU Fuchao, et al. Regional moment-independent sensitivity analysis with its applications in engineering [J/OL]. *Chinese Journal of Aeronautics*, 2017, 30 (3): 1031–1042. http://dx.doi.org/10.1016/j.caj.2017.04.006.

[38] Institute of Biochemistry and Cell Biology, Shanghai Institute for Biological Sciences, Chinese Academy of Sciences. *Cell Research* [J]. 2018, 28 (4). Institute of Biochemistry and Cell Biology, Shanghai Institute for Biological Sciences, Chinese Academy of Sciences (CAS) and Springer Nature, 2018.

[39] Institute of Biochemistry and Cell Biology, Shanghai Institute for Biological Sciences, Chinese Academy of Sciences. *Cell Research* [J]. 2017, 27 (12). Institute of Biochemistry and Cell Biology, Shanghai Institute for Biological Sciences, Chinese Academy of Sciences (CAS) and Springer Nature, 2017.

[40] Institute of Biochemistry and Cell Biology, Shanghai Institute for Biological Sciences, Chinese Academy of Sciences. *Cell Research* [J]. 2016, 26 (4, 10). Institute of Biochemistry and Cell Biology, Shanghai Institute for Biological Sciences, Chinese Academy of Sciences (CAS) and Springer Nature, 2016.

[41] Changchun Institute of Optics, Fine Mechanics and Physics, Chinese Academy of Sciences (CAS). *Light Science & Application* [J]. 2017, 6 (3, 4). Changchun Institute of Optics, Fine Mechanics and Physics, Chinese Academy of Sciences and Springer Nature, 2017.

[42] Changchun Institute of Optics, Fine Mechanics and Physics, Chinese Academy of Sciences (CAS). *Light Science & Application* [J]. 2016, 5 (1). Changchun Institute of Optics, Fine Mechanics and Physics, Chinese Academy of Sciences and Springer Nature, 2016.

[43] The Nonferrous Metals Society of China, General Research Institute for Nonferrous Metals (GRINM). *Rare Metals* [J]. 2018, 37 (1). GRINM Bohan (Beijing) Publishing Co., Ltd. and Springer, 2018.

[44] The Nonferrous Metals Society of China, General Research Institute for Nonferrous Metals (GRINM). *Rare Metals* [J]. 2014, 33 (3). Editorial Office of Rare Metals, 2014.

[45] The Chinese Anti-Cancer Association. *Cancer Biology & Medicine* [J]. 2016, 13 (2). The Chinese Anti-Cancer Association and ELSEVIER, 2016.

[46] Cold and Arid Regions Environmental and Engineering Research Institute, Chinese Academy of Sciences; Science Press; The Geographical Society of China. *Sciences in Cold and Arid Regions* [J]. 2016, 8 (5). Science Press, 2016.

[47] The Institution of Engineers Australia. *Australian Journal of Water Resources* [J]. 2013, 17 (1). Engineering Media for Engineers Australia, 2013.

[48] Chinese Mechanical Engineering Society. *Chinese Journal of Mechanical Engineering* [J]. 2012, 25 (1)-. Beijing: Editorial Office of Chinese Journal of Mechanical Engineering and Springer-Verlag Berlin Heidelberg, 2012.

[49] Oxford Journals. *Annals of Botany* [J]. 2007, 99 (5). Bristol, UK: Editorial Office of Annals of Botany, 2007.

[50] The European Federation of Neurological Societies. *European Journal of Neurology* [J]. 2007, 14 (9). Edinburgh, UK: Blackwell Publishing, 2007.

[51] Chinese Academy of Sciences (CAS), National Natural Science Foundation of China (NSFC). *SCIENCE CHINA Technological Sciences* [J]. 2011, 54 (7). Beijing: Science China Press; Heidelberg: Springer, 2011.

[52] Science Press, Springer Science, Business Media. *Journal of Computer Science and Technology* [J]. 2008, 23 (2). Beijing: Editorial Office of Journal of Computer Science and Technology, 2008.

[53] Chinese Academy of Medical Sciences, ELSEVIER. *Chinese Medical Sciences Journal* [J]. 2011, 26 (2). Beijing: Editorial Office of Chinese Medical Sciences Journal, 2011.

[54] The Geological society of China. *Acta Geological Sinica* [J]. 2008, 82 (2). Beijing: Editorial Office of Acta Geological Sinica, 2008.

[55] Polish Academy of Sciences committee of Machine Design. *The Archive of Mechanical Engineering* [J]. Warszawa: Warszawska Drukarnia Naukowa PAN, 2009, LVI (4).

[56] 国家技术监督局. 量和单位: GB 3100~3102—1993 [S]. 北京: 中国标准出版社, 1994.

[57] 中华人民共和国国家质量监督检验检疫总局, 中国国家标准化管理委员会. 信息与文献 参考文献著录规则: GB/T 7714—2015 [S]. 北京: 中国标准出版社, 2015.

[58] 张磊. 工业设计论文选题与质量分析 [C]//第22届全国工业设计学术年会暨2017国际智能创新高峰论坛, 广州, 2017-12-22-24.

[59] 李达, 李玉成, 李春艳. SCI论文写作解析 [M]. 北京: 清华大学出版社, 2012.

[60] 论文写作之应该如何区分摘要和结论 [OL]. [2019-03-15]. http://blog.sina.com.cn/s/blog_148124e9a0102xkbb.html.

后 记
POSTSCRIPT

  笔者已出版多部科技论文写作专著，社会反响较好，同时用户也普遍反映目前更缺少专门针对研究生学术论文、英文论文写作的实用教材，期望笔者日后能写出更有针对性和更加适用的教材。为满足这种社会需求，笔者先尝试撰写了《SCI论文写作与投稿》这部教材。

  SCI论文写作涉及的方面很多，本书只是完成了它的内容篇，侧重论文的内容与结构。而它的语言篇，侧重论文的语言表达，将在另一本著作讲述，书名先暂定《英语科技论文语法、词汇与修辞》。

  按原来的构想，为方便读者阅读，本书初稿中对所有英文实例给出了中文译文，但因这些中文译文篇幅较多，考虑到本书的读者主要是硕士、博士研究生，其英文水平通常较高，给出中文译文反而可能多余，因此在最终定稿时，将这部分内容删除了。另外，本书用中文来讲述英文写作，在中英文混合模式下，容易从中文的视角来讲述英文，进而产生偏差。如果改用英文来写，恐怕是一个不错的方案，但纯英文教材对中国学生使用可能不太方便，因此还是用中文写成了现在的版本。

  不管怎样，笔者撰写的第一部教材还是问世了，欣慰之情不溢言表！

  在本书付梓之际，笔者由衷感谢美国密西西比州立大学刘宇澄（Yucheng Liu）教授、英国布鲁内尔大学程凯（Kai Cheng）教授和科技导报社副社长、副主编史永超编审为本书作序，感谢名刊主编宋天虎、白雨虹研究员和程磊编审，大学校长、博导刘清友教授，高校博（硕）导杜雪、李振波、王秋惠教授，行业协会领导李琛高级工程师为本书撰写推荐语，感谢好友张磊副主编、张凌云编辑，青年学者邓星桥、岳彩旭、秦红玲、窦金花、卢文娟、冯旭、赵宁、刘雪老师为本书内容完善或语病修改提出的宝贵意见，感谢机械工业出版社营销销售中心李双雷副主任、高等教育分社韩效杰副社长为本书选题献计献策，感谢机械工业信息研究院（机械工业出版社）学术媒体中心主任、《机械工程学报》常务副主编王淑芹编审及有关领导为本书撰写给予的帮助和勉励！

  最后，感谢家人孟晓丽教授级高工在本书撰写过程中给予的默默支持！

梁福军
2019-6-18